A CASEBOOK ON
DELICT

A CASEBOOK ON DELICT

William J. Stewart, LL.B., LL.M., N.P.
Partner; MacMillans, Solicitors, Glasgow

W.GREEN /Sweet & Maxwell
EDINBURGH
1997

First edition, 1991
Second edition, 1997

© 1997
W. GREENS & SON LTD

ISBN 0 414 01188 0

A catalogue record of this book is available from the British Library

Typeset by Trinity Typesetting, Edinburgh
Printed and bound in Great Britain by the Cromwell Press, Wiltshire

For
Hugh and Jackie

and

for the new addition
since the last edition-
Rachel

PREFACE TO SECOND EDITION

The huge expansion in student numbers since the first edition probably means that more students will want to be able to have access to case materials without queuing for a seat in the library. The book has the same core. Its aims and objectives remain the same. However I have (1) up-dated the commentary to reflect developments here and in England; (2) substituted some more relevant extracts — for example cases relating to the manual handling regulations; (3) included a few unreported cases (ideas for others welcome); (4) started the book with a contextual chapter which should at the same time allow quite a bit about the law of damages to be learned; (5) updated the bibliography of relevant articles which with effort should be helpful for students, teachers and practitioners (who in smaller firms find books such as this useful as a pocket library and statute book).

I am grateful to Noel Keenan of Greens for his work in helping me put this edition together; to Angela McCreadie and Frank McGuire, solicitor, Glasgow, for helping with Chapter 1; and to the clients, staff and Gerry at MacMillans for coping with the recent absences; to Alison for research and for her support; and to LWWS for the laughs.

The law is as at January 1, 1997.

PREFACE TO FIRST EDITION

This book is a learning aid for any law student who does not have ready access to the case reports. For law students who have daily access and the time to consult the reports, the book may still be a useful learning aid when revising notes and reading textbooks. It is also a teaching tool — allowing lectures or tutorials to proceed on the basis of a core of information. Delict is still a subject which is essentially in the cases, so it is particularly difficult to understand as a series of rules. Those statutes most important to an understanding of the law are included as extracts. Many other statutes have importance in delict, and most of these are reproduced in Appendix A from the *Parliament House Book*. I hope that this will make the book more useful, even though it might have been desirable, had more space been available, to extract and comment upon these. In any event the inclusion of the statutes together with the absence of introductory text might make the book suitable for use in open-book examinations.

It is not by any means comprehensive, although its scope is deliberately wide. There will be cases some consider to be essential reading that are not included, and some included that some or many will consider should not be here at all. To either critic it need only be pointed out that the author of a work such as this is his own Roy Plomley (or Sue Lawley as the case may be). On the other hand, just as no man is an island, a book such as this must be as useful as possible to as many students as possible. Thankfully there is, as yet, no standard curriculum in the universities — lecturers and teachers can use those they like and provide those cases they prefer themselves for their students. Students, as learners, can and should read such other cases as their studies suggest are appropriate.

The book is therefore intended to provide a large proportion of the cases and statutes needed to understand this subject, cases referred to not only in my own *Introduction to Scots Law of Delict* (1989) [now *Delict* (2nd ed., 1993)], but also in the other works which students are likely to use to study the subject, such as Volume II of Walker's *Principles* or the chapters on Reparation and Verbal Injury in Gloag and Henderson's *Introduction to the Law of Scotland* [or Thomson's *Liability*]. To facilitate this use of the casebook I have not written introductory sections, as in Weir's excellent *Casebook*, my own general view being set out in *Introduction*.

The structure of the book broadly follows *Introduction to the Scots Law of Delict*. At the end of a given passage or series of extracts I have included comments. These either raise hypotheticals, refer to English cases, or refer to periodical literature. Sometimes reference is made to the appropriate passages in *Introduction.*

I have avoided the inclusion of any English materials and concentrated on Scots materials alone. There are three excellent English books — Weir, Hepple and Matthews, and Kidner (for details see Select Bibliography), in which the leading English cases can be found and which no student of Scots law would be wasting money in purchasing. At first sight this exclusion of English cases may appear an astonishing approach to delict where, at least in relation to negligence, both systems are said to be in harmony. On the other hand, it is clear from the approach of the courts in daily practice, as opposed to academic articles, that generally Scottish authority is preferred in the Scottish courts — most certainly so outwith negligence. It might be thought to be somewhat hypothetical but I have dealt with the leading English cases which *are* regularly cited through their *reception* by Scottish courts. Providing the book is used in the context of further reading and/or instruction, no substantial distortion should thereby result. In choosing extracts I have tried to make sure, where Scottish cases have adopted important dicta from leading English cases, that these are extracted. Naturally the student must read these English cases in the reports or the excellent English casebooks. This tendency to legal patriotism (or xenophobia) extends to statutes where I have tried to confine myself to statutes specially applying to Scotland, despite the fact that the Westminster parliament is as much that of Scotland as that of the rest of the United Kingdom. An exception has been made for the Consumer Protection Act 1987 in view of its European pedigree. So far as other statutes are concerned a number will be found discussed in the cases and often repeated *verbatim* therein.

This work was produced in a relatively short period of time largely thanks to the use of my portable personal computer (Amstrad PPC512) which augmented the technology already specified in *Introduction,* the data being downloaded to my Tandy 1000 whose 215K Ram is beginning to creak. Strathclyde University and Professor Paterson are as ever committed to the full use of technology in the law, and an Intelligent character-reader was available to me had I chosen to use it. On this occasion I declined to use the technology, only because I thought that it would have been psychologically unfortunate: to have had the full text on disk would have meant chopping away judicial wisdom, to actually choose the words that must go into the text encourages critical selection. Thus the intelligent character-reading (the data input on the portable) was done by Morag King (now Blair) expertly, efficiently and cheerfully. I am obliged to her, and to MacMillans, solicitors, Glasgow, for their co-operation.

I am grateful to Pino de Emidio [now at the Bar], solicitor, Glasgow, who commented on a draft of the Foreword.

I am very grateful to Jim Logie, formerly lecturer in law at Dundee University and presently a solicitor with Dorman Jeffrey, solicitors, Glasgow [now at the Scottish Office]. He kindly gave of his time to read the draft and make valuable and useful comments as a result of which the book is better. I should also like to thank my fellow tutors in delict at the university here, who have offered many helpful comments.

Finally, it is a pleasure to thank Peter Nicholson, Mr Hendry and the rest of the team at Greens for their assistance in getting this project to press in its present form.

The law is at June 1, 1990, although it was clearly necessary to take account of developments in July. Some later points have been included in the proofs.

ACKNOWLEDGMENTS

The following have kindly given permission to use copyright materials—

The Incorporated Council of Law Reporting.
The Linklater Estate.
Guardian Newspaper Ltd: *The Guardian.*
Her Magesty's Stationary Office.
The Scotsman Publications Ltd: *The Scotsman* and *Scotland on Sunday.*
The Scottish Law Commission.
Scottish Media Newspapers Ltd: *Evening Times* and *The Herald.*
Sweet & Maxwell Ltd.
T and T Clark Ltd.

CONTENTS

Preface to the Second Edition vii
Preface to First Edition ix
Acknowledgments xiii
Using this Book xvii
Foreword: A Case for a Table xix
Alphabetical Table of Cases xxiii
Alphabetical Table of Statutes xxxi
Chronological Table of Cases and Statutes xxxiii

1. Reform and Debate 1
2. The Institutional Writers — Terminology 67
3. Wrongful Interference with the Person 80
4. Breach of Confidence 91
5. Wrongful Use of Land 98
6. Wrongful Interference with Goods 120
7. Economic Delicts 135
8. Negligence: Duty 161
9. Negligence: Causation 182
10. Negligence: Standard of Care 192
11. Negligence: Remoteness 206
12. Third Party Intervention 213
13. Economic Loss 237
14. Liability of Public Bodies 275
15. Statutory Duty and Eurorep. 289
16. Occupiers' Liability 319
17. Product Liability 329
18. Animals 340
19. Employers' Liability 353
20. Defences 361
21. Verbal Injury 389
22. Vicarious Liability and some Special Parties 415
23. Private International Law — Jurisdiction and
    Claim of Law in Delict 434
24. Proof and Damages 444

Appendix 455
Selected Bibliography 549
Index 561

USING THIS BOOK

Each extract is numbered and often cross-references will be to the extract number instead of the page number, thus "See Ext. 24." There then follows a "Comment" section which will generally do one or more of four things: (1) refer to articles or other cases; (2) pose hypothetical problems to make the reader think about the extract; (3) refer to the law of England; or (4) refer to relevant passages of *Delict* (2nd ed., 1993). Again for the sake of simplicity I have tried to keep references to the law of England to Baker on *Tort*, Winfield and Jolowicz on *Tort*, or Weir's *Casebook on Tort*, which are my own favourite English books.

While this book is not designed as a companion to *Delict*, I thought it right to make easy cross-reference possible. Such references are made as follows, *viz.* "*Delict*, 5.07)" — *i.e.* the paragraph numbers have one decimal divider as opposed to the paragraphs in this book which have two, *viz.* "5.2.9."

Where an extract has footnotes these are generally not reproduced unless the sense of the whole extract might be lost or the reference is very important. When footnotes are included, they are incorporated in the text in square brackets. Where cases are cited in extracts of reports which do not note the citation in the body of the text but elsewhere, I have taken the liberty of including the full citation the first time the case is mentioned.

Where I have missed out parts of a report and continued without starting a new paragraph there will be three dots like this ... — with the text continuing on.

The paragraphs in this book do not necessarily reflect paragraphs in the original work. This is the greatest liberty that has been taken with the original material. I have, however, tried to be faithful to the original by making paragraph breaks according to the logic of the extract.

The numbering of paragraphs has a number of intended purposes. The first is to break up the text. One of the reasons students find the reading of judgments repellent is partly their length but perhaps also the appearance of a judgment as a large block of continuous prose without figure, diagram nor direct speech. The fragmentation of the text encourages a "one-step-at-a-time" approach to reading, and hopefully raises the chance of students reading the whole extract. Secondly, it is easier to make a quick and appropriate cross-reference. This is beneficial for at least two reasons: (i) it enhances the value of the book as a teaching tool — in the middle of a lecture, seminar or tutorial it should be possible to refer to the dictum of Lord Blank at x.y.z. with a fair chance that the student should have the text in sight fairly quickly; (ii) it should be possible to cross-refer to the casebook in other books.

Most of the cases in the book are appellate decisions. The heading of the extract for the sake of simplicity reveals the court in which the case is heard: H.L. — House of Lords; C.A. — English Court of Appeal; I.H. — Inner House; O.H. — Outer House; S.A. — Sheriff Court appeal, from sheriff to sheriff principal or, pre-1971, sheriff-substitute to sheriff. In addition I have added the word "appellant" in brackets after the party initiating the appeal. Again, pleading ease of exposition, I have done this even where, in the case of appeal from the Outer to the Inner House, the correct term should be reclaimer.

The book concludes with an Appendix which brings together parts of the *Parliament House Book* which bear upon the subject.

The Selected Bibliography should be used to locate further reading on most topics.

FOREWORD: A CASE FOR A TABLE
(Not to be Read by Students)

This book has a chronological table of cases, which does not normally appear in Scottish nor indeed Anglo-American textbooks, and it is that table and some associated comments in the book which are explained here. (The dates are the dates of publication in the reports — sometimes this may result in considerable distortion where a case is reported many years after it is decided: such as, for example, *Bonthrone*, Ext. 45).

There is almost always a chronological table of statues but seldom (or never) a chronological table of cases. Why should this be? Perhaps it would be better to begin with a preliminary question — why are these tables there at all? The obvious answer is that they are there to help the reader find cases and statutes to which (s)he may wish to refer — these cases and statutes are after all the prime source of the law. So far so good with the alphabetical table of cases. So long as one is aware of the name of the case, location (placing) is possible. To be even more helpful the cases could be listed as often they are in volumes of the law reports, by the defender's name, *viz.* 'Fish, Fiss v."

Is it likely, however, that the reader will know the year of a statute, rather than its short title? There are no data available. A small, unrepresentative and statistically insignificant sample of colleagues and students suggested that it is the name of the statute which is most likely to be recalled rather than simply a date and a subject-matter. Tony Weir's casebook helpfully lists the statutes alphabetically (although it does not list them chronologically).

If we, at least tentatively, discard location as the primary purpose of the table of statutes, what might be another explanation? The ordering might be based upon our interpretative strategies. Before the introduction of short titles the Acts were ordered according to their appearance in the regnal years and indeed still reflect the continuing outpouring of Parliament — as it happens. This method of recording, although inconvenient for the purposes of locating references in a text, does however, quadrate with the accepted strategy of interpretation of legislation. The task is to discover the intention of Parliament and Parliament's intentions. Parliament legislates temporally (and of course, spiritually) forward in time, repealing previous legislation, and accordingly statutes must be located in time rather than in text. Early Scots statutes could become the subject of tacit repeal by desuetude — contrary usage over time. In modern times, time is still of the essence. As Paterson and Bates say: "Where a later Act is inconsistent with an earlier one, but does not expressly amend or repeal it, the courts will normally apply the later Act. The earlier legislation is considered to have been impliedly amended or repealed by the later legislation (*e.g. Vauxhall Estates Ltd v. Liverpool Corporation* [1932] 1 K.B. 733; *Ellen St Estates Ltd v. Minister of Health* [1934] 1 K.B. 590)." (p. 313.) Thus the chronological table of statutes adds something to our reading of the text.

This is in direct contrast to the table of cases. Helpful as it is in locating a citation, it adds nothing to our understanding. Even if cases were ranked according to their place in the hierarchy, this would be of some value. They are not — the humblest example from a single inferior court sits arrogantly beside the weightiest pronouncement of our Supreme Court.

So the alphabetical model is not essential, nor is it of any special assistance in reading. It does do one thing. By its presence, it displaces one alternative and that alternative would be a chronological table, locating each case, not in the text, but in time. Even within the most orthodox tradition of interpretation some degree of diachronic reading may be permitted (see Paterson and Bates, "*Cessante ratione cessat ipsa lex*," pp. 341–345. See, however, Rodger, "The Strange demise of Hyslops v. Gordon" in *Obligations In Context*, p. 1 at p. 5). However, a diachronic reading is probably to some extent subversive — it questions the authority of the text and requires an interpretative strategy which is beyond that of traditional textual exegesis.

Is there value, then, in having such a chronological table? It is submitted that there is. It is at least another option in reading cases even within the most traditional method. T.B. Smith seems — correctly, it is submitted — to have considered that indexing was important in developing the present doctrine of precedent: "It may be suggested that several causes concurred in developing doctrines of strict precedent in the Scottish judicial process ... it may be observed that soon after the court divided law reporting in Scotland was greatly improved and developed ... Associated with actual reporting, was the work devoted in the early years of the nineteenth century to compiling useful indexes to the decisions, so that they might be traced when required" (quoted, Paterson and Bates at p. 324). It also allows the reader to use Professor Walker's "Table of Significant Events in legal history," *Scottish Legal System* (5th ed.), pp. 165–184.

So, beyond simply locating in time, there is the need to see the rule in a case in its legal context. This view can be seen in Twinning and Miers: "Any test for determining the *ratio decidendi*, which suggests, explicitly or implicitly, that a case can be interpreted in isolation, without reference to other cases, is unrealistic and misleading. As the courts hand down new decisions, so the range of plausible interpretations of an earlier case may change over time" (quoted, Paterson and Bates at p. 331).

More radically, a chronological table is a reminder that an unpicking of the full historical context might provide an insight which will allow some wider understanding of the law. An example of such an exercise in the law of tort is the article by Davies, "The Road from Morocco: Polemis, Donoghue, No-Fault" (1982) 45 M.L.R. 534.

Finally, a diachronic reading of the law is one of the opportunities presented by a chronological table. As Goodrich puts it: "The key to any form of hermeneutics is its sense of history or of tradition. Throughout the various stages of its development, from the Renaissance to the nineteenth century, the consistent concern of hermeneutics has been with the recovery and reconstruction of ancient texts and alien meanings. Hermeneutics ... is best comprehended as 'historical consciousness', as a method which reflects upon and draws up the rules for recollecting and interpreting documents deemed to be of historical significance ...' (Goodrich, *Reading the Law*, 5.2.1).

It goes without saying that a textbook which had such a table would offer the reader the opportunity to test the views of the textbook on the history and development of the subject discussed.

Those then are the opportunities. There are, however, all sorts of threats inherent in what might be considered an historical contextual approach, such as might be encouraged by the existence of a chronological table. Professor E. D. Hirsch, Jr., sets out three relativistic fallacies in relation to historical perspectives in reading which have to be considered (Extract 14, *Modern Criticism and Theory* (ed. Lodge, 1988)).

The first fallacy is the fallacy of the inscrutable past. This is where it is assumed that the historical subject's views of his or her time are so obscure that they cannot be fathomed save by an élite who, through an act of historical sympathy, can attempt a reading. This does not seem prevalent in the law save in connection perhaps with Roman law certainly so far as the counter-movement which suggests that as the past is inscrutable then it is better to distort the past in an interesting and relevant way rather than distort and deaden it under the pretence of historical reconstruction — reminiscent in Scots law of the approach of T. B. Smith to Roman law (see *Short Commentary*, pp. 19–24).

The second fallacy is relevant to any attempted historical reconstruction of a legal past — the fallacy of the homogenous past. This assumes that everyone who lived in a given period shared a common perspective imposed by a common culture. The temptation to fall into it must be strong in law, where often the privileged texts are scripted by a relatively homogeneous élite of a very similar background, education and experience. Hirsch — quite correctly, it is submitted

— accepts that to speak of the "Victorian frame of mind" is a useful heuristic device: so too for the legal reader are similar statements like the Warren court, the inter-war courts, the great nineteenth-century decisions, etc. The third fallacy — and for Hirsch the most important — is the fallacy of the homogenous present-day perspective. This fallacy occurs when, particularly in criticism, the past is commented upon and their explicitly or implicitly compared with the present day in such a way that an assumption is made about the reader's historical perspective. In this way the critic writes his reader.

In addition to a chronological table I have provided the merest thumbnail sketch of what was happening on or around the very day the litigants dragged their weary feet up the steps to the font of justice. Obviously history cannot be reconstructed in this way. This is not the aim. Instead it is there as a simple reminder (especially for 18-year-olds who may not even have studied history at all), of the law as part of a wider social discourse.

It is hoped that the reader (including disobedient students) is convinced that a chronological table is worthwhile, not just in this law book but in all others. If not, at least the book can be used by the delict adept as a parlour game perhaps called "Trivial Lawsuits" — *viz.* "What case was decided in the same year as Maurice Chevalier died?"

ALPHABETICAL TABLE OF CASES

Ext./
Para.

Akram v. Commission for Racial Equality, 1994 G.W.D. 22–1372 .... 7.8.3
Alcock v. Chief Constable, South Yorkshire Police [1992] 1 A.C. 310 .... 8.4.4
Alford v. National Coal Board, 1951 S.L.T. 163 .... 22.5.17
Allan v. Barclay (1863) 2 M. 873 .... Ext. 48; 8.6.2; 10.7.5; 11.3.5;
                                                11.3.8; 11.3.9; 13.7.4; 13.7.5
Allen v. Flood [1898] A.C. 1 .... 7.5.20
Aloe Coal Co. v. Clark Equipment Co. (1987) 816 F. 2d. 110 .... 17.4.2
Anderson v. Glasgow D. C., 1987 S.L.T. 279 .... 20.12.8
——v. Lothian Health Board, 1996 Rep. L.R. 88 .... Ext. 60
——v. Marshall (1835) 13 S. 1130 .... 3.1.3
Angus v. Glasgow Corporation, 1977 S.L.T. 205 .... 22.2.3
Anns v. Merton London B. C. [1978] A.C. 728 .... 121.43; 13.1.6; 13.2.3; 13.2.6; 13.3.17;
                                 13.3.19; 13.3.25; 13.3.26; 13.3.27; 13.6.8;
                                 14.1.20; 14.1.30; 14.2.2; 15.4.2; 17.4.2
Argyll and Clyde Health Board v. Strathclyde R.C., 1988 S.L.T. 381 ...... Ext. 22; 5.10.1
Att.-Gen. v. Guardian Newspapers Ltd (No. 2) [1988] 3 W.L.R. 776 .... 4.3.6

Bain v. Fife Coal Co., 1935 S.C. 681 .... 19.1.5–7
Baker v. Willoughby [1970] A.C. 467 .... 10.8.2
Bankhead v. McCarthy, 1936 S.L.T. 144 .... 20.6.9
Banque Financière de la Cité SA v. Westgate Insurance Co. [1989] 2 All E.R. 952 ..... 13.2.6
Black v. Fife Coal Co., 1912 1 S.L.T. 20 .... 15.2.2
Blackburn v. Sinclair, 1984 S.L.T. 368 .... 13.10.2
Bolam v. Friern Hospital Committee [1957] 2 All E.R. 118 .... 9.4.5
Bonthrone v. S. of S. for Scotland, 1987 S.L.T. 34 .... Ext. 56
Borders R.C. v. Roxburgh D.C., 1989 S.L.T. 837 .... 5.4.2
Bourhill v. Young, 1942 S.C.(H.L.) 78 .... Ext. 40; 9.1.3; 9.1.8;
                                       11.3.5; 11.3.9; 18.1.3
Bowen v. Paramount Builders [1977] 1 N.Z.L.R. 394 .... 13.3.19; 17.4.2
Bradford (Mayor of) v. Pickles [1895] A.C. 587 .... 5.12.3; 5.13.2
Bravado Merchandising Services Ltd v. Mainstream Publishing (Edinburgh)
    Ltd, 1995 G.W.D. 39–1921 .... 7.4.4
British Motor Trade Association v. Salvadori [1949] Ch. 556 .... 7.9.2
——v. Gray, 1951 S.L.T. 247 .... Ext. 37
——v. Naylor, 1950, unreported 7.9.2
British Road Services v. Slater [1964] 1 W.L.R. 498 .... 5.10.5
Broder v. Saillard (1876) 2 Ch.D. 692 .... 5.1.8
Brown v. Rolls Royce, 1960 S.C.(H.L.) 22 .... 9.4.7
Brown's Trustees v. Hay (1898) 25 R. 1112 .... 6.2.3
Burnie Port Authority v. General Jones Pty Ltd (1994) 179 C.L.R. 520 .... 5.2.6
Burns v. North British Ry. Co., 1914 S.C. 754 .... 24.3.5

Caledonian Ry. Co. v. Greenock Corporation, 1971 2 S.L.T. 67 .... 5.1.7; 5.2.5
——v. Warwich (1897) 25 R.(H.L.) 1 .... 8.1.9
Cambridge Water Co. v. Eastern Counties Water Plc [1994] 2 A.C. 264 .... 5.2.6
Campbell v. Muir, 1908 S.C. 387 .... 5.13.2
——v. Kennedy (1864) 3 M. 121 .... Ext. 23; 5.7.4; 5.7.6

Canadian Pacific Ry. Co. v. Lockhart [1942] A.C. 591 .... 22.1.2
Candlewood Navigation Corp. Ltd v. Mitsui O.S.K. Lines Ltd [1986] A.C. 1 .... 13.5.2;
                                                                         13.9.4–5; 13.9.10
Caparo Industries v. Dickman [1990] 2 W.L.R. 358 .... 13.2.6
Carniner v. Northern and London Investment Trust [1951] A.C. 885 .... 5.10.5
Carrick Furniture House Ltd v. Paterson, 1978 S.L.T. (Notes) 48 .... 12.1.11
Carrick Jewellery Ltd v. Ortak, 1989 G.W.D. 35–1624 .... 7.2.3
Castle v. St Augustine Links (1922) 38 T.L.R. 615 .... 5.4.3
Caswell v. Powell Duffryn Associated Collieries [1940] A.C. 152 .... 9.3.2
Cattle v. Stockton Waterworks Co. (1875) L.R. 10 Q.B. 453 .... 12.1.44
Cavanagh v. Goodfreys of Dundee, February 28, 1996, unreported 19.6.2
Cellular Clothing Co. v. Maxton & Murray [1899] A.C. 326 .... 7.1.13
Christie v. Davey [1893] 1 Ch. 316 .... 5.12.3
Cleghorn v. Taylor (1856) 18 D. 664 .... 5.5.4–6; 5.7.2–6; 5.8.2; 5.10.5
Clunis v. Camden Health Authority [1996] T.L.R. 752 .... 20.9.2
Crawford v. Hill (1830) 5 Mor. 215 .... 6.2.3
Creswell v. Sirl [1948] 1 K.B. 241 .... 13.5.6
Crofter Hand Woven Harris Tweed Co. v. Veitch, 1942 S.C.(H.L.) 1 ...... Ext. 35; 7.9.5
Crotty v. McFarlane, January 27, 1891, unreported .... Ext. 86
Cunningham v. Philips (1868) 6 M. 926 .... 21.13.11
Curran v. Northern Ireland Co-owernship Housing Association Ltd [1987]
     A.C. 778 .... 14.2.2
Cushing v. Peter Walker & Sons Ltd [1941] 2 All E.R. 693 .... 5.10.5
Cuthbert v. Linklater, 1935 S.L.T. 94 .... Ext. 82
Cutler v. Wandsworth Stadium Ltd [1948] 1 K.B. 291 .... 15.2.3; 15.4.2

D & F Estates v. Church Commissioners [1988] 3 W.L.R. 368 .... 13.2.6; 13.5.7;
                                                            13.5.11–12; 13.6.2; 13.6.4; 17.4.3
Daily Mirror Newspapers Ltd v. Gardner [1968] 2 Q.B. 762 .... 7.10.2
Dalhanna Knitwear Co. Ltd v. Mohammed Ali, 1967 S.L.T. (Sh. Ct.) 74 .... 6.2.2
Dann v. Hamilton [1939] 1 K.B. 509 .... 20.6.9
Dash Ltd v. Philip King Tailoring, 1989 S.L.T. 39 .... 7.2.4
Davenport v. Corinthian Motor Policies at Lloyds, 1991 S.L.T. 774 .... Ext. 93
Davie v. Magistrates of Edinburgh, 1953 S.C. 34 .... 11.3.7
Defreitas v. O'Brien [1995] T.L.R. 86 .... 9.4.5
Denny v. Supplies and Transport Co. Ltd [1950] 2 K.B. 374 .... 17.4.4
De Silva v. Otto 1986 (S.) S.A. 538 (T) 18.4.4
Devine v. Colvilles, 1969 S.L.T. 154 .... Ext. 95
Donald v. Rutherford, 1984 S.L.T. 70 .... 20.12.8
Donoghue v. Stevenson, 1932 S.C.(H.L.) 31 .... Ext. 39; 5.2.3; 6.3.7; 6.3.10; 7.3.6;
                                                      9.1.8; 12.1.12; 12.1.16; 12.1.29;
                                                        13.3.12–28; 13.5.7–12; 13.7.6;
                                                       17.2.1; 17.4.3; 17.4.4; 22.9.3
Duff v. Highland and Islands Fire Board, 1995 S.L.T. 1362 .... 14.2.3
Dulieu v. White & Sons [1901] 2 K.B. 669 .... 8.3.8; 8.3.12
Dumbreck v. Addie & Sons (Collieries) Ltd, 1929 S.C.(H.L.) 51 .... 16.2.1; 16.3.2
Dunlop v. McGowans, 1979 S.C. 22 .... 20.10.2; 20.11.2
Dutton v. Bognor Regis U.D.C. [1972] 1 Q.B. 373 ... 13.3.17–19; 13.6.4; 14.2.2; 15.4.2
Dynamco v. Holland & Hannen & Cubitts (Scotland) Ltd, 1971 S.C. 257 .... Ext. 54

E. v. Dorset C. C. [1994] 3 W.L.R. 853 .... 14.2.3
East River Steamship Corpn. v. Transamerica Delaval (1986) 106 S.Ct. 2295 ... 17.3.4;
                                                                                             17.4.2
Eisten v. North British Ry. Co. (1870) 8 M. 980 .... 2.7.3
Elliot v. J. & C. Finney, 1989 S.L.T. 606 .... Ext. 79
English v. Wilsons and Clyde Coal Co., 1937 S.C.(H.L.) 46 .... Ext. 70
Evans v. Glasgow D. C., 1978 S.L.T. 17 .... 12.1.11; 12.1.42
—v. Stein (1904) 7 F. 65 .... 22.5.4

Evren Warnink v. Townend & Son Ltd [1979] A.C. 731 .... 7.2.5; 7.3.6
Ewing v. Mar (1851) 14 D. 314 .... 3.2.3

F.C. Finance Ltd v. Brown & Son, 1969 S.L.T. (Sh.Ct.) 41 .... Ext. 29; 6.2.3
Fairlie v. Carruthers, 1996 S.L.T. (Sh.Ct.) 56 .... Ext. 69; 6.10.3; 18.2.4
Fanton's Case [1932] 2 K.B. 309 .... 19.1.5
Farr v. Butters Bros. & Co. [1932] 2 K.B. 606 .... 16.2.1; 17.4.4
Faulds v. Townsend (1861) 23 D. 437 .... 6.3.7
Feely v. Co-op. Wholesale Ltd, 1990 S.L.T. 547 .... 16.2.1
Fergusson (Alex.) & Co. Ltd v. Matthews, McClay & Manson Ltd,
    1989 S.L.T. 795 .... 7.4.4
Findlay v. Blaylock, 1937 S.C. 21 .... Ext. 36; 7.9.5
Fleming v. Gemmill (1907) 15 S.L.T. 691 .... 13.9.4
——v. Hislop (1886) 13 R. (H.L.) 43 .... 5.1.8
Forbes v. Dundee C. C., 1997 G.W.D. 11–450 .... 14.2.3
Forsyth v. A. F. Stoddard & Co. Ltd, 1995 S.L.T. 51 .... 20.12.8
Fowler v. Tierney, 1974 S.L.T. (Notes) 23 .... 20.6.10
Fraser v. Greater Glasgow Health Board, 1996 Rep. L.R. 58 .... Ext. 59
Froom v. Butcher [1976] Q.B. 286 .... 20.4.2
Frost v. Chief Constable, South Yorkshire Police [1995] T.L.R. 379 .... 8.4.8

G.A. Estates Ltd v. Caviapen Trustee Ltd (No. 1), 1993 S.L.T. 1037 .... 5.2.5
Gault v. Philip, 1984 S.L.T. 28 .... 3.3.8
Gee v. Metropolitan Ry. Co. (1873) 8 Q.B. 161 .... 24.3.5
Gemmell v. Bank of Scotland, Nov. 11, 1996, unreported 6.4.5
Gillon v. Chief Constable, Strathclyde Police, 1995 G.W.D. 31–1618;
    1996 Rep. L.R. 165 .... 12.2.5
Glanna v. Glasgow Corporation, 1950 S.L.T. 2 .... 15.2.2
Goh Choon Seng v. Lee Kim Soo [1925] A.C. 550 .... 22.1.2
Gold v. Haringey Health Authority [1987] 3 W.L.R. 649 .... 9.4.5
Goldman v. Hargrave [1967] 1 A.C. 645 .... 12.1.35
Gordon v. Grampian Health Board, 1991 S.C.L.R. 213 .... 24.7.3
Gorebridge Co-operative Society v. Turnbull, 1952 S.L.T. (Sh. Ct.) 91 .... 6.2.2
Gourock Ropework Co. Ltd v. Greenock Corporation, 1966 S.L.T. 125 .... 5.1.10
Graham v. David P. Hall, 1996 S.L.T. 596 .... 8.4.7
—— (Thomas) & Co. Ltd v. Church of Scotland General Trustees,
    1982 S.L.T. (Sh.Ct.) 26 .... 12.1.11; 12.1.36
Grant v. Australian Knitting Mills [1936] A.C. 85 .... 8.2.6; 17.4.4
Gray v. Dunlop, 1954 S.L.T. (Sh. Ct.) 75 .... 5.9.3–4
Greater Nottingham Co-operative Society v. Cementation Piling and
    Foundations Ltd [1988] 3 W.L.R. 396 .... 13.5.9–12

Haig & Co. v. Forth Blending Co., 1954 S.C. 35 .... Ext. 33; 7.2.3–5
Hall v. Fairfield Shipbuilding Co., 1964 S.C.(H.L.) 72 .... 15.3.10
Hallet v. Nicholson, 1979 S.C. 1 .... 14.1.22
Hambrook v. Stokes Bros. [1925] 1 K.B. 141 .... 8.3.3–13; 8.4.2
Hamilton v. Fife Health Board, 1993 S.L.T. 624 .... Ext. 92
Hanlon v. Cuthbertson, 1981 S.L.T. (Notes) 57 .... 20.5.2
Harris v. Abbey National plc, 1996 G.W.D. 33–1993 .... 6.4.5
——v. Wyre Forest D.C. [1989] 2 W.L.R. 790 .... 13.2.4
Hart v. Frame (1839) McL. & Rob. 595 .... 9.3.3
Hay, Feb. 13, 1801 (F.C.) 6.5.7
——v. Littlejohn (1666) Mar. 13974 .... 5.8.2
Haynes v. Harwood [1935] 1 K.B. 146 .... 12.1.16; 12.1.32; 12.1.43
Heaven v. Pender (1883) 11 Q.B.D. 503 .... 8.1.4; 8.1.22–23

Hedley Byrne & Co. Ltd *v.* Heller & Partners Ltd [1964] A.C. 465 .... 6.3.10; 13.1.1;
                                    13.1.8; 13.2.3; 13.2.4; 13.2.6; 13.3.3;
                            13.3.17; 13.3.20; 13.3.21; 13.3.25; 13.6.8; 17.4.2
Henderson *v.* John Stuart (Farms) Ltd, 1963 S.C. 245; 1963 S.L.T. 22 ... Ext. 67; 18.5.6
—*v.* Merrett Syndicates [1995] 2 A.C. 145 .... 13.2.2
—*v.* Chief Constable, Fife Police, 1988 S.L.T. 361 .... Ext. 18
Hewitt *v.* Edinburgh and District Lathsplitters Association (1906) 14 S.L.T. 489 ..... 7.11.2
Hill *v.* Chief Constable, West Yorkshire Police [1988] 2 W.L.R. 1049 ...... 14.2.2; 14.2.3
Hodge & Sons *v.* Anglo American Oil Co. (1922) 12 Ll.L.Rep. 183 .... 8.1.9
Holywood Silver Fox Farm *v.* Emmett [1936] 2 K.B. 468 .... 5.12.3
Home Office *v.* Dorset Yacht Co. [1970] A.C. 1004 .... 12.1.12; 12.1.16; 12.1.19;
                                    12.1.22; 12.1.29; 12.1.31; 13.1.6;
                            13.3.16–19; 14.1.18–19; 14.1.30; 14.2.2
Hotson *v.* East Berkshire Health Authority [1987] A.C. 750 .... 10.2.4
Hughes *v.* Lord Advocate, 1963 S.L.T. 150 .... Ext. 41; 12.1.11
Hunter *v.* British Steel Corporation, 1980 S.L.T. 31 .... Ext. 71
—*v.* Hanley, 1955 S.C. 200 .... Ext. 43

I.R.C. *v.* Muller & Co.'s Margarine Ltd [1901] A.C. 217 .... 7.3.6
Inglis *v.* London Midland and Scottish Ry. Co., 1941 S.C. 551 .... Ext. 96

J.E.B. Fasteners Ltd *v.* Marks, Bloom & Co. [1981] 3 All E.R. 289 .... 13.2.3
Jackson *v.* Harrison (1978) 138 C.L.R. 438 .... 20.8.3; 20.8.6; 20.8.7
Jag Shakti (The) 13.9.7
James Burrough Distilleries plc *v.* Speymalt, 1989 G.W.D. 1867. .... 7.4.4; 23.5.2
Jobling *v.* Associated Dairies Ltd [1982] A.C. 794 .... 10.8.2
Joel *v.* Morison (1834) 6 C. & P. 501 .... 22.1.3
Johnston *v.* Orr Ewing (1882) 7 App. Cas. 219 .... 7.1.10–12
Johnstone *v.* Traffic Commissioners, 1990 S.L.T. 409 .... 14.2.3
Jones *v.* Dept. of Employment [1988] 2 W.L.R. 493 .... 14.2.2
—*v.* Hulton & Co. [1909] 2 K.B. 444, aff. (H.L.) Dec. 6, 1909 .... 21.5.1; 21.5.5
Junior Books *v.* The Veitchi Co., 1982 S.L.T. 492 .... Ext. 52; 12.1.43;
                                    13.5.1–12; 13.6.2–4; 17.4.2

Kalfelis *v.* Bankhous Schröder (189/87); [1988] E.C.R. 5565 .... 23.1.10; 21.1.12–15
Kay *v.* I.T.W. Ltd [1968] 1 Q.B. 140 .... 22.5.17
Kay's Tutor *v.* Ayrshire and Arran Health Board, 1987 S.L.T. 577 .... Ext. 44
Keenan *v.* Rolls-Royce, 1970 S.L.T. 90 .... 19.3.3
Kelly *v.* Edinburgh D.C., 1983 S.L.T. 593 .... 9.4.4
Kennedy *v.* Glenbelle, 1996 S.L.T. 1186 .... 2.11.2; 5.4.2; 5.6.2; 5.10.1
Kerr *v.* Earl of Orkney (1857) 20 D. 298 .... 5.1.3–10; 20.1.4
King *v.* Liverpool C. C. [1986] 1 W.L.R. 890 .... 12.1.42
Kirby *v.* National Coal Board, 1959 S.L.T. 7 .... 22.1.2; 22.5.13
Kirkcaldy D. C. *v.* Household Manufacturing Ltd, 1987 S.L.T. 617 ..... 2.10.2–4; 23.2.2

Lord Advocate *v.* Scotsman Publications Ltd, 1989 S.L.T. 705 .... Ext. 20
Laing *v.* Tayside Health Board, 1996 Rep. L.R. 51 .... 24.6.2
Lamb *v.* Camden L.B.C. [1981] 2 All E.R. 408 .... 12.1.42
Lamond *v.* Glasgow Corporation, 1968 S.L.T. 291 .... 5.4.3
Lane *v.* Holloway [1968] 1 Q.B. 379 .... 3.1.4–5
Lang Brothers Ltd *v.* Goldwell, 1982 S.L.T. 309 .... Ext. 22
Launchbury *v.* Morgans [1973] A.C. 127 .... 22.4.2
Laurent *v.* Lord Advocate (1869) 7 M. 607 .... 5.7.4
Leask *v.* Burt, 1893 1 S.L.T. 270 .... 3.3.4
Lees *v.* Dunkerley Bros. [1911] A.C. 5 .... 15.1.6
Le Lievre *v.* Gould (1893) 1 Q.B.D. 503 .... 8.1.23
— *v.* — (1893) 1 Q.B. 491 .... 8.1.5

Leigh & Sillivan Ltd v. Aliakmon Shipping Co. Ltd [1986] A.C. 785 .... 12.1.43; 13.5.2; 13.9.7–10
Levin v. Caledonia Produce (Holdings) Ltd, 1975 S.L.T. (Notes) 69 .... 4.1.2
Lindley v. Rutter [1981] 1 Q.B. 128 .... 3.3.13
Lloyds Bank v. Bundy [1974] 3 W.L.R. 501 .... 13.4.4
London and South of England Building Society v. Stone [1983] 1 W.L.R. 1242 ...... 13.1.11
London Passenger Transport Board v. Upson [1949] A.C. 155 .... 15.4.2
Longworth v. Coppas International (U.K.) Ltd, 1985 S.L.T. 111 .... 19.2.2
Lonrho plc v. Fayed [1989] 2 All E.R. 65 .... 7.10.4
— v. Shell Petroleum Ltd [1982] A.C. 173 .... 7.6.2
Lumley v. Guy (1853) 2 E. & B. 216 .... 7.5.20

McAulay v. Dunlop, 1926 S.L.T. 341 .... 22.5.17
McCaig v. Langan, 1964 S.L.T. 121 .... 20.6.9
MacColl v. Hoo, 1983 S.L.T. (Sh. Ct.) 23 ....Ext. 24
Macdonald v. Glasgow Western Hospitals Board, 1954 S.L.T. 226 .... 14.1.27–28
McElroy v. McAllister, 1949 S.C. 110 .... 23.5.1
Macfarlane v. Black & Co. (1887) 14 R. 870 .... 21.3.3; 21.13.9
McGhee v. National Coal Board, 1983 S.L.T. 14 .... Ext. 46, 10.1.6–8; 24.6.3
McGlone v. British Railways Board, 1966 S.L.T. 2 .... Ext. 63; 16.5.4; 16.5.8
McGowan v. Lord Advocate 1972 S.L.T. 188 .... 24.7.3
— (and Mullen) v. Barr & Co., 1929 S.C. 461 .... 8.1.14; 8.1.24
McGregor v. Shepherd (1946) 62 Sh.Ct.Rep. 139 .... 3.1.2
Mackay v. Borthwick, 1982 S.L.T. 265 ....Ext. 75
— v. McCankie (1883) 10 R. 537 .... 21.1.1
McKendrick v. Sinclair, 1972 S.L.T. 110 .... 2.7.2; 3.1.4
Mackersie v. Dickson (1848) 11 D. 4 .... 3.2.3
McKew v. Holland & Hannen & Cubitts (Scotland) Ltd, 1970 S.L.T. 68 .... Ext. 47
McKillen v. Barclay Curle & Co. Ltd, 1967 S.L.T. 41 .... Ext. 49
M'Laren v. Caldwell's Paper Mill Co. Ltd, 1973 S.L.T. 158 .... 24.8.2
McLaren v. Ritchie, July 8, 1856, unreported .... Ext. 85
McLaughlan v. Craig, 1948 S.L.T. 483 .... 5.1.6–8; 18.1.5
McLaughlin v. O'Brien [1983] A.C. 410 .... 8.4.3–5
— v. Orr Pollock & Co. (1894) 22 R. 38 .... 21.13.9; 21.13.12
McMullan v. Lochgelly Iron and Coal Co., 1933 S.C.(H.L.) 64 .... Ext. 57
McNair v. Don & Co. (1932) 48 Sh. Ct. Rep. 6.4.5
McNeil Estates v. Faulds of Girvan, 1992 G.W.D. 1–42 .... 17.2.4
MacRae v. Henderson, 1989 S.L.T. 523 .... 9.4.4
Mains v. Uniroyal Englebert Tyres Ltd, 1995 S.L.T. 1115 .... 15.7.4
Maloco (and Smith) v. Littlewoods Organisation Ltd, 1987 S.L.T. 425 .... Ext. 50; 9.2.2; 13.5.2
Marc Rich & Co v. Bishop Rock Ltd [1996] 1 A.C. 211 .... 14.2.3
Martin v. Bell Ingram, 1986 S.L.T. 575 ....Ext. 51
Mason v. Orr (1901) 4 F. 220 .... 3.2.3
May and Burdett (1846) 9 Q.B. 101 .... 20.1.7
Merkur Island Shipping Corp. v. Laughton [1983] 2 A.C. 570 .... 7.10.2; 7.10.4
Mersey Docks and Harbour Board v. Coggins and Griffith (Liverpool) [1947] A.C. 1 ....22.5.18
Middleton v. Douglas, 1991 S.L.T. 726 .... 2.11.2
Miller v. Glasgow D. C., 1989 S.L.T. 44 .... 2.11.2
Milligan v. Henderson, 1915 S.C. 1030 .... 18.1.7
Mills v. Winchester Diocesan Board [1989] 2 All E.R. 317 .... 13.2.6
Mitchell v. Crassweller (1853) 13 C.B. 237 .... 22.1.3
— v. McCulloch, 1976 S.C. 1 .... Ext. 75; 23.6.1
Mogul Steamship Co. v. McGregor, Gow & Co. (1888) 21 Q.B.D. 544 .... 7.5.7–10
Monk v. Warbey [1935] 1 K.B. 75 .... 15.2.2; 22.4.2
More v. Boyle, 1967 S.L.T. (Sh. Ct.) 38 ....Ext. 27

Morris v. Murray, 1990 N.L.J. 1459 .... 20.7.4
Morrison v. J. Kelly & Sons Ltd, 1970 S.L.T. 198 .... 24.7.3
Morrison Steamship Co. Ltd v. Greystoke Castle [1947] A.C. 265 .... 13.2.6; 13.3.14
Muir v. Cumbernauld and Kilsyth D. C., 1993 S.L.T. 287 .... 10.6.3
Muirhead v. Industrial Tank Specialities [1985] 3 All E.R. 705 ...... 8.2.5; 13.5.2; 13.6.5
Mull Shellfish Ltd v. Golden Lea Produce Ltd, 1992 S.L.T. 703 .... 13.10.4
Mullen (and McGowan) v. Barr & Co., 1929 S.C. 461 .... 8.1.14; 8.1.24
Munro v. Morrison, 1980 S.L.T. (Notes) 87 .... 3.3.15
Murphy v. Brentwood D. C. [1990] 3 W.L.R. 414 ..... 13.2.6; 13.6.4; 14.2.2; 15.4.2; 17.4.3
Mustard v. Paterson, 1923 S.C. 142 .... Ext. 30

Nacap Ltd v. Moffat Plant Ltd, 1987 S.L.T. 221 .... 13.9.6; 13.9.10; 13.10.2
Nimmo v. Alexander Cowan & Sons Ltd, 1967 S.C. (H.L.) 79; 1967 S.L.T. 277 ...... Ext. 58;
                                                                                      15.7.4; 16.2.2
Noble's Trs. v. Economic Forestry (Scotland) Ltd, 1988 S.L.T. 662 .... 5.4.2
North Pacific Steamship Co. Ltd v. Canadian National Ry. [1992]
    91 D.L.R. (4th) 289 .... 13.10.4
North Scottish Helicopters Ltd v. United Technologies Corpn. Inc.,
    1988 S.L.T. 77 .... Ext 55
Norwich Union Insurance Society v. Covell Matthews Partnership,
    1987 S.L.T. 452 .... 13.5.12; 13.6.3

O'Donnell v. Murdoch McKenzie & Co., 1967 S.C.(H.L.) 63 .... Ext. 97
O'Hara v. Central S.M.T. Co., 1941 S.C. 754 .... 24.3.6
Okehampton (The) 13.9.10
Oliver v. Saddler & Co., 1929 S.C. (H.L.) 94 .... 8.1.8
O'Neil v. Coyle, 1995 G.W.D. 21–1185 .... 18.4.2
Ormrod v. Crosville Motor Services [1953] 1 W.L.R. 1120 .... 22.3.2; 22.4.2
Oropesa (The) [1943] P. 32 .... 10.7.5
Overseas Tankship (U.K.) Ltd v. Morts Dock & Engineering Co. Ltd [1961]
    A.C. 388 (The Wagon Mound No. 1) 11.3.6

Pacific Associates v. Baxter [1989] 2 All E.R. 159 .... 13.2.6
Page v. Smith [1995] 2 W.L.R. 655 .... 8.4.6; 11.4.4
Palmer v. Wick, etc., Co. Ltd (1894) 2 S.L.T. 91 .... Ext. 15
Park v. Tractor Shovels, 1980 S.L.T. 94 .... Ext. 90
Paterson v. Welch (1893) 20 R. 744 .... Ext. 84; 21.13.4; 21.13.13
Payton & Co. v. Snelling, Lampard & Co. [1901] A.C. 308 .... 7.1.12
Pegasus Security Ltd v. Gilbert, 1989 G.W.D. 26–1186 .... 7.4.4
Peggie v. Clark (1868) 7 M. 89 .... 3.3.4
Pepper v. Hart [1993] A.C. 593 .... 1.12.1
Perl (P.) (Exporters) Ltd v. Camden L.B.C. 12.1.31; 12.1.43
Perry v. Sidney Phillips & Son [1982] 1 W.L.R. 1297 .... 13.1.11
Pirelli General Cable Works Ltd v. Oscar Fabler & Partners [1983] 2 A.C. 1 .. 20.10.2;
                                                                                      20.10.5
Pitts v. Hunt [1991] 1 Q.B. 24 .... 20.8.5
Polemis (The) (1942) 3 K.B. 560 .... 11.3.9
Polemis and Furness, Withy & Co, Re [1921] 3 K.B. 560 .... 8.3.9–10; 11.3.6
Porter v. Strathclyde R.C. unreported 10.6.3
Pullar v. Window Clean, 1956 S.L.T. 17 .... 15.2.2

Quackenbush v. Ford Motor Co. (1915) 167 App. Div. 433, N.Y., S.C. 17.4.2
Quinn v. Leatham [1901] A.C. 495 .... 7.5.16; 7.5.20; 7.5.21; 7.9.6; 7.11.2

R.H.M. Bakeries (Scotland) Ltd v. Strathclyde R.C., 1985 S.L.T. 214 . Ext. 21; 5.3.3–8;
                                                                     5.10.1; 5.10.5; 21.6.4

Ramsay v. MacLay (1890) 18 R. 130 .... Ext. 81
Read v. J. Lyons & Co. Ltd [1947] A.C. 156 .... 5.1.6
Reavis v. Clan Line Steamers, 1925 S.C. 725 .... 13.7.5
Renfrew Golf Club v. Ravenstone Securities Ltd, 1984 S.L.T. 170 .... Ext. 78
Richards v. Great Eastern Ry. (1873) 28 L.T. 711 .... 24.3.5
Ritchie v. Purdie (1833) 11 S. 771 .... Ext. 26
Rivtow Marine Ltd v. Washington Iron Works (1973) 40 D.L.R. (3d) 530 .... 13.3.25;
                                                                                                                          17.4.2
Robbie v. Graham & Sibbald, 1989 S.L.T. 870 .... 13.3.5
Roberts v. Ramsbotton [1980] 1 All E.R. 7 .... 22.8.2
Robertson v. Forth Road Bridge (No. 1), 1994 S.L.T. 566 .... 8.4.6
— v. Forth Road Bridge (No. 2), 1994 S.L.T. 568 .... 8.4.6
— v. Turnbull, 1982 S.L.T. 96 .... 14.1.9
Roe v. Wade, 410 US 113 (1973) 22.9.4
Rookes v. Barnard [1964] A.C. 1129 .... 3.1.5; 7.11.1–2
Rose v. Colville's Ltd, 1950 S.L.T. (Notes) 72 .... Ext. 72
Ross v. Associated Portland Cement Manufacturers [1964] 1 W.L.R. 768 ..... 24.5.1; 24.5.4
— v. Bryce, 1972 S.L.T. (Sh.Ct.) 76 .... Ext. 17
— v. S. of S. for Scotland, 1990 S.L.T. 13 .... 14.2.3
Rossleigh v. Leader Cars, 1987 S.L.T. 355 .... 7.10.2
Rowling v. Takaro Properties [1988] 2 W.L.R. 418 .... 13.2.6; 14.2.23
Roxburgh v. Seven Seas Engineering Ltd, 1980 S.L.T. (Notes) 49 .... 4.1.3; 5.1.6
Russell v. F. W. Woolworth & Co. Ltd, 1982 S.L.T. 428 .... 2.10.2; 2.10.4; 23.2.2
Rylands v. Fletcher (1868) L.R. 3 H.L. 330 .... 5.1.3–10; 5.2.6; 18.1.4–6

S.C.M. Ltd v. W. J. Whittall [1971] 1 Q.B. 337 .... 13.7.7
S.S. Baron Vernon v. S.S. Metagama, 1928 S.C.(H.L.) 21 .... 10.7.5
Saed v. Waeed, 1996 S.L.T. (Sh.Ct.) 39 .... 6.4.5
Scala Ballroom Ltd v. Ratcliffe [1958] 1 W.L.R. 1057 .... 7.6.3
Scobie v. Steele & Wilson Ltd, 1963 S.L.T. (Notes) 45 .... Ext. 89
Scott v. EDL Pipeworks, 1995 S.L.T. 561 .... 19.6.2
— v. London and St Katherine Docks Co. (1865) 3 H. & C. 596 .... 24.1.2
Scott's Trustees v. Moss (1889) 17 R. 32 .... 12.1.16
Scott Lithgow v. G.E.C. Electrical Products, 1992 S.L.T. 244 .... Ext. 16; 13.6.1–4
Sedleigh Denfield v. O'Callaghan [1940] A.C. 880 .... 5.1.8
Seixo v. Provezende (1865) L.R. 1 Ch. 192 .... 7.1.10
Shields v. Shearer, 1914 1 S.L.T. 360; 1913 2 S.L.T. 68 .... 3.3.4
Sidaway v. Bethlem Royal Hospital [1985] A.C. 871 .... 9.4.5
Sim v. Stretch (1936) 52 T.L.R. 669 .... 21.13.10
Simaan Construction Co. v. Pilkington Glass Ltd (No 2) [1988] 2 W.L.R. 761 ..... 13.5.2–10
Sime v. Sutcliffe Catering (Scotland) Ltd, 1990 S.L.T. 687 .... 22.6.3
Simpson & Co. v. Thomson (1877) 5 R.(H.L.) 40 .... 13.7.4–5; 13.9.5; 13.9.9
Sinclair v. Falkirk D. C., 1995 G.W.D. 40–2099 .... 16.4.4
Sion v. Hampstead Health Authority [1994] 5 Med. L.R. 170 .... 8.4.4
Six Constructions Ltd v. Humbert (32/88); [1989] E.C.R. 341 .... 23.1.10, 23.1.12
Slater v. Clay Cross Co. Ltd [1956] 2 Q.B. 264 .... 16.5.8
Smith v. Bush (Etric S.) [1989] 2 W.L.R. 790 .... 13.2.4–6
— v. Jenkins (1970) 117 C.L.R. 397 .... 20.8.3
— v. Leech Brain & Co. Ltd [1962] 2 Q.B. 405 .... 11.3.6
— v. Leurs (1945) 70 C.L.R. 256 .... 12.1.31
— (and Maloco) v. Littlewoods Organisations Ltd, 1987 S.L.T. 425 .... Ext 50;
                                                                                                                        9.2.2; 13.5.2
Sorrell v. Smith [1925] A.C. 700 .... 7.5.17; 7.5.21
Sparham-Souter v. Town and Country Developments (Essex) Ltd [1976]
     Q.B. 858 .... 13.3.17; 20.10.2
Squires v. Perth and Kinross D. C., 1986 S.L.T. 301 .... 2.1.12; 12.1.39–41; 12.2.4
Stansbie v. Troman [1948] 2 K.B. 48 .... 12.1.31; 12.1.43

Steel v. Glasgow Iron and Steel Co., 1944 S.C. 237 .... 11.3.9
Steele v. Scottish Daily Record and Sunday Mail Ltd, 1970 S.L.T. 53 .... Ext 87
Stephen v. Scottish Boatowners Mutual Insurance Association, 1989 S.L.T. 52 .... 9.4.4
Stewart v. H. A. Brechin & Co., 1959 S.L.T. (Notes) 45 .... 13.1.11; 13.1.12
—v. London, Midland and Scottish Ry. Co., 1944 S.L.T. 13 .... 2.7.3
Stevenson v. A. J. Stephen (Builders) Ltd, 1995 G.W.D. 21–1145 .... 17.4.3
Storey v. Ashton, (1869) L.R. 4 Q.B. 476 .... 12.1.3
Stovin v. Wise [1996] 3 W.L.R. 388 .... 14.2.3

Tate & Lyle Foods and Distribution Ltd v. G.L.C. [1983] 2 A.C. 509 .... 13.5.2–4
Taylor v. Shieldness Product Ltd [1994] PIQR 329 .... 8.4.4
Taylorson v. Somerset Health Authority [1993] 4 Med. L.R. 34 .... 8.4.4
Telfer v. Glasgow D.C., 1974 S.L.T. (Notes) 51 .... 16.2.2
Tennent v. Earl of Glasgow (1864) 2 M.(H.L.) 22 .... Ext. 73
Thomson v. Sinclair, 1992 G.W.D. 8–439 .... 17.2.4
— (D.C.) & Co. v. Deakin [1952] 2 All E.R. 361 .... 7.10.2
Titchener v. British Railways Board, 1984 S.L.T. 192 .... Ext. 64; 20.7.3
Torquay Hotel Co. Ltd v. Cousins [1969] 2 Ch. 106 .... 7.10.2
Torrack v. Corpamerica Inc. (1958) 144 A 2d. 703 .... 12.1.37
Treadwells' Drifters Inc. v. RCL Ltd, 1993 G.W.D. 26–161 .... 7.4.4
Tredget and Tredget v. Bexley Health Authority [1994] 5 Med.L.R. 178 .... 8.4.4
Twomax Ltd v. Dickson McFarlane & Robinson, 1983 S.L.T. 98 .... 13.2.3

Vine Products Ltd v. MacKenzie & Co. Ltd [1969] R.P.C. 1 .... 7.3.7
Vyner v. Waldenbert Brothers [1946] K.B. 50 .... 10.3.3

Waddell v. Roxburgh (1894) 21 R. 883 .... 21.13.13
Wagon Mound (The), see Overseas Tankships (U.K.) Ltd v. Morts Dock &
    Engineering Co. Ltd [1961] A.C. 388 .... 10.3.7–9; 11.3.6
Walker v, Pitlochry Motor Co., 1930 S.C. 565 .... 8.4.3
Wallace v. Glasgow D.C. 1985 S.L.T. 23 .... 16.2.2
Ward v. Chief Constable, Strathclyde Police, 1991 S.L.T. 292 .... 14.2.3
Wardlaw v. Bonnington Castings, 1956 S.C.(H.L.) 26 .... Ext. 45; 10.5.4–6; 19.6.2
Watt v. Jamieson, 1954 S.L.T. 56 .... 5.1.8–9
Waugh v. Ayrshire Post Ltd (1894) 21 R. 326 .... 21.13.13
—v. James K. Allan Ltd, 1964 S.C.(H.L.) 102 .... Ext. 91
Weir v. Wyport, 1992 S.L.T. 579 .... Ext. 77
Weld-Blundell v. Stephens [1920] A.C. 956 .... 12.1.30
Weller & Co. v. Foot and Mouth Disease Research Institute [1966] 1 Q.B. 569 .... 13.7.7
Western Bank Liquidators v. Douglas (1860) 22 D. 447 .... 5.9.5
Wickham Holdings Ltd v. Brooke House Motors Ltd [1967] 1 W.L.R. 295 ... 6.2.3; 6.4.3
Williams v. A. & W. Hemphill Ltd, 1966 S.C.(H.L.) 31 .... Ext. 88; 22.5.13
—v. Natural Life Health Foods, January 9, 1997, unreported 22.4.2
Wilsher v. Essex Area Health Authority [1988] A.C. 1074 .... 10.2.4; 10.6.3
Wilson v. Merry & Cunninghame (1868) 6 M. (H.L.) 84 .... 19.1.8
—v. McCaffrey, 1989 G.W.D. 1–37 .... 14.2.3
Winkfield (The) [1902] P. 42 .... 13.9.10
Winnick v. Dick, 1984 S.L.T. 185 .... Ext. 76
Wooldridge v. Summer [1963] 2 Q.B. 43 .... 20.7.4
Wragg v. D. C. Thomson & Co. Ltd, 1909 2 S.L.T. 315 and 409 .... Ext. 83
Wringe v. Cohen [1940] 1 K.B. 229 .... 5.10.5

X v. Bedfordshire County Council [1995] 3 All E.R. 353 .... 14.2.3

Yeun Kun Yeu v. Att.-Gen. of Hong Kong [1988] A.C. 175 .... 13.2.6; 13.6.5;
                                                                            14.2.2; 14.2.3
Young v. Bankier Distillery Co. (1983) 20 R. (H.L.) 76 .... 5.13.2
— (John) & Co. Ltd v. O'Donnell, 1958 S.L.T. (Notes) 46 .... 22.5.18

ALPHABETICAL TABLE OF STATUTES

Animals (Scotland) Act 1987 .... Ext. 32, 5.2.3; 5.10.3;
          6.10.3; 18.2.3; 18.3.1; 18.4.3; 18.5.3

Building (Scotland) Act 1959 .... 14.2.3

Civil Evidence (Scotland) Act 1988 .... 24.2.2; 24.7.3
Civil Jurisdiction and Judgments Act 1982 .... 23.1.11
Coal Mines Act 1911 .... 15.1.2–9; 19.1.2; 19.1.5
Congenital Disabilities (Civil Liability) Act 1976 .... 17.1.8
Conspiracy and Protection of Property Act 1875 .... 3.3.8
Consumer Protection Act 1987 .... 5.10.3; 8.2.6; 17.1.1; 16.3.1 *et seq.*
Criminal Justice (Scotland) Act 1980 .... 3.3.5; 3.3.7; 12.1.11; 12.1.15

Damages (Scotland) Act 1976 .... 1.12.1; 22.9.2–7
Damages (Scotland) Act 1993 .... 1.12.1
Dangerous Wild Animals Act 1976 .... 18.3.2
Defamation Act 1952 .... 21.6.3
Defamation Act 1996 .... 21.6.4

Factories Acts 1937 .... 19.5.1
Factories Acts 1961 .... 15.3.1–10; 16.2.2; 19.3.2 *et seq.*
Fatal Accidents Act 1976 .... 17.1.8

Guard Dogs Act 1975 .... 18.3.3

Hire Purchase Act 1964 .... 6.3.4; 6.3.13
Hotel Proprietors Act 1956 .... 6.7.1; 6.7.8

Law Reform (Contributory Negligence) Act 1945 .... 17.1.8; 18.3.2; 20.3.1
Law Reform (Husband and Wife) Act 1984 .... 7.8.2
Law Reform (Personal Injuries) Act 1948 .... 19.2.2

National Health Service (Scotland) Act 1972 .... 14.1.3–28

Occupiers' Liability (Scotland) Act 1960 .... 5.2.3; 16.1.1; 16.2.1–3;
          16.3.1–4; 16.5.1–4; 16.5.8; 16.5.4; 19.8.5

Police (Scotland) Act 1967 .... 3.3.4; 3.3.10
Prescription and Limitation (Scotland) Act 1973 .... 20.10.5; 20.12.5
Private International Law (Miscellaneous Provisions) Act 1995 .... Ext. 94
Public Health Act 1936 .... 15.4.2

Road Traffic Act 1972 .... 20.6.1–10; 20.12.1; 22.4.2

Security Services Act 1989 .... 4.4.2
Sewerage (Scotland) Act 1968 .... 5.1.–3; 5.1.11

Trade Disputes Act 1906 .... 7.5.1; 7.11.1
Trade Marks Act 1905 .... 7.5.2

Trespass (Scotland) Act 1865 .... 3.3.1–4

Unfair Contract Terms Act 1977 .... 13.2.5

Workmen's Compensation Act 1925 .... 15.1.1; 15.1.10

CHRONOLOGICAL TABLE OF CASES
AND STATUTES

1660   Charles II restored to throne
Hay v. Littlejohn (1666)

1800   Napoleon Bonaparte became First Consul of French Republic
Hay (1801)

1830   First passenger railway opened - first fatal injury
Crawford v. Hill (1830)
Ritchie v. Purdie (1833)
Joel v. Morison (1834)
Anderson v. Marshall (1835)
Hart v. Frame (1839)

1840   Paganini died
May and Burdett (1846)
Mackersie v. Dickson (1848)
Pupils Protection (Scotland) Act 1849

1850   Liszt conducted premiere of Wagner's *Lohengrin*
Ewing v. Mar (1851)
Lumley v. Guy (1853)
Mitchell v. Crassweller (1853)
Cleghorn v. Taylor (1856)
McLaren v. Ritchie (1856)
Kerr v. Earl of Orkney (1857)

1860   Abraham Lincoln elected President
Western Bank Liquidators v. Douglas (1860)
Faulds v. Townsend (1861)
Allan v. Barclay (1863)
Campbell v. Kennedy (1864)
Tennent v. Earl of Glasgow (1864)
Trespass (Scotland) Act 1865
Scott v. London and St Katherine Docks Co. (1865)
Seixo v. Provezende (1865)
Peggie v. Clark (1868)
Cunningham v. Philips (1868)
Rylands v. Fletcher (1868)
Wilson v. Merry & Cunninghame (1868)
Laurent v. Lord Advocate (1869)
Storey v. Ashton (1869)

1870   Prussia defeated France in Franco-Prussian war
Eisten v. North British Ry. Co. (1870)

Gee v. Metropolitan Ry. Co. (1873)
Richards v. Great Eastern Ry. (1873)
Conspiracy and Protection of Property Act 1875
Cattle v. Stockton Waterworks Co. (1875)
Broder v. Saillard (1876)
Simpson & Co. v. Thomson (1877)

1880   War declared on Britain by the Boers
Johnston v. Orr Ewing (1882)
Heaven v. Pender (1883)
Mackay v. McCankie (1883)
Fleming v. Hislop (1886)
Macfarlane v. Black & Co. (1887)
Mogul Steamship Co. v. McGregor, Gow & Co. (1888)
Judicial Factors (Scotland) Act 1889
Scott's Trustees v. Moss (1889)

1890   Sherman Anti-trust Act passed in USA
Ramsay v. MacLay (1890)
Crotty v. McFarlane (1891)
Leask v. Burt (1893)
Paterson v. Welch (1893)
Christie v. Davey (1893)
Le Lievre v. Gould (1893)
Waddell v. Roxburgh (1894)
McLaughlin v. Orr Pollock & Co. (1894)
Palmer v. Wick, etc., Co. Ltd (1894)
Waugh v. Ayrshire Post Ltd (1894)
Merchant Shipping Act 1894
Bradford (Mayor of) v. Pickles (1895)
Caledonian Ry. Co. v. Warwich (1897)
Allen v. Flood (1898)
Brown's Trustees v. Hay (1898)
Cellular Clothing Co. v. Maxton & Murray (1899)

1900   Mafeking relieved
Quinn v. Leatham (1901)
I.R.C. v. Muller & Co.'s Margarine Ltd (1901)
Dulieu v. White & Sons (1901)
Mason v. Orr (1901)
Payton & Co. v. Snelling, Lampard & Co. (1901)
Winkfield (The) (1902)
Evans v. Stein (1904)
Trade Marks Act 1905
Trade Disputes Act 1906
Hewitt v. Edinburgh Lathsplitters Assn. (1906)
Fleming v. Gemmill (1907)
Campbell v. Muir (1908)
Jones v. Hulton & Co. (1909)
Wragg v. D. C. Thomson & Co. Ltd (1909)

1910   Ballet Russe opened in Paris
Coal Mines Act 1911
Lees v. Dunkerley Bros. (1911)

Black v. Fife Coal Co. (1912)
Burns v. North British Ry. Co. (1914)
Shields v. Shearer (1914)
Milligan v. Henderson (1915)
Quackenbush v. Ford Motor Co. (1915)

1920   Bolsheviks defeat White Army
Weld-Blundell v. Stephens (1920)
Re Polemis and Furness, Withy & Co. (1921)
Castle v. St Augustine Links (1922)
Hodge & Sons v. Anglo American Oil Co. (1922)
Mustard v. Paterson (1923)
Workmen's Compensation Act 1925
Reavis v. Clan Line Steamers (1925)
Goh Choon Seng v. Lee Kim Soo (1925)
Sorrell v. Smith (1925)
Hambrook v. Stokes Bros. (1925)
McAulay v. Dunlop (1926)
S.S. Baron Vernon v. S.S. Metagama (1928)
Dumbreck v. Addie & Sons (Collieries) Ltd (1929)
Mullen (and McGowan) v. Barr & Co. (1929)
Oliver v. Saddler & Co. (1929)

1930   Amy Johnston flew solo to Australia
Walker v. Pitlochry Motor Co. (1930)
Fanton's Case (1932)
Donoghue v. Stevenson (1932)
Farr v. Butters Bros. & Co. (1932)
McNair v. Don & Co. (1932)
McMullan v. Lochgelly Iron and Coal Co. (1933)
Haynes v. Harwood (1935)
Bain v. Fife Coal Co. (1935)
Monk v. Warbey (1935)
Cuthbert v. Linklater (1935)
Bankhead v. McCarthy (1936)
Sim v. Stretch (1936)
Holywood Silver Fox Farm v. Emmett (1936)
Grant v. Australian Knitting Mills (1936)
Findlay v. Blaylock (1937)
English v. Wilsons and Clyde Coal Co. (1937)
Dann v. Hamilton (1939)

1940   Dunkirk evacuated
Sedleigh Denfield v. O'Callaghan (1940)
Wringe v. Cohen (1940)
Caswell v. Powell Duffryn Associated Collieries (1940)
O'Hara v. Central S.M.T. Co. (1941)
Cushing v. Peter Walker & Sons Ltd (1941)
Inglis v. London Midland and Scottish Ry. Co. (1941)
Bourhill v. Young (1942)
Polemis (The) (1942)
Canadian Pacific Ry. Co. v. Lockhart (1942)
Crofter Hand Woven Harris Tweed Co. v. Veitch (1942)
Oropesa (The) (1943)

Stewart v. London, Midland and Scottish Ry. Co. (1944)
Steel v. Glasgow Iron and Steel Co. (1944)
Law Reform (Contributory Negligence) Act 1945
Smith v. Leurs (1945)
McGregor v. Shepherd (1946)
Vyner v. Waldenbert Brothers (1946)
Mersey Docks and Harbour Board v. Coggins and Griffith (1947)
Read v. J. Lyons & Co. Ltd (1947)
Morrison Steamship Co. Ltd v. Greystoke Castle (1947)
Law Reform (Personal Injuries) Act 1948
McLaughlan v. Craig (1948)
Creswell v. Sirl (1948)
Cutler v. Wandsworth Stadium Ltd (1948)
Stansbie v. Troman (1948)
McElroy v. McAllister (1949)
London Passenger Transport Board v. Upson (1949)
British Motor Trade Association v. Salvadori (1949)

1950   Communist North Korea invaded South
British Motor Trade Association v. Naylor (1950)
Ghannan v. Glasgow Corporation (1950)
Denny v. Supplies and Transport Co. Ltd (1950)
Rose v. Colville's Ltd (1950)
Alford v. National Coal Board (1951)
British Motor Trade Association v. Gray (1951)
Carniner v. Northern and London Investment Trust (1951)
Defamation Act 1952
Thomson (D.C.) & Co. v. Deakin (1952)
Gorebridge Co-operative Society v. Turnbull (1952)
Davie v. Magistrates of Edinburgh (1953)
Ormrod v. Crosville Motor Services (1953)
Watt v. Jamieson (1954)
Gray v. Dunlop (1954)
Macdonald v. Glasgow Western Hospitals (1954)
Haig & Co. v. Forth Blending Co. (1954)
Hunter v. Hanley (1955)
Hotel Proprietors Act 1956
Slater v. Clay Cross Co. Ltd (1956)
Wardlaw v. Bonnington Castings (1956)
Pullar v. Window Clean (1956)
Occupier's Liability Act 1957
Bolam v. Friern Hospital Committee (1957)
Torrack v. Corpamerica Inc. (1958)
Kirby v. National Coal Board (1959)
Young (John) & Co. Ltd v. O'Donnell (1958)
Scala Ballroom Ltd v. Ratcliffe (1958)
Building (Scotland) Act 1959
Stewart v. H. A. Brechin & Co. (1959)

1960   East German border closed
Occupiers' Liability (Scotland) Act 1960
Brown v. Rolls Royce (1960)
The Wagon Mound (1961)
Factories Act 1961

Overseas Tankship (U.K.) v. Morts Dock & Eng. Co. (1961)
Smith v. Leech Brain & Co. Ltd (1962)
Offices, Shops and Railway Premises Act 1963
Wooldridge v. Summer (1963)
Hedley Byrne & Co. Ltd v. Heller & Partners Ltd (1964)
Scobie v. Steele & Wilson Ltd (1963)
Hughes v. Lord Advocate (1963)
Henderson v. John Stuart (Farms) Ltd (1963)
Hire Purchase Act 1964
Hall v. Fairfield Shipbuilding Co. (1964)
McCaig v. Langan (1964)
Rookes v. Barnard (1964)
Ross v. Associated Portland Cement Manufacturers (1964)
British Road Services v. Slater (1964)
Waugh v. James K. Allan Ltd (1964)
Weller & Co. v. Foot and Mouth Disease Research Inst. (1966)
Gourock Ropework Co. Ltd v. Greenock Corpn. (1966)
McGlone v. British Railways Board (1966)
Williams v. A. & W. Hemphill Ltd (1966)
Police (Scotland) Act 1967
Wickham Holdings Ltd v. Brooke House Motors Ltd (1967)
More v. Boyle (1967)
McKillen v. Barclay Curle & Co. Ltd (1967)
Goldman v. Hargrave (1967)
Nimmo v. Alexander Cowan & Sons Ltd (1967)
Dalhanna Knitwear Co. Ltd v. Mohammed Ali (1967)
O'Donnell v. Murdoch McKenzie & Co. (1967)
Sewerage (Scotland) Act 1968
Lane v. Holloway (1968)
Kay v. I.T.W. Ltd (1968)
Lamond v. Glasgow Corpn. (1968)
Daily Mirror Newspapers Ltd v. Gardner (1968)
F.C. Finance Ltd v. Brown & Son (1969)
Torquay Hotel Co. Ltd v. Cousins (1969)
Vine Products Ltd v. MacKenzie & Co. Ltd (1969)
Devine v. Colvilles (1969)

1970   Janis Joplin, Jimmy Hendrix deceased
     Keenan v. Rolls-Royce (1970)
     Morrison v. J. Kelly & Sons Ltd (1970)
     Smith v. Jenkins (1970)
     Baker v. Willoughby (1970)
     McKew v. Holland & Hannen & Cubitts (Scotland) Ltd (1970)
     Steele *v.* Scottish Daily Record and Sunday Mail Ltd (1970)
     Home Office v. Dorset Yacht Co. (1970)
     Caledonian Ry. Co. v. Greenock Corpn. (1971)
     S.C.M. Ltd v. W. J. Whittall (1971)
     Dynamco v. Holland & Hannen & Cubitts (Scotland) Ltd (1971)
     National Health Service (Scotland) Act 1972
     Road Traffic Act 1972
     McKendrick v. Sinclair (1972)
     McGowan v. Lord Advocate (1972)
     Ross v. Bryce (1972)
     Dutton v. Bognor Regis U.D.C. (1972)

Prescription and Limitation (Scotland) Act 1973
Launchbury v. Morgans (1973)
McLaren v. Caldwell's Paper Mill Co. Ltd (1973)
Roe v. Wade (1973)
McGhee v. National Coal Board (1973)
Rivtow Marine Ltd v. Washington Iron Works (1973)
Fowler v. Tierney (1974)
Lloyds Bank v. Bundy (1974)
Telfer v. Glasgow D.C. (1974)
Guard Dogs Act 1975
Levin v. Caledonia Produce (Holdings) Ltd (1975)
Dangerous Wild Animals Act 1976
Fatal Accidents Act 1976
Congenital Disabilities (Civil Liability) Act 1976
Froom v. Butcher (1976)
Mitchell v. McCulloch (1976)
Damages (Scotland) Act 1976
Sparham-Souter v. Town and Country Dev. Ltd (1976)
Unfair Contract Terms Act 1977
Bowen v. Paramount Builders (1977)
Angus v. Glasgow Corporation (1977)
Anns v. Merton London B.C. (1978)
Carrick Furniture House Ltd v. Paterson (1978)
Jackson v. Harrison (1978)
Evans v. Glasgow D.C. (1978)
Sale of Goods Act 1979
Hallet v. Nicholson (1979)
Dunlop v. McGowans (1979)
Evren Warnink v. Townend & Son Ltd (1979)

1980   Solidarity established in Poland
Criminal Justice (Scotland) Act 1980
Limitation Act 1980
Munro v. Morrison (1980)
Roberts v. Ramsbotton (1980)
Roxburgh v. Seven Seas Engineering Ltd (1980)
Hunter v. British Steel Corpn. (1980)
Park v. Tractor Shovels (1980)
J.E.B. Fasteners Ltd v. Marks, Bloom & Co. (1981)
Lamb v. Camden L.B.C. (1981)
Lindley v. Rutter (1981)
Hanlon v. Cuthbertson (1981)
Civil Jurisdiction and Judgments Act 1982
Lonrho v. Shell Petroleum Ltd (1982)
Jobling v. Associated Dairies Ltd (1982)
Graham & Co. Ltd v. Church of Scotland Gen. Trs. (1982)
Lang Brothers Ltd v. Goldwell (1982)
Perry v. Sidney Phillips & Son (1982)
Junior Books v. The Veitchi Co. (1982)
Mackay v. Borthwick (1982)
Russell v. F. W. Woolworth & Co. Ltd (1982)
Robertson v. Turnbull (1982)
Twomax Ltd v. Dickson McFarlane & Robinson (1983)
Tate & Lyle Foods and Distribution Ltd v. G.L.C. (1983)

London and South of England Building Society v. Stone (1983)
Young v. Bankier Distillery Co. (1983)
Pirelli Cable Works Ltd v. Oscar Fabler & Ptnrs. (1983)
Merkur Island Shipping Corpn. v. Laughton (1983)
McLaughlin v. O'Brien (1983)
Kelly v. Edinburgh D.C. (1983)
MacColl v. Hoo (1983)
Law Reform (Husband and Wife) Act 1984
Blackburn v. Sinclair (1984)
Gault v. Philip (1984)
Renfrew Golf Club v. Ravenstone Securities Ltd (1984)
Titchener v. British Railways Board (1984)
Donald v. Rutherford (1984)
Winnick v. Dick (1984)
Wallace v. Glasgow D.C. (1985)
Longworth v. Coppas International (U.K.) Ltd (1985)
Muirhead v. Industrial Tank Specialities (1985)
R.H.M. Bakeries (Scotland) Ltd v. Strathclyde R.C. (1985)
Sidaway v. Bethlem Royal Hospital (1985)
Leigh & Sillivan Ltd v. Aliakmon Shipping Co. Ltd (1986)
Candlewood Navigation Corp. Ltd v. Mitsui O.S.K. Lines Ltd (1986)
De Silva v. Otto (1986)
East River Steamship Corpn. v. Transamerica Delaval (1986)
Martin v. Bell Ingram (1986)
King v. Liverpool C.C. (1986)
Squires v. Perth and Kinross D.C. (1986)
Consumer Protection Act 1987
Animal (Scotland) Act 1987
Aloe Coal Co. v. Clark Equipment Co. (1987)
Kirkcaldy D. C. v. Household Manufacturing Ltd (1987)
Anderson v. Glasgow D.C. (1987)
Curran v. N.I. Co-Owernship Housing Assn. Ltd (1987)
Maloco (and Smith) v. Littlewoods Organisation Ltd (1987)
Norwich Union Ins. Soc. v. Covell Matthews Partnership (1987)
Nacap Ltd v. Moffat Plant Ltd (1987)
Rossleigh v. Leader Cars (1987)
Gold v. Haringey Health Authority (1987)
Hotson v. East Berkshire Health Authority (1987)
Kay's Tutor v. Ayrshire and Arran Health Board (1987)
Bonthrone v. S. of S. for Scotland (1987)
Civil Evidence (Scotland) Act 1988
Yeun Kun Yeu v. Att.-Gen. of Hong Kong (1988)
Greater Nottingham Co-op. Soc. v. Cementation Piling Ltd (1988)
Kalfelis v. Bankhous Schröder (1988)
Rowling v. Takaro Properties (1988)
D & F Estates v. Church Commissioners (1988)
Simaan Construction Co. v. Pilkington Glass Ltd (No 2) (1988)
Jones v. Dept. of Employment (1988)
Hill v. Chief Constable, West Yorkshire Police (1988)
Att.-Gen. v. Guardian Newspapers Ltd (No. 2) (1988)
Noble's Trs. v. Economic Forestry (Scotland) Ltd (1988)
Wilsher v. Essex Area Health Authority (1988)
Argyll and Clyde Health Board v. Strathclyde R.C. (1988)
North Scottish Helicopters Ltd v. United Technologies Corpn. Inc. (1988)

Craigie v. North Scotland Hydro Board (1988)
Henderson v. Chief Constable, Fife Police (1988)
Security Services Act 1989
Robbie v. Graham & Sibbald (1989)
Harris v. Wyre Forest D.C. (1989)
Mills v. Winchester Diocesan Board (1989)
Banque Financière de la Cité SA v. Westgate Ins. Co. (1989)
Pacific Associates v. Baxter (1989)
Miller v. Glasgow D.C. (1989)
Wilson v. McCaffrey (1989)
Borders R.C. v. Roxburgh D.C. (1989)
Lonrho plc v. Fayed (1989)
Elliot v. J. & C. Finney (1989)
Carrick Jewellery Ltd v. Ortak (1989)
Dash Ltd v. Philip King Tailoring (1989)
Fergusson (Alex.) & Co. Ltd v. Matthews, McClay & Manson Ltd (1989)
Pegasus Security Ltd v. Gilbert (1989)
James Burrough Distilleries plc v. Speymalt (1989)
Stephen v. Scottish Boatowners Mutual Insurance Association (1989)
MacRae v. Henderson (1989)
Porter v. Strathclyde R.C. (1989)
Lord Advocate v. Scotsman Publications Ltd (1989)
Six Constructions Ltd v. Humbert (1989)
Smith v. Bush (Eric S.) (1989)

1990   Professor David Walker retired
Caparo Industries v. Dickman (1990)
Ross v. S. of S. for Scotland (1990)
Murphy v. Brentwood D.C. (1990)
Feely v. Co-op. Wholesale Ltd (1990)
Johnstone v. Traffic Commissioners (1990)
Morris v. Murray (1990)
Middleton v. Douglas (1991)
Pitts v. Hunt (1991)
Davenport v. Corinthian Motor Policies at Lloyds (1991)
Gordon v. Grampian Health Board (1991)
Ward v. Chief Constable, Strathclyde Police (1991)
McNeil Estates v. Faulds of Girvan (1992)
Alcock v. Chief Constable, South Yorkshire Police (1992)
Thomson v. Sinclair (1992)
Weir v. Wyport (1992)
Mull Shellfish Ltd v. Golden Lea Produce Ltd (1992)
North Pacific Steamship Co. Ltd v. Canadian National Ry. (1992)
Damages (Scotland) Act 1993
Muir v. Cumbernauld and Kilsyth D.C. (1993)
Gibson v. Strathclyde R.C. (1993)
Pepper v. Hart (1993)
Hamilton v. Fife Health Board (1993)
Treadwells' Drifters Inc. v. RCL Ltd (1993)
G.A. Estates Ltd v. Caviapen Trustee Ltd (No. 1) (1993)
Taylorson v. Somerset Health Authority (1993)
Robertson v. Forth Road Bridge (No. 1) (1994)
Robertson v. Forth Road Bridge (No. 2) (1994)
Sion v. Hampstead Health Authority (1994)

Taylor v. Shieldness Product Ltd (1994)
Tredget and Tredget v. Bexley Health Authority (1994)
Akram v. Commission for Racial Equality (1994)
Burnie Port Authority v. General Jones Pty Ltd (1994)
Cambridge Water Co. v. Eastern Counties Water Plc (1994)
E. v. Dorset C.C. (1994)
Private International Law (Miscellaneous Provisions) Act 1995
Scott v. EDC Pipeworks (1995)
Stevenson v. A. J. Stephen (Builders) Ltd (1995)
X. v. Bedfordshire C.C. (1995)
O'Neil v. Coyle (1995)
Page v. Smith (1995)
Mains v. Uniroyal Englebert Tyres Ltd (1995)
Defreitas v. O'Brien (1995)
Bravado Merchandising Serv. v. Mainstream (1995)
Duff v. Highland and Islands Fire Board (1995)
Forsyth v. A. F. Stoddard & Co. Ltd (1995)
Frost v. Chief Constable, South Yorkshire Police (1995)
Henderson v. Merrett Syndicates (1995)
Sinclair v. Falkirk D.C. (1995)
Defamation Act 1996
Damages Act 1996
Kennedy v. Glenbelle (1996)
Laing v. Tayside Health Board (1996)
Saed v. Waeed (1996)
Stovin v. Wise (1996)
Cavanagh v. Goodfreys of Dundee (1996)
Clunis v. Camden Health Authority (1996)
Fraser v. Greater Glasgow Health Board (1996)
Gemmell v. Bank of Scotland (1996)
Graham v. David P. Hall (1996)
Anderson v. Lothian Health Board (1996)
Fairlie v. Carruthers (1996)
Harris v. Abbey National plc (1996)
Marc Rich & Co. v. Bishop Rock Ltd (1996)
Williams v. Natural Life Health Foods (1997)
Forbes v. Dundee C.C. (1997)

Chapter 1

CONTEXT DEBATE AND REFORM

Introduction

Pressure for reform

1. David Cameron, "Rough justice for victims of asbestos"
Scotland on Sunday, July 30, 1989

1.1.1 'The case of the Glasgow-born electrician, who was 47 when he died, is typical of the tragedy unfolding in Scotland, as more and more men fall victim every year to mesothelioma, cancer of the lung medically proven to result from asbestosis.

One compensation specialist alone reports handling 30 cases this year. The only official figures for Scotland are from 1983, when 70 mesothelioma cases were reported. Experts say the figure now will be considerably higher.

Lawyers, doctors and cancer care workers are highly-critical of the Scottish legal system, claiming that it is failing to act in the best interests of the victim, and running against natural justice. An immediate review of the process is desperately needed, they say.

. . . . . .

1.1.2 John Riley had spent 25 years working for a variety of firms throughout the west of Scotland. Although as an electrician he did not work directly with asbestos, he was regularly exposed to its dust as sheets of the material, used as insulation, were cut away for him to work in schools, factories and offices.

But it was not until November 1987 that he suspected that something was wrong. His GP was uncertain of the cause of his pain and distress, and sent him to a specialist in Dundee. There, he was told it was possible he had a tumour in the lung, but it was much more likely that he was suffering from tuberculosis, and was given treatment for this.

Riley's wife, Deborah, said: "When John failed to respond to the treatment for TB, we began to move from doctor to doctor and hospital to hospital, looking for someone who could tell us exactly what was wrong with him. No-one could."

It was not until October last year that the couple were finally referred to an asbestosis specialist, who confirmed their worst fears. The diagnosis came too late, and five days later John Riley died.

His widow says: "There should have been someone we could have been sent to immediately who could have diagnosed his condition at the outset. Then he could have fought for his compensation with dignity.

"As it was, we were pushed from pillar to post and despite the fact that in the last stages of his illness, John was unable to get about, we were always denied mobility allowance and other social security benefits because there was no confirmed diagnosis."

1.1.3 Mrs Riley is now preparing complaints against the various health authorities from which she sought help, and her husband's case study is in the hands of her lawyers with a view to possible court action in the future.

However, Ted Rushworth maintains that the odds are heavily stacked against the victim from the outset. In the first instance, it is extremely difficult to diagnose mesothelioma. There are only a handful of doctors with specialist knowledge of asbestos-related diseases working in Scotland — virtually all in the Glasgow area.

Their whereabouts are not generally known to the average general practitioner. And, in any case, the majority of GPs, when presented with chest complaints, think first of smoking and lack of exercise as the most likely causes. They are not schooled in thinking to ask about their patients' industrial background, where they might find the vital early warning clues to asbestosis.'

2. **Joan McAlpine, "Insurers accused of delaying asbestos payments"**
Scotsman, March 1, 1990

1.2.1 'Insurance firms are dragging their heels over payments to Scottish victims of asbestos-related diseases, a lawyer claims, writes Joan McAlpine.

Thousands of men who contracted the disease while working with the deadly substance in the heavy industries as long as 30 years ago have still not received a penny, says David Stevenson of Edinburgh, who deals with most claims from Scottish workers.

They fear their wives and families will be left with next to nothing because, under Scots law, when they die their compensation claim dies with them.

John Moody, a former lagger and an asbestosis victim, told *The Scotsman* yesterday: "If I know my family is secure, I could die happy tonight."

Mr Moody, from Nitshill, Glasgow, and Mr Stevenson, appear tonight on BBC Scotland's *Focal Point* documentary, during which the allegations are made. The programme is subtitled *Slow Death: Dead Slow Justice.*

The programme says that now evidence has been uncovered to show that when cases do get to court, awards by Scottish judges are less generous than those of their English and Welsh counterparts.

Scottish doctors have also failed to recognise the link between asbestos and lung cancer, a connection which is acknowledged in the rest of Britain.

Mr Stevenson describes the tactics that insurance companies use to avoid paying out quickly: "It is not uncommon to be presented, within two or three weeks of a case being heard, with further written details throwing doubt on all sorts of medical issues. In those circumstances the cases are adjourned."

Yet they are settled, usually months later, he says, on exactly the same terms as they might have been in the first place. "It is difficult to avoid the conclusion again that that is a classic delaying tactic which simply puts off the evil day so far as the insurer is concerned," said Mr Stevenson.

1.2.2 Mr Moody, who is 59 but looks like he is in his 70s, becomes breathless after walking a few yards. He already has several growths in his chest and has been told he is likely to contract mesothelioma, the asbestos-related cancer that kills within months.

He is terrified of dying before he can make sure his wife Agnes is financially secure. "All I want is enough money to buy our council house so my wife has some collateral."

He has been pursuing his case for three years. If he dies before it is settled, his wife will be able to claim only "loss of society", which carries an award of about £10,000, compared with up to £60,000 which John could get for pain and suffering while he is alive.

"I worked for loads of different employers with every colour of asbestos. I would be covered in it but I never had any protection, not even a pair of gloves. Nobody said anything about the danger."

The company responsible for most asbestos claims in Scotland is the Iron Trades Insurance Company, which refused to comment on the programme. Mr Stevenson claims he has had to resort to litigation in every case involving Iron Trades.

James Roxburgh, of Biggart Baillie Gifford, Iron Trades' solicitors, said he believed the company had "worked with the greatest of expedition" in its dealings with claims.

The programme also discloses comparative work by researchers at Oxford University which shows that awards in Scotland are lower than England. The same team found that Scottish doctors, unlike those in England, were not linking incidences of lung cancer with asbestos.

The Law Commission is reviewing the Scots law which leaves widows with a pittance. But even if the law is changed, it will probably come too late for John Moody and many like him.'

3. The Scottish Law Commission

The Effect of Death on Damages
(Discussion Paper No. 89)

PART I

INTRODUCTION

Our remit

1.3.1   [1.1] On 14 September 1989 we received a reference on behalf of the Secretary of State for Scotland, under section 3(1)(e) of the Law Commissions Act 1965:

> "To consider the case for amending the law of damages in Scotland having regard to the possibility that there may be an incentive inherent in the present law for a defender to postpone making settlement or reaching proof until after the death of the pursuer in order to minimise the amount of any compensation to be paid."

. . . . . .

Survey of legal firms

1.3.2   [1.4] As a first step we decided to gather some basic facts from selected legal firms with substantial experience of handling claims for personal injuries. We prepared a short questionnaire with the assistance of the Central Research Unit. After piloting it in one of the target firms, we posted it to some 45 firms in Aberdeen, Edinburgh and Glasgow, chosen with the advice of the Law Society of Scotland. We also carried out interviews with five solicitors who have extensive reparation practices. Unfortunately, only 15 firms (33%) responded to the postal questionnaire. Nevertheless, those who did respond, and those who willingly gave time to be interviewed, provided us with a large amount of information which greatly assisted our deliberations. We draw on this as appropriate in what follows.

1.3.3   [1.5] The numbers of personal injury claims currently being processed by the firms responding to our questionnaire varied from less than 100 to more than 500. Generally, the firms were fairly evenly distributed across the range. One or two were handling between 1,000 and 2,000 claims. Most of the firms seem to act either mainly for claimants (10) or mainly for defenders (4).

Statistics of claims

1.3.4   [1.6]It is difficult to estimate accurately how many personal injury claims might be under way at any given time. In the five years from 1984 to 1988 9,427 personal injury actions were raised in the Court of Session and the sheriff courts (ordinary causes). [Figures taken from Civil Judicial Statistics returns.] At the end of 1988 3,376 such actions were pending. On the basis of the replies to our questionnaire it seems that about 80% of all claims may be settled without court action. [Estimates ranged from 50% to 90%.] Assuming this figure is approximately accurate, we may have 15,000 to 20,000 claims currently being processed, with 9,000 to 10,000 new claims entering the system every year.

1.3.5 [1.7] These projections can only be approximate, since they rest on estimates. Also, they do not take account of summary cause actions in the sheriff courts, or actions under the small claims procedure which, it seems, is increasingly used for personal injury claims. And of course some claims may be settled without the involvement of solicitors. The numbers are therefore likely to be even larger than we suppose. Whatever the defects of our statistics, we are clearly concerned with very large numbers of claims. Hence there is always a risk that too heavy demands may be made of the courts. When that happens delay in settling claims cannot be avoided. Nor can the possibility be excluded that the delay might be exploited.

Claims in respect of death

1.3.6 [1.8] In the first instance, we are concerned with claims in respect of death, more particularly where the victims die after raising an action but before proceedings are completed. The firms returning our questionnaire report 1,202 claims in respect of death during the five-year period 1985–89. Some 70 deaths (6%) occurred after an action was raised but before proof. Work-related accidents (other than those attributable to industrial disease) caused 53.5% of the 1,202 recorded deaths, road traffic accidents 29.0% and industrial disease 13.9%. The corresponding figures for deaths during legal proceedings are 2.9%, 11.4% and 74.3%. The table in the appendix contains more details.

1.3.7 [1.9] The questionnaires also record 43 current cases where there is a serious risk that the claimant might die before his claim can be resolved. Of these 30 (70%) involve industrial disease. Already 19 (44%) of the 43 claims were in court. This is comparable with what happens where claims are made in respect of death. The rate of settlement without court action seems to be lower for death claims (29% as against an estimated rate of 80% over all claims). The corresponding rates of settlement after an action is raised but before proof are closer. On the basis of our figures 82% of recorded actions in respect of death settled before proof compared with an estimated 90% over all actions. Claims in respect of death do not seem to take significantly longer to resolve than other claims. This applies both to claims settled without court action and claims settled after an action is raised but before proof.

1.3.8 [1.10] Again we must urge caution when using these statistics. Not only is our sample small but our questionnaire is not detailed enough to eliminate the possibility of double counting. As we have already mentioned, firms seem to act mainly for claimants or mainly for defenders. We cannot tell how far 'claimants' firms' and 'defenders' firms', or out-of-Edinburgh firms and Edinburgh firms, are reporting the same cases. A more detailed survey would have taken too long and imposed an unrealistic burden on busy practitioners. We therefore rejected that course. Nevertheless, the results of our limited survey have helped us to appreciate the nature of the problem, which is clearly significant quantitatively as well as qualitatively. Even halving the recorded total, we are probably concerned with more than 100 deaths per year. [See para 1.8. The figures may have been distorted by recent mass disasters.] It is difficult to know what proportion of these might be deaths which are delayed or protracted, as opposed to instantaneous: our overall figure for 1985–89 was 6%. Certainly, most deaths are likely to follow closely on the injuries causing them, for example death in a road accident. We hope, however, that this discussion paper will elicit more precise quantitative information from insurers, as well as trade unions and employers' associations.

An incentive to delay?

1.3.9 [1.11] One of our main concerns when we circulated our questionnaire was to find out how far solicitors agreed with the premise of our remit. We have made the point briefly that delayed (or intervening) death can reduce the total damages payable in respect of a claim. Our remit presupposes that this creates an incentive to postpone settlement where a claimant is likely to die. It is a serious matter to suggest that litigation might be deliberately manipulated to exploit the possibility of a claimant dying before his claim can be resolved. We therefore determined to make no such assumption without canvassing the views of experienced practitioners.

1.3.10 [1.12] In our questionnaire we specifically asked:

> "Do you agree —
> 'that there may be an incentive in the present law for a defender to postpone making settlement or reaching proof until after the death of the pursuer in order to minimise the amount of any compensation to be paid?'
> If so, why do you think this?"

All but one of those who returned the questionnaire, or were interviewed, agreed that there might indeed be such an incentive. But no firm claimed to have any evidence of tactical delay being used as a deliberate policy, although several criticised the practices of defenders in a general way. An equal number of firms, however, stated expressly that deliberate delay was quite unheard of in their experience. Problems of proof were said to be the principal cause of delay. The difficulty of negotiating settlements with multiple defenders was also mentioned. On the basis of our survey, therefore, we can only say that there may be at least an inducement to delay inherent in the present law. We cannot say that there is hard evidence that the state of the law has been or is being exploited. Nevertheless, we think that it is sufficient to justify reform that there is even this possible inducement.

. . . . . .

PART II

THE PRESENT LAW AND ITS CONSEQUENCES WHEN A CLAIMANT DIES BEFORE HIS CLAIM IS RESOLVED

. . . . . .

The injured person's claim while alive

1.3.11 [2.2] Broadly, there are two main heads of damages. First, the injured person is entitled to compensation for patrimonial loss. In essence this is pecuniary loss and comprises such items as loss of past or future earnings, loss of employability, outlays and expenses, eg medical expenses. In addition, statute provides for "reasonable remuneration" by way of damages for "necessary services" rendered to an injured person by a relative; and for damages in respect of an injured person's inability to render to a relative personal services which meet certain criteria.

1.3.12 [2.3] The second main head of damages is called solatium. This is compensation for pain and suffering, generally described as non-pecuniary loss in contrast with patrimonial loss, which is more naturally measured by money. Damages by way of solatium may be awarded for physical pain, loss of limbs or physical functions, disfigurement, disease, impairment of bodily powers or senses, wounded feelings and various sorts of mental damage.

The effect of death on the injured person's claim

1.3.13 [2.4] If the injured person dies before his claim is resolved, his right to claim damages is transmitted to his executor, but only in part. No claim can be made by the executor for patrimonial loss which is attributable to any period after the injured person's death. Further, the right to claim damages by way of solatium is completely extinguished. These provisions are contained in section 2 of the Damages (Scotland) Act 1976:

> "(1) Subject to subsection (3) below there shall be transmitted to the executor of a deceased person the like rights to damages in respect of personal injuries sustained by the deceased as were vested in him immediately before his death; and for the purpose of enforcing any such right the executor shall be entitled to bring an action or, if an action for that purpose had been brought by the deceased before his death and had not been concluded before then, to be sisted as pursuer in that action.
>
> (3) There shall not be transmitted to the executor of a deceased person any right to damages in respect of personal injuries sustained by the deceased and vested in the deceased as aforesaid, being a right to damages —
>
> (a) by way of solatium;
> (b) by way of compensation for patrimonial loss attributable to any period after the deceased's death,
>
> and accordingly the executor shall not be entitled to bring an action, or to be sisted as pursuer in any action brought by the deceased before his death, for the purpose of enforcing any such right."

For the purpose of section 2 it is irrelevant whether the injured person's death was caused by his injury or was due to intervening natural causes unconnected with the injury.

The claims of the injured person's relatives

1.3.14 [2.5] Where the injured person dies as a result of his injury, whether immediately or after some time, certain relatives may claim compensation for the loss they suffer through his death. Again there are two heads of damages.

1.3.15 [2.6] The first is damages for certain forms of patrimonial loss. Such damages comprise —

(a) compensation for loss of support suffered since date of death, or likely to be suffered, as a consequence of the death;
(b) payment in respect of the reasonable expense incurred in connection with the deceased's funeral;
(c) payment of a reasonable sum in respect of the loss of personal services obtainable on payment but which the deceased might otherwise have rendered gratuitously.

1.3.16 [2.7] The second head of damages covers non-patrimonial loss arising from deprivation of the deceased's society. Such an award is called a "loss of society award" and may be claimed by relatives who are members of the deceased's "immediate family":

> "1(4) If the relative is a member of the deceased's immediate family (within the meaning of section 10(2) of this Act) there shall be awarded … such sum of damages, if any, as the court thinks just by way of compensation for the loss of such non-patrimonial benefit as the relative might have been expected to derive from the deceased's society and guidance if he had not died; and a sum of damages such as is mentioned in this subsection shall be known as a 'loss of society award'."

Under this head compensation has been given for grief caused by the death and for distress in contemplating the suffering of the deceased before death. These elements are comparable with the solatium which dependants could claim for grief and sorrow under the pre-1976 law. But we doubt whether such compensation, in particular compensation for pre-death distress, can be justified on a strict reading of the 1976 Act. The loss of society award is compensation for lost non-patrimonial benefits which might have accrued to the claimant if the deceased had not died. In other words, the award looks to the future not the past. We will return to this issue.

1.3.17 [2.8] The relative's patrimonial and non-patrimonial claims are separate claims and are evaluated independently of each other. It is expressly provided that the non-patrimonial claim is not transmitted to an executor, if the claimant dies. By implication, the patrimonial claim is transmitted, so far as it relates to the period of survival after the death of the injured person. Both these claims under section 1 of the Damages (Scotland) Act 1976 are quite distinct from any claim the executor of the injured person may have under section 2, as previously described. This is expressly provided by section 4:

> "4. A claim by the executor of a deceased person for damages under section 2 of this Act is not excluded by the making of a claim by a relative of the deceased for damages under section 1 of this Act; nor is a claim by a relative of a deceased person for damages under the said section 1 excluded by the making of a claim by the deceased's executor for damages under the said section 2."

The problem posed in our remit

1.3.18 [2.9] Our remit requires us to consider how claims for damages are affected when a (potential) claimant dies before he can pursue his claim to its conclusion. Our preliminary statement of the problem was that delayed (or intervening) death can have the effect of reducing the total damages recoverable from the defender. Now that we have described the general legal provision for damages, we can locate the difficulty more precisely. It is principally that the injured person's claim for solatium is extinguished by his death and cannot be taken up by his executor. His immediate family, who would normally inherit his estate, are therefore deprived of any benefit they might otherwise have had from the non-patrimonial claim. This can seem very arbitrary, especially if the injured claimant dies just before legal proceedings are concluded, as has happened. It is also a situation which can be exploited by defenders, although we have no firm evidence that this is happening. Plainly, however, it constitutes an inducement to delay settling some claims.

1.3.19 [2.10] Of course, the deceased's claim for patrimonial loss to date of death is not lost. And, where the death is attributable to the injury, new claims emerge which the deceased's relatives can pursue in their own right. It might seem, therefore, that the deceased's immediate family is well provided for, at least in the more common case of wrongful death. Compensation for patrimonial loss before the deceased's death can be recovered by his executor for the benefit of those who inherit his estate; patrimonial loss thereafter can be compensated by an award for loss of support; and the claim for solatium will be replaced by a claim for loss of society.

1.3.20 [2.11] Even so, the injured person's family is still likely to be worse off as a result of his untimely death. This is partly because of differences in the methods of calculating the elements of patrimonial loss. Net prospective earnings which are lost count in full when calculating the living claimant's entitlement. Only the proportion which, on evidence of past practice, would have been used to support the family enters the calculation of loss of support. But the main reason for the discrepancy is that damages for loss of society tend to be rather less generous than awards of solatium for serious injury.

. . . . . .

1.3.21 [2.14] It is perhaps reasonable to assume that injuries which are serious enough eventually to cause death would attract payments of solatium at the higher levels, if the victim survived. This proposition can be illustrated by considering asbestos-related disease, which first drew attention to the problem we are now considering. Several asbestos-related conditions affecting the lungs are recognised. Mesothelioma is invariably fatal, and the problem of delay is acute as far as this condition is concerned. We are told that the average period of survival after diagnosis is about a year and that 80% of those afflicted die within two years and virtually all within three years. Asbestosis can also result in death, but it varies in its degree of severity. Pleural plaques are less serious, except that they may indicate a risk that the graver conditions will develop. The question whether asbestos dust may cause lung cancer and gastro-intestinal cancer is still a matter of debate.

1.3.22 [2.15] In recently reported English cases payments of £20,000 and £32,000 were made for pain, suffering and loss of amenities, (broadly equivalent to solatium in Scotland) in respect of asbestosis; and payments of £24,800 and £28,000 in respect of mesothelioma. In a Scottish case reported in 1987, in the sheriff court, solatium of £15,100 was awarded to a pursuer for asbestosis where the resultant disability had been assessed at 10%. More recently, in the Court of Session, it was said when awarding interim damages that "solatium [for asbestosis] on a conservative basis could lie between £15,000 and £20,000". Solicitors whom we interviewed and firms responding to our questionnaire anticipated payments of solatium around £30,000 for victims of mesothelioma who survived until their claims were settled. There was also general agreement that asbestosis might attract payments between £20,000 and £30,000, depending on its severity. Present levels of solatium for pleural plaques, £1,500–£3,000, were regarded as nominal. The pleural plaques were thought to be important as evidence of exposure to asbestos dust and, as mentioned, as indicating vulnerability to the graver conditions. Accordingly, there seems to be a move towards using these less serious conditions as a ground for claiming provisional damages under section 12 of the Administration of Justice Act 1982.

1.3.23 [2.16] From the foregoing it is obvious that if a victim of mesothelioma, for example, dies before his claim is resolved, this has serious financial consequences for his family. The solatium, perhaps up to £30,000, is lost. Further, that loss is likely to be only partially offset by any ensuing claims for loss of society. These are unlikely to amount altogether to more than £20,000, unless perhaps the deceased's family includes numerous (young) children, as well as a spouse. In fact, victims of asbestos-related disease tend to be elderly and this may further reduce the payment(s) to be expected for loss of society. In such cases, too, there might be minimal or even no compensation payable for loss of support. One solicitor, who is very experienced in these cases, told us that no client of his had ever received more than £15,000 for loss of society, and that payments of less than £10,000 were not uncommon. In other words, the intervening death of the claimant in the most unfavourable circumstances could lead to a significant saving for the defender as far as non-patrimonial damages are concerned. It is this possibility which constitutes the incentive to delay settling claims and which is now causing public concern.

. . . . . .

PART IV

OPTIONS FOR REFORM

Introduction

1.3.24   [4.1] Our starting point is that reform is almost certainly required to deal with the problem of the injured person who survives to initiate a claim but whose life is seriously at risk. It is clear, as we have tried to bring out in Part II, that the present law may provide a significant financial incentive to delay in such cases. Virtually all of those who participated in our preliminary survey agree. It is equally clear that the claims which concern us are more numerous than was anticipated in the mid 1970s and we do not see this as a temporary problem. Certainly, the numbers of asbestos-related claims which are presently causing concern are likely to decline eventually. [Most of the participants in our survey thought this was unlikely to happen before the turn of the century.] But we expect that occupational and environmental hazards will continue to generate new causes of action of a similar sort. Apart from that, there is always likely to be a small core of familiar injuries, road traffic injuries for example, where the problem of delayed death cannot be ignored. In these circumstances we think it would be wrong to be too concerned about disputed allegations of deliberate delay. It is surely a sufficient reason for reform that there is always a risk of delay in the court system, because it is vulnerable to excessive demand. The potential for exploitation is there. It is only sensible, therefore, to try to eliminate any financial incentive there may be within the system itself to exploit delay. Precisely what sort of reform is needed is less clear.

1.3.25   [4.2] One possibility which may seem obvious is procedural reform. An expedited optional procedure for some reparation actions already exists in the Court of Session. Perhaps some extension or modification of such a procedure would solve the problem. This approach, however, is problematic. Any expedited procedure is necessarily subject to limitations. It may not be suitable for cases involving complicated facts which are difficult to prove. And at least some of the cases which give rise to the problem we are concerned with fall into just that category. We conclude, therefore, that the problem cannot be solved by procedural change alone, though no doubt the existing special procedures will sometimes provide a solution in particular cases.

1.3.26   [4.3] Similarly, we are reluctant to recommend the introduction of *ad hoc* remedies for special categories of claims. For example, it was suggested to us in the course of our survey, that penal rates of interest should be applied to damages to discourage late settlement in asbestos-related claims. This would be at the discretion of the court. We recognise that late settlements, and indeed litigation generally, are stressful for claimants, particularly claimants suffering from a painful and possibly terminal disease. Nevertheless, we have reservations about such a remedy. As said in the preceding paragraph, the cases for which the remedy was suggested are quite often complex. There may be difficulties in establishing a claimant's employment record, where that extends over many years and many employers. There may be problems of causation and medical diagnosis. Such issues are inevitably time-consuming, and will often only be clarified finally in the intensive process of preparing for proof. Our view, therefore, is that we should look for a more fundamental solution to the problem. How then should we set about this?

. . . . . .

Is solatium inherently personal?

1.3.27 [4.5] It is undoubtedly a primary presupposition underlying the scheme of the 1976 Act that the right to claim solatium is inherently personal. In other words, solatium is intended to solace the injured person. We appreciate the reasons for that view. There is, as has often been observed, something odd about the idea of compensating one person for another person's suffering. On the other hand, this view is not the only one that can be taken. We have already pointed to an earlier view which regarded a claim for solatium as a patrimonial asset, transmissible on death like a claim for debt. There are considerable attractions in this view too. It is somewhat surprising and apparently unjust that the amount recoverable by a family and payable by a wrongdoer should depend to such an extent on the precise date of death. The question, as we see it, is not the inherent nature of solatium but whether or not, as a matter of policy, the right to claim ought to be transmissible to an executor.

1.3.28 [4.6] Certainly, the rule now established in Scotland has also been adopted in numerous Commonwealth jurisdictions. But it is notably not the rule in England and Wales. It is therefore not obvious that death should necessarily terminate the right to claim solatium in all circumstances.

. . . . . .

1.3.29 [4.7] We are impressed by this divergence of views. Clearly the proposition that death should necessarily terminate a claim for solatium in all circumstances is not beyond question. Indeed, it is difficult to understand why it was accepted almost without question in Scotland in the 1970s. Certainly, there were weaknesses in the arguments used to justify the rule as it then stood. And the English approach, which was the obvious alternative, had some rather unattractive features at the time, though these have now gone. Even so, this hardly accounts for the manner in which the alternative approach was dismissed in the 1973 Report. It may be, therefore, that the initial view taken of solatium was reinforced by other presuppositions which also tended to discourage a more detailed assessment of alternatives.

. . . . . .

Our proposals: First option

1.3.30   [4.16] What then are our proposals for reform? One option would be to allow a claim for solatium to survive for the benefit of the deceased's estate. There are strong arguments for this option, which we are inclined to favour. It is the solution adopted in England and Wales and it may seem anomalous to maintain a distinction between the two jurisdictions in this respect. Indeed, the fact that there is such a distinction has featured prominently in the demand for reform. Counter-arguments about the personal nature of solatium are not necessarily conclusive. Whether a claim for solatium should be transmissible is a matter of policy on which a decision could be taken either way. Nor do we see any element of over-compensation where dependants receiving compensation in their own right also take the deceased's estate and benefit from his claim for solatium. In the mid-1970s it seemed arbitrary that a claim for solatium should survive merely because the claimant raised an action before he died. It could be said to be just as arbitrary that a claim should now fall merely because death intervenes before legal proceedings can be concluded. Perhaps it is easier to accept the latter, on the theoretical view that solatium is purely personal, when a disqualifying event seems unlikely. We now know that it is commoner than once seemed likely, and we cannot ignore that knowledge.

1.3.31   [4.17] On the other hand, the view that the right to claim solatium ought to be personal to the injured party cannot be rejected out of hand. It could well appear unjust to allow strangers or remote relatives to recover a windfall from someone whom the deceased himself would not have wished to sue. There is perhaps something in the principle that one person should not, in general, be compensated for another person's suffering.

1.3.32   [4.18] We invite views on the following proposals:

1.   Should a claim for solatium in respect of personal injuries survive for the benefit of the deceased claimant's estate?

2.   If it were provided that a claim for solatium in respect of personal injuries should survive for the benefit of a deceased claimant's estate, and the dependant who inherits any part of the estate also

receives compensation in his own right, that compensation should be paid without deduction in respect of the benefit derived from the deceased's claim.

. . . . . .

Second option

1.3.33 [4.23] A second possibility would be to preserve the principle that solatium is personal and does not transmit on death but to increase the claims of the immediate family. Such an increase appears to us to be justifiable on two grounds. First, it would ensure that in many cases the wrongdoer would have no incentive to delay settlement. Second, it would remove what appears to us to be a defect in the present law. As we tried to bring out in Part III, the deceased's immediate family may sustain certain injuries to feelings which seem to us not to be compensated appropriately in present practice. Arguably, the emotional distress and grief which a person may suffer while and after a close relative dies are not given due weight by the courts. And there can be few injuries more serious as far as a family is concerned than the death of one of its members. Whether death follows immediately on injury or is delayed, the loss is final. Further, if we are correct in our interpretation of section 1(4) of the Damages (Scotland) Act 1976, even the present limited recognition of distress and grief may rest on a precarious juridical foundation.

1.3.34 [4.24] Our second option for reform might therefore be achieved by reformulating the heads of non-patrimonial loss under which the members of a deceased's immediate family would be entitled to recover damages. These would be:

    (a)   loss of society as in section 1(4) of the 1976 Act;
    (b)   grief and sorrow at the deceased's death;
    (c)   where to their knowledge the deceased had undergone pain and suffering before death, distress and anxiety in contemplating his suffering.

Under head (c), the longer the deceased's suffering had continued, the greater would be the relatives' claim. As a result of such a reformulation, depending on the amounts awarded, the relatives' claims could equal or even exceed the solatium which would have been due to the deceased. This result would be more readily achieved if, consistently with section 1(4), the courts were to award "compensation" under each head of damages. That would involve a clear departure from the pre-1976 law, which commonly described such damages as an acknowledgement of injury to feelings, rather than as reparation or compensation. Accordingly, while a substantial acknowledgement rather than a nominal award was called for, there was a tendency to say that it should be confined within comparatively modest limits. It is not entirely clear that the present law has eradicated the effects of that approach.

1.3.35   [4.25] Other methods of increasing the immediate relatives' claims could also be considered. The simplest would be to provide that a relative could recover in name of non-patrimonial loss only a fixed sum specified by statute. Here compare section 1A of the Fatal Accidents Act 1976, which provides a remedy of damages for "bereavement" in England and Wales. The remedy is available only to the surviving spouse of the deceased, or to the parent(s) of a deceased minor who was never married. The damages are a fixed sum of £3,500, which is variable by statutory instrument and may soon be increased to £5,000 or £10,000. Introducing a similar provision into Scots law might go some way to meet the objection that it is distasteful to conduct a judicial inquiry into the feelings of a grieving family. To some extent it would also harmonise the laws of Scotland and England as to the amount of damages for non-patrimonial loss which is recoverable in such cases. On the other hand, it would be undesirable to import the limitation of the remedy to those two classes of claimants, given the definition of the deceased's immediate family in the Damages (Scotland) Act 1976. And even the sum of £10,000 would appear to some people in Scotland to be unacceptably low. For our part we do not favour a single tariff designed to compensate all non-patrimonial losses by the immediate family. Certainly, if such an option were to be pursued, considerable modification of the English provision would be required. For example, it would probably be necessary to devise a tariff which allocated different sums to different classes of claimant, perhaps placing children, if not others, in bands according to age. It would certainly be necessary, as regards quantum and qualification, to ensure that any such tariff was no less generous than the present provision in Scotland.

1.3.36   [4.26] As an alternative to a single tariff, a system of separate tariffs could be introduced. The three elements of non-patrimonial loss — pre-death distress and anxiety, grief and sorrow at death, and loss of society — could be specified and a tariff devised for each, or perhaps only certain of them. It may be that pre-death distress and anxiety would be the least suitable for the application of a tariff, since much would depend on variable but ascertainable factors: for example, the nature and duration of the deceased's suffering, or the extent to which the claimant was in his company. On the other hand, grief and sorrow at death and loss of society are very difficult to quantify. And it is not easy to justify variations in awards under these heads to relatives of similar age who are identically related to the deceased. It is also unfortunate that a surviving relative, such as a widow, may have to give —

> "the usual general evidence indicative of the acuteness of the pain and grief which she has suffered and the gravity of the wound to her feelings."

We believe that for many pursuers this is at best an embarrassment and at worst an ordeal. Tariffs for awards in respect of grief and sorrow at death and loss of society could resolve problems of quantification and eliminate the leading of evidence. Clearly, tariffs could not distinguish between insincere and unusually devoted relatives who might otherwise receive awards smaller or more substantial than the average. But such cases are perhaps less common than those in which tariffs might be expected to have the advantages mentioned. The tariffs could no doubt be linked to the age of the claimant and his or her legal relationship with the deceased. However, while we recognise the possible advantages, we would be reluctant to recommend the introduction of such a system.

1.3.37   [4.27] Our predecessors also rejected the option of a tariff of compensation for loss of society. Their grounds were that it would soon become out of date; and that if it attempted to deal with the many complex situations which might arise, it would be both arbitrary and unwieldy. We agree with the latter; the former, however, is relatively unproblematic. We envisage that if a tariff or tariffs were to be introduced, provision would be made for both index-linking and variation by statutory instrument. This would enable regular updating and, if appropriate, more radical review of the level or levels initially set. It is not so easy to deal with the criticism that a tariff is an arbitrary and unwieldy instrument in complex situations. As we have indicated, some stratification by relationship and age could be imposed. But this is crude at best. Accordingly, we have yet to be persuaded that the advantages which tariffs provide are sufficient to compensate for their obvious defects.

1.3.38   [4.28] We recognise, however, that tariffs have seemed attractive to some...

1.3.39   [4.30] The second option, however it might be achieved, may be thought to have several advantages. First, it would be entirely consistent with the principle that the deceased's claims and the surviving relatives' claims are juridically distinct. Awards to relatives for non-patrimonial loss would be designed to compensate their real and continuing suffering rather than the past suffering of the deceased. Under the first option the deceased's transmissible claim for solatium might confer a windfall benefit on remote relatives or strangers. But under the second option awards would be made to compensate pursuers for their own distress, and would not enable them to benefit from the distress someone else. Second, in its most acceptable form where awards would continue to be variable, it would require the court to make a specific award for each element of non-patrimonial loss. Thus, any under-valuation of any element which may occur in current practice would be avoidable. Third, in at least some cases where a claimant was suffering from a dust-related disease, the second option might significantly alleviate the mischief of the possible incentive to delay settlement.

1.3.40 [4.31] On the other hand, it must be recognised that the second option would not necessarily be a complete answer to all the problems which might arise. First, assuming awards remain variable, its effectiveness would depend greatly on how much the courts chose to award in respect of each distinct element of non-patrimonial loss. The legislation would give the courts a means of dealing with the mischiefs of possible incentive to delay settlement of injured persons' claims and under-valuation of relatives' claims. But it would be for the courts to apply it effectively. Second, enhancing relatives' claims would not introduce any incentive to settle quickly, or reduce any possible incentive to delay settlement, where there were no relevant claims.

1.3.41 [4.32] We invite views on the following questions:

4(1) As an alternative to making claims for solatium transmissible, should the non-patrimonial claims of the deceased's immediate family be enhanced?

(2) If so, should this be done —

(a) by reformulating the heads of non-patrimonial loss under which members of the deceased's immediate family would be entitled to claim damages as —
(i) loss of society;
(ii) grief and sorrow at the deceased's death; and
(iii) where to their knowledge the deceased had undergone pain and suffering before death, distress and anxiety in contemplating his pain and suffering; or

(b) by introducing a tariff for —
(i) all non-patrimonial loss; or
(ii) any of elements (i)–(iii) under 2(a) above, and if so, which; or

(c) by some other means, for example by setting a minimum payment for loss of society?

Third option

1.3.42 [4.33] So far we have presented our first and second options as if they were mutually exclusive. We have expressed a preference for the first option, in the form of making claims for solatium transmissible without conditions. We have also discussed several variants of the second option of enhancing the claims of the deceased's immediate family. While no one of these greatly attracts us, we regard the variants which involve tariffs as the least satisfactory. As a final possibility we should consider combining the second option with the first. That might have its attractions, particularly if consultees were to favour restricting the transmissibility of claims for solatium. It is also arguable, quite independently of any question of enhancement, that the present law regulating loss of society should be restated, if only for clarification. Consultees are therefore invited to consider whether they would support combining the first and second options, with or without qualifications; and if with qualifications, to specify what qualifications they would wish.

1.3.43   [4.34] We invite views on the following question:

> 5.   Should the second option of enhancing the claims of the deceased's immediate family (in any of its variants) be combined with the first option of making claims for solatium transmissible (with or without conditions); and if so, with what qualifications?

4. The Scottish Law Commission Report on The Effect of Death on Damages
(Scot. Law Com. No. 134)

Part I Introduction

The impact of delay

1.4.1   [1.18] Our point is that delay of one sort or another probably cannot be wholly eliminated. There are too many potential causes of delay, and therefore an ever-present possibility of exploitation. We must also recognise that delay has a differential impact on the parties in dispute. The typical claimant, who would prefer to receive damages sooner rather than later, becomes increasingly vulnerable as time goes on. Accordingly, there is mounting pressure on the claimant to settle quickly, preferably without resort to litigation, which is widely regarded as most stressful for those not accustomed to it. The English study previously referred to concludes that the ordinary bargaining process generally favours defenders. If that is so, the claimant whose life is seriously at risk must be the most vulnerable of all claimants. He or she is aware of impending death and its effect on the value of the claim; is concerned about the future welfare of his or her family; and for these very reasons is poorly equipped to withstand the normal hurly-burly of bargaining, even without tactical manoeuvring by the defender. In such circumstances it is difficult to justify legal rules which add to the pressure on the claimant and invite exploitation.

Capricious effects of the present rules

1.4.2   [1.19] In considering the effect of death on damages, we are primarily concerned with the case where death is attributable to the fault giving rise to the claim. But similar considerations apply where death intervenes naturally and is wholly unconnected with the circumstances of the claim. Although this is unlikely to be a frequent occurrence, our consultees did in fact report two recent cases. Again, the effect of intervening death is to reduce the damages payable. Further, because the death has no causal connection with the injury, the deceased's family have no claims in their own right. Their claim depends on their right to inherit the deceased's estate and is restricted to recovering the pecuniary loss suffered by the deceased before death. This is a most capricious effect of the present rules and another argument for reform. One of our consultees makes the point tellingly:

> "The principal reason for my interest was that I very recently had a case where a client of mine suffered a serious injury in a road traffic accident and then died of unconnected causes before the claim could be settled or had been brought into court. The reason it had not been brought into Court was that the negotiations were going well and there was no need to sue. By the time of my client's unfortunate death the [damages] had been more or less agreed and the delay related to the calculation of [pecuniary] loss. After the death the [pecuniary] loss claim was resolved and a payment of that at least was made to the widow."

. . . . . .

Part II How the present rules operate

The loss of society award: Its nature and purpose

1.4.3 [2.21] The new loss of society award was conceived as being rather different from the traditional concept of solatium for dependants. It was to be made for reason other than that of assuaging the grief and sorrow of the claimant. Its basis was to be much wider. It was consequently thought that awards would be more varied in their amounts than solatium for dependants under the pre-1976 law. The underlying assumption seems to have been that the wider basis would encourage more generous awards. This has not happened. Awards have settled in practice at the modest levels described above. To that extent the expectations in 1973 have not been fulfilled. In fact, after allowing for inflation, current levels of compensation to relatives for non-patrimonial loss seem very little changed from pre-1976 levels. For example, awards quoted as typical in our memorandum in 1972 range from £1,250 to £1,500 for a widow and from £600 to £750 for a child: that is, after adjustment to 1991 values, from £10,000 to £12,100 and from £4,900 to £6,100 respectively. We have noted that the current negotiating base is probably in the range £10,000–£12,000 for a widow and £5,000–£6,000 for a child.

1.4.4 [2.22] When a person is injured and dies his or her immediate family may be said to sustain non-patrimonial injury in three ways.

First, where to their knowledge the injured person has undergone suffering before death, they experience distress and anxiety in contemplating that suffering. Second, they suffer grief and sorrow at the death. Third, they are deprived of the person's society and guidance in the future. But compensation for only one of these sources of injury to feelings is provided for in the Damages (Scotland) Act 1976, namely, deprivation of the deceased's society and guidance. Solatium for grief and sorrow was of course awarded before the 1976 Act came into effect. It was also said that in the assessment of solatium it was legitimate to consider —

> "the laceration of the feelings of the widow and family in contemplating the pain and suffering to which the deceased was exposed before death actually supervened."

In our view this is clearly distinct from both grief and sorrow at the death and deprivation of the deceased's society in the future.

The loss of society award: Its reception by the courts

1.4.5 [2.23] Notwithstanding the terms of the 1976 Act, all three sources of injury to feelings have been taken into account in awards for loss of society. And such awards are now the only competent awards for the immediate family's non-patrimonial loss. In certain cases the courts appear to have equated loss of society with solatium. But the extent to which there is now any judicial consensus on the matter is not altogether clear. Differing views have been expressed in the two cases in which section 1(4) of the 1976 Act has been considered by the Inner House, namely, *Dingwall v Walter Alexander & Sons (Midland) Ltd* 1982 SC(HL) 179 and *Donald v Strathclyde Passenger Transport Executive* 1986 SLT 625. We must therefore examine these decisions more closely.

Dingwall v Walter Alexander & Sons (Midland) Ltd

1.4.6 [2.24] In *Dingwall* Lord Jauncey said in the Outer House:

> "By abolishing awards of *solatium* the section clearly removes grief and sorrow as a factor to be considered. On the other hand, by substituting the alternative imponderables of the benefits flowing from society and guidance the section constitutes a new claim which differs in degree rather than in principle from the former claim for *solatium*... . I conclude ... that the use of the word 'compensation' in the subsection was not intended to effect an approach to loss of society awards different in principle to that which formerly prevailed in relation to *solatium*, albeit there may be some difference in degree and albeit younger children through the deprivation of a parent's society and guidance for a longer period than older children are likely to receive larger awards than their elder brothers and sisters."

Lord Jauncey found the defenders liable to the pursuers and awarded damages for, amongst other things, loss of society.

1.4.7 [2.25] The defenders appealed on the question of liability and the pursuers took advantage of the appeal to present argument on the question of damages. The Second Division found for the defenders on the question of liability, but also discussed fully, albeit *obiter*, the pursuers' submissions on damages. The majority (Lord Justice-Clerk Wheatley and Lord Kissen) thought that the loss of society awards should be increased by one-third. Lord Robertson, dissenting on this point, did not consider that the Lord Ordinary's figures for loss of society could be successfully challenged. The argument before the Court proceeded on the basis that both parties were agreed that solatium as such had been abolished and replaced by a loss of society award. The pursuers founded on the use of the word "compensation" in section 1(4) as contrasting with the traditional judicial concept of solatium attracting only an "acknowledgement payment". The defenders submitted that in recent years the concept of solatium had been judicially expanded to comprehend what had now become a loss of society award. Accordingly, awards of damages for solatium made before the passing of the 1976 Act would be a proper guideline for loss of society awards.

1.4.8 [2.26] Lord Justice-Clerk Wheatley expressed the opinion that with the abolition of solatium and the substitution of a loss of society award it must be presumed that something different was intended. He said:

> "The old basis has been abolished and a new one has been introduced. That new basis seems to me to increase the considerations to be taken into account. Loss of society and guidance covers more aspects of family relationship than grief and sorrow, although grief and sorrow may be an inevitable consequence of the loss of society and guidance. Moreover, any limitation or restriction in the amount of the award to an acknowledgement or a token payment has been removed, and when compensation is substituted for such an award it means compensation in the normal use of the word. Accordingly, in my opinion, when a judge has to determine compensation for a loss of society award under the new legislation he must look at the relationship which existed between the parties involved, their respective ages, the circumstances in which they lived with respect to each other, and any other relevant factor, and from the weighing-up of these factors determine what in the exercise of his judgment an appropriate award of compensation should be for the loss of society and guidance and what that involves to the individual pursuer, once again keeping in mind the imponderables. On that approach, pre-Act awards can provide no necessary criteria."

1.4.9 [2.27] Lord Kissen agreed that the loss of society awards should be increased by one-third. His reasons, however, were expressed rather differently:

"My view is that Parliament were simply re-stating the meaning of *solatium* by substituting for it other words in English which have a clearer meaning and are in line with what the Courts latterly considered *solatium* to include. On the other hand, in so re-stating it and using the word 'compensation', I think that Parliament intended the Courts to exercise discretion in this matter on a more generous basis although it is not easy to calculate 'compensation' on such a matter. I would have awarded one-third more to each of the pursuers than the Lord Ordinary did if I had to award damages."

1.4.10 [2.28] Lord Robertson, dissenting on this point, said:

"Although it is clear that Parliament intended to get rid of the old conception of *solatium*, and substitute therefor a more modern concept of loss of society, I am not convinced that the change in substance is material."

Later he said:

"… my conclusion is that the Act of 1976 has not in fact effected any alteration in the law in regard to this head of claim. I regard section 1(4) and (7) rather as simplifying the statement of the law as it has existed, by abolishing the word *'solatium'* as a legal word not understood by laymen, and by simply translating it into the more common and easily understood language of section 1(4). So I am of opinion that the concept of grief and sorrow clearly contemplated in the old word *'solatium'* is not excluded from an award for the loss of a deceased's 'society and guidance'. So, too, I do not consider that the word 'compensation' in section 1(4) widens the scope of an award for loss of society, which was in any event embraced under the head of *solatium* before the Act… .

I agree accordingly with the Lord Ordinary that section 1(4) does not affect an approach to loss of society awards different in principle to that which formerly prevailed in relation to *solatium*."

Donald v Strathclyde Passenger Transport Executive

1.4.11 [2.29] *Donald* was an appeal by the pursuers from the sheriff court on the question of the damages awarded to them as parents for the loss of society of their son. The pursuers' counsel initially submitted that wider considerations entered into an award of damages for loss of society; and that such awards should therefore tend to be larger than pre-1976 awards of solatium made in similar circumstances. Subsequently, counsel departed from this submission, although it could have been supported by reference to Lord Justice-Clerk Wheatley's opinion in *Dingwall*. Counsel's final position appears to have been that awards for loss of society should not be less than awards of solatium would have been in similar circumstances. Counsel for the respondents argued that the

compensation provided for loss of society under the 1976 Act was
something less than an award of solatium would have provided. Grief
and distress at the time of death could no longer form an element
in an award of damages, solatium having been expressly abolished
by section 1(7). For these reasons an award in respect of loss of
society should in most cases be smaller than an award of solatium
would have been.

1.4.12   [2.30] The Court said:

> "In our opinion it would be very strange if Parliament, in enacting
> the Act of 1976, had intended to take away a head of damages in
> respect of the death of a child which a parent had previously enjoyed.
> Counsel's references to *Kelly v Glasgow Corporation* and the well known
> and oft quoted passage in the opinion of Lord Russell in that case at
> p. 501, as to what is comprehended by an award of solatium, and also
> the opinion of Lord Dunedin in the seven judge case of *Black v North
> British Railway Co* ... confirm our opinion that solatium has never
> been a mere token payment, that it always could take into account
> the loss of society of a parent or child, and the guidance given by the
> one to the other. In our opinion there is nothing in s. 1(4) of the Act
> of 1976 which requires the court to make a larger award or a smaller
> award in respect of loss of society than it would have made in respect
> of solatium. The award made must be such as to compensate the
> claimant, in so far as money can, for the loss of the relative in question.
> Counsel for the respondents retreated from his initial submission after
> a discussion of the cases of *Kelly* and *Black*, and said that it was good
> enough for him to submit that an award in respect of loss of society
> was not bound to be greater than an award of solatium in similar
> circumstances would have been. He was content to rest his submissions
> on that basis.
>
> As counsel appeared to agree between them that awards of solatium
> could be looked at when trying to assess what a reasonable award for
> loss of society should be in this case, there is no need for us to consider
> in detail the provisions of s. 1(4) of the Act of 1976. Nor is it necessary
> to consider the opinion of the Lord Justice-Clerk in the case of
> *Dingwall*. In his opinion in that case his Lordship seemed to suggest
> that awards in respect of loss of society should be greater than awards
> in respect of solatium to the extent of one-third, because what he
> called 'the new basis' had increased the considerations to be taken
> into account. It has to be noted however that when his Lordship came
> to describe these considerations, there were none of them which would
> have been irrelevant in making an assessment for solatium (see the
> opinion of the Lord Justice-Clerk at [p 209] of the report). It has to
> be remembered that these observations of the Lord Justice-Clerk were
> obiter, but they have been frequently referred to. An opportunity may
> yet be afforded for reconsidering them, but we are of opinion that
> this is not it."

The loss of society award: Some conclusions

1.4.13 [2.31] In view of the judicial opinions quoted, the present state of the law as to the content of a loss of society award is difficult to determine. Lord Justice-Clerk Wheatley in *Dingwall* was of the opinion that "the new basis" increased the considerations to be taken into account. It seems clear that the First Division in *Donald* were not satisfied that that was so. They were content to proceed on the basis of an agreement between counsel which, at least in effect, corresponded with Lord Robertson's view in *Dingwall*. The third view is that of Lord Kissen in *Dingwall*, that section 1(4) had restated the meaning of solatium in English but had intended the courts to make more generous awards than before.

1.4.14 [2.32] It appears to us that it is of the essence of a loss of society award, as defined in section 1(4) of the Damages (Scotland) Act 1976, that it should look to the future. Section 1(4) provides that it is to consist of damages —

> "by way of compensation for the loss of such non-patrimonial benefit as the relative might have been expected to derive from the deceased's society and guidance if he had not died."

Neither grief and sorrow nor, more particularly, pre-death distress and anxiety can easily be brought within that description. Certainly it was originally envisaged that a loss of society award would be given for reasons other than that of assuaging the grief and sorrow of the claimant. Accordingly, including such elements of compensation within a loss of society award does not appear to us to have a secure juridical foundation. We also think it is probable that these elements have been undervalued when taken into account.

1.4.15 [2.33] However that may be, the restrictive approach adopted by the courts has undoubtedly had serious consequences. The claims of the injured person for solatium and of the immediate family for loss of society, if the injured person dies, are generally not of comparable value. This runs counter to the assumptions underlying the reforms in 1976. Indeed, precisely the problem we are now concerned with was then recognised, though perhaps not fully appreciated. The new form of award was thought to be sufficient in itself:

> "It was suggested to us that there might be a growing tendency to delay the settlement of claims by living pursuers if the right to solatium were extinguished on death. We doubt this because, in the normal case at least, there would be more substantial claims by the deceased's dependants."

With hindsight, we can now see that the problem is rather more complex.

Part III Principles and Policy

· · · · · ·

Is the right to claim solatium a patrimonial asset?

· · · · · ·

1.4.16 [3.17] [S]olatium was not always regarded prior to 1976 merely as solace for injury. Consider, for example, the case of *Dalgleish v Glasgow Corporation* 1976 SC 32, which was decided under the pre-1976 law. That case concerned a child who was rendered comatose by her injuries. The Lord Ordinary was prepared to contemplate an award of solatium in these circumstances, though in fact he held that liability was not established. On reclaiming, by which time the child had died, the Inner House took the same view with regard to solatium, while also affirming that liability was not established. It was said:

> "It is accepted that the fact that the victim may not derive any personal or financial benefit from the award is irrelevant."

Such an approach seems at odds with the view that solatium is purely personal and only intended to solace the injured claimant.

Transmissibility: A question of policy?

1.4.17 [3.18] It seems anomalous that a claim for solatium should be assignable *inter vivos*, and transmissible to a trustee in bankruptcy, but not transmissible to an executor. Some justification can be offered for distinguishing between assignability and transmissibility as such on the view that solatium is inherently personal. Assignability has a cash value which the injured person can realise. Control of the claim remains with the injured person unless and until it is assigned. Transmissibility, on the other hand, may involve loss of control over the claim and cannot be so easily translated into money's worth. We are not satisfied that that is a sound argument. It does not provide a convincing reason for distinguishing between an executor and a trustee in bankruptcy so far as transmissibility is concerned. Nor does it account for the approach adopted in *Dalgleish*, where personal benefit to the injured person was considered irrelevant.

1.4.18 [3.19] The fact is that a claim for solatium combines both personal and patrimonial elements. In some cases the personal elements predominate, in others the patrimonial elements. We therefore conclude that the question whether a right to claim solatium should be transmissible cannot be answered merely by analysing the nature of solatium. The question, as we see it, is whether or not or to what extent, as a matter of policy, the right should transmit.

The relative's non-patrimonial award

1.4.19   [3.20] Our starting point is that there should continue to be an award akin to the present loss of society award. And here we are not merely stating the obvious. Prior to our report in 1973 serious consideration was given to abolishing such awards and instead allowing the deceased's claim for solatium to survive. That scheme was rejected, however, on the ground that the then dependant's claim for solatium was too well established to be discarded without substituting some alternative. And, if one of these rights had to go, as was assumed, it was thought better as a matter of principle to retain the dependant's right; for this would emphasise the continuing loss of the living rather than the past loss of the dead.

1.4.20   [3.21] It was accordingly part of the general policy in our report in 1973 to place less emphasis on past suffering. And it was consonant with such a policy that the new award should be strongly orientated towards future or continuing loss arising from deprivation of the deceased's society and guidance. However, as we tried to bring out in Part II, elements of past suffering have now been incorporated into the concept of "loss of society" — somewhat dubiously in our view. At the very least, therefore, if we are to retain a non-patrimonial award for relatives, we must clarify the conditions under which it can be made.

1.4.21   [3.22] It is a separate question whether we should go further. It would be possible, for example, to enhance the loss of society award. We received many complaints from consultees that current awards are too low. Arguably, the emotional distress and grief which a person may suffer while and after a close relative dies are not given due weight by the courts. Nor is there sufficient recognition that there can be few injuries more serious as far as a family is concerned than the death of one of its members. And, of course, it is the discrepancy between loss of society awards and awards of solatium which creates the financial incentive to delay. If loss of society awards were more generous that incentive might be reduced.

1.4.22   [3.23] In fact, in Discussion Paper No 89 we did suggest that loss of society awards might be enhanced as an alternative to making solatium transmissible. We also suggested how this might be done, for example by setting tariffs or minima. Significantly, our suggestion was criticised on the basis that, realistically, enhancement could only be achieved through tariffs or minima, which the critic regarded as generally undesirable. We are inclined to agree, and we would be reluctant to recommend the introduction of such a scheme.

1.4.23   [3.24] Certainly our consultees rejected tariffs and minima conclusively, if not unanimously. They attached great importance to preserving the discretion of the courts when making awards of damages. This was thought to provide essential flexibility and sufficient certainty. There was no confidence that a system of tariffs could be devised which would both operate fairly and take account of the widely varying circumstances of individual families. We agree, though we do recognise that tariffs may have advantages. Systematic quantification is not easy when injury and loss cannot be readily measured in money. We also accept that a tariff system could save close relatives of the deceased from the ordeal of giving evidence on the nature and degree of their suffering. Undeniably, there is something distasteful about conducting a judicial inquiry into the feelings of a grieving family. Nevertheless we are not persuaded that the advantages which tariffs may provide are sufficient to compensate for their defects.

1.4.24 [3.25] Other reforms were also suggested by our consultees. For example, several proposed that the class of relatives who qualify for non-patrimonial awards should be extended. Various extensions were suggested, most commonly that siblings should be included within the class. We have considerable sympathy with these proposals. We are not however prepared to make recommendations at present. In our view such matters should be considered in a wider context than that of our current remit. Accordingly, we intend to give further thought in due course to the possibility of undertaking a more extensive review of the law of damages.

Duplication of damages

1.4.25 [3.26] As mentioned, it was assumed prior to our report in 1973 that a choice must be made between allowing the deceased's claim for solatium to survive and retaining the relative's non-patrimonial award. We have commented on one aspect of the policy which guided that choice, namely, that compensation should be directed primarily to real continuing loss rather than past suffering. But another major concern was that duplication of damages or over-compensation should be avoided. So a primary objective in our report in 1973 was to separate clearly the claims of a deceased's executors and those of his or her dependants. The main reason for this was the much criticised case of *Darling v Gray & Sons*. That case established that a dependant's right of action was excluded if the deceased's executor had taken up an action of damages for patrimonial loss and solatium instituted by the deceased. One of the reasons for the decision was that to admit the dependant's right of action in these circumstances would entail duplication of damages. In recommending the abolition of the rule in *Darling*, it was said:

> "This approach should not lead to duplication of damages if other Recommendations in this Report are accepted, namely that the deceased's claim for solatium should not transmit to the executors, and that the executors' right to insist in the deceased's claim should be limited to patrimonial loss attributable to the period up to his date of death."

In other words, the proposal that the right to claim solatium should terminate on death was linked to the aim of preventing duplication of damages.

1.4.26 [3.27] A similar concern was manifest in some of the suggestions made by our consultees. For example, it was proposed that relatives should be allowed to elect between pursuing their own non-patrimonial claims and taking the benefit of the deceased's claim for solatium. Again, it was thought incompatible to allow the deceased's claim for solatium to survive and at the same time compensate a relative for distress caused by seeing the deceased suffer. In both cases the aim is to avoid over-compensation.

1.4.27 [3.28] We entirely agree that it is a proper aim to prevent duplication of damages. But seeking to set off the deceased's claim against the relative's claim is misconceived. The two claims are juridically quite distinct. Allowing the deceased's claim for solatium to survive as part of his or her estate cannot involve duplication of damages just because a relative who receives compensation in his or her own right may also take the estate. This principle was clearly established in *Dick v Burgh of Falkirk* which overruled *Darling v Gray & Sons* a few months before the Damages (Scotland) Act 1976 came into force.

. . . . . .

Part IV Reform

Preliminary

1.4.28 [4.1] In this part we develop our specific recommendations for reform in light of the principles discussed in Part III. Our general policy is clear. It is not our purpose to carry out a comprehensive review of the Damages (Scotland) Act 1976. Our aim is limited to correcting a perceived defect in the present law. Otherwise we recommend change only where it seems necessary as part of a coherent solution to the problem posed in our remit.

1.4.29 [4.2] In our recommendations we try to ensure so far as possible that claimants in Scotland will not be disadvantaged in comparison with their counterparts in England and Wales. That seems to us to be a necessary objective in this area of the law. It is no part of our policy, however, to try to equalise awards of damages in the two jurisdictions, even if that were possible. That is a more general issue which our remit does not address. We also recognise that, as far as the law of tort or delict is concerned, the two legal systems have very different historical starting points and have developed very differently. This limits the possibilities of assimilation by piecemeal reform.

Can the problem be solved by enhancing the relative's non-patrimonial award?

1.4.30 [4.3] We have accepted as a first principle that we must retain an award akin to the present loss of society award. One solution to our problem, therefore, might be simply to enhance that award. In this way the relatives' claims might substantially offset the loss of solatium when a claimant dies while pursuing the claim. We might thereby counter the incentive to delay settlement in at least some cases.

1.4.31 [4.4] Such a solution may be thought to have several advantages. Arguably, it would entail minimal interference with the structure of the current legislation. It would be entirely consistent with the principle that the deceased's claim and the surviving relatives' claims are juridically distinct. Non-patrimonial awards to relatives would be designed to compensate their real and continuing suffering and not the past suffering of the deceased. In other words, relatives would be compensated for their own suffering and would not benefit from someone else's suffering. There might also be procedural advantages. Any dispute would most likely be confined to the relatives' claims, concerning which evidence would be readily available. The deceased's executor would be concerned only with the deceased's claim for patrimonial loss, which is generally amenable to objective assessment and therefore perhaps less likely to become the subject of prolonged dispute or litigation. Finally, as we have noted, the solution of enhancing relatives' awards as an alternative to allowing claims for solatium to survive attracted significant support among our consultees. Those favouring the solution, though not a majority, included both legal academics and legal practitioners, perhaps most notably the Faculty of Advocates. The Law Society of Scotland was divided, a clear indication that the issues are controversial and tend to arouse strong reactions.

1.4.32 [4.5] We are not convinced, however, that a solution along these lines would work. Certainly it would not be a complete answer to all the problems which might arise. Enhancing relatives' claims would not introduce any incentive to settle quickly, or reduce any incentive to delay settlement, where there were no appropriate claims. Nor would it assuage the sense of injustice where the claimant dies from extraneous causes and the immediate family consequently have no claims. Most importantly, the success of the solution would depend on devising a mode of enhancement which would ensure that the courts made appropriate awards. We doubt if this can be done.

1.4.33 [4.6] In Discussion Paper No 89 we suggested that the loss of society award might be reformulated to distinguish expressly elements of emotional suffering, including distress and anxiety caused by seeing the deceased suffer before death. Our idea was that the longer the deceased's suffering had continued the greater would be the relatives' non-patrimonial claim. As a result of such a reformulation, depending on the amounts awarded, the relatives' non-patrimonial claims could equal or even exceed the solatium which would have been due to the deceased. But, so long as awards were discretionary, the effectiveness of the solution would depend greatly on how much the courts chose to award in respect of the several elements of suffering. The legislation would give the courts a means of dealing with the mischiefs of possible incentive to delay and under-valuation of relatives' non-patrimonial claims. It would be for the courts to apply it effectively. Doubts were expressed on this count both by solicitors participating in our preliminary survey and by our commentators. We share these doubts. Certainly, we could not compel enhancement merely by reformulating the award, though we could possibly reinforce the reformulation by introducing a tariff or a system of tariffs or minima. As we mentioned, however, there was widespread resistance among our consultees to the introduction of any such scheme. We therefore conclude that our problem cannot be solved effectively by seeking to enhance relatives' non-patrimonial awards.

Solatium: Transmissibility

1.4.34   [4.7] If the problem cannot be tackled effectively through the relative's non-patrimonial award, the only real alternative is to allow a right to claim solatium to transmit to the claimant's executor. That is not to say there are no independent grounds for adopting this solution. There are strong arguments in its favour. It is the solution favoured by a majority of our commentators, though not by an overwhelming majority. It is also the solution adopted in England and Wales and it may seem anomalous to maintain a distinction between the two jurisdictions in this respect. Indeed, the fact that there is such a distinction has featured prominently in the demand for reform in Scotland. There are of course counter-arguments about the personal nature of solatium, but we do not regard them as conclusive. Whether a right to claim solatium should be transmissible is a matter of policy on which a decision could be taken either way. Nor do we see any element of over-compensation where relatives receiving compensation in their own right also take the deceased's estate and benefit from the deceased's claim for solatium. In the mid-1970s it seemed arbitrary that a claim for solatium should survive merely because the claimant had raised an action. It could be said to be just as arbitrary that a claim should survive merely because the claimant had raised an action. It could be said to be just as arbitrary

that a claim should now fall merely because death intervenes before
legal proceedings can be concluded. Perhaps it is easier to accept the
latter, on the theoretical view that solatium is purely personal, when a
disqualifying event seems unlikely. We now know that it is commoner
than once seemed likely, and we cannot ignore that knowledge.

1.4.35 [4.8] On the other hand, the personal elements of a claim
for solatium cannot be wholly ignored. It could well appear unjust to
allow strangers or remote relatives or even creditors to recover a
windfall from someone whom the deceased might have elected not
to sue. Indeed, several consultees who were generally in favour of
transmissibility suggested that benefit should be confined to members
of the deceased's immediate family. Doubts were also expressed about
extending the principle of transmissibility to claims in respect of injury
arising from defamation or other verbal injury or injury to reputation.
Such claims were clearly regarded, at least by some commentators, as
being of a peculiarly personal nature.

1.4.36 [4.9] We do not favour confining the benefit of transmissibility
as suggested. It seems to us that if a claim for solatium is allowed to
survive, it should survive for the benefit of the claimant's estate and
those who take it, without qualification. We do accept, however, that
defamation and injury to reputation generally may give rise to special
considerations. Here the principle of election is particularly important
and more must be said about that. With that reservation, we think
the correct starting point for reform is to allow the right to claim
solatium in respect of personal injury to transmit to the claimant's
executor.

1.4.37 [4.10] We accordingly recommend:

  1. Subject to such qualifications as are contained in subsequent
      recommendations, any right to damages by way of solatium vested
      in a claimant in consequence of personal injury should transmit
      to his or her executor in the same manner as the corresponding
      right to damages by way of compensation for patrimonial loss
      transmits under the present law.

                        . . . . . .

Quantification of damages

1.4.38 [4.11] Under our scheme what is transmitted to the deceased's
executor is the right to damages vested in the deceased immediately
before death. The damages payable to the executor must therefore
be quantified by reference to the period ending immediately before
the deceased's death. It is important to appreciate just what this means
in relation to a claim for solatium. The claim which survives is not
necessarily the full claim as it might have been pursued by the

deceased. In the case of the living claimant part of the damages payable by way of solatium may well reflect future pain and suffering or future loss of faculties or amenities. And that part may well be much the larger part of the claim. We are proposing that, when a right to damages transmits, account is taken only of pain or suffering or loss of faculties or amenities endured before death. In other words, a claim for solatium is to be treated exactly as a claim for patrimonial loss is treated under the present law. This may seem so obvious as to be hardly worth saying. But it could have a very substantial effect on the value of a claim. Clearly, the shorter the period between injury and death, the smaller the claim for solatium is likely to be.

1.4.39   [4.12] We recommend:

2. When a right to damages by way of solatium transmits to an executor, the damages payable to the executor should be quantified by reference to the period ending immediately before the deceased's death.

. . . . . .

The elements of solatium

1.4.40   [4.13] In Part II we described the threefold classification of damages by way of solatium as compensation for —

(a) pain and suffering;
(b) loss of faculties and amenities;
(c) loss of expectation of life.

These elements are analytically distinct in the sense that not every element need be present in every case. Thus, in *Dalgleish* the injured child was comatose. An award of damages for pain and suffering would therefore have been inappropriate. The necessary awareness was lacking. In contrast, awareness is not a prerequisite of an award of damages for loss of faculties and amenities or loss of expectation of life. It is not however the practice of the Scottish courts to allocate separate sums to these analytically distinct elements of solatium. The general view is that one sum is awarded for solatium:

"This view is reinforced by what was said in the unreported opinion of the First Division in the case of *Keith v Fraser and Others* where the Lord Ordinary had awarded separate sums in assessing solatium … it is stated that the court felt: 'bound to say that in our opinion, the course the Lord Ordinary was persuaded by counsel to adopt in considering solatium cannot be justified in authority or practice. It involved, in effect, a division of what is truly an indivisible head of damages into several parts which are no more than representative of certain of the elements which should properly be considered together in the assessment of the claim for solatium. As a general rule we are in no doubt that solatium should be considered and assessed as a single entity...' ."

1.4.41 [4.14] There is another ground on which the elements of solatium can be distinguished. Pain and suffering and loss of faculties and amenities are, or may be, continuing states. Loss of expectation of life, as opposed to awareness of that loss, is a once-and-for-all consequence of injury. In other words, a claim for pain and suffering or for loss of faculties and amenities may become more valuable the longer the effects of injury persist. A claim for loss of expectation of life is treated differently. Damages for such loss are said to be restricted to a conventional sum, though the practice of awarding a single sum for solatium makes it difficult to know what the conventional sum is.

1.4.42 [4.15] These distinctions have implications if a right to damages by a way of solatium is allowed to transmit. The executor to whom the right transmits would have the task of proving the extent of the deceased's suffering in disputed cases. This may well be a difficult task on occasion in absence of evidence from the deceased. And the shorter the period of survival after injury the more difficult it is likely to be. In the extreme case of instantaneous or near-instantaneous death there are unlikely to be provable claims for pain and suffering or loss of faculties and amenities. But could the executor pursue a claim for loss of expectation of life in these circumstances? One of our consultees argued strongly that this would indeed follow if a right to claim solatium was allowed to transmit without qualification. He clearly regarded any such consequence as unacceptable.

1.4.43 [4.16] The point is well taken. There may be some justification for allowing a claim for lost life expectancy to survive as an element in a larger claim, which the court must assess on a substantive rather than a conventional basis. But it seems very artificial to allow the claim to survive in the case of instantaneous or near-instantaneous death, where it may be the only non-patrimonial claim which can be made by the deceased's executor. It is in just such circumstances that the court's way of assessing the claim is most likely to exacerbate rather than assuage the distress of the deceased's relatives. Conversely, the courts are likely to come under pressure to change the present basis of assessing the claim. How are they to respond? Arguably, the present law provides little guidance and our recommendations could make an already unsatisfactory situation worse. We therefore conclude that special provision is required for loss of expectation of life, if only to avoid confusion.

Loss of expectation of life

1.4.44 [4.17] It is worth noting that under the present law loss of expectation of life is taken into account when assessing the patrimonial loss of the living claimant. Section 9 of the Damages (Scotland) Act 1976 applies where a pursuer's "expected date of death is earlier than it would have been if he had not sustained the injuries". In that case the court can assume a normal lifespan when assessing patrimonial loss. The question now is: How should loss of expectation of life be treated in the case of a deceased claimant whose executor is pursuing a claim for solatium?

1.4.45 [4.18] One possibility, perhaps the simplest option, would be not to allow a claim for solatium for loss of expectation of life to survive. The claim is insignificant in practice. While the basis of assessment remains conventional, such a claim is always likely to be swamped by the typically much larger claims for pain and suffering and loss of faculties and amenities. If there are no larger claims, as might well be the case where death is instantaneous or near-instantaneous, is there any merit in preserving the merely conventional claim? Here we can cite the Canadian example. Among the various provinces, even where claims for non-pecuniary loss are allowed to survive, claims for loss of expectation of life tend to be excluded. But this solution seems altogether too arbitrary. We cannot consistently defend applying different rules in respect of different heads of non-patrimonial damages.

1.4.46 [4.19] In England and Wales loss of expectation of life has been abolished as a separate head of general (non-patrimonial) damages, on a recommendation of the Law Commission. The court can however take into account any suffering caused by awareness of lost life expectancy when making an award for pain and suffering. Section 1(1) of the Administration of Justice Act 1982 provides:

> "1(1)   In an action under the law of England and Wales … for damages for personal injuries —
>
> (a) no damages shall be recoverable in respect of any loss of expectation of life caused to the injured person by the injuries; but
> (b) if the injured person's expectation of life has been reduced by the injuries, the court in assessing damages in respect of pain and suffering caused by the injuries, shall take account of any suffering caused or likely to be caused to him by awareness that his expectation of life has been so reduced."

1.4.47 [4.20] We are much attracted by this approach. It offers the possibility of a systematic treatment of solatium for loss of expectation of life without making an arbitrary distinction between the living claimant and the deceased claimant. It also means that the present conventional basis of assessment could be replaced by a flexible assessment, which could take individual circumstances more fully into account. In effect, loss of expectation of life would be compensated as an aspect of pain and suffering; that is, mental suffering caused by awareness of loss would be compensated. Admittedly, adopting this approach would overturn the law as established in *Dalgleish v Glasgow Corporation*. The comatose victim would no longer have a claim for loss of expectation of life, though the larger claim for loss of faculties and amenities would be unaffected. We think that is an acceptable price to pay for putting the claim for loss of expectation of life on a more realistic basis.

1.4.48 [4.21] We therefore recommend:

    3.   Damages by way of solatium for loss of expectation of life should be recoverable only where the injured person is aware of the loss and suffers in consequence.

······

Conditions for transmissibility?

1.4.49 [4.22] Given our recommendation that, in principle, a right to damages by way of solatium should transmit, we must now consider whether it should transmit unconditionally or subject to conditions. We have already considered and rejected a suggestion made by some of our consultees that the benefit of the deceased's claim should be confined to the immediate family. But other conditions may be apposite.

1.4.50 [4.23] For example, under the pre-1976 rule it was a condition for transmissibility that the deceased should have raised an action while alive. As we explained in Part III, justification for the rule rested on the view that solatium was inherently personal. It was a corollary of this view that legal action was the prerogative of the injured person. It was for the injured person to elect to sue or not to sue. The same idea appears in association with the doctrine of litiscontestation, which was also used to justify the pre-1976 rule. Raising an action was regarded as an unequivocal intimation to the alleged wrongdoer that the claim had not been waived:

> "If the ground on which the exception is based is that by raising an action the deceased sufferer has provided evidence of his having made up his mind to seek reparation, it would be an easy step to the position that his election might be established by some other evidence, on the view that there is no reason in principle why, in seeking evidence of a concluded election, one should discriminate between raising an action and intimating that an action is to be raised. It is only a matter of degree.
>
> If, on the other hand, there is some inherent virtue in a public and significant act, like the raising of an action, which distinguishes it in kind from the mere private and equivocal act of intimating an intention to the opposite party, then it is open to say that the Court in *Leigh's Executrix* did more than just develop an existing principle. In my view, the raising of an action is different in kind from the intimation of an intention to

do so. An action convenes the defender before a Court of law with certain inevitable consequences; short of some form of abandonment it is irrevocable. On the negative side, it shows that the ground of action has not been waived. Intimation of a claim has no such effect; it may be no more than a manoeuvre or a threat; it carries no consequences, it involves the intimator in no risks. It is not even conclusive on whether the sufferer has decided not to waive his ground of action. The defender need do nothing, indeed, he may never hear anything further.

Since the decision of the House of Lords in *Stewart*, it must be taken that the rationale of the exception is the institution of an action, as such, and not that the raising of the action is evidence of an election to vindicate the ground of action."

1.4.51 [4.24] We are obviously not concerned to maintain this particular view of solatium. But we do recognise that there are personal elements in a claim for solatium and that the principle of election may be one such element of continuing importance. Certainly it suggests pertinent questions. For example, should an executor have an unfettered discretion to pursue a claim for solatium which the deceased did not pursue, and might never have pursued? It is easy to imagine circumstances where the deceased would have been unwilling to raise an action. Perhaps, therefore, special provision is needed to ensure that the deceased's intention to pursue a claim is properly attested before action is taken by an executor. Again, how far should an executor be liable to beneficiaries if he fails to investigate and follow up potential claims? Should an executor be protected by being required to pursue only those claims where the deceased's intention to sue has been appropriately manifested before death; or can we simply assume that a claim for solatium is no different from a claim for pecuniary loss? If no special provision is required for the latter, none may be required for the former.

1.4.52 [4.25] These questions may point to a need for conditions qualifying transmissibility in the case of claims for solatium. On the other hand, imposing such conditions may itself cause further difficulties. If some act by the deceased while alive is to be a prerequisite of transmissibility, what happens if an injured person is incapacitated by the injury and unable to act? Would special provision be required for someone to act on his or her behalf; or would the ordinary law of curatory suffice?

1.4.53 [4.26] We put these issues to consultation in Discussion Paper No 89. The clear consensus among our commentators, with only a small minority dissenting, was that if a right to claim solatium was allowed to transmit, it should transmit unconditionally. As one commentator put it:

"… we do not consider it appropriate that a condition be attached that the deceased, while alive, either intimate a claim or raise an action.

The reason for this is that in many of the most tragic cases, for example, cases of persons suffering from Mesothelioma … diagnosis of the cause of the illness is only made subsequent to death at post-mortem and in consequence no claim is anticipated until this diagnosis is made."

1.4.54   [4.27] Of course conditions could be imposed subject to yet further qualifications to cater for such eventualities. But this would entail a statutory scheme of some complexity. And, arguably, such a scheme would merely provide alternative and perhaps even more artificial cut-offs than the present law. More particularly, a condition that the deceased should have raised an action while alive seems more likely to provoke early litigation than to encourage settlement. It seems to us, therefore, to be quite sufficient to rely on the established principles of prescription and limitation. We see no point in trying to devise an elaborate scheme of conditions for general application, when on the evidence of our consultation any such scheme would attract little support. We do however think that there may be an argument for imposing conditions in the case of claims arising from defamation or other verbal inquiry or other injury to reputation. We examine this special case separately.

4. Fiona Montgomery, "New bill will help asbestos families"
Evening Times, October 21, 1992

1.5.1   'A new Bill will help families of Scots asbestosis victims.

Under it, they will be able to claim compensation — even after the victim has died.

The Labour-sponsored Bill, which will ensure Scots families have the same rights as those in England to claim compensation, should be law by the summer.

Clydeside Action on Asbestos today welcomed the news but said many families will still lose out.

. . . . . .

1.5.2   Ministers have agreed with the Bill's sponsors, Lord MacAulay and Brian Wilson, that the law will be backdated to cover deaths on or after July 16 this year, the day of its first reading.

The Damages (Scotland) Bill will have its second reading in the House of Lords next week.

Mr Wilson accepted there would be dispute over the retrospective date but said: "The first priority is to get a Bill on to the Statute Book."

But campaigners at CAA had hoped it would be backdated further.

. . . . . .

1.5.3   Secretary John Docherty said: "It is good news for future widows and widowers but it should really go back 20 years.

"There should be parity with the English."

Until now the rights of families to compensation has died with the victim causing them considerable stress when they are very ill.

It is estimated the law change could benefit relatives by £30,000–£40,000.

Today, Glasgow widow Bridget Coyle (60) spoke of her disappointment at the backdating.

. . . . . .

1.5.4   Her husband James died from mesothelioma in 1990 and so the new Bill would not help her win compensation.

She said: "It is very unfair."

Mr Wilson added that he expected the Bill to cover about 100 cases per year.

He said: "We welcome Government support although we also have to accept its constraints.

"The fact that our Bill is now underway should relieve some of the strain and worry for those at an advanced stage of their illness."'

5. John Robertson, "£15,000 for widow of asbestos victim"
The Scotsman, May 21, 1993

1.6.1   'The widow of a french polisher who died of asbestos-related cancer after working in a Clyde shipyard during the Second World War, was awarded £15,000 damages yesterday.

A judge rejected a defence by Ernest Rennie's bosses that steps to protect workers from asbestos dust had not been necessary for french polishers who worked in a clean atmosphere. Lord Cameron said that they would still have been at risk of inhaling the dust from other areas of the ship.

1.6.2   Mr Rennie, originally from Clydebank, lived with his wife, Margery, in Portsmouth. He was 75 when he died of mesothelioma in 1990.

During the war, he worked for John Brown (Shipbuilders) and Mrs Rennie sued the firm's successors, Upper Clyde Shipbuilders, at the Court of Session.

1.6.3   Lord Cameron said UCS conceded that precautions to protect workers against asbestos dust had not been taken in Mr Rennie's case. He accepted that french polishers on board ships at that time would have taken all steps to see that their work area was clear of dust, but was satisfied that Mr Rennie had been exposed to significant amounts of asbestos dust where insulation work was taking place.

"I also consider that there was ample evidence to suggest that even within the cabins the atmosphere would be dusty, even though the surfaces upon which they were to work had been cleaned."'

6. Sarah Wilson, "New law will bring damages to asbestos victims"
The Scotsman, October 22, 1992

1.7.1 'Relatives of asbestosis victims in Scotland are to be made eligible for compensation since Government support has been won for a parliamentary bill aimed at bringing Scots law into line with the rest of the UK.

The bill, designed to end the anomaly that forbids compensation claims in Scotland to continue after the death of a victim, was introduced into the House of Lords by a Labour peer, Lord Macaulay of Bragar, QC.

The Damages (Scotland) Bill will allow the Scottish courts to award compensation to relatives, taking account of the pain and suffering of the victim. Until now, the right to that compensation died with the victim.

According to the Law Society of Scotland, this could mean a difference of £30,000–£40,000 in compensation, per case.

1.7.2 The Scottish Law Commission had recommended changes to the law in March and even suggested that there was an incentive under existing arrangements for the insurance companies to delay settlements or spin out the litigation until a victim died.

Brian Wilson, Labour MP for Cunninghame North, said yesterday that a new law should be on the statute books by next summer. "We have reached an agreement with the Government to allow retrospective claims for people who died on or before 16 July 1992," he added.

But while the legislation will help many people, it has come too late for the relatives of Peter Boyle, a former Clydeside shipyard worker who died of an asbestos-related disease last February. They will not be eligible for compensation.

Jim Kelman, the author who is also a member of Clydeside Action on Asbestos, cautiously welcomed the new law saying: "Anything that helps the victims and their families cannot be a bad thing.

"But I don't understand why the cut-off date has to be in July. I don't see why the families of people who died before that date should be penalised. Why can't they set it back 25 years?"'

7. John Mullin, "From dust to dust"
The Guardian, November 12, 1992

1.8.1 'There were eight of them. In a tiny office on the banks of the Clyde, they talked with calm dignity and controlled fury. They were talking of death. Bert Connor said simply: "We're all terminal here. Come back in a year, and there might be four of us still here."

Five days later, Peter Boyle, a quietly spoken man, was dead. He had a heart attack after climbing two flights of stairs at Glasgow City Halls to give his support to people like him, workers dying from asbestos-related illnesses.

Sufferers, who contracted the disease by breathing the asbestos fibres, believe the failure of Glasgow's city fathers to offer alternative premises or make available a goods lift showed what little clout they have. They see themselves as the forgotten victims of Britain's industrial past.

Most of those who die from asbestosis, a lung fibrosis which eventually squeezes the breath from its victims, or mesothelioma, a supposedly rare cancer caused by asbestos fibres, used to work in heavy industry, including shipbuilding, where asbestos, a highly effective flame resistant material, was widely used. Most of the disease blackspots are around the ports. Workers used to play with the asbestos, kicking it up and throwing it at each other.

Asbestosis guarantees a horrible death. As well as breathlessness, one of its early signs is an inability to have sex. Harry McCluskey, 65, a lagger who was one of the so-called white mice because he was covered every day in asbestos dust, said: "What kind of man can I be to my wife now? I can't even bend down to tie my own shoelaces."

In a tiny bedroom in Dalmuir, on the western outskirts of Glasgow, and in the heart of the shipbuilding on the Clyde, Tommy Allan has faded away from 18 to 8 stone. He has confounded doctors by surviving as long as he has. The last time he left his small flat was 18 months ago to attend a former workmate's funeral. He knows the next time he leaves it will be to his own.

. . . . . .

1.8.2 Asbestos is still being used by British manufacturers, albeit under stringent conditions. But the asbestos linked diseases could still spread. Buildings throughout the country contain the material, and there are fears that safety practices will be forgotten when the time comes for them to be demolished. There are worries about asbestos disposal. One example makes the point. Glasgow councillors claim asbestos was left to blow around the playground at St Sixtus primary school during removal work.

Firms using asbestos 50 years ago knew at least some of the dangers of asbestos as workers, unmasked and in ignorance, carried on handling it. Two thousand years ago, Romans used to dispense masks made from pig bladders to workers in contact with asbestos. The annual report of the Chief Inspector of Factories for 1968 stated: "The evil effects of asbestos dust have also attracted my attention. A microscopic examination of this mineral dust which was made by HM Medical Inspector clearly revealed the sharp, glass-like, jagged nature of the particles, and where they are allowed to rise and remain suspended in the air of a room, in any quantity, the effects have been found to be injurious, as might have been expected."

. . . . . .

1.8.3 Problems with compensation claims are exemplified in confidential board minutes of almost 40 years ago from Turner & Newall, one of Britain's main asbestos companies. Claims were coming in even then, although most settled before getting to court. From 1943–55, the company paid out £75,006 in compensation. Payments were around £1,500, including costs. In the past two years, Turner & Newall, still working with asbestos, has paid out about £28 million in compensation.

But complacency elsewhere continues today. No one is carrying out post-graduate medical research in this country, either to find a cure or a treatment to delay death after diagnosis. Nor is there a hospice anywhere in Britain dedicated to those in the terminal stages of asbestos-related diseases.

Claiming disability benefits is a slow, laborious business. It can even involve extra health risks. The Department of Social Security requires a biopsy on those seeking to claim about £117 a week for disability. A biopsy can trigger off the disease, according to research carried out in Western Australia, where an asbestos mine destroyed a whole community. CT scans, a safer method, cost £300 each.

The system is loaded even more heavily against sufferers seeking compensation, particularly north of the border. When he died, Mr Boyle, a 58-year-old former shipyard worker, was within four days of a cash settlement after asbestosis forced him to give up his work. Under Scottish law, his claim dies with him. His wife, Ethel, and three children, will get only a fraction of the small sum Mr Boyle could have expected had he lived long enough to sign the papers.

The difficulties of mounting a legal fight are illustrated by Pat McCrystal, aged 68, who has been told he will die from mesothelioma by Christmas. The former shipwright was determined to see his fight through to court. He wanted to pursue the issue of liability, and to create a legal precedent, but his efforts have been frustrated.

He rejected a first offer from his previous employers of £18,000, then a second of £22,000. The money was increased to £50,000, which he again declined. He was determined to go to court. "Had I got to argue in court, insurance companies would have thrown the employers to the wolves, like they did in the United States. And that would have meant something would have to be done." But he says his counsel withdrew from the case minutes before last month's court case was due to begin because the lawyer's advice had been rejected.

Mr McCrystal was told legal aid would not be extended to another counsel. If he wanted justice, he should go to Parliament. Facing death within three months, he accepted the £50,000.

"I was diagnosed just before last Chrsitmas. So what do I do? Do I just go home and watch the candle burning out? I've gone on a cancer diet plan. Nobody in this country knows about it. I've put on some weight. I would be an ideal guinea pig for somebody to study the benefits of this, but nobody wants to know.

"Nobody is interested in anything about this condition: the employers, the lawyers, the medical profession, the DSS. They are not in the business of saving life or making what's left of it easier. They are in the business of saving money. The whole episode that morning I accepted the money was a charade. I am flabbergasted at the scale of the blackmail.

"I feel cheated out of my retirement. I left school in 1937 and worked hard ever since. I've been building a yacht for four years. It's called Govan Maid. It won't be launched until next spring. I probably won't be around to see it."

For Tommy Allan, there is simply a wait for death. Mr Allan is aged 73, older than most victims of asbestos. He has confounded the doctors who diagnosed mesothelioma four years ago. Two years was thought to be the longest anyone could survive after the illness was identified.

. . . . . .

1.8.4   With an evenness of tone which belies his anger, Mr Forrest says: "I was just annoyed that the employers knew perfectly well of the dangers, and we were never told. You never think of it at the time, but I'm so angry now."

Lord Macaulay of Bragar is shortly to introduce a Bill in the House of Lords in order to close the compensation loophole in Scotland and allow families from north of the border to continue to make claims after the death of the affected person. Campaigners say it will cut down on what they call procrastination by employers in settling debts.

They also hope the move might spark more generous awards in Scotland. Clydeside Action on Asbestos believes compensation claims in Scotland are around one half of what a person in England might expect. A Southampton man diagnosed as suffering from 10 per cent asbestosis recently received more than £100,000 compensation last month, twice what Mr McCrystal received.

. . . . . .

1.8.5   A third factor which is bound to focus attention on the issue are the financial problems now hitting Lloyd's of London. American insurers have refused for several years to accept premiums from companies seeking to protect themselves from lawsuits, so Lloyd's syndicates have picked up many of the risks. Lloyd's have already paid out about $1 billion in such claims, according to Robin Jackson, of Centre Right, co-ordinator of many of the asbestos-related claims. But they are now receiving 2,000 claims a month, mostly from the United States.

That could mean further serious losses for Lloyd's. The irony is not lost on Bert Connor, chairman of Clydeside Action on Asbestos. "No aristocrat has ever died from this disease. How strange it would

be if something were done now only because some of those greedy
sods at Lloyds start losing cash. Those names are trying to make a
financial killing. All we were doing was going to work.'"

8. Damages (Scotland) Bill [H.L.]
Second Reading, October 28, 1992

1.9.1 'Lord Macaulay of Bragar: It may be helpful if I explain briefly
something of the background and purpose of the Bill. The purpose
of the Bill is to give effect to the recommendations of the Scottish
Law Commission contained in its report *The Effect of Death on Damages*
which was published earlier this year. The Bill makes amendments to
the Damages (Scotland) Act 1976 to deal with a pressing concern
about the unintended effect of that legislation on claims which arise
in particular from terminal industrial diseases and asbestos-induced
disease... As I have indicated, the reference to the commission
reflected a growing concern in legal circles and in the public mind
about the effects of the Damages (Scotland) Act 1976 on claims arising
from terminal industrial diseases.

. . . . . .

1.9.2 The principal change which the Bill, if enacted, would make
to the present law of damages in Scotland is set out in Clause 3. This
would enable the deceased's right to solatium to transmit to his
executor for the benefit of the deceased's estate. Such a claim would
be competent over and above any claim that relatives would be able
to bring in their own right. By enabling the claim for solatium to
transmit to the deceased's executor, the Bill would remove what has
been perceived to be an injustice in the present law in Scotland and,
indeed, as I understand it, it will bring the law into line with that in
England which has existed for some time. It would also relieve
claimants from the anxiety that they presently face from the harrowing
knowledge that, if their claims are not settled before they die, their
dependants will be financially worse off.

1.9.3 The Bill retains, but seeks to clarify, the non-patrimonial award,
presently known as a loss of society award in Section 1(4) of the
Damages (Scotland) Act 1976, for relatives of a deceased person. The
loss of society award remains available to relatives over and above the
transmission to the executor of a right to claim solatium which the
deceased would have received had he survived. The loss of society
award was conceived as being different from the traditional concept
of solatium — for pain and suffering — for dependants. When the
concept was introduced under the Damages (Scotland) Act in 1976,
itself based on a Scottish Law Commission report, it was envisaged
that the award would be made for reasons other than assuaging the

grief and sorrow of the claimant and that its basis would be much wider. The underlying assumption was that the wider basis would encourage the courts to make more generous awards. In practice, this has not happened.

When a person dies through injury his immediate family may be said to sustain non-patrimonial injury in three ways. First, where to their knowledge the injured person has undergone suffering before death, they experience distress and anxiety in contemplating that suffering. Secondly, they suffer grief and sorrow at the death. Thirdly, they are deprived of the person's society and guidance in the future. Compensation is, however, provided in the Damages (Scotland) Act 1976 only for the deprivation of the deceased's society. Notwithstanding the terms of the 1976 Act, all three sources of injury to feelings which I have outlined have probably in practice been taken into account by the court in most cases when awards are made for loss of society. Clause 1 of the Bill, by itemising these three elements, therefore seeks to provide a secure legislative foundation for the assessment of awards. In assessing an award the court will not be required to ascribe specifically any part of the award to any of the three elements — the stress and anxiety, grief and sorrow, and loss of non-patrimonial benefit — set out in the clause. But if the Bill passes, the award can be scrutinised in the light of the legislative foundation set out in the Bill.

A consequence of enacting Clause 1 is that it will no longer be appropriate to refer to a "loss of society award". The Bill accordingly provides for the removal of the reference to "loss of society" in the 1976 Act. More significantly, it is hoped that the very fact of reformulating the award may act as an incentive to the courts to make more generous awards than at present apply.

. . . . . .

1.9.4   Under the present law loss of expectation of life attracts a small conventional award of solatium. Awareness of that loss by the injured person is not currently a prerequisite for entitlement to the award. This provision creates difficulties if claims for solatium are to be allowed to survive, as the Bill provides for. The executor to whom the right transmits would have the task of having to prove the extent of the deceased's suffering in disputed cases. This may be a difficult task on occasions in the absence of evidence from the deceased; and the shorter the period of survival after injury the more difficult it is likely to be. Clause 5 of the Bill therefore provides that no damages by way of solatium for loss of expectation of life shall be recoverable except where the expectation of life has been reduced and the injured person was or is likely to become aware of that reduction. Under the provisions proposed in Clause 5, the courts would, in assessing solatium, be required to have regard to the extent to which the injured person has suffered or is likely to suffer as a consequence of that awareness. Such loss would be compensated as an aspect of pain and suffering and claims for solatium in that regard will survive accordingly.

1.9.5 Those are the principal provisions of the Bill. Its other provisions are in the main of a technical nature which your Lordships may consider could most appropriately be considered at a later stage if your Lordships agree that the Bill receive a Second Reading today.

1.9.6 I should like to raise one final important matter. The provisions in the Bill relating to the transmissibility to the deceased's executor of rights to solatium have effect only where death occurs after the date of commencement of the Bill. As I mentioned earlier, some of those who have contracted asbestos-related diseases will have only a very short time to live. Indeed there may be some who will not live to see the enactment of this Bill which I have introduced with the express purpose of providing some benefit to them and their family. To ensure that as many families as possible will benefit from the provisions of the Act, I propose to bring forward an amendment at Committee stage which, if accepted by your Lordships, will enable the new rights of transmissibility to executors to apply in cases where the death of the injured person occurred on or after the date of the introduction of the Bill — namely, 16th July 1992 — provided that these rights cannot be exercised if the claim is time barred, or has been settled, or judicially determined.

1.9.7 In all such legislation there must be a cut-off point which is normally the date of the passing of the legislation. Because of the nature of the diseases we are dealing with in this legislation I have thought it proper to introduce an element of retrospection which, among other things, will ease the burden on surviving victims and their families. I should advise your Lordships that I have held discussions with the noble and learned Lords, the Minister of State, Lord Fraser of Carmyllie, and the Lord Advocate, Lord Rodger of Earlsferry, who have informed me that they would support the principle of such an amendment. I hope that my amendment will gain your Lordships' support when it is brought forward in Committee.

1.9.8 In providing for the transmission of solatium to an executor of the deceased injured person and in reformulating the present loss of society award and allowing it to be transmitted to the executor of a deceased relative, the Bill will significantly improve the financial position of those unfortunate enough to lose a close family member through personal injury. By enabling a claim for solatium to transmit to the executor of the victim, the provisions of the Bill will help to relieve the added anxiety which he or she and the immediate family suffer in the knowledge that if the victim dies before the action for damages is settled or completed his family will be worse off. The report of the Scottish Law Commission on which the Bill's provisions are based has been widely welcomed and supported. I trust that the Bill will receive the support of your Lordships' House.

. . . . . .

1.9.9   Lord Cocks of Hartcliffe: My Lords, I rise briefly to thank my noble friend Lord Macaulay of Bragar for introducing and moving the Second Reading of the Bill and taking us through its provisions. In another place I was sponsored by one of the major trade unions which has been involved in this field, especially in the asbestos-related diseases to which my noble friend referred. We should place on record not only personal gratitude but also the gratitude of many of the trade union members, particularly the full-time trade union officers who have had to deal with these very harrowing cases mentioned by my noble friend. I should like to point out how very much it is appreciated that the law is being brought into line with that which applies in the rest of the country and that this anomalous situation will be remedied.

I welcome my noble friend's suggestion about an amendment to be tabled in Committee. I hope that will be carried through. Given the background to the Bill, I am sure that your Lordships will wish to ensure that it passes through the House with the maximum speed.

1.9.10   Lord Carmichael of Kelvingrove: My Lords, I rise merely to say that the Bill before us has, so far as I know, been brought forward by the Scottish Law Commission, is supported by two distinguished QCs, and I understand that my noble friend Lord Macaulay of Bragar and the noble and learned Lord the Lord Advocate also support it. Therefore, it is difficult for someone like myself as a non-legal person to make any comment on the Bill. However, I think that the explanation given by my noble friend Lord Macaulay will be a great help to laymen such as myself. As my noble friend said, the Bill covers a complex area of law. Listening to the speech, inevitably, a great deal of it seemed to be what I think we would call "lawyers' speak" in terms of people like me.

There is but one point I should like to raise. Again, it is possible that it may become even more complicated. As a layman, it seems to me that there is a possibility of a great deal of legal discussion. I have in mind Clause 5 as regards the solatium of loss of expectation of life. That struck me as being a matter which could raise a great deal of argument, discussion and debate. Of course, there may be legal precedents for it and if the noble and learned Lord the Lord Advocate or my noble friend tells me so, then I shall accept it. However, I imagine that there must be a point at which the person who is claiming the damages becomes aware of the fact that he is likely to die relatively soon. I should like some clarification on that point. At what stage will this add or subtract from the final decision as regards the award given by the tribunal of the court? As I said, there may be a simple way of assessing the situation, but it seems to me to be one of the points that could cause a great deal of disturbance.

. . . . . .

1.9.11   The Lord Advocate (Lord Rodger of Earlsferry): My Lords, the Government warmly welcome the Bill … In respect of the remarks made by the noble Lord, Lord Carmichael, I believe it is right to add that Clause 5 seeks to deal with what is a very difficult head of damages; and, indeed, with the acuteness of the layman looking at the problem, the noble Lord has actually pointed out the very area which is most difficult and which has always given difficulty to the courts when assessing that particular head of damages. I say that because, for the very reason indicated by the noble Lord, it is difficult for a court to put a figure upon what the damages should be for the loss of expectation of life. One of the aspects of that difficulty is, for example, to decide to what extent the award should be made only when the person has been aware of the fact that he is losing life. That kind of aspect is dealt with in Clause 5. As I said, it is a difficult area and the clause is designed to try to clarify that aspect of the law.

1.9.12   I turn now to Clause 3 and the rest of the Bill. The first thing which may strike your Lordships — and it has already been referred to by the noble Lord, Lord Carmichael — is that the Bill is couched in rather complex and legal language. But although there are dry technicalities, the issues at stake are very important and affect the every-day lives of many men and women. Even in very legal language, the Bill is tackling an important and sensitive issue.

It may seem somewhat surprising to your Lordships that Parliament is being asked to make an important change of principle in the law of damages which was set down as recently — I use the word "recently" as lawyers would — as 16 years ago. The reason behind that is that the provisions adopted in 1976 have given rise to criticism in practice. The key point is that under the 1976 Act any right to damages for pain and suffering dies with the victim and cannot be pursued by the victim's executor. That is a very strict and absolute rule. It means that even where the victim has raised proceedings for damages in respect of pain and suffering, his executor cannot pursue those aspects of the claim.

It is this provision which gave rise to the suspicion mentioned by the noble Lord, Lord Macaulay, that defenders and their insurers could delay cases in the hope that the victim would die. I have to say that the Law Commission did not find any evidence that that actually happened, but clearly there is a potential inducement here. It is right to notice that that problem did not really exist in Scots law before 1976. Under the law which applied before 1976 an executor could pursue a claim for past pain and suffering in cases where the victim had raised proceedings before his death. It was the 1976 Act which changed that. So in allowing executors to continue such proceedings raised by victims, the provisions of Clauses 3 and 4 of this Bill really just restore Scots law to the position that existed before 1976 and remove a specific problem created at that time.

1.9.13 Actually, the Bill goes further and indeed it goes beyond anything which existed in Scotland before 1976. Clause 4 specifically allows an executor to raise an action for damages for pain and suffering even though the victim had not done so during his lifetime. Before 1976 the Scottish courts held that suffering of this kind was really personal to the victim and that, if he had not begun proceedings, then his executor should not be able to do so since in effect none of the beneficiaries of such a claim would themselves have suffered pain. Clearly there is some force in that argument and the Scottish Law Commission has rehearsed the issues on both sides of it, but in the end they have rightly said that it is simply a matter of policy. They have recommended that the policy be to allow executors to pursue all such claims, whether or not the deceased had begun proceedings.

As I have already indicated, the Government accept the Commission's closely-argued recommendations. However defensible the present provision may be as a matter of pure legal theory, there is no doubt that relatives of victims who have suffered grievous pain find it frankly offensive that the law seems to set that pain and suffering at nought just because the victim has died.

. . . . . .

1.9.14 There is one other point which I would mention, and it has already been raised by the noble Lord, Lord Macaulay. He indicated that he has discussed with my nobel and learned friend Lord Fraser and myself his wish to introduce a clause allowing the new rules of transmissibility to apply where the injured person has died since the date of introduction of the Bill. I think it is right that I should say a few words about that aspect.

My right honourable friend the Secretary of State has received a number of representations arguing that the Bill is somewhat unsatisfactory in its present form, in that it will mean that where a claimant dies after enactment his estate will enjoy the benefits of the Bill, but where the claimant has died prior to enactment, his estate will not. It has been suggested that such a state of affairs will lead to resentment and added distress for families who are continuing their claims for compensation under the previous rules and who are denied the benefits of the new provisions because of lack of retrospection.

I think it is right to say that we all deeply sympathise with such families. It is also right to say that, unfortunately, there is no easy and neat solution which will guarantee fairness in every case. Whether there is retrospective provision or not, I fear there will always be a degree of unfairness to someone where one case is viewed against another.

1.9.15 In seeking a solution which is fair not only to pursuers but to defenders, it is necessary to bear a number of factors in mind. First, it would be wrong in principle to reopen cases where a settlement has been reached either by agreement or by judicial determination. Secondly, to allow, say, the new rules to apply to any case which has not been settled or judicially determined, irrespective of when death occurred, would be a major departure from the legal principle that like cases should be treated in the same way. Such wide-ranging retrospection could produce unfairness where those who have brought forward and settled their claims quickly are penalised, whereas those who have delayed doing so could be rewarded. That would not seem to be fair or acceptable.

However, as a means of ensuring that as many families as possible can benefit from the new rules while keeping within the acceptable bounds of legal policy, we felt able to indicate to the noble Lord, Lord Macaulay, that we would support an amendment to the Bill, as he has indicated. This would provide that, if the Bill passes into law, the new provisions relating to transmissibility of rights to executors will apply where the death of the person concerned occurred on or after the date when the Bill was introduced into your Lordships' House (16th July 1992), provided of course that those rights cannot be exercised if the claim is time-barred or has been settled or judicially determined.

1.9.16 I can confirm to your Lordships' House that such a degree of retrospection would be of a type which is not unfamiliar and would not be objectionable in terms of legal principles. It also means that all the victims who are alive today will be entitled to benefit from its provisions. Although I have touched on only a few points, the Government have considered the Bill as a whole, and I am happy to commend it to your Lordships' House.

1.9.17 **Lord Macaulay of Bragar**: My Lords, I am grateful to the noble Lords who have made a contribution to the debate from the various aspects of their experience. I agree with the noble Lord, Lord Carmichael, that perhaps Clause 5 raises some difficult problems. That will be looked at closely again in the light of the observations he has made. Although this Bill is a short one, it is important, as must be obvious from what the noble and learned Lord the Lord Advocate has said. It will represent a progressive step forward in Scots law, and I ask your Lordships to give the Bill a Second Reading.'

9. **Damages (Scotland) Bill [H.L.]**
Committee, November 11, 1992

1.10.1 'Lord Macaulay of Bragar': My Lords, I beg to move that the House do now resolve itself into Committee on this Bill.

. . . . . .

1.10.2   **The Earl of Selkirk** had given notice of his intention to move Amendment No. 1:

Page 1, line 12, leave out ("from the deceased's society and guidance").

The noble Earl said: I am not going to talk about this amendment at all. We are at a late hour and there are very few Members present for a Bill of outstanding importance. I question whether further discussion at this stage is really worthwhile. I suggest that we take a further look at the report which we have in front of us.

. . . . . .

1.10.3   **Lord Macaulay of Bragar** moved Amendment No. 4:

Page 1, line 16, at end insert:

("(2) At the beginning of subsection (5) of that section there shall be added the words "Subject to subsection (5A) below,".

(3) After subsection (5) of that section there shall be inserted the following subsection —

"(5A) Where a deceased has been awarded a provisional award of damages under section 12(2) of the Administration of Justice Act 1982, the making of that award does not prevent liability from arising under this section but in assessing for the purposes of this section the amount of any loss of support suffered by a relative of the deceased the court shall take into account such part of the provisional award relating to future patrimonial loss as was intended to compensate the deceased for a period beyond the date on which he died.".").

The noble Lord said: Take the case of a shipyard worker of 40 years of age who has contracted asbestosis as a result of working with that substance. His doctor tells him that he has scars on his lungs and that he is unfit for any gainful employment. The doctor also reveals that there is a risk of mesothelioma developing at an unspecified future date.

Faced with a complete loss of future earnings, the claimant seeks advice from his lawyer who decides that the best course for the claimant is to raise an action for provisional damages in terms of Section 12 of the Administration of Justice Act 1982. The action is raised and the pursuer recovers solatium in respect of the injury to his lungs and he is awarded a sum representing loss of earnings for a period of future time. The court awards these damages as provisional damages under, and in terms of, Section 12 of the 1982 Act. In a year or two after the provisional award has been made mesothelioma develops and causes the claimant's death before he has an opportunity to return to court to finalise his award.

Two questions arise. The first is: do the provisions of Section 1(2) of the 1976 Act prevent a claim being made by the relatives? Section 1(2) should not preclude the raising of an action by the relatives on his death. In part, this amendment is intended to remove any doubt as to that. The second question is whether there is a possibility that there could be an overlap of the loss of earnings awarded as a provisional award under the 1982 Act to the claimant and the loss of support which may be claimed by the relatives under Section 1(4) of the 1976 Act. It would appear that this might well arise as there could be a potential overlap of patrimonial damages where the deceased has obtained in his provisional award of damages a sum representing his entire loss of earnings throughout his life. In such a case it would be inequitable that the defender should also be liable to pay the relatives damages for loss of support resulting from the deceased's death. If this had not been a provisional award of damages, the payment of such an amount for patrimonial loss would have discharged the defender's liability and thus prevented the relatives claim from arising.

To obviate the possibility of double damages being paid, the amendment enables the court to take into account in considering the relatives' claim such part of the provisional award relating to future patrimonial loss as was intended to compensate the deceased for any period beyond the date on which he died. I hope you will agree that this amendment clarifies the existing law and provides a solution which is fair both to the relatives and to the defender. I beg to move.

1.10.4 Baroness Carnegy of Lour: I am sure that it was a very full description of the amendment that the noble Lord gave. It is not easy for a lay person to follow that kind of description. Can he tell the Committee whether this amendment comes from any particular body? Is this a Law Commission second thought about the Bill, or does it come from any particular direction? It would help the Committee to understand what is happening. I do not think it was mentioned at Second Reading. I was not able to be here but I have read the *Hansard* report and I do not remember that aspect being mentioned.

1.10.5 Lord Macaulay of Bragar: To be honest at this stage, I cannot be precise; but I think it arises out of the report of the Scottish Law Commission on the effect of death on damages.

1.10.6 The Lord Advocate (Lord Rodger of Earlsferry): Perhaps I could help my noble friend Lady Carnegy. This particular amendment derives from I shall not say a second thought but a further thought by the Scottish Law Commission and a letter from Lord Davidson on this matter. It was realised that if this particular amendment was not brought in, a difficulty would arise where someone died after a part of the procedure had been gone through, and that while alive that person had recovered a sum of money which would include a sum for future loss of earnings for a period beyond that period when he actually died.

Therefore, when he had died and his relatives then came to bring their claim, and that claim being for a loss of dependency during the period after his death, it was seen that there would be a possibility of double counting, so to speak. In order to take account of that matter, the chairman of the Scottish Law Commission wrote, and this is an amendment deriving from the Scottish Law Commission.

1.10.7   The Earl of Selkirk moved Amendment No. 5:

Page 2, line 9, leave out ("not").

The noble Earl said: This is an important point. The Bill would delete that on the death of a certain person the executors will be fully informed. The executors should be fully informed. In a way it is a small point but they may be interested in a variety of matters and all sorts of things may be concerned relating to the property of the man who died. His relatives and friends should be acquainted as to how they stand. For that reason this should remain and the word "not" should be taken out. It seems to me to be fair to the persons concerned and that that is the best way to handle it.

1.10.8   Lord Rodger of Earlsferry: I am not sure that I understood the noble Earl, Lord Selkirk, when he said that he thought that the relatives should be informed of a certain matter, and he thought that if the amendment was not carried, the effect would somehow or other be to deprive the relatives or the executor of some information. I think that what the noble Earl said perhaps rested on a misunderstanding of the purpose of Clause 3(2). I shall explain what the effect of Amendments Nos. 5 and 6 would be.

The idea of the amendment of the Law Society was that not only claims for solatium but also claims for patrimonial loss in the period after the deceased's death should transmit to an executor on the death of the deceased injured person. The existing Section 2(3)(b) of the Act, which is re-enacted by what will become Section 2(2), is intended to prevent the duplication of damages. But Section 2(3)(b) does much more than that because it actually expresses one of the fundamental purposes behind the Act and rests on a principle which has been part of Scots law for — I put it at the very lowest — at least 100 years. The principle is that compensation is directly related to the loss suffered.

When a claimant dies the situation is radically changed, and in the new situation the claims of the deceased's executor and the claims of the surviving relatives are quite distinct. The claim of the executor is one for compensation for losses which have been suffered by the deceased up until the date of his death. Thereafter, the deceased having died, he can suffer no more and it is a matter of compensating relatives for their losses after the deceased's death. That is the basic structure of the legislation. This amendment would completely undermine it.

I should add that with the introduction of the new rules on transmissibility, which is the whole point of the Bill, the family should be substantially better off than it was formerly. In addition to solatium, which would come via the executor, the relatives enjoy the right of loss of support suffered since death or likely to be suffered as well as the reformulated loss of society award relating to non-patrimonial benefits.

The effect of the amendment would be particularly unacceptable if the deceased died leaving no dependants who can make a claim for loss of support. It could then happen that some beneficiary who might be a very remote relative would receive a windfall sum of damages which would apparently be designed to compensate the deceased for earnings which he could not make because he was dead. Such a concept verges on the grotesque.

There may indeed be a case for a further and wider review of the current law on damages, as the noble Earl suggested, but this amendment would represent a fundamental departure from the present law and would raise much wider issues such as the possible use of structured settlements or actuarial methods for calculating damages. No change such as is envisaged by Amendments Nos. 5 or 6 could possibly be contemplated without wide-ranging consultation and without seeking the advice of the Scottish Law Commission. I underline the fact that the Bill has been prepared by the Scottish Law Commission. Bearing those matters in mind, I ask the noble Earl to withdraw the amendment.

1.10.9   The Earl of Selkirk: I hate to say this but I could not understand the noble and learned Lord the Lord Advocate. I did not follow his argument. He said that the relatives should get other things, which is exactly what I am trying to do. If a man is killed, one would expect his wife and children to get something. Who would give it to them? The executors would receive it and it would be up to them to hand it on.

I listened as carefully as I could to what the noble and learned Lord said. If he can tell me that that is what will happen, I shall not press the point further. I realise that the Bill is not finished and is still in a somewhat immature state. But if that is not what it does, I think it is wrong. The relatives must get those things. It may be a house, a handkerchief, tables or chairs, but that is what they should have. There is no protection if the word "not" is left in. The noble and learned Lord may show that I am wrong but that is my reading of the Bill as it stands.

1.10.10 Lord Rodger of Earlsferry: I am sure that it is my fault if the noble Earl did not follow my explanation. I can assure him that the Bill as it stands does not take away anything from the relatives. On the contrary, the effect of the Bill will be to increase what is claimable by the executor. As the noble Earl rightly said, the executors would pass it on to the people entitled to it.

Under the present law the executor can claim only for damages suffered by way of patrimonial loss by the estate up until the date of the man's death. The executor cannot recover damages for the pain and suffering which the man has suffered up until the present date. The effect of the Bill will be that from now on the executor will have a claim which will relate not only to the loss suffered but also to the pain and suffering which the man experienced before his death. The effect of the noble Earl's amendment would be to go much further than that — this is where I take issue with it — and to undermine the principle underlying the whole of our law of damages and say that, in addition to that, a sum will be awarded for earnings which he would have had after his death. What happens under law is that the estate does not get earnings after the man's death but the relatives get a sum which represents what they would have been expected to get if he had lived. That is a just and fair way of proceeding. It is certainly the way the law has been up until now.

It may be that I have not made the matter sufficiently clear. I should be more than happy to discuss it with the noble Earl between now and Report stage. If he has any doubts or hesitations at that stage I have no doubt that he will raise the matter again. I ask him to withdraw the amendment at this stage.

1.10.11 The Earl of Selkirk: I do not have doubts on the laying down of the law by the Lord Advocate on any account. I would not for a moment press this point. But what I am saying is that I do not understand how the damages of a man who has been killed can possibly transfer to his relatives. That seems to be one of the things the noble and learned Lord said, but I may not be right. I am sure that the noble and learned Lord has taken the point; he has asserted that without the "not" he gets the point. If he says that, I am prepared to withdraw the amendment.

1.10.12 Lord Carmichael of Kelvingrove moved Amendment No. 7:

Page 2, leave out lines 28 to 33 and insert:

""Enforcement by executor of rights transmitted to him.

2A.—(1) For the purpose of enforcing any right transmitted to an executor under section 1A or 2 of this Act the executor shall be entitled —

(a) to bring an action; or

> (b)　to be sisted as pursuer if an action for that purpose has been
> brought by the deceased but has not been concluded before his
> death.").

The noble Lord said: After the discussion between the Lord
Advocate and the noble Earl, Lord Selkirk, I approach this fairly simple
amendment with a certain temerity. The amendment is proposed by
the Law Society of Scotland. Its purpose is to restructure Clause 4 and
is for clarification purposes only. The Law Society of Scotland considers
that Clause 4 as presently worded is unclear. It has therefore asked
me to put forward this amendment which is certainly simpler in terms
of words. As to whether it is as clear legally, I await the Lord Advocate's
comments. I beg to move.

1.10.13　Lord Macaulay of Bragar: I am grateful to my noble friend
Lord Carmichael of Kelvingrove for bringing the matter before the
Committee. In dealing with the amendment, I should put on record
the fact that we are grateful to the Law Society for the careful and
constructive approach that it has taken to what is a most important
Bill and one which is demanded by the people of Scotland. In this
case, I am prepared to give my noble friend an assurance that the
principle behind the amendment is acceptable. It will require a little
redrafting but that will not change the spirit of the amendment;
indeed, I think that it will make it much clearer. With that assurance,
I hope that my noble friend will see fit to withdraw the amendment.

1.10.14　Lord Carmichael of Kelvingrove: I know that my noble friend
Lord Macaulay of Bragar has spent much time on the Bill and had
many discussions with the Law Society. Therefore, until we reach
Report stage, I am certainly happy to withdraw the amendment.

1.10.15　Lord Macaulay of Bragar moved Amendment No. 11 ...
The noble Lord said: In my remarks during the Second Reading
debate I informed noble Lords that it was my intention to bring forward
an amendment to Clause 6 of the Bill which would enable the new
rights of transmissibility to executors to apply in cases where
the death of the injured person occurred on or after the date of
introduction of the Bill in this Chamber — namely, 16th July 1992 —
subject to certain provisions and, in particular, provided that those rights
could not be exercised if the claim was time-barred (obviously, by the
passage of time as set out in law) or had been settled, or judicially
determined in a court. The amendment seeks to give effect to that
undertaking. The clause is necessarily somewhat complex in its
structure. It may assist Members of the Committee if I explain its
principal provisions...

No doubt that explanation sounds very technical — indeed, it is
very technical — but it was correct to put it on record so that people,
especially lawyers, who read the report of the debate will understand

the purpose of the amendment. I trust that Members of the Committee will agree that, in effect, the solution of suspending the running of the prescription period in the last section that I mentioned represents a reasonably fair means of dealing with what we all hope will be a small number of claims arising in that interim period.

As the noble and learned Lord the Lord Advocate remarked on Second Reading, whether there is retrospection or not, there will always be a degree of unfairness to someone when one case is viewed against another. It is not possible to reopen cases where settlement has been made; nor, for the reasons explained by the noble and learned Lord, is it possible to change the rules for ongoing cases, irrespective of when death occurred. However, if the amendment is accepted by the Committee, it should provide some degree of comfort to those currently suffering from a terminal industrial disease. Should such people die before the Bill is enacted, it will ensure that their families will, nevertheless, be able to benefit from the improved provisions. That is the main objective behind the Bill. I beg to move.

1.10.16 Baroness Carnegy of Lour: As the noble Lord has explained to me the reason behind the amendment, I understand it very well. I have also read his Second Reading speech and that of my noble and learned friend the Lord Advocate. I understand that the amendment has been put forward for reasons of compassion and sympathy for certain people who will be on the wrong side of the cut-off line when the Bill becomes enacted.

As I understand it, the intention is to backdate part of the clause to the date of the Bill's First Reading. On Second Reading, I believe that both the noble Lord and my noble and learned friend said that there were precedents for the provision. As a lay person, it seems to me to be extremely strange that one can arbitrarily fix the date when the Bill received its First Reading as the date after which people are able to take advantage of the Bill's provisions. I wonder whether the noble Lord, Lord Macaulay, or my noble and learned friend can tell me what kind of precedents there are in this respect? Are they numerous? It seems very strange. I wonder whether it is good law.

1.10.17 Lord Macaulay of Bragar: I thank the noble Baroness for raising the point which, of course, interests us all. The reason for taking the provision back to First Reading is that the House sets its face against retrospective legislation in principle, and we had to strike a balance. There has to be a cut-off point at some stage, and we believed that we were doing the best that we could and being as fair as we could by making the First Reading what the noble Baroness has called the arbitrary date. I describe it as the most reasonable date that we could think of in all the circumstances.

1.10.18 Baroness Carnegy of Lour: Does the noble Lord know what precedents there are?

1.10.19   Lord Macaulay of Bragar: I cannot quote a precedent. Each Bill has to be considered on its own merits. Perhaps the noble and learned Lord the Lord Advocate can give some precedents.

1.10.20   Lord Rodger of Earlsferry: I do not believe that I can put my hand on a precedent at the moment, but I am aware in general terms that there are Bills which have been given effect from the date of First Reading. That is done on the broad principle that from that stage onwards the people who have an interest in the possible effects of the Bill are, so to speak, put on notice as to the effect that it will have. That is the reasoning underlying the choice of the date. It might be helpful if I were to write to my noble friend and give her details of some examples. I can assure her that this has been done in the past.

I am grateful to the noble Lord, Lord Macaulay, for the care that he has given to this provision and others and also, of course, to the Law Society of Scotland which has taken an interest in the Bill and has discussed various aspects of it with him and the noble Lord, Lord Carmichael. I am grateful to everyone involved.'

10. Damages (Scotland) (No. 2) Bill
Second Scottish Standing Committee, January 27, 1993

RIGHTS OF RELATIVES OF A DECEASED PERSON

1.11.1   Mr Brian Wilson (Cunninghame North): As the Bill received its Second Reading as a formality, it may help members of the Committee if I take the opportunity to explain something of its background and purpose. My involvement arises from the fact that I was drawn number 19 in the private Members' ballot and I thought that it would be useful to introduce such a measure.

. . . . . .

1.11.2   Dr Norman A. Godman (Greenock and Port Glasgow): Has my hon. Friend sought advice from his legal friends about the restrictions that may be placed upon claims such as those that he has described by the imposition of changes in the rules of access to civil legal aid? Trade unions have become involved in many asbestosis cases but some claimants are not trade union members. Where do they stand? Do they have to appeal to a lawyer to take on a speculative case?

1.11.3   Mr Wilson: My hon. Friend has touched on an important question. It is self-evident that improvements in the law are of value only if people have access to the law to seek the necessary redress. I hope to clarify that matter before the end of our proceedings, but my hon. Friend has made that point well.

In setting out the background to the Bill, it is appropriate to point out that we are dealing with an anomaly in the law of Scotland that has caused a great deal of grief, unhappiness and additional pressure to families that are already in the saddest of circumstances. I am grateful for the support that the Bill has received, and I hope that it can go through its detailed consideration today. I know that hon. Members will want to contribute to the discussion and to refer to the experience of their constituents. If we proceed with the Bill, I have no doubt that a useful and important social reform will be achieved for Scotland.

1.11.4   Mr Menzies Campbell (Fife, North-East): I should declare an interest as I am still a member of the Faculty of Advocates and the Bill involves access to the law and, indeed, the terms of the law of Scotland.

I approach this matter not so much from the point of view of constituents but as someone who has, in professional practice, acted on behalf of both pursuers and defenders, although in reality it has been on behalf of insurance companies that have taken up the case of defenders who have been sued. I have little doubt that the overall provisions of the Bill, especially clause 1, go a long way to filling the lacuna that has existed since the last substantial change in the law in 1976.

At the heart of the matter is the tactic that is based on the belief that it is in the interests of defenders in civil litigation to put off for as long as possible the day of judgment — literally and metaphorically — when the case comes to court. There have been cases in which a defence, while not dilatory in the technical sense, has been conducted perfectly properly and within the law in such a way as to draw matters out for as long as possible in the hope that as a consequence of delay circumstances might arise where the actual sum of money recovered from the defenders — in practice, the insurance company — would be reduced. That has undoubtedly led to injustice. It has certainly led to a lack of equity. The Bill passed through the other place with remarkable speed and with all party support and goes a long way towards dealing with that lack of equity.

1.11.5   Dr Godman: May I seek some free legal advice from the hon. Gentleman? Judging from his experience, does he agree that some of these cases are difficult to determine? I referred to a lawyer taking a case on a speculative basis. Given the difficulty of determining such cases, some lawyers may be unwilling to act for someone on a speculative basis, especially if access to legal aid is denied to that person.

1.11.6   Mr Campbell: The hon. Member for Greenock and Port Glasgow (Dr Godman) is not a lawyer but often shows a remarkable perception of how the law operates, and particularly of how it could be improved. He has raised an important point. Causation has to be established based on the merits of the case: do fault and negligence lie with the defenders and did that fault give rise to the condition from which the individual is suffering? In the case of someone who suffers from asbestosis, that may be an extremely difficult issue of fact to determine. It may require substantial investigation and the employment of expert witnesses. To put it colloquially, it may require a lot of leg work among former employees who worked with the person who contracted the disease who is seeking compensation.

Lawyers who take cases on a speculative basis are inclined to take on the more straightforward cases — for instance, to act for a passenger in a motor car that was involved in an accident. Self-evidently, the passenger was not at fault; either one or both drivers were at fault, and the lawyer will know that he is bound to win against someone. The recovery of fees and outlays is not at risk.

With a case as complicated as a claim for asbestosis, however lawyers may sometimes not be prepared to risk the expenditure involved because of the difficulty of establishing the merits of the claim, never mind the damages. That is why the comment of the hon. Member for Greenock and Port Glasgow to the hon. Member for Cunninghame, North (Mr Wilson) was well taken. There is no point in improving the law, making it more equitable and just, if the level of access to the law is not maintained. That is why, when the legal aid proposals come before a Standing Committee, perhaps chaired by you, Mr Martin, the Government should not expect the same unanimity or sweetness and light as we are likely to see today. I do not want to stray into those matters, Mr Martin, because even your tolerance might be exhausted.

We are dealing with complicated matters, but we should remember that they are of deep significance to those whose lives are affected. The claim of a widow of a person who had contracted asbestosis will be truncated unless the Bill is enacted. What we do today may be of material significance to that widow. I doubt whether she would understand the intricacies of the law, but the changes that the Bill seeks to bring about may have substantial consequences for her quality of life.

The assessment of damages is not an empirical science, it is an art. Some judges are more generous than others, as one can see from reading *Scots Law Times* or other records of decided cases. The more clear signposts there are, the more uniform will be the awards. One cannot create circumstances in which a tariff could be used, but with clear signposts, such as clause 1, which shows under what heads damages may be recovered as compared to loss of society, which was imprecise and gave rise to varying interpretations, the better chance there will be of people being treated justly. Awards would thus be comparable with awards that others obtained in similar cases.

. . . . . .

1.11.7   Dr Godman: I am sorry. I dashed into the Committee helter-skelter from the debate on the Floor of the House, where I was hoping to speak on the exclusion of the social chapter from the Maastricht treaty.

I shall conclude my remarks, but I reiterate that problems remain regarding what seems to many people to be restricted access to legal assistance in pursuing a claim.

1.11.8   Mr Menzies Campbell: The hon. Gentleman referred to the fact that many people receive legal assistance from their trade union. However, he should know, if he does not already, that, because of the decline in membership and the increase in applications for legal aid, several trade unions have adopted a more restrictive approach in deciding whether trade union members are automatically entitled to legal support. Although trade unions have supported their members in the past, and many cases have been milestones in the evolution of the law of damages and the law of delict in Scotland, that support can no longer be taken for granted because of the internal economic difficulties experienced by trade unions. So it is all the more significant that access to legal services may be reduced as a result of restricting the availability of legal aid.

1.11.9   Dr Godman: I am grateful to the hon. and learned Member for Fife, North-East for that contribution. He has stated a regrettable fact of life for many trade unions. I well recall listening to a case in Edinburgh, in which a trade union member, who had been injured in an accident at work, was represented by a man whom, I am told, is one of the finest QCs in the land. Trade unions have had to introduce restrictions but, from the cases that I have encountered at my surgery, I understand that the unions are doing their best to protect the interests of dying and terminally ill trade union members in as comprehensive a way as possible...

1.11.10   Mr Tony Worthington (Clydebank and Milngavie): I also welcome the Bill and congratulate my hon. Friend the Member for Cunninghame, North on introducing it. It will be a boon for my constituents. I also congratulate organisations such as Clydeside Action on Asbestos that successfully kept this issue before us. It is a transparently just Bill that has all-party agreement...

The Scottish Law Commission's work has been valuable. It has led to today's debate and the attempt to change the law. However, I am disturbed about the way in which the Law Commission formed its contributions. Its survey into the problem was based on the issue of delay. For the reason that I have just given, I do not think that delay is the central issue. The law is unjust whether there is an attempt to delay or not. Many claims are likely to be posthumous. In the case of mesothelioma, 36 per cent. of sufferers were discovered only when they died.

The commission conducted a survey of 45 firms that specialised in this area of law about what was right or wrong with the law. Only 15 firms replied. Of those, the Law Commission conceded that there would have been double counting — one would have acted for the defendant, another for the claimant. The Law Commission was wrong to make no attempt to approach the consumers of the law.

Clydeside Action on Asbestos and concerned individuals could go to the Law Commission. But surely we should recognise that the law is for people other than just lawyers. If we are considering how the law operates, we should ask those people who have been through the legal process for their view of how the law worked. My major point is that, in many cases, the law comes in only at the end of the very long process that people have to go through before they can submit claims. We should examine that whole process, not just the end part, which is when, or if, a claim gets through the court. When the Minister replies, I would like him to tackle the issues that have already been raised at least twice, of access to the law and of how changes to civil legal aid will affect such people.

1.11.11 I would like to illustrate the difficulties that people experience when they pursue a claim. That process is immensely difficult because we are talking about a disease, the potential for which may have been acquired 20 or 30 years ago. To demonstrate the cause of that disease, it is necessary to prove one's employment record. It is difficult to obtain such a record from the Government's Contributions Agency as it currently operates. A constituent came to see me about obtaining his employment record. I hope that the Minister will be able to reply to me about this matter on another occasion. The reply from the Contributions Agency was, that Mr X's claim that "he claimed compensation for the onset of industrial deafness in September 1991 may well be correct, but this office only became aware of the claim when we received a letter from his solicitor on 12 June 1992." His solicitors "are aware that it can take up to six months to prepare an employment history and, as it happens, we are now ready to reply." That request for employment history — crucial to being able to establish a claim for having contracted an industrial disease which led to death — took seven months for the Contributions Agency to process. Only then was my constituent able to take the case forward to prepare it for court.

That case as I have mentioned, concerned industrial deafness, but it could have concerned asbestosis. My constituents had initiated events 19 months before even receiving his employment record from the contributions agency. The hon. and learned Member for Fife, North-East highlighted the difficulty of making a case. Although the legal change is valuable, it takes us, only a little way towards giving people affected by such diseases a better deal...

I deeply value today's debate and the Bill, but this is just the first stage in better treating people who acquired such awful diseases. It is not about bargaining between equals but about a situation in which some have knowledge and others are ignorant; some have wealth and others are debarred from law.

There are more difficult cases in which people are convinced that others have died from an occupational disease. I am aware of such a case at the moment in which much evidence suggests that a man contracted cancer of the larynx because of exposure to asbestos, but, as yet, that is not recognised as an occupational disease. I am sure that my hon. Friend the Member for Greenock and Port Glasgow is aware of similar cases. Many people are struggling to obtain recompense from the state for occupationally acquired diseases. At some stage, we shall have to reconsider no-fault compensation. What matters is not who was to blame but the suffering that has been caused.

I want to express my appreciation to my hon. Friend the Member for Cunninghame, North for introducing the Bill. I hope that it will not result in our feeling that the way in which such cases are dealt with is adequate: it is not and there is a long way to go.

1.11.12 The Parliamentary Under-Secretary of State for Scotland (Lord James Douglas-Hamilton): I warmly congratulate the hon. Member for Cunninghame, North on introducing the Bill, which is important in proving the financial position of relatives of asbestosis sufferers and of other comparable conditions. That in turn will help the peace of mind of those whose relatives suffer.

It was refreshing to hear speeches of support from the hon. and learned hon. Member for Fife, North-East and from the hon. Members for Greenock and Port Glasgow and for Clydebank and Milngavie. Under the rules governing the Register of Members' Interests I was advised that if the issue of insurance arose I should mention an interest. That is because I left Lloyds in 1985 …

Two of the syndicate accounts from 1980 and 1985 are still open and relate to asbestosis claims in America, but the possibility that they might include Scottish claimants cannot be totally excluded …

The hon. Members for Greenock and Port Glasgow and for Clydebank and Milngavie mentioned access and whether the proposed changes in legal aid will restrict access to the courts. That is a separate debate, but I shall reply briefly. We believe that, in practice, access will not be restricted because the majority of claims are made through trade unions. The purpose of the proposed changes is to ensure continuation of reasonable access to legal aid for the most needy while controlling the rate of growth in legal aid expenditure, which has been substantial. We see no reason why, in the few cases in which unions are not giving support and legal aid is not available, lawyers will not be willing to take on cases on a speculative basis. In any case, the Bill does not restrict access to the courts and I shall ensure that the hon. Members' comments are passed to my right hon. Friend and Minister of State for his consideration.

Transitional and Retrospective Provisions

1.11.13   Mr Wilson: [M]uch of the pressure for change in the law has come from organisations such as Clydeside Action and Asbestos, which represents people who have contracted asbestos-related diseases. Some of those people have only a short time to live. It would be unfortunate for them to be cruelly tantalised by the prospect of a Bill that would ensure that their dependants would benefit — but only if they live long enough to see it enacted.

That would be unacceptable and, with Lord Macaulay of Bragar, who successfully oversaw the passage of the Bill in another place, I had discussions with the Government to ensure that as many families as possible could benefit from the Bill. I commend to the Committee the solution that was reached. It was that the new rights of transmissibility to executors should apply when the death of the injured person will come on, or after, the date of the Bill's introduction, which was 16 July 1992. That was agreed, provided that the right cannot be exercised if a claim is time barred, had been settled or judicially determined.

In reaching that solution, it was necessary to consider various factors. First, it was recognised that it would be wrong in principle to re-open cases where settlement had been reached either by agreement or by judicial determination. Secondly, to allow the new rules to apply to cases that had not been settled or judicially determined, irrespective of when death occurred, would be a major departure from the established legal principle that life cases should be treated in the same way. Such a wide ranging retrospective provision could lead to unfairness, whereby those who had settled their claims quickly would be penalised, and those who had delayed so doing could be rewarded.

Unfortunately, there is no easy or neat solution that will guarantee fairness in each case. Whether or not there is retrospective provision, someone will always suffer some unfairness when one case is reviewed against another. Clause 6, however, should ensure that as many families as possible benefit from the new rules, while keeping within the acceptable bounds of legal policy.

The Lord-Advocate has confirmed that the retrospection under clause 6 is of a type that is not unfamiliar in legislation and, in legal principles is not objectionable. It ensures that victims who are alive today can be sure that, if the Bill is enacted, their estates will benefit from its provisions. The solution is not perfect. No death has occurred since the Bill was introduced. If it had, we would be in the invidious position of death before enactment, thus depriving those involved of the benefits of the Bill.

I am a little surprised that there was not more reaction to that aspect of the Bill. Clearly, some people will be bitter about it. Although everyone would like historic cases to be dealt with, campaigning organisations accept that such retrospection would not be acceptable to Parliament. It would have certainly made the progress of the Bill more difficult. Therefore, the solution was the best that was available in the circumstances. I am grateful for the flexibility that has been shown by the Government.

1.11.14   Mr Menzies Campbell: If the hon. Gentleman had been minded to push for more retrospection than is proposed in the Bill, he would have experienced insurmountable problems that might have prevented it from becoming law. He has struck a neat balance between what is achievable and what is just. To re-open a raft of cases that may have been settled on an entirely different basis of law would not be tolerated by Parliament. Therefore, the hon. Gentleman is to be commended for what one might describe as his pragmatism.

1.11.15   Mr Wilson: On a point of order, Mr Martin. This is the only stage in the Bill's progress that offers me the opportunity to place on record my appreciation of everyone's efforts in getting the legislation this far. Everyone has worked to the end that the Bill should be enacted in the minimum possible time. I hope that Third Reading will be on Friday. According to the advice given to me by officials, people are waiting day by day for the Bill to pass into law. The sooner it does so, the sooner claims can be settled. Friday is the first available date.

The initiative for the Bill came from the Scottish Law Commission. I place on record my appreciation of its work. It would be to the benefit of the government of Scotland and would enhance our proceedings if reports from the Scottish Law Commission were more frequently translated into legislation. I believe that 15 reports are outstanding, some of which date back to 1985, including a report on the law on succession ...

1.11.16   Lord James Douglas-Hamilton: Further to that point of order, Mr Martin. I thank the hon. Gentleman. When the Bill came before the previous Parliament, it was thought to be important that the Scottish Law Commission should consider it. If I remember correctly, the commission had considered it earlier but had not come to a conclusion. It was important that it should consider the measure again. It has done so, and the hon. Gentleman has done a service to the House.

1.11.17   The Chairman [Mr Michael J. Martin]: I thank the hon. Member for Cunninghame, North for his kind remarks. I wish him well with the Bill.

It has been a pleasure to chair the Committee. There used to be an asbestos factory in my constituency — fortunately, it has transferred to non-asbestos materials — so some people there suffer from that terrible disease. The hon. Member's remarks brought back memories of my apprenticeship. I remember that the metal was full of oil and grease. We did not want to work with it, so we thought that it was marvellous when jobs came up with white asbestos board because it was clean. Little did we know how dangerous that material was. Thank God, people do not have to work with it now unless they are properly protected. I hope that all goes well for the hon. Member. The Bill will benefit many people in Scotland.

I thank the Clerk, *Hansard* and the security officers for their help.'

COMMENT

1.12.1 The story speaks for itself. Since *Pepper v. Hart* [1993] A.C. 593, some of the foregoing materials might well be cited in argument in interpretation of the 1993 Act. (Reprinted in the Appendix and as amending the 1976 Act). This is one of the better examples of law reform. The impetus came from outside the profession. It involved and displays the valuable work of the Law Commission. It also reveals that Law Commission legislation, such as the 1976 Act, will need review. Politics were largely kept out of it but readers will have seen that there are themes of employer verses employee and rich verses poor running through some of the texts. The difficulty of non-lawyers in following such legislation is clear.

CHAPTER 2

THE INSTITUTIONAL WRITERS; TERMINOLOGY

The Institutional writers

11. Stair Institutions
Bk. I, Tit. 9

2.1.1 '[I,9,Pr.] Amongst obligations obediential we have placed these which are by delinquence; because they arise without any convention, consent, or contract, either particularly, or only by virtue of any positive law; and therefore, they must needs have their original from the authority and will of God, and of our obedience due thereto. For though they do proceed from our fact, and from our will, whence that fact is voluntarily committed, yet it is not from our contracting will: and, therefore, these obligations do not receive their effect, and measure, or extent, by our will.

2.1.2 [I,9,1] That obligations of delinquence are introduced by the law of nature, the suffrage of all men and all nations will evince, who do everywhere acknowledge the reparation of damages, and punishment of crimes and injuries, as having by nature a clear evidence and sharp sense thereof; and thereupon can, without reluctancy, concur with the magistrate in the punishment of citizens, and enemies by the sword.

But it may be doubted how the law of nature, which is perpetual, and had place chiefly in innocency, can prescribe any thing in relation to delinquency or malefice which was not to be found in that condition. This will be easily cleared, if it be considered that, though man was made in the state of innocency, yet he had a natural instability, for which God did warn and arm him; and though the principal and direct law of nature did teach man to love his neighbour as himself, yet he could not but by consequence know, (though he had stood in innocency, as the angels do), that any who acted against that royal law of love by doing evil to his neighbour, and taking away from him that which is his, ought to repair him, and to be liable to divine justice, which is that certification which God put upon his natural law, as he did more expressly upon the forbidden fruit, *morte morieris*.

2.1.3 [I,9,2] The obligation of delinquence then, is that where unto injury or malefice doth oblige, as the meritorious cause thereof. And it is twofold: either that which relateth to God, or that which relateth to man. The former is the obligation of punishment, pain, or penalty: for unto God there can properly no reparation be made by the creature, whose duty and service is due to him; so that to him the creature is obliged to underly the punishment. In reference to man is the obligation of repairing his damage, putting him in as good condition as he was in before the injury; and this only is man's part for himself. For the inflicting of punishment is for God, in so far as it is authorized or allowed by him; but it is not for, or from man of himself: "Revenge is mine; and I will repay it," saith the Lord. [Rom. xii, 19.] ... So in delinquence the power of exaction of reparation of his damage is man's for himself, but the power of exacting punishment is in God.

· · · · · ·

2.1.4 [I,9,3] Damage is called *damnun, à demendo*, because it diminisheth or taketh away something from another, which of right he had *l.3.ff. de damn. inf.* [D.39,2,3]... . It is not every damage that raiseth this obligation; for some damages may be just, as these which are inflicted by way of punishment, and others may have their reparation arising from contracts, whereby, though a delinquence may arise in non-performance of the contract, yet the original cause of the obligation is the contract. Some also arise from deeds or things, the non-performance whereof is a delinquence; as in the obligations of restitution and recompence. But here are only understood obligations which originally arise from delinquencies as the first cause thereof.

2.1.5 [I,9,4] Delinquence in the Roman law [Inst. IV,I,pr.] is reduced into these four, *furtum, rapina, damnum, injuria*; wherein we shall not insist, but follow private delinquences, and obligations and actions thence arising, as they are known by the terms in our law, in so far as they use to be civily prosecute ... therefore, it shall in general suffice here to consider, that, according to several rights and enjoyments, damages and delinquences may be esteemed ... As first, life, members, and health; which, though they be inestimable, and can have no price, *l.3. ff. si quad. paup.* [D.9,1,3], yet, there are therewith incident damages, and that either *lucrum cessans* or *damnum emergens.* So the life of any being taken away, the damage of these who were entertained and maintained by his life, as his wife and children may be repaired, see *Cuja.* [Jacques Cujas] *Obs. 14.c.4.* So likewise the loss any man hath by the expenses of his cure or the loss of his labour, and industry in his affairs, is also reparable *d.l.3. si quad. paup.* [D.9,1,3].

2.1.6 Next to life is liberty; and the delinquences against it are restraint and constraint: And though liberty itself be inestimable, yet the damage sustained through these delinquences are reparable.

2.1.7   The third is fame, reputation, and honour, which is also in some way reparable ... *First,* by making up the damage that is inferred in men's goods by the hurt of their fame, whereby their gain ceaseth, in that being repute such persons they are disenabled for their affairs. As if a merchant be called a bankrupt, it may not only hinder his traffick, but make all his creditors fall upon him suddenly to his ruin. So if a man be called a cheater, deceiver or the like, it disables him to manage his affairs, men being unwilling to meddle with such. And if a man, being about to marry, be called impotent, or infected with any noisome disease, he may be damnified in his match and tocher. Such actions upon injurious words, as they may relate to damage in means, are frequent and curious among the English; but with us there is little of it accustomed to be pursued though we own the same grounds, and would proceed to the same effects with them, if questioned. *Secondly,* damage in fame or honour is repaired by homage, acknowledgment or ignominy put upon the delinquent. *Thirdly,* by equivalent honour and vindication of the injured. Slander is competent to be judged by commissaries; and therefore a decreet of the commissaries of Edinburgh, upon a pursuit for slander and defamation, decerning the slanderer to make acknowledgement of the injury before the congregation, and to pay an hundred pounds Scots to the party, and as much to the poor, was sustained by the lords, February 5, 1669, Deans *contra* Bothwell [I Stair 598; M. 7577].

2.1.8   The fourth interest that may be damnified, is our content, delight, or satisfaction; and especially by the singular affection to, or our opinion of, the value or worth of any thing that owners have, in which consideration it is said, that every thing is to every man as he esteemeth it.

. . . . . .

2.1.9   The last damage is in goods and possession; the redress whereof is more clear, because the things themselves are more valuable and estimable. In all reparations the natural fruits and profits of the things taken away come in as part thereof; and in many cases, the industrial fruits and profits which the owner might have had, at least to make thereof.

Reparation is either by restitution of the same thing, in the same case, that it would have been in if it had remained with the owner, and this is most exact; or, where that cannot be, by giving the like value, or that which is nearest to make up the damage, according to the desire of the damnified. And if none be found fitter, reparation must be made in money, which is the common token of exchange and hath in it the value of every thing estimable.

. . . . . .

2.1.10   [I,9,5] Hence also is that famous edict of the praetor in the Roman law, *Nautrae, caupones, stabularii, quod salvum fore receperunt,*

nisi restituant, in eos judicium dabo [D.4,9,I,pr.]; by which the masters
of taverns, stables, or ships, are liable for restitution of the damages
that may be sustained by their servants, or any other that shall happen
to be there for the time, in what is brought aboard upon the account
of their employments ... but these obligations are rather introduced
by statutory law for common utility, than by natural obligation.

· · · · · ·

2.1.11   Hence we shall insist no further, but come to the obligations
by delinquence, which are civilly cognoscible by our custom, according
to their known names and titles in our law; which though they do
rather signify the acts or actions, whereby such obligations are incurred
or prosecute, than the obligations themselves, yet will they be sufficient
to hold out both.

2.1.12   [I,9,6] These are either general, having no particular name
or designation: and such are pursued under the general names of
damage and interest. Which hath as many branches and specialties,
as there can be valuable and reparable damages: besides those of a
special name and nature, which are chiefly these, assythment,
extortion, circumvention, spuilzie, intrusion, ejection, molestation,
breach of arrestment, deforcement, contravention, forgery, which
comes in more properly in the process of improbation [IV, 20,5, *infra*].'

COMMENT

2.2.1   Clearly Stair's concept of delict is a product of his time. Seldom, when the
Institutions are being cited, either in courts or in writings, are the full passages cited
which reveal the religious foundation of the work. To do so makes the passages
cited open to question in a more secular society. Stair was a natural lawyer; the present
times are perhaps more positivist. Naturally much has been written about the context
within which Stair wrote: see particularly Professor Walker's introduction to the
tercentenary edition of the *Institutions* the *Stair Tercentenary Studies* (Stair Society); and
Volume 26 of the *Juridical Review* (1981) which contains a number of most accessible and
valuable articles.

2.2.2   Stair's contribution, as usual, is one of rationalisation and collection. The analysis
of delict as non-contractual would not be questioned today. Other points of note are
(1) the refusal to allow penal damages [2.1.3]; (2) the rejection of the divisions of the
Roman law [2.1.5]; (3) the division of the law according to the interests of the individual
[2.1.5–8]; (4) the reception of the edict of the praetor [2.1.10 and see Ext. 30]; (5) the
existence of a catalogue of recognised delicts but the acceptance that there can be
obligations with no name or designation [2.1.11].

12. Erskine Institutes
Bk. III, Tit. I

2.3.1   '12. Obligations arising from delinquency are also obediential.
And though the consideration of crimes and delicts, in so far as they
draw after them the resentment of public justice, falls under tit.

"Crimes", it may be proper to mention in this place some rules concerning the obligation under which a delinquent is brought to indemnify the private party, or make-up to him the damage he suffered by the wrong, with respect, first, to the nature of the delinquency; secondly, to the extent of the damage; and, thirdly, to those who are liable to repair it.

2.3.2 13. *Alterum non laedere* is one of the three general precepts laid down by Justinian, which it has been the chief purpose of all civil enactments to enforce. In consequence of this rule, every one who has the exercise of reason, and so can distinguish between right and wrong, is naturally obliged to make up the damage befalling his neighbour from a wrong committed by himself. Wherefore every fraudulent contrivance or unwarrantable act by which another suffers damage, or runs the hazard of it, subjects the delinquent to reparation. Thus a party resiling after subscribing a marriage-contract, without giving a good reason for it, was condemned to the payment of the expense disbursed by the other party in wedding-clothes, and other preparations for marriage; Wrong may arise not only from positive acts of trepass or injury, but from blameable omission or neglect of duty. Thus a jailor by whose negligence a prisoner for debt suffered to escape, becomes liable to the creditor in the sum due, though the creditor receives no immediate damage by that omission, and only loses one of the chances which he had before of recovering the debt by the *squalor carceris*. Thus, also, a clerk of court who has through carelessness lost the writings of a party which were produced in process, must make up to the sufferer his damage. This obligation to repair the loss of another, supposes some wrong committed by the party obliged; for no person ought to be subjected to the reparation of damage who has not by some culpable act or omission been the occasion of it; One draining marshy grounds, will not be obliged to repair the damage the proprietor of an inferior tenement may thereby sustain by having a greater quantity of water thrown upon his grounds, because that is a lawful act of property. And, on the same ground, if what has brought on the damage be merely accidental, the person suffering has no remedy. As to the second head, every thing by which a man's estate is lessened, is damage or loss.

. . . . . .

2.3.3 15. … As to the persons liable to repair the damage, it is he who does the wrong that must repair it; and whoever gives a mandate or order for doing it is held as the doer.'

COMMENT

2.4.1 This passage is remarkable for laying down a general principle of recovery for harm. It is even wider in its potential application than Stair's general view which was still influenced by the patchwork of remedies and nominate delicts which had developed in Scotland.

2.4.2 The example of the jailor is actually quite exciting and far from uncontroversial. It raises a point in connection with economic loss, which is generally difficult to recover (*Delict*, 5.20–5.30). Wilkinson and Forte in their article, "Pure Economic Loss — A Scottish Perspective", 1985 J.R. 1, cast light on his head of liability at page 6: "Cases in which creditors successfully sued a jailor or magistrates for negligence in allowing the release or escape of a debtor and so depriving the creditors of the incentive for payment afforded by *squalor carceris*, were, as already mentioned, cited by Erskine and are apt examples of liability for pure economic loss. Their true ground, however, although not always disclosed on the face of the report, lay in the acts of sederunt which expressly created this liability. They are therefore, cases of specific statutory provision for the recovery of pure economic loss rather than examples of any general doctrine." They also go on to point out that a similar action known to the Roman law in respect of the compassionate release of a slave may not have been based on the *lex aquilia*, which is one of the foundations of liability in Scots law. In cases like the release of a prisoner, the loss is economic because the chance of payment of a debt was greatly increased by having the debtor in prison, in that his friends or relatives would try to pay the debt. Richard Wagner was able to obtain payment of his debt by alerting his friends to his imminent imprisonment (see B. Millington, *Wagner* (1984), pp. 24–25). A student of law might find Chapters 41 to 47 of the *Pickwick Papers* a worthwhile read on the topic of *squalor carceris*, Mr Pickwick very soon being disabused by Sam Weller and his own experience of his first notion that, "imprisonment for debt is scarcely any punishment at all." The loss in this case is certainly not to the pursuer's person or property, and in that sense is economic.

2.4.3 The footnotes in Erskine provide more common examples of liability. Interestingly, Erskine comments on the liability of the coach-driver for the overturning of the coach due to his fault or negligence, pointing out that there is also an obligation *ex contractu*. This attitude was important in supporting the decision in *Donoghue* (Ext. 39. See especially 8.1.15).

2.4.4 Consider the passage concerning drainage (2.3.2) with Chapter 5.

13. **Bell, Principles**
8th Edition (1885), Chapter XVII

"Of Reparation of Injuries"

2.5.1 '543. General Rule.—The rights of individuals, either to property or to personal liberty, safety, or reputation, are not only protected by penal law, but in civil law they furnish, when invaded, ground of action for reparation. This class of civil remedies has by lawyers been divided into actions grounded on delict, and actions grounded on something short of delict, but which, to the purposes of civil reparation, is so considered — *quasi* delict.

. . . . . .

2.5.2 544. Delict.—(1.) *Nature of it.*—A delict is an offence committed with an injurious, fraudulent, or criminal purpose. Criminal law looks to the prevention of delict by punishment, example, and terror, without any view to indemnification; while civil jurisprudence, looking only to indemnification, without regard to punishment or example, raises for this purpose, by construction of law, an obligation to repair the damage occasioned by the delict.

. . . . . .

2.5.3 533. *Quasi Delict.*—(1.) *Nature of it.*—Gross negligence or imprudence, though it should bear no such character of fraud, malice, or criminal purpose as to subject the person to criminal cognisance, is, as a ground for an action for damages, held as a delict, to the effect of making the person guilty of the imprudence or negligence liable to indemnify the person who suffers by the fault. These are by lawyers called *quasi* delicts ... (2.) *Collision of Ships*—... It is a *quasi* delict or negligence when a man unintentionally, *i.e.* without malice or fraud, but from want of care, interferes with the rights of another so as to cause him to suffer loss ... (3.) *Keeping dangerous Dogs, etc.*—Carelessness in the keeping of a dangerous dog (or other animal,) or in the management of fire-arms, subjects to damages in reparation ... (4.) *The use of diligence* (as arrestment, etc., in security) is always *periculo petentis*; and where injury arises, will entitle to reparation if nimious or groundless. (5.) *Carelessness of Public Officers.*—Carelessness on the part of public officers, magistrates, or road trustees, or their managers or workmen, has in Scotland been held to render them liable as trustees for reparation, with relief against the trust fund, though not in their private capacities.

. . . . . .

2.5.4 554.(6.) *Responsibility of Master for Servant.*—One is liable for the faults or gross negligence of those in his employment or under his command, according to the rules already laid down.'

COMMENT

2.6.1 These first three extracts give a "fast-forward" view of the development of delict. Stair's major contribution could well have been the separation of delict from the concept of punishment, one of the marks of a modern system of civil liability. Erskine's version of the law is very significant in that it states the law in very broad terms, supporting a general principle of recovery. Bell's treatment, as in much else that Bell wrote, indicates an English influence — the identification of certain categories of case where recovery is permitted, with the corollary that cases outwith the recognised categories become more of a problem.

2.6.2 A student with an interest in the history and development of delict would be well served by reading from the following: Sheriff McKechnie, "Delict and *Quasi*-delict" Stair Society, Vol. 20; Professor Walker, "The Development of Reparation" (1952) 64 J.R. 101; and the much more lively and equally scholarly multi-instalment article by Professor Black, "A Historical Survey of Delictual Liability on Scotland for Personal Injuries and Death" (1975) 8 C.I.L.J.S.A. 46, 189, 316; (1976) 9 C.I.L.J.S.A. 57. Extract 25 contains much of historical interest. In McKenzie and Evans-Jones, "The Development of Remedies for Personal Injury and Death" in *The Civilian Tradition in Scots Law*, Stair Society (1995), the "general action" for damages for delict is pushed back and said to originate in Stair, being a manifestation of the *jus commune.*

2.6.3   Scots law has some difficulty, in common with other systems, in dealing with remedies. Assythment (2.1.12) was formally abolished by the Damages (Scotland) Act 1976. Lawburrows was recently used in an attempt to control the local constabulary. This was supremely ironic in that it was perhaps increased policing which made the need for private recourse to this remedy ever less necessary (see Stewart, 1988 S.L.T. (News) 181 and the letters at 199). The position of spuilzie is not clear, (see Rodger, "Spuilzie in the Modern World", 1970 S.L.T. (News) 33 and Ext. 28).

Terminology

14. T. B. Smith, "Designation of Delictual Actions: Damn Iniuria Damn"
1972 S.L.T. (News) 125

2.7.1   'For well over 20 years the present writer has protested against the abuse of terminology which has latterly been tolerated and encouraged in the Scottish courts in certain delictual actions — in particular the designation of a relative's action in respect of death of a victim caused by *culpa* of the defender as an "*actio injuriarum*," and the designation of an action as "verbal injury" when patrimonial loss rather than affront must be averred. This was not a protest based on pedantry but because erroneous designation so confuses the study of the law of delict for intrants to the profession of law as to induce either mental confusion or contempt for the system or both.

. . . . . .

2.7.2   It has been a humiliating experience, having traced from Roman to modern times the development in Europe of the Aquilian action for damages (*damnum injuria datum*) based on *culpa* and having traced the development of the *actio injuriarum* or delict of "injury" (real or verbal) for affront — with references to all the Scottish Institutional writers, Scottish decisions and treatises until the late 19th century and comparative materials — to have to add at the end: "But I must warn you that in Parliament House today totally different meanings have been attached latterly to the expressions '*actio injuriarum*' and 'verbal injury' which conform neither to the history of our law nor to the generally received understanding of lawyers for over 15 centuries throughout the civilised world" … One day, [the writer] ventured to hope, the abuse of terminology, which has long been recognised as such by lawyers with a pretence to scholarship, would be disapproved judicially. In fact this has been one of the side-effects of *McKendrick* v. *Sinclair* (House of Lords, 1972 S.L.T. 110; in the Court of Session, 1971 S.L.T. 17 and 234). *Laus Dominis!*

2.7.3   Lord Reid, with whose speech Lord Morris concurred, explained the decline of assythment as follows: "The reason was that by the end of the 18th century a new remedy began to emerge for the quasi-delict of negligence and that remedy was also available for delict" ... Lord Reid's references to "quasi-delict of negligence" clearly indicates the Aquilian action. The *actio injuriarum* was essentially a delict involving *dolus* or intent. (As for the equiparation of quasi-delict with negligence in the context of the Aquilian action, this has the blessing of Heineccius, and the present writer need not rehearse his views on this particular terminology.)... By 1950 at least three Lord Presidents had followed uncritically Lord President Inglis' inexplicable lapse in terminology (if correctly reported) in *Eisten v. N.B. Railway Co.* (1870) 8 M. 980, and neither counsel nor scholar had ventured to question it. Lord President Cooper might have welcomed such questioning. Later in his speech, Lord Kilbrandon, after citing *Stewart v. L.M.S. Railway Co.* (1944 S.L.T. 13, at pp. 20–21) states: "It has been repeatedly pointed out by scholars (see, *e.g.* Professor T. B. Smith, *Studies Critical and Comparative*, at p. 78) and Lord Macmillan in a later passage in the same speech seems himself to agree, that the correct analogue is not the *actio injuriarum*. This was truly based on insult or affront; it survives in our forms of action which are included under the classification of verbal injury — see Professor Walker, 1970 J.R. 157... . The Roman ancestor of our action of reparation is *Lex Aquilia* as was forcibly pointed out by Sheriff McKechnie in his chapter in the *Introduction to Scottish Legal History*, Stair Society, Vol. 20, at pp. 267–277."

2.7.4 The proper scope of the *actio injuriarum* of Roman law and systems derived from it — including Scots law — has always been to deal with those many situations where there has been deliberate affront to the pursuer (or negligence so gross as to be the equivalent of intent) and the pursuer's feelings have consequently been hurt. Damages are for non-patrimonial loss (*solatium*), and the malicious purpose of the defender is always relevant. The broad divisions of this action, described in our Institutional writers, are "real injury" and "verbal injury", as Lord Kilbrandon had recently stressed extra-judicially as well as judicially ("The Law of Privacy in Scotland" (1971) 2 Camb.L.R. 35). Erroneous invocation of the expression *actio injuriarum* in connection with the action brought by relatives in respect of the death of a dependant caused by negligence may indirectly result in distortion of other branches of the law — in particular defamation and *convicium*. Moreover, in the context of the action in respect of causing death by negligence, it is at least possible that false inferences may be drawn relying on analogy with the Roman *actio injuriarum*.

2.7.5 In the true *actio injuriarum*, solatium is given (as in Roman law) for feelings hurt by affront; in the action in respect of *culpa* causing injury or death solatium is given (as a result of Germanic and Canon law influences) in respect of pain or grief — the "pacifying of rancour" having been transmuted into *solatium doloris* ...

The most distinguished contemporary scholar working in this field, Professor Robert Feenstra of Leiden, has written: "Speaking of *Lex Aquila* in general ... in spite of some early attempts in the fifteenth and sixteenth century, the coping stone had to be put on by Grotius. Grotius states generally that 'fault' creates the obligation to make good the loss ... In working out this principle he largely makes use of the texts on the *Lex Aquilia* on the one hand, but on the other hand he introduces ideas from customary law and theological writers" ...

Professor R. G. McKerron (a Scotsman who taught in Aberdeen University) has written in his classic treatise on *Delict* [in South Africa] as follows: "Although the action by which the right of the dependants is asserted has its roots in early Germanic custom and was unknown to the civil law, it came to be regarded by most of the Roman-Dutch writers as a species of *actio utilis* under the *Lex Aquilia.*'"

15. Palmer (Appellant) v. Wick and Pulteneytown Steam Shipping Co. Ltd
(1894) 2 S.L.T. 91

2.8.1 A man was killed by equipment used while moving a ship's cargo. His widow sued (1) the shipowner on the basis of his fault in having supplied unfit tackle, and (2) the stevedore on the basis that he had overloaded the tackle recklessly.

2.8.2 'LORD CHANCELLOR: ... It is not necessary in this appeal to decide whether there can be any right to contribution in the case of a delict proper when the liability has arisen from a conscious and therefore moral wrong, nor even whether in every case of *quasi*-delict a delinquent may obtain relief against his co-delinquent, though I see, as at present advised, no reason to differ from the opinion, which I gather my noble and learned friend Lord Watson holds, that such a right may exist... . It was urged that the person seeking relief might be the more culpable of the delinquents; but it is just as likely that he should be less culpable. In selecting from which of his co-debtors he will obtain payment, the creditor would be guided usually by considerations wholly independent of the relative culpability of those from whom he may recover it.

. . . . . .

2.8.3 LORD WATSON: At the bar of the House the appellant mainly relied on the proposition, which he endeavoured to establish by authority, that, by the law of Scotland, there can be no right of contribution among persons who are jointly responsible for the civil consequences of any delict or *quasi*-delict. Delicts proper embrace all breaches of the law which expose their perpetrator to criminal punishment. The term *quasi*-delict is generally applied to any violation of the common or statute law which does not infer criminal consequences, and does not consist in the breach of any contract, express or implied. Cases may and do often occur in which it is exceedingly difficult to draw the line between delicts and *quasi*-delict. The latter class, as it has been developed in the course of the present century, covers a great variety of acts and omissions, ranging from deliberate breaches of the law, closely bordering upon crime, to breaches comparatively venial and involving no moral delinquency.

. . . . . .

2.8.4   LORD HALSBURY: The difficulty which has arisen is, I think, one of words. The word "tort" in English law is not always used with strict logical precision. The same act may sometimes be treated as a breach of contract and sometimes as a tort. But "tort" in its strictest meaning, as it seems to me, ought to exclude the right of contribution which would imply a presumed contract to subscribe towards the commission of a wrong. It seems to me, therefore, that the distinction between classes of torts or quasi-delicts and delicts proper is reasonable and just, though I doubt whether in dealing with an English case one would be at liberty to adopt such a distinction.'

COMMENT

2.9.1   Decided: June 5, 1894.
  Oct. (1893): Marcel Proust graduated in Law.
  March: Gladstone resigned over Irish Home Rule

2.9.2   See the sequel to Ext. 14 at 1984 S.L.T. (News) 85.

2.9.3   It may have been noticed by the careful reader that the term "*quasi*-delict" was used at 2.5.3 and 2.8.3. The usage is examined later in the book in an extract dealing with a remedy known to the Roman law under the heading "*quasi*-delict." Simply put, until relatively recently, cases of intentional wrongdoing were known as delicts, whereas lesser cases including negligence cases were known as cases of *quasi*-delict. The preferred usage is now probably to reserve the term, "*quasi*-delict" for cases involving the old Roman remedies. Nonetheless, the term *quasi*-delict in its sense as denoting unintentional harm cases has some limited sanction in the context of the law relating to jurisdiction.

16. Scott Lithgow Ltd v. GEC Electrical Products Ltd (O.H.)
1992 S.L.T. 244

2.10.1   The following extract relates to the claim of the pursuer against a sub-contractor based in England who allegedly supplied defective goods albeit not to the pursuers directly.

2.10.2   LORD CLYDE: It was assumed by the third defenders that the pursuers were seeking to found upon s. 1 of the Law Reform (Jurisdiction in Delict) (Scotland) Act 1971. That section requires that the delict forming the cause of action should have been committed in Scotland. It was submitted under reference to *Kirkcaldy District Council* v. *Household Manufacturing Ltd.* [1987 S.L.T. 617] that "delict" here means injuria and not damnum, and under reference to *Russell* v. *F. W. Woolworth & Co. Ltd.* [1982 S.L.T. 428] that it was sufficient that there had been a material breach of duty inside Scotland. Reference was made to the grounds of fault alleged against the third defenders. Condescendence 13 discloses that the breach of duty is a failure to carry out their subcontract work in a proper manner. In particular there is an alleged failure to wire the switchboards subcontracted to these defenders in such a way as not to cause damage to the wire and an alleged failure to check and inspect their work during construction to ascertain whether damage had been sustained. It was then submitted that none of these breaches of duty was committed in Scotland. It is not averred that they were, and from their address in the instance and the pursuers' reference to supply to the pursuers in Scotland it appears that the third defenders were not within Scotland. Counsel for the third defenders thus agreed that the delict was committed in England.

2.10.3 Counsel for the pursuers explained that they claimed a jurisdiction in Scotland under the Act of 1971. Junior counsel argued first that it was sufficient that the damnum by itself occurred in Scotland. He founded upon the recognition by Lord Allanbridge in *Kirkcaldy District Council* v. *Household Manufacturing Ltd.* at p. 620 that the word "delict" can have a wider as well as a narrower meaning, the wider meaning comprehending both injuria and damnum. He founded upon the reference in the Act to the delict "forming the cause of action" and submitted that for a cause of action there must be both injuria and damnum. If injuria alone was intended the Act should have read "forming part of the cause of action". Albeit with some courteous reticence, he was constrained to submit that Lord Allanbridge's preference for the so called narrower view was incorrect and that the word "committed" should be construed widely so as to embrace both injuria and damnum.

2.10.4 I am quite satisfied that this argument is not sound. I am not wholly persuaded that the word "delict" admits of the wider meaning which has been suggested. No illustrations of this wider meaning were given in argument and I note that Lord Allanbridge in the *Kirkcaldy* case in explaining the wider meaning (at p. 620B) states: "The fundamental concept of the law of delict is breach of legal duty causing unjustifiable harm". It may be that the phrase "the law of delict" may import the element of damnum as an ingredient in a claim based on wrongdoing, but the word "delict" by itself seems to me to connote wrong-doing by itself. In s. 1 (3) of the Act "delict" is defined to include quasi-delict but no mention is made of damnum. I respectfully adopt Lord Allanbridge's conclusion based on the word "committed" which seems to me correct. That verb sits more easily with the construction of delict as injuria than with the inclusion of damnum. Further, as counsel for the third defenders pointed out, it may be possible to raise proceedings in some cases of quasi-delict without any damnum having occurred (Walker on *Delict*, p. 40). Nor am I persuaded that "cause of action" includes both injuria and damnum. The precise meaning of the expression was not explored in argument but it may well be that the cause of action is the wrong on which the action is based and the happening of damage creates a right of action. Further to that, if, as Lord Murray explains in *Russell* v. *Woolworth*, 1982 S.L.T. at p. 430, the purpose of the Act was to extend the pre-existing common law which required the additional step of personal service and that law proceeded upon the requirement of material injuria in Scotland, it seems to me the more difficult to reach the conclusion that the Act intends the Scottish court to have jurisdiction simply where the damnum was sustained in Scotland. On this branch of the argument counsel for the pursuers' proposition went so far as to claim that it was sufficient that damnum on its own occurred in Scotland. That requires not simply the construction of "the delict" as including damnum but as meaning damnum by itself. That seems to me to be an impossible interpretation of the Act and I have little difficulty in rejecting this branch of the argument.'

COMMENT

2.11.1   Decided: November 14, 1989.
   Nov. 10: Berlin wall breached.
   Nov. 24: Dubrek returns to Czechoslovakia.
   Dec. 5: Margaret Thatcher survives leadership challenge — from Sir Anthony Meyer.

2.11.2   In *Miller* v. *City of Glasgow District Council*, 1989 S.L.T. 44 (I.H.) a question arose as to whether an action for re-instatement had prescribed in terms of the Prescription and Limitation (Scotland) Act 1973, s. 6(1), Sched. 1, para. 1d, relating to obligations "to make reparation". The court said: 'In our opinion counsel for the pursuer approached the question at issue in the correct way. The first matter to consider is the generally accepted meaning of the word "reparation" in the law of Scotland. From the authorities to which we were referred it is apparent that the word is used in the sense of "reparatio injuriarum", and is a pecuniary remedy which the law of Scotland affords for a loss caused by a wrong. It is not a remedy which the law of Scotland affords for breach of contract. A breach of contract, if established, attracts an award of damages, the damages being the remedy for the breach. In this connection it is relevant and interesting to note that the extinction of a s. 6 obligation arising from a liability to make reparation, and of a s. 6 obligation arising from a breach of contract, are referred to in para. 1 of Sched. 1 to the Act under separate subparagraphs, namely subparas. (*d*) and (*g*).'

   In the course of debate reference was made to the Shorter Oxford English Dictionary, Glegg on *Reparation*, Sir Thomas Smith's *Short Commentary* and Gloag and Henderson. See also *Middleton* v. *Douglass*, 1991 S.L.T. 726.

   In *Kennedy* v. *Glenbelle*, 1996 S.L.T. 1186, the Lord President said: "According to the law of Scotland liability in reparation for damages arises either ex contractu or ex delicto."

2.11.3   The 1971 Act discussed above is no longer the applicable statute: see Chapter 23.

CHAPTER 3

WRONGFUL INTERFERENCE WITH THE PERSON

Assault

17. Ross v. Bryce (Appellant)
1972 S.L.T. (Sh.Ct.) 76 (S.A.)

3.1.1 'The Sheriff Principal (Margaret H. Kidd, Q.C.): This appeal is in a summary action of reparation for assault in which the pursuer claimed damages of £150. The sheriff, after hearing evidence which was not recorded, found the assault upon the pursuer proved but modified the sum of £150 claimed to £75 on the ground that the pursuer had by his actions provoked the assault. The solicitors for both parties agreed that in the circumstances the findings-in-fact of the sheriff were not open to question and that the appeal was restricted to the question whether on the findings-in-fact the sheriff was entitled to reach the conclusions in law which resulted in his award to the pursuer of £75 damages. The appeal is at the instance of the defender, for it was maintained that since the sheriff had found that there was provocation by the pursuer no award of damages should have been granted. The solicitor for the pursuer took advantage of the appeal, as it was conceded he was entitled to do, to argue that having found that the assault had taken place the sheriff should have granted decree for the full sum of £150, as he was not entitled in assessing damages to take into consideration that the assault had been provoked.

. . . . . .

3.1.2 It is a strange fact that after the thirties of last century no case of reparation for assault appears to have been reported until *McGregor* v. *Shepherd* (1946) 62 Sh.Ct.Rep. 139 which the sheriff cited in his note. In his argument the solicitor for the defender drew analogies from the criminal law to the effect that in a case of assault it was always for the court to weigh up whether the force used in retaliation was excessive. In the present case the sheriff found that the pursuer, who is a gamekeeper, had, prior to April 25, 1970 when the assault took place, been resentful that the defender was tenant of a country cottage near Laggan by Newtonmore. On that evening the pursuer and a friend who had been drinking in Newtonmore drove in a car to a piece of waste ground very close to the defender's cottage about 10.45 p.m. The pursuer got out of the cottage and a fight ensued. In the course of this fight the pursuer was struck on the head by the defender with a blunt instrument as a result of which he required to have 13 stitches inserted by a doctor in Newtonmore about an hour after the fight. The defender sustained no injury.

· · · · · ·

3.1.3 Both solicitors referred me to a number of cases and textbooks all of which I have considered. There is no doubt that from early times assault has been in Scots law a ground of action in the civil as well as the criminal court—indeed Bell in his *Principles*, para. 2028, states: "Everyone who lives under the protection of the law has an absolute right to the safety of his person; and wherever this right is invaded there is in Civil law a provision for redress of injury, as well as in penal law a punishment for the crime." On the other hand all the early cases state that provocation sounds in reduction of damages. In *Anderson* v. *Marshall* (1835) 13 S. 1130 Lord President Hope stated to the jury: "No verbal provocation whatever can justify a blow … But, as verbal provocation is a good ground for mitigating damages, and as the pursuer does not come before you with clean hands, I should conceive that sufficient reparation would be made in this case by a small award of damages"— and the jury awarded one shilling.

3.1.4 Accordingly, I agree with the sheriff's approach to the case and I see no reason to interfere with his decision. In maintaining that the full award of £150 should be granted to the pursuer my attention was directed to the comparatively recent case of *Lane* v. *Holloway* [1968] 1 Q. B. 379. In that case a very savage attack was made by the defendant upon the plaintiff who was a much older man. It was established that the plaintiff had made derogatory remarks about the defendant's wife and that after a relatively slight blow from the plaintiff the defendant inflicted grievous injury upon him. There the appeal court increased the award of the lower court from £75 to £300 and expressed views which seemed to indicate that in the law of England provocation in an action of assault would not mitigate damages. While I accept that decisions of the Court of Appeal in England warrant the greatest respect in the field of reparation, the development of the law in Scotland has followed different paths—and indeed is based on different principles. It may thus be dangerous in some cases to follow English precedents. As the late Sheriff Hector McKechnie pointed out in the sound and careful article on reparation in Vol. XII of *Green's Encyclopaedia of the Laws of Scotland* (which article was recently commended by Lord Kilbrandon in *McKendrick and Others* v. *Sinclair*, 1972 S.L.T. 109 at p. 120): "The insistence upon a basis of wrongdoing and the generality of right to redress are characteristic features which distinguish the law of this country from that of England." Again Sheriff McKechnie states: "In England an action is based on *damnum*, in

Scotland on *culpa*." The fact that the underlying principle of Scots law in actions of reparation for intentional wrong is based upon *culpa* is the reason why a pursuer in such an action must come into court with clean hands.

3.1.5 In an action for assault, accordingly, if he has been guilty of provocation then he cannot fully succeed and so the court is entitled to reduce the damages which would otherwise have been awarded. This is precisely the course which the learned sheriff adopted. Reverting to the case of *Lane* v. *Holloway* (*supra*) the difference of approach in that English law emphasises the element of *damnum* is clearly seen in the opinion of Lord Justice Salmon, at p. 392, where he states: "some of the older English authorities and some of the Commonwealth cases appear to fall into the error which until recently has by no means been eliminated that damages for tort were partly to punish the defendant. We now know certainly since *Rookes* v. *Barnard* [1964] A.C. 1129 that they are nothing of the kind, that they are purely compensatory—with the exception of course of exemplary damages." Whatever may be the law of England in regard to provocation in civil actions of damages for assault, I am satisfied that in the law of Scotland provocation on the part of the pursuer is an element which the court is entitled to consider in its discretion to modify the award of damages accordingly.'

COMMENT

3.2.1 Decided: July 3, 1972.
   Bobby Fisher arrived in Iceland for World Chess Championship.
   May 24: Glasgow Rangers won European Cup Winners' Cup.

3.2.2 What basis could there be, other than that stated, for reducing damages in such a case?

3.2.3 For other Scottish cases, see *Delict*, 2.2–2.3. It is not a "fact" (3.1.2) that there are no reported cases for reparation for assault between 1830 and 1946. There are lots, *e.g. Mason v. Orr* (1901) 4 F. 220, and cases cited therein. And, equally significant, *Ewing v. Mar* (1851) 14 D. 314 and *MacKersie v. Dickson* (1848) 11 D. 4.

3.2.4 The next extract deals with the particular question of wrongful detention, but is also notable for its principle-based approach to the matter of interference with personality.

Detention and imprisonment

18. Henderson v. Chief Constable, Fife Police
1988 S.L.T. 361

3.3.1 'Two medical laboratory scientific officers (MLSOs) employed by a health board participated along with 10 other MLSOs in a "work in" at a hospital laboratory in furtherance of an industrial dispute. Proceeding under the Trespass (Scotland) Act 1865, the police broke down the door of the laboratory and arrested all of the MLSOs and transported them to the police station where the seven women were put in an interview room and the five men were held in the cell passage. Their names and addresses were taken and they were cautioned and charged. Thereafter they were all placed in cells to allow the police to check certain matters. Before being placed in the cells the men were asked to remove certain articles of clothing and the women were asked to remove their brassières as a matter of routine. The two MLSOs sought damages from the chief constable. The male pursuer was handcuffed by the police and at the proof it was conceded that the handcuffing was unjustified. The pursuers sought damages for wrongful arrest and detention, for the removal of the brassière of the female pursuer, and for the handcuffing of the male pursuer.

. . . . . .

3.3.2 LORD JAUNCEY: Rather than attempt to summarise the pursuers' cases as pleaded, of which some parts are no longer insisted in, I think it is more appropriate to narrate the propositions which counsel for the pursuers developed in his closing speech.

3.3.3 As I understood it, these four propositions embodied the issues which I have to determine, but these issues are further narrowed by certain concessions made in their closing submissions by counsel. The pursuers accepted that the chief constable was, on the evidence presented to him, fully entitled to consider that patient care was likely to be jeopardised unless Dr Barrie and others obtained access to the laboratory on the morning of September 25. Counsel further stated that the pursuers were no longer maintaining that the chief constable was not justified in proceeding under the Trespass (Scotland) Act 1865. For his part counsel for the defender accepted that the handcuffing of Mr Jones was, on the evidence, unjustified.

3.3.4 Before considering in more detail the evidence which bears upon the pursuers' four propositions it is proper to look at the laws which must be applied. The starting point is the Trespass (Scotland) Act 1865, of which s. 4 provides *inter alia* that a person who commits an offence against the Act, "may, if found in the act of committing the same by any... constable be apprehended and detained." The section also provides for the case where a person is charged with an offence but not taken into custody. It is clear that a police officer who finds a person in the act of committing an offence has a discretion either to arrest and detain or to charge and summon to appear. It is the law applicable to the exercise of that discretion with which this case is concerned. As a general rule the common law will jealously protect the liberty of the subject from undue interference. Thus no one should be deprived of his liberty without a warrant from a magistrate unless the circumstances fall within certain well-defined exceptions to the rule (*Leask* v. *Burt* (1893) 1 S.L.T. 270, Lord Young at p. 270). Similarly where a discretionary power to arrest is given to police officers they are "not entitled to overstep the necessity or reasonable requirements of the particular case" (*Peggie* v. *Clark* (1868) 7 M. 89, Lord Deas at p. 93). To exercise a discretionary power to arrest in circumstances where such arrest was neither reasonable nor necessary would amount to undue interference or tampering with the liberty of the subject (see Lord Kinloch at p. 94 in *Peggie* v. *Clark*). The pursuers aver that their arrest and subsequent detention was wrongous and unlawful, in other words, that the exercise of discretion to arrest was wrongly exercised. In that situation the onus of establishing these matters rests upon them (*Shields* v. *Shearer*, Lord Salvesen, 1913 2 S.L.T. at p. 71; Lord Shaw of Dunfermline, 1914 1 S.L.T. at p. 362). So much for the common law... . What I do have to decide is whether in exercising that discretion the police officers concerned took the steps required of them under s. 17 of the Police (Scotland) Act 1967 — steps which I am informed are not required of English constables by English legislation.

3.3.5 Much discussion centred round the question of the powers possessed by police officers to remove persons who were present in premises without the consent of the owner. It was argued by the pursuers that a police officer was entitled to remove an individual from premises at the request of the owner and that this occurred frequently in practice, for example at football matches or in domestic disputes, when the person removed was simply told to go away without any further action being taken. While such a course of action by police officers may in many cases be very sensible I was referred to no basis in law for their taking such action. In my view the defender is correct in maintaining that if a police officer wishes to remove a person from premises because the occupier has never granted or has withdrawn permission to remain he is only entitled in law to take one of three courses of action, namely: (1) he may leave the premises at the same time requiring the person to remain with him while he verifies any name and address which has been given (s. 1 (2) of the Criminal Justice (Scotland) Act 1980); (2) he may detain him under s. 2 of the Criminal Justice (Scotland) Act 1980; (3) he may arrest him. Whatever be the position in practice I do not consider that a constable has a right in law to remove someone from premises for the sole purpose of terminating his presence there... . In view of the pursuers' concession that the chief constable was fully entitled to consider that patient care was likely to be jeopardised if Dr Barrie and others did not obtain access to the laboratory on the morning of September 25, it is unnecessary for me to consider a good deal of the evidence relating to events prior to the chief constable being asked by Dr Gardiner to take action. I should add that in the light of the evidence led in this case I have no doubt that the pursuers' concession was properly made.

. . . . . .

Proposition 1

Arrest

3.3.6   When the chief constable decided to take action in response to Dr Gardiner's request he gave instructions to Borrer that those in the laboratory who did not leave voluntarily were to be arrested and removed... At the time the decision to arrest was made the state of knowledge of the senior police officers present at the hospital may be summarised as follows. (1) They did not know precisely how many people were in the laboratory but assumed that there were about a dozen. (2) They only knew of the identity of Low and Wilson. The chief constable from past experience in industrial disputes was not prepared to exclude the possibility that persons other than MLSOs might have been in the laboratory. Borrer assumed that all the people in the laboratory were MLSOs but could not exclude the possibility that there might be other people. (3) Those inside the laboratory had refused to allow entry to the police officers or indeed to talk to them except through locked doors — a situation which the chief constable described as unique in his experience of industrial disputes. They had also indicated politely and defiantly that they were prepared to stay inside the laboratory for an indefinite period.

A further factor which supervened the decision to arrest but preceded the actual arrest was the refusal of those inside the laboratory to unlock the door at 6.05 a.m. thereby rendering it necessary for the police to break it open in order to obtain entry, an act which was unlikely to advance patient care.

Borrer was pressed as to why after entering the laboratory the police did not merely caution and charge the persons therein and inform them that the matter would be reported to the procurator fiscal. His view was that there would have been no guarantee that those persons would have left the premises. The chief constable also felt that if they were not removed from the hospital they might return to the laboratory — he expressed these views in the light of past experience with picket lines.... In these circumstances once the chief constable had concluded that action must be taken to restore the use of the laboratory to the health board it followed that the most effective way of doing this was to remove the persons therein from the laboratory and its vicinity.

3.3.7   It was argued that this removal could have been achieved by action under either s. 1 or s. 2 of the Criminal Justice (Scotland) Act

1980. So far as s. 1 is concerned it was said that police officers could have required an individual to remain with them while they verified his or her name and address. The officers would have then left the laboratory with the individual in company and Dr Barrie, who was outside the laboratory, could have identified each individual. This suggested procedure is open to two objections, namely: (1) it would not have achieved the object of removing the individual from the laboratory and its vicinity; and (2) although Dr Barrie would have been able to say whether or not each individual worked in the laboratory he did not know the surnames of all the MLSOs and there is no evidence that he knew their addresses. The senior police officers who gave evidence all disapproved of the practice of using civilians to identify suspects except where no other alternative existed. In all the circumstances I do not consider that either the chief constable or Chief Superintendent Borrer can be criticised for not acting under s. 1. So far as s. 2 is concerned the justification for operating this procedure is to facilitate investigations into (a) the offence and (b) whether or not the individual should be reported... . Again I do not consider that the chief constable and the chief superintendent can be criticised for concluding that s. 2 procedure was not appropriate in the circumstances. If I am correct in concluding that there are only three ways in which a police officer is entitled in law to remove from premises a person who is there without the consent of the occupier it follows that in this case arrest was the most appropriate way. However, that is further than it is necessary to go because the pursuers must show that in this case arrest was unreasonable and unnecessary and this I consider that they have completely failed to do.

3.3.8 I was referred to *Galt* v. *Philp*, 1984 S.L.T. 28, which was an appeal by stated case to the High Court of Justiciary by the procurator fiscal in Kirkcaldy against a decision of the sheriff in a prosecution of the 12 MLSOs under the Conspiracy and Protection of Property Act 1875. In that case Lord Cameron at p. 39 expressed regret that action had been taken with such precipitancy and so little apparent consideration for the issues involved. I make no comment upon that dictum in other proceedings but I think it fair to state that on the evidence which was presented to me I would find it very difficult to pass such strictures on the action of the chief constable. Indeed it was clear that he was most reluctant to involve the police in any positive action and it was only when it became obvious that there was a serious risk that Dr Barrie would not have timeous access to his cultures with resultant risk to patient care that he was persuaded to act.

Detention

3.3.9 The pursuers then argued that even if their arrest in the laboratory was justified there was no reason or necessity to detain them after they had been removed therefrom. Their names and addresses could then have been taken and the matter reported to the procurator fiscal. In the aide-mémoire which is issued to all officers under the heading "Procedure on arrest, rights of accused" there appears the following passage: "Immediately on arrest, or as soon as practicable therefore, police officer must, (a) administer formal caution, (b) inform accused of reason for arrest, (c) take accused to suitable police station, (d) at police station read rights to accused, (e) carry out set procedure and complete necessary forms."

3.3.10   … However, I think that the pursuers are justified in arguing that the laying down of a normal procedure would not of itself absolve a police officer from his duty to comply with s. 17 of the Police (Scotland) Act 1967. It may well be that the laid down procedure is appropriate in most cases but that does not mean that a police officer is entitled to follow it slavishly without regard to the application of s. 17 to the particular circumstances of the case with which he is dealing. Thus the reasonableness of and necessity for removal to a police station after arrest must always depend upon circumstances… . I do not consider that the pursuers have shown that their removal to the police station was in the circumstances unreasonable and unnecessary. It follows that I reject the pursuers' first proposition.

. . . . . .

Proposition 2

3.3.11   Borrer explained that from the moment of arrest in the laboratory it had been his intention that the arrestees should be released once the normal checks had been carried out and no impediment to their release disclosed thereby… . The detention book showed that cautioning and charging started about 6.47 a.m. and finished about 7.15 a.m. Thus, if individuals were placed in the cells immediately after being cautioned and charged their time therein must have varied from about one and a half to two hours. The checks which had to be carried out were threefold, namely: (1) an identity check which could probably have been from the voters' roll; (2) an outstanding warrant check which is carried out as invariable practice; and (3) a check for previous convictions. The last two checks were carried out by police headquarters at Dysart after the names and addresses had been passed thereto by teleprinter. Borrer considered that it would have taken about an hour to carry out these checks on all 12 arrestees … I did not understand the pursuers in the end of the day to be maintaining … that they were detained for an unreasonable time at the police station but rather that if it was reasonable to detain them it was unreasonable that such detention should be in cells… .

3.3.12   In this case it was said there was no reason for adopting the normal procedure of placing arrested persons in cells pending a decision as to their release particularly as the women had already spent some 30 minutes without incident in the interview room with two or three police officers prior to being placed in the dells. If it was degrading to lock persons up in cells and if there was space available to hold them otherwise than in cells it was unreasonable not to make use of that other space... . Even allowing for the fact that the 12 arrestees were intelligent, articulate people I do not consider that the pursuers have demonstrated that the police officers acted unreasonably and unnecessarily in placing them in the cells for the relatively short space of time required to carry out the necessary checks. I did not understand the pursuers to argue that if they were justifiably placed in the cells they should not have been searched. I therefore reject the pursuers second proposition.

Proposition 3

3.3.13   This relates solely to the removal of Mrs Henderson's brassière. She was asked to remove this article of clothing before entering the cell in a manner which suggested that she was expected to comply with the request. She did so. There was a good deal of discussion with the police witnesses about certain circulars issued by the Scottish Home and Health Department dealing with the removal of clothing from persons about to be detained in cells. I do not consider that the precise terms of these circulars, nor which circular was current in September 1982 are relevant to this case. It was clear that the invitation to Mrs Henderson to remove her brassière was given as matter of course to all female detainees in Fife at the time. The justification advanced for this practice was that it prevented the detainee doing harm to herself or to any police officer who might enter the cell. Since the removal against her will of an undergarment from a woman must constitute an invasion of her liberty, I must therefore consider whether Mrs Henderson has demonstrated that such invasion was in the circumstances unjustified. The mere fact that the police officers concerned were acting in accordance with normal practice would not necessarily mean that what they did was justifiable in law if the particular circumstances did not require that normal practice be followed (*Lindley* v. *Rutter* [1981] 1 Q.B. 128, Donaldson L.J. at p. 132).

Prior to her entering the cell Mrs Henderson had been entirely co-operative with the police, she had made no attempt to escape and there was no suggestion that she was exhibiting any signs of mental unbalance such as would lead someone to think that she might do herself or anybody else harm. When she was put in the cell she asked but was not told how long she was going to be kept there. The police officers who put her in the cell must have been aware that she was an intelligent woman who had behaved in a co-operative and rational manner while in police custody. If they had told her that she was merely being detained while checks were being carried out I do not consider that they would have had any reasonable grounds for believing that she would harm herself or anyone else. In these circumstances I consider that Mrs Henderson has established that the request to remove her brassière was an interference with her liberty which was not justified in law, from which it follows that she has a remedy in damages. I should perhaps add that the researches of counsel had disclosed no Scottish case in which it had been held that removal of clothing forcibly or by requirement could constitute a wrong but since such removal must amount to an infringement of liberty I see no reason why the law should not protect the individual from this infringement just as it does from other infringements and indeed as the law of England did in very similar circumstances in *Lindley* v. *Rutter.*

Proposition 4

3.3.14   In view of the defender's concession I do not require to consider this.'

COMMENT

3.4.1   Decided: November 4, 1987.
  Sept. 4: Mattheus Russ jailed for four years in Moscow.
  Oct. 13: Ronson charged in Guinness affair.

3.4.2   The law of delict represents the common law's most significant protection of liberty. For a discussion in context and other relevant cases, see especially Chapter 4 of Ewing and Finnie, *Civil Liberties in Scotland: Cases and Materials* (2nd ed., 1988). Since the first edition I had a case where a television production company allegedly filmed my client without permission. On sending them a copy of this case they settled for a similar sum without admission of liability. Was that a wise decision? See paragraph 21.14.2 *et seq.* for references to privacy.

3.4.3   Do you think the decision would have been any different if one of the pursuers had been an unintelligent, inarticulate striking miner who had been asked to remove his string vest?

CHAPTER 4

BREACH OF CONFIDENCE

19. Scottish Law Commission
Report No. 90

4.1.1 '2.11. Apart from contract, express or implied, certain Scottish authorities suggest that an obligation of confidence may arise by virtue of the relationship of the parties and that the breach of such obligation is actionable as delict under Scots law. The position is obscure, not least because the decisions in some earlier cases, while bearing strong similarities to a delictual approach, were in fact decided on principles of common law copyright, which extended to unpublished material.

. . . . . .

4.1.2 2.13. The existence of an extra-contractual obligation of confidence was the basis of the decision in the case of *Levin* v. *Caledonia Produce (Holdings) Ltd.*, 1975 S.L.T. (Notes) 69. The pursuer concluded for damages for breach of contract and, alternatively, if there was no breach of contract, for damages for breach of confidence. Lord Robertson held that the pursuer's case based on breach of contract was irrelevant and fell to be dismissed. With regard to the pursuer's conclusion relating to breach of confidentiality he allowed proof before answer and said: "It was well settled in law that a relationship of trust or confidence may exist independently of contract, such as to entitle one party to restrain the other from disclosing, using or publishing something communicated under cover of confidence." Though the judgment as reported presents certain difficulties, the decision is in consonance both with earlier Scottish and more recent English authority that obligations of confidence may arise by virtue of the relationship of the parties.

4.1.3 2.14. In the later case of *Roxburgh* v. *Seven Seas Engineering Ltd.*, 1980 S.L.T. (Notes) 49, however, Lord Robertson appears to have envisaged that, before a third party can be liable, the relationship of the original parties must be a specific one (such as between employer and employee, doctor and patient). The decision also suggests that there must have been some kind of agreement or undertaking to maintain confidentiality between them. The case was one in which a partner of a firm sought to interdict the divulging by a third party of information disclosed to him by another partner of the firm. Lord Robertson recalled interim interdict on the ground that the petition was irrelevant. He said: "In order to state a relevant case based upon breach of confidentiality a pursuer or petitioner must aver primarily an agreement to treat the material as confidential and a relationship giving rise to the duty. Here there is no such relationship and no basis for any such agreement. The respondents have no relationship with the petitioner giving rise to any such duty. Whatever may be thought of the propriety or morals of the respondents' actions, they have in my opinion committed no wrong in law against the petitioner.'"

COMMENT

4.2.1 The Law Commission took the view that if legislation were required it should supplement, rather than replace, the existing law. The obligation under the draft Bill would have extended further than the original confider to encompass any person to whom or to whose interests the information in question related. Proposed defences would include: "that the use or disclosure of the information was in the public interest"; "in the absence of any agreement or undertaking … that the information was at the time of its use or, as the case may be, the disclosure, public knowledge." Whatever the nature of the right, the draft Bill in clause 5 provided for a right to reparation or alternatively (but not in addition) a right to an accounting of profits, if the breach was "knowing and deliberate".

Confidence and the reception in Scotland of "Spycatcher"
(*Att.-Gen. v. Guardian Newspapers Ltd* (No. 2) [1988] 3 W.L.R. 776)

20. **Lord Advocate (Appellant) v. The Scotsman Publications Ltd**
1989 S.L.T. 705 (H.L.)

4.3.1 'PETITION FOR INTERDICT.

The Lord Advocate presented a petition to the court seeking interdict of The Scotsman Publications Ltd., the editor of *The Scotsman* and "any other person having notice of said interlocutor" from publishing any of the content of a book called *Inside Intelligence* written and distributed by Anthony Cavendish, which contained information concerning the British security and intelligence services. Scottish Television plc and George Outram & Co. Ltd., publishers of the *Glasgow Herald,* entered the process as persons having notice of the proposed interdict … The Lord Ordinary refused the application for interim interdict … The petitioner reclaimed. The reclaiming motion was heard by the Second Division on 15, 16, 17, 18, 22 and 23 March 1988. On 8 April 1988 the Second Division *refused* the reclaiming motion. (Reported 1988 S.L.T. 490).

. . . . . .

4.3.2 LORD KEITH OF KINKEL: Mr Anthony Cavendish was employed by the British secret intelligence service (M.I.6) from 1948 to 1953. After leaving the service he remained on close terms with some continuing members of it, in particular Sir Maurice Oldfield, who was head of M.I.6 from 1973 to 1977. In 1987 Mr Cavendish sought authorisation from the government for publication of a book of memoirs which included some information about his period of service with M.I.6 and his association with Sir Maurice Oldfield. The book was called *Inside Intelligence*. Authorisation to publish it was refused. Mr Cavendish then had 500 copies of the book printed at his own expense, and at Christmas 1987 distributed 279 copies of it to various private individuals. Following representations made to him on behalf of the Crown, Mr Cavendish on 30 December 1987 gave an undertaking not to distribute any more copies of the book without first giving 14 days' notice.

4.3.3 Apparently a copy of the book came into the hands of the *Sunday Times* newspaper, which published an article about it on 27 December 1987... A copy of *Inside Intelligence* also came into the possession of *The Scotsman* newspaper, having apparently been handed over to it by one of the original recipients. On 5 January 1988 *The Scotsman* published an article which included some of the material contained in the book. The first respondents, publishers of *The Scotsman*, were requested on behalf of the Lord Advocate to give an undertaking that they would not publish any material which if published in England would be in breach of the injunction granted against Times Newspapers Ltd. They refused to give such an undertaking, and thereupon the Lord Advocate launched the present petition against the publishers and the editor of *The Scotsman* in the Court of Session... . [The] Lord Ordinary on 23 February 1988, following a lengthy hearing, refused the Lord Advocate's application for interim interdict. His interlocutor was affirmed by the Second Division (Lord Ross, Lord Justice-Clerk, Lord Dunpark and Lord McDonald) on 8 April 1988. The Lord Advocate now appeals, with leave of the Second Division, to your Lordships' House.

4.3.4 The grant or refusal of interim interdict is a discretionary matter, so that in order to succeed the appellant must demonstrate that the court below in some way misdirected themselves in law or that their discretion was exercised unreasonably. The ground upon which the appellant seeks interdict is that of confidentiality. It is averred that Mr Cavendish as a former member of the secret intelligence service remains under a lifelong obligation of confidentiality owed to the Crown as regards information which came into his possession as such a member, and further that as regards information communicated to him after his retirement by other members of the service he is under the same obligation of confidentiality as affected those other members. *The Scotsman* article of 5 January 1988 is said to contain material revealed by Mr Cavendish in breach of his obligation. The appellant goes on to aver, in stat. 7 of his petition: "The averments were to the effect that the Crown was reasonably apprehensive that Cavendish would publish further information: that others would further publish it to the prejudice of the administration of justice. Such publication was averred to be contrary to the national interest on the basis that other secret services would lose confidence in the UK service; other former agents might publish; morale would be affected." [His Lordship continued:] It is the appellant's case that the duty of confidence which was incumbent upon Mr Cavendish in relation to relevant information contained in his book is incumbent also upon the respondents, who received that information knowing that it had been revealed by Mr Cavendish in breach of his own obligation.

4.3.5   In the course of the argument for the appellant before the Second Division it became clear, as apparently it had not been before the Lord Ordinary, that the Crown did not maintain that *Inside Intelligence* contained any information disclosure of which was capable of damaging national security. From that point of view the whole contents of the book were entirely innocuous. So the grounds upon which the Second Division refused interim interdict were different from those relied on by the Lord Ordinary, which in the circumstances need not be examined. The judges of the Second Division, having considered such authorities upon the law of confidentiality as existed in the Scottish *corpus juris*, came to the conclusion that Scots law in this field was the same as that of England, in particular as respects the circumstances under which a person coming into possession of confidential information knowing it to be such, but not having received it directly from the original confider, himself comes under an obligation of confidence. That conclusion was, in my opinion, undoubtedly correct. While the juridical basis may differ to some extent in the two jurisdictions, the substance of the law in both of them is the same. If it had not been for the acceptance by counsel for the appellant that further publication of the information contained in the book would not be prejudicial to national security, the Second Division would have been disposed to grant interim interdict. They would not, at the interlocutory stage, have been prepared to hold that such limited publication as had already taken place had placed the contents of the book in the public domain to such an extent that a restriction on further publication would serve no useful purpose.

. . . . . .

4.3.6   At the time of the decision by the Second Division the *Spycatcher* case had passed through the stages of trial before Scott J. and appeal

to the Court of Appeal: *Att.-Gen.* v. *Guardian Newspapers Ltd. (No. 2)*
[1988] 2 W.L.R. 805; [1988] 3 W.L.R. 776. The decision on appeal
to your Lordships' House, which affirmed the Court of Appeal, was
given on 13 October 1988. That decision authoritatively established
that a member or former member of the British security or
intelligence service owes a lifelong duty of confidentiality to the
Crown which renders him liable to be restrained by injunction or
interdict from revealing information which came into his possession
in the course of his work. Disclosure of such information is by its
nature damaging to national security and there is no room for close
examination of the precise manner in which revelation of any
particular information would cause damage. A publisher or other
person acting on behalf of the member or former member of the
service was held to be subject to similar restraint. It was the prospect
of damage to the public interest which necessitated the fetter on
freedom of speech, and the House accepted the principle that in
general the Crown was not in a position to insist on confidentiality
as regards governmental matters unless it could demonstrate the
likelihood of such damage being caused by disclosure. I said at [1988]
3 W.L.R., pp. 782–783: "In so far as the Crown acts to prevent such
disclosure or to seek redress for it on confidentiality grounds, it must
necessarily, in my opinion, be in a position to show that the disclosure
is likely to damage or has damaged the public interest. How far the
Crown has to go in order to show this must depend on the
circumstances of each case. In a question with a Crown servant
himself, or others acting as his agents, the general public interest in
the preservation of confidentiality, and in encouraging other Crown
servants to preserve it, may suffice. But where the publication is
proposed to be made by third parties unconnected with the
particular confidant, the position may be different. The Crown's
argument in the present case would go the length that in all
circumstances where the original disclosure has been made by a
Crown servant in breach of his obligation of confidence any person
to whose knowledge the information comes and who is aware of the
breach comes under an equitable duty binding his conscience not
to communicate the information to anyone else irrespective of the
circumstances under which he acquired the knowledge. In my
opinion that general proposition is untenable and impracticable,
in addition to being unsupported by any authority. The general rule
is that anyone is entitled to communicate anything he pleases to
anyone else, by speech or in writing or in any other way. That rule is
limited by the law of defamation and other restrictions similar to
these mentioned in article 10 of the Convention for the Protection
of Human Rights and Fundamental Freedoms (1953) (Cmnd. 8969).
All those restrictions are imposed in the light of considerations of
public interest such as to countervail the public interest in freedom
of expression. A communication about some aspect of government

activity which does no harm to the interests of the nation cannot, even where the original disclosure has been made in breach of confidence, be restrained on the ground of a nebulous equitable duty of conscience serving no useful practical purpose."

4.3.7   This passage recognises that there may be some circumstances under which a third party may come into possession of information, originally confidential, which has been revealed by a crown servant in breach of his own duty of confidence, and yet may not be liable to be restrained from passing it on to others. In *Spycatcher* itself the circumstances which resulted in the defendant newspaper not being restrained from publishing and commenting on material contained in the book were that it had been disseminated worldwide to the extent of over 1,000,000 copies and that it was freely available in this country. In that situation it was impossible for the Crown to demonstrate that further publication by the defendants would add to any extent to the damage to the public interest which had already been brought about.

. . . . . .

4.3.8   [The] appellant has not pleaded a good arguable prima facie case that further publication by the respondents would do any material damage to the public interest. If a proof were allowed, any opinion evidence on the lines of stat. 7 of the petition, such as was given by Sir Robert Armstrong in the *Spycatcher* case, would be given on the basis that the contents of the book were innocuous. The court would not be proceeding on the normal prima facie footing that any book about his work by a former member of the security or intelligence service was directly prejudicial to national security. Further, as the Lord Justice-Clerk pointed out, the sort of indirect prejudice which is described in paras. (a) to (e) of stat. 7 is brought about by the known fact of publication by a former member of the service, not by its extent.

4.3.9   It was argued for the appellant that dismissal of this appeal would have the effect that any newspaper which received an unsolicited book of memoirs by a present or former member of the security or intelligence service would be free to publish it. That is not so. If there had been no previous publication at all and no concession that the contents of the book were innocuous the newspaper would undoubtedly itself come under an obligation of confidence and be subject to restraint. If there had been a minor decree of prior publication, and no such concession, it would be a matter for investigation whether further publication would be prejudicial to the public interest, and interim interdict would normally be appropriate.'

COMMENT

4.4.1 Decided: July 6, 1989.
June 4: Massacre at Tiananmen Square.
June 21: Police arrested 250 hippies on their way to Stonehenge.
June 28: Prince of Wales considered English taught "bloody badly".
July 3: National Dock Labour Scheme abolished.

4.4.2 Lord Keith is a Scots lawyer and this is a Scots appeal. It would thus be difficult
to suggest that Scots law is not now as stated above. On the other hand, it would have
been more satisfying if some intimation could have been given of the legal basis of the
duty in question. The writer is not yet fully convinced that this obligation, on a third-
party confidant, although clearly obediential, is properly delictual. If it is an equitable
duty, there is a possibility that it is an obligation *sui generis*. Liability to pay money as a
result of publishing information received from a primary confidant might better be
considered as a restitutionary obligation than as based on delict, the wrongdoing being
the basis for calling on the defender to disgorge the profits he made by his wrongdoing.
The particular relationship involved has been affected by the Security Services Act
1989 and the Official Secrets Act 1989. See generally Dickinson (1989) 34 J.L.S.S.

For an analysis of the various issues (from the point of view of English law) see, Goff
and Jones, *The Law of Restitution* (4th ed., 1993) Chap. 36.

CHAPTER 5

WRONGFUL USE OF LAND

Nuisance

21. R.H.M. Bakeries (Scotland) Ltd v. Strathclyde Regional Council (Appellants)
1985 S.L.T. 214 (H.L.)

5.1.1 'Bakery premises were flooded as the result of the collapse of a sewer, which was under the operation and control of the local authority. Food and packing materials stored in the bakery premises were damaged. The bakery raised an action of damages against the local authority on the grounds of (a) nuisance at common law and (b) breach of statutory duty under s. 2 of the Sewerage (Scotland) Act 1968. The action was dismissed as irrelevant by the sheriff and appealed to the sheriff principal who allowed a proof before answer. The Second Division held that the defences were irrelevant and granted decree *de plano*. The defenders appealed.

. . . . . .

5.1.2 LORD FRASER OF TULLYBELTON: This appeal raises a question as to the principle on which the owner or occupier of land in Scotland (the defender) is liable at common law for damage to his neighbour's land caused by an agency, in this case sewage, which escapes from an artificial work on the defender's land. A secondary question arises as to the liability of a defender which is a public authority acting under statutory powers.... . In their common law case, they do not aver that the damage to their bakery was caused by any fault on the part of the local authority, either in failing to take reasonable care to maintain the sewer, or in failing to repair it promptly after it had collapsed, or in any other way. Their case at common law on record is that the flooding was, or possibly was caused by, a nuisance for which the local authority are "strictly liable". Their case under the Sewerage (Scotland) Act 1968 is that by s. 2 of that Act the local authority were under a duty to maintain the sewer, and that "said duty [was] absolute". A faint attempt was made by counsel for R.H.M. to argue that his pleadings were sufficient to found a case of fault at least by relying on the brocard *res ipsa loquitur*. In my opinion the attempt was hopeless on the pleadings as they stand, and we were not moved to allow them to be amended... The first issue is, and has always been, whether the local authority are liable at common law for the damage caused by flooding, even if it occurred without fault on their part, or whether they are only liable if they were to some extent at fault. The second issue is, and always been, whether the local authority are liable for breach of the provisions of the Sewerage (Scotland) Act 1968, s. 2 requiring them to maintain the sewer, even if they have used all reasonable care and skill to maintain it.

. . . . . .

5.1.3 The Second Division (Lord Justice-Clerk (Lord Wheatley), Lord Robertson and Lord Dunpark) allowed an appeal from the sheriff principal, held the defences irrelevant and granted decree *de plano* for the sum sued for. The Division held by majority (Lord Dunpark dissenting) that R.H.M.'s averments of nuisance at common law were relevant and unanimously that their averments of breach of s. 2 of the Act of 1968 were relevant. I consider first the question of liability at common law. The argument in this House resolved itself largely into an analysis of the legal basis of the decision in *Kerr* v. *Earl of Orkney* (1857) 20 D. 298 and later Scottish cases in the same field. Inevitably the argument touched also upon the decision of this House in *Rylands* v. *Fletcher* (1868) L.R. 3 H.L. 330 and later English cases in the same field. But no question of English law is raised in this appeal so far as it relates to common law, and I disclaim any intention of deciding one.

. . . . . .

5.1.4 It is convenient to start with *Kerr* v. *Earl of Orkney* which for long has been regarded as a landmark decision in this field. Unfortunately the legal basis on which it rests has been the subject of much discussion and, I humbly think, some misunderstanding. The facts were that the defender, the Earl of Orkney, had built a dam on his land in Ayrshire across a stream on which the pursuer had a mill about half-a-mile lower down. Four months after the dam had been completed, there were several days of heavy rain, the dam burst, the waters in the pond behind it escaped and the stream, augmented by those waters, swept away the pursuer's house and his mill. Not surprisingly the defender was held to be liable in damages to the pursuer. The question is as to the exact basis on which he was found to be liable.

. . . . . .

5.1.5 When *Kerr* v. *Earl of Orkney* reached the Inner House, the Lord Justice-Clerk (Hope) began his opinion with a general statement which seems to lay down a rule of strict liability and has been so understood in later cases... . The only exception which he would have admitted was a *damnum fatale* or act of God. But later in his opinion he appears to rest it upon the view that the defender was at fault ... I am of opinion that the true basis of the decision in *Kerr* v. *Earl of Orkney* was *culpa* on the part of the defender.

. . . . . .

5.1.6   In *McLaughlan v. Craig*, 1948 S.L.T. 483, Lord President Cooper emphatically rejected the proposition that an owner of property acted at his peril, which he described (at p. 610) as "that 'coarse and impolitic idea'" — a description which he borrowed from Lord Simonds in *Read* v. *J. Lyons & Co. Ltd.* [1947] A.C. 156 at p. 181 who in turn attributed it to Holmes J. in America... . The doubt about whether *culpa* is the essential basis in Scots law for the liability of the proprietor of land to a neighbour arises from the fact that the English decision in *Rylands* v. *Fletcher* has sometimes been referred to as if it were authoritative in Scotland. In my opinion, with all respect to eminent judges who have referred to it in that way, it has no place in Scots law, and the suggestion that it has, is a heresy which ought to be extirpated.

. . . . . .

5.1.7   The only decision which might create some difficulty on this part of the appeal is *Caledonian Railway Co.* v. *Greenock Corporation*, 1917 2 S.L.T. 67, where several members of this House referred to *Kerr v. Earl of Orkney* and approved of the first part of Lord Justice-Clerk Hope's opinion, cited above, in which he seemed to apply the rule of strict liability to a person who interferes with the flow of a stream. In the *Caledonian Railway* case the defender, in order to improve a public park, had altered the course of a burn by enclosing the burn in a culvert and filling in the valley through which the burn had previously flowed. There are certainly dicta in some of the speeches which could be read as supporting a rule of strict liability — see Lord Finlay L.C. at pp. 69–70. *Rylands* v. *Fletcher* was mentioned but not relied upon for the decision; indeed, it was distinguished by Lord Finlay L.C. at p. 70, on the grounds that it related merely to the storage of water and did not affect the question of liability for interference with the course of a natural stream. But there are other parts of the speeches which can be read as founding liability on *culpa*.... But whatever may be the basis of the decision in the *Caledonian Railway* cases, the decision is not directly applicable to the facts of the instant appeal, which are not concerned with diverting the flow of a natural stream. Accordingly I do not consider that it is an authority which inhibits your Lordships from deciding that the local authority in this appeal will only be liable if they are shown to have been at fault. It may be that the case should be regarded as laying down a special rule applicable only to the case of a person who interferes with the course of a natural stream. If so, it is contrary to a general principle of the law of Scotland and, in my opinion, the rule should not be extended beyond the precise facts of that case.

5.1.8 I come now to the two recent decisions which were mainly relied upon by the Second Division. The first of these is *Watt v. Jamieson*, 1954 S.L.T. 56, which was a decision by Lord President Cooper sitting in the Outer House. Having regard to his rejection of strict liability in *McLaughlan v. Craig* in 1948, it would be surprising if he had accepted that principle in *Watt* in 1954...

The facts in *Watt*, which I take form the [*Session Cases*] rubric, were that "In an action of damages brought by the owner of a flat in a tenement against the owner of a flat in an adjoining tenement, the pursuer averred that damage had been caused to his flat through the discharge into a vent in the mutual gable of sulphur-impregnated water vapour from a gas water-heater installed by the defender in his flat. In answer to the pursuer's plea of nuisance, the defender maintained that the action was irrelevant in respect that the user complained of involved only a normal, natural and familiar use of dwellinghouse property in a burgh." All that the case decided was that it was not a relevant defence to say that the defender's use of his property was a normal and familiar one. But the Lord President went on to say (1954 S.L.T. at p. 57): " ... The modern view of nuisance is, I think, more accurately founded upon such cases as *Broder v. Saillard* (1876) 2 Ch. D. 692, *Fleming v. Hislop* 13 R. (H.L.) 43, and *Sedleigh Denfield v. O'Callaghan* [1940] A.C. 880, and this modern view is formulated in such textbooks as Salmond on *Torts* (11th ed.), at p. 259, and Burn-Murdoch on *Interdict*, p. 228. From these and other pronouncements I deduce that the proper angle of approach to a case of alleged nuisance is rather from the standpoint of the victim of the loss or inconvenience than from the standpoint of the alleged offender; and that, if any person so uses his property as to occasion serious disturbance or substantial inconvenience to his neighbour or material damage to his neighbour's property, it is in the general case irrelevant as a defence for the defender to plead merely that he was making a normal and familiar use of his own property. The balance in all such cases has to be held between the freedom of the proprietor to use his property as he pleases, and the duty on a proprietor not to inflict material loss or inconvenience on adjoining proprietors or adjoining property; and in every case the answer depends on considerations of fact and of degree ... The critical question is whether what he was exposed to was *plus quam tolerabile* when due weight has been given to all the surrounding circumstances of the offensive conduct and its effects. If that test is satisfied, I do not consider that our law accepts as a defence that the nature of the user complained of was usual, familiar and normal. Any type of use which in the sense indicated above subjects adjoining proprietors to substantial annoyance, or causes material damage to their property, is *prima facie* not 'reasonable' use."

. . . . . .

5.1.9 [Lord Fraser continued:] In a case when the only remedy sought was interdict the position might be different; I think that a defender might be liable to be interdicted from using some artificial work on his land, even although he had no personal responsibility for putting it there in the first place and had not begun to use it, if there was a reason to believe that he was likely to use it in the future. But that question does not arise here. Accordingly, I do not regard Lord President Cooper's opinion in *Watt* v. *Jamieson* as giving any support to the view that a defender is liable for damages for nuisance merely *ex dominio* and without fault on his part... . For these reasons I am of opinion that the majority of the Second Division came to the wrong conclusion on the common law case.

. . . . . .

5.1.10 I wish to add two further comments on this part of the case. The first is that the view that I have just expressed does not by any means imply that, in a case such as this, a pursuer cannot succeed unless he avers the precise nature of the fault committed by the defender which caused the accident. It would be quite unreasonable to place such a burden on a pursuer, who in many cases will have no knowledge, and no means of obtaining knowledge, of the defender's fault. As a general rule it would, in my opinion, be relevant for a pursuer to make averments to the effect that his property has been damaged by a flood caused by an event on the defender's land, such as the collapse of a sewer which it was the defender's duty to maintain, that properly maintained sewers do not collapse, and that the collapse is evidence that the defender had failed in his duty to maintain the sewer. The onus will then be on the defender to explain the event in some way consistent with absence of fault on his part. As a general rule the defences available will be limited to proving that the event was caused either by the action of a third party for whom he was not responsible, as the defender did in *Gourock Ropework Co. Ltd.* v. *Greenock Corporation*, 1966 S.L.T. 125 or by a *damnum fatale*. My second comment is that I do not believe that there is much difference in the practical result between the law as laid down in *Rylands* v. *Fletcher* and the law as laid down according to my understanding of *Kerr* v. *Earl of Orkney* ... But as the parties have chosen to litigate the question, and as they presumably consider it to be important to them, I think they are entitled to have it decided. In my opinion it should be decided in favour of the local authority.

5.1.11   I come now to the case based on breach of statutory duty. The averments of R.H.M. on this matter are as follows: "Separatim in terms of s. 2 of the Sewerage (Scotland) Act 1968, it is the duty of every local authority including the defenders, inter alia to maintain all sewers vested in them. *Said duty is absolute*" (emphasis added)… Lord Robertson read s. 2 of the Act of 1968 as imposing an absolute duty to maintain the sewer. I doubt whether that is correct, having regard to the fact that the section also imposes duties to inspect and to repair. The former would be unnecessary if the duty to maintain was absolute, and the latter seems to imply that some degree of disrepair is to be expected and permitted, and thus to negative an absolute duty to maintain. But whether that is right or not, I am of opinion, on the authorities, that the duty to maintain under s. 2 was not absolute.'

COMMENT

5.2.1   Decided: January 24, 1985.
(1984)
Dec. 10: IRA bomb Grand Hotel, Brighton.
Oct. 31: Indira Gandhi assassinated.
Nov. 6: Ronald Reagan re-elected President.
Dec. 14: Arthur Scargill fined for obstruction. Bob Geldof and others record *Do they know it's Christmas?*

5.2.2   For a long time it was accepted (by some quite reluctantly) that nuisance was a separate head of liability and that liability for nuisance was strict — that is, there could be liability without fault on the part of the defender. For those who took the view that Scots law had come to be based on a principle of *culpa*, this was a major exception (although some tried to define the problem away by having a wider view of *culpa*). Thankfully, the problem has been substantially resolved by this decision. This case can also be taken as giving some support to the *culpa* theory of liability (*Delict*, 1.13).

5.2.3   This chapter deals with the obligations imposed by the law upon landowners or occupiers, other than those imposed by the general law of negligence (see especially Chap. 12) or the Occupiers Liability (Scotland) Act 1960 (see Chap. 16). The trend is to explain all of these on the basis of fault, but that may be over-ambitious. These delicts are of long standing and reflect a community view of what is wrong. Unlike *Donoghue*-type (Ext. 39) neighbours, who are not necessarily neighbours at all, many of these following cases *do* depend upon the persons concerned living next to each other. The obligations arise by force of law and not of consent, but are personal to the person using the land. They are thus clearly delictual obligations, but the obligations exist mainly to protect interests in land. The Roman *quasi*-delicts, two of which are dealt with here (Chap. 5, 4 and 5 and *Delict*, 2.21–22), are problematic and obviously to protect the public rather than a neighbouring property owner. Physical invasion of property is dealt with by trespass. Long-term interference is covered by the old delicts of ejection and intrusion (*Delict*, 2.9). The Animals (Scotland) Act 1987 (Ext. 68) (*Delict*, 7.23–7.33) provides neighbours, inter alios, with the protection of strict liability for certain damage, which often in reality will be caused by neighbouring animals.

5.2.4   The system of feudal tenure in Scotland allows many disputes between neighbours to be resolved by reference to the title deeds. Sometimes neighbours are each bound by a set of conditions imposed upon them by the feudal superior, quite often a building developer. Providing title and interest can be established, each neighbour may rely on the conditions against the others. Many practical problems are solved by local authorities exercising their powers under the common lease. However, as seems often to be the rôle of delict now, it remains as a safety net, to give access to the courts when other means fail.

5.2.5 Even though the House of Lords did not overrule *Caledonian Railway Co.*, and accordingly it still stands as high authority, it might not be prudent to rely on strict liability in a case in point unless absolutely necessary. See the discussion of the Roman Actio *aquae pluviae arcendae* in Johnston, "Owners and neighbours: from Rome to Scotland" in *The Civil Law Tradition in Scotland*, Stair Society (Evans-Jones ed. 1995), p. 180. A culvert features in the interesting case *G.A. Estates Ltd v. Caviapen Trustees Ltd (No. 1)*, 1993 S.L.T. 1037.

5.2.6 The law of England still has difficulties with the question of how far fault or negligence is crucial to liability in damages. Some of the difficulty is attributed to a particular passage of a Scots Lord of Appeal, Lord Reid. (See generally, Chap. 14 of Winfield and Jolowicz on *Tort* (13th ed., 1989), esp. pp. 382–387.) In *Cambridge Water Co v. Eastern Counties Leather Plc* [1994] 2 A.C. 264 the House of Lords accepted that the remoteness of damage test in tort applied to *Rylands* liability. Lord Goff accepted that *Rylands* was a species of nuisance. The High Court of Australia has now accepted that *Rylands* is "absorbed by the principles of ordinary negligence": *Burnie Port Authority v. General Jones Pty Ltd* (1994) 179 C.L.R. 520.

5.2.7 Paragraphs 5.1.2 and 5.1.11 are relevant to statutory duty (Chap. 15). Paragraph 5.1.10 is relevant to the question of proof (Chap. 24).

22. **Argyll and Clyde Health Board v. Strathclyde Regional Council**
1988 S.L.T. 381 (O.H.)

5.3.1 'LORD MCCLUSKEY: This case raises an important question of relevancy, not least because there could be other cases arising out of similar circumstances.... It was discovered that a 16-inch diameter water main pipe, owned by the defenders and running under the surface of a field, had burst. Water from the burst main flooded the pursuers' premises and the pursuers incurred financial loss in repairing the damage and reinstating the premises. The pursuers aver that they "are unable to specify which or which combination of... factors caused the burst." It is averred, however, that there had been no interference with the pipe "whether by act of man or God". It is also said that the weather conditions had not been unusual, and that there had been no activities in the vicinity of the burst such as to cause it or contribute to it. It is not in dispute that the pipe was laid at the end of the 19th century.... It is further averred that: "Each of said factors could be prevented only by persons authorised by the defenders" and that the defenders "would alone be in a position to ascertain the likelihood of a pipe, of an age which they alone would be able to record and check, being subjected to such corrosion and to judge the foreseeable effect thereof, whether alone or in combination with any of the above factors"... Article 3 of the condescendence contains the only averments of fault. It is plain from these averments that the pursuers are resting their cases upon culpa. It is not suggested that there is a strict liability or any breach of statutory duty.

. . . . . .

5.3.2 The critical averments are: "It was their duty to take reasonable care to see said water mains had been laid and was maintained (including maintenance by way of replacement if such was considered necessary or appropriate) in such condition that it would not burst. In respect that water mains which are properly laid and properly maintained do not burst, the defenders failed in said duties. But for the defenders' said failure in duty, said loss and damage would not have occurred."

. . . . . .

5.3.3 The defenders argued that there could be no liability *ex dominio*; fault was an essential requisite of liability. It appears to me that proposition is undeniably sound. I refer to *R.H.M. Bakeries (Scotland) Ltd.* v. *Strathclyde Regional Council* [Ext. 21] ... The pursuers pointed to the fact that the case made in art. 3 of the condescendence was a case of *culpa*. I approach the case on the basis that it is necessary to aver facts and circumstances from which fault can be inferred. The pursuers' submission was that this was exactly what had been done. The defenders said that there was no sufficient averment of fault ... It is important nonetheless to note that in that case the House of Lords decided no more than that the common law case was irrelevant because it excluded any reference to fault on the part of the defenders (a secondary question, as to the interpretation of the relevant statute, does not arise here).

5.3.4 An argument that liability could be established without proof of fault was rejected. The pursuers, however, in defence of the form of their pleadings, founded upon a passage from the speech of Lord Fraser of Tullybelton at p. 219, with which the other members of the committee agreed: that passage reads as follows: [his Lorship referred *inter alia* to the passage in *R.H.M. Bakeries* [5.1.10] beginning "The first is that ..." and ending "damnum fatale", in which Lord Fraser made comments on what should be averred and proved. He continued]: "This passage is obiter but, in my respectful opinion, it properly expresses the law ... [Lord Fraser] is not, in my view, saying that a bald averment, "that properly maintained sewers do not collapse" is by itself sufficient in such a context to shift the onus to the defender to explain the collapse in some way consistent with absence of fault on the defenders' part. He is indicating the essential legal context of such a case; he is not saying that no more need be said in order to make the case sufficiently specific so as to be relevant for inquiry at a proof... Accordingly the question which I have to decide appears to me not to be a question of the law applicable, but a question as to the adequacy of the pleadings in the light of the Scottish tradition and current practice. To test the relevancy of the pursuers' pleadings it is necessary to ask whether or not the pursuers, if they prove no more than what is averred, are entitled to succeed. But it goes further than that. Pursuers must also give sufficient specification of what they intend to prove.

. . . . . .

5.3.5 Exactly how much specification is needed will certainly vary from case to case ... If the pursuer avers a state of facts which, if proved, will be eloquent of negligence unless the defenders can by averment and proof exclude an inference of negligence, then the pursuer's pleadings will be relevant for inquiry, even in the absence of any precise or complete account therein as to the cause of the accident. This is the situation most commonly encountered in cases where the pursuer hopes to be able to rely on the brocard *res ipsa loquitur*. In such a case the pursuer avers a fact, usually the fact of the accident itself, or the appearance of a defect which caused the accident, and the proper inference from the happening of the accident, or the manifestation of the defect, is that it would not have occurred unless there had been fault on the defender's part.

. . . . . .

5.3.6 Undoubtedly, therefore, a case may still be dismissed on the ground of relevancy, not only where it is clear that a ground which is unsound in law has been pled (as in *R.H.M. Bakeries (Scotland) Ltd.*) but also in any case where, although the law is clear enough, the pursuer has not given adequate and fair notice of the facts which he intends to prove, being facts which, if proved, would yield the inference of fault ... In order to pass the test of relevancy the pursuers must give adequate notice in their pleadings of facts which either infer a specific fault or are so eloquent of some unspecified fault on the part of the defenders that, in the absence of any acceptable alternative explanation (alternative in the sense of excluding fault), *res ipsa loquitur*, and the court would be entitled to infer that the cause of the loss, injury and damage must have been some fault on the part of the defenders... I do not consider that Lord Fraser of Tullybelton was, in the passage quoted, attempting to give pleaders a lesson in how to frame pleadings.

. . . . . .

5.3.7 So there is a hiatus in these pleadings: There is no averment as to what kind of maintenance would have been appropriate or even possible, with the result that the court is provided with no canon for judging what falls short of "proper". The pursuers do not offer to prove what is meant by "proper": the defenders have no notice of what it means... Indeed the defenders themselves aver that, when the internal corrosion occurs in a pipe, that involves the build-up of a considerable deposit on the internal surface of the pipe which results in a reduction of the effective diameter and, therefore, of the carrying capacity of the pipe, a circumstance which can be identified... In my opinion it is essential for the pursuers in a case of this character to specify what is meant by the words "properly maintained".

. . . . . .

5.3.8 It is not for me (any more than it was for Lord Fraser of Tullybelton in *R.H.M. Bakeries* [Ext. 1]) to attempt to draft the pleadings that might be appropriate. But it is obvious enough that the pursuers could seek expert evidence as to how such old pipes might be examined for signs of impending failure, and evidence as to how other water authorities, wherever situated, inspect, monitor and maintain such pipes. If such evidence were obtained it would be possible and proper to aver both what is meant by "proper" maintenance and also that the defenders could not have carried out such maintenance or the pipe in question would not have failed. With such pleadings, fair notice would be given. Without them fair notice would not be given ... I therefore consider that their pleadings are irrelevant for want of specification and I shall dismiss the action.'

COMMENT

5.4.1   Decided: December 4, 1987
    Oct. 19: "Black Monday" stock market crash.
    Oct. 23: Lester Piggot jailed for three years.
    Nov. 8: Enniskillen remembrance ceremony bombed by IRA.
    Nov. 11: Van Gogh's *Irises* sold for a record $53.9 Million.
    Dec. 3: *Crockford's* preface criticises Archbishop Runcie.

5.4.2   The working through of the R.H.M. restatement is not easy. As can be seen from this extract what must be averred and proven is a matter for concern. The method of approach in this extract was expressly approved in *Noble's Trs. v. Economic Forestry (Scotland) Ltd*, 1988 S.L.T. 662, and by reference in *Borders Regional Council v. Roxburgh District Council*, 1989 S.L.T. 837. In *Borders Regional Council* a case was raised in negligence against a number of defenders and in nuisance against the first defender, the neighbouring heritable proprietor. The first defenders, the district council, had allowed the second-named defenders, the Scottish Development Agency, to do building work on their (the first named defenders') land which was adjacent to that of the pursuers. The following averment made by the pursuer was held to be irrelevant: "the said damage sustained by [the pursuers] was caused or materially contributed to by nuisance on the part of the first-named defenders as occupiers and proprietors of the neighbouring ground. They were responsible for the hazardous work undertaken in excavating the trench for the foundation of the stair where their ground bordered on [the pursuers' property]. In the course of this operation they disturbed the support and fabric of [the pursuers' property] and thereby caused damage." Lord Dervaird held that this did not aver *culpa* and effectively approved the defenders' view that the averment actually proceeded on the basis that liability in nuisance rested solely on ownership of land. The negligence case failed against both the first and second-named defenders. The pursuers continued the cause to amend against the consulting engineers involved and the contractors involved were content to let the case proceed to a proof before answer. For a well-received and erudite treatment of the law of Nuisance, see N. R. Whitty, "Nuisance", Vol. 14, *Stair Encyclopaedia*. An important comment which might assist concerned pleaders can be found in a review at 1990 J.R. 117 at 121. It is by a reviewer identified only by initials — J.A.D.H.! See also *Kennedy v. Glenbelle*, 1995 G.W.D. 7–398 in which Lord Abernethy held that although *R.H.M. Bakeries* decided that nuisance was based on *culpa* this was not to say that it was the same as negligence. This view was endorsed and expanded by the aforementioned J.A.D.H. in his (then) new incarnation as Lord President when the case came before the Inner House 1996 S.L.T. 1186 — this case ought to be read.

5.4.3 Some sports provide good examples of nuisances and the interrelation of nuisance and negligence: see *Castle v. St Augustine Links* (1922) 38 T.L.R. 615 and *Lamond v. Glasgow Corp.*, 1968 S.L.T. 291.

23. **Campbell v. Kennedy (Appellant)**
(1864) 3 M. 121 (I.H.)

5.5.1 'Archibald Campbell, musical instrument dealer in Glasgow, raised an action in the sheriff court of Lanarkshire against Thomas Kennedy, the proprietor of a flat situated two storeys above the pursuer's shop, concluding for payment of £33 11s. as the damage sustained by the pursuer... through the bursting or insufficiency of a water-pipe in the defender's flat, "all through the culpable carelessness or recklessness, or negligence of the defender or others (whose names and designations are to the pursuer unknown) for whom the defender is responsible".

Kennedy admitted that some damage had been done to the pursuer's property "through the accidental escape of water in a house belonging to the defender," but denied that there was any negligence or want of care on the part of the defender or anybody for whom he was responsible.

· · · · · ·

5.5.2 LORD BENHOLME: ... But I cannot help thinking that there was another matter of fact in his Lordship's view in pronouncing this judgment, which ought also to have been stated. I mean the fact of *culpa*, or negligence; and I would, therefore, propose to add to the findings in fact, another finding, *viz.*, "That through the negligence of the defender, the said pipe had been allowed to remain in an insufficient or defective state." Some such finding is necessary in order to make the findings in fact quadrate with the findings in law. It was not enough to say that the premises in which the defective pipe existed were the defender's property and that they were the cause of the damage. I have no doubt but that the Lord Ordinary held that, to infer responsibility for damage, there must be *culpa*. It may have been that the duties of property are so generally recognised, and that it is so well known, that one of these duties is to keep one's property in such a state that it shall not injure neighbours, that the Lord Ordinary may have felt justified in assuming that the fact of damage inferred negligence, and, therefore, responsibility. But I think it is of great importance that there should be no mistake as to the true ground of liability. There is another reason why this matter of fact should be distinctly embodied in a finding; and that is, that the court of appeal might find it difficult to affirm our finding in law for want of a sufficient basis of fact. I am, therefore, of opinion that we must make up our minds on the question, whether negligence has or has not been established... .

5.5.3 This circumstance, together with the nature of the leakage which caused the damage, suggest to my mind the idea of a very thin pipe being gradually worn away, rather than of leakage occasioned by a sudden force of water. There is a very general understanding, founded in common sense, that it is the duty of the proprietor of an upper flat of a house to see that the water-pipes are kept in a secure state. Now it appears to me that the evidence here is sufficient to shew some failure of this duty on the part of the defender, and I think that he is liable for the damage thereby occasioned.

I know of no decision inconsistent with this view of the law. If a case should arise in which it appeared that the property had occasioned damage, whilst the proprietor was exempt from all *culpa* or negligence, I am not prepared to say that he would be responsible.

5.5.4 LORD NEAVES: ... My view of the law is, that the possession of property infers certain duties, and that a proprietor is bound to follow a reasonable and prudent course of administration, so as not to injure his neighbours. But it is quite a different thing to say that if, notwithstanding this prudent management, an injury is caused to the property of a neighbour, a proprietor is responsible. There are obligations which arise *ex contractu*, and *quasi ex contractu* and *ex delicto*, and *quasi ex delicto*, but I never heard of an obligation arising merely *ex dominio*.

The case of *Cleghorn* [(1856) 18 D. 664] only settled this principle, that when a proprietor employs a tradesman to do something to his property, he is responsible to his neighbours for injury caused by the insufficiency of the work. I think that the opinions delivered in that case are to be read as applicable to that case... .

5.5.5 LORD COWAN: On the proof, I am satisfied that some degree of blame is shewn to have been attachable to the proprietor for allowing the pipe, the bursting of which caused the damage, to remain in the state in which it is proved to have been... I think it unnecessary to consider what liability would legally have attached to the owner, supposing such fault did not exist, and was not to be inserted as an additional finding into the interlocutor... .

5.5.6 LORD JUSTICE-CLERK [Inglis]: ... But I go farther, and hold that no action for reparation of damage so caused can be relevant, unless negligence or *culpa* of some description is averred. The remedy of an action for reparation is confined to cases of breach of contract, and of damage caused by delinquency. I cannot find any example of a claim for reparation being allowed in any other case and, except in the recent case of *Cleghorn*... I know of no trace of authority for a different doctrine. The various kinds of delinquency which will sustain a claim of reparation are exceedingly numerous. They are generally of the inferior sort of delinquencies, which consist in the breach of natural or obediential obligations, and not of the greater delinquencies, which are commonly called crimes. The case before us is one of the former class. The brocard which sets forth the duty of a proprietor is, *sic utere tuo ut alienum non laedas*; and the only ground on which the owner of property can be made liable is a breach of that obediential obligation. But there can be no such breach, without fault of some kind, either of omission or commission. I cannot, therefore, hold that the mere fact of ownership, upon which the interlocutor proceeds, is in itself a ground of liability...

The next question is, whether there is sufficient evidence to establish *culpa* in the case before us? It is a very narrow case, and I have great difficulty in holding negligence established. At the same time I am not prepared to dissent.'

COMMENT

5.6.1 Decided: Nov. 25, 1864.
Oct. 30: Denmark surrenders Schleswig and Holstein to Bismarck's Prussians.
Nov. 8: Abraham Lincoln re-elected President.
Nov. 25: British ambassador at Washington resigned due to ill-health.

5.6.2 Is this the kind of case of unspecified fault which Lord McCluskey might have had in mind in *Argyll* (Ext. 22)? Notice the *Kennedy v. Glenbelle* view clearly remarked upon at 5.5.6 "negligence or *culpa* of some description" over 100 years ago. See *Dewar v. Lothian,* May 30, 1996, unreported, for an application of *Kennedy v. Glenbelle* to facts similar to those in this extract.

Roman quasi-delicts and land use

24. **MacColl v. Hoo (Appellant)**
1983 S.L.T. (Sh. Ct.) 23 (S.A.)

5.7.1 'The owner of a motor car damaged by a slate which had been blown off the roof of a nearby house sought damages from the owner of the house. On the agreed facts no negligence on the defender's part could be inferred. The pursuer successfully contended that she was nonetheless entitled to damages on the ground that as owner and occupier of the property the defender had an absolute liability for its maintenance in a safe condition. The defender appealed to the sheriff principal... .

5.7.2 THE SHERIFF PRINCIPAL (R. A. Bennett, Q.C.): ... The sheriff held, in my opinion correctly, that the stated facts did not disclose any negligence on the part of the defender and appellant, but he felt himself constrained by the case of *Cleghorn* v. *Taylor* (1856) 18 D. 664 to hold that the defender and appellant as owner and occupier had an absolute liability for the maintenance of his property in a safe condition. In that case the owner of heritable property was held liable to a neighbour when a chimney-can fell a few days after it had been erected on the owner's instructions by the workmen of the master slater. The sheriff took the view that the ratio of the case was binding upon him.

5.7.3 A close examination of that case reveals, to my mind, that it is not in point. The jury's verdict did not find negligence on the part of the defender, but held that the chimney-can was put up in "insecure and insufficient manner" by the workmen. It seems to me that the judgment of the Second Division, in holding that the proprietor of the building was liable to his neighbour, proceeded on the basis that the master slater was an employee of the defender and not an independent contractor. This is clearest, perhaps, from the judgment of Lord Wood at p. 669 where he said: "the tradesman was to be considered as in the service of the party employing him, although he was not to be paid by day's wages but at the ordinary rates chargeable for the work to be done. And it may be observed that that is the footing on which the employment in the present instance must be taken to have stood, it not being found that the work was engaged to be done for any positive sum, as in a proper contract." Lord Justice-Clerk Hope, at p. 667, contrasts liability of a proprietor for the tradesmen "whom he himself selects and employs" and his liability for the "personal and wrongous acts of a contractor, and in the course of the execution of his work". In short, *Cleghorn* v. *Taylor* is not a case of strict or absolute liability but a case of the liability of a heritable proprietor for the acts of an employee... .

5.7.4 In the case of *Laurent* v. *Lord Advocate* (1869) 7 M. 607 Lord Inglis (by this time Lord President) reiterated his view at p. 610. His Lordship said: "An operation carried on by a proprietor within burgh, which is either in its own nature unlawful, or which, though lawful in itself, is executed in a reckless, unskilful or negligent manner, whereby injury is done to his neighbour, is a wrong in law, for which reparation is due... the principle is clear. There must be fault, or, in other words, delinquency or wrong, on the part of the defender of the action of reparation to render him liable to the pursuer in damages." He goes on to point out that the only doubt that ever was thrown on this clear doctrine arose inter alia from a misunderstanding of some obiter dicta observations of Lord Justice-Clerk Hope and Lord Wood in *Cleghorn* v.

Taylor— "a misunderstanding which I think was satisfactorily explained and removed in the judgment of the Second Division in *Campbell* v. *Kennedy*".

5.7.5 The legal position is in my opinion correctly summed up in Glegg on *Reparation* (4th ed.) at p. 19: "The correct Scottish rule would still seem to be that liability depends on negligence… In *Cleghorn* v. *Taylor*, it was laid down that the proprietor of a building was liable for damage caused by its defective condition, though he did not and could not have known of the defect. That decision has been the subject of adverse criticism and cannot now be accepted as an authority in support of absolute liability."

5.7.6 The sheriff sought support for the opposite view from Professor Walker's *Law of Delict in Scotland* (2nd ed.) at pp. 286 to 288, where after examining *Cleghorn* v. *Taylor* and *Campbell* v. *Kennedy* he submits that such a case would properly fall within the principle of the *actio de positis vel suspensis* without the need to prove or to presume or impute fault. I cannot, with respect, agree with this conclusion. The Roman *actio*, as the professor points out, lay where a person kept something placed or suspended over a public way and it caused damage by falling. In such a case there was penal liability and an obligation to take down a thing which might do harm if it fell but no liability in reparation. Hume (*Lect.*, III, 186) indicates that this head of quasi-delict is recognised in Scotland, but the terms in which he writes are consistent with the doctrine that civil liability depends upon proof of negligence. In any event, in my opinion the modern view must prevail that there can be no liability without negligence, and it is significant that there is no decision (with the doubtful exception of *Cleghorn* v. *Taylor*) of any Scottish case which would support an absolute liability on the part of the proprietor of heritable property in any such circumstances. Accordingly, in the absence of findings of which negligence on the part of the defender could be established, I am of opinion that he must be assoilzied.'

COMMENT

5.8.1 Decided: March 5, 1982.
Feb. 5: Laker Airways collapsed.
Feb. 17: Thelonious Monk died.
Feb. 24: Greenland voted to leave EEC.

5.8.2 The case at first instance was the subject of a critical and learned note — "Householders' Liabilities" — by Professor Gordon at (1982) 27 J.L.S. 253. The learned professor starts by mentioning the general rule that there is no liability *e dominio solo*. He states his general view of liability in delict in Scotland as depending upon *res ipsa loquitur*. His main task is to question the use of *Cleghorn* at first instance, and he takes the view that it is best accepted as authority for the vicarious liability of certain employed tradesmen — the view which found favour with the sheriff principal. Being a professor of Roman law, the reader is treated to another possible Roman source of a special liability: "Alternatively or additionally, he [Lord Wood] may have had in mind the Roman rules on *damnum infectum*. These latter imposed on a proprietor, the state of whose property threatened damage to a neighbour, an obligation to give a promise, with security, that he would make good any damage which did occur." And later the learned professor continues: "If he [Lord Wood] were thinking of *damnum infectum*, which was indeed referred to in one of the cases quoted to the court, *Hay v. Littlejohn* (1666) Mor. 13974, Roman law required a neighbour to take preventive action in order to provide a remedy for damage if damage did occur. In *Hay v. Littlejohn* itself, where it was stated that the Roman rules on this matter did not apply and that the Scots law did not require such preventive action, it was nevertheless clearly held that the defender in the case, whose ruinous house (well-named 'The Tower of Babylon') had caused the damage complained of, was at fault in not taking steps to prevent damage." The article gives four reasons for the non-applicability of the Roman law. (1) The action was for a penalty, not damages; (2) the action lay against the occupier, not the owner; (3) the Roman law did not apply to bits of a building falling off — that was covered by *damnum infectum*; (4) there is the possibility that the Roman action required the defender to have knowledge of the placing of the item. Accordingly the judgment on appeal, reversing the sheriff, is a vindication of the professor's views. He also makes interesting comments on the other Roman *quasi*-delict particularly relevant to heritage, the *actio de effusis vel dejectis*, a discussion of which follows. Anyone particularly interested in this area might want to follow up Professor Gordon's citation of the following two articles: Watson, "The *Actio de Postitis ac Suspensis*" (1963) 1 *Mélanges Meylan* 379; Birks, "The Problem of *Quasi*-delict", 22 C.L.P. 164. And see Johnston, "Owners and Neighbours: From Rome to Scotland" in *The Civil Law Tradition in Scotland*, Stair Society (Evans-Jones ed. 1995).

5.8.3 The next extract is from another academic reaction to a Scottish sheriff court decision. Yet it goes further and deals with a general terminological problem: the meaning of "*quasi*-delict".

25. Stein, "The Actio de Effusis vel Dejectis and the Concept of Quasi-Delict in Scots Law"
(1955) 4 I.C.L.Q. 356

5.9.1 'About 5 p.m. on an August afternoon, a boy, aged eleven, was walking past a common lodging house in Glasgow, when someone emptied a vessel containing urine on him from an upper window. His father as tutor, raised a small debt action in the sheriff court against the registered keeper and the occupier of the lodging house. The claim for damages was based on the grounds: (1) negligence consisting in a breach of the corporation bye-laws for common lodging houses; (2) absolute liability; (3) nuisance. It succeeded on none of these grounds... .

5.9.2 Our interest in the decision lies in the rejection of the second ground. This was in effect an assertion that the praetorian *actio de effusis vel dejectis* of the Roman law is part of Scots law. This action was an *actio in factum* for double the damage, and lay against the occupier of the house whence that which caused the damage had been thrown or poured. It was not necessary to show that he had been negligent in any way. *Culpa* was "conclusively presumed" [Buckland, *Textbook of Roman Law*, p. 598, n. 22]. In contrast to the general rule in delict, if several families shared one house or flat, and the *patresfamilias* were therefore all liable, satisfaction by one freed the others from liability. In Justinian's *Institutes*, the householder's obligation was classified as one of these *quae quasi ex delicto nascuntur.*

5.9.3 For the legal historian *Gray* v. *Dunlop*, 1954 S.L.T. (Sh. Ct.) 75 suggests two problems. First, was the *actio de effusis vel dejectis* ever received into Scots law?, and secondly, this action having enforced one of the four original obligations *quasi ex delicto*, when and how did the current idea of *quasi*-delict, as "actionable negligence" arise?

The actio de effusis vel dejectis

· · · · · ·

5.9.4 But in the middle of the eighteenth century, Scots law was still in a formative period ... After 10 p.m. it was the practice to pour waste matter in the street in order that it might be swept away by official scavengers at 7 a.m. the following morning. But what if the hour were anticipated and the refuse poured out by day? Contemporary Roman-Dutch law, with which mid-eighteenth century Scots lawyers were generally familiar, gave an action in such circumstances. Grotius, in c. 38 of the *Jurisprudence of Holland*, gives as one of the "wrongs by construction of law", "when from a man's dwelling something is thrown or poured on a public way, whereby someone suffers damage" ...

Bankton cautiously refrained from committing himself too precisely. That he favoured the reception of the action is more likely when the other two passages are considered. These were not before the court in *Gray v. Dunlop*.

The concept of quasi-delict

(a) Quasi-delict today

5.9.5 *Quasi*-delict as understood in Scotland today, is well described by Bell in his *Principles* [see Chap 2, 3]... But it is clear that so far as concerns the reparation of damage done, there is no difference between delict and *quasi*-delict. Lord Justice-Clerk Inglis (as he then was) in *Liquidators of Western Bank* v. *Douglas* (1860) 22 D. 447 [at p. 475] stated as much with his customary clarity: "Some writers in our law have made a distinction between delicts and *quasi*-delicts as a ground for civil action of reparation, giving the former name to these graver offences which might form the object of criminal proceedings, and the latter to those which will only found a claim to pecuniary reparation of damage sustained. But this distinction is of little importance to the present case, for we are of opinion that the same measure of reparation is due, on the same conditions and by the same form of action, whether the cause of the damage be the one kind of delict or the other. *Crassa negligentia equiparatur dolo*" ... Modern French law has a similar distinction between delict and *quasi*-delict ... The expressions occur in a rubric of a chapter of the *Code Civil* and in articles 1310 and 1370, but are nowhere defined. This is because the compilers of the Code were so familiar with Pothier's definitions that they considered any further definitions unnecessary.

· · · · · ·

(b) Quasi-delict in the seventeenth and eighteenth centuries

· · · · · ·

5.9.6 The most influential academic jurist of the eighteenth century, as David Balfour learned when a student in Leiden, was Johan Heineccius (1681–1741). In his *Elementa Juris Civilis, secundum ordinem Institutionum* (1727) he adopts the clear-cut distinction of Calvin's *Lexicon Juridicon*, equating delict with *dolus* and *quasi*-delict with *culpa*... Stair, in his *Institutions* (1681), quotes the fourfold classification of obligations in Justinian's *Institutes*, but criticises it because it "insinuates no reason of the cause or rise of these distinct obligations, as is requisite in a good and distinct division", and prefers the twofold classification into obligations obediential and by engagement. Among the former is the obligation by delinquence, defined as "that whereunto injury or malefice doth oblige, as the meritorious cause thereof".

· · · · · ·

5.9.7 We do not know for certain what induced Bell to adopt this notion, but we can suggest a likely source. It will be remembered that Bell's definition is essentially that of Heineccius. Not only was the latter's *Elementa Juris Civilis* prescribed reading for the Scots who went overseas to learn their legal principles; it was also used in the law schools of Scotland. Sir Walter Scott relates how as a student, together with his friend William Clerk, "in the course of two summers we went, by way of question and answer, through the whole of Heineccius's Analysis of the Institutes and Pandects". An edition of the *Elementa* of the *Institutes* was printed in Edinburgh in 1780. During the Napoleonic War copies became so scarce that the demands of the Scottish *cupida legum juventus* drove the price up to 30 shillings a copy. So a new edition, whose editor (Ninian Little) claimed to have restored the original text of Heineccius, and which contained additional notes from the 1789 Leipzig edition of Christian Biener, was published in Edinburgh in 1822. This was the very year in which Bell was appointed to the chair at Edinburgh, and when he would be preparing his lectures. (The *Principles* were published seven years later.) It would not be surprising if he used what had for long been respected as a student's manual as the source of some of his basic concepts, and more particularly as the source of his concept of *quasi*-delict.'

COMMENT

5.10.1 If there is no strict liability, would it be possible to argue for the sort of inferred *culpa* of which Lord Fraser spoke in *R.H.M. Bakeries* (Ext. 21)? Would that be subject to the pleading difficulties set out in *Argyll and Clyde Health Board* (Ext. 22)? Is it another example of non-negligent non-intentional fault — see *Kennedy v. Glenbelle*, 1986 S.L.T. 1186.

5.10.2 Is it possible that the *actio de effusis vel dejectis* should be treated as received into the law but not the *actio de positis vel suspensis*? In view of Professor Gordon's comments in the article referred to in para. 5.8.2, the answer should perhaps be "yes". He points out that the *actio de effusis vel dejectis* did give damages and that liability was indeed strict.

5.10.3 Is the view that there should be no liability without fault still the modern view, in the light of the enactment of the Animals (Scotland) Act 1987 and the Consumer Protection Act 1987 (Ext. 68 and Ext. 66)?

5.10.4 The Stein article seems to have been approved by most other academics. It is also an example of just how important is our civilian heritage. See generally *The Civilian Tradition in Scotland*, Stair Society (Evans-Jones ed. 1995).

5.10.5 English law seems to suffer from similar difficulties in relation to facts which might fall under the scope of the *actio de positis vel suspensis*. In *Wringe v. Cohen* [1940] 1 K.B. 229, the Court of Appeal laid down a rule of strict liability: "If, owing to want of repair, premises on a highway became dangerous and, therefore, a nuisance and a passer-by or an adjoining owner suffers damage by their collapse, the occupier ... is answerable whether he knew or ought to have known of the danger or not." This rule has not been applied liberally (see *British Road Services v. Slater* [1964] 1 W.L.R. 498; *Cushing v. Peter Walker & Sons Ltd* [1941] 2 All E.R. 693; *Carriner v. Northern and London Investment Trust* [1951] A.C. 88). The following comments of the learned editor of the 13th edition of Winfield and Jolowicz recall the point made in the foregoing comment. "In effect, it would seem that *Wringe v. Cohen* sets a standard somewhere between strict liability and ordinary fault liability. The plaintiff need only show that the defendant had control over the defective premises and that the injury resulted from their dangerous condition. This gives rise to a presumption that the defendant has failed in his duty of inspection and repair which can only be rebutted by proof that the accident was inevitable, *i.e.* it was not, nor could have been, avoided by reasonable inspection. From a substantive point of view, *Wringe v. Cohen* differs from ordinary liability in negligence because the occupier is liable for the default of his independent contractor" (pp. 417–418). How does this compare with a post-*R.H.M.* view of *Cleghorn v. Taylor*?

Use of land *aemulationem vicini*

26. Ritchie (Appellant) v. Purdie
(1833) 11 S. 771

5.11.1 [From the summary in the report] 'Mr Purdie acquired a flat or floor in No. 46, being the fourth story from the foundation ... Mrs Mary Ritchie was proprietrix of a flat in No. 50, being also the fourth storey from the foundation. But the floor of her house was a few feet lower than the floor of Purdie's; and as the landing-place of the staircase was on the same level with Mrs Ritchie's floor there was an ascent of a few steps from the landing place to the door of Purdie, which was situated in the mutual gable. In Mrs Ritchie's titles, her house was described as "bounded on the east by the mutual gable between it and a tenement built by John Brough"; and it was disponed, "together with free ish and entry to the said dwelling-house and others, the common stair of the said tenement, and the privilege of the space or area at the foot of the common stair, which is declared to be the joint property of the whole proprietors of the said tenement"; ... Mrs Ritchie's husband, who was a teacher of elocution, conceiving that it would be more convenient to open a separate communication between the school-room and the common stair, so that the classes might enter at once to the school-room, in place of going in at the same door with the family, and passing through a lobby in the interior of the house, struck out a door in the north side of the staircase ... It was averred by Ritchie that the mode in which this had been done showed it to have been part of the original plan of the house to provide for a door being opened there, if occasion required.

. . . . . .

5.11.2 Pleaded by Mrs Ritchie and Husband... 2. Even if Purdie had a right of common property, he could not object to the alteration made, which is truly *innocuae utilitatis*. In the original plan of the house, a place for the door had been filled in with brick, so as prospectively to facilitate the present alteration. The change is not in the mutual gable, but solely in the wall belonging to Mrs Ritchie and nobody has the least interest to complain except the party in the same tenement above if he can show that any damage or danger results to his house from it. The opposition of Mr Purdie is an attempt to use a right of property in *emulationem vicini*, and ought to be repressed.

. . . . . .

5.11.3 LORD BALGRAY: I think this is a plain case, to any party who has inspected the premises, as I have now done. The wall in which the operation has been made is no part of the mutual gable in which Mr Purdie claims a right of common property. It is a wall wholly within the tenement No. 50, in which Mrs Ritchie's house is situated being a species of partition wall, for subdividing that tenement internally. Upon inspecting it, I see that it has formed part of the original plan of the building, that a doorway should be left there ... But I cannot perceive any lawful interest on the part of Mr Purdie, a proprietor of the contiguous tenement, to challenge the operation.

5.11.4 LORD CRAIGIE: I take the same view.... It is a maxim of the law of Scotland, *malitiis non est indulgendum*; and the Court should not permit the malice of a neighbour to stop an operation beneficial to another party, and not injurious to any one.

5.11.5   LORD GILLIES: I entertain the same opinion. It is a valuable rule of our law that a man cannot use his property *in emulationem vicini*. He may attempt to do so by positive acts, and this is the most common form perhaps in which such an abuse of the right of property is attempted. But he may also attempt it, as in this instance, negatively, by endeavouring to restrain the rights of his neighbour, to the injury of that neighbour, and without any benefit whatever to himself. In this case, as well as in the other, the Court will refuse their sanction to the nimious and emulous enforcement of a right to the hurt of another.

5.11.6   LORD PRESIDENT (Hope): I am of the same opinion with the rest of the Court. This alteration is not the cause of attracting a school to the stair, for the school is there already. But if it should be so, it is a perfectly lawful use of property to convert any part of it into a school-room.'

COMMENT

5.12.1   Decided: June 21, 1833.
   March 22: Zollverein signed.
   May 5: Brahms born.

5.12.2   Have you ever heard anyone other than a lawyer say "nimious and emulous"?

5.12.3   Another fine arts pedagogue was at the centre of a case raising a similar point in England. In *Christie v. Davey* [1893] 1 Ch. 316 the plaintiff taught music. His neighbour reacted to this exercise of the plaintiff's profession by beating on trays, whistling and shrieking. An injunction was granted restraining the defendant. However, the law in England, as stated in *Mayor of Bradford v. Pickles* [1895] A.C. 587 is that a bad motive cannot make wrongful an act otherwise legal. This case is discussed in the next extract [Ext. 16]. In more recent times *Christie v. Davey* has been followed (*Holywood Silver Fox Farm v. Emmett* [1936] 2 K.B. 468). There is an interesting discussion of these cases in Winfield and Jolowicz (1989), pp. 392–393 which suggests a limited *ratio* for *Mayor of Bradford*.

27. **More v. Boyle**
1967 S.L.T. (Sh. Ct.) 38 (S.A.)

5.13.1   'THE SHERIFF (R. H. McDonald, Q.C.): In 1926 four semi-detached dwelling-houses were erected by the same firm of builders on the south side of Irvine Road, Kilmarnock, west of Loanfoot Avenue. Of these Nos. 86 and 88 form one building with a mutual gable, and Nos. 90 and 92 another. The pursuers are the present proprietors of Nos. 88, 90 and 92. The defender is the present proprietor of No. 86. The titles are silent as to the manner in which water-drainage and other services are to be laid on to the respective properties. It is admitted, however, that when the houses were built a water supply pipe was laid from the main supply pipe in Loanfoot Avenue through the garden ground at the rear of No. 86, thence through the garden ground at the rear of Nos. 88, 90 and 92. From this pipe where it passed through the garden ground at the rear of each house a branch pipe with a stop-cock was led at right-angles to supply each house. This arrangement continued until 1964. It appears that in that year a leak occurred in the system within the defender's property. It is not clear from the pleadings whether this was in the main pipe or the branch pipe, but it is apparent that the defender tried to get the pursuers to bear a proportion of the cost of repairing the leak, and this they refused to do. The defender freely admits that thereafter he excavated the ground in his garden and partially closed the water pipe supplying the pursuers' houses. Approximately 14 days later he closed the pipe completely and cut off the water supply altogether.

5.13.2 In the present action the pursuers claim damages from the defender for loss, injury and damage sustained by them due to his actings. They maintain that the defender's interference with the water pipe was a misuse of property *in aemulationem vicini* which resulted in loss to them and so entitled them to damages. It was submitted by counsel for the defender that the doctrine of *aemulatio vicini* was no longer part of the law of Scotland, having been expressly disowned as such by Lord Watson in *Mayor of Bradford* v. *Pickles* [1895] A.C. 587, at p. 597. In that case, Lord Watson said in terms that no use of property which would be legal if due to a proper motive, can become illegal because it is prompted by a motive which is improper. This observation, which was *obiter* so far as the law of Scotland is concerned, has been very widely criticised. Two years earlier, Lord Watson himself in *Young* v. *Bankier Distillery Co.* (1893) 1 S.L.T. 204 had, by implication at least, recognised the existence of the doctrine of *aemulatio vicini* in the law of Scotland. In my opinion the dictum of Lord Watson in *Bradford* v. *Pickles (supra)* is inconsistent with principle as expressed by the Institutional writers... and as applied in numerous cases. For a detailed exposition of these I refer to the article on Reparation by the late Sheriff McKechnie in Green's *Encyclopaedia of the Law of Scotland*, vol. XII, at paras. 1077 and 1078, the reasoning in which I am content to adopt. Moreover, in a case subsequent to *Bradford* v. *Pickles* the Court of Session recognised the existence in the law of Scotland of the doctrine of *aemulatio vicini* (*Campbell* v. *Muir* (1908) 15 S.L.T. 737). Finally, I note that Lord Watson's dictum is doubted or rejected by Gloag and Henderson in their *Introduction to the Law of Scotland* (6th edition), at p. 397; by Professor T. B. Smith in his *Short Commentary on the Law of Scotland* at p. 662; and by Professor Walker in his work on the *Law of Delict in Scotland*, vol. II, at pp. 992–994. In my judgment, therefore, the clear weight of authority is that the doctrine of *aemulatio vicini* is still part of the law of Scotland in an appropriate case.

. . . . . .

5.13.3   I am unwilling to accept that the defender may escape the consequences of his actings by suggesting that they may have incidentally caused a benefit to himself by interrupting the running of prescription. He could have achieved the same result by other means without causing the hardship which his actings must have involved. For these reasons, I am of opinion that the pursuers' case based upon the defender having acted *in aemulationem vicini* is relevant and I shall allow inquiry on this branch of the case.'

COMMENT

5.14.1   Decided: October 3, 1966.
   May 6: Moors murderers jailed.
   July 30: West Germany failed to win football World Cup Final.
   Aug. 3: Lenny Bruce died.

5.14.2   Is the doctrine of *aemulationem vicini* in keeping with the times? What other laws achieve the same or a similar purpose?

5.14.3   What repercussions can you think of for the rest of the law if the doctrine were often to be applied? How would it deal with businesses in competition? Should it be restricted to land? Or to individual rather than corporate hatred? Should it be restricted to *vicini* in a literal sense of neighbours rather than an Atkinian sense (para. 8.1.5)?

5.14.4   See Johnston, "Owners and Neighbours: From Rome to Scotland" in *The Civil Law Tradition in Scotland*. This contains a detailed investigation of *aemulationem vicini*. The form does not appear in the Corpus Juris. Johnston indicates it was used in early competition cases: *Falconer v. Laird of Glenbervie* (1642) Mor. 4146; *Farquarson v. Earl of Aboyne* (1679) Mor. 4147; *Mays of Stirling v. Murray* (1706) Mor. 4148. (See Chap. 7.)

CHAPTER 6

WRONGFUL INTERFERENCE WITH GOODS

28. Scottish Law Commission
Memorandum 31 (1976)

6.1.1 'Spuilzie was or is the only possessory action recognised by Scots law in relation to moveables, and it is a matter of controversy as to whether, or to what extent, it has fallen into disuse … [It] combines elements of restitution and reparation. It asserts the principle *spoliatus ante omnia est restituendus*. It is partly penal in that the pursuer can himself estimate the value of the property of which he was deprived, and claim "violent profit", *i.e.* such profit as could have been made from the moveables by use of utmost industry.

. . . . . .

6.1.2 Erskine writes [III,vii,16]: "Actions of spuilzie suffer a triennial prescription. Spuilzie is the taking away or the triennial prescription. Spuilzie is the taking away or the intermeddling with moveable goods in the possession of another, without either the consent of the other, or the order of law. When a spuilzie is committed, action lies against the delinquent, not only for restoring to the former possessor the goods or their value, but for all the profits he might have made of these goods, had it not been for the spuilzie."

. . . . . .

6.1.3 Professor D. M. Walker considers that the action for spuilzie is still competent and discusses it fully in his treatise on *Delict* (he gives more weight to recent sheriff court decisions than we should ourselves) as to a lesser extent has Dr J. J. Gow in his book on *The Law of Hire Purchase*. Walker believes that the action of damages for spuilzie is in substance a remedy against a person who comes to be in possession of goods, the possession of which he is not entitled to retain, who fails to implement his *quasi*-contractual obligation to restore them to the person truly entitled thereto.

. . . . . .

6.1.4 In recent years there have been several efforts, especially in connection with wrongful disposal of goods possessed on hire-purchase, to invoke the remedy of spuilzie in the sheriff courts — or to describe the owner's remedy as a modern version of spuilzie. Moreover, since Scots law recognises that possession may be either "civil" or "natural", it has been suggested that hire-purchase companies may find in spuilzie a remedy as effective as the tort of conversion in English law.

. . . . . .

6.1.5 It seems to us, therefore, that the law regarding spuilzie is in need of clarification or reform, and we are provisionally of opinion that radical reform is desirable. If spuilzie as such were to be abolished this would leave unaffected the other remedies available for wrongful appropriation or disposal of moveables — the remedy of restitution against the *mala fide* former possessor, or a delictual action based on *culpa* or an order for restoration of possession under the existing powers of the Court of Session and sheriff court.

. . . . . .

6.1.6 However, the invocation of ancient remedies of uncertain scope is not necessarily the ideal solution for modern wrongs. It seems to us that the delict of spuilzie, of uncertain competence and scope, should probably be expressly abolished, and consideration be given to what, if any, action or actions should be introduced in its place.

. . . . . .

6.1.7 We should not favour introducing into Scots law the equivalent of the English tort of conversion, which may involve the defender's liability if he has asserted innocently a right over goods inconsistent with an owner's right, or has dealt with goods in a way inconsistent with that right, even if in ignorance of it. Such situations are, we think, adequately covered by our law of restitution and recompense. However, in view of the difficulty of proving economic loss in actions of delict, we think that there may well be a case for restating the principle of "violent profits" in the cases where a possessor (not necessarily an owner) had been deprived of or excluded from natural possession (as contrasted with civil possession) by the intentional act of the defender.'

COMMENT

6.2.1 A full and fascinating entry relating to the term "spuilzie" can be found in the *Scottish National Dictionary* (1965), pp. 499–500, under "Spuilyie". It is clear that although the term "spuilzie" refers to a remedy, it was also a term or word in common usage relating to the actual carrying off of moveables. This is perhaps the most neglected area of the law of delict. The law of negligence naturally will solve many cases, but the nature of moveable property is such that, in many cases, it might be difficult to establish the necessary proximity between the wrongdoer and the person suffering the loss. Some instances of this difficulty are apparent in the section of this book dealing with secondary economic loss. The poverty of our law in this respect is not assisted by the fact that, as a matter of procedure, cases for the recovery of moveable property are dealt with by way of summary cause, making debate on pleadings unlikely and avoiding the need for stating the precise legal basis of the claim.

Spulzie is the closest Scotland has to a developed remedy for wrongful interference in interests in moveable property. The complication is that property can be recovered from another person on three identifiable grounds: (1) as a punishment or reparation for his having wrongfully obtained it; (2) because it still, as a matter of the law of property, belongs to the pursuer; and (3) because the item, although it belongs in the law of property to the defender, should be made over to the pursuer. Only the first truly concerns the law of delict, but the remedy known as spulzie satisfied various needs. See *Gorebridge Co-operative Society Ltd v. Turnbull*, 1952 S.L.T. (Sh.Ct.) 91 and *Dalhanna Knitwear Co. Ltd v. Mohammed Ali*, 1967 S.L.T. (Sh.Ct.) 74.

6.2.2 Until the subject has been fully explored it would be regrettable to dump one of our indigenous creations. More work has to be done. The Scottish Law Commission stated that the law was in need of clarification. In a very interesting piece on the subject Rodger leaves the task of identifying the law to someone with more time (see 1970 S.L.T. (News) 33). Nonetheless he made two very important points in relation to one of the sheriff court cases in the context of hire-purchase: *F.C. Finance Ltd v. Brown & Son*, 1969 S.L.T. (Sh.Ct.) 41. The first is that it is by no means certain that the measure of recovery in a case of wrongful interference, certainly where the decision is not based on a specialty of spulzie, is the value of the goods. To select such a measure is to provide the pursuer with a windfall. Rodger preferred the measure to be limited to the loss which will normally be the balance outstanding on the hire-purchase contract, and in this he was approving Lord Denning's approach in *Wickham Holdings Ltd v. Brooke House Motors Ltd* [1967] 1 W.L.R. 295. The second point relates to title to sue in spulzie action. He quite properly showed concern at the learned sheriff's *obiter* adoption of a right to possess as a sufficient title. The true position is not yet clear and, until it should be so, Rodger's suggestion that in the absence of direct authority in hire-purchase cases there is nothing to prevent a court, by analogy with land-leasing cases, holding that the civil possession of the lessor-seller is sufficient title, might usefully be followed.

Rodger did not take issue with the actual basis of liability in *F.C. Finance v. Brown* on appeal. Although neither duty nor *culpa* gets a mention, the ground of the decision is the fault of an employee in dealing with the car without safeguarding the rights of the owner in the knowledge of the owner's position. On the other hand, once one expresses the *ratio* in this way, the danger of the bar on economic loss cases appears. The loss is however primary, in that the property belongs to the pursuer. An interesting demonstration of the implications of the absence of an intelligible and developed law in this area for wider aspects of commercial law can be seen in MacQueen (1989), pp. 34–36.

6.2.3 A more general authority is *Browns Trs. v. Hay* (1898) 25 R. 1112 in which a person who "borrowed" papers to "leak" them to the Revenue was held liable for ultroneous use. Actual detention is also actionable as where a person delayed a coach going to a funeral: *Crawford v. Hill* (1830) 5 Mor. 215.

29. F.C. Finance v. Langtry Investment Co. Ltd (Appellant)

1973 S.L.T. (Sh.Ct.) 11 (S.A.)

6.3.1 'THE SHERIFF PRINCIPLE (Sir Allan G. Walker, Q.C.): Both the parties to this action are hire-purchase finance companies; and they have concurred in asking the court to decide the case upon the agreed facts as disclosed by the parties' pleadings, and without a proof. The agreed facts appear to be as follows.

6.3.2 On or about June 15, 1966, the pursuers entered into a hire-purchase agreement with Mr Robert Allan in relation to a motor car, and it was a condition of the agreement that the vehicle was, and would remain, the property of the pursuers until Mr Allan had paid all the instalments thereunder and had exercised his option to purchase. The vehicle was registered with H.P. Information Ltd. H.P. Information Ltd is a company limited by guarantee and operating on a basis of service and not of profit, its function, as a protective organisation being to record by identification numbers the ownership of *inter alia* motor vehicles let on hire purchase agreements.

. . . . . .

6.3.3 One of the objects of the company is to prevent the wrongful disposal of any motor vehicle on which an unpaid hire-purchase balance is still outstanding. A finance company may telephone before buying a vehicle in order to ascertain whether or not the vehicle is on record, or inquiries may be made by post or telex. When a hire-purchase interest has been noted against such a vehicle, the inquirer is informed at once by telephone, and the information is confirmed in writing.

6.3.4 Mr Allan paid certain instalments under his hire-purchase agreement with the pursuers, and there is still a balance of £169.57$\frac{1}{2}$ due thereunder. Without the knowledge or permission of the pursuers, and without any lawful authority, he sold the vehicle on January 1, 1967 to a motor dealer, Mr I. R. McKay, who traded as Medwin Motors at an address in Glasgow. It was found after inquiry that Mr McKay was a man of straw, and meantime Mr Allan has emigrated to Canada. Further inquiries by the pursuers later revealed that the vehicle was registered in the name of Mr Matthew Kennedy, who informed the pursuers that he had purchased it on January 11, 1967, from Medwin Motors through a hire-purchase agreement with the defenders. The defenders purchased the vehicle from Medwin Motors for the sum of £295 on or about the last-mentioned date. The pursuers have now lost their title to the vehicle because Mr Kennedy is an innocent private purchaser in terms of Pt. III of the Hire Purchase Act 1964, and the pursuers are thus unable to recover the vehicle from him. Mr Kennedy will acquire, or has acquired, a title to the vehicle by completing the payments due under his hire-purchase agreement with the defenders.

. . . . . .

6.3.5 The sum sued for is £295, this being the price paid for the vehicle by the defenders to Medwin Motors. The parties, however, are now agreed that if the defenders are found liable in payment to the pursuers of the value of the vehicle, that value, for the purpose of this action, will be £169.57½ which is the equivalent of the outstanding balance of instalments due by Mr Allan to the pursuers under his hire-purchase agreement with them. It is also agreed between the parties that the profit earned by the defenders from their transaction with the vehicle was £50, and that if the defenders are found not to be liable in payment to the pursuers of the value of the vehicle, decree will be granted against them for payment of the last-mentioned sum.

6.3.6 The pursuers base their claim for payment of the value of the vehicle upon two independent grounds, neither of which, in relation to hire-purchase agreements, appears to have been the subject of decision in any earlier case. The pursuers maintain, in the first place, that they have suffered loss to the extent of the value of the vehicle as a result of the defenders' negligence, the defenders having been in breach of a duty of care which they owed to the pursuers, and being liable in damages as a result. In the second place, and separately, the pursuers maintain that the defenders are bound to pay to the pursuers the value of the vehicle on the basis, or on the analogy, of the doctrine of *specificatio*.

. . . . . .

6.3.7 It is probable that, but for the decision in *Donoghue* v. *Stevenson*, 1932 S.L.T. 317, and what was said by Lord Atkin in that case, it would not have occurred to the pursuers to base a claim such as this upon the ground of negligence, although the possibility of such claim was suggested by Lord Ardmillan's opinion in *Faulds* v. *Townsend* (1861) 23 D. 437, at p. 439, his decision being supported on appeal.

. . . . . .

6.3.8 The pursuers in this action maintain that they were at all relevant times the defenders' neighbours, and that the defenders owed them a duty of care. They aver that, before acquiring a vehicle from small individual dealers such as Medwin Motors, and re-hiring it to a private individual so as to render it irrecoverable by the true owner, they had a duty to take reasonable steps to check that it did not belong to another finance company by inquiring about the history of the car from H.P. Information Ltd. If, they aver, the defenders had shown reasonable care and had made such inquiries, they would have discovered that the pursuers were true owners of the vehicle and that Medwin Motors had no title to it, and the pursuers' loss would have been avoided.

6.3.9 Before considering the submissions of the counsel for the pursuer, I propose to refer to two submissions made by counsel for the defenders which in my opinion, must be rejected. It was submitted, in the first place, that negligence based upon neighbourliness had no place in the field of commerce, and that one finance company can never have any duty of care towards a rival finance company, in respect of the property of that company… It was also submitted that it was of no interest to the defenders to discover, when buying a vehicle from Medwin Motors, whether or not some other finance company was the true owner, because of a practice whereby the dealer, in this case Medwin Motors, paid to the finance company who were the true owners the balance of instalments due to them under any hire-purchase agreement affecting the vehicle. It was said that, in accordance with this practice, the defenders were entitled to expect that Medwin Motors would pay to the pursuers the sum now sued for, with the result that the defenders would obtain the good title to the vehicle which otherwise they would not have had. If such a practice in fact exists, it is clearly, in my opinion, an improper practice. Nobody, it appears to me, is entitled to intromit with stolen property, and to justify his intromission by an assertion that he hopes that some other person will recompense the true owner in respect of his loss.

· · · · · ·

6.3.10   I am not convinced that the facts to which the sheriff refers were in themselves sufficient to impose upon the defenders a duty to inquire about the ownership of the vehicle. In *Hedley Bryne & Co. Ltd.* v. *Heller & Partners Ltd.* [1963] 2 All E.R. 575, Lord Devlin, at p. 601, said: "Nor indeed is there any general duty to be careful in action. The duty is limited to those who can establish some relationship of proximity such as was found to exist in *Donoghue* v. *Stevenson.*" There is, in my opinion, no general duty resting upon a prospective purchaser of a motor car to inquire into the title of the offerer unless the circumstances impose upon him a special duty to be careful. Had there been no special circumstances in this case which ought to have made the defenders suspicious of any offers by Medwin Motors, the mere fact that the offerers were small individual dealers, would not, in my opinion, be sufficient to impose upon finance companies, such as the defenders, a duty to make a special inquiry.

· · · · · ·

6.3.11   In this case, however, there appears to me to be a special circumstance… The defenders themselves aver, and this is admitted by the pursuers, that in earlier transactions with Medwin Motors, vehicles, to their knowledge, were offered to them by Medwin Motors which were the subject of subsisting hire-purchase agreements with other finance companies, with the result that Medwin Motors were not the true owners of these vehicles and were unable to give a good title to them. The defenders ought therefore to have been aware that the general presumption of innocence did not apply to the dealings of Medwin Motors with vehicles which they offered for sale. In these circumstances, in my opinion, a duty of care towards the pursuers arose in this case, and it included a duty to make inquiry about the antecedents of the vehicle in question. They failed to discharge this duty and the pursuers suffered loss thereby. For these reasons I agree with the sheriff's decision, although I have arrived at the same result in a different way.

6.3.12 In my opinion the pursuers are also entitled to succeed in respect of the other ground of claim. In Brown, *Sale of Goods* pp. 145, 146 the author describes the normal rights of an owner of goods which have been stolen against any other person who has acquired them from or through the thief. If the other person purchased or re-sold the article *mala fide*, the owner may recover from him its value. If, on the other hand, the other person acquired and re-sold the article *bona fide*, the owner may recover from that other person any profit which the latter obtained as a result of the re-sale. There is, however, a third possible situation which the author describes as follows: "The Scottish rule assumes that the *bona fide* purchaser acquiring without title has in good faith passed on the goods to a third party, against whom the true owner may proceed for recovery. But the purchaser may have himself used the goods, or he may have subjected them while in his own hands to a process by which their character and description is changed. In either case restitution is impossible, and the first purchaser, having in effect become proprietor of the goods, is liable to the true owner for their value."

. . . . . .

6.3.13 In my opinion, the principle of the doctrine of *specificatio* applies exactly to the circumstances surrounding the defenders' transactions with the vehicle in question in this action. When the defenders entered into a hire-purchase agreement in respect of this vehicle with Mr Kennedy, who was a private purchaser acting in good faith and without notice of the earlier hire-purchase agreement they brought into operation the provisions of s. 27(1) and (3) of the Hire Purchase Act 1964, which had the effect of giving to themselves *inter alios* a title as owner of the vehicle, with the result that Mr Kennedy also will become the owner of the vehicle when he completes his payments under the second hire purchase agreement. The defenders, therefore, have intromitted with the pursuers' vehicle in such a way as to deprive the pursuers of their title as owners and to deny to them their right to recover possession of the vehicle from the defenders themselves or from its present possessor... For these reasons I am of the opinion that the pursuers are also entitled to succeed upon their second ground of claim.'

COMMENT

6.4.1 Decided: March 28, 1972.
  Jan. 1: Maurice Chevalier died.
  Jan. 22: Edward Heath signed Treaty of Brussels.
  March 25: Direct rule imposed on Northern Ireland.

6.4.2 The question still remains as to what the solution would have been if it had not been possible to find fault — if, for example, there had been no previous experience of dealing with Medwin Motors.

6.4.3 This case is of little help on the damages point made by Rodger. The sheriff principal seems to be awarding the value of the car. Because of an agreement by the parties, the value for the purpose of the action was said to be a sum (roughly) equivalent to the outstanding payments. The sheriff, however, had expressly approved the decision in *Wickham Holdings*.

6.4.4 We now have a treatise on the Scots law of corporal moveables — see Carey Miller, *Corporal Moveables in Scotland* (1991).

6.4.5 Deliberate interference causing intentional harm is not a negligence case and should not be argued as such as was done — it is submitted wrongly done — in *Saeed v. Waeed*, 1996 S.L.T. (Sh.Ct.) 39 and *Gemmell v. Bank of Scotland* Clasgow Sheriff Court, November 11, 1996, unreported. As the learned sheriff said in the latter case many such cases are simple. See *McNair v. Don and Co.* (1932) 48 Sh.Ct.Rep. 99. See also *Harris v. Abbey National plc*, 1996 G.W.D. 33–1993 for another spuilzie argument resolved on a different basis (this time gratuitous deposit).

The Praetorian Edict and the Hotel Proprietors Act

30. **Mustard v. Paterson (Appellant)**
1923 S.C. 142

6.5.1 'LORD JUSTICE-CLERK (Alness): Though this case involves but a small sum of money, it raises questions of importance and difficulty, and, to aid us in its decision, we have had the advantage of an able and elaborate argument from the Bar. The action relates to the death of a horse, which the pursuer, a farmer, entrusted for some hours, in accordance with an existing arrangement, to the care of the defender, who is the lessee of a stable. The horse was delivered by the pursuer to the defender in a sound condition, and was restored to the pursuer in such a state that, on the advice of a veterinary surgeon, he was obliged to destroy it.

. . . . . .

6.5.2 The first question which we have to decide is whether a stabler falls within the Praetor's Edict "*Nautae, caupones, stabularii*". The Edict is in these terms: "*nautae, caupones, stabularii, quod cujusque slavum fore receperint, nisi restituent, in eos judicium dabo*". Its necessity arose from the opportunities for collusion between persons falling within the categories alluded to and their servants, guests, or others — opportunities which in the view then taken,

justified the imposition of a high standard of care upon them. No
doubt the liability imposed is a stringent one, and accordingly the
Edict must be strictly construed. The defender maintained that,
while the Edict unquestionably covered the case of an innkeeper
who afforded accommodation to a guest and also to his horse, it
did not apply to the case of a stabler who merely accommodated a
horse. For that distinction there appears to be no warrant in the
commentators upon Roman Law, whose works were cited to us and
with a detailed reference to which I think it unnecessary to trouble
your Lordships. The dictionaries to which we were referred yield
the same result.

. . . . . .

6.5.3 I am of opinion that stablers as such as well as innkeepers,
according to the law of Scotland, fall within the ambit of the Edict.
The views of our institutional writers are, I think, clearly to this effect...
I am unable on a survey of these passages to adopt the view urged on
us by the defender that our custom has not received the Edict to the
effect of including within its ambit *stabularii*, or that it applies only to
travellers. Bankton, for example... says: "The edict was principally
intended for the security of the necessaries that passengers and
travellers have along with them for their journey or passage: but it
likewise concerns ... all manner of things which innkeepers, stablers,
or masters of ships receive in the exercise of their respective callings
or occupations." I will only add that the principle upon which the
Edict was applied to innkeepers appears to me to apply with equal
force to stablers.

. . . . . .

6.5.4 As regards cases decided in England, they must be handled
with care. Indeed, I am disposed to think that they are irrelevant to
the issue. For it is, I think, clear that the Edict was not incorporated in
the law of England in the same manner as it has been in the law of
Scotland... Assuming then that the defender is within the ambit of
the Edict, *quid juris*? I think it is plain that he can only escape liability
by proving that the injury to the horse confided to his care arose
from inevitable accident, or from the action of the King's enemies.
The onus is, I think, on the defender to prove this. If so, I am clearly
of opinion that he has failed to discharge it. Indeed, he has not made
the attempt. It was suggested in argument by the defender that all
that he had to prove, in order to escape liability, was that he had
taken all usual precautions. I cannot accept that view, if for no other
reason then that, if it were sound, the Edict would confer no advantage
whatever upon a depositor. It was faintly argued by the defender that
the Edict was confined to a case of loss, and did not cover a case of
damage. I consider the argument untenable, and unsupported by

authority. Accordingly I reach the conclusion that, inasmuch as the Edict applies to the defender, and inasmuch as he has not succeeded in proving and has not even attempted to prove, that he falls within the well-known exceptions to it, he is liable to the pursuer in damages.

. . . . . .

6.5.5 LORD ANDERSON: It is said that the law of Scotland has *adopted* the Edict, but perhaps that is not quite an accurate mode of expressing what has been done. If a legal system like ours desires to borrow from the law of another country, this may be done in one of two ways: — (1) By formal and express adoption by means of an Act of Parliament. A noted example of this mode is found in the Act 1567, cap. 14, which borrows the ancient Jewish Law embodied in the 18th Chapter of Leviticus. (2) The other method is by the establishment of customary law similar to that which is copied. That is the method which has been followed with reference to the Edict in this country.

6.5.6 Where formal adoption by statute takes place, it will be necessary to ascertain exactly what the law was which has been assimilated. Had the Edict been adopted in this way, it would have been necessary to determine what the law of Rome was as set forth in the Edict, and, in particular, what was the signification in that law of the term *stabularii*. But, where the second method of appropriation is followed, the system which borrows may expand or circumscribe what is borrowed. Thus the law of England, if it has copied the Edict, does not exact the extreme degree of diligence prescribed by the Edict from a livery stable keeper... Again, both in England and Scotland, the scope of the Edict has been expanded so as to embrace public carriers by land as well as by water. These considerations, in my opinion, make the question purely academic as to what was the meaning of the term *stabularii* in the law of Rome. Our business is to ascertain, not what was the law of Rome, but what is the law of Scotland. I have no hesitation however in stating on this point that, in my opinion, the term *stabularii* meant, or at all events included, livery stable keepers. The epoch of the Pretorian Edict (367 B.C. till the reign of Hadrian, when the whole Edict was revised and consolidated by Salvius Julianus) included the period at the latter end of the Republic and beginning of the Empire, when the wealth and luxury of Rome had reached their zenith. I have no doubt that livery stables unassociated with inns then existed, and the Praetor designed to apply to the keepers of these the provisions of the Edict. There were, in such establishments, opportunities for dishonesty equal to those which offered themselves to carriers and innkeepers... The evidence that an alleged custom is part of our common law is to be derived (1) from the institutional treatises on the law of Scotland, and (2) from the decisions of the Court which declare the common law. Of our institutional writers Stair, Bankton, Erskine, and Bell, have each something to say regarding the Edict.

. . . . . .

6.5.7   The only other point taken by the defender's counsel on the Edict was that it did not apply to loss as the result of accident. This contention is not well founded, as both the law of Rome and that of Scotland make those to whom the Edict applies responsible for loss as the result of accident as well as by theft. As to the law of Rome, Gaius put the matter quite conclusively — (D.IV.ix.5) "*Quaecunque de furto diximus, eadem et de damno debent intellegi; non enim dubitari oportet, quin is, qui salvum fore recipit, non solum a furto, sed etiam a damno recedere videatur.*" As to the law of Scotland, Erskine (*Inst.*, III,i,28) makes it plain that damage as well as loss by theft is covered by the provisions of the Edict; and Bell (Comm.,i,499) says expressly that there is responsibility if the deposited goods have perished "or have suffered injury by inevitable accident". The case of *Hay* (Feb. 13, 1801, F.C.) is a direct authority to the same effect.'

COMMENT

6.6.1   Decided: Nov. 23, 1922.
   Oct. 19: Lloyd George resigned as Prime Minister. Bonar Law took over.
   Nov. 5: Discovery of Tutankamun's tomb.
   Nov. 15: First regular news broadcast by BBC.
   Nov. 22: Marcel Proust buried. Ravel's *Pavane pour une enfante défunte* played.

6.6.2   The case explains fairly well the history and nature of this head of liability. The Edict was the collected body of law given by the holders of a magistracy in ancient Rome. It applies in modern law to innkeepers and carriers in addition to the stable-keepers mentioned in the foregoing extract. See Stair's view at 2.1.10.

6.6.3   The next extract shows a modern amendment of one of the heads of edictal liability. Similar changes have been made in respect of carriers, but these are now usually dealt with under the head of the contract of carriage (see Walker, *Prin.*, Chaps. 4.17–4.19). Nothing has been done in respect of stablers. There may not be many in the High Street, but should they be worse off than garage mechanics?

31. The Hotel Proprietors Act 1956
(4 & 5 Eliz. 2, c. 62)

6.7.1   'An Act to amend the law relating to inns and innkeepers.

6.7.2   1.—(1) An hotel within the meaning of this Act shall, and any other establishment shall not, be deemed to be an inn; and the duties, liabilities and rights which immediately before the commencement of this Act by law attached to an innkeeper as such shall, subject to the provisions of this Act, attach to the proprietor of such an hotel and shall not attach to any other person.

6.7.3   (2) The proprietor of an hotel shall, as an innkeeper, be under the like liability, if any, to make good to any guest of his any damage to property brought to the hotel as he would be under to make good the loss thereof.

6.7.4   (3) In this Act, the expression "hotel" means an establishment held out by the proprietor as offering food, drink and, if so required, sleeping accommodation, without special contract, to any traveller presenting himself who appears able and willing to pay a reasonable sum for the services and facilities provided and who is in a fit state to be received.

6.7.5   2.—(1) Without prejudice to any other liability incurred by him with respect to any property brought to the hotel, the proprietor of an hotel shall not be liable as an innkeeper to make good to any traveller any loss or damage to such property except where —
    (*a*) at the time of the loss or damage sleeping accommodation at the hotel had been engaged for the traveller; and
    (*b*) the loss or damage occurred during the period commencing with the midnight immediately preceding, and ending with the midnight immediately following, a period for which the traveller was a guest at the hotel and entitled to use the accommodation so engaged.

6.7.6   (2) Without prejudice to any other liability or right of his with respect thereto, the proprietor of an hotel shall not as an innkeeper be liable to make good to any guest of his any loss of or damage to, or have any lien on, any vehicle or any property left therein, or any horse or other live animal or its harness or other equipment.

6.7.7   (3) Where the proprietor of an hotel is liable as an innkeeper to make good the loss of or any damage to property brought to the hotel, his liability to any one guest shall not exceed fifty pounds in respect of any one article, or one hundred pounds in the aggregate, except where —
    (*a*) the property was stolen, lost or damaged through the default, neglect or wilful act of the proprietor or some servant of his; or
    (*b*) the property was deposited by or on behalf of the guest expressly for safe custody with the proprietor or some servant of his authorised, or appearing to be authorised, for the purpose, and, if so required by the proprietor or that servant, in a container fastened or sealed by the depositor; or
    (*c*) at a time after the guest had arrived at the hotel, either the property in question was offered for deposit as aforesaid and the proprietor or his servant refused to receive it, or the guest or some other guest acting on his behalf wished so to offer the property in question but, through the default of the proprietor or a servant of his, was unable to do so:
    Provided that the proprietor shall not be entitled to the protection of the subsection unless, at the time when the property in question

was brought to the hotel, a copy of the notice set out in the Schedule to this Act printed in plain type was conspicuously displayed in a place where it could conveniently be read by his guests at or near the reception office or desk or, where there is no reception office or desk, at or near the main entrance to the hotel.

. . . . . .

SCHEDULE

Notice

LOSS OF OR DAMAGE TO GUESTS' PROPERTY

6.7.8 Under the Hotel Proprietors Act 1956, an hotel proprietor may in certain circumstances be liable to make good any loss of or damage to a guest's property even though it was not due to any fault of the proprietor or staff of the hotel.

This liability however —

(*a*) extends only to the property of guests who have engaged sleeping accommodation at the hotel;

(*b*) is limited to £50 for any one article and a total of £100 in the case of any one guest, except in the case of property which has been deposited, or offered for deposit, for safe custody;

(*c*) does not cover motor-cars or other vehicles of any kind or any property left in them, or horses or other live animals.

This notice does not constitute an admission either that the Act applies to this hotel or that liability thereunder attaches to the proprietor of this hotel in any particular case.'

COMMENT

6.8.1 This Act does not alter the basis of liability which is still that of the Edict — it merely controls its application. What is today's equivalent of £50 in 1956?

6.8.2 The next head that follows replaces many older statutes. It is interesting to note that the first chapter of the *Lex Aquilia*, which is of course so important in the development of Scots law, related to slaves and four-footed animals classified as cattle. Thus the distinction between different kinds of beast has a long history in the law: the Romans found pigs, elephants and camels difficult to classify.

32. **The Animals (Scotland) Act 1987**
(1987 c. 9)

6.9.1 '3.—(1) … where an animal strays on to any land and is not then under the control of any person, the occupier of the land may detain the animal for the purpose of preventing injury or damage by it…

6.9.2 4.—(1) Subject to subsection (2) below, in any civil proceedings against a person for killing or causing injury to an animal, it shall be a defence for him to prove —

(*a*) that he acted—

(i)   in self-defence;

(ii)   for the protection of any other person; or

(iii)   for the protection of any livestock and was one of the persons mentioned in subsection (3) below; and

(*b*) that within 48 hours after the killing or injury notice thereof was given by him or on his behalf at a police station or to a constable.

6.9.3   (2) There shall be no defence available under subsection (1) above to a person killing or causing injury to an animal where the killing or injury—

(*a*) occurred at or near a place where the person was present for the purpose of engaging in a criminal activity; and

(*b*) was in furtherance of that activity.

6.9.4   (3) The persons referred to in subsection (1)(*a*)(iii) above are—

(*a*) a person who, at the time of the injury or killing complained of, was a keeper of the livestock concerned;

(*b*) the owner or occupier of the land where the livestock was present; and

(*c*) a person authorised (either expressly or impliedly) to act for the protection of the livestock by such a keeper of the livestock or by the owner or occupier of the land where the livestock was present.

6.9.5   (4) A person killing or causing injury to an animal ("the defender") shall be regarded, for the purposes of this section, as acting in self defence or for the protection of another person or any livestock if, and only if—

(*a*) the animal is attacking him or that other person or that livestock and (whether or not the animal is under the control of anyone) the defender has reasonable grounds for believing that there are no other practicable means of ending the attack; or

(*b*) the defender has reasonable grounds for believing—

(i)   that the animal is about to attack him, such person or livestock and that (whether or not the animal is under the control of anyone) there are no other practicable means of preventing the attack; or

(ii)   that the animal has been attacking a person or livestock, is not under the control of anyone and has not left the vicinity where the attack took place, and that there are no other practicable means of preventing a further attack by the animal while it is still in that vicinity.

6.9.6   (5) In subsection (4) above "attack" or "attacking" includes "harry" or "harrying".

6.9.7   (6) In this section—
"livestock" means any animal of a domestic variety (including in
particular sheep, cattle and horses) and, while they are in captivity,
any other animals.'

COMMENT

6.10.1   A preliminary difficulty here is what the nature of the action would be to
which a defence is given. Negligence is not in point, but *culpa* in the sense of fault
encompassing deliberate intentional causing of harm is relevant. Damage and interest
would clearly cover the case of destruction. Wrongful detention of a sheep (moveable
property) might be in the sphere of spuilzie.

6.10.2   This section is typical of much modern legislation which requires to be read
in its entirety. Something is given in one section, sub-section or sub-subsection, and
taken away in another or others.

6.10.3   "Attack" and "harry" have been judicially considered in the context of s. 1(3):
Fairlie v. Carruthers, 1996 S.L.T. (Sh.Ct.) 56 (Ext. 69).

6.10.4   Nothing has (yet?) come of the consultation paper issued in May 1991 by the
Lord Chancellor's Department "Compensation for Road Traffic Accidents", which
considered the imposition of strict liability in road traffic accidents.

CHAPTER 7

ECONOMIC DELICTS

Passing-off

33. John Haig & Co. v. Forth Blending Co.
1954 S.C. 35 (O.H.)

7.1.1 'LORD HILL WATSON: The action is one for "passing off" and, before discussing the facts, I propose to deal with the law applicable to a case of this nature.

7.1.2 1. No man has a right to sell his goods as though they were the goods of another, or, to express this principle more fully, one man is not entitled to sell his goods under such circumstances, by the name, or the packet, or the mode of making up the article, or in such a way as to induce the public to believe that they are the manufacture of someone else…

7.1.3 2. In order to obtain redress in an action for passing off, the trader who sues must prove that his goods are known to and recognised by the public, or by a particular section of the public who deal in that type of goods, by a particular name, mark, get-up or other accompaniment, which is associated in their minds with his goods alone. It is immaterial whether the name or mark is a registered trade name or a registered trade mark, or whether the get-up includes a registered design, or whether the actings of the trader who is sued do or do not constitute infringement…

7.1.4 3. The actings of the trader who is sued must satisfy the court that there is a likelihood of the public or the particular section of the public being misled into thinking that the goods are the goods of the trader who sues. It is not essential that the trader who sues should prove actual instances of confusion having taken place, but, if such are proved, the court will more readily grant interdict…

7.1.5 4. A trader has no property in a trade name, trade mark or particular get-up. The object of the action is to protect the goodwill of the trader who sues. Goodwill, being invisible, is represented by visible symbols such as trade names, trade marks, get-up and other accompaniments associated with the goods of a particular trader. Every article which is sold by such a trade name or bears such a trade mark, get-up or accompaniment has behind it an element of the particular trade's goodwill and reputation, and a rival or second trader, by adopting that trade name, trade mark, get-up or accompaniment, or a substantial part of it, with the result that the public are misled into thinking that the goods of the second trader are the goods of the first trader, commits an actionable wrong and appropriates to himself part of the goodwill of the first trader...

7.1.6 5. The get-up of goods comprises the size and shape of the package or container, labels and wrappers, the dress in which the goods are offered to the public. No trader, by adopting and using a particular style of get-up, thereby acquires a right to prevent a rival or second trader using the same or a similar get-up, unless the get-up of the first trader has become so associated in the minds of the public with the first trader's goods as to be distinctive of the goods of the first trader and no other. It is unusual that any single feature of the get-up of goods is so associated with a particular trader's goods is that a second trader cannot make use of it, but, if it is proved that a single feature of a trader's get-up is so peculiar that it above all else catches the eye and is retained in the memory of the purchasing public, and that the purchasing public recognise the goods of the trader by this one feature alone, then a second trader may be prevented from adopting this peculiar feature of the first trader's get-up and so misleading the public. A part of the article sold which is useful may, if peculiar, be part of the get-up of the goods and may become associated with and distinctive of a particular trader's goods...

7.1.7 It may be that there is no reported case in Scotland or England in which one particular and peculiar feature of the get-up of goods had become associated with and distinctive of a particular trader's goods so as to found an action of passing off, but the proposition which I have stated appears to me to follow from, and to be merely an example of the fundamental principle stated in my first proposition. It is quite impossible to lay down and enumerate all the possible ways in which one trader may pass off his goods as the goods of another, and cases dealing with trade names, trade marks or get-up are all just examples of particular methods of passing off.

7.1.8 6. In dealing with ordinary cases where articles are sold to the public whole and unopened you must look at the get-up as a whole, and you must treat the labels on the goods fairly in ascertaining whether or not the public is likely to be misled... but to place the articles side by side is not always the right test... The member of the public who falls to be considered is a person with reasonable apprehension and proper eyesight...

7.1.9 7. A container such as a bottle may be part of the get-up of goods of a trader if it is of a peculiar shape which catches the eye and is retained in the memory of the ordinary purchaser and is associated in the mind of the purchasing public with the goods of that particular trader alone and no other...

7.1.10   8. If the goods of the trader have, from the peculiar mark or get-up which he has used, become known in the market by a particular name, the adoption by a rival or second trader of any mark or get-up which will cause his goods to bear the same name in the market is a violation of the rights of the first trader — *Seixo* v. *Provezende* [(1865) L.R. 1 Ch. 192], *per* Lord Cranworth, L.C. at p. 197; *Johnston* v. *Orr Ewing* (1882) 7 App. Cas. 219, where the goods of the plaintiffs had become known in the Indian market as "Two Elephants" yarn.

7.1.11   9. No trader, however honest his personal intentions, has a right to adopt and use so much of his rival's established get-up as will enable any dishonest trader or retailer into whose hands the goods may come to sell them as the goods of his rival... Counsel for the respondents disputed this proposition. He pointed out that the *dicta* in the cases mentioned dealt with trade marks and not get-up. This is correct, but, in my opinion, the proposition follows from the ratio of these *dicta*. Counsel for the respondents maintained that an innocent trader should not be held responsible for the actings of a fraudulent retailer.

7.1.12   ... [Counsel for the respondents] further maintained that... [the] facts and circumstances of each case decide whether it falls within one set of *dicta* or the other. If the innocent trader enables the dishonest retailer to carry out a fraud upon the purchasers having regard to the market in which the goods are sold and the type of customer who buys, then he may be interdicted. In *Johnstone* v. *Orr Ewing* the trader who was interdicted adopted a ticket for his goods depicting two elephants which differed in certain respects from the two elephant ticket which was the established mark of the trader who sued, but the fact that both tickets depicted two elephants enabled a dishonest retailer to mislead the ignorant customer in the Indian market by displaying to them the ticket. The second trader accordingly supplied the dishonest retailer with a weapon with which he was able to perpetrate the fraud. In the case of *Payton & Co.* v. *Snelling, Lampard & Co.* [1901] A.C. 308 the two labels on the tins of coffee were distinct in respect that one bore the name "Royal" and the other "Flag", and the dishonest retailer, in order to carry out the fraud, would require to hide the tin and the label from the customer. The customer, when he made the purchase, would get the tin into his own hands and would see the difference in the labels, and the chances of deception would be remote.

7.1.13   10. The actings of a trader who copies a rival's established get-up need not be fraudulent and he need have no intention of obtaining any benefit from his rival's goodwill and reputation — indeed he may be ignorant of his existence — but, if the result of his innocent actings is that the public are likely to be misled, he will be interdicted — Lord Halsbury, L.C., in *Cellular Clothing Co.* v. *Maxton & Murray* (1989) 1 F. (H.L.) 29 at p. 31. If, however, the court is satisfied that the trader who is sued intended to obtain some benefit from his rival's established get-up and was thus fraudulent, the court will be more ready to grant interdict.'

COMMENT

7.2.1   Decided: Oct. 1, 1953.
  July 27:   Korean conflict ended.
  Sept. 12: John Kennedy married Jacqueline Bouvier.

7.2.2   This delict is explained in *Delict.*, 3.7–13. It is well defined but yet capable of extension. The Scottish contribution is not only jurisprudential. The Scotch Whisky Association is active throughout the world protecting the distinctiveness of our national drink from unjustifiable encroachment.

7.2.3   This case was applied in *Carrick Jewellery Ltd v. Ortak*, 1989 G.W.D. 35–1624. Perhaps with Glasgow being European City of Culture in 1990, something of an industry in artefacts in the style of one of the city's most renowned designers had been nurtured. The pursuers in this case made and sold "The Rennie Mackintosh Collection" of jewellery, using a stylised typeface. The defenders also sold similar jewellery, calling it "The Rennie Mackintosh Collection", in which the word "Mackintosh" was in a similar style to that of the pursuers. The defenders' argument was that the public would associate the produce with Charles Rennie Mackintosh the artist, rather than the pursuers. Lord Sutherland held that a name like Mackintosh, following the *Haig* case, could become sufficiently associated with a trader. However, he only interdicted the defenders from using the stylised typeface and not the name "Rennie Mackintosh Collection". These words merely described a style. The implication was that the defenders would have to alter their catalogue in time for Christmas. The possible sting for the pursuers was that the court pointed out that if they were unsuccessful at a later and full hearing for perpetual interdict, then they might well be liable for the expenses of the interim proceedings because interim interdict is always sought *periculo petentis*, at the pursuer's risk.

7.2.4   Some question as to the precise general applicability of *Haig* might have been raised by the Inner House in *Dash Ltd v. Philip King Tailoring*, 1989 S.L.T. 39. In this case counsel argued that the confusion which was said to exist in the case was only such as to amount to the *possibility* of confusion, whereas the *Haig* case required a likelihood of confusion. Lord McDonald, giving the opinion of the court, stated that the *Haig* case dealt with the similarity of goods rather than names, as was the issue in the case at Bar, and accordingly was not in point. The court did however consider that in the case before it, if the test were likelihood, it had been met. There seems no reason why the principles expounded in *Haig* should not apply to names as much as get-up — the test should be the same. Neither is it clear that there is much value in the semantic distinction made. If the court is saying that possibility is the test then there is, it is submitted, little doubt that they would be compelled to explain it later as meaning a "real possibility" or "possible in a real sense", because, after all, anything is possible. "Likelihood", it is submitted, is still the better verbal formulation. At all costs, let it be hoped that this area of the law is not to be treated to the multiplicity of verbal formulations of chance such as have bedevilled both third-party intervention cases (see Chap. 12) and the question of remoteness of contract damages (see Woolman, *Contract* (2nd ed., 1994), pp. 147–150).

7.2.5   The *Haig* case is a classic passing-off case, where one trader was using a design in such a way as to create confusion in a buyer's mind as to the identity of the manufacturer: to suggest that his (the defender's) goods were those of the pursuer. The next extract is a more striking case, and according to H. L. MacQueen in "Wee McGlen and the Action of Passing-off", 1982 S.L.T. (News) 225, is quite a step forward. It is also something of a reception of *Erven Warnink v. Townend (Hull) Ltd* [1979] A.C. 731.

34. **Lang Brothers Ltd (Appellants) v. Goldwell Ltd**
1982 S.L.T. 309 (I.H.)

7.3.1   'THE LORD JUSTICE-CLERK (Wheatley): The petitioners, who are the reclaimers in this reclaiming motion, seek to interdict the respondents from passing off as having been produced wholly in Scotland any alcoholic drink, containing in part whisky, which is not composed entirely of alcoholic beverages distilled, brewed or fermented in that country. Despite the generality of the terms of the proposed interdict it seems to be primarily directed towards a beverage called "Wee McGlen", produced by the first-named respondents in England and advertised and marketed by both respondents in England and Scotland. This beverage is said to consist of ginger wine blended with Scotch malt whisky.

7.3.2   The petitioners are blenders of Scotch whisky. The first-named petitioners blend and bottle all their products in Glasgow. The second-named petitioners blend their whisky in South Queensferry and label the blended Scotch whisky, which is bottled by them in West Germany, Switzerland, USA, Australia and New Zealand, as Scotch whisky. It is a matter of agreement that Scotch whisky is a description which applies only to whisky which has been distilled in Scotland; that it is recognised throughout the world that no other alcoholic drink is entitled to be called Scotch whisky than a blend of a number of distillates each of which separately is entitled to the description of Scotch whisky; that considerable reputation and goodwill attaches to whisky distilled in Scotland and that this reputation and goodwill extends to blended Scotch whisky; and that the name "Scotch" is universally recognised to attach to these products and that it is well known that Scotland is the country where they are distilled. The petitioners further aver, although these averments are not admitted by the respondents, that by the reason of the quality of the product Scotch whisky has achieved a pre-eminence throughout the world in the market for alcoholic drinks; that the association of these products with Scotland is a factor of great importance in promoting the sale of the petitioners' blended Scotch whisky wherever these products are sold, since it is by means of indicating the country of their origin that the said reputation and goodwill are employed (*i.e.* put to use or exploited); that the public throughout the world has come to rely on indications of the country of origin when used in relation to alcoholic beverages, and has come to expect that where such indications of the country of origin are used the beverage is the product of that country, *i.e.* that it was distilled, brewed or fermented there, and has the quality to be expected of that product, and that the public throughout the world has come to rely on the use of the word "Scotch" or other indications of Scottish origin by name or get-up when used in relation to whisky as meaning only whisky distilled in Scotland and as implying the quality of excellence which such whisky is recognised to possess.

7.3.3   The petitioners aver that the admixture in the respondents' produce "Wee McGlen" consists of ginger wine and Scotch malt whisky, the ginger wine being made in England in the premises of the first-named respondents by fermenting grape juice there then adding ginger essence obtained from Jamaica. They further believe and aver that the ingredients of the product are no more than about one part of Scotch malt whisky to eight parts of ginger wine. The sources of their complaint are the contents of the label on the bottle and the contents of an advertisement in a trade newspaper. Sample bottles and copies of the newspaper were lodged as productions, and they give a better appreciation of the complaints than the mere description on record. The label on the bottle has a tartan background and features a thistle as a device. At the top there is printed "Goldwell". Immediately under that in large yellow letters there is printed "Wee McGlen". Underneath that in slightly smaller but still large print appears "A Whisky Mac". Below that, in yet smaller but still distinct print on three separate lines are (1) "Ginger Wine", (2) "Blended with" and (3) "Scottish Malt Whisky". At the foot of the bottle the words "not less than 26⁰ Proof Spirit" are printed in smaller but still distinct lettering. On one edge the words "Goldwell" (Scotland) Ltd. Edinburgh" are similarly printed. The newspaper advertisement contains a reproduction of the bottle with the label showing and a caricature of a be-tartaned Scotsman to whom are attributed the words "Haste ye back for another Wee McGlen. The drink the trade has been asking for — Whisky Mac in a baby bottle."

. . . . . .

7.3.4   It is not a classical case of passing off in that it is not said that the respondents are passing off their product as that of the petitioners. The petitioners' complaint is that the "set up" of the label on the bottle and of the advertisement is such as to mislead the public into thinking that the whole ingredients of "Wee McGlen" are Scottish. It was said that the whole "Scottishness" of the "set up" was able to give this impression. The description of the contents of the product "Ginger Wine Blended with Scottish Malt Whisky" in all the surrounding circumstances suggests or at least is liable to create the impression in the minds of the public that both the ginger wine and the malt whisky are "Scottish". This was not so, as the ginger wine was

English, and the description was thereby misleading. Accordingly, when it became known that the reference to ginger wine was false and misleading the source of origin in all respects would fall under suspicion. This was liable to raise suspicion or cast doubts on the origin of the whisky as well, and diminish reliance on "Scotch whisky" which would affect the goodwill of the petitioners' business. I pause to observe that in this connection there may or may not be significance in the words "A Whisky Mac" which appear largely both in the label on the bottle and in the advertisement, but it is not for me at this stage to attempt to evaluate the significance, if any, of what that is …

7.3.5   As hereinbefore noted, this is not a classical passing off case. Nor is it averred in terms that the misleading misrepresentation could cast doubt or suspicion on the authenticity of the Scottish malt whisky in the "Wee McGlen" bottles. What is said is in general terms, *viz.* that the effect of the misrepresentation is that it is likely to endanger the reputation and goodwill which attaches to Scotch whisky because of its Scottish origin, since it is liable to dilute the distinctiveness of indications of Scottish origin when used in relation to alcoholic beverages. This, I suppose, could conceivably cover the Scottish malt whisky in the "Wee McGlen" bottles.

7.3.6   The *Warnink* case was said by petitioners' counsel to be a watershed in this branch of the law, just as the case of *Donoghue* v. *Stevenson* was a watershed in the law of negligence. I do not feel constrained to express any views on the validity of that comparison, whatever doubts I may have on its validity, since petitioners' counsel maintained that their averments cover the tests laid down in *Warnink* by Lord Diplock and Lord Fraser of Tullybelton respectively. Nor do I require to canvass the development of this chapter of the law, because that was exhaustively done in *Warnink*. The petitioners' complaint here is the damage to their reputation and goodwill by the respondents' alleged misrepresentation. In *Warnink* Lord Diplock adopted the words of Lord Macnaghten in *Inland Revenue Commissioners* v. *Muller & Co.'s Margarine Ltd.*, [1901] A.C. 217 at pp. 223–224 in explaining the concept of goodwill in law, which he said was a broad one: "It is the benefit and advantage of the good name, reputation, and connection of a business. It is the attractive force which brings in custom." The manner in which goodwill can be affected can occur in a variety of ways. Lord Diplock at p. 742 stated that the previous cases make it possible to identify five characteristics which must be present in order to create a valid cause of an action for passing off; "(1) a misrepresentation, (2) made by a trader in the course of trade, (3) to prospective customers of his or ultimate consumers of goods or services supplied by him, (4) which is calculated to injure the business or goodwill of another trader (in the sense that this is a reasonably foreseeable consequence), and (5) which causes actual damage to a business or goodwill of the trader by whom the action is brought or (in a *quia timet* action) will probably do so."

. . . . . .

7.3.7 Lord Fraser of Tullybelton at pp. 755–756 (in referring to the sherry case of *Vine Products Ltd* .v. *MacKenzie & Co. Ltd.* [1969] R.P.C. 1 and the judgment of Cross J. therein) said: "But the decision is in my opinion soundly based on the principle underlying the earlier passing off actions, which is distinctive of the product or class of products sold by him in the course of his business. It is essential for the plaintiff in a passing off action to show at least the following facts: (1) that his business consists of, or includes, selling in England a class of goods to which the particular trade name applies; (2) that the class of goods is clearly defined, and that in the minds of the public, or a section of the public, in England, the trade name distinguishes that class from other similar goods; (3) that because of the reputation of the goods, the goodwill attaches to the name; (4) that he, the plaintiff, as a member of the class of those who sell the goods, is the owner of goodwill in England which is of substantial value; (5) that he has suffered or is really likely to suffer, substantial damage to his property in the goodwill by reason of the defendants selling goods which are falsely described by the trade name to which the goodwill is attached. Provided the conditions are satisfied... I consider that the plaintiff is entitled to protect himself by a passing off action." There is ample authority for the proposition that the law of Scotland does not differ from the law of England in this field of law. While it was accepted by petitioners' counsel that there were differences between the fourth and fifth characteristics adumbrated by Lord Diplock and the fifth characteristic adumbrated by Lord Fraser of Tullybelton, they submitted that their averments in art. 8 of the closed record, when read along with the other relevant averments in their pleadings, were sufficient to meet the requirements of either test. While, in my opinion, the petitioners' averments could have been more clearly and definitely framed in this regard, there is sufficient in them to satisfy these requirements, provided of course that the ultimate test of relevancy is satisfied.'

COMMENT

7.4.1 Decided Feb. 29, 1980.
Dec. 24 (1979): Russia invaded Afghanistan.
Jan. 18: Sir Cecil Beaton died.
Feb. 12: Lake Placid Winter Olympics opened.

7.4.2 What is the difference between the fourth and fifth characteristics adumbrated by Lord Diplock and the fifth characteristic adumbrated by Lord Fraser of Tullybelton?

7.4.3 The Lord Justice-Clerk (Wheatley) was very much a Scotsman. The Inner House sits in Edinburgh which is in Scotland. Why do you think he described Scotland as "that" country instead of "this" country at 7.3.1?

7.4.4 For more comment see MacQueen (1983) and Stewart Q. (1983). Passing-off actions are not uncommon, although they may not always be significant enough to merit a full report. For some recent examples see *Pegasus Security Ltd v. Gilbert*, 1989 G.W.D. 26–1186; *Alexander Fergusson & Co. Ltd v. Mathews McClay & Manson Ltd*, 1989 S.L.T. 795; *James Burrough Distilleries plc v. Speymalt Whisky Distributors Ltd*, 1989 S.L.T. 561. If you like pop music, are amused at how seriously people can take themselves and would like to see trade mark legislation in action: see *Bravado Merchandising Services Ltd v. Mainstream Publishing (Edinburgh) Ltd*, 1995 G.W.D. 37–1921. For passing off pop music see *Treadwell's Drifters Inc. v. RCL Ltd*, 1993 G.W.D. 26–1641. See also Waelde, C., "Wet? Wet — a little mystery unrecorded", 1996 S.L.T. (News) 1.

Treadwell's Drifters has been reported by request: 1996 S.L.T. 1048. Lord Osborne (Obiter) accepted the definition of the delict by Lord Oliver in *Reckitt & Colman Products Ltd v. Borden Inc.* [1990] 1 W.L.R. 491 at 499 (1996 S.L.T. at 1057K–1058D and 1062A).

Conspiracy

35. **Crofter Hand Woven Harris Tweed Co. (Appellants) v. Veitch**
1942 S.C.(H.L.) 1

7.5.1 'LORD CHANCELLOR (Viscount Simon): The appellants are seven producers of tweed cloth in the island of Lewis in the Outer Hebrides. Their business is carried on by purchasing yarn which they give out to the crofters for weaving in their own homes, so that the appellants may sell the tweed so woven. The respondent, Mr Veitch, is the Scottish Area Secretary of the Transport and General Workers' Union, which is a trade union, and the respondent, Mr Mackenzie, is the Stornoway Branch Secretary of the Union. The appellants are seeking interdict against the two respondents in order to stop what is called an "embargo" imposed by their order or inducement upon all yarn arriving for the appellants at the port of Stornoway, which is the main port on the island and is connected by a service of steamers with the mainland, and upon certain tweeds despatched by the appellants from that port.

In argument before this House it was conceded that no issue is involved which might bring into the case any provision of the Trade Disputes Act 1906. The respondents are sued as individuals and not in any representative capacity. The question is whether the appellants have established that the respondents have committed a delict or tort at common law against them by thus interfering with their trade. It was not suggested that, as regards the law applicable to the present action, there was any material difference between the Scottish law of delict and the English law of tort...

7.5.2 The description "Harris Tweed" was originally applied to woollen cloth, which was not only woven by hand-looms in the cottages of the Outer Hebrides, but was also woven out of yarn spun by hand in the islands. (The trade-name "tweed" is not, it appears, derived from the river near which the cloth-weaving industry of Galashiels and neighbouring towns is established: it is a transformation, now nearly a century old, of the word "twill".) Moreover, "Harris Tweed" was hand-finished in the islands. It was thus a hand-produced and island-produced product throughout, and in 1911 a company limited by guarantee was registered under the name of the Harris Tweed Association Limited, which obtained a Trade Mark (referred to as the "Stamp") under section 62 of the Trade Marks Act, 1905, to apply to Harris Tweed which satisfied these conditions. After a time, the hand-spinning of wool into yarn ceased to be commercially practicable, and in 1934 the conditions of the Trade Mark were varied, with the result that it could apply to tweed hand-woven by the islanders in their own homes out of yarn spun in island spinning mills, and finished in the island mills instead of by hand...

7.5.3   Ninety per cent of the spinners in the mills are members of the Transport and General Workers' Union — the same trade union as that to which all the Stornoway dockers belong. The percentage of trade-unionists among the weavers in the cottages is much smaller. The officials of the Union desired that none but members of their Union should be employed, but when this was asked of the millowners in 1935, together with a rise in spinners' wages, the answer of the mills was that this was in existing circumstances impossible, and that a reduction in wages was more likely, owing (as was alleged) to the cut-throat competition of independent producers of cloth such as the appellants, who obtained their supplies of yarn from the mainland at a cheaper price than that charged by the mills. Cloth made out of mainland yarn could not carry the "Stamp", though it could be sold as Harris Tweed as having been woven in the island.

7.5.4   How far there really was injurious competition may be seriously questioned, but there is no evidence that the Union officials did not believe it, and what is clear is that the union official then mainly concerned, a Mr Buchan, set himself to assist in establishing a minimum selling price for island cloth, and that he, and after him Veitch, conceived that it would benefit their Union members if conditions of collective bargaining could be established in the island between employers and employed. To this end, Mr Buchan in 1935 proposed to Mr Skinner, the Secretary of the Mill-Owners' Association, a scheme whereby the trade union could "provide definite safeguards to the successful operation of a minimum selling price", and added that "the only argument that price-cutters will ever understand and appreciate will be the joint power of the employers and this Union to put them out of business if they refuse loyally to abide by minimum selling prices as fixed from time to time by the Harris Tweed Producers' Association... ." A long and complicated story of discussions and interviews followed, at the end of which the effort to secure by negotiations minimum prices and the use of none but island-spun yarn failed.

7.5.5 The appellants have strenuously argued that there was a combination between Mr Veitch and Mr Skinner to impose the embargo and in particular rely on Mr Veitch's letter to Mr Mackenzie of January 19, 1938 requesting the latter to give instructions to the dockers, which contains the significant sentence: "This action will complete our deal with the employers and we will have 100 per cent. membership, not only in their mills but also in the weaving section." My own view is in accord with that of the Lord Ordinary (with which at least one member of the Inner House, Lord Wark, was disposed to agree) that, suspicious as the circumstances are, there is not sufficient evidence to establish that Mr Skinner was combining with the respondents to impose the embargo; he was aware of the intention to impose it and he approved of it and was apparently willing to concede 100 per cent membership to the Union if his trade rivals were put out of business or compelled to buy yarn from the mills, but I am not prepared to hold that the respondents struck at the appellants because of a bargain so to do between Mr Skinner and themselves.

7.5.6 Such being the facts of this case as I take them to be, the question to be decided is whether the appellants have proved that the respondents are liable to them for illegal conspiracy. In other words, is it proved that the two respondents combined together "to injure" the appellants in the way of their trade, and that the appellants have suffered damage from the respondents' illegal action? Conspiracy, when regarded as a crime, is the agreement of two or more persons to effect any unlawful purpose, whether as their ultimate aim, or only as a means to it, and the crime is complete if there is such agreement, even though nothing is done in pursuance of it. (I am omitting consideration of those cases on the borderland of illegality, where the combination was held to amount to a criminal conspiracy because the purpose aimed at, though not perhaps specifically illegal, was one which would undermine principles of commercial or moral conduct.) The crime consists in the agreement, though in most cases overt acts done in pursuance of the combination are available to prove the fact of agreement. But the tort of conspiracy is constituted only if the agreed combination is carried into effect in a greater or lesser degree, and damage to the plaintiff is thereby produced. It must be so, for, regarded as a civil wrong, conspiracy is one of those wrongs (like fraud or negligence) which sound in damage, and a mere agreement to injure, if it was never acted upon at all and never led to any result affecting the party complaining, could not produce damage to him.

7.5.7 The distinction between the essential conditions to be fulfilled by the crime and the tort respectively are conveniently set out by Lord Coleridge, C.J., in his judgment in *Mogul Steamship Co.* v. *McGregor, Gow & Co.* (1888) 21 Q.B.D. 544. "In an indictment it suffices if the combination exists and is unlawful, because it is the combination itself which is mischievous, and which gives the public an interest to interfere by indictment. Nothing need be actually done in furtherance of it... It is otherwise in a civil action: it is the damage which results from unlawful combination itself with which the civil action is concerned... once more, to state the proposition somewhat differently with a view to some of the arguments addressed to me, the law may be put thus. If the combination is unlawful, then the parties to it commit a misdemeanour, and are offenders against the State: and if, as the result of such unlawful combination and misdemeanour, a private person receives a private injury, that gives such person a right of private action."

. . . . . .

7.5.8 The appellants, therefore, in order to make out their case have to establish (a) agreement between the two respondents; (b) to effect an unlawful purpose; (c) resulting in damage to the appellants. As regards (c), there can here be no doubt. Instructing or persuading the dockers at Stornoway to refuse to handle imports of mainland spun yarn arriving for delivery to the appellants was an interference with the appellants' normal source of supply, which was bound to damage their business. Still more, perhaps was it an injury to the appellants to prevent by these means the sending of their unfinished cloth to the mainland. Indeed, it is one of the most serious aspects of this case, and an aspect that I deplore, that the action taken against the appellants not merely put pressure on them to adopt new arrangements but might well destroy their business altogether without offering any *locus poenitentiae*. Whether this consideration affects the ultimate conclusion must be considered hereafter. I am equally satisfied about (a)... The Lord Ordinary, after a full and careful hearing, came to the conclusion of fact that the immediate purpose of Mr Veitch and Mr McKenzie was to force producers to come to an agreement regarding the selling price of tweed and the exclusive use of island-spun yarn. The means adopted necessarily inflicted injury on the petitioner..." Questions (a) and (c) are, therefore, conclusively disposed of. The only difficulty in the case arises under (b).

7.5.9 What exactly is meant, in this branch of the law, by a combination to effect an unlawful purpose?... It seems to me that the subject may be usefully approached by beginning with some preliminary propositions not in themselves, I think, open to challenge at this time of day. In stating these propositions I shall try to distinguish between "damage" and "injury" following the stricter diction, derived from the civil law, which more especially prevails in Scottish jurisprudence. So used, "injury" is limited to actionable wrong, while "damage" in contrast with injury, means loss or harm occurring in fact, whether actionable as an injury or not. "An intent to injure," said Bowen L.J. in the *Mogul* case, "in strictness means more than an intent to harm. It connotes an intent to do wrongful harm." First, then, apart from the effects of combination, it is clear that (1) if A is damaged by the action of B, A nevertheless has no remedy against B, if B's act is lawful in itself and is carried out without employing unlawful means. In such a case A has to endure *damnum absque injuria*. (2) It makes no difference to the above proposition that B in so acting had the purpose of damaging A. A bad motive does not *per se* turn an individual's otherwise lawful act into an unlawful one. (3) If C has an existing contract with A and B is aware of it, and if B persuades or induces C to break the contract with resulting damage to A, this is, generally speaking, a tortious act for which B will be liable to A for the injury he has done him. In some cases, however, B may be able to justify his procuring of the breach of contract, *e.g.* a father may persuade his daughter to break her engagement to marry a scoundrel... The father's justification arises from a moral duty to urge C that the contract should be repudiated. So far there is, I apprehend, little to dispute about. But if the act which damages A is not that of a single individual, but is due to a combination of two or more persons, then it is no longer possible to say that motive or purpose is immaterial.

. . . . . .

7.5.10 Lord Bramwell, in the *Mogul* case, observed that it had been objected that it was strange that that should be unlawful if done by several which is not unlawful if done by one, and he offered some suggestions as an explanation. The view that the explanation is to be found in the increasing power of numbers to do damage beyond what one individual can do is open to the obvious answer that this depends on the personality and influence of the individual. In the play, Cyrano de Bergerac's single voice was more effective to drive the bad actor Montfleury off the stage than the protests of all the rest of the audience to restrain him. The action of a single tyrant may be more potent to inflict suffering on the continent of Europe than a combination of less powerful persons. Bowen L.J., when the *Mogul* case was before the Court of Appeal, observed: "The distinction is based on sound reason, for a combination may make oppressive or dangerous that which if it proceeded only from a single person would be otherwise, and the very fact of the combination may show that the object is simply to do harm, and not to exercise one's own just rights."

. . . . . .

7.5.11 On this question of what amounts to an actionable conspiracy "to injure" (I am assuming that damage results from it), I would first observe that some confusion may arise from the use of such words as "motive" and "intention..." It is much safer to use a word like "purpose" or "object". The question to be answered, in determining whether a combination to do an act which damages others is actionable, even though it would not be actionable if done by a single person, is not "did the combiners appreciate, or should they be treated as appreciating, that others would suffer from their action?" but "what is the real reason why the combiners did it?" Or, as Lord Cave puts it: "What is the real purpose of the combination?" The test is not what is the natural result to the plaintiffs of such combined action, or what is the resulting damage which the defendants realise or should realise will follow, but what is in truth the object in the minds of the combiners when they acted as they did. It is not consequence that matters but purpose.

. . . . . .

7.5.12   Next it is to be borne in mind that there may be cases where the combination has more than one "object" or "purpose". The combiners may feel that they are killing two birds with one stone, and, even though their main purpose may be to protect their own legitimate interests, notwithstanding that this involves damage to the plaintiffs, they may also find a further inducement to do what they are doing by feeling that it serves the plaintiffs right. The analysis of human impulses soon leads us into the quagmire of mixed motives, and even if we avoid the word "motive" there may be more than a single "purpose" or "object". It is enough to say that, if there is more than one purpose actuating a combination, liability must depend on ascertaining the predominant purpose. If that predominant purpose is to damage another person and damage results, that is tortious conspiracy. If the predominant purpose is the lawful protection or promotion of any lawful interest of the combiners (no illegal means being employed), it is not a tortious conspiracy, even though it causes damage to another person.

7.5.13   It may well be that in this corner of the law it is not possible to lay down with precision an exact and exhaustive proposition like an algebraical formula which will provide an automatic answer in every case that may arise by substituting the actual instance for generalisation... I am content to say that, unless the real and predominant purpose is to advance the defendants' lawful interest in a matter where the defendants honestly believe that those interests would directly suffer if the action taken against the plaintiffs was not taken, a combination wilfully to damage a man in his trade is unlawful. Although most of the cases have dealt with trade rivalry in some form or other, I do not see why the proposition as to the conditions under which conspiracy becomes a tort should be limited to trade competition. Indeed, in its original sense, conspiracy as a tort was a combination to abuse legal procedure... I have used the word "directly" without seeking to define its boundaries as an indication that indirect gains... would not provide a justification.

7.5.14   In the present case, the conclusion, in my opinion, is that the predominant object of the respondents in getting the embargo imposed was to benefit their trade union members by preventing under-cutting and unregulated competition, and so helping to secure the economic stability of the island industry. The result they aimed at achieving was to create a better basis for collective bargaining, and thus directly to improve wage prospects. A combination with such an object is not unlawful, because the object is the legitimate promotion of the interests of the combiners... I agree with Lord Fleming when he says in his judgment that it is not for a court of law to consider in the connection the expediency or otherwise of a policy adopted by a trade union... I move that this appeal be dismissed with costs.

7.5.15 VISCOUNT MAUGHAM: It seems to me, therefore, and with the greatest deference to those who perhaps think otherwise, a mistake to hold that combinations to do acts which necessarily result in injury to the business or interference with the means of subsistence of a third person are not actionable provided only the true or predominant motive was not to injure the plaintiff and that no unlawful means are used. For instance, the object of the combination may be a dislike of the religious views or the politics or the race or the colour of the plaintiff, or a mere demonstration of power by busybodies. Again, the person joining in the combination may have been induced so to act by payment of money or by some other consideration. There is, I think, no authority to be found which justifies the view that a combination of such a character, causing damage to the plaintiff, would be lawful... But I will add that, when the question of the real purpose is being considered, it is impossible to leave out of consideration the principle that men are in general to be taken as intending the direct consequences of their acts...

7.5.16 It is worthwhile to note that *Quinn* v. *Leathem* [1901] A.C. 495 is an example of a mixed motive; for there the defendants, being officials and members of a trade union, combined to call out the union workmen of the plaintiff Leathem if he would not discharge sone non-union men in his employment, and also to call out the union workmen of a customer of Leathem called Munce if he did not cease to deal with Leathem. It is true that there was a finding of the Belfast jury that what the defendants had done was done with malice in order to injure the plaintiff; but it can scarcely have been in doubt that one at least of the motives actuating the defendants was the benefit of their trade union. As Lord Lindley remarked: "That they [the defendants] acted as they did in furtherance of what they considered the interests of union men may probably be fairly assumed in their favour." The facts as set out in detail in Lord Brampton's speech show clearly that the whole dispute between Leathem and the trade union originated in Leathem's refusal to dismiss non-union workmen. It must, however, be assumed from the findings of the jury that the main object or purpose of the defendants was to punish or injure Leathem, and that this was "malicious" whatever the precise evidence of malice may have been. It was never suggested by anyone that, if the defendants' act were at least partly in furtherance of trade union interests, that would be a defence to the action.

7.5.17   LORD WRIGHT: As I read the authorities, there is a clear and definite distinction which runs through them all between what Lord Dunedin in *Sorrell* v. *Smith* [1925] A.C. 700 calls "a conspiracy to injure" and "a set of acts dictated by business interests". I should qualify "business" by adding "or other legitimate interests", using the convenient adjective not very precisely. It may be a difficult task in some cases to apply this distinction. It depends largely on matters of fact, but also on a legal conception of what is meant by "intention to injure". The appellants contend that there was here an intention to injure, even though it is negatived that the respondents were actuated by malice or malevolence.

7.5.18   In effect, it was said, the union were bribed by the mill owners to victimise the appellants in their trade by the promise of help in the matter of the union membership, which was entirely foreign to the question of the importation of yarn. These considerations, it was said, constituted "malice" in law even if there was not malevolence, and prevented the respondents from justifying the injury which they wilfully did to the appellants' trade, because they could not assert any legitimate interest of their union which was relevant to the action taken. Actual malevolence or spite was, it was said, not essential.

. . . . . .

7.5.19   Before I refer to the authorities, there are some preliminary observations which I desire to make. I shall avoid the use of what Lord Bowen described as the "slippery" word "malice" except in quotations. When I want to express spite or ill-will, I shall use the word malevolence. When I want to express merely intentional tortious conduct I shall use the word wrongful. As the claim is for a tort, it is necessary to ascertain what constitutes the tort alleged. It cannot be merely that the appellants' right to freedom in conducting their trade has been interfered with. That right is not an absolute or unconditional right. It is only a particular aspect of the citizen's right to personal freedom, and like other aspects of that right is qualified by various legal limitations, either by statute or by common law. Such limitations are inevitable in organised societies where the rights of individuals may clash. In commercial affairs each trader's rights are qualified by the right of others to compete.

. . . . . .

7.5.20   In the present case the respondents are sued for imposing the "embargo" which corresponds to calling out the men on strike. The dockers were free to obey, or not to obey, the call to refuse to handle the appellants' goods. In refusing to handle the goods they did not commit any breach of contract with anyone; they were merely exercising their own rights. But there might be circumstances which rendered the action wrongful. The men might be called out in breach of their contracts with their employers, and that would be clearly a wrongful act as against the employer, an interference with his contractual right, for which damages could be claimed not only as against the contract-breaker, but against the person who counselled or procured or advised the breach. This is the principle laid down in *Lumley* v. *Guy* (1853) 2 E. & B. 216 which Lord Macnaghten in *Quinn* v. *Leathem* defined to be "that a violation of legal right committed knowing is a cause of action, and that it is a violation of legal right to interfere with contractual relations recognised by law if there be no sufficient justification for the interference". That is something substantially different from a mere interference with a person's qualified right to exercise his free will in conducting his trade. A legal right was violated and needed justification, if it could be justified... In *Allen* v. *Flood* [1898] A.C. 1 this House was considering a case of an individual actor, where the element of combination was absent. In that case, it was held, the motive of the defendant is immaterial. Damage done intentionally and even malevolently to another thus, it was held, gives no cause of action so long as no legal right of the other is infringed.

. . . . . .

7.5.21   Thus for the purpose of the present case we reach the position that, apart from combination, no wrong would have been committed. There was no coercion of the dockers. There were no threats to them. They were legally free to choose the alternative course which they preferred. In *Quinn* v. *Leathem* a wide meaning was given to words like threats, intimidation or coercion, especially by Lord Lindley, but that was not the *ratio decidendi* adopted by the House. These words, as R. S. Wright pointed out in his book on Criminal Conspiracy, are not terms of art and are consistent either with legality or illegality. They are not correctly used in the circumstances of a case like this... There is nothing unlawful in giving a warning or intimation that, if the party addressed pursues a certain line of conduct, others may act in a manner which he will not like and which will be prejudicial to his interests, so long as nothing unlawful is threatened or done. In Lord Buckmaster's words in *Sorrell* v. *Smith*: "A threat to do an act which is lawful cannot, in my opinion, create a cause of action, whether the act threatened is to be done by many or by one." No doubt the use of illegal threats or the exercise of unlawful coercion would create by itself a cause of action, but there was nothing of the sort in this case.

. . . . . .

7.5.22 A conspiracy to injure involves *ex vi termini* an intention to injure, or more accurately, a common intention and agreement to injure. Both "intention" and "injure" need definition. The word "injure" is here used in its correct meaning of "wrongful harm" — *damnum cum injuria*, not *damnum absque injuria*. That obviously raises the question, when is the harm wrongful?

. . . . . .

7.5.23 We live in a competitive or acquisitive society, and the English common law may have felt that it was beyond its power to fix by any but the crudest distinctions the metes and bounds which divide the rightful or the wrongful use of the actor's own freedom leaving the precise application in any particular case to the jury or judge of fact. If further principles of regulation or control are to be introduced, that is matter for the legislature. There are not many cases in which the court has had to consider these problems. Actions of this character are not of everyday occurrence like actions for negligence.'

COMMENT

7.6.1. Decided: Dec. 15, 1941.

Oct. 23: Première of Walt Disney's *Dumbo*.

Nov. 13: *Ark Royal* sunk.

Dec. 7: Japan bombed US fleet at Pearl Harbor and declared war on USA and Britain (after the bombing).

Dec. 11: Hitler and Mussolini declared war on USA.

7.6.2 For a time in England it was thought that a predominant motive to harm was a requirement even in unlawful means cases (*Lonrho v. Shell Petroleum* [1982] A.C. 173), but that was denounced in *Lonrho plc v. Al-Fayed* [1991] 3 W.L.R. 188.

7.6.3 The race point mentioned in passing at 6.5.15 arose, but in a sense in reverse in the case of *Scala Ballroom (Wolverhampton) Ltd v. Ratcliffe* [1958] 1 W.L.R. 1057. The plaintiffs decided to exclude coloured persons from their places of entertainment. The Musicians' Union had a policy against racial discrimination and indicated that its members would not perform where a colour bar was in force. It was accepted in the Court of Appeal that furthering the interests of the union, which had many coloured members, could be held to be the predominant purpose.

7.6.4 Cyrano de Bergerac mentioned at 7.5.10 was a French satirist (1619–55). His fame rests more upon Edmond Rostand's play *Cyrano de Bergerac* written in 1897. He (Cyrano) had a big nose. People still find this amusing: See, *e.g.* Fred Schepisi's film *Roxanne* (U.S. 1987). The story has again attained enormous popularity: *Cyrano de Bergerac* un film de Jean-Paul Rappeneau (1990), starring Gerard Depardieu.

Wrongful inducement to breach contract

36. Findlay (Appellant) v. Blaylock
1937 S.C. 21

7.7.1 'THE LORD PRESIDENT (Normand): 'In this case the pursuer, a young woman of 23 years of age, sues the father of a man, whom at one time she was engaged to marry, for damages, alleging against him that he wrongfully induced his son, then a minor, to break off his engagement with her. The pursuer and the defender's son had fixed a date on which the marriage was to take place. The father wrote to the pursuer's father a letter in which he complained that he was aggrieved and annoyed that the proposal that a marriage should take place had been put forward without his permission or consent, or even without it being brought to his notice by the proper people concerned. He also stated that he strongly resented this action, and suggested that probably the father of the pursuer was not "aware of the above facts".

7.7.2 The real complaint is that the defender maliciously used his position as father of Peter Blaylock to incite and coerce him to break his promise of marriage with the pursuer. It is further said that the defender wrongfully and maliciously and without reasonable or probable cause used his position as employer of his son to incite and coerce him to break his promise of marriage and provided him with funds to fly from Scotland. When the pursuers' counsel was asked where the particular specification relating to this coercion was to be found, we were referred to another averment that the father had dismissed the boy from his employment with himself. I do not understand how such a dismissal, which was operative notwithstanding that the boy had broken off the engagement, can have been regarded as an inducement to break off the engagement. It appears to me that the record, which contains averments of malice in general terms, contains no particular averment from which any obliquity of motive can be inferred.

. . . . . .

7.7.3 It is no doubt true that, if a person, knowing that another person has a contractual relation with a third party, induces that person to break that contractual relation, he may be liable to the third party whose contract in consequence of his action is thereby breached. There are illustrations of that both in Scotland and in England...

7.7.4 I think it is the duty of a father to consider whether a marriage, which his son proposes to contract, is one which he should encourage or discourage. If a father decides to dissuade his son from entering into a proposed marriage, it should reasonably be presumed that his dissuasion is brought to bear in the exercise of his parental duty to guide his son in a matter of such vital importance to his future happiness. Accordingly, if the dissuasion is to be said to have been inconsistent with his parental duty, and to have been actuated by motives which were oblique and not related to his son's future welfare, or if it is to be said that the dissuasion was exercised merely in order to inflict an unwarrantable wrong upon the woman to whom the son was engaged — these allegations must be supported by clear and specific averments of facts and circumstances from which the wrongful motive and malice may be inferred. It is not necessary to decide in this case what facts and circumstances would have to be specified in order that a relevant case might be made, and I am assuming rather than deciding that it would be possible in a case of this sort for a father to render himself liable for damages for inducing his son to break a promise of marriage.

· · · · · ·

7.7.5   LORD MONCRIEFF: The pursuer goes on to aver, or the defender admits, that the father turned his son out of his house, turned him out of his employment and sent him to England. These are, however, stated to have been completed and not conditional acts, and, accordingly, while they may have punished the offending son, cannot (so far as the pursuer explains them) be supposed to have influenced him towards a breach of his engagement. On the general ground that I find no relevant averment as against a father of a wrongful act, I agree with your Lordship that the second plea in law stated by the defender should be sustained.'

COMMENT

7.8.1   Decided: October 29, 1936.
>   Aug. 8: Jesse Owens won the first of four medals at Munich Olympics.
>   Sept. 21: Frank Hornby, inventor of Meccano, died.
>   Oct. 5: Jarrow Hunger March began.
>   Oct. 27: Wallis divorced Ernest Simpson.

7.8.2   Since the Law Reform (Husband and Wife) Act 1984, s. 1, a promise to marry no longer has effect under the law of Scotland to create any rights or obligations. Would a case like *Findlay* be decided differently today?

7.8.3   Read *Akram v. Commission for Racial Equality*, 1994 G.W.D. 22–1372, in which this case was distinguished. Do you agree it properly could be? If so, why? If not, why not?

37. British Motor Trade Association v. Gray
1951 S.L.T. 247

7.9.1   The following is the deed referred to in the report:

'THIS DEED made the   day of   19
Between   of   in the County of
(hereinafter called "The Owner") of the first part, and The British
Motor Trade Association" of the second part, and
of
(hereinafter called "the dealer") of the third part.

Whereas:

A. The dealer has sold and delivered to the owner the motor vehicle
(hereinafter called "the said vehicle").

B. The Association is an association of manufacturers and dealers
engaged in the motor industry whose objects are to protect the
interests of the motor trade and to safeguard the purchasing public
and for this purpose, *inter alia*, to prevent price inflation of motor
vehicles and of which Association the dealer is a member.

C. As part of the consideration for the said sale the owner agreed
with the dealer that he would upon the said vehicle being delivered
to him by the dealer enter into such covenants with the Association
and the dealer as are hereinafter contained.

Now this Deed Witnesseth and it is hereby agreed as follows:

1. The owner hereby covenants with the Association and (as a
separate covenant) with the dealer that he will not during the period
of twelve months from the date hereof without the consent in writing
of the Association which consent shall not be unreasonably withheld
use the said vehicle or permit the same to be used for any purpose
whatever other than for the private, professional or trade purposes of
the owner so that (without prejudice to the generality of the foregoing)
the owner shall not during the said period without the consent in
writing of the Association sell, give, pledge, hire (whether by way of
hire purchase or otherwise) or (whether by way of hire purchase or
otherwise) or otherwise deal with the said vehicle in any manner
whereby the property therein is or may be transferred to any other
person.

2. The owner hereby covenants with the dealer that he will for every
breach of the covenant on the part of the owner hereinbefore
contained pay to the dealer as and by of liquidated damages and not
as a penalty (but without prejudice to any other right or remedies of
the dealer hereunder) the sum of £

In Witness whereof the owner has hereunto set his hand and seal
the day and year first above written.

Signed, Sealed and Delivered by the above-named owner in the
presence of

Witness.

. . . . . .

7.9.2 'LORD PRESIDENT (Cooper): This action is a virtual replica of
British Motor Trade Association v. *Salvadori* [1949] Ch. 556, and *British*

Motor Trade Association v. *Naylor* [1950] unreported, in both of which the Association were successful in parallel circumstances in obtaining in England protection against organised infringement of the familiar motor car "covenant" scheme, introduced by them with the object of ensuring reputable trading in new cars... It is unnecessary to rehearse the features of the scheme or the obvious evils which it was designed to frustrate. I single out from the petitioners' averments the salient points of their indictment against the respondent. He is a motor car dealer in business in Glasgow, and therefore presumably familiar with the conditions under which the post-war market in cars is conducted. In February 1948 he was placed upon the Association's "stop list" by reason of his conduct in breach of the rules relating to price protection; and this involved that no member of the Association (which means no reputable car manufacturer, importer or dealer), would thereafter do business with him. Between April 1948 and November 1949 he knowingly purchased nine different vehicles in breach of current covenants prohibiting the sales, one of the sellers who sold in breach of covenant being a person named Mark Hutchison. In addition, while acting in concert with Mark Hutchison, he knowingly purchased five further vehicles from Mark Hutchison in breach of current covenants. The full details regarding the acquisition of these 14 cars will only be discovered at a proof, but the averments sufficiently disclose a deliberate course of conduct, pursued over an extended period, and involving the carrying on as a business venture of what I may describe as a "black market" in cars, in wilful defiance of the Association's covenant scheme. The acceptance of the respondent's argument would mean that the respondent and others like-minded to himself are entitled so to proceed and that the law is powerless to interfere. I do not think that it is.

7.9.3 The main issues which emerged from the admirable arguments presented to us came to be reduced to two in number: (1) Is the contract embodied in the covenant illegal as being in restraint of trade? and (2) Even if it is not, have the petitioners relevantly averred a good cause of action by Scots law?

. . . . . .

7.9.4 (1)... The typical contract in restraint of trade is a contract by which some restriction is imposed which tends to deprive the community of the labour, skill or talents of men in the employments or capacities in which they might be most useful to the public as well as to themselves, and which may be on that account contrary to public policy. Now the motor car covenant imposes no restraint upon any trader. It is a contract between trader and customer and the customer is envisaged not as a person who buys for re-sale by way of trade, but as a person who buys in order himself to use and consume the subject of sale. The only restraint imposed by the covenant is a restraint on such a customer, and the covenant is neither more nor less than an effort by the whole body of car manufacturers and dealers to ensure that, during the present emergency conditions of the market, they will only supply new cars to persons who will use them, and that they will not supply new cars to speculators who wish to turn them over at inflated prices. I am unable to hold that such a contract is in restraint of trade so far as the parties to the contract are concerned... Doubtless it is an incidental (and deliberate) consequence of the taking of covenants from all purchasers of new cars that the second-hand market is *pro tanto* restricted; but that is a consequence and in my view a beneficial consequence of the policy adopted by the association, and not a direct result of any individual contract.

. . . . . .

7.9.5   (2) The second issue raises at the outset a point of importance which the respondent felt unable to argue but to which nevertheless I desire to avert, *viz.* whether it is or may be an actionable wrong in Scotland for a third party to induce the breach of such a contract as that now in question. In England the answer is clearly in the affirmative; but in Scotland it so happens that until recently the only illustrations of the rule were found in relation to contracts of service, and the view has been hazarded that with us the doctrine is confined to the contract of service, and finds its origin in the primitive rights of property once recognised in the services of a servant and originally in the servant or serf himself (*Encyclopaedia of the Laws of Scotland*, Vol. xii, p. 534). But the rule is subjected to no such limitation as formulated in Glegg on *Reparation* (3rd ed., p. 261), and in *Findlay* v. *Blaylock*, 1936 S.L.T. 596, the rule was extended to promise of marriage. Lord Normand said in general terms: "It is no doubt true that if a person knowing that another person has a contractual relation with a third party, induces that person to break that contractual relation, he may be liable to the third party whose contract in consequence of his action is thereby breached. There are illustrations of this both in Scotland and in England," and his Lordship then went on to cite from one of the leading English decisions. Lord Fleming and Lord Moncrieff proceeded upon the same view. In *Crofter Hand Woven Harris Tweed Co.*, 1942 S.C. (H.L.) 1, 1943 S.L.T. 2, several of the learned Lords, in dealing with a related question, assumed that a wider rule applied to Scotland. In these circumstances I am prepared to affirm expressly that it is only by accident that the Scottish illustrations have centred around the contract of service and the wrong of "harbouring servants" that these are only instances of the wider rule, and that on principle the wider rule as more fully developed in England, must be considered as part of the law of Scotland. It remains to consider the precise form and limitations of the wider rule, for even our own decision of *Findlay* v.

Blaylock (*supra*) shows that in some situations a third party may lawfully induce the breach of a contract between two other persons.

7.9.6. The classic pronouncement on the subject is in the speech of Lord Macnaghten in *Quinn* v. *Leathem* [1901] A.C. 495 at p. 510, where he said that "a violation of legal right committed knowingly is a cause of action, and ... it is a violation of legal right to interfere with contractual relations recognised by law if there be no sufficient justification for the interference ...

7.9.7 The suggestion that "sufficient justification" for the respondent's conduct can be found in his own self-interest seems to me to be manifestly untenable, for such an exception would empty the rule of all intelligible content. Equally it is plain as a matter of averment that the petitioners have a legal interest to claim the remedy which they seek in the fact that they are a trade union which is deeply concerned in maintaining and enforcing as uniformly as possible the scheme they have devised for the benefit of their members and of the public generally — indeed that the covenant scheme may fairly be described as their *raison d'être* — and that the respondent's efforts to break the scheme, if successful, must inevitably inflict damage upon them.'

COMMENT

7.10.1   Decided: Jan. 26, 1951.
     Nov. 28, 1950: Chinese forces attacked U.S. forces in Korea.
     Dec. 25: Coronation Stone stolen from Westminster Abbey.
     Jan. 27, 1951: Meat ration cut to its lowest ever (4 ozs. per person), partly as a result of difficulties with Argentina.

7.10.2   In *Rossleigh v. Leader Cars*, 1987 S.L.T. 355, Lord Mayfield accepted that the foregoing case was the leading authority on the topic. In doing so he effectively rejected some post-*B.M.T.A.* English decisions. He did not accept the view expressed in inter alia *Daily Mirror Newspapers Ltd v. Gardner* [1968] 2 Q.B. 762, that "turning a blind eye" to the existence of the contract might be sufficient unless the actings "are tantamount to enable the court to conclude that such actings were in effect intentional" (at p. 360). Accordingly, although Lord President Cooper equiparated the law in Scotland and the law in England in *B.M.T.A.*, it is not completely safe to assume that Scots courts will accept every development in England. The most significant case in England may be *D.C. Thomson & Co.v. Deakin* [1952] Ch. 646, decided very shortly after the foregoing extract. This case is the root of some very sophisticated distinctions, particularly that between the three forms of committing the tort, *viz.* (1) direct persuasion; (2) direct intervention and (3) indirect intervention. Indirect intervention, it seems, may be very indirect, for in the House of Lords case, *Merkur Island Shipping Co. v. Laughton* [1983] 2 A.C. 570, the interference was some three steps removed from the contract. *D.C. Thomson* is also the source of the requirement that in cases of intervention rather than persuasion there must be the use of some independently unlawful means.
     A further extension took place in *Torquay Hotel Co. Ltd v. Cousins* [1969] 2 Ch. 106, in which there was technically no breach of contract because the parties had provided an exclusion where delivery was prevented as a result of circumstances outside their

control. It is enough that the defender prevents or hinders performance of the contract. (See generally, *Delict*, 3.18–3.20, and for a fuller explanation Winfield and Jolowicz, pp. 497–408.)

7.10.3 Is it all curious that a case dealing with an unsuitable engagement should assist in a matter of commerce? If not, why?

7.10.4 In England a tort of interference with trade by unlawful means is in the course of being developed. See *Merkur Island Shipping Corp. v. Laughton* [1983] 2 A.C. 570 at pp. 609–610; see also *Lonrho plc v. Fayed* [1989] 2 All E.R. 65, affirmed in the House of Lords [1992] 1 A.C. 448. No sign yet of it immigrating. For a full and illuminating account with reference to the relevant periodical literature, see Winfield and Jolowicz, pp. 521–526. Lord Wedderburn considers it to exist albeit of uncertain ambit. See Clark and Lindsell (17th ed.), p. 1244.

Intimidation: The reception of Rookes v. Barnard [1964] 1 All E.R. 367

38. J. T. Cameron, "Intimidation and the Right to Strike"
1964 S.L.T. (News) 81

7.11.1 'The case of *Rookes* v. *Barnard* [1964] 1 All E.R. 367, has already given rise to much discussion and will presumably continue to be discussed for a long time… . The facts can be quite briefly stated. As the jury found, Barnard and others conspired to threaten strike action by members of the union of which they were officials and by so threatening strike action induced B.O.A.C. to dismiss the appellant, Rookes. No breach of contract was committed by B.O.A.C. as against Rookes; all that was done was to terminate his employment in a perfectly normal manner. Rookes, however, alleged that Barnard and the other defendants had intimidated B.O.A.C. by the threat of strike action and that this intimidation by causing B.O.A.C. to terminate his employment had caused damage to him. The House of Lords held that there does exist such a tort as intimidation, that it had been committed in the present case, and that although the parties were involved in a trade dispute, those who had committed the tort were not protected by the Trade Disputes Act 1906. The reason for this last decision is that the Trade Disputes Act only protects persons who act jointly or in a conspiracy when the act which is done is one which would be lawful if done by an individual alone. The House of Lords held that intimidation could be committed by an individual and, therefore, that what was done was not something which would have been lawful if done by one person alone.

. . . . . .

Intimidation and Scots law

7.11.2 The authorities on which the tort of intimidation, even in its old and narrow form, is based, are entirely English… It is true that in

Hewit v. *Edinburgh and District Lathsplitters Association* (1906) 14 S.L.T. 489, a workman who had been dismissed from his employment as a result of threats of strike action made by officials of an unregistered trade union was held to have a good cause of action. The case, however, was decided in the Outer House and accepted as the relevant principle of law the decision in *Quinn* v. *Leathem* [1901] A.C. 495: in other words, it was decided on the basis of conspiracy rather than on intimidation as such. It can, however, be accepted that a wrong of the kind envisaged by the judges in *Rookes* v. *Barnard* falls within the generality of the Scottish rule of reparation. As is well known the general principle of Scots law is that a remedy exists and damages can be recovered for wrongful interference with person, property or freedom, and intimidation could easily be regarded as a species of *culpa*, though not as a separate tort. It does not seem that there is any objection in principle either to making intimidation by means of physical violence a wrong sounding in damages or to extending that wrong to cover threats of breach of contract as envisaged in *Rookes* v. *Barnard*. The general observations which led Lord Reid to approve of the extension of the English tort of intimidation are equally good ground for applying the general Scottish principle of reparation to such a case. It is for this reason that it is particularly important to note the element of policy and of deliberate extension in the case of *Rookes* v. *Barnard* itself. Indeed such a principle is perhaps even more appropriate in Scots law which has had a tendency to award damages for deliberate injury, even where the injurer was acting in pursuance of some legal right. (See McKechnie in *Encyclopaedia*, Vol. xii.). Further, the tendency in the law connected with trade disputes and the like has always been in Scotland to follow the English authorities. It may, therefore, safely be assumed that a wrong of the same kind as or parallel to the tort of intimidation will be recognised by the Scottish courts. Questions as to the scope of the wrong, of course, arise in Scotland as much as in England, and are no easier to solve.'

COMMENT

7.12.1   There have been no reported Scottish cases dealing with intimidation. It is, however, generally accepted that the view expressed above is accurate. Nonetheless, on a topic like this and despite the common market between the two jurisdictions, there is room for taking a distinctively Scottish view, if one exists. Professor Walker has approved the principle, basing it upon the Roman *actio quod metus causa* and cases collected in *Morison's Dictionary*. See generally, *Delict.*, 3.21–3.22 and Winfield and Jolowicz, pp. 508–513 for a full discussion and citation of English authority.

CHAPTER 8

NEGLIGENCE: DUTY

39. **McAlister or Donoghue (Appellant) v. Stevenson**
1932 S.C.(H.L.) 31

8.1.1 'On April 9, 1929, Mrs Mary McAlister or Donoghue brought an action against David Stevenson, aerated water manufacturer, Paisley, in which she claimed £500 as damages for injuries sustained by her through drinking ginger beer which had been manufactured by the defender.

8.1.2 The pursuer averred, *inter alia*: (Cond. 2) "at or about 8.50 p.m. on or about August 26, 1928, the pursuer was in the shop occupied by Francis Minchella, and known as Wellmeadow Café, at Wellmeadow Place, Paisley, with a friend. The said friend ordered for the pursuer ice cream, and ginger beer suitable to be used with ice cream as an iced drink. Her friend, acting as aforesaid, was supplied by the said Mr Minchella with a bottle of ginger beer manufactured by the defender for sale to members of the public. The said bottle was made of dark opaque glass, and the pursuer and her friend had no reason to suspect that the said bottle contained anything else than the aerated water. The said Mr Minchella poured some of the said ginger beer from the bottle into a tumbler containing the ice cream. The pursuer then drank some of the contents of the tumbler. Her friend then lifted the said ginger beer bottle and was pouring out the remainder of the contents into the said tumbler when a snail, which had been, unknown to the pursuer, her friend, or the said Mr Minchella, in the bottle, and was in a state of decomposition, floated out of the said bottle. In consequence of the nauseating sight of the snail in said circumstances, and of the noxious condition of the said snail-tainted ginger beer consumed by her, the pursuer sustained the shock and illness hereinafter condescended on. The said Mr Minchella also sold the pursuer's friend a pear and ice. The said ginger beer bottle was fitted with a metal cap over its mouth. On the side of the said bottle there was pasted a label containing, *inter alia*, the name and address of the defender, who was the manufacturer... (Cond. 3) "The shock and illness suffered by the pursuer were due to the fault of the defender."

. . . . . .

8.1.3 Lord Atkin: The question is whether the manufacturer of an article of drink sold by him to a distributor, in circumstances which prevent the distributor or the ultimate purchaser or consumer from discovering by inspection any defect, is under any legal duty to the ultimate purchaser or consumer to take reasonable care that the article is free from defect likely to cause injury to health. I do not think a more important problem has occupied your Lordships in your judicial capacity, important both because of its bearing on public health and because of the practical test which it applies to the system under which it arises. The case has to be determined in accordance with Scots law, but it has been a matter of agreement between the experienced counsel who argued this case, and it appears to be the basis of the judgment of the learned judges of the Court of Session, that, for the purposes of determining this problem, the laws of Scotland and of England are the same. I speak with little authority on this point, but my own research, such as it is, satisfies me that the principles of the law of Scotland on such a question as the present are identical with these of English law, and I discuss the issue on that footing. The law of both countries appears to be that, in order to support an action for damages for negligence, the complainant has to show that he has been injured by the breach of a duty owed to him in the circumstances by the defendant to take reasonable care to avoid such injury.

. . . . . .

8.1.4 It is remarkable how difficult it is to find in the English authorities statements of general application defining the relations between parties that give rise to the duty. The courts are concerned with the particular relations which come before them in actual litigation, and it is sufficient to say whether the duty exists in those circumstances. The result is that the courts have been engaged upon an elaborate classification of duties as they exist in respect of property, whether real or personal, with further divisions as to ownership, occupation, or control, and distinctions based on the particular relations of the one side or the other, whether manufacturer, salesman or landlord, customer, tenant, stranger, and so on... To seek a complete logical definition of the general principle is probably to go beyond the function of the judge, for the more general the definition the more likely it is to omit essentials or to introduce non-essentials. The attempt was made by Brett, M.R., in *Heaven* v. *Pender* (1883) 11 Q.B.D. 503 in a definition to which I will later refer. As framed, it was demonstrably too wide, although it appears to me, if properly limited, to be capable of affording a valuable practical guide.

. . . . . .

8.1.5 The liability for negligence, whether you style it such or treat it as in other systems as a species of "*culpa*", is no doubt based upon a general public sentiment of moral wrongdoing for which the offender must pay. But acts or omissions which any moral code would censure cannot, in a practical world, be treated so as to give a right to every person injured by them to demand relief. In this way rules of law arise which limit the range of complaints, and the extent of their remedy. The rule that you are to love your neighbour becomes in law, you must not injure your neighbour; and the lawyer's question, Who is my neighbour? receives a restricted reply. You must take reasonable care to avoid acts or omissions which you can reasonably foresee would be likely to injure your neighbour. Who, then, in law, is my neighbour? The answer seems to be — persons who are so closely and directly affected by my act that I ought reasonably to have them in contemplation as being so affected when I am directing my mind to the acts or omissions which are called in question. This appears to me to be the doctrine of *Heaven v. Pender* as laid down by Lord Esher (then Brett, M.R.), when it is limited by the notion of proximity introduced by Lord Esher himself and A. L. Smith, L.J., in *Le Lievre v. Gould* [1893] 1 Q.B. 491.

8.1.6 I draw particular attention to the fact that Lord Esher emphasises the necessity of goods having to be "used immediately" and "used at once before a reasonable opportunity of inspection". This is obviously to exclude the possibility of goods having their condition altered by lapse of time, and to call attention to the proximate relationship, which may be too remote where inspection even of the person using, certainly of an intermediate person, may reasonably be interposed... There will no doubt arise cases where it will be difficult to determine whether the contemplated relationship is so close that the duty arises. But in the class of case now before the court I cannot conceive any difficulty to arise... It is said that the law of England and Scotland is that the poisoned consumer has no remedy against the negligent manufacturer. If this were the result of the authorities, I should consider the result a grave defect in the law, and so contrary to principle that I should hesitate long before following any decision in that effect which had not the authority of this House. I would point out that, in the assumed state of the authorities, not only would the consumer have no remedy against any one other than the manufacturer, and, except in the case of a consumer who was also a purchaser, no contract and no warranty of fitness, and, in the case of the purchase of a specific article under its patent or trade name (which might well be the case in the purchase of some articles of food or drink), no warranty protecting even the purchaser-consumer... I confine myself to articles of common household use, where everyone, including the manufacturer, knows that the articles will be used by other persons than the actual ultimate purchaser — namely, by members of his family and his servants, and in some cases his guests. I do not think so ill of our jurisprudence as to suppose that its principles are so remote from the ordinary needs of civilised society and the ordinary claims it makes upon its members as to deny a legal remedy where there is obviously a social wrong.

. . . . . .

8.1.8 A very recent case which has the authority of this House is *Oliver* v. *Saddler & Co.*, 1929 S.C.(H.L.) 94. In that case a firm of stevedores employed to unload a cargo of maize in bags provided the rope slings by which the cargo was raised to the ship's deck by their own men using the ship's tackle, and then transported to the dockside by the shore porters, of whom the pursuer was one. The porters relied on examination by the stevedores, and had themselves no opportunity of examination. In these circumstances this House, reversing the decision of the First Division, held that there was a duty owed by the stevedore company to the porters to see that the slings were fit for use, and restored the judgment of the Lord Ordinary, Lord Morison, in favour of the pursuer. I find no trace of the doctrine of invitation [invitation to use a chattel] in the opinion expressed in this House, of which mine was one; the decision was based upon the fact that the direct relation established, especially the circumstances that the injured porter had no opportunity of independent examination, gave rise to a duty to be careful.

. . . . . .

8.1.9 I do not find it necessary to discuss at length the case dealing with duties where the thing is dangerous, or, in the narrow category, belongs to a class of things which are dangerous in themselves. I regard the distinction as an unnatural one so far as it is used to serve as a logical differentiation by which to distinguish the existence or non-existence of a legal right. In this respect I agree with what was said by Scrutton, L.J., in *Hodge & Sons* v. *Anglo-American Oil Co.* (1922) 12 Ll.L.Rep. 183 at p. 187, a case which was ultimately decided on a question of fact. "Personally, I do not understand the difference between a thing dangerous in itself, as poison, and a thing not dangerous as a class, but by negligent construction dangerous as a particular thing. The latter, if anything seems the more dangerous of the two; it is a wolf in sheep's clothing instead of an obvious wolf." [Lord Atkin then proceeded to distinguish two cases, one of which was] *Caledonian Railway Co.* v. *Mulholland or Warwick* (1897) 25 R.(H.L.) 1, in which the appellant railway company were held not liable for injuries caused by a defective brake on a coal wagon conveyed by them to a point in the transit where their contract ended, and where the wagons were taken over for haulage for the last part of the journey by a second railway company, on which part the accident happened. It was held that the first railway company were under no duty to injured workmen to examine the wagon for defects at the end of their contractual haulage. There was ample opportunity for inspection by the second railway company. The relations were not proximate.

. . . . . .

8.1.10 It is always a satisfaction to an English lawyer to be able to test his application of fundamental principles of the common law by the development of the same doctrine by the lawyers of the courts of the United States. In that country I find that the law appears to be well established in the sense in which I have indicated. The mouse had emerged from the ginger beer bottle in the United States before it appeared in Scotland, but there it brought liability upon the manufacturer... If your Lordships accept the view that this pleading discloses a relevant cause of action, you will be affirming the proposition that by Scots and English law alike a manufacturer of products, which he sells in such form as to show that he intends them to reach the ultimate consumer in the form in which they left him, with no reasonable possibility of intermediate examination, and with the knowledge that the absence of reasonable care in the preparation or putting up of the products will result in an injury to the consumer's life or property, owes a duty to the consumer to take that reasonable care.

It is a proposition which I venture to say no one in Scotland or England who was not a lawyer would for one moment doubt. It will be an advantage to make it clear that the law in this matter, as in most others, is in accordance with sound common sense. I think that this appeal should be allowed.

. . . . . .

8.1.11 LORD THANKERTON: ... The duties which the appellant accuses the respondent of having neglected may be summarised as follows: (a) that the ginger beer was manufactured by the respondent or his servants to be sold as an article of drink to members of the public (including the appellant), and that accordingly it was his duty to exercise the greatest care in order that snails would not get into the bottles, render the ginger beer dangerous and harmful, and be sold with the ginger beer; (b) a duty to provide a system of working his business which would not allow snails to get into the bottles, and, in particular, would not allow the bottles when washed to stand in places to which snails had access; (c) a duty to provide an efficient system of inspection which would prevent snails from being in the sealed bottles; and (d) a duty to provide clear bottles so as to facilitate the said system of inspection. There can be no doubt, in my opinion, that, equally in the law of Scotland and the law of England, it lies upon the party claiming redress in such a case to show that there was some relation of duty between her and the defender which required the defender to exercise due and reasonable care for her safety... It is necessary for the pursuer in such an action to show that there was a duty owed to her by the defender, because a man cannot be charged with negligence if he has no obligation to exercise diligence... We are not dealing here with a case of what is called an article *per se* dangerous, or one which was known by the defender to be dangerous, in which cases a special duty of protection or adequate warning is placed upon the person who uses or distributes it.

8.1.12 The present case is that of a manufacturer and a consumer, with whom he has no contractual relation, of an article which the manufacturer did not know to be dangerous; and, unless the consumer can establish a special relationship with the manufacturer, it is clear, in my opinion, that neither the law of Scotland nor the law of England will hold that the manufacturer has any duty towards the consumer to exercise diligence... I am aware that the American courts, in the decision referred to by my noble and learned friend Lord Macmillan, have taken a view more favourable to the consumer.

8.1.13 The special circumstances from which the appellant claims that such a relationship of duty should be inferred may, I think, be stated thus, namely, that the respondent, in placing his manufactured article of drink upon the market, has intentionally so excluded interference with, or examination of, the article by any intermediate handler of the goods between himself and the consumer that he has, of his own accord, brought himself into direct relationship with the consumer, with the result that the consumer is entitled to rely upon the exercise of diligence by the manufacturer to secure that the article shall not be harmful to the consumer... In my opinion, the existence of a legal duty under such circumstances is in conformity with the principles of both the law of Scotland and the law of England. The English cases demonstrate how impossible it is to catalogue finally, amid the ever-varying types of human relationships, those relationships in which a duty to exercise care arises apart from contract, and each of these cases relates to its own set of circumstances, out of which it was claimed that the duty had arisen.

. . . . . .

8.1.14 The cases of *Mullen* and *McGowan*, 1929 S.C. 461, which the learned judges of the Second Division followed in the present case, related to the facts similar in every respect, except that the foreign matter was a decomposed mouse. In these cases the same court (Lord Hunter dissenting) held that the manufacturer owed no duty to the consumer. The view of the majority was that the English authorities excluded the existence of such a duty, but Lord Ormidale (at p. 471) would otherwise have been prepared to come to a contrary conclusion. Lord Hunter's opinion seems to be in conformity with the view I have expressed above... I am therefore of opinion that the appeal should be allowed, and that the case should be remitted for proof, as the pursuer did not ask for an issue.

8.1.15 LORD MACMILLAN: ... At your Lordship's bar counsel for both parties to the present appeal, accepting, as I do also, the view that there is no distinction between the law of Scotland and the law of England in the legal principles applicable to the case, confined their arguments to the English authorities... [In] the discussion of the topic which now engages your Lordship's attention two rival principles of the law find a meeting place where each has contended for supremacy. On the one hand, there is the well-established principle that no one other than a party to a contract can complain of a breach of that contract. On the other hand, there is the equally well-established doctrine that negligence apart from contract gives a right of action to the party injured by that negligence — and here I use the term negligence, of course, in its technical legal sense, implying a duty owed and neglected. The fact that there is a contractual relationship between the parties, which may give rise to an action for breach of contract, does not exclude the co-existence of a right of action founded on negligence as between the same parties, independently of the contract, although arising out of the relationship in fact brought about by the contract. Of this the best illustration is the right of the injured railway passenger to sue the railway company either for breach of contract of safe carriage or for negligence in carrying him. And there is no reason why the same set of facts should not give one person a right of action in contract and another person a right of action in tort.

. . . . . .

8.1.16 Where, as in cases like the present, so much depends upon the avenue of approach to the question, it is very easy to take the wrong turning. If you begin with the sale by the manufacturer to the retail dealer, then the consumer who purchases from the retailer is at once seen to be a stranger to the contract between the retailer and the manufacturer and so disentitled to sue upon it. There is no contractual relation between the manufacturer and the consumer; and thus the plaintiff, if he is to succeed, is driven to try to bring himself within one or other of the exceptional cases where the strictness of the rule that none but a party to a contract can found on a breach of that contract has been mitigated in the public interest, as it has been in the case of a person who issues a chattel which is inherently dangerous or which he knows to be in a dangerous condition. If, on the other hand, you disregard the fact that the circumstances of the case at one stage include the existence of a contract for sale between the manufacturer and the retailer, and approach the question by asking whether there is evidence of carelessness on the part of the manufacturer, and whether he owed a duty to be careful in a question with the party who had been injured in consequence of his want of care, the circumstance that the injured party was not a party to the incidental contract of sale becomes irrelevant, and his title to sue the manufacturer is unaffected by that circumstance. The appellant in the present instance asks that her case be approached as a case of delict, not as a case of breach of contract... I rather regard this type of case as a special instance of negligence where the law exacts a degree of diligence so stringent as to amount practically to a guarantee of safety.

. . . . . .

8.1.17   The law takes no cognisance of carelessness in the abstract. It concerns itself with carelessness only where there is a duty to take care and where failure in that duty has caused damage. In such circumstances carelessness assumes the legal quality of negligence, and entails the consequences in law of negligence. What then are the circumstances which give rise to this duty to take care? In the daily contacts of social and business life, human beings are thrown into, or place themselves in, an infinite variety of relations with their fellows; and the law can refer only to the standards of the reasonable man in order to determine whether any particular relation gives rise to a duty to take care as between those who stand in that relation to each other. The grounds of action may be as various and manifold as human errancy; and the conception of legal responsibility may develop in adaptation to altering social conditions and the changing circumstances of life. The categories of negligence are never closed. The cardinal principle of liability is that the party complained of should owe to the party complaining a duty to take care, and that the party complaining should be able to prove that he has suffered damage in consequence of a breach of that duty. Where there is room for diversity of view, it is in determining what circumstances will establish such a relationship between the parties as to give rise, on the one side, to duty to take care, and, on the other side, to a right to have care taken. To descend from these generalities to the circumstances of the present case, I do not think that any reasonable man, or any 12 reasonable men, would hesitate to hold that, if the appellant establishes her allegations, the respondent has exhibited carelessness in the conduct of his business. For a manufacturer of aerated water to store his empty bottles in a place where snails can get access to them, and to fill his bottles without taking any adequate precautions, by inspection or otherwise to ensure that they contain no deleterious foreign matter, may reasonably be characterised as carelessness, without applying too exacting a standard.

. . . . . .

8.1.18 Now, I have no hesitation in affirming that a person, who for gain engages in the business of manufacturing articles of food and drink intended for consumption by members of the public in the form in which he issues them, is under a duty to take care in the manufacture of these articles. That duty, in my opinion, he owes to those whom he intends to consume his products... It is sometimes said that liability can only arise where a reasonable man would have foreseen, and could have avoided, the consequences of his act or omission. In the present case the respondent, when he manufactured his ginger beer, had directly in contemplation that it would be consumed by members of the public. Can it be said that he could not be expected as a reasonable man to foresee that, if he conducted his process of manufacture carelessly, he might injure those whom he expected and desired to consume his ginger beer? The possibility of injury so arising seems to me in no sense so remote as to excuse him from seeing it... The recognition by counsel that the law of Scotland applicable to the case was the same as the law of England implied that there was no special doctrine of Scots law which either the appellant or the respondent could invoke to support her or his case; and your Lordships have thus been relieved of the necessity of a separate consideration of the law of Scotland. For myself, I am satisfied that there is no speciality of Scots law involved, and that the case may safely be decided on principles common to both systems. I am happy to think that in their relation to the practical problem of everyday life which this appeal presents, the legal systems of the two countries are in no way at variance, and that the principles of both alike are sufficiently consonant with justice and common sense to admit of the claim which the appellant seeks to establish.

. . . . . .

8.1.19 The burden of proof must always be upon the injured party to establish that the defect which caused the injury was present in the article when it left the hands of the party whom he sues; and that the circumstances are such as to cast upon the defender a duty to take care not to injure the pursuer. There is no presumption of negligence in such a case as the present, nor is there any justification for applying the maxim *res ipsa loquitur*. Negligence must be both averred and proved... I am accordingly of the opinion that this appeal should be allowed.

8.1.20 LORD BUCKMASTER (dissenting) (read by Lord Tomlin): The facts of this case are simple... As a result she alleged, and at this stage her allegations must be accepted as true, that she suffered from shock and severe gastro-enteritis... The foundation of her case is that the respondent, as the manufacturer of an article intended for consumption and contained in a receptacle which prevented inspection, owed a duty to her as consumer of the article to take care that there was no noxious element in the goods, and that he neglected such duty and is consequently liable for any damage caused by such neglect. After certain amendments, which are now immaterial, the case came before the Lord Ordinary, who rejected the first plea in law of the respondent and allowed a proof. His interlocutor was recalled and the action dismissed by the Second Division of the Court of Session, from whose judgment this appeal has been brought.

8.1.21   Before examining the merits two comments are desirable:— (1) that the appellant's case rests solely on the ground of a tort based not on fraud but on negligence; and (2) that throughout the appeal the case had been argued on the basis, undisputed by the Second Division and never questioned by counsel for the appellant or by any of your Lordships, that the English and the Scots law on the subject are identical. It is therefore upon the English law alone that I have considered the matter, and, in my opinion, it is on the English law alone that, in the circumstances, we ought to proceed.

. . . . . .

8.1.22   The dicta of Brett, M.R., in *Heaven* v. *Pender* [1883] 11 Q.B.D. 503 at p. 509 are rightly relied on by the appellant. The material passage is as follows: "The proposition which these recognised cases suggest, and which is, therefore, to be deduced from them, is that whenever one person is by circumstances placed in such a position with regard to another that everyone of ordinary sense who did think would at once recognise that if he did not use ordinary care and skill in his own conduct with regard to those circumstances he would cause danger of injury to the person or property of the other, a duty arises to use ordinary care and skill to avoid such danger... Let us apply this proposition to the case of one person supplying goods or machinery, or instruments or utensils, or the like, for the purpose of their being used by another person, but with whom there is no contract as to the supply. The proposition will stand thus: Whenever one person supplies goods, or machinery, or the like, for the purpose of their being used by another person under such circumstances that everyone of ordinary sense would, if he thought, recognise at once that unless he used ordinary care and skill with regard to the condition of the thing supplied or the mode of supplying it, there will be danger of injury to the person or property of him for whose use the thing is supplied, and who is to use it, a duty arises to use ordinary care and skill as to the condition or manner of supplying such thing. And, for neglect of such ordinary care or skill whereby injury happens, a legal liability arises to be enforced by an action for negligence. This includes the case of goods, etc., supplied to be used immediately by a particular person or persons or one of a class of persons, where it would be obvious to the person supplying, if he thought, that the goods would in all probability be used once by such persons before a reasonable opportunity for discovering any defect which might exist, and where the thing supplied would be such a nature that a neglect of ordinary care of skill as to its condition or the manner of supplying it would probably cause danger to the person or property of the person for whose use it was supplied, and who was about to use it. It would exclude a case in which the goods are supplied under circumstances in which it would be a chance by whom they would be used or whether they would be used or not, or whether before there would probably be means of observing any defect, or where the goods would be of such a nature that a want of care or skill as to their condition or the manner of supplying them would not probably produce danger of injury to persons or property. The cases of vendor and purchaser and lender and hirer under contract need not be considered, as the liability arises under the contract, and not merely as a duty imposed by law, though it may not be useless to observe that it seems difficult to import the implied obligation into the contract except in cases in which if there were no contract between the parties the law would accordingly to the rule above stated imply the duty."

. . . . . .

8.1.23 In [*Le Lievre v. Gould* [1893] 1 Q.B.D. 503] Lord Esher seems to have qualified to some extent what he said in *Heaven* v. *Pender*, for he says this (at p. 497): "But can the plaintiffs rely upon negligence in the absence of fraud? The question of liability for negligence cannot arise at all until it is established that the man who has been negligent owed some duty to the person who seeks to make him liable for his negligence. What duty is there when there is no relation between the parties by contract? A man is entitled to be as negligent as he pleases towards the whole world if he owes no duty to them. The case of *Heaven* v. *Pender* has no bearing upon the present question. That case established that, under certain circumstances, one man may owe a duty to another even though there is no contract between them. If one man is near to another, or is near to the property of another, a duty lies upon him not to do that which may cause personal injury to that other, or may injure his property"... In my view, therefore, the authorities are against the appellant's contention; and, apart from authority, it is difficult to see how any common law proposition can be formulated to support her claim.

. . . . . .

8.1.24 In *Mullen* v. *Barr & Co.*, 1929 S.C. 461, a case indistinguishable from the present excepting upon the ground that a mouse is not a snail, and necessarily adopted by the Second Division in their judgment, Lord Anderson says this (at p. 479): "In a case like the present, where the goods of the defenders are widely distributed throughout Scotland, it would seem little short of outrageous to make them responsible to members of the public for the condition of the contents of every bottle which issued from their works. It is obvious that, if such responsibility attached to the defenders, they might be called on to meet claims of damages which they could not possibly investigate or answer." In agreeing, as I do, with the judgment of Lord Anderson, I desire to add that I find it hard to dissent from the emphatic nature of the language with which his judgment is clothed. I am of the opinion that this appeal should be dismissed, and I beg to move your Lordships accordingly.'

COMMENT

8.2.1 Decided: May 26, 1932.
March 2: Charles Lindbergh's son kidnapped.
April 10: Hindenburg defeated Hitler in presidential election.
May 10: French president Doumer assassinated.

8.2.2 Mr Minchella's Wellmeadow Cafè no longer stands. To find out more about the lawyer who put the question to which Lord Atkin refers at 8.1.5 read (or re-read) Luke 10, 25–35. To read more about the potential liability of a person following the moral lead of the volunteer in Luke 10, 30 see Cullen, W.D., "The Liability of the Good Samaritan", 1995 J.R. 20. See also para 12.1.19.

8.2.3 Read Alan Rodger's reconstruction of the facts of the case and his attempt to sketch a life of Mrs Donoghue at 1988 C.L.P. 1. As he points out, the friend, according to one of the speeches in the House, was a woman. Harlow at p. 40, perhaps anticipating Mrs Donoghue's future matrimonial problems, has the friend of the opposite sex — indeed a "young man". See also Heuston at (1957) 20 M.L.R. 2. See Lord Rodgers "Lord MacMillan's Speech in *Donoghue v. Stevenson*" (1992) 108 L.Q.R. 236 for an earlier "Scottish" draft (March 1932). The article explores the reasons for a difference in the final version. (See 8.1.3; 8.1.11; 8.1.15; 8.1.20.)
Lord Rodger's biographical approach has been followed by Professor W. W. McBryde. "Donoghue v. Stevenson: The story of the 'snail in the bottle' case," in *Obligations in Context* (1990), p. 13.

8.2.4 What exactly is the *ratio* of the case?

8.2.5 One *ratio* of the case covers personal injury or damage to property. If the consumer suffers economic loss, then different rules apply: see particularly *Muirhead v. Industrial Tank Specialties* [1985] 3 All E.R. 705.

8.2.6 A Mrs Donoghue today would rely instead upon the Consumer Protection Act 1987, Pt. 1 (Ext. 65; *Delict*, 7.12–22). However, where property damaged is not worth £275, the common law applies. There is no fixed liability level for a personal injuries case. In common law cases the evidential burden established in *Grant v. Australian Knitting Mills* [1936] A.C. 85 will be of value.

40. Bourhill (Appellant) v. Young
1942 S.C.(H.L.) 78

8.3.1 'The facts established at a proof before the Lord Ordinary were briefly as follows: On October 11, 1938 John Young, riding a motor bicycle, overtook and passed on its near side a tramway car which was halted at a stopping place upon a main road. A motor car, coming along the main road from the opposite direction, turned to its right and crossed in front of the tramway car in order to enter a side road which joined the main road some 40 or 50 feet away from the stopping place and from the front of the stationary tramway car. The motor cyclist was driving too fast and without due care, and ran into the motor car just as it was about to enter the side road. The collision was wholly due to his negligence and resulted in his death. The pursuer, who was a fishwife, had been a passenger on the tramway and had got down and gone round the front of the tramway car to the off-side of the driver's platform to get her creel, which she had left there. At the moment of the collision she was standing on the road with her back to the tramway car getting the creel on to her back. She did not see and could not have seen, the collision, but she proved that the noise of the collision had produced in her a fright or terror which resulted in nervous shock, but she explained in her record "that the pursuer's terror did not involve any element of reasonable fear of immediate bodily injury to herself". Averments that injury to her back and the still-birth of a child were due to what happened were not, in the opinion of the Lord Ordinary, established... The defender did not dispute that the pursuer had sustained a nervous shock which had affected her business, and the House decided that the argument on liability should be completed before any question as to the extent of the pursuer's injuries was considered.

. . . . . .

8.3.2 LORD RUSSELL OF KILLOWEN: ... In considering whether a person owes to another a duty a breach of which will render him liable to that other in damages for negligence, it is material to consider what the defendant ought to have contemplated as a reasonable man. This consideration may play a double rôle. It is relevant in cases of admitted negligence (where the duty and breach are admitted) to the question of remoteness of damage, *i.e.* to the question of compensation not to culpability, but it is also relevant in testing the existence of a duty as the foundation of the alleged negligence, *i.e.* to the question of culpability not to compensation.

. . . . . .

8.3.3 We heard a lengthy argument addressed to the questions whether *Hambrook* v. *Stokes Brothers* [1925] 1 K.B. 141 was rightly decided, and if so, whether the decision was in accordance with the law of Scotland as expounded in the numerous Scottish decisions cited to us. In the view which I have taken of the present case it is unnecessary to express a final view upon these questions. I will only say that, as at present advised, I see no reason why the laws of the two countries should differ in this respect, and I prefer the dissenting

judgment of Sargant L.J. to the decision of the majority in *Hambrook* v.
Stokes Brothers. It was said by counsel for the appellant that it was
impossible to affirm the interlocutor under appeal without
disapproving of the decision in *Hambrook* v. *Stokes Brothers*. I do not
agree, for the simple reason that in that case the negligence, which
was the basis of the claim, was admitted, whereas in the present case
we are affirming because John Young was guilty of no negligence in
relation to the appellant.

8.3.4 LORD MACMILLAN: It is established that the appellant suffered
in her health and in her ability to do her work by reason of the shock
which she sustained when a motor cycle ridden by the deceased John
Young collided with a motor car in her vicinity. The question for decision
is whether the respondent, as representing the late John Young, can be
rendered accountable at law for what the appellant has suffered.

It is no longer necessary to consider whether the infliction of what
is called mental shock may constitute an actionable wrong. The crude
view that the law should take cognisance only of physical injury
resulting from actual impact has been discarded, and it is now well
recognised that an action will lie for injury by shock sustained through
the medium of the eye or the ear without direct contact... But in the
case of mental shock there are elements of greater subtlety than in
the case of an ordinary physical injury, and these elements may give
rise to debate as to the precise scope of legal liability.

8.3.5 Your Lordships have here to deal with a common law action
founded on negligence... She can recover damages only if she can
show that in relation to her the late John Young acted negligently. To
establish this she must show that he owed her a duty of care which he
failed to observe, and that, as a result of this failure in duty on his
part, she suffered as she did... In dealing with a case of alleged
negligence it is thus necessary to ascertain, first, what in the
circumstances was the duty of the person alleged to be in fault, and,
second, to whom that duty was owed.

8.3.6 The late John Young was riding a motor bicycle in an
Edinburgh street. What duty then was incumbent on him? It cannot
be better or more succinctly put than it was by Lord Jamieson in the
Second Division in the present case, when he said that "the duty of a
driver is to use proper care not to cause injury to persons on the
highway or in premises adjoining the highway."

. . . . . .

8.3.7 The duty to take care is the duty to avoid doing or omitting to
do anything the doing or omitting to do which may have as its
reasonable and probable consequence injury to others, and the duty
is owed to those to whom injury may reasonably and probably be
anticipated if the duty is not observed.

There is no absolute standard of what is reasonable and probable. It must depend on circumstances and must always be a question of degree. In the present instance the late John Young was clearly negligent in a question with the occupants of the motor car with which his cycle collided. He was driving at an excessive speed in a public thoroughfare and he ought to have foreseen that he might consequently collide with any vehicle which he might meet in his course, for such an occurrence may reasonably and probably be expected to ensue from driving at a high speed in a street. But can it be said that he ought further to have foreseen that his excessive speed, involving the possibility of collision with another vehicle, might cause injury by shock to the appellant? The appellant was not within his line of vision, for she was on the other side of a tramway car which was standing between him and her when he passed, and it was not until he had proceeded some distance beyond her that he collided with the motor-car... I am of opinion with the majority of the learned judges of the Second Division that the late John Young was under no duty to the appellant to foresee that his negligence in driving at an excessive speed and consequently colliding with a motor car might result in injury to her; for such a result could not reasonably and probably be anticipated. He was therefore, not guilty of negligence in a question with the appellant.

8.3.8   This is sufficient for the disposal of the case and absolves me from considering the question whether injury through mental shock is actionable only when, in the words of Kennedy J., the shock arises from a reasonable fear of immediate personal injury to oneself (*Dulieu* v. *White & Sons* [1901] 2 K.B. 669) which was admittedly not the case in the present instance. It also absolves me from considering whether, if the late John Young neglected any duty which he owed to the appellant which, in my opinion, he did not, the injury of which she complains was too remote to entitle her to damages.

· · · · · ·

8.3.9   On the second point it was argued that once an act is properly characterised as negligent, that is to say, as a breach of a duty of care owed to a particular person, then the party at fault is liable to that person for everything that directly follows from the negligent act, whether or not it could have been foreseen as a natural and probable result of the negligent act. For this *Re Polemis and Furness, Withy & Co.* [1921] 3 K.B. 560 was cited. Whether the law there laid down is consonant with the law of England it will be for this House to pronounce when the occasion arises. As at present advised, I doubt if it is the law of Scotland, and I could cite ample authority to the contrary, but, again, this is not a point which I deem it necessary to discuss now. I am, accordingly, for affirming the decision of the Second Division of the Court of Session and dismissing the appeal.

· · · · · ·

8.3.10 Lord Wright: ... The present case, like many others of this type, may, however, raise the different question whether the appellant's illness was not due to her peculiar susceptibility. She was eight months gone in pregnancy. Can it be said, apart from everything else, that it was likely that a person of normal nervous strength would have been affected in the circumstances by illness as the appellant was? Does the criterion of reasonable foresight extend beyond people of ordinary health or susceptibility, or does it take into account the peculiar susceptibilities or infirmities of these affected which the defendant neither knew of nor could reasonably be taken to have foreseen?... One who suffers from the terrible tendency to bleed on slight contact, which is denoted by the term "a bleeder", cannot complain if he mixes with the crowd, and suffers severely, perhaps fatally, from being merely brushed against. There is no wrong done there. A blind or deaf man who crosses the traffic on a busy street cannot complain if he is run over by a careful driver who does not know of, and could not be expected to observe and guard against, the man's infirmity. These questions go to "culpability, not compensation": as Bankes L.J. said in the *Polemis* case. No doubt, it has long ago been stated and often restated that, if the wrong is established, the wrongdoer must take the victim as he finds him. That, however, is only true, as the *Polemis* case shows, on the condition that the wrong has been established or admitted. The question of liability is anterior to the question of the measure of the consequences which go with the liability.

8.3.11 What is now being considered is the question of liability, and this, I think, in a question whether there is duty owing to members of the public who come within the ambit of the act, must generally depend on a normal standard of susceptibility... It is here, as elsewhere, a question of what the hypothetical reasonable man, viewing the position, I suppose *ex post facto*, would say it was proper to foresee... The lawyer likes to draw fixed and definite lines and is apt to ask where the thing is to stop. I should reply it should stop where in the particular case the good sense of the jury or of the judge decides... I may add that the issue of duty or no duty is, indeed, a question for the court, but it depends on the view taken of the facts.

. . . . . .

8.3.12 I have carefully considered all the authorities cited, and it may well be that some day this House will have to examine the exact meaning and effect of what Kennedy J. said in *Dulieu* v. *White & Sons.* He was, he said, inclined to think that there was at least one limitation: "the shock where it operates through the mind must be a shock which arises from a reasonable fear of immediate personal injury to oneself." That statement, if meant to lay down a rigid rule of law, has been overruled by the Court of Appeal in *Hambrook* v. *Stokes Brothers*, which now lays down the English law unless it is set aside by this House. As at present advised, I agree with that decision.

8.3.13 In *Hambrook* v. *Stokes Brothers* the defendant's lorry was left unattended and improperly braked at the top of a steep and narrow street with the engine running, with the result that it started off by itself and ran violently down the hill, putting the plaintiff in fear for the safety of her children, whom she had just left, and thereby causing a serious illness and ultimately her death.'

COMMENT

8.4.1 Decided: Aug. 5, 1942.

June 7: U.S. Navy won the battle of Midway against the Japanese.

June 10: Himmler killed entire male population of Lidice, near Prague, as a reprisal for the assassination of Heydrich.

July 2: Churchill wins vote of censure over conduct of war by 450 votes.

8.4.2 The plaintiff (the deceased's husband) recovered in *Hambrook v. Stokes*.

8.4.3 Lord Porter mentioned and impliedly accepted the decision in *Walker v. Pitlochry Motor Co.*, 1930 S.C. 565, where damages were recovered for shock on the sight of injury caused to a near relative. Accordingly, and in any event, Scots lawyers can accept the slightly more pro-pursuer decision of *McLaughlin v. O'Brian* [1983] A.C. 410, which is now one of the leading authorities on the particular topic of nervous shock. That case does no more than apply the same principle. What it did do, though, was dispel the possibility that it should invariably be the case that a person should be within the area of the actual incident. It also made it quite clear that the floodgates argument is not one which should be immediately applied (see *Delict*, 5.15–5.19). Accordingly *McLaughlin* was influential in *Junior Books* (Ext. 52). In *McLaughlin* Lord Wilberforce in particular tried to give an indication of cases which would in general not be foreseeable as being too remote. Harm to strangers, incidents happening distant in time or space and shock resulting from media other than one's own senses might not be within the scope or ambit of the defender's duty.

8.4.4 The guidelines set out in *McLaughlin* were tested in the most recent House of Lords examination of nervous shock: *Alcock v. Chief Constable of South Yorkshire Police* [1992] 1 A.C. 310 (*Delict*, 5.19). It decided that the category of plaintiffs is not limited to parents and children and husbands and wives. A fiancé was within the category of allowed closeness — a brother and a brother-in-law were not. Generally presence at the locus is required and seeing an event on television as in this case (a disaster at the Hillsborough football stadium) is inadequate. Teff has convincingly argued that comments in *Alcock* have brought about a perceived need for the pursuer to have experienced a sudden shock rather than an accumulation of events, making some aftermath cases difficult even for closely related parties. Teff, H., "The requirement of 'sudden shock' in liability for negligently inflicted, psychiatric damage" [1996] Tort L.R. 44, citing *inter alia Taylor v. Somerset Health Authority* [1993] 4 Med. L.R. 34; *Taylorson v. Shieldness Product Ltd* [1994] PIQR 329; *Sion v. Hampstead Health Authority* [1994] 5 Med. L.R. 170; *Tredget and Tredget v. Bexley Health Authority* [1994] 5 Med. L.R. 178. What do you think of "sudden shock"?

8.4.5 The House of Lords turned to the topic once more in *Page v. Smith* [1995] 2 W.L.R. 644. The plaintiff was in a car crash. He did not suffer personal injury. His ME syndrome got worse after the accident. It was held that as a "primary" victim the *McLaughlin/Alcock* rules did not require to be considered. Do you agree that there are primary and secondary victims? What do you think of Lord Keith's dissent? See also Brodie, D., "Primary and Secondary Nervous Shock", 1995 Rep. B. 5–2.

8.4.6   Consider the case of the workers whose workmate was blown off the Forth Road Bridge. *Robertson v. Forth Road Bridge (No. 1)*, 1994 S.L.T. 566; *(No. 2)* 1994 S.L.T. 568; and in the Inner House, 1996 S.L.T. 263. It attempts to apply *Alcock*.

After proof before answer it was held that there was not a sufficient tie of affection between employees. In one case they had known each other for years and had gone out socially. The fact the pursuers were co-employees did not affect the result. The pursuers did not take part in the precise operation which resulted in the deceased being blown from the bridge. But they were all working together at the time. Have you any sympathy with Lord Cowie's near dissent?

Reconsider this case in light of *Page v. Smith* [1995] 2 W.L.R. 644.

8.4.7   The term most often used in discussion is no longer "nervous shock" but Post Traumatic Stress Disorder. (See Bibliography, p. 549.) An attempt to defend a case because the illness was "grief" rather than PTSD failed: *Vernon v. Bosley*, 1996 April 4, C.A.

The condition has to be caused by the accident rather than anger at the defenders: *Graham v. David A. Hall*, 1996 S.L.T. 596. The opinion in *Whyte v. Nestlé*, March 5, 1997, unreported, contains a review of PTSD.

8.4.8   The policemen who attended the Hillsborough incident giving rise to *Alcock* (8.4.4) claimed for their shock. In *Frost v. Chief Constable of South Yorkshire Police* [1995] T.L.R. 379 the claim failed because officers were meant to be tough enough. But in June 1996 it was reported (*The Times*, June 4, 1996) that settlements were made with 14 officers for £1.2 million damages. The chairman of the Hillsborough Families' Support Group, who lost two daughters in the tragedy said, "I'm gutted and I've had several families on to me who are appalled." How would you explain to him that the result is legally correct? Lawyers who had not argued a PTSD case in a certain way were sued but escaped liability by showing that the former client was only a secondary victim: *McFarlane v. Wilkinson* [1997] T.L.R. 69.

41. Hughes (Appellant) v. Lord Advocate
1963 S.L.T. 150 (H.L.)

8.5.1   'LORD REID: I am satisfied that the Post Office workmen were in fault in leaving this open manhole unattended; and it is clear that if they had done as they ought to have done this would not have happened. It cannot be said that they owed no duty to the appellant. But it has been held that the appellant cannot recover damages.

It was argued that the appellant cannot recover because the damages which he suffered were of a kind which was not foreseeable. That was not the ground of judgment of the First Division or of the Lord Ordinary and the facts proved do not, in my judgment, support that argument. The appellant's injuries were mainly caused by burns; and it cannot be said that injuries from burns were unforeseeable. As a warning to traffic the workmen had set lighted red lamps round the tent which covered the manhole; and if boys did enter the dark tent it was very likely that they would take one of these lamps with them. If the lamp fell and broke, it was not at all unlikely that the boy would be burned, and the burns might well be serious. No doubt it was not to be expected that the injuries would be as serious as those which the appellant in fact sustained. But a defender is liable, although the damage may be a good deal greater in extent than was foreseeable. He can only escape liability if the damage can be regarded as differing in kind from what was foreseeable.

8.5.2 So we have (first) a duty owed by the workmen, (secondly) the fact that if they had done as they ought to have done there would have been no accident, and (thirdly) the fact that the injuries suffered by the appellant, though perhaps different in degree, did not differ in kind from injuries which might have resulted from an accident of a foreseeable nature. The ground on which this case has been decided against the appellant is that the accident was of an unforeseeable type. Of course, the pursuer has to prove that the defender's fault caused the accident, and there could be a case where the intrusion of a new and unexpected factor could be regarded as the cause of the accident rather than the fault of the defender. But that is not this case. The cause of this accident was a known source of danger, the lamp; but it behaved in an unpredictable way.

The explanation of the accident which has been accepted, and which I would not seek to question, is that, when the lamp fell down the manhole and was broken, some paraffin escaped, and enough was vaporised to create an explosive mixture which was detonated by the naked light of the lamp. The experts agree that no one would have expected that to happen: it was so unlikely as to be unforeseeable. The explosion caused the boy to fall into the manhole: whether his injuries were directly caused by the explosion or aggravated by fires which started in the manhole, is not at all clear. The essential step in the respondent's argument is that the explosion was the real cause of the injuries, and that the explosion was unforeseeable.

8.5.3 The only authority cited to us from which the respondent can derive any assistance is *Muir* v. *Glasgow Corporation*, 1943 S.C. (H.L.) 3, 1944 S.L.T. 60…; This accident was caused by a known source of danger, but caused in a way which could not have been foreseeable, and in my judgment that affords no defence. I would, therefore, allow the appeal.

8.5.4 Lord Morris of Borth-y-Gest: It is within common experience and knowledge that children may be allured by, and tempted to play and meddle with, objects which for others would have no special attraction. In such playing or meddling children may be heedless of danger and may bring neither method nor reason nor caution to bear. If by the exercise of reasonable foresight there can be avoidance of the risk that as a result of being so allured children may get themselves hurt, it is not over-exacting to require such foresight, and where a duty is owed, such reasonable and practicable measure as foresight would prompt.

When shortly after 5 p.m. on Saturday, November 8, 1958 the appellant (then aged eight) and his companion (then aged 10) were in Russell Road, Edinburgh, they could not resist the opportunity of exploring the unattended canvas shelter. In and around it they found aids to exploration readily at hand. Within the canvas shelter or tent was the uncovered manhole. Nearby was a section of a ladder. Nearby also there were lighted lamps. Pursuing their boyish whims they must have thought that as a place for play it was bounteously equipped. Furthermore, somewhere outside the tent they found a rope and a tin can (which apparently were no part of the Post Office material). The ladder and the rope and a lamp proved helpful in exploring the hole and the chamber below the road. In all this, however, as anyone might have surmised, was the risk that in some way one of the boys might fall down the hole or might suffer some burns from a lamp. The lamps were doubtless good and safe lamps when ordinarily handled, but in the hands of playful, inquisitive or mischievous boys, there could be no assumption that they would be used in a normal way.

8.5.5 Exercising an ordinary and certainly not an overacting degree of precaution the workmen should, I consider, have decided when the tea break came, that someone had better be left in charge who could repel the intrusion of inquisitive children. If, of course, there was no likelihood that children might appear, different considerations would apply. But children did appear; and I find no reason to differ from the conclusion of the Lord Ordinary that the presence of children in the immediate vicinity of the shelter was reasonably anticipated. No questions as to trespassing have been raised before your Lordships.

When the children did appear they found good scope for moments of adventure. Then came disaster for the pursuer. A risk that he might in some way burn himself by playing with a lamp was translated into reality. In fact he was very severely burned. Though his severe burns came about in a way that seems surprising, this only serves to illustrate that boys can bring about a consequence which could be expected but yet can bring it about in a most unusual manner and with unexpectedly severe results. After the pursuer tripped against the lamp and so caused it to fall into the manhole, and after he contrived to be drawn into or to be blown into or to fall into the manhole, he was burned. His burns were however, nonetheless burns, although there was such an immediate combustion of paraffin vapour that there was an explosion. The circumstances that an explosion as such would not have been contemplated does not alter the fact that it could reasonably have been foreseen that a boy who played in and about the canvas shelter, and played with the things that were thereabouts, might get hurt and might in some way burn himself. That is just what happened. The pursuer did burn himself, though his burns were more grave than would have been expected. The fact that the features or developments of an accident may not reasonably have been foreseen does not mean that the accident itself was not foreseeable. The pursuer was, in my view, injured as a result of the type or kind of accident or occurrence that could reasonably have been foreseen.

8.5.6   In my view, there was a duty owed by the defenders to safeguard the pursuer against the type or kind of occurrence which in fact happened and which resulted in his injuries; and the defenders are not absolved from liability because they did not envisage "the precise concatenation of circumstances which led up to the accident". For these reasons I differ with respect from the majority of the First Division and I would allow the appeal.'

COMMENT

8.6.1   Decided: February 21, 1963.
  Dec. 21, 1962: Nassau agreement for Polaris submarines concluded.
  Feb. 4, 1963: Two journalists jailed for not revealing sources.

8.6.2   This is a particularly difficult case to categorise. Some of the dicta seem to relate to remoteness of injury, *i.e.* the inquiry whether or not the harm is not within the concept of proximity and particularly the foreseeability required for a duty to exist, and it is in that connection that it is included here. It does, however, raise another issue, or another two issues: those of causation and remoteness of damage which are treated elsewhere. Lord Reid's speech, for example, seems to be directed more toward remoteness of damage. The case is probably best thought of as relevant to both inquiries. However, as a Scottish case, if it had been about remoteness of damage then one would have expected the usual mis-citation of *Allan v. Barclay* (Ext. 48)! Reasonable foreseeability can enter into both inquiries. Reasonable foreseeability also enters into the test of the standard of care (see Chap. 9). However, none of the speeches seem to treat it as such a case — why not?

Chapter 9

NEGLIGENCE: STANDARD OF CARE

42. Muir and Others v. Corporation of Glasgow (Appellants)
1943 S.C.(H.L.) 3

9.1.1 'William Muir, as tutor and administrator-at-law of his pupil daughter, Eleanor Muir, and others, as tutors and curators for their children, brought an action against the Corporation of the City of Glasgow in which they concluded for payment of certain sums as damages in respect of personal injuries sustained by their children in an accident caused, as they averred, by the negligence of an employee of the corporation, the manageress of a tea-room belonging to the corporation... In the King's Park, Glasgow, the Corporation of the City of Glasgow provided for the use of the public a tea-room and shop under the charge of a manageress. On June 15, 1940, a picnic party of Milton Free Church went to the park intending to have a tea picnic in the open air, taking their supplies with them. Owing to a breakdown in the weather, they obtained the manageress's permission, in return for a small payment, to have their picnic in the tea-room. Entrance to the tea-room was obtained through the shop, the public part of which was nothing more than a narrow passage bounded on one side by the wall of the building and a doorway opening into the park, and on the other by the counter, at which sweets and similar products were sold to the public. The picnic party got boiling water for their tea-urn from a neighbouring shelter, where boiling water was supplied by the corporation to picnic parties, and two members of the party proceeded to carry the urn containing the boiling tea towards the tea-room. The urn was about 16 inches high and about 15 inches in diameter. It was a cylinder of metal about one-eighth of an inch thick, with a lid which was in position. It weighed about 100 lb. with the quantity of tea which it contained. The handles were about 18 inches apart. At the time, the passage or shop was full of children, actual or prospective purchasers of sweets and ice-cream. The bearers of the urn had got through the doorway and into the passage when, for some cause not clearly explained, the urn was dropped and upset, and a number of the children were scalded. The manageress, who knew that the urn would be carried through the shop, had at the time her back to the doorway and was dealing with a refrigerator, and no one warned her that the urn was approaching. One only of the bearers was examined as a witness and he deponed that, owing to the narrowness of the passage, he and his colleague, a man McDonald, could not walk side by side; that he asked the children to stand aside, which they did; and that he suddenly felt that his companion's end of the urn had been dropped.

. . . . . .

9.1.2 LORD THANKERTON: The pursuers averred that, for a long time, the defenders had allowed and encouraged picnic parties to bring their urns and food into the tea-rooms. It is not now disputed that the present occasion was the first one on which that had occurred ... On a careful consideration of the opinions in the courts below, it appears to me to be accepted by the parties and by all the learned judges that there rested on Mrs Alexander, as representing the appellants, a duty to take reasonable care for the safety of the children who had come on to the premises to purchase sweets and ices.

. . . . . .

9.1.3 I shall state the test by which, in my opinion, the standard of care is to be judged, and this I will do by two quotations from the recent decision of this House in the Scottish case of *Bourhill* v. *Young*, 1942 S.C.(H.L.) 78. I take from my own opinion (at p. 83), that the duty is to take "such reasonable care as will avoid the risk of injury to such persons as he [in that case as a motor cyclist] can reasonably foresee might be injured by failure to exercise such reasonable care," and from the opinion of my noble and learned friend Lord Macmillan (at p. 88): "The duty to take care is the duty to avoid doing or omitting to do anything the doing or omitting to do which may have as its reasonable and probable consequence injury to others, and the duty is owed to these to whom injury may reasonably and probably be anticipated if the duty is not observed." In my opinion, it has long been held in Scotland that all that a person can be held bound to foresee are the reasonable and probable consequences of failure to take care, judged by the standard of the ordinary reasonable man. I am unable to agree with Lord Carmont (1942 S.C. at p. 140) that the appellants could be made liable "even if it were proved that the actual damage to the invitees happened through the tea-urn being spilt in a way that could not reasonably have been anticipated." Further, this is essentially a jury question, and, in cases such as the present one, it is the duty of the court to approach the question as if it were a jury, and a Court of Appeal should be slow to interfere with the conclusions of the Lord Ordinary. The court must be careful to place itself in the position of the person charged with the duty, and to consider what he or she should have reasonably anticipated as a natural and probable consequence of neglect, and not to give undue weight to the fact that a distressing accident has happened or that witnesses in the witness-box are prone to express regret, *ex post facto*, that they did not take some step, which it is now realised would definitely have prevented the accident... I also am of the opinion that Lord Moncrieff is not justified in regarding the event as demonstrating the risk, and that, in particular, because there is no evidence as to why McDonald let go his handle, but I will deal with this aspect of the case later — in other words, what event it was that caused the accident.

. . . . . .

9.1.4   There is no evidence that it was any want of care on the part of McDonald that caused the accident, or that the children hustled him and caused him to let go... I am not prepared to find that the careful carriage of the tea-urn past the dozen or so children in the wider end of the passage involved such an obvious danger as would have been foreseen as a natural and probable consequence of such carriage by an ordinary reasonable person which would lead him to clear the children out of the passage, but, further, let me make it quite clear that, even on the contrary view, I would hold that the respondents must fail here, as they have not proved what the event was that caused the accident. If the truth were that the accident was caused by some unexpected physical failure on McDonald's part, it is not enough for the pursuers to say that, if the children had been removed, the accident could not have happened. That would be to make Mrs Alexander, on behalf of the appellants, an insurer... The appeal should be allowed.

9.1.5   LORD MACMILLAN: The degree of care of the safety of others which the law requires human beings to observe in the conduct of their affairs varies according to the circumstances. There is no absolute standard, but it may be said generally that the degree of care required varies directly with the risk involved. Those who engage in operations inherently dangerous must take precautions which are not required to persons engaged in the ordinary routine of daily life. It is, no doubt, true that in every act which an individual performs there is present a potentiality of injury to others. All things are possible, and, indeed, it has become proverbial that the unexpected always happens, but, while the precept *alterum non laedere* requires us to abstain from intentionally injuring others, it does not impose liability for every injury which our conduct may occasion. In Scotland, at any rate, it has never been a maxim of the law that a man acts at his peril. Legal liability is limited to those consequences of our acts which a reasonable man of ordinary intelligence and experience so acting would have in contemplation... The standard of foresight of the reasonable man is, in one sense, an impersonal test. It eliminates the personal equation and is independent of the idiosyncrasies of the particular person whose conduct is in question. Some persons are by nature unduly timorous and imagine every path beset with lions. Others, of more robust temperament, fail to foresee or nonchalantly disregard even the most obvious dangers. The reasonable man is presumed to be free both from over-apprehension and from over-confidence, but there is a sense in which the standard of care of the reasonable man involves in its application a subjective element. It is still left to the judge to decide what, in the circumstances of the particular case, the reasonable man would have had in contemplation, and what, accordingly, the party sought to be made liable ought to have foreseen. Here there is room for diversity of view, as, indeed, is well illustrated in the present case. What to one judge may seem far-fetched may seem to another both natural and probable.

. . . . . .

9.1.6   The question, as I see it, is whether Mrs Alexander, when she was asked to allow a tea-urn to be brought into the premises under her charge, ought to have in mind, that it would require to be carried through a narrow passage in which there were a number of children, and that there would be a risk of the contents of the urn being spilt and scalding some of the children. If, as a reasonable person, she ought to have had these considerations in mind, was it her duty to require that she should be informed of the arrival of the urn, and, before allowing it to be carried through the narrow passage, to clear all the children out of it in case they might be splashed with scalding water?... It was not in itself an inherently dangerous thing and could be carried quite safely and easily by two persons exercising ordinary care. A caterer, called as a witness on behalf of the pursuers, who had large experience of the use of such urns, said that he had never had a mishap with an urn while it was being carried... For some unexplained reason, McDonald loosened hold of the other hand, the urn tilted over, and some of its contents were spilt, scalding several of the children who were standing by. The urn was not upset, but came to the ground on its base.

9.1.7   In my opinion, Mrs Alexander had no reason to anticipate that such an event would happen as a consequence of granting permission for a tea-urn to be carried through the passage-way where the children were congregated, and, consequently, there was no duty incumbent on her to take precautions against the occurrence of such an event. I think that she was entitled to assume that the urn would be in charge of responsible persons (as it was) who would have regard for the safety of the children in the passage (as they did have regard), and that the urn would be carried with ordinary care, in which case its transit would occasion no danger to bystanders. The pursuers have left quite unexplained the actual cause of the accident. The immediate cause was not the carrying of the urn through the passage but McDonald's losing grip of his handle. How he came to do so is entirely a matter of speculation. He may have stumbled, or he may have suffered a temporary muscular failure. We do not know, and the pursuers have not chosen to enlighten us by calling McDonald as a witness. Yet it is argued that Mrs Alexander ought to have foreseen the possibility, nay, the reasonable probability of an occurence the nature of which is unascertained... The only ground on which the view of the majority of the learned judges of the First Division can be justified is that Mrs Alexander ought to have foreseen that some accidental injury might happen to the children in the passage if she allowed an urn containing hot tea to be carried through the passage, and ought, therefore, to have cleared out the children entirely during its transit, which Lord Moncrieff describes as "the only effective step." With all respect, I think that this would impose on Mrs Alexander a degree of care higher than the law exacts.

· · · · · ·

9.1.8 LORD WRIGHT (read by Lord Clauson): That the appellants owed a duty to the children is not open to question. Your Lordships are not, therefore, on this occasion exercised by the problem which was presented recently in *Bourhill* v. *Young*, which was whether the person injured came within the limits of foreseeable harm from the dangerous acts complained of. Here the children were on the appellants' premises in full view of Mrs Alexander, the appellants' responsible servant, and were plainly liable to be injured, if the place in which they were was rendered dangerous to them by Mrs Alexander's act in consenting to the urn being carried through the place. The question thus is whether Mrs Alexander knew or ought to have known that what she was permitting involved danger to the children. It is not a question of what Mrs Alexander actually foresaw, but what the hypothetical reasonable person in Mrs Alexander's situation would have foreseen. The test is what she ought to have foreseen. I may quote again, as in *Bourhill's* case, Lord Atkin's words in *Donoghue* v. *Stevenson*: "You must take reasonable care to avoid acts or omissions which you can reasonably foresee would be likely to injure your neighbour." On this occasion the children were "the neighbours". The act or omission to be avoided was creating a new danger in the premises by allowing the church party to transport the urn. If that issue is decided against the appellants, they must be held responsible in the action.

· · · · · ·

9.1.9 Thus, in the present case the appellants are not primarily concerned with the manner in which the members of the church party carried the urn, as they would have been if these members had been servants or agents. The two men were mere licensees in the matter. The appellants were not directly responsible for their acts. If they are to be held responsible, it must be because, by the permission which Mrs Alexander, their manageress, gave to the members of the church party, they created an unusual danger affecting the invitees, in particular, the children… It is not, of course, a question of what she actually thought at the moment, but what the hypothetical reasonable person would have foreseen. That is the standard to determine the scope of her duty. This involves the question: Was the operation of carrying the tea-urn something which a reasonable person in Mrs Alexander's position should have realised would render the place in which it was performed dangerous to the children in the circumstances? This is the crucial issue of fact and the acid test of liability.

9.1.10 A distinction has been drawn in some cases between things intrinsically dangerous or dangerous *per se* and other things which are not dangerous in the absence of negligence. The correctness or value of that distinction has been doubted by eminent judges. I think, however, that there is a real and practical distinction between the two categories. Some things are obviously and necessarily dangerous unless the danger is removed by appropriate precautions. These are things dangerous *per se*. Other things are only dangerous if there is negligence. It is only in that contingency that they can cause danger. Thus, to introduce, not a tea-urn, but a savage animal, such as a lion or tiger, into the passageway would have been of the former class.

9.1.11 LORD ROMER: … For, with all respect to Lord Carmont, I am unable to agree with the opinion that he expressed (1942 S.C. at p. 140) to the effect that, if it were the duty of the appellants to see that the children were not in the passageway in order to prevent the children being subjected to a risk that should have been within the contemplation of the appellants, "there would be no escape from liability even if it were proved that the actual damage to the invitees happened through the tea-urn being spilt in a way that could not reasonably have been anticipated." I cannot think for instance, that, if the accident had been occasioned by a portion of the ceiling falling down on McDonald owing to a defect in it of which they neither knew or ought to have known, the appellants could have been made liable, even if it had been their duty (and I see no reason to suppose that it was) to remove the children altogether from the passage to avoid the risk of Taylor and McDonald being jostled as they carried the urn along. In such a case the breach of this last-mentioned duty would not have been the cause of the accident to the children. It might have been a *causa sine qua non*. It certainly would not have been the *causa causans*.'

COMMENT

9.2.1 Decided: April 16, 1943.
  Jacques Mornard sentenced to 20 years' imprisonment for killing Trotsky, including six months for carrying an ice-axe.

Feb. 6: Errol Flynn acquitted of *Moorov*-like rape charges.
March 2: R.A.F. dropped 900 tons of bombs on Berlin city centre.
March 28: Rachmaninov died.

9.2.2 Eleanor Muir's case is also discussed by Rodger, at 1988 C.L.P. 1. Once you have read the case of *Smith v. Littlewoods* (Ext. 51), consider whether you think *Muir* would be decided differently today. If so, why? If not, why not?

9.2.3 Why is there held to be a duty of care at all in this case?

Persons professing special skills

43. **Hunter (Appellant) v. Hanley**
1955 S.C. 200

9.3.1 'LORD PRESIDENT (Clyde): This is a note of exceptions, brought before us by the pursuer in an action against a doctor for professional negligence. The case was tried before Lord Patrick and a jury, and a verdict for the defender was obtained. The case arose out of the breaking of a hypodermic needle when the defender was giving the pursuer the 12th of a series of injections of penicillin. One of the grounds of fault alleged against the defender was that the type of needle employed on the occasion in question was not strong enough, and that "any doctor possessing a fair and average knowledge of his profession would have known this." A question therefore arose at the trial regarding what was the normal and usual practice in regard to the type of needle required. In the course of his charge to the jury, Lord Patrick directed them as follows on this matter: "There must be such a departure from the normal and usual practice of general practitioners as can reasonably be described as gross negligence. I could use from cases of high authority in the House of Lords, Scots cases, much stronger adjectives than that, but all that I will say to you in conclusion on the general topic is that there must be a serious departure from a normal practice, if that normal practice has been proved, and the serious departure must involve a substantial and serious fault." Counsel for the pursuer excepted to this direction, and requested the judge to direct the jury that there must be a departure from normal practice which involves fault. This direction his Lordship refused to give. I am clearly of the opinion that he was right in so refusing, as the direction asked for is plainly too vague to assist the jury at all. The question still remains, however, as to whether the direction actually given is sound in law. The reference to "gross negligence" in the direction given no doubt springs partly from the fact that the words are employed throughout her pleadings by the pursuer in regard to the allegations she makes of deviation from the alleged practice, and, form that point of view, her pleadings certainly leave much to be desired in the way of fair notice of the case she now makes.

. . . . . .

9.3.2 To succeed in any action based on negligence, whether against a doctor or against anyone else, it is of course necessary to establish a breach of that duty to take care which the law requires, and the degree of want of care which constitutes negligence must vary with the circumstances — *Caswell* v. *Powell Duffryn Associated Collieries* [1940] A.C. 152 *per* Lord Wright at pp. 175–176. But where the conduct of a doctor, or indeed any professional man, is concerned, the circumstances are not so precise and clear-cut as in the normal case. In the realm of diagnosis and treatment there is ample scope for genuine difference of opinion and one man clearly is not negligent merely because his conclusion differs from that of other professional men, nor because he has displayed less skill or knowledge than others would have shown. The true test for establishing negligence in diagnosis or treatment on the part of a doctor is whether he has been proved to be guilty of such failure as no doctor of ordinary skill would be guilty of it acting with ordinary care — Glegg, *Reparation* (3rd ed.), p. 509. The standard seems to be the same in England — Salmond, *Torts* (11th ed.), p. 511. It is a tribute to the high standard in general of the medical profession in Scotland that there are practically no decisions on this question in the reported cases.

. . . . . .

9.3.3 An analogy, however, is afforded by a series of decisions mostly pronounced many years ago, in regard to allegations of professional negligence on the part of law agents advising their clients... In all these cases mere errors in interpreting the law or lack of knowledge of the law are not treated as constituting negligence. As the Lord Chancellor put it in *Hart* v. *Frame* (1839) McL. & Rob. 595 at p. 614: "Professional men, possessed of a reasonable portion of information and skill according to the duties they undertake to perform, and exercising that they so possess with reasonable care and diligence in the affairs of their employers, certainly ought not to be liable for errors in judgment, whether in matters of law or of discretion... In several of the opinions in these cases the words "gross negligence" are used. The use of such a criterion as the test of liability has been more than once criticised... But the compendious description "gross negligence", "*culpa lata*", "*crassa negligentia*" has frequently been adopted, in deciding Scottish appeals in the House of Lords, as the test of liability of trustees claiming protection under an immunity clause in the trust deed... I am not therefore prepared to say that the concept of gross negligence forms no part of the law of Scotland today.

9.3.4   In relation, however, to professional negligence, I regard the phrase "gross negligence" only as indicating so marked a departure from the normal standard of conduct of a professional man as to infer a lack of the ordinary care which a man of ordinary skill would display. So interpreted, the words partly describe what I consider the sound criterion in the matter, although, strictly viewed, they might give the impression that there are degrees of negligence.

It follows from what I have said that in regard to allegations of deviation from ordinary professional practice — and this is the matter with which the present note is concerned — such a deviation is not necessarily evidence of negligence. Indeed it would be disastrous if this were so, for all inducement to progress in medical science would then be destroyed. Even a substantive deviation from normal practice may be warranted by the particular circumstances. To establish liability by the doctor where deviation from normal practice is alleged, three facts require to be established. First of all it must be proved that there is a usual and normal practice; secondly it must be proved that the defender has not adopted that practice; and thirdly (and this is of crucial importance) it must be established that the course the doctor adopted is one which no professional man of ordinary skill would have taken if he had been acting with ordinary care. There is clearly a heavy onus upon a pursuer to establish these three facts, and without all three his case will fail. If this is the test, then it matters nothing how far or how little he deviates from the ordinary practice. For the extent of deviation is not the test. The deviation must be of a kind which satisfies the third of the requirements just stated.

In these circumstances the direction given in the present case does not, in my view, accurately set out the legal criterion for liability and the jury's verdict therefore cannot stand.'

COMMENT

9.4.1   Decided: February 4, 1955.
Nov. 29, 1954: Sir George Robey died.
Jan. 19, 1955: Amnesty given to Kenyan Mau Mau terrorists.

9.4.2   Note that this was a jury case. These are now uncommon in civil matters. Accordingly, there is less opportunity for having judges state their precise view of the way the law has to be applied to any given facts. A single judge could just make up his mind as a juryman without articulating the test in great detail. In his note he would need only to refer to *culpa* to be unimpeachable.

9.4.3   This case arguably makes it a general rule that professions are judged by the conduct of their profession. But it is getting ever more difficult to determine just what that profession is because of the division of functions in modern society. Thus soon bank clerks might be doing conveyancing — should they be judged by the standard of the late Professor Halliday or that of the average bank clerk or building society clerk? Should a solicitor advising a client on investing the lump-sum damages he has just recovered be judged by the standard of his fellow-solicitors, of his fellow-solicitors who conduct investment business, or of a bank manager, building society manager or stockbroker? (See generally, *Delict*, 5.3–5.14).

9.4.4 *Hunter* was accepted by both sides as laying down the proper test in *Kelly v. Edinburgh D.C.*, 1983 S.L.T. 593 — a case involving architects. The Second Division in *Stephen v. Scottish Boatowners Mutual Insurance Association*, 1989 S.L.T. 52, refused to apply *Hunter* as the test applicable in an inquiry as to whether a ship's captain had exercised "all reasonable endeavours" to save his ship in terms of a policy of insurance. Lord Mayfield considered the applicability of *Hunter* to a case involving a liquidator in *MacRae v. Henderson*, 1989 S.L.T. 523: "It was further submitted by counsel for the defender that the standard of care to be applied was to be related to the standard of the ordinary liquidator. That was a submission based on *Hunter v. Hanley*. That was a case concerning an allegation of deviation from normal practice of a doctor. It was held that it had first to be proved that there was a usual and normal practice; that the defender had not adopted that practice; that it had to be established that the course adopted was one which no professional man of ordinary skill would have taken if he had been acting with ordinary care. In my view, however, the circumstances of this case do not put the liquidator in the same category as the professional man in *Hunter*. In the circumstances of this case the liquidator had to exercise reasonable care to protect interests by ingathering debts in the particular circumstances of the present liquidation. The circumstances of the present case are not such that the pursuers were bound to rely on the practice or standard of the ordinary liquidator" (at p. 526). Did this statement assist the pursuer or defender? Why?

9.4.5 *Hunter* was approved in England in *Bolam v. Friern Hospital Management Committee* [1957] 2 All E.R. 118 by McNair J.: "It is just a question of expression. I myself would prefer to put it this way, that he is not guilty of negligence if he has acted in accordance with a practice accepted as proper by a responsible body of medical men skilled in that particular art. I do not think there is much difference in sense. It is just a different way of expressing the same thought. Putting it the other way round, a man is not negligent, if he is acting in accordance with such a practice, merely because there is a body of opinion who would take a contrary view." *Bolam* and a later (and important) House of Lords case, *Sidaway v. Bethlem Royal Hospital* [1985] A.C. 871, were considered in *Gold v. Haringey Health Authority* [1987] 3 W.L.R. 649. The Court of Appeal held that the *Bolam* test applied to a doctor giving contraceptive advice. Following *Sidaway*, it was held that a doctor's duty was not to be dissected into parts. The test was whether the advice would have been given in the way that it was by a responsible body of medical opinion. Consideration has been given to the number of doctors who constitute a body of opinion. In *Defreitas v. O'Brien* [1995] T.L.R. 86 it was held that a small band of specialists could constitute a body of opinion.

9.4.6 Is the absence in the law reports of cases dealing with the alleged negligent conduct of a given profession a measure of the excellence of that profession or the craftiness of its liability insurers?

9.4.7 There are really two issues dealt with in *Hunter*. One is the principal issue of the standard of care. It certainly seems to be agreed by most commentators that it is a special standard, on the basis that the reasonable man cannot do brain surgery or nuclear physics, and to set the standard at his level would have the effect of acquitting many bungling professionals. The second issue, which is not dealt with in this book, is the question of whether factually there has been a breach of a duty. The issue of deviation from common practice relates to this question. While at one time common practice was thought to be a matter of law, it is now simply part of the factual structure which allows a decision to be made: *Brown v. Rolls Royce*, 1960 S.C. (H.L.) 22.

9.4.8 Prof. Norrie has contributed a number of very valuable studies on the question of medical negligence in Scotland: 1985 S.L.T. (News) 289; 1985 J.R. 145; 1986 S.L.T. (News) 145. See also Sutherland, L., "A Single Standard of Care", 1995 Rep. B. 6–11; Griffith, J.R., "Medical Negligence", 1995 S.L.P.Q. 25.

CHAPTER 10

NEGLIGENCE: CAUSATION

Causation

44. Kay's Tutor (Appellant) v. Ayrshire and Arran Health Board
1987 S.L.T. 577 (H.L.)

10.1.1 'LORD KEITH OF KINKEL: On November 28, 1975 the appellant's son Andrew Stuart Kay, then aged two years and five months, was admitted to Seafield Children's Hospital, Ayr, which was under the management of the respondent board. His admission had been sought by his general practitioner because she suspected that he was suffering from meningitis, following an infection of the upper respiratory system... The general practitioner had treated the respiratory infection with ampicillin administered orally... On admission to hospital Andrew was found to be seriously ill. He was treated with benzyl penicillin and sulphadiazine administered intravenously. A specimen of C.S.F. was taken... This led to a confirmed diagnosis of pneumococcal meningitis, a most virulent form of the disease. The consultant paediatrician in charge of the case, Dr McClure, instructed that 10,000 units of penicillin be injected intrathecally, that is to say by way of lumbar puncture into the subarachnoid space containing the C.S.F. The reason for this procedure was to bring about that the penicillin might most readily reach the infected meninges and attack the bacteria which were causing the disease. The injection was carried out shortly after noon on that day by Dr Adam-Strump, a senior house officer. By mistake he injected about 300,000 units of penicillin instead of 10,000 units. This rapidly produced toxic effects. The child went into convulsions and later developed a degree of hemiparesis, that is to say paralysis on one side of his body. Dr Adam-Strump realised his mistake immediately, and remedial measures were urgently instituted. These were successful in saving the child's life and by December 1 the immediate ill-effects of the overdose appeared to have been surmounted. A rapid recovery from the meningitis also followed. He was discharged from hospital on December 24. His parents before then had begun to suspect that he was suffering from deafness. This proved to be the case. He was suffering and still suffers from profound bilateral deafness.

10.1.2   The appellant, as Andrew's tutor and administrator-at-law, raised the present action against the respondent board on November 20, 1978, claiming damages on his behalf on the ground of vicarious liability for negligence of Dr Adam-Strump. The board admitted liability, but contended that the consequences of Dr Adam-Strump's negligence were limited to the convulsions and hemiparesis from which Andrew suffered immediately following the overdose of penicillin. They denied that the overdose had resulted in any residual disability and, in particular, that it had caused Andrew's deafness. They lodged a tender on that basis.

. . . . . .

10.1.3   The board led the evidence of a number of specialists... They ascribed the deafness wholly to the meningitis, a disease of which it is a common sequela. The Lord Ordinary decided that his deafness had been contributed to by the overdose... He awarded damages of £102,000. The board reclaimed, and their motion for review, the present appellants at that stage being represented by counsel, was heard by the First Division (the Lord President, Lord Grieve and Lord Kincraig) who on December 18, 1985 allowed it, holding that Andrew's deafness had not been proved to have been related causally to the overdose. They reduced the damages to £7,275. It appears that this sum did not beat the board's tender, since the appellant was awarded expenses being found due to or by either party after that date.

10.1.4   The principal reason why the First Division decided as they did was that they found the Lord Ordinary, in holding proved a causal connection between the overdose and the deafness, to have proceeded on a theory of causation propounded by himself, which had not been spoken to by any of the medical witnesses and had not been suggested to any of them so that they might express an opinion on its validity... The Lord Ordinary's theory was that the convulsions from which Andrew suffered following the overdose involved the firing of neurones in the cerebral cortex; that this resulted in an enhanced demand by the neurones for oxygen; that the defence mechanisms of the body against the toxins produced by the pneumococcal bacteria required for their efficiency an ample supply of oxygen in the blood; that because of the demands of the firing neurones the oxygen available to the defence mechanisms was reduced; and thus that the toxins were less effectively combatted, which enabled them to damage the auditory nerve and produce the deafness. In the argument before your Lordships' House, counsel for the appellant rightly accepted that this theory of the Lord Ordinary could not be supported.

. . . . . .

10.1.5   "There was an overall decline in [Andrew's] condition which suggests a resultant weakening of his powers of resistance to the disease…" None of the witnesses suggested, nor was it suggested to any of them, that the cyanosis, breathlessness and lapse into coma had the effect of weakening the child's powers of resistance to the toxins generated by the pneumococci… One of the steps which [the Lord Ordinary] took in forming this view was to hold that it had not been proved that Andrew was deaf before the overdose was administered. As the judges of the First Division pointed out, the evidence likewise did not enable a finding to be made that he was not deaf before the overdose. There was in truth, no evidence either way. The factor is of some significance because medical knowledge indicates that deafness, if it materialises as a sequela of meningitis, is likely to do so at an early stage of the disease… Though no firm inferences can be drawn, if the disease was already past its peak when the overdose was administered, and thus past the stage when deafness is most likely to occur, it is not easy to see, once the Lord Ordinary's untenable theory is rejected, how the overdose can be held to have increased the prospects of deafness… Medical knowledge, as revealed in the course of the evidence, clearly demonstrates that deafness is a common sequela of meningitis. Statistics indicate that it occurs in about a third of all cases of pneumococcal meningitis.

· · · · · ·

10.1.6 Counsel for the appellants placed some reliance on *McGhee* v. *National Coal Board*, 1973 S.L.T. 14. In my opinion the decision does not assist the present appellant. Had there been acceptable medical evidence here that an overdose of penicillin administered intrathecally was known to increase the risk that meningitis, which the penicillian was intended to treat, would cause deafness, the decision would have been in point. It would be immaterial that medical science was unable to demonstrate the precise mechanism whereby the risk was increased. But as it is, there is in the instant case no such medical evidence. It is true that there are few recorded cases of overdoses of penicillin intrathecally administered for the purpose of treating actual or suspected meningitis. But the paucity of such cases, none of which supports the suggested causal connection, cannot in itself make good the lack of appropriate evidence.

10.1.7 LORD MACKAY OF CLASHFERN: [Counsel for the appellant] went on to submit that the evidence showed that an overdose of penicillin increased the likelihood of neurological damage in the person affected by pneumococcal meningitis, that permanent deafness was a particular kind of neurological damage, that the mechanisms bringing deafness about were not sufficiently clear to enable a confident explanation of them to be furnished and that by a development of the decision of your Lordships' House in *McGhee* v. *National Coal Board*, proof that the overdose of penicillin materially increased the risk of neurological damage was sufficient to establish that the overdose had made a material contribution to the neurological damage which, in fact, resulted, namely deafness, and thus to entitle the appellant to succeed. This formulation was devised in order to elide the difficulty that the basis upon which the Lord Ordinary had concluded that the overdose of penicillin materially increased the risk of deafness involved reliance on the theory which he himself had advanced that the body's defensive mechanisms had been rendered less effective by the overdose than otherwise they would have been to offer resistance to the toxins attacking the auditory nerve.

In this formulation, counsel derived assistance for the proposition that an overdose of penicillin materially increased the risk of neurological damage from the study of the results in the recorded cases of intrathecal overdoses of penicillin. There were 12 such cases reported. In eight the result was death, in two the result was complete recovery after the initial experience of neurological damage and in the remaining two cases the patient suffered neurological damage which was permanent although not deafness.

. . . . . .

10.1.8 In my opinion, it is not right to ask whether it materially increased the risk of neurological damage when the evidence available distinguishes between different kinds of neurological damage. As I have said, the evidence upon which this part of counsel's submission depends is the record of the cases of overdose to which I have referred. In none of those who survived an overdose, and the number of cases is very small, was the particular type of neurological damage which results in deafness found to have occurred. I cannot accept that it is correct to say that because evidence shows that an overdose of penicillin increases the risk of particular types of neurological damage found in these cases that an overdose of penicillin materially increases the risk of a different type of neurological damage, namely that which causes deafness, when no such deafness has been shown to have resulted from such overdose. Apart from Mr Williams' evidence that, in his opinion, deafness was caused in Andrew by direct effect of penicillin on the auditory nerve, which opinion the Lord Ordinary felt unable to accept as establishing the appellant's case in the light of the other evidence, there was no evidence accepted by the Lord Ordinary that penicillin in overdose or otherwise had caused or contributed to deafness. It is not necessary to consider in this case whether, if the appellant had a sufficient factual basis for the argument which he advanced based upon the decision of this House in *McGhee's* case, his submission was correct since, in my opinion, the essential factual foundation for the submission is missing.

The result is that, in the light of the whole evidence, the appellant has not established that the overdose of penicillin had any causal connection with the deafness which Andrew now suffers. That deafness must, on the weight of the evidence, be held to have resulted solely from his pneumococcal meningitis and his claim for damages in respect thereof accordingly fails.'

COMMENT

10.2.1   Decided: May 14, 1987.
   April 1: Keith Best, M.P. (Con.), admitted making illegal multiple share-applications.
   April 16: Harvey Proctor, M.P. (Con.), arrested on indecency charge.
   April 23: Prime Minister confirmed that former head of MI5, Maurice Oldfield, was a homosexual.
   May 8: Gary Hart withdrew from Presidential race as a result of Donna Rice affair.

10.2.2   This case became something of a *cause célèbre*. As Lord Ackner said in the House of Lords: "If sympathy alone could be a valid basis for awarding the appellant's son, Andrew Stuart Kay, damages to compensate for his many and serious disabilities, then this claim would have given rise to no argument. Everybody who has or will read about his case cannot but be moved by the tragedy which has befallen him and his family."
   Was this "playing to the gallery"? The law reports are crammed full of tragedies — some perhaps even more enormous (if there is a scale of tragedies) than this case. Certainly for a lawyer it is no more tragic than many other cases that turn up in the waiting-room. See also Lord Wright at p. 12 in *Muir v. Glasgow Corporation*, 1943 S.C.(H.L.) 3.

10.2.4   In *Wilsher v. Essex Area Health Board* [1988] A.C. 1074 it was made clear that the court has to decide whether the breach of duty was a cause or not, the onus being on the plaintiff. The House of Lords, in *Hotson v. East Berkshire Health Authority* [1987] A.C. 750, decided that causation in fact is really an all-or-nothing exercise — either the breach of duty is a cause or it is not. It is not therefore appropriate to adjust damages to reflect the degree of causal effect of the breach of duty.

10.2.5   Causation is sometimes described as a matter of "common sense". It will come as little surprise that there is little evidence of a unanimous community view of common sense — see Mullany, N.J., "Common Sense Causation — an Australian View", 1992 O.J.L.S. 431.

45. Wardlaw v. Bonnington Castings (Appellants)
1956 S.C.(H.L.) 26

10.3.1   'LORD REID: The respondent was employed by the appellants for eight years in the dressing shop of their foundry in Leith, and while employed there he contracted the disease of pneumoconiosis by inhaling air which contained minute particles of silica. He ceased work on May 12, 1950. The Lord Ordinary (Lord Wheatley) held the appellants liable for this and awarded £2000 damages. The First Division by a majority (Lord Carmont and Lord Russell, the Lord President dissenting) adhered to the interlocutor of the Lord Ordinary.

The appellants produce steel castings. These are made by pouring molten metal into moulds which consist of sand with a very high silica content. When the casting has cooled, it is freed from sand so far as possible and then annealed. The annealed casting has a certain amount of the sand adhering to it or burnt into it, and the surface of the casting is somewhat irregular. It is then necessary to remove these irregularities and smooth the surface of the casting, and in the course of doing this any adhering sand is removed. This is done in the dressing-shop by three types of machine. In two of these machines, floor grinders and wing grinders, the means employed are grinding wheels made of carborundum, and in the third a hammer or chisel is driven by compressed air so that it delivers some 1800 blows per minute. There are several of each type of machine in the dressing-shop and all of them produce dust, part of which is silica, from the sand which they remove. The particles of this sand are originally sufficiently large not to be dangerous, because it is only exceedingly small particles of silica which can produce the disease-particles which are invisible except through a powerful microscope. But either in the annealing process or by the working of these machines or at both stages (the evidence on this is inconclusive) a number of the original particles are broken up, and the dust produced by all these machines contains a certain proportion of the dangerous minute particles of silica.

. . . . . .

10.3.2 Throughout his eight years in the appellant's service, the respondent operated one of these pneumatic hammers, and he admits that he cannot complain in so far as his disease was caused by the dust from his own or the other pneumatic hammers. As there was no known means of collecting or neutralising this dust, and as it is not alleged that these machines ought not to have been used, there was no breach of duty on the part of the appellants in allowing this dust to escape into the air.

. . . . . .

10.3.3 But the respondent alleges, and is admitted, that a considerable quantity of dust escaped into the air of the workshop from the swing grinders, because the dust-extraction plant for these grinders was not kept free from obstruction as it should have been. It frequently became choked and ineffective... It is admitted for the appellants that they were in breach of this Regulation [reg. 1 of the Grinding of Metals (Miscellaneous Industries) Regulations 1925], in that for considerable periods dust from the swing grinders escaped into the shop where the respondent was working owing to the appliances for its interception and removal being choked and therefore inadequate. The question is whether this breach of the Regulation caused the respondent's disease. If this disease results from his having inhaled part of the noxious dust from the swing grinders which should have been intercepted and removed, then the appellants are liable to him in damages: but, if it did not result from that, then they are not liable.

The Lord Ordinary and the majority of the First Division have dealt with this case on the footing that there was an onus on the defenders, the appellants, to prove that the dust from the swing grinders did not cause the pursuer's disease. This view was based on a passage in the judgment of the Court of Appeal in *Vyner* v. *Waldenbert Brothers* [1946] K.B. 50, *per* Scott L.J. at p. 55.

. . . . . .

10.3.4 It would seem obvious in principle that a pursuer or plaintiff must prove not only negligence or breach of duty but also that such fault caused or materially contributed to his injury, and there is ample authority for that proposition both in Scotland and in England. I can find neither reason nor authority for the rule being different where there is breach of statutory duty. The fact that Parliament imposes a duty for the protection of employees has been held to entitle an employee to sue if he is injured as a result of breach of that duty. But it would be going a great deal further to hold that it can be inferred from the enactment of a duty that Parliament intended that any employee suffering injury can sue his employer merely because there was a breach of duty and it is shown to be possible that his injury may have been caused by it. In my judgment, the employee must in all cases prove his case by the ordinary standard of proof in civil actions; he must make it appear at least that on a balance of probabilities the breach of duty caused or materially contributed to his injury.

. . . . . .

10.3.5 I think that the position can be shortly stated in this way. It may be that, of the noxious dust in the general atmosphere of the shop, more came from the pneumatic hammers than from the swing grinders, but I think it is sufficiently proved that the dust from the grinders made a substantial contribution. The respondent, however, did not only inhale the general atmosphere of the shop: when he was working his hammer, his face was directly over it, and it must often have happened that dust from his hammer substantially increased the concentration of noxious dust in the air which he inhaled. It is therefore probable that much the greater proportion of the noxious dust which he inhaled over the whole period came from the hammers. But on the other hand some certainly came from the swing grinders, and I cannot avoid the conclusion that the proportion which came from the swing grinders was not negligible. He was inhaling the general atmosphere all the time, and there is no evidence to show that his hammer gave off noxious dust so frequently, or that the concentration of noxious dust above it when it was producing dust was so much greater than the concentration in the general atmosphere, that special concentration of dust could be said to be substantially the sole cause of his disease... In my opinion, it is proved not only that the swing grinders may well have contributed but that they did in fact contribute a quota of silica dust which was not negligible to the pursuer's lungs and therefore did help to produce the disease... I am therefore of the opinion that this appeal should be dismissed.'

COMMENT

10.4.1 Decided: March 1, 1956.
Oct. 31: Princess Margaret decided not to marry Group-Captain Townsend and cited the Church's teaching that marriage is indissoluble.
Nov. 28: State of emergency declared in Cyprus.
Dec. 14, 1955: Gaitskell beat Bevan and Morrison for Labour leadership (in opposition).
Feb. 27, 1956: Coloured voters to be removed from electoral roll in South Africa.

10.4.2 This case also bears on the questions of statutory liability (Chap. 15) and proof (Chap. 24).

10.4.3 What is the opposite of "not negligible"?

46. McGhee (Appellant) v. National Coal Board
1973 S.L.T. 14 (H.L.)

10.5.1 'LORD REID: The appellant was employed for many years by the respondents as a labourer at their Prestongrange brickworks. His normal work was emptying pipe kilns. On March 30, 1967 (a Thursday), he was sent to empty brick kilns. Working conditions there were much hotter and dustier than in the pipe kilns. On Sunday, April 2, he felt extensive irritation of his skin. He continued to work on the Monday and Tuesday and then went to his doctor who put him off work and later sent him to a skin specialist. He was found to be suffering from dermatitis.

He sued the respondents for damages alleging breaches on their part of common law duties to him. After proof before answer the Lord Ordinary assoilzied the respondents. On March 17, 1972 the First Division refused a claiming motion.

It is now admitted that the dermatitis was attributable to work which the appellant did in the brick kilns. The first ground of fault alleged against the respondents is that the kilns ought to have been allowed to cool "sufficiently" before the appellant was sent to remove the bricks for them. I agree with the Scottish courts that this contention fails; the pleadings lack specification and the evidence is much too vague to prove any breach of duty.

10.5.2 The other ground of fault alleged raises a difficult question of law. It is said in condescendence 3: "It was their duty to take reasonable care to provide adequate washing facilities including showers, soap, and towels to enable men to remove dust from their bodies. In each and all of said duties incumbent on them the defenders failed and so caused said disease. Had the defenders fulfilled said duties incumbent on them the pursuer would not have contracted the disease." Originally the defence was twofold: (i) a denial of any such duty, and (ii) an argument that the disease was of a non-occupational character. But the Lord Ordinary decided against the respondents in both of these matters and the respondents accept these findings. So the respondents' defence in the Inner House and before your Lordships has taken the unusual form that breach of duty is admitted, and that it is admitted that the disease is attributable to the work which the appellant performed in the brick kiln, but that it has not been proven that failure to carry out the admitted duty caused the onset of the disease.

10.5.3 The medical witnesses are in substantial agreement. Dermatitis can be caused, by repeated minute abrasion of the outer horny layer of the skin followed by some injury to or change in the underlying cells, the precise nature of which has not yet been discovered by medical science. If a man sweats profusely for a considerable time the outer layer of his skin is softened and easily injured. If he is then working in a cloud of abrasive brick dust, as this man was, the particles of dust will adhere to his skin in considerable quantity and exertion will cause them to injure the horny layer and expose to injury or infection the tender cells below. Then, in some way not yet understood, dermatitis may result... Washing is the only practicable method of removing the danger of further injury.

. . . . . .

10.5.4 It was held in the Court of Session that the appellant had to prove that his additional exposure to injury caused by his having to bicycle home unwashed caused the disease, in the sense that it was more probable than not that this additional exposure to injury was the cause of it. I do not think that is the proper approach. The Court of Session may have been misled by the inadequacy of the appellant's pleadings. But I do not think that it is now too late to re-examine the whole position.

It has always been the law that a pursuer succeeds if he can show that fault of the defender caused or materially contributed to his injury. There may have been two separate causes, but it is enough if one of the causes arose from fault of the defender. The pursuer does not have to prove that this cause would of itself have been enough to cause him injury. That is well illustrated by the decision of this House in *Wardlaw* v. *Bonnington Castings Ltd.*, 1956 S.C.(H.L.) 26, 1956 S.L.T. 135. There the pursuer's disease was caused by an accumulation of noxious dust in his lungs. The dust which he had inhaled over a period came from two sources. The defenders were not responsible for one source, but they could and ought to have prevented the other. The dust from the latter source was not in itself sufficient to cause the disease, but the pursuer succeeded because it made a material contribution to his injury.

. . . . . .

10.5.5 The respondents seek to distinguish *Wardlaw's* case (*supra*) by arguing that then it was proved that every particle of dust inhaled played its part in causing the onset of the disease, whereas in this case it is not proved that every minor abrasion played its part.

In the present case the evidence does not show — perhaps no one knows — just how dermatitis of this type begins. It suggests to me that there are two possible ways. It may be that an accumulation of minor abrasions of the horny layer of the skin is a necessary precondition for the onset of the disease. Or it may be that the disease starts at the one particular abrasion and then spreads, so that multiplication of abrasions merely increases the number of places where the disease can start and in that way increases the risk of its occurrence.

10.5.6 I am inclined to think that the evidence points to the former view. But in a field where so little appears to be known with certainty I could not say that is proved. If it were, then this case would be indistinguishable from *Wardlaw's* case, but I think that in cases like this we must take a broader view of causation. The medical evidence is to the effect that the fact that the man had to cycle home caked with grime and sweat added materially to the risk that this disease might develop. It does not and could not explain just why that is so. But experience shows that it is so. Plainly that must be because what happens while the man remains unwashed can have a causative effect though just how the cause operates is uncertain. I cannot accept the view expressed in the Inner House that once the man left the brick kiln he left behind the causes which made him liable to develop dermatitis. That seems to me quite inconsistent with a proper interpretation of the medical evidence. Nor can I accept the distinction drawn by the Lord Ordinary between materially increasing the risk that the disease will occur and making a material contribution to its occurrence.

There may be some logical ground for such a distinction where our knowledge of all the material factors is complete. But it has often been said that the legal concept of causation is not based on logic or philosophy. It is based on the practical way in which the ordinary man's mind works in the everyday affairs of life. From a broad and practical viewpoint I can see no substantial difference between saying that what the defenders did materially increased the risk of injury to the pursuer and saying that what the defender did made a material contribution to his injury.

I would therefore allow this appeal.

10.5.7 LORD SIMON OF GLAISDALE: In the circumstances of the present case, the possibility of a distinction existing between (a) having materially increased the risk of contracting the disease, and (b) having materially contributed to causing the disease may no doubt be a fruitful source of interesting academic discussions between students of philosophy. Such a distinction is, however, far too unreal to be recognised by the common law. I would accordingly allow the appeal.'

COMMENT

10.6.1 Decided: Nov. 1, 1972.
Nov. 7: Nixon won presidential election.
Oct. 10: Betjeman appointed Poet Laureate.
Oct. 9: End of U.C.S. work-in.
Sept. 12: Icelandic gunboat sank two British trawlers in Cod War.
Sept. 5: Black September murdered Israeli athletes at Olympic Games.

10.6.2 What does this case actually decide? (See Wilson, "A Note on Causation", 1976 S.L.T. (News) 193.) *Wardlaw* and *McGhee* clearly make it easier for a pursuer to satisfy the law's requirements. Is the distinction in para. 10.5.6 important? Is it necessary?

10.6.3 This case has now been fully reconsidered in England, particularly in *Wilsher v. Essex Area Health Authority* [1988] A.C. 1074. All that case does is to prevent *McGhee* being used to undermine the need for causation. It has been explained now as being an instance of an inference from primary facts.
 Nonetheless it has recently been applied in its proper context in *Porter v. S.R.C.*, 1991 S.L.T. 446. Employers of a nursery assistant were held liable because they had a policy of leaving the food spilled by children to be cleared up at the end of the meal session. A system of mopping-up immediately a spill occurred would have materially diminished the risk. See also *Muir v. Cumbernauld and Kilsyth D.C.*, 1993 S.L.T. 287.

10.6.4 Two very useful articles on the particular topic of causation in medical negligence cases but which deal with the broader issues are Logie, "Proof of Causation in Medical Negligence Cases", 1988 S.L.T. (News) 25 and Phillips, "Further Reflections on Medical Causation", 1988 S.L.T. (News) 325. Mr Logie suggests that the all-or-nothing approach to causation is perhaps not appropriate where difficult causation issues arise and that a more creative approach could be considered. Do you agree? What are the alternative approaches? Consider what Mr Phillips calls the *Brachtenbach* approach (discussed by Lord Mackay in *Hotson*). Do you think that the use of statistical evidence depends upon whether there are cumulative or mutually exclusive multiple causes? Why? See also Griffiths, J.R., "Medical Negligence", 1995 1 S.L.P.Q. 25 at 31 *et seq.* Phillips, A. F., "Lost Chances in Delict", 1995 J.R. 401.

Novus actus interveniens

47. McKew (Appellant) v. Holland & Hannen & Cubitts (Scotland) Ltd
1970 S.L.T. 68 (H.L.)

10.7.1 'LORD REID: The appellant sustained in the course of his employment trivial injuries which were admittedly caused by the fault of the respondents. His back and hips were badly strained, he could not bend, and on several occasions his left leg suddenly "went away from" him. I take this to mean that for a short time he lost control of his leg and it became numb. He would have recovered fully from his injuries in a week or two but for a second accident in which he suffered a severe fracture of his ankle. The question in this case is whether the respondents are liable for the damage caused by this second accident. If they are so liable, then damages have been agreed at £4915: if they are not so liable, then damages are agreed at £200, the sum awarded in the Court of Session.

Some days after the first accident the appellant was offered the tenancy of a flat in Succouth Street, Glasgow. He went to inspect it, accompanied by his wife and child and a brother-in-law. The flat is approached by a steep stair between two walls and there was no handrail.

. . . . . .

10.7.2 The main argument for the respondents is that the second accident was not the direct or natural and probable or foreseeable result of their fault in causing the first accident.

In my view the law is clear. If a man is injured in such a way that his leg may give way at any moment he must act reasonably and carefully. It is quite possible that in spite of all reasonable care his leg may give way in circumstances such that as a result he sustains further injury. Then that second injury was caused by his disability which in turn was caused by the defender's fault. But if the injured man acts unreasonably he cannot hold the defender liable for injury caused by his own unreasonable conduct. His unreasonable conduct is *novus actus interveniens*. The chain of causation has been broken, and what follows must be regarded as caused by his own conduct and not by the defenders' fault or the disability caused by it. Or one may say that unreasonable conduct of the pursuer and what follows from it is not the natural and probable result of the original fault of the defender or of the ensuing disability. I do not think that foreseeability comes into this. A defender is not liable for every consequence which a reasonable man could foresee. What can be foreseen depends almost entirely on the facts of the case, and it is often easy to foresee unreasonable conduct or some other *novus actus interveniens* as being quite likely. But that does not mean that the defender must pay for damage caused by the *novus actus*. It only leads to trouble if one tries to graft on to the concept of foreseeability some rule of law to the effect that a wrongdoer is not bound to foresee something which in fact he could readily foresee as quite likely to happen. For it is not at all unlikely or unforeseeable that an active man who has suffered such a disability will take some unreasonable risk. But if he does he cannot hold the defender liable for the consequences.

10.7.3 So, in my view, the question here is whether the second accident was caused by the appellant doing something unreasonable. It was argued that the wrongdoer must take his victim as he finds him and that applies not only to a thin skull but also to his intelligence.

But I shall not deal with that argument because there is nothing in the evidence here to suggest that the appellant did something which a moment's reflection would have shown him was an unreasonable thing to do.

He knew that his left leg was liable to give way suddenly and without warning. He knew that this stair was steep and that there was no handrail. He must have realised, if he had given the matter a moment's thought, that he could only safely descend the stair if he either went extremely slowly and carefully so that he could sit down if his leg gave way, or waited for the assistance of his wife and brother-in-law. But he chose to descend in such a way that when his leg gave way he could not stop himself. I agree with what the Lord Justice-Clerk says at the end of his opinion, and I think that this is sufficient to require this appeal to be dismissed.

10.7.4 But I think it right to say a word about the argument that the fact that the appellant made to jump when he felt himself falling is conclusive against him. When his leg gave way the appellant was in a very difficult situation. He had to decide what to do in a fraction of a second. He may have come to a wrong decision: he probably did. But if the chain of causation had not been broken before this by his putting himself in a position where he might be confronted with such an emergency, I do not think that he would put himself out of court by acting wrongly in the emergency unless his action was so utterly unreasonable that even on the spur of the moment no ordinary man would have been so foolish as to do what he did. In an emergency it is natural to try to do something to save oneself and I do not think that his trying to jump in this emergency was so wrong that it could be said to be more than an error of judgment. But for the reasons already given I would dismiss this appeal.

10.7.5 LORD GUEST: I would have difficulty in faulting the Lord Ordinary's view. If the appellant was believed — and the Lord Ordinary bases his judgment upon his evidence — he performed a not inconsiderable acrobatic feat in jumping down 10 steps clear. "The grand rule," said Lord Kinloch in *Allan* v. *Barclay* (1864) 2 M. 873), "on the subject of damages is that none can be claimed except such as naturally and directly arise out of the wrong done; and such therefore as may reasonably be supposed to have been in the view of the wrongdoer."

This has been elaborated, discussed and explained in future cases but never improved upon. If, on the other hand, the action which resulted in the injury was "something unaccountable, a new cause which disturbs the sequence of events, something which can be described as either unreasonable or extraneous or extrinsic the chain of causation is broken" (*The Oropesa* [1943] P. 32, Lord Wright at p. 39). In *S.S. Baron Vernon* v. *S.S. Metagama*, 1928 S.C.(H.L.) 21,

Viscount Haldane at p. 25, states that damages are recoverable if they are the natural and reasonable result of the negligence and it will assume this character if it can be shown to be such a consequence as in the ordinary course of things would flow from the negligence. "Reasonable human conduct is part of the ordinary course of things."

If the appellant jumped, as found by the Lord Ordinary, I cannot regard this as reasonable human conduct. But whether this is to judge the appellant's conduct in too-fine scales I would regard the Lord Justice-Clerk's ground of judgment as equally satisfactory... He had the experience of his leg giving way. Yet he chose without assistance, without hanging on to the wall, to commence to descend those steep stairs holding his young daughter by the hand.'

COMMENT

10.8.1 Decided: Nov. 26, 1969.
Nov. 24: Apollo 12 arrived back on Earth.
Oct. 21: Edward Heath appointed Margaret Thatcher shadow education spokeswoman.
Oct. 5: First episode of *Monty Python's Flying Circus* broadcast.

10.8.2 This case is often usefully considered with two English House of Lords cases. In *Baker v. Willoughby* [1970] A.C. 467 the plaintiff had sustained an injury to his leg as a result of the defender's carelessness. Before the case came to hearing he changed jobs, but was unfortunate enough to be shot in a robbery. His injuries were so severe that his left leg was amputated. The defendants tried to have the amount of damages reduced in that the damages they would have had to pay for future loss had been overtaken by events. The House of Lords refused to allow the defendants the reduction due to the injuries sustained at the hands of the robbers. In *Jobling v. Associated Dairies Ltd* [1982] A.C. 794 the House of Lords came to a conclusion which seemed contrary to the reasoning of *Baker*. This time, before the trial, the plaintiff developed a condition quite naturally which would render him unfit for work. The defendants accordingly tried to claim that they should not pay damages in respect of his future loss which was not going to be caused by their carelessness but would have happened in any event. The House of Lords agreed with the defendants. This makes it difficult to be sure of the distinction between the cases: could it be the difference between subsequent tortious or delictual causes, neutral causes and natural causes?

10.8.3 For the "grand rule" mentioned by Lord Guest, see the next extract. (Ext. 48.)

Chapter 11

NEGLIGENCE: REMOTENESS

The grand rule

48. Allan v. Barclay
(1864) 2 M. 873 (I.H.)

11.1.1 '[From the report]: This was an action at the instance of John Allan, brewer, Airdrie, against Andrew Barclay, engineer, Kilmarnock, concluding for £50. It was averred that, on September 22, 1863, an engine belonging to the defender had broken down on the public road and was left in an oblique position across the road; that the engine might have been easily moved into a recess at the side of the road, where it would have done no damage; that it was not removed, but allowed after dark to continue lying across the road, with a large fire or other blaze of light burning on the engine to mark the place, and that William Hill, a carter in the service of the pursuer, came opposite the engine with his horse and cart, and his horse being frightened by the glare, shied, and upset Hill and the horse and cart into the ditch, Hill receiving personal injuries, and the horse and cart being damaged. The pursuer further averred — "Through the occurrences above set forth, the said William Hill sustained very serious injuries, in consequence of which he has since been utterly unable to prosecute his work, in the capacity aforesaid as servant to the pursuer. The services of the said William Hill were of the utmost importance to the pursuer, as being acquainted with the pursuer's business, and with his customers, he was instrumental, to a very great extent, both in maintaining and in extending it. The pursuer, by being deprived of these services, and not having been able to supply the place of his servant by another person of the same qualification, and the same knowledge of his business, has sustained serious loss, which he cannot estimate at less than £30... The defender objected to the relevancy of the action; and the Lord Ordinary reported the case on the adjustment of issues.

11.1.2 LORD KINLOCH: In the present case there is the further objection that the action is not sued by the person who was injured by the accident, but by a person to whom he was servant, and in its primary conclusion claims reparation for the loss of the individual's services during the time he was laid up by his injuries. It is contended by the defender that this is a remote or consequential damage, of which the law will not take cognisance... Again there appeared no sound analogy derivable from the recognised claim of damages against a person who seduces an apprentice or servant to break his contract of service, and leave his place. The injurious act is then directly committed against the master, and the damages claimed for loss of service are the direct results of the act. The difficulty in the present case is, that the injury done the servant was in its own nature not committed against him in that capacity, nor aimed, directly or indirectly, against the master. It was *tanquam quilibet* that the servant was injured. It is not alleged to have been even known to the defender, before or at the time of the accident, that Hill was the servant of the pursuer; and the *quasi*-contract of reparation could not be said to have been made with him in that character.

. . . . . .

11.1.3 The Lord Ordinary inclines strongly to the opinion that a claim such as that now made is not sanctioned by our law. If the claim be competent to a master, it is, by parity of reason, competent to everyone, in whatever relation, who can show himself to have suffered loss by the physical incapacitation of another. Nor is it easy to say where the claim of reparation will stop. The person injured may be a worker in a manufactory, where the loss of his services causes a cessation of the labours of half-a-dozen others; the want of the services of these may impede those of hundreds; the work may be entirely stopped; an order, involving thousands of pounds, may be prevented from being executed. Many other illustrations may be figured.

11.1.4 The grand rule on the subject of damages is, that none can be claimed except such as naturally and directly arise out of the wrong done; and such, therefore, as may reasonably be supposed to have been in the view of the wrongdoer. Tried by this test, the present claim appears to fail. The personal injuries of the individual himself will be properly held to have been in the contemplation of the wrongdoer. But he cannot be held bound to have surmised the secondary injuries done to all holding relations with the individual, whether that of a master, or any other.

. . . . . .

11.1.5 [In the First Division] LORD PRESIDENT: This appears to be a new proposal in the law of Scotland; but apart altogether from that, I do not think we have facts alleged relevant to infer any claim of damage. It is not said what agreement for service there was between the sufferer and his master and the allegations of loss are so vague that we cannot recognise them.

. . . . . .

11.1.6   LORD DEAS: There is no instance of an action of this kind, but I do not think it is necessary to inquire whether such an action could never be maintained, because here I do not find any allegation of a contract of service for any specified period, not even for a week or a day — nor any relevant statement of damage resulting to the master.'

COMMENT

11.2.1   Decided: March 15, 1864.
      Nov. 20, 1863: Gettysburg Address.
      Dec. 23: W. M. Thackeray died.

11.2.2   Do you think Lord Kinloch meant to say *quasi*-contract, or did he mean to say *quasi*-delict? If his conception of the issue were contractual, might his thinking have been coloured by the law on contract damages where the test is one of foreseeability as a real possibility? (See Woolman, *Contract*, pp. 147–150.)

11.2.3   What is the *ratio decidendi* of this case? What accordingly is the status of the grand rule?

11.2.4   The most important point to make is that the case, even though included here, is truly concerned with culpability rather than remoteness of damage — the reason is that it has *become* the most used verbal formulation in the Scots courts. Remoteness issues overlap with causation issues also. The three issues culpability, causation and remoteness are, however, conceptually distinct.

The thin skull rule

49. **McKillen v. Barclay Curle & Co. Ltd, (Appellants)**
1967 S.L.T. 41

11.3.1   "THE LORD PRESIDENT (Clyde): This is an action by a plumber's mate against his employers who are shipbuilders. On November 7, 1961 he sustained injuries while he was working on a ship in the course of construction in the defenders' shipyard, and he claims damages from them on the ground that their fault caused the injuries. The accident happened when he was in course of descending a three-step staging. The fault alleged is that the middle step on which he slipped was defective, and caused him to fall. It is unnecessary to examine this aspect of the case further, as the Lord Ordinary held fault to be established and the defenders have acquiesced in this finding.

11.3.2   The main issue before the Lord Ordinary and the only issue before us was concerned with the measure of damages. When he fell the pursuer fractured a rib. This rib was strapped up for about three weeks, and when the strapping was removed the pursuer was sent to the Knightswood Chest Clinic, as there appeared to be some congestion at the base of his left lung. In the summer of 1953 it had been diagnosed that the pursuer was suffering from a patch of tuberculosis in the upper part of his left lung. But in November 1953 and in subsequent X-ray examinations in 1954, 1955 and 1957 the condition had become inactive. There had been no further X-ray examinations of his lung after 1957 prior to the accident on November 7, 1961. On admission after his accident to the chest clinic his lungs were again examined by X-ray on December 13, 1961 and an active tuberculosis infection of the left lung was found at its base.

. . . . . .

11.3.3 In order to relate the tuberculosis at the base of the left lung causally with the accident the pursuer admittedly must establish two things, first of all a causal relation between the fracture of the rib and the congestion of the lung, and secondly a causal relation between the congestion and the reactivation of tuberculosis.

The pursuer's own doctor... expresses the view in evidence that he does not believe that the injury to the ribs caused the congestion. The only other medical witness who expresses an opinion on the matter differs from this conclusion and did form the view that the injury to the ribs and the congestions were causally related. On this preliminary matter, therefore, the doctors differ, and it follows that this essential link in the chain is not established. The Lord Ordinary nowhere suggests that either of these doctors is unreliable or in error, and in the light of this flat contradiction in their testimony it would not be proper to infer that the pursuer has linked up the congestion, and anything which may have followed from it and the accident... Even if [the second doctor's] evidence can be read as meaning that it is more probable than not that the inflammation to which the fracture gave rise reactivated the tuberculosis, that evidence stands alone and uncorroborated. This in itself is fatal to the pursuer's success... In my opinion, therefore, the pursuer has not proved a causal connection between his injury and the reactivation of tuberculosis in his lung.

. . . . . .

11.3.4 I come now to the last matter argued to us, namely the remoteness of damage following from the tuberculosis reactivation. The defenders contended that even if the evidence showed (contrary to their contention) that the tuberculosis which because active in December 1961 was a consequence of the accident, the pursuer was not entitled to damage in respect of it. The defenders, so they contended, were only liable for damage which is reasonably foreseeable, and although the damage to the rib would fall within that category, the outbreak of tuberculosis would not. On the view which I take of the facts, it is strictly not necessary for me to deal with this issue, but in the light of the full argument presented to us upon it I feel it only right to express my views upon it.

11.3.5 In my opinion it has never been the law of Scotland that a man guilty of negligence towards another is only liable for the damage in respect of physical injuries which a reasonable man would foresee as likely to follow from it. On the contrary it has always been the law of Scotland as I understand it that once a man is negligent and injures another by his negligence he is liable for all damage to the injured man which naturally and directly arises out of the negligence. He must take his victim as he finds him, and if his victim has a weak heart and dies as a result of the injury the negligent man is liable in damages for his death even although a normal man might only in the same circumstances have sustained a relatively trivial injury. The principle of Scots law was laid down as long ago as 1864 by Lord Kinloch in *Allan* v. *Barclay* (1863) 2 M. 873, at p. 874, and his statement of the law has never since been controverted. The doctrine of reasonable foreseeability with all its subtle ramifications may be applied in determining questions of liability (see *Bourhill* v. *Young*, 1942 S.C.(H.L.) 78; *Muir* v. *Glasgow Corp.*, 1943 S.C.(H.L.) 3). It has no relevance once liability is established and the measure of damage is being determined.

. . . . . .

11.3.6 We were referred to several English decisions which seem to disclose inconsistencies *inter se* (*Re Polemis and Furness Withy & Co.* [1921] 3 K.B. 560; *Wagon Mound* [1961] A.C. 388). I do not find it necessary to examine these in detail. I am content to accept the position in England now as set out by Lord Parker C.J. in *Smith* v. *Leech Brain & Co. Ltd.* [1962] 2 Q.B. 405 at p. 415, where he recognises that whatever may have been the position at the time, the law in England in this matter is now precisely in conformity with the law of Scotland — namely that a tortfeasor takes the victim as he finds him. Had I considered therefore that the pursuer has established a causal connection between the injury to his ribs and the reactivation of tuberculosis I should have held that the defenders were liable in damages in respect of both the rib injury and the reactivation.

11.3.7 LORD GUTHRIE: ... In my opinion it is clear from the passage quoted [from *Davie* v. *Edinburgh Magistrates*, 1953 S.C. 34] that the Lord President [Cooper] had not in mind a case like the present, in which the essential fact is a matter of technical science, namely, whether the reactivation of the pursuer's tuberculosis was, according to medical science, a consequence of his fractured rib. If the essential fact in dispute is a matter of technical science, then it cannot be established by the uncorroborated testimony of a single expert witness.

11.3.8 The Lord Ordinary's opinion and the debate before us were largely taken up with the discussion of English cases on the law of damages, and the decision of the Privy Council in *The Wagon Mound* [1961] A.C. 388. I do not think it is necessary to consider these cases, since the rule of Scotland law is well settled. It was stated by Lord Kinloch in *Allan* v. *Barclay, supra,* in terms which have since been frequently quoted with approval... If the accident reactivated the tuberculosis then the reactivation arose naturally, in the ordinary course of nature, out of the defenders' negligence, and was the direct consequence of it... This particular pursuer has a weak chest, and his weak chest was injured by the defenders' negligence. There is no ground for holding that a reasonable man would have assumed that the pursuer had a sound pair of lungs, and no justification for limiting an award in his favour to the amount which would have been due to another person with a stronger constitution. I think that it is well settled in our law, that, if negligence is established, the wrong-doer must take his victim as he finds him.

11.3.9   LORD MIGDALE: It is conceded that the doctrine of reasonable foreseeability can be invoked where a pursuer is seeking to establish liability against an alleged wrong-doer (see *Bourhill* v. *Young* (*supra*), *Muir* v. *Corporn. of Glasgow* (*supra*). The contention here is whether that doctrine can be invoked after liability has been established, to restrict the amount of damages. This contention was put forward on the assumption that the tubercular infection was the direct and natural consequence of the injury. The defenders maintained that even on that basis they were not liable to pay compensation in respect of that part of the pursuer's disability because they did not know of his earlier condition and could not reasonably foresee that a fall on the step would give rise to tuberculosis. It was argued to us that the effect of the Privy Council decision in *The Wagon Mound* [1961] A.C. 388 was that the defender was not liable for damage which he could not have reasonably foreseen. I do not propose to embark on the contentious sea which has beaten upon the earlier decision in *Re Polemis* [1942] 3 K.B. 560. It concerns English law. I will content myself with saying that there is a formidable body of opinion to support the view that the rule laid down in *Re Polemis* (*supra*) was not and is not the law of Scotland. I would refer to what was said by Lord Russell of Killowen and by Lord MacMillan in *Bourhill* v. *Young* (*supra*), at pp. 85 and 89 and by Lord Justice-Clerk Cooper in *Steel v. Glasgow Iron and Steel Co.,* 1944 S.C. 237 at p. 248, where he says that "the rule of the reasonable and probable consequence is the key which opens several locks... maybe whether the damages claimed are too remote." On the other hand I know of no case of personal injury where damages have been refused where they flowed directly from the injury but could not be reasonably foreseen. It may be that the doctrine of reasonable foreseeability gives way in the class of personal injuries to the other rule that a wrong-doer must take his victim as he finds him.

But I prefer the view that the doctrine of reasonable foreseeability does extend to the measure of damages and can be invoked by a defender if the damages are too remote, but not in a case of personal injuries. In such a case the wrong-doer is liable in reparation for the loss, injury and damage which flow naturally and directly from his wrongful act, because he ought to have had in contemplation that his victim might be a sickly person whose health was such that a fall would start off complications which would not be likely to afflict a person in normal health.

That is what Lord Kinloch said in the case of *Allan* v. *Barclay* at p. 874 [his Lordship quoted the grand rule at 11.1.4] ... This statement of the law has stood unchallenged for over 100 years and is still sound. The wrong-doer must pay for the injuries suffered by his victim provided they arise naturally and directly from the wrongful act, because he ought to have contemplated that he might be an unusually frail person or one afflicted with a latent trouble liable to be reactivated.

11.3.10 LORD CAMERON: ... I do not think it is necessary or even helpful to support a conclusion on this matter by reference to English authorities. It may be that in this matter the law of England has reached the same conclusion as the law of Scotland, but I do not find it helpful in determining what is the law of Scotland to endeavour first to discover what is the law of England, when Scottish authority is plain and of long and undoubted standing.

I therefore agree that this reclaiming motion should be disposed of as your Lordship in the chair had proposed.'

COMMENT

11.4.1   Decided: November 26, 1965.
   Oct. 7: Post Office Tower in London opened.
   Oct. 14: Bertrand Russell tore up Labour party card over Vietnam war.
   Nov. 11: Ian Smith declared UDI in Rhodesia.

11.4.2   Do you agree that it is reasonably foreseeable that a person you bump into will be especially frail? Would it help to know what proportion of the general population were especially frail? Who should insure for such an accident: should most people insure against an accident befalling them or against being liable to another? What form of insurance is the most common in the general population? Would the law treat differently two men each with thin skulls, and each of whom did not wear a crash helmet or reinforced hat, if one of them was aware of his condition?

11.4.3   Do you agree with the treatment of English precedent at 11.3.10?

11.4.4   What if a person is suffering from chronic fatigue syndrome and it gets worse when you bang into the car he is driving? See *Page v. Smith* [1995] 2 W.L.R. 644.

Chapter 12

THIRD PARTY INTERVENTION

50. Smith (Appellant) v. Littlewoods Organisation Ltd; Maloco (Appellant) v. Littlewoods Organisation Ltd
1987 S.L.T. 425

12.1.1 'Lord Keith of Kinkel: I have had the advantage of considering in draft the speeches to be delivered by my noble and learned friends Lord Mackay of Clashfern and Lord Goff of Chieveley. I agree with them, and for the reasons they give would dismiss these appeals.

12.1.2 Lord Brandon of Oakbrook: It is axiomatic that the question whether there has been negligence in any given case must depend on the particular circumstances of that case. That being so, I do not think that these appeals can in the end be determined by reference to other reported cases in which the particular circumstances were different, even though some degree of analogy between such other cases and the present one can legitimately be drawn. Nor do I think that it is possible, however helpful it might otherwise be, to lay down any general principle designed to apply to all cases in which the negligence alleged against a person involves the unauthorised acts of independent third parties on premises owned or occupied by that person. The particular facts of the present case appear to me to raise two, and only two, questions, on the answers to which the determination of the appeal depends.

The first question is what was the general duty owed by Littlewoods, as owners and occupiers of the disused cinema, to the appellants, as owners and occupiers of other buildings near to the cinema? The answer to that question is, in my view, that Littlewoods owed to the appellants a duty to exercise reasonable care to ensure that the cinema was not, and did not become, a source of danger to neighbouring buildings owned or occupied by the appellants.

12.1.3 The second question is whether that general duty encompassed a specific duty to exercise reasonable care to prevent young persons obtaining unlawful access to the cinema, and, having done so, unlawfully setting it on fire. The answer to that question, in accordance with general principles governing alike the law of delict in Scotland and the law of negligence in England, must depend on whether the occurrence of such behaviour was reasonably foreseeable by Littlewoods if they had known the activities of young persons observed by certain individuals in the locality. But they did not know of such activities because the individuals concerned did not inform either Littlewoods or the police of them, nor did the police themselves observe them. In the absence of information about such activities, either from the individuals referred to or from the police, I am of opinion that the occurrence of the behaviour in question was not reasonably foreseeable by Littlewoods. I conclude, therefore, that the general duty of care owed by Littlewoods to the appellants did not encompass the specific duty referred to above. For these reasons I would dismiss the appeals.

12.1.4   LORD GRIFFITHS: I agree so fully with the statement and evaluation of the facts appearing in the speech of my noble and learned friend, Lord Mackay of Clashfern, that I can state my own reasons for dismissing these appeals very shortly... Listening to the seductive way in which counsel for the appellants developed his argument on the facts step by step, as described by Lord Mackay, I was reminded of the fable of the prince who lost his kingdom but for the want of a nail for the shoe of his horse. A series of foreseeable possibilities were added one to another and, hey presto, there emerged at the end the probability of a fire against which Littlewoods should have guarded. But, my Lords, that is not the common sense of this matter.

The fire in this case was caused by the criminal activity of third parties upon Littlewoods' premises. I do not say that there will never be circumstances in which the law will require an occupier of premises to take special precautions against such a contingency but they would surely have to be extreme indeed. It is common ground that only a 24-hour guard on these premises would have been likely to prevent this fire, and even that cannot be certain, such is the determination and ingenuity of young vandals.

There was nothing of an inherently dangerous nature stored in the premises, nor can I regard an empty cinema stripped of its equipment as likely to be any more alluring to vandals than any other recently vacated premises in the centre of a town... In short so far as Littlewoods knew, there was nothing significantly different about these empty premises from the tens of thousands of such premises up and down the country. People do not mount 24-hour guards on empty properties and the law would impose an intolerable burden if it requires them to do so save in the most exceptional circumstances. I find no such exceptional circumstances in this case and I would accordingly dismiss the appeals.

12.1.5   LORD MACKAY OF CLASHFERN: ... "Littlewoods" purchased the Regal Cinema in the centre of Dunfermline from its previous owners with entry on May 31, 1976. Littlewoods' intention was to demolish the cinema within a short time and replace it by a supermarket. On July 5, 1976, in consequence of a fire which began in the cinema, a café and billiard saloon, which lay close to the cinema on the west, known as the Café Maloco, was seriously damaged and St Paul's Church, which lay also to the west but at a slightly greater distance from the cinema, was so substantially damaged that it had to be demolished... The appellants' claimed against Littlewoods for the damage done to their properties, alleging that the damage was caused by negligence on part of Littlewoods. Littlewoods in turn claimed that, if they were at fault, the Chief Constable of Fife Constabulary or his officers were also at fault and he should be held liable to make a contribution to the award made against Littlewoods. The Lord Ordinary held that the claims had been established. Littlewoods accepted the decision relating to the chief constable but reclaimed against the awards which had been made against them. The First Division of the Inner House of the Court of Session (1986 S.L.T. 272) unanimously allowed the reclaiming motions and recalled the Lord Ordinary's interlocutors.

12.1.6   The cinema comprised a substantial brick-built auditorium with a balcony at the north end and a flat timber and felt covered roof on a steel frame... To the east of the cinema entrance in the High Street there was a passageway, known as Macpherson's Close, which ran down the length towards the south on the east side of the main building... Macpherson's Close was regularly used by the public as a short cut from Canmore Street to the High Street... The main building of the cinema had a number of exits or fire doors with locking bars, designed to be opened only from the inside which were set in the walls of the cinema.

The last showing of a film in the cinema took place on May 29, 1976. Although legal entry was given on May 31, 1976, the keys were not handed over to Littlewoods until about June 14. During that period the previous owners employed contractors to remove fittings and equipment from the cinema which were worth taking away but which were of no interest to Littlewoods... From about the end of the third week in June 1976 the cinema remained empty and unattended by any persons employed by or giving services to Littlewoods.

The evidence established that children began to overcome the security of the cinema building by breaking into it in one way or another in the period of about four days when Littlewoods contractors were doing preliminary work inside the premises during or towards the end of the third week in June 1976. Although these contractors locked and secured the premises when they finished work each night, they discovered on their return in the morning clear signs that the premises had been forcibly entered. Some of the fire doors had been forced open from inside and the locking bars had been broken. The contractors then had to secure the doors which had been so affected by tying them with rope to the stage. When they finished their work they left the premises as secure as they could make them. Thereafter the security of the premises was again overcome by children and young persons, and children and young persons resorted to the premises with increasing regularity for play, horseplay, and pleasure of making a mess and breaking whatever they could find to break. The Lord Ordinary held that it was amply established that the first few days of July 1976 anyone with half an eye who made use of Macpherson's Close would have seen that the main building of the cinema was no longer lockfast and was being regularly entered by unauthorised persons. Paper and débris was scattered about the auditorium and in Macpherson's Close outside the building débris increased, consisting of bricks, glass and old films. During the time that the Littlewood's contractors were working inside the main building one of the contractors' employees saw lengths of old cinema film lying in Macpherson's Close and noticed signs of someone having attempted to set fire to them. The type of film used in the cinema was non-inflammable and no fire had occurred. About the end of June, Mr Scott, who was the beadle of St Paul's Church and of another church in the vicinity, saw signs of someone having tried to light a fire inside the building. His attention had been attracted because some children had run out of the building as he approached. When he went inside, he found that the carpet, where oil has been spilled on it, was burning. He put it out very easily by stamping on it and told Mr Kerr, the session clerk of St Paul's, about it. Neither Mr Scott nor anyone else informed the police or Littlewoods about any of these matters... On July 5, 1976 about 6.30 p.m. a large ceramic sink from a toilet on the top floor of the main building of the cinema landed on the roof of the billiard saloon in Café Maloco. It was thrown from a window on the west side of the cinema by boys of 13 or 14 years of age. The police were called and detained two boys. Between 8.00 and 9.00 p.m. on the same day a passer-by noticed three teenagers come out Macpherson's Close and soon after she saw smoke coming from the close. The police and the fire brigade were called but the fire which started in the south-west corner of the balcony soon engulfed the whole building... The Lord Ordinary concluded — and there was no challenge to the correctness of his conclusion — that the fire which started on July 5, 1976 was deliberately started by children or teenagers and that the teenagers that the passer-by saw emerging from Macpherson's Close shortly before the smoke started to come out were probably responsible. Apart from the contractors employed by Littlewoods, to whom I have referred, the only person employed by Littlewoods who gave evidence was a member of the architectural department who was responsible for the design and supervision of the construction of buildings for the company. He visited the cinema about the middle of June and according to his evidence it was secure at that time.

12.1.7 The claims are based on the allegation that Littlewoods, as owners and occupiers of the Regal Cinema, had a duty to take reasonable care of the safety of premises adjoining; that they knew or ought to have known that a disused cinema would be a ready target for vandals; and they knew or ought to have known that their cinema was, in fact, the subject of extensive vandalism and that if they did not take steps to prevent the entry of vandals they would cause damage not only to their own property, whether by fire or otherwise, but further such fire might spread and cause damage to adjoining properties. In these circumstances, it was claimed that Littlewoods had a duty to take reasonable care to keep and maintain the premises lockfast, to cause frequent and regular inspection to be made and to lock and board up any doors and windows found to be open or smashed and to employ a caretaker to watch over the premises and to prevent the entry of vandals. In the course of hearing before your Lordships counsel for the appellants accepted that, in the light of the evidence, the only precaution that was likely to be effective in preventing the entry of vandals was to arrange for a 24-hour watch to be maintained on the premises. Littlewoods, while accepting that as owners and occupier of the premises they had a duty to take reasonable care of the safety of premises adjoining, strenuously denied that they owned the duties on which these claims are founded.

12.1.8 The Lord Ordinary, after examining the authorities, concluded that whether such duties were owned by Littlewoods or not depended on the answer to the question: "Bearing in mind that [Littlewoods] had no control over the children and teenagers, was it reasonably foreseeable by [Littlewoods] that, by failing to keep the cinema lockfast and to inspect it regularly during the last half of June and the first few days of July 1976, children and young persons would not only enter it, but start a fire?" He considered that it was appropriate that he should treat this as a jury question and try to answer it as a jury would. He says: "In the absence of any evidence about the lighting of fires, it would have been difficult to say that it was very likely that children and young persons breaking into these premises would start a fire, but in the present instance there is evidence that on two occasions shortly before 5th July 1976 witnesses saw signs of someone having tried to start a fire... . I accept that there is a very narrow dividing line in the circumstances of this case between bare foreseeability and reasonable foreseeability, but having applied my mind to that problem I have reached the conclusion that the lighting of a fire in the premises by children or teenagers was in the circumstances reasonably foreseeable"...

12.1.9 Before the First Division it was accepted by the appellants that, on the evidence, Littlewoods had no knowledge of the attempts to start fires to which the Lord Ordinary referred in the passage I have quoted and that, accordingly, in considering whether Littlewoods were bound reasonably to foresee that as a consequence of their inaction a fire would be started in their building and not only engulf it but cause damage to buildings nearby, these required to be left out of account unless it could be said that they had a duty to know of them. If they had not such a duty, the Lord Ordinary's decision on this crucial matter was open for review by the judges of the First Division. The judges of the First Division unanimously concluded that the question was at large for their consideration and that in the circumstances it had not been shown that it was reasonably to be foreseen by Littlewoods that if they took no steps to discourage widespread use of the cinema by youngsters, including vandals, one or more of them, or some other intruder, would be likely deliberately to set fire to the building or deliberately to set fire in such place as would be likely to engulf the building.

12.1.10 Counsel for the appellants in his very persuasive submissions to your Lordships suggested that this crucial question should be approached in stages. First, he submitted that by reason of the particular features of this building it was reasonably foreseeable by Littlewoods that young persons were likely to be attracted to the building and would attempt to overcome such security as there was and would attempt to gain entry. The second submission was that it was reasonably foreseeable that if the building was insecure and remained insecure it would be entered. Further, it was reasonably foreseeable that a proportion of such young persons would be intent on causing damage within the building which might have an effect on adjoining property. The fourth step in the argument was that it was reasonably foreseeable that such damage would include damage by fire which, being unpredictable, was likely to take hold of the fabric of the building. And the final step in the logical progression was that it was reasonably foreseeable that if the fire took hold of the building it would engulf the building and, since the building was large, the fire would readily spread to adjoining properties.

. . . . . .

12.1.11 Counsel for the appellants referred to three decisions in which conduct of this kind had come to the notice of the courts: *Evans* v. *Glasgow District Council*, 1978 S.L.T. 17, in which it was alleged that one of the forms vandalism had taken in that case was that ignited material had been dropped through damaged floors of a flat above the pursuer's premises with the consequence that the contents of these premises were destroyed almost entirely; *Carrick Furniture House Ltd.* v. *Paterson*, 1978 S.L.T. (Notes) 48, in which it was alleged that persons had entered and deliberately set fire to the premises in question; and thirdly, *Thomas Graham & Co. Ltd.* v. *Church of Scotland General Trustees*, 1982 S.L.T. (Sh.Ct.) 26, in which vandals had entered a church and set it on fire. Counsel for the appellants also referred to the Criminal Justice (Scotland) Act 1980, s. 78... He further referred to *Hughes* v. *Lord Advocate*, 1963 S.C.(H.L.) 31 as demonstrating the unpredictability of children's behaviour as factor to be taken into account in dealing with a question such as is raised here.

12.1.12 Counsel for the appellants submitted further, and anticipating what might be argued against him, that although the actions that caused the fire were those of vandals over whom Littlewoods had no control, his case was founded on the need that arose in consequence of the likely results of allowing vandals into the building to take precautions to keep them out. The test of whether such precautions should be taken was, in counsel for the appellant's submission, whether it was reasonably foreseeable by Littlewoods that if they did not take these precautions it was a substantial risk that the neighbouring properties would be damaged. He referred particularly to *Dorset Yacht Co. Ltd.* v. *Home Office* [1970] 1 A.C. 1004, and to the speech of Lord Reid at p. 1027, where referring to the well-known passage (at p. 580) in Lord Atkin's speech in *Donoghue* v. *Stevenson* [Ext. 39], Lord Reid said: "[It] should I think be regarded as a statement of principle. It is not to be treated as if it were a statutory definition. It will require qualification in new circumstances. But I think that the time has come when we can and should say that it ought to apply unless there is some justification or valid explanation for its exclusion"... Rather, said counsel for the appellants, one should take account of actions of third parties over whom the defender has no control in considering the consequences of acts or omissions on the defender's part. He referred in support of this submission to the later passages in Lord Reid's speech where he dealt with this question. As an illustration of this approach being taken in Scotland, he referred to *Squires* v. *Perth and Kinross District Council*, 1986 S.L.T. 30, in which jewellers successfully sued building contractors who were working in a flat above their shop for not adequately securing the flat against entry by thieves. A thief entered the jewellers' premises through the flat by climbing up a drain pipe at the back of the property to which he obtained access by climbing over a building. A substantial quantity of jewellery was stolen.

12.1.13 Counsel for Littlewoods submitted that on the findings of fact in the present case Littlewoods had not established, applying the test of reasonable foreseeability, the existence of a risk sufficient to have obliged Littlewoods to adopt in advance of the catastrophic fire the only one of the prescribed remedies that might have avoided that occurrence, namely, having the premises watched all the time. He also advanced a broader proposition that the policy of the law should deny these claims, first, because they involved an unwarranted invasion of the basic right of a person to use his property as he pleased and, secondly, because affirming these claims implied potential obligations on those who leave property unoccupied for a comparatively short time that would be unduly heavy having regard to the purpose intended to be served. Or, putting the matter another way, he submitted that the law should put the responsibility for securing the safety and security of property against vandals on the owner or occupier of the property and not on neighbouring owners or occupiers from whose property damage by vandals and thieves might be caused… He pointed out that there was no evidence that this building was in any way a special fire hazard, nor was there evidence that this part of Dunfermline was specially subject to vandalism.

. . . . . .

12.1.14 In approaching these rival submissions it has to be borne in mind that the damage to the neighbouring properties, upon which the claims against Littlewoods are founded, is damage by fire or otherwise resulting from vandalism in Littlewoods' premises. A duty of care to prevent this damage is the only duty alleged to be incumbent upon Littlewoods relevant to this case. From this it follows that unless Littlewoods were bound reasonably to anticipate and guard against this danger, they had no duty of care, relevant to this case, requiring them to inspect their premises…

12.1.15 As I have said, the Lord Ordinary's answer to the basic question in the case depended, and depended critically, on his assumption that Littlewoods were to be taken as aware of the evidence relating to the attempt to start a fire in the lane with the abandoned film and to the smouldering carpet which Mr Scott extinguished. It is plain from the way in which the Lord Ordinary expresses his opinion that, had it not been for his reliance upon the evidence against Littlewoods, he would not have found against them. There was no evidence that Littlewoods knew of these matters. Unless they had a duty to inspect, there is no basis on which it can be alleged that they ought to have known of them. Since the only basis on which any relevant duty of care is said to arise is that damage to neighbouring properties was to be anticipated unless it were exercised, in considering whether such damage should have been anticipated one cannot assume that any of the relevant duties should have been performed. I conclude that the Lord Ordinary was not entitled to assume that Littlewoods should have known of these matters. The First Division concluded, as I have said that the matter was at large for their consideration. In my opinion, their Lordships of the First Division applied their minds to the correct question.In my opinion, the question whether, in all the circumstances described in evidence, a reasonable person in the position of Littlewoods was bound to anticipate as probable, if he took no action to keep these premises lockfast, that, in a comparatively short time before the premises were demolished, they would be set on fire with consequent risk to the neighbouring properties is a matter for the judges of fact to determine... The cases to which counsel for the appellants drew attention in his argument, and section 78 of the Act of 1980, illustrate that a consequence of this kind, if premises are left unoccupied, is a possibility, but the extent to which such an occurrence is probable must depend on the circumstances of the particular case. While no doubt in this case, as the judges in the courts below have found, it was probable that children and young persons might attempt to break into the vacated cinema, this by no means establishes that it was a probable consequence of its being vacated with no steps being taken to maintain it lockfast that it would be set on fire with consequent risk of damage to neighbouring properties. A telling point in favour of Littlewoods is that, although Littlewoods' particulars were shown on a board prominently displayed at the front of the premises, no one made any protest to them about the state of the premises or indicated to them any concern that, unless they took some action neighbouring premises were at risk... Neither is there evidence that the police were ever informed of the situation with regard to the cinema.

. . . . . .

12.1.16 This is sufficient for the disposal of this appeal but in view of the general importance of some of the matters raised in the parties' submissions it is right that I should add some observations on these.

First, counsel for the appellants urged us to say that the ordinary principle to be deduced from Lord Atkin's speech in *Donoghue* v. *Stevenson* should apply to cases where the damage in question was caused by human agency. It is plain from the authorities that the fact that the damage, upon which a claim is founded, was caused by a human agent quite independent of the person against whom a claim in negligence is made does not, of itself, preclude success of the claim, since breach of duty on the part of the person against whom the claim is made may also have played a part in causing the damage. In dealing with the submission in *Dorset Yacht Co. Ltd.* v. *Home Office* that the claim must fail because there was a general principle that no person can be responsible for damage caused by the acts of another who is not his servant nor acting on his behalf, Lord Reid, having quoted from *Haynes* v. *Harwood* [1935] 1 K.B. 146 and from *Scott's Trustees* v. *Moss* (1889) 17 R. 32 said at p. 1030: "These cases show that, where human action forms one of the links between the original wrongdoing of the defendant and the loss suffered by the plaintiff, that action must at least have been something very likely to happen if it is not to be regarded as *novus actus interveniens* breaking the chain of causation. I do not think that a mere foreseeable possibility is or should be sufficient, for then the intervening human action can more properly be regarded as a new cause than as a consequence of the original wrongdoing. But if the intervening action was likely to happen I do not think that it can matter whether that action was innocent or tortious or criminal. Unfortunately, tortious or criminal action by a third party is often the 'very kind of thing' which is likely to happen as a result of the wrongful or careless act of the defendant. And in the present case, on the facts which we must assume at this stage, I think that the taking of a boat by the escaping trainees and their unskilful navigation leading to damage to another vessel were the very kind of thing that these Borstal officers ought to have seen to be likely."

. . . . . .

12.1.17 It was accordingly not critical whether the test was foreseeability of that damage as likely or very likely. At the state at which Lord Reid used the phrase "very likely", he was giving his view on what the two cases he had cited showed... When Lord Reid turns to state his own position, he does so on the basis that the intervening action was likely to happen. In *Muir* v. *Glasgow Corpn.*, 1943 S.C.(H.L.) 3, the issue was whether the defenders' manageress was negligent in allowing two members of a picnic party to bring a tea urn along a passage in her tearoom without taking certain precautions. The damage in question, in that case, might therefore have arisen from the conduct of the two persons carrying the tea urn, who were not employees of the defenders nor in any way accountable to them. The test of liability set out by Lord Macmillan in *Bourhill* v. *Young* [1942] A.C. 92 at p. 104, namely: "The duty to take care is the duty to avoid doing or omitting to do anything the doing or omitting to do which may have as its reasonable and probable consequence injury to others and the duty owed to those to whom injury may reasonably and probably be anticipated if the duty is not observed" [Lord MacKay emphasised the word "probably" in the foregoing quotation] was expressly used by Lord Thankerton and Lord Macmillan. Lord Wright said at p. 16: "As to negligence, the two men (who were carrying the urn) were not their [*i.e.* the defenders'] servants. They were not responsible for their acts. That the men should be negligent in so simple an operation was not likely to happen. It was a mere possibility, not a reasonable probability. The men, if negligent, were, no doubt, responsible for their own negligence, but from the standpoint of the appellants the risk of negligence was a mere unlikely accident which no responsible person in [the manageress's] position could naturally be expected to foresee."

. . . . . .

12.1.18 It is true, as has been pointed out by Oliver L.J. in *Lamb* v. *Camden L.B.C.* [1981] Q.B. 625 at p. 642, that human conduct is particularly unpredictable and that every society will have a sprinkling of people who behave most abnormally. The result of this consideration, in my opinion, is that where the only possible source of the type of damage or injury which is in question is agency of a human being for whom the person against whom the claim is made has no responsibility, it may not be easy to find that as a reasonable person he was bound to anticipate that type of damage as a consequence of his act or omission. The more unpredictable the conduct in question, the less easy to affirm that any particular result from it is probable and in many circumstances the only way in which a judge could properly be persuaded to come to the conclusion that the result was not only possible but reasonably foreseeable as probable would be to convince him that, in the circumstances, it was highly likely. In this type of case a finding that the reasonable man should have anticipated the consequence of human action as just probable may not be a very frequent option. Unless the judge can be satisfied that the result of the human action is highly probable or very likely, he may have to conclude that all the reasonable man could say was that it was a mere possibility. Unless the needle that measures the probability of a particular result flowing from the conduct of a human agent is near the top of the scale, it may be hard to conclude that it has risen sufficiently from the bottom, to create the duty reasonably to foresee it.

12.1.19 In summary I conclude, in agreement with both counsel, that what the reasonable man is bound to foresee in a case involving injury or damage by independent human agency, just as in cases where such agency plays no part, is the probable consequences of his own act or omission, but that, in such a case, a clear basis will be required on which to assert that the injury or damage is more than mere possibility. To illustrate, it is not necessary to go further than the decision of this House in *Dorset Yacht Co. Ltd.* v. *Home Office* where I consider that all the members of the majority found such a possible basis in the facts that the respondents' yacht was situated very close to the island on which the Borstal boys escaped from their custodians, that the only effective means of avoiding recapture was to escape by the use of some nearby vessel, and that the only means of providing themselves with the means to continue their journey was likely to be theft from such nearby vessels. These considerations so limited the options open to the escaping boys that it became highly probable that the boys would use, damage or steal from one or more of the vessels moored near the island.

12.1.20 The matter is further illustrated by *Thomas Graham & Co. Ltd.* v. *Church of Scotland General Trustees*, 1982 S.L.T. (Sh.Ct.) 26 in which Sheriff Macvivar, Q.C., found that the area in which the defenders' church lay was subject to vandalism on a large scale, that on an inspection of the church in which representatives of the owners of the church took part shortly before the final fire evidence existed of small fires having already been lit in its interior and that, on that inspection, the official reporting to the local authority concerned with public safety had reported that the building should be demolished since it constituted a serious fire hazard. Sheriff Macvicar concluded that by not taking the very obvious and inexpensive precaution of securing the side door of the church, by which apparently access had been taken, the defenders had failed in their duty to take reasonable care for the safety of their neighbour's property... On Sheriff Macvicar's findings, the empty church building constituted a serious fire hazard unless it were effectively secured against further trespass.

12.1.21 Before leaving cases relating to fires, I should mention *Evans* v. *Glasgow District Council*, 1978 S.L.T. 17 and *Carrick Furniture House Ltd.* v. *Paterson*, 1978 S.L.T. (Notes) 48... In the first of these, *Evans*, the defenders had demolished premises which adjoined the pursuers' premises which were also leased from the defenders, and in doing so had damaged the lock securing the pursuers' doors which had been replaced with inadequate locks. The pursuers suffered loss as a result of (1) theft of goods by the persons who broke the new and inadequate locks; (2) fire caused by vandals dropping lighted materials through gaps left by the defenders in floorboards above the pursuers' premises and (3) water which escaped from the defenders' premises as a result of vandals interfering with the plumbing there... Lord Wylie said, at p. 19: "In such circumstances there was a general duty on owners or occupiers of property, particularly property of the tenement type, where they chose to leave it vacant for any material length of time, to take reasonable care to see that it was proof against the kind of vandalism which was calculated to affect adjoining property." In my view that amounted only to a decision that depending on the facts as they emerged, a duty of the scope alleged might be incumbent on owners or occupiers of such property in some circumstances that fell within the allegations made by the pursuers. *Carrick Furniture* which followed is explicable on the same ground.

· · · · · ·

12.1.22 *Lamb* v. *Camden, L.B.C.* [1981] Q.B. 625, was a decision that a workman, damaging a water pipe with his pick in such a way that settlement was occasioned to the foundations of the plaintiff's house, was not reasonably bound to foresee, as a consequence of that for which he and his employers should be liable, damage done to the plaintiff's house by squatters who obtained access because the house was not adequately secured against their entry when it was empty in order that repairs might be carried out. Both Lord Denning M.R. and Oliver L.J. dealt fully with the speech of Lord Reid in *Dorset Yacht Co. Ltd.* v. *Home Office*, to which I have already referred, and concluded that the was propounding "highly likely" as the degree of probability required before liability for the wrongful act of a third party could be established against a defendant. It will be apparent that my understanding of Lord Reid's speech, in its context, is somewhat different from theirs. While I do not consider that it is correct to base the decision in *Lamb* v. *Camden L.B.C.* on a proposition as a matter of policy that no wrongdoer could ever be liable for outrageous or anti-social conduct that had followed his wrongdoing and had contributed to the damage resulting therefrom, I respectfully and entirely agree with the result to which the Court of Appeal came in that case, and particularly with the reasons for it expressed by Oliver L.J. where he said at p. 643: "I confess that I find it inconceivable that the reasonable man wielding his pick in the road in 1973 could be said reasonably to foresee that his puncturing of a water main would fill the plaintiff's house with uninvited guests in 1974."

12.1.23 The next case referred to was *P. Perl (Exporters) Ltd.* v. *Camden L.B.C.* [1984] Q.B. 342, in which the plaintiffs were tenants of the defendants who used the basement of the demised premises in accordance with the lease for the storage of garments. The defendants were also owners of the adjoining premises. These premises had a broken lock on the front door. Unauthorised persons were often seen on those premises and burglaries had also taken place there, but the defendants had done nothing about complaints regarding lack of security. During a weekend, intruders entered the basement of the premises adjoining the plaintiffs from their basement. The plaintiffs brought an action against the defendants claiming damages for negligence. The Court of Appeal held that the claim failed... My noble and learned friend, Lord Goff of Chieveley, as Robert Goff L.J., gave the third judgment... "I know of no case where it has been held, in the absence of a special relationship, that the defendant was liable in negligence for having failed to prevent a third party from wrongfully causing damage to the plaintiff."

Earlier he had made reference to *Stainsbie* v. *Tronman* [1948] 2 K.B. 48 in which a decorator, who had contracted to carry out work in the plaintiff's home, went out for a time when no one else was in the house, leaving the door unsecured. In consequence, a thief entered and removed some of the plaintiff's property from the house and the plaintiff succeeded in recovering damages against the decorator. There was in that case no special relationship between the decorator and thief although there was a contract between the decorator and the plaintiff... That case proceeded on the basis that the decorator was liable because it was "as a direct result of his negligence that the thief entered by the front door."... On the other hand, if a thief, instead of confining his attention to the house whose door it was, bored a hole through the wall into the house next door, and stole items from the adjoining proprietor, assuming the first house was in a terrace or semi-detached, I consider that the decorator would not be liable in respect of the adjoining proprietor's loss, in the absence of the circumstances from which this was shown to be reasonably foreseeable... In some sense a thief who goes through one proprietor's property in order to reach the adjoining property of his neighbours creates a special relationship between himself and the first proprietor as a user of the first proprietor's land. In my opinion, therefore, the reason that in the circumstances of *P. Perl (Exporters) Ltd.* v. *Camden L.B.C.* no duty was owed by the defendants to Perl was that the defendants were not bound as reasonable occupiers to foresee that, if they took no steps to improve the security of their property, a probable consequence of that was that thieves would first unlawfully enter their property and then, by making an entry into the property of Perl for the purpose of stealing goods belonging to Perl.

12.1.24 The somewhat analogous case of *Squires* v. *Perth and Kinross District Council,* to which I have already referred, was... decided by an application of what, in my opinion, was the correct test. Like Lord Dunpark, I have the greatest difficulty in seeing, in view of the mode of entry which the thief actually used, that the alleged breach of duty was in any way related to the particular manner in which the theft occurred.

． ． ． ． ． ．

12.1.25 Cases of theft where the thief uses a neighbour's premises to gain access to the premises of the owners of the stolen goods are, in my opinion, in an important respect different from cases of fire such as that with which your Lordships are concerned in the present appeal. In the case of fire, a hazard is created on the first occupier's premises and it is that hazard which operating from the first occupier's premises creates danger to the neighbouring properties... There is also a sense in which neighbouring proprietors can independently take action to protect themselves against theft in a way that is not possible with fire. Once the fire had taken hold in Littlewoods' building, St Paul's proprietors could not be expected to take effective steps to prevent sparks being showered over on their property. On the other hand, in [*Squires*] there was no reason why the pursuers, if they had anticipated the risk of theft as sufficiently serious, should not have had a burglar alarm which would prove effective to warn of burglars whatever their mode of entry although this would not, of itself, prevent their entry.

12.1.26 When the question is whether or not the duty to take a particular precaution is incumbent on a defendant, the probability of the risk emerging is not the only consideration, as was pointed out by Lord Reid [who], giving the opinion of the board in *Overseas Tankship (U.K.) Ltd.* v. *Miller Steamship Co. Pty.* in reference to *Bolton* v. *Stone* (1951) A.C. 850, said at pp. 642–643: "The House of Lords held that the risk was so small that in the circumstances a reasonable man would have been justified in disregarding it and taking no steps to eliminate it. But it does not follow that, no matter what the circumstances may be, it is justifiable to neglect a risk of such a small magnitude. A reasonable man would only neglect such a risk if he had some valid reason for doing so, *e.g.* that it would involve considerable expense to eliminate the risk. He would weigh the risk against the difficulty of eliminating it... ." In my opinion, this observation demonstrates that when the word "probable" is used in this context in the authorities, it is used as indicating a real risk as distinct from a mere possibility of danger. It is not used in the sense that the consequence must be more probable than not to happen before it can be reasonably foreseeable... My Lords, I think it is well to remember, as Lord Radcliffe pointed out in *Bolton* v. *Stone* at pp. 868–869: "[A] breach of duty has taken place if they show the appellants guilty of a failure to take reasonable care to prevent the accident. One may phrase it as 'reasonable care' or 'ordinary care' or 'proper care' — all these phrases are to be found in decisions of authority — but the fact remains that, unless there has been something which a reasonable man would blame as falling beneath the standard of conduct that he would set for himself and require of his neighbour, there has been no breach of legal duty."

12.1.27 Counsel for the respondent's broad submission does not therefore add anything to his narrow submission in the circumstances of this case since, in my opinion, no undue burdens are put upon property occupiers by the application of the principle of *Donoghue* v. *Stevenson*, nor is there any undue interference with the freedom of a person to use his property as he pleases.

In my opinion, these appeals should be refused...

12.1.28 LORD GOFF OF CHIEVELEY: The Lord President founded his judgment on the proposition that the defenders, who were both owner and occupiers of the cinema, were under a general duty to take reasonable care for the safety of premises in the neighbourhood.

Now if this proposition is understood as relating to a general duty to take reasonable care *not to cause damage* to premises in the neighbourhood (as I believe that the Lord President intended it to be understood) then it is unexceptionable. But it must not be overlooked that a problem arises when the pursuer is seeking to hold the defender responsible for having failed to prevent a third party from causing damage to the pursuer or his property by the third party's own deliberate wrongdoing. In such a case, it is not possible to invoke a general duty of care to prevent third parties from causing such damage. The point is expressed very clearly in Hart and Honoré, *Causation in the Law* (2nd ed.), where the authors state at pp. 196–197: "The law might acknowledge a general principle that whenever the harmful conduct of another is reasonably foreseeable, it is our duty to take precautions against it... . But, up to now, no legal system has gone so far as this." The same point is made in Fleming, *Law of Torts* (6th ed., 1983), where it is said at p. 200: "there is certainly no general duty to protect others against theft or loss."

. . . . . .

12.1.29 Why does the law not recognise a duty of care to prevent others from suffering loss or damage caused by the deliberate wrongdoing of third parties? The fundamental reason is that the common law does not impose liability for what are called pure omissions. If authority is needed for this proposition, it is to be found in the speech of Lord Diplock in *Dorset Yacht Co. Ltd.* v. *Home Office*, where he said at p. 1060: "The very parable of the Good Samaritan which was evoked by Lord Atkin in *Donoghue* v. *Stevenson* illustrates, in the conduct of the priest and of the Levite who passed by on the other side, an omission which was likely to have as its reasonable and probable consequence damage to the health of the victim of the thieves but for which the priest and Levite would have incurred no civil liability in English law."

. . . . . .

12.1.30 Another statement of principle, which has been much quoted, is the observation of Lord Sumner in *Weld-Blundell* v. *Stephens* [1920] A.C. 956 when he said at p. 986: "In general... even though A is in fault, he is not responsible for injury to C which B, a stranger to him, deliberately chooses to do." This dictum may be read as expressing the general idea that the voluntary act of another, independent of the defender's fault, is regarded as a *novus actus interveniens* which, to use the old metaphor, "breaks the chain of causation". But it also expresses a general perception that we ought not be held responsible in law for the deliberate wrongdoing of others. Of course, if a duty of care is imposed to guard against deliberate wrongdoing by others, it can hardly be said that the harmful effects of such wrongdoing are not caused by such breach of duty. We are therefore thrown back to the duty of care. But one thing is clear, and that is that liability in negligence for harm caused by the deliberate wrongdoing of others cannot be founded simply upon foreseeability that the pursuer will suffer loss or damage by reason of such wrongdoing. There is no such general principle. We have therefore to identify the circumstances in which liability may be imposed.

. . . . . .

12.1.31 For example, a duty of care may arise from a relationship between the parties, which gives rise to an imposition or assumption of responsibility upon or by the defender, as in *Stansbie* v. *Tronman* where responsibility was held to arise from a contract... Again, the defender may be vicariously liable for the third party's act: or he may be held liable as an occupier to a visitor on his land. Again, as appears from the dictum of Dixon J. in *Smith* v. *Leurs* (1945) 70 C.L.R. 256 at p. 262, a duty may arise from a special relationship between the defender and the third party, by virtue of which the defender is responsible for controlling the third party: see, for example, *Dorset Yacht Co. Ltd.* v. *Home Office.* More pertinently, in a case between adjoining occupiers of land, there may be liability in nuisance if one occupier causes or permits persons to gather on his land, and they impair his neighbour's enjoyment of his land. Indeed, even if such persons come on to his land as trespassers, the occupiers may, if they constitute a nuisance, be under an affirmative duty to abate the nuisance. As I pointed out in *P. Perl (Exporters) Ltd.* v. *Camden L.B.C.* at p. 359, there may well be other cases.

12.1.32 These are all special cases. But there is a more general circumstance in which a defender may be held liable in negligence to the pursuer, although the immediate cause of the damage suffered by the pursuer is the deliberate wrongdoing of another. This may occur when the defender negligently causes or permits to be created a source of danger, and it is reasonably foreseeable that third parties may interfere with it and, sparking off the danger, thereby cause damage to persons in the position of the pursuer. The classic example of such a case is, perhaps, *Haynes* v. *Harwood* [1935] 1 K.B. 146, where the defendant's carter left a horse-drawn van unattended in a crowded street, and the horses bolted when a boy threw a stone at them. A police officer who suffered injury in stopping the horses before they injured a woman and children was held to be entitled to recover damages from the defendant.

· · · · · ·

12.1.33 We are concerned in the present case with an allegation that the defenders should be held liable for the consequences of deliberate wrongdoing by others who were trespassers on the defenders' property. In such a case it may be said that the defenders are entitled to use their property as their own and so should not be held liable if, for example, trespassers interfere with dangerous things on their land. But this is, I consider, too sweeping a proposition... Let me give an example of circumstances in which an occupier of land might be held liable for damage so caused. Suppose that a person is deputed to buy a substantial quantity of fireworks for a village fireworks display on Guy Fawkes' night. He stores them, as usual, in an unlocked garden shed abutting on to a neighbouring house. It is well known that he does this. Mischievous boys from the village enter as trespassers and, playing with the fireworks, cause a serious fire which spreads to and burns down the neighbouring house. Liability might well be imposed in such a case; for, having regard to the dangerous and tempting nature of fireworks, interference by naughty children was the very thing which, in the circumstances, the purchaser of the fireworks ought to have guarded against.

12.1.34   But liability should only be imposed under this principle in cases where the defender has negligently caused or permitted the creation of a source of danger on his land, and where it is foreseeable that third parties may trespass on his land and spark it off, thereby damaging the pursuer or his property. Moreover, it is not to be forgotten that, in ordinary households in this country, there are nowadays many things which might be described as possible sources of fire if interfered with by third parties, ranging from matches and firelighters to electric irons and gas cookers and even oil-fired central heating systems. These are commonplaces of modern life; and it would be quite wrong if householders were to be held liable in negligence for acting in a socially acceptable manner. No doubt the question whether liability should be imposed on defenders in a case where a source of danger on his land has been sparked off by the deliberate wrongdoing of a third party is a question to be decided on the facts of each case, and it would, I think, be wrong for your Lordships' House to anticipate the manner in which the law may develop: but I cannot help thinking that cases where liability will be imposed are likely to be very rare.

12.1.35   There is another basis upon which a defender may be held liable for damage to neighbouring property caused by a fire started on his (the defender's) property by the deliberate wrongdoing of a third party. This arises where he has knowledge or means of knowledge that a third party has created or is creating a risk of fire, or indeed has started a fire, on his premises, and then fails to take such steps as are reasonably open to him (in the limited sense explained by Lord Wilberforce in *Goldman* v. *Hargrave* [1967] 1 A.C. 645 at pp. 663–664 to prevent any such fire from damaging neighbouring property... . I observe that in *Goldman v. Hargrave* such liability was held to sound in nuisance; but it is difficult to believe that, in this respect, there can be any material distinction between liability in nuisance and liability in negligence.

12.1.36   I turn to the authorities... In the second case, *Thomas Graham & Co. Ltd.* v. *Church of Scotland General Trustees*, Sheriff Macvicar, Q.C., held that the defenders, who were occupiers of a disused church, were liable to the pursuers whose neighbouring property suffered damage by reason of a fire started in the church by unknown vandals. He relied *inter alia* on the facts that the church was situated in an area of Glasgow which was subject to vandalism on a large scale; that, to the knowledge of the defenders, on a number of previous occasions vandals had entered the church and caused damage there;... I incline to the opinion that this case can best be classified under the second of the two heads of liability to which I have referred, on the basis that the defenders had the means of knowledge that a risk of fire had been created or was being created by third parties on their land, yet they did nothing to prevent such risk of fire from damaging neighbourhood property.

. . . . . .

12.1.37 But a case more similar to the two Scottish cases to which I have referred is perhaps the American case of *Torrack* v. *Corpamerica Inc.* (1958) 144 A. 2d 703, where it was alleged that the defendants' derelict property was frequented by children and vagrants and had been condemned by the fire marshal as a fire menace, and that thereafter a fire was deliberately started by a third person on the property which spread to and damaged the plaintiff's neighbouring property; there the defendants' motion for summary judgment was denied. In so holding, Judge Christie relied on earlier cases to the same effect.

. . . . . .

12.1.38 Turning to the facts of the present case, I cannot see that the defenders should be held liable under either of these two possible heads of liability. First, I do not consider that the empty cinema could properly be described as an unusual danger in the nature of a fire hazard. As the Lord President pointed out at p. 276: "There was nothing about the building, so far as we know from the evidence, to suggest that it could easily be set alight." This conclusion was, in my judgment, entirely justified on the evidence in the case; and it is, I consider, fatal to any allegation that the defenders should be held liable on the ground that they negligently caused or permitted the creation of an unusual source of danger in the nature of a fire hazard.

Nor can I see that the defenders should be held liable for having failed to take reasonable steps to abate a fire risk created by third parties on their property without their fault. If there was any such fire risk, they had no means of knowing that it existed... As the Lord President observed at pp. 276–277: "My experience of life, which I am entitled to bring to bear as a juryman would, has not taught me that empty buildings, to which vandals gain access, are likely to be set on fire by them."

12.1.39 In the course of his argument before your Lordships, [counsel for the appellants] placed reliance upon the decision of the Inner House of the Court of Session in *Squires* v. *Perth and Kinross District Council*. That was a case concerned not with liability in respect of a fire hazard, but with liability in respect of a theft by a burglar who had gained access to the pursuers' jeweller's shop through a flat above which was empty because it was being renovated by building contractors who were held to be in occupation of the flat... It was a remarkable feature of the case that the burglar himself, one Sneddon, gave evidence at the trial; and it transpired from his evidence that, although his attention was drawn to the possibility of breaking into the jeweller's shop through the empty flat by seeing the scaffolding and open windows of the flat facing the High Street, he in fact approached the flat from behind, climbing over a building of about 12 to 15 ft. high overall. He found the door to the yard behind the shop and flat unsecured, but nevertheless climbed over a wall into the yard and then climbed a drainpipe to a balcony, from which he entered the flat through a door which was open. Having entered the flat, he broke into the jeweller's shop through the floor of the flat and the ceiling of the shop. In these circumstances, assuming that the defenders were in breach of duty in leaving the flat insecure, I feel, with all respect, serious doubts about the decision on the issue of causation, since it is difficult to imagine that an experienced and practised housebreaker, as Sneddon was held to be, would have been deterred from entering the flat even if the door on the balcony had been secured. I am not surprised therefore to find that Lord Dunpark has had the same doubts (see at p. 49). Furthermore, I find it difficult to understand why the question of contributory negligence on the part of the pursuers was not considered. The pursuers were just as aware of the risk as the defenders were; yet, although (as was found) an alarm system is often fitted to the roof of premises such as those of the pursuers, and is relatively inexpensive, they did not take this precaution. They seemed to have assumed that, although it was their shop which was likely to attract thieves, they were entitled to rely on the contractors working above. I do not think that that can be right.

12.1.40   In truth the case raises a more fundamental question, which is whether an occupier is under a general duty of care to occupiers of adjacent premises to keep his premises lockfast in order to prevent thieves entering his premises and thereby gaining access to the adjacent premises.

. . . . . .

12.1.41   It is not difficult to multiply these homely examples of cases where a thief may gain access to a house or flat which is not lockfast — for example, where an old lady goes out to spend the day with her married daughter and leaves a ground floor window open for her cat; or where a stone-deaf asthmatic habitually sleeps with his bedroom window wide open at night; or where an elderly gentleman leaves his french windows open when he is weeding at the bottom of the garden, so that he can hear the telephone. For my part, I do not think that liability can be imposed on an occupier of property in negligence simply because it can be said that it is reasonably foreseeable, or even (having regard, for example, to some particular temptation to thieves in adjacent premises) that it is highly likely that, if he fails to keep his property lockfast, a thief may gain access to his property and thence to the adjacent premises. So to hold must presuppose that the occupier of property is under a general duty to prevent thieves from entering his property to gain access to neighbouring property, where there is a sufficient degree of foresight that this may occur. But there is no general duty to prevent third parties from causing damage to others, even though there is a high degree of foresight that they may do so. The practical effect is that everybody has to take such steps as he thinks fit to protect his own property, whether house or flat or shop, against thieves... He has to form his own judgment as to the precautions which he should take, having regard to all the circumstances of the case, including (if it be the case) the fact that his premises are a jeweller's shop which offers a special temptation to thieves. I must confess that I do not find this practical result objectionable. For these reasons I consider, with all respect, that *Squires* v. *Perth and Kinross District Council* was wrongly decided.

12.1.42   The present case is, of course, concerned with entry not by thieves but vandals. Here the point can be made that, whereas an occupier of property can take precautions against thieves, he cannot (apart from insuring his property and its contents) take effective precautions against physical damage caused to his property by a vandal who has gained access to adjacent property and has there created a source of danger which has resulted in damage to his property by, for example, fire or escaping water. Even so, the same difficulty arises... The practical effect is that it is the owner of the damaged premises (or, in the vast majority of cases, his insurers) who is left with a worthless claim against the vandal, rather than the occupier of the property which the vandal entered (or his insurers) a conclusion which I find less objectionable than one which may throw an unreasonable burden upon ordinary householders. For these reasons, I consider that both *Lamb* v. *Camden L.B.C.* and *King* v. *Liverpool C.C.* were rightly decided; but I feel bound to say, with all respect, that the principle propounded by Lord Wylie in *Evans* v. *Glasgow D.C.* at p. 19, *viz.* that there is "a general duty on owners or occupiers of property... to take reasonable care to see that it [is] proof against the kind of vandalism which was calculated to affect adjoining property" is, in my opinion, too wide.

12.1.43   I wish to emphasise that I do not think that the problem in these cases can be solved simply through the mechanism of foreseeability. When a duty *is* cast upon a person to take precautions against the wrongdoing of third parties, the ordinary standard of foreseeability applies; and so the possibility of such wrongdoing does not have to be very great before liability is imposed. I do not myself subscribe to the opinion that the liability for the wrongdoing of others is limited because of the unpredictability of human conduct. So, for example, in *Haynes* v. *Harwood*, liability was imposed although it cannot have been at all likely that a small boy would throw a stone at the horses left unattended in the public road; and in *Stansbie* v. *Tronman* liability was imposed although it cannot have been at all likely that a thief would take advantage of the fact that the defendant left the door on the latch while he was out. *Per contra*, there is at present no general duty at common law to prevent persons from harming others by their deliberate wrongdoing, however foreseeable such harm may be if the defender does not take steps to prevent it.

. . . . . .

12.1.44   In preparing this opinion, I have given careful consideration to the question whether *P. Perl (Exporters) Ltd.* v. *Camden L.B.C.*, in which I myself was a member of the Court of Appeal, was correctly decided. I have come to the conclusion that it was, though on rereading it I do not think that my own judgment was very well expressed... It is very tempting to try to solve all problems of negligence by reference to an all-embracing criterion of foreseeability, thereby effectively reducing all decisions in this field to questions of fact. But this comfortable solution is, alas, not open to us. The law has to accommodate all the untidy complexity of life, and there are circumstances where considerations of practical justice impel us to reject a general imposition of liability for foreseeable damage. An example of this phenomenon is to be found in cases of pure economic loss, where the so-called "floodgates" argument (an argument recognised by Lord Blackburn as long ago as 1875 in *Cattle* v. *Stockton Waterworks Co.* at p. 457, the force of which is accepted not only in common law countries but also in civil law countries such as the Federal Republic of Germany), compels us to recognise that to impose a general liability based on a simple criterion of foreseeability would impose an intolerable burden upon defendants. I observe that in *Junior Books Ltd.* v. *Veitchi Co. Ltd.* some members of your Lordships' House succumbed, perhaps too easily, to the temptation to adopt a solution based simply upon "proximity". In truth, in cases such as these, having rejected the generalised principle, we have to search for special cases in which upon narrower but still identifiable principles, liability can properly be imposed. That is the task which I attempted to perform in *Leigh and Sillivan Ltd.* v. *Aliakmon Shipping Co. Ltd.* by identifying a principle of transferred loss — a principle which has not, so far, achieved recognition by other members of your Lordships' House. As the present case shows, another example of this phenomenon is to be found in cases where the plaintiff has suffered damage through the deliberate wrongdoing of a third party; and it is not surprising that once again we should find the courts seeking to identify specific situations in which liability can properly be imposed. Problems such as these are solved in Scotland, as in England, by means of the mechanism of the duty of care; though we have nowadays to appreciate that the broad general principle of liability for foreseeable damage is so widely applicable that the function of the duty of care is not so much to identify cases where liability is imposed as to identify those where it is not (see *Anns* v. *Merton L.B.C.* (at p. 752 by Lord Wilberforce)). It is perhaps not surprising that our brother lawyers in France find themselves able to dispense with any such concept, achieving practical justice by means of a simple concept of "*faute*". But since we all live in the same social and economic environment, and since the judicial function can, I believe, be epitomised as an educated reflex of facts, we find that, in civil law countries as in common law countries, not only are we beset by the same practical problems, but broadly speaking we reach the same practical solutions. Our legal concepts may be different, and may cause us sometimes to diverge; but we have much to learn from each other in our common efforts to achieve practical justice founded upon legal principle.

For these reasons I would dismiss this appeal.'

COMMENTS

12.2.1 Decided: Feb. 5, 1987.
Dec. 23, 1986: Andrei Sakharov freed.
Jan. 12, 1987: Prince Edward resigned from Marines.
Jan. 20: Terry Waite kidnapped.
Feb. 5: SOGAT stopped picketing Wapping.

12.2.2 Is there a divergence between the views of Lords Mackay and Goff? If not, what is the law according to both of them? If there is a divergence, what is it and does it matter?

12.2.3 Is the reluctance to accept foreseeability really due to a reluctance to go beyond the fact that the intervention is, in most cases, criminal and that to make another liable somehow or other lets the criminal off, or at best, makes an innocent person pay for another's crime? See Stuart, 1984 S.L.T. (News) 45, Forensis, 1986 J.L.S. p. 406, P. W. Ferguson, 1987 S.L.T. (News) 233. See *Cunningham v. Reading Football Club* [1991] T.L.R. 153.

12.2.4 Can *Squires* be safely ignored on the basis that very seldom will evidence be available from the thief? On what other view might it be ignored?

12.2.5 Is the brocard that there should be no liability *ex domino soli* at the back of this decision? Is the law looking after the institution of private property at the expense of victims? And see the earlier and similar Scottish case *Hosie v. Arbroath*. What about the Bobbie hit by a flying footballer — should the occupiers be liable? See *Gillon v. Chief Constable, Strathclyde Police*, 1995 G.W.D. 31–1618; 1996 Rep.L.R. 165.

12.2.6 In Scotland the concept of *negotiorum gestio* is recognised — *i.e.* the obligation to pay someone who helps out unasked — the very Good Samaritan referred to by Lord Goff. Is it thus possible that a system recognising that someone may be permitted to render a service unasked and place the recipient under an obligation to pay might also encourage people to take care that their property does not become a source of injury to others? (See also para 8.2.2.) See Howarth "My Brothers' Keeper etc." (1994) 14 L.S. 88. What is the difference between misfeasance and non-feasance? Why, if at all, is it important?

12.2.7 See the article by Mr Logie at 1988 J.R. 77 for a full discussion of this case.

12.2.8   The author once received the following correspondence. (The names have been changed.)

"The Jericho Building Co.,
Somewhere St.,
SOMETOWN.

The Occuper,
20 Birks Quad,
SOMETOWN.

Dear Sir/Madam,

Re: Property at 24 Birks Quad

We have been awarded the contract to stone-clean and floodlight the property at the above. As the building adjoins your own building in Birks Quad, we enclose a copy of a Noddytown Police circular for your attention.

Assuring you of our best attention,

Yours faithfully,
Jericho Builders
GIDEON TRUMPET (Director)."

The following circular was attached:

"Vulnerability due to scaffolding

In a short time scaffolding will be erected in the vicinity of your premises in order to carry out essential work.

Noddytown police advise that your premises could be more vulnerable during this time.

While the contractor will take every precaution to limit this hazard, please consider the security of your premises.

Windows are particularly vulnerable, and it is suggested that key-operated window locks are fitted.

If any further information or clarification on crime prevention is required, please contact your police crime prevention officer through your local police office.

CHIEF CONSTABLE PLOD."

Do you think the chief constable has been reading the law reports? If he has, do you think he has understood the case law properly? Even if he has, imagine the contractor does not "take every precaution" but utilises reasonable care — would the chief constable be liable for his statement? If so, why? If not, why not?

12.2.9   For a case where *Maloco* seems to have been used to support a finding of liability, see *Fry's Metals Ltd v. Durastic Ltd*, 1991 S.L.T. 689. What if a person leaves the keys in the ignition of their unlocked car? (See *Topp v. London County Bus Ltd* [1993] 3 All E.R. 448 (C.A.).) What if a patient decides to commit suicide *G's C.B. v. Grampian Health Board*, 1994 G.W.D. 152.

CHAPTER 13

ECONOMIC LOSS

Primary economic loss — the reception of Hedley Byrne v. Heller & Partners

51. Martin v. Bell-Ingram (Appellants)
1986 S.L.T. 575

13.1.1 'THE LORD JUSTICE-CLERK (Ross): In this action, the pursuers sought damages from the defenders for alleged negligence. In 1979, the pursuers were considering the purchase of a house at Newmiln, by Tibbermore, Perthshire. They approached a building society with a view to obtaining a loan to finance the proposed purchase, and the building society requested the defenders, who are a firm of chartered surveyors, to produce a survey report. The defenders proceeded to inspect the subjects and they issued their report thereon on October 18, 1979. The report drew attention to slight damp penetration adjacent to the chimney flues, and recommended that a roof plumber be instructed and any remedial work be carried out. The said report also noted a ceiling crack which was not considered serious. The report made no reference to any sagging or other structural instability in the roof of the said subjects. The subjects were valued in the sum of £35,000, and it was reported that they provided a suitable security for mortgage purposes. On receipt of the report, the building society reported the terms of the report to the pursuers. The pursuers proceeded to purchase the said subjects at a price of £33,500, the bargain being concluded on October 22, 1979.

13.1.2 Subsequently, in January 1981, the defenders carried out a further inspection of the said subjects for the building society in connection with an additional advance which the pursuers were obtaining and again nothing was said by the defenders regarding any defect in the roof. Later, in April 1981, the pursuers exposed the said subjects for sale at an asking price of £48,500. After a proposed purchaser had the subjects inspected by the defenders, he indicated to the pursuers that the defenders' report to him had revealed a serious roof sag. Thereafter the pursuers had various remedial works carried out to the roof, but they encountered difficulty in selling the subjects, which were ultimately sold for £39,000. The pursuers' case is that they have suffered loss and damage as a result of fault and negligence on the part of the defenders.

13.1.3 So far as the merits are concerned, the crucial question is whether the defenders owed a duty to the pursuers. Whether or not any duty was owed depends on the circumstances... It is normal practice for the surveyor to convey the terms of his report by telephone to the building society, and for the building society to convey the terms of the report to the prospective purchaser or his solicitor. The surveyor is aware that the terms of his report will be conveyed to the prospective purchaser or his solicitor. The surveyor is aware that the terms of his report are critical to the prospective purchaser's decision as to whether or not to offer to purchase the subjects in question;... as a matter of invariable practice, the report indicates not only such defects as may affect the value of the subjects, but also such defects as may affect the decision of the prospective purchaser as to whether or not he will pursue his interest in buying the house.

. . . . . .

13.1.4 Before the sheriff, the pursuers argued that the defenders had a duty to take reasonable care to disclose the existence of the defect to the building society in terms of their contract and that they owed a co-extensive duty of care in the circumstances to prospective purchasers such as the pursuer. The sheriff explained in his note that this was because the evidence clearly indicated that the existence of the defect was a matter which would materially affect the value of the property. That was the pursuers' principal submission. They had an alternative case on the following basis: esto the defect in question was one which did not require to have been disclosed by the defenders in terms of the duty referred to above, nonetheless since the defenders chose to go outwith what they maintained was the strict letter of their contract with the building society, they did so at their peril and accordingly were under a duty to exercise reasonable care in a question with the pursuers.

13.1.5 Senior counsel also underlined important concessions which the defenders made regarding the relationship between the defenders as surveyors and the pursuers as prospective purchasers. In particular he reminded us that the following passage in finding B2 was accepted: "the surveyor is aware that the terms of his report are conveyed to the purchaser. Where a purchaser requires a mortgage to finance the purchase of a house, the terms of the report by the surveyor are critical to the purchaser's decision as to whether or not to offer for said house, and at what price. The surveyor is aware of this."

13.1.6 In the context of the foregoing findings, senior counsel referred to the speech of Lord Wilberforce in *Anns* v. *Merton L.B.C.* [1978] A.C. 728 at p. 751: "Rather the question has to be approached in two stages. First one has to ask whether, as between the alleged wrongdoer and the person who has suffered damage, there is a sufficient relationship of proximity of neighbourhood such that, in the reasonable contemplation of the former, carelessness on his part may be likely to cause damage to the latter — in which case a *prima facie* duty of care arises. Secondly, if the first question is answered affirmatively, it is necessary to consider whether there are any considerations which ought to negative, or to reduce or limit the scope of the duty or the class of person to whom it is owed or the damage to which a breach of it may give rise; see *Dorset Yacht* [1970] A.C. 1004, *per* Lord Reid at p. 1027." In the present case senior counsel accepted that the pursuers had satisfied that first stage, and that a *prima facie* duty of care arose, and that *prima facie* there was a breach of that duty. In that situation, senior counsel submitted that two questions arose under the second stage referred to by Lord Wilberforce. In the first place, he submitted that one consideration which negatived a duty of care in this instance was the existence of a disclaimer. In the second place he submitted that there were other considerations which limited the extent of duties owed...

13.1.7 On November 13, 1979 (after the bargain had been concluded) the building society sent a written offer of an advance of funds to the pursuers for mortgage purposes. In terms of this written offer of advance of funds, one of the conditions (cond. E) stated *inter alia* [his Lordship quoted the terms of the conditions and continued:] The sheriff has found as a fact that the terms of the disclaimer were not communicated to the pursuers in any form before November 13, 1979. Senior counsel... also stressed that he was not seeking to rely on evidence to the effect that similar provisions appear in offers of advance from building societies, nor on any custom or course of dealing which might enable it to be said that the pursuer knew or should have known that clauses of this type were customarily incorporated within building society reports. He also stressed that he was not seeking to rely on any principle of law to the effect that knowledge of this matter on the part of the pursuers' solicitor should be attributed to the pursuers as principals. What senior counsel did contend was this. Looked from the point of view of a surveyor, when he communicates his report verbally to the building society, he knows that an offer to advance with a disclaimer is likely to follow. Senior counsel submitted that, in these circumstances, the existence of the disclaimer in the building societies' printed form which was used for an offer of advance was part of the background which enabled one to say that the surveyor was not undertaking a duty of care to the prospective purchaser when he was providing information to the building society.

13.1.8 In my opinion, this contention on behalf of the defenders is without substance... [There] was no evidence that the defenders ever assumed that the pursuers would be aware that the defenders were performing their duties against the background relied upon by senior counsel. Counsel referred us to various passages in speeches delivered in *Hedley Byrne & Co. Ltd.* v. *Heller & Partners Ltd.*, [1964] A.C. 465. In that case the information provided by the respondents was expressly stated to be "without responsibility". It was held that the respondents by these words had effectively disclaimed any assumption of a duty of care. It is clear, however, that to be effective the disclaimer must be brought to the notice of the party against whom it is pleaded. In the present case the defenders were well aware that the prospective purchasers would rely on both the report which was conveyed orally and the written report, and if they wished to rely on any disclaimer in regard to these reports they should have taken steps to bring the existence of the disclaimer to the attention of the prospective purchaser such as the pursuers. This they did not do. In these circumstances I am of opinion that the existence of the disclaimer in the written offer of advance did not serve to negative the *prima facie* duty of care which arose when the defenders reported both orally and in writing as to the result of their survey of the subjects.

13.1.9 As regards senior counsel for the defenders' second argument, this was directed to what the sheriff described as the pursuers' subsidiary argument, and this related to the scope of the duty which the defenders owed to the pursuers... In view of the concessions made by senior counsel for the defenders, it is clear that the sag in the roof was a defect which would affect the value of the subjects and which should have been referred to in a report to the building society by the defenders if they had been exercising reasonable care. In that way it would have been brought to the attention of the pursuers.

. . . . . .

13.1.10 For myself, I find it difficult to envisage a defect which would be liable materially to affect the pursuers' decision in respect of the purchase of the house which would not also affect the value of the house. Senior counsel for the pursuers, however, submitted that the evidence revealed that there were some defects which might affect a prospective purchaser but might not affect the value of the subjects... In my opinion, in the light of the evidence, the sheriff was entitled to make the findings in fact and in law which he made, and in particular to make finding in fact and in law (2).

13.1.11 It was not disputed that, where the negligence consists of the failure of surveyors to detect a defect in the building, the proper measure of damages is the difference between the price paid as representing the market price of the subjects on the basis of the report, and the market price which the subjects would have fetched on the basis of their actual condition: *Stewart* v. *H. A. Brechin & Co.; Perry* v.

Sidney Phillips & Son, 1959 S.L.T. (Notes) 45; *London and South of England Building Society* v. S*tone,* [1983] 1 W.L.R. 1242. Counsel for the pursuers accepted that the difference in value fell to be assessed as at the date of the sale. As at that date the market value of the subjects when they were understood to have no defect was the price which the pursuers paid, namely £33,500. No evidence however was led as to what their value would have been at that date on the basis that they suffered from a sag in the roof. In that situation the defenders' submission was that there was no sufficient evidence from which the proper measure of damages could be calculated. The sheriff rejected that submission and proceeded to assess the damages upon a broad basis. He founded on the fact that, as Lord Cameron had stated in *Stewart* v. *H. A. Brechin & Co.,* the question is largely a jury one. He assessed the difference in value between the market value for property with the defect and the market value without defect as £2,500. In my opinion, senior counsel for the pursuers was well-founded in contending that the sheriff's approach on this matter was a reasonable one.

13.1.12   Moreover, the sheriff had regard to the evidence of repairs as a cross-check. Although the cost of repairs is not *per se* the proper measure of damages in a claim of this kind, it is legitimate to have regard to what repairs have cost. "No doubt the actual expenditure proper incurred may be a guide in calculating the amount of damages, but the extent to which it is a useful guide must depend upon the circumstances of the particular case" (*Stewart* v. *H. A. Brechin & Co.,* 1959 S.L.T. (Notes) at p. 46).'

COMMENT

13.2.1   Decided: March 14, 1986.
   Feb. 16: Dr Soares became first civilian president in Portugal for 60 years.
   Feb. 25: Corazon Aquino sworn as new President of Philippines.
   March 2: Australia Bill given the Royal Assent.
   March 14: Sir Huw Wheldon died.

13.2.2   Economic loss in its many different forms is at the heart of many of the most difficult contemporary discussions of liability in delict. The most useful intellectual activity which can assist in understanding what the law might be is to identify and attempt to categorise the different types of economic losses. It does, however, have to be accepted that policy plays a very great part in economic loss cases because of the effect of delict in resource allocation and loss distribution. The most valuable distinction (and that adopted in this chapter) is that made by Wilkinson and Forte in 1985 J.R. 1 between primary economic loss, where the pursuer is directly injured "in his pocket"; and secondary economic loss, where some damage is done to the person or property of another which causes the pursuer an economic loss. (See *Delict,* 5.20–5.30.) For the use of the terminology of "Relational loss" see Hogg K., "Relational loss, the Exclusory Rule and the High Court of Australia" (1995) 3 Tort L.Rev. 26. There are all sorts of other distinctions which can be made in attempting to locate and explain the many cases — see Cane, P., "Contract Tort and the Lloyd's Débâcle in *Consensus ad idem* (1996), p. 96 for a "delictual theory", a "transitional theory" and an "equitable theory" to be found in the speeches in *Henderson v. Merrett Syndicates* [1995] 2 A.C. 145.

13.2.3   This case clearly established *Hedley Byrne*-type liability in Scotland. *Hedley Byrne* and *Anns* had been considered before in *Twomax Ltd v. Dickson McFarlane & Robinson*, 1983 S.L.T. 98. In that case, concerning the liability of accountants and auditors in respect of accounts relied upon by a non-contracting party, Lord Stewart in the Outer House cited the Wilberforce trilogy dictum (see 12.1.6 above) with approval and decided in favour of the pursuers on the basis of a duty arising on the basis of proximity, reasonable foreseeability of loss and the pursuers' reliance, reasonably to be expected by the defenders. He found assistance in, *inter alia*, the English case of *J.E.B. Fasteners Ltd v. Marks, Bloom & Co.* [1981] 3 All E.R. 289. For further cases see the rest of this chapter: also para. 2.4.2.

13.2.4   One of the crucial points in this case was that it was not argued that conveyancing or house-buying practice should be considered in establishing the duty. That could have been for any reason. Certainly the author's recollection of conveyancing practice at the time was that every solicitor warned every purchaser before concluding missives to the effect that this was to be one of the most important purchases in the buyer's life, that the survey obtained had been for the lender's valuation purposes only and that the potential purchaser should most seriously consider contracting for and paying for a full structural survey, which if incorrect, would probably provide a right of action. What do you think the result of the case would have been if this point had been made? At the time of writing surveyors take emphatic steps to make solicitors (and thus house buyers!) aware of the scope of their activity. Another interesting topic which arose after *Martin* is the quantification of damage. The basic approach can be seen in the extract at 13.1.11–12. However, there was a collapse in property values in the 1990s meaning that when lenders sold under standard securities the properties fetched much less than valuation or the sum lent. Who ought to be responsible for the drop in lending? The courts answers can be tracked in *Banque Bruxelles Lambert v. Eagle Star* [1995] 2 All E.R. 769; *Leeds Permanent Building Society v. Walker, Fraser & Steele*, 1995 S.L.T. (Sh.Ct.) 72; *Mortgage Express Ltd v. Dunsmuir Reid and Smith*, January 25, 1996, unreported. In *South Australia Asset Management Corporation v. York Montague* and associated cases, [1996] 3 W.L.R. 87, the House of Lords has decided that BBL was wrongly decided (the case could not be overruled because it had settled. See also Paul Wade's article (1995 4 Rep. Bul. 2) which raises the interesting point as to contributory negligence on the part of the lender. The keen student will notice that some of the cases are contractual — does that or should that make a difference?

13.2.5   The Scottish provisions of the Unfair Contract Terms Act 1977 did not, as did the English provisions, expressly restrict the use of non-contractual disclaimers. Criticism of this position by academics found judicial support in the judgment of Lord Weir in *Robbie v. Graham & Sibbald*, 1989 S.L.T. 870. In this case an action against surveyors by purchasers was dismissed on the procedure roll, it being held that the loan application form signed by or on behalf of the applicants which contained *inter alia* the following phrases: "the survey is limited and may not reveal defects that a more detailed survey would discover"; "neither the society nor the surveyor gives any warranty regarding the report's accuracy" and perhaps most damagingly, "the surveyor does not accept responsibility to applicants or to any other person". Quite clearly those phrases, and the last in particular, were likely to be as effective as the disclaimer in *Hedley Byrne* itself, subject to any evidence about how it was or was not brought to the attention of the party affected by it. The disclaimer not being contractual appeared not to be struck at by the Scottish part of the Act, whereas in England the Act would and has been used to control a broadly similar sort of notice. See the joined appeals: *Smith v. Eric S. Bush and Harris v. Wyre Forest D.C.* [1989] 2 W.L.R. 790.

However, see the curious case decided by the First Division *Melrose v. Davidson & Robertson*, 1993 S.C.L.R. 365. The facts were essentially similar to *Martin*. However the case came up after the Act came into force *but* did not apply as it came into force *after* the relevant events took place. The court held that the arrangement between the potential borrower and the lenders to pay for the survey report was contractual thus activating section 15(2) of the unamended Act as relating "to services of whatever kind". Thus the unamended section 16 applied as that section did not have to be read where it referred to "a term of a contract" only to a contract between the parties to the action. The defenders would have been able to rely on the disclaimer and the principle *ius quasitum tertio*. Thus the Act applied and the disclaimer was struck down. With respect the 15 2 (c) decision seems wrong — it was an application in a process which leads to an offer — that was its commercial importance and the likely understanding of the parties. The language of section 16 supports the second argument and the point was not argued for the defender. Lord President Hope adopted the approach to the fair and reasonableness test in such a case of Lord Griffith in *Smith v. Bush,* although the defenders did not suggest it was fair and reasonable. In *Smith* it was considered that there was a difference between commercial valuations and those of modest houses for owner occupation.

13.2.6   As indicated in *Delict* (5.40), Lord Keith with Lord Bridge were active in restating liability, particularly in relation to economic loss and foreseeability generally. The House as a whole came to a new and far less mechanical view of negligence. Lord Bridge in *Caparo Industries v. Dickman* [1990] 2 W.L.R. 358, took the opportunity expressly to approve Lord Keith's efforts: "But since *Anns* a series of decisions of the Privy Council and speeches delivered by Lord Keith of Kinkel, had emphasised the inability of any single general principle to provide a practical test which could be applied to every situation." Lord Bridge, after considering the authorities of which *Martin* is an example, including *Hedley Byrne* itself and *Smith v. Eric S. Bush,* stated that "the salient feature of all those cases was that the defendant giving advice or information was fully aware of the transaction which the plaintiff had in contemplation, knew that the advice or information would be communicated to him, and knew that it was likely that the plaintiff would rely on that advice or information in deciding whether or not to engage in the transaction in contemplation." Accordingly Lord Bridge and a unanimous House concluded that the auditors of a public company's accounts owed no duty of care to members of the public at large who relied on the accounts to buy shares. This refusal of the existence of a duty of care is ultimately on the basis that it would not be fair, just and reasonable to impose one. It would not be fair, just and reasonable to impose a duty where a statement is put into general circulation and could be relied on by strangers for all sorts of purposes. The Privy Council cases of *Rowling v. Takaro Properties* [1988] 2 W.L.R. 418 and *Yuen Kun Yeu v. Attorney-General, Hong Kong* [1988] 1 A.C. 175 and the House of Lords' decision *D. & F. Estates v. Church Commissioners* [1988] 3 W.L.R. 368 are now required reading for those wishing to appreciate the change in emphasis brought about (principally) by Lords Keith and Bridge. See also *Banque Financière de la Cité v. Westgate Ins. Co.* [1989] 2 All E.R. 952; *Pacific Associates Inc. v. Baxter* [1989] 2 All E.R. 159; and *Mills v. Winchester Diocesan Board* [1989] 2 All E.R. 317.

In *Murphy v. Brentwood* [1990] W.L.R. 414, the House of Lords was able to resolve some of the problems that they had perceived troubled the law of negligence, particularly in relation to economic loss. These matters are dealt with elsewhere in the book, but the House also reconsidered *Hedley Byrne*-type liability. This "Full Bench" of seven, while departing from the landmark decision of *Anns v. Merton,* made it clear that *Hedley Byrne* and its issue are established law. Indeed, the talk of assumption of responsibility in some of the more recent cases seems to have dissolved in favour of the "traditional" reliance-orientated interpretation of *Hedley Byrne* (see Lord Keith at pp. 427, 429; Lord Bridge at p. 439): "The House has already held in *D. & F. Estates* that a builder, in the absence of any contractual duty or of a special relationship of proximity introducing the *Hedley Byrne* principle of reliance, owes no duty of care in tort in respect of the quality of his work" (Lord Bridge at p. 440 and see also p. 441). Lord Oliver (at p. 443) clearly distinguishes *Hedley Byrne*-type cases as based on reliance and as having nothing to do with the now discredited *Dutton/Anns* reasoning: "Secondly, in neither case it was possible to allege successfully that the plaintiffs had relied on the proper performance by the defendant of its Public Health Act duties so as to invoke the principles expounded in *Hedley Byrne & Co Ltd v. Heller & Partners Ltd* ... In the course of his speech in *Anns* at pp. 768–769 Lord Salmon was at pains to emphasise that the claim had nothing to do with reliance." And the same point is made even more emphatically later by Lord Oliver at p. 445: "The decision of this House in *Morrison*

Steamship Co. Ltd v. Greystoke Castle (Cargo Owners) [1947] A.C. 265 demonstrates that the mere fact that the primary damage suffered by a plaintiff is pecuniary is no necessary bar to an action in negligence given the proper circumstances (in that case, what was said to be the 'joint venture' interest of shipowners and the owners of cargo carried on board) and if the matter remained in doubt that doubt was conclusively resolved by the decision of this House in *Hedley Byrne & Co. Ltd v. Heller & Partners Ltd* at p. 517, where Lord Devlin convincingly demonstrated the illogicality of a distinction between financial loss caused directly and financial loss resulting from physical injury to personal property." (See Lord Jauncey at p. 452.) In other societies people may take a different view of reliance upon the building authorities. See the Privy Council advice in *Invercargill City Council v. Hamlin* [1996] 2 W.L.R. 367. See Brodie, D., "Subsidiarity and Subsidence", 1996 Rep. LB 9–3.

52. Junior Books v. The Veitchi Co. (Appellants)
1982 S.L.T. 492 (H.L.)

13.3.1 'LORD FRASER OF TULLYBELTON: I have had the advantage of reading in draft the speech of my noble and learned friend, Lord Roskill, and I am in full agreement with his conclusion and with the reasons on which he bases it. I also gratefully adopt his summary of the facts. It is enough for me to say that the appellants (defenders) are specialist sub-contractors who laid composition flooring in a factory that was built for the respondents (pursuers) at Grangemouth between September 1969 and May 1970. The respondents aver that the floor is defective, owing to failure by the appellants to take reasonable care in laying it, and that it will have to be replaced. There was no contractual relationship between the appellants and the respondents, and for some reason that has not been explained, the respondents have not taken legal proceedings against the main contractors with whom they did have a contractual relationship. The respondents have raised this action against the appellants, claiming damages which consist mainly of the direct and indirect cost of replacing the floor, the action being founded on averments that the appellants were negligent in laying the floor. At the present stage of relevancy these averments must be taken as true. The appeal raises an important question on the law of delict or, strictly speaking, *quasi*-delict, which is not precisely covered by authority. The question is whether the appellants having (as must at this stage be assumed) negligently laid a floor which is defective, but which has not caused danger to the health or safety of any person nor risk of damage to any other property belonging to the owner of the floor, may in the circumstances averred by the respondents be liable for the economic loss caused to them by having to replace the floor.

. . . . . .

13.3.2 As I agree with my noble and learned friend, Lord Roskill, that the appeal fails, I only add to his speech in order to deal in my own words with two important matters that arise. The first is the concern which has been repeatedly expressed by judges in the United Kingdom and elsewhere that the effect of relaxing strict limitations upon the area of liability for delict (tort) would be, in the words of Cardozo J., to introduce "liability in an indeterminate amount for an indeterminate time to an indeterminate class". This is the "floodgates" argument, if I may use the expression as a convenient description, and not in any dismissive or question-begging sense. The argument appears to me unattractive, especially if it leads, as I think it would in this case, to drawing an arbitrary and illogical line just because a line has to be drawn somewhere. But it has to be considered, because it has had a significant influence in leading judges to reject claims for economic loss which were not consequent upon physical danger to persons or other property of the pursuer/plaintiff.

. . . . . .

13.3.3 Whether the defender's knowledge of the identity of the person likely to suffer from his negligence is relevant for the present purpose may with respect be doubted and it seems to be contrary to the views expressed in *Hedley Byrne & Co. Ltd.* v. *Heller & Partners Ltd.* [1964] A.C. 465 by Lord Reid at p. 482 and by Lord Morris of Borth-y-Gest at p. 494. But it is not necessary to decide the question in this appeal because the appellants certainly knew, or had the means of knowing, the identity of the respondents for whom the factory was being built. So, if knowledge of the respondents' identity is a relevant test, it is one that the appellants can satisfy. They can also satisfy most, if not all, of the other tests that have been suggested as safeguards against opening the floodgates. The proximity between the parties is extremely close, falling only just short of a direct contractual relationship. The injury to the respondents was a direct and foreseeable result of negligence by the appellants.

. . . . . .

13.3.4 It would surely be wrong to exclude from probation a claim which is so strongly based, merely because of anxiety about the possible effect of the decision upon other cases where the proximity may be less strong. If and when such other cases arise they will have to be decided by applying sound principles to their particular facts. The present case seems to be to fall well within limits already recognised in principle for this type of claim, and I would decide this appeal strictly on its own facts. I rely particularly on the very close proximity between the parties which in my view distinguishes this case from the case of producers of goods to be offered for sale to the public.

13.3.5 The second matter which might be thought to justify rejecting the respondents' claim as irrelevant is the difficulty of ascertaining the standard of duty owed by the appellants to the respondents. A manufacturer's duty to take care not to make a product that is dangerous sets a standard which is, in principle, easy to ascertain. The duty is owed to all who are his "neighbours". It is imposed upon him by the general law, and is in addition to his contractual duties to other parties to the contract. It cannot be discharged or escaped by pleading that it conflicts with his contractual duty. But a duty not to produce a defective article sets a standard which is less easily ascertained because it has to be judged largely by reference to the contract.

. . . . . .

13.3.6 A building constructed in fulfilment of a contract for a price of £100,000 might justly be regarded as defective, although the same building constructed in fulfilment of a contract for a price of £50,000 might not. Where a building is erected under a contract with a purchaser, then provided the building, or part of it, is not dangerous to persons or to other property and subject to the law against misrepresentation, I see no reason why the builder should not be free to make with the purchaser whatever contractual arrangements about the quality of the product the purchaser wishes. However jerry-built the product, the purchaser would not be entitled to damages from the builder if it came up to the contractual standard. I do not think a subsequent owner could be in any better position, but in most cases he would not know the details of the contractual arrangements and, without such knowledge, he might well be unable to judge whether the product was defective or not. But in this case the respondents, although not a party to the contract with the appellants, had full knowledge of the appellants' contractual duties, and this difficulty does not arise. What the position might have been if the action had been brought by a subsequent owner is a matter which does not have to be decided now.

. . . . . .

13.3.7 Lord Keith of Kinkel: I am of the opinion that the respondents have stated a proper case for inquiry into facts, and that the Lord Ordinary and the Second Division were therefore right to allow a proof before answer. I would accordingly dismiss the appeal.

Having thus reached a conclusion in favour of the respondents upon the somewhat narrow ground which I have indicated, I do not consider this to be an appropriate case for seeking to advance the frontiers of the law of negligence upon the lines favoured by certain of your Lordships. There are a number of reasons why such an extension would, in my view, be wrong in principle. In the first place, I am unable to regard the deterioration of the flooring which is alleged in this case as being damage to the respondent's property such as to give rise to a liability falling directly within the principle of *Donoghue* v. *Stevenson*.

. . . . . .

13.3.8 They supplied them with a defective floor. Such an act can, in accordance with the views I have expressed above, give rise to liability in negligence in certain circumstances. But it does not do so merely because the flooring is defective or valueless or useless and requires to be replaced. So to hold would raise very difficult and delicate issues of principle having a wide potential application. I think it would necessarily follow that any manufacturer of products would become liable to the ultimate purchaser if the product, owing to negligence in manufacture was, without being harmful in any way, useless or worthless or defective in quality so that the purchaser wasted the money he spent on it… To introduce a general liability covering such situations would be disruptive of commercial practice, under which manufacturers of products commonly provide the ultimate purchaser with limited guarantees usually undertaking only to replace parts exhibiting defective workmanship and excluding any consequential loss. There being no contractual relationship between manufacturer and ultimate consumer, no room would exist, if the suggested principle were accepted, for limiting the manufacturer's liability. The policy considerations which would be involved in introducing such a state of affairs appear to me to be such as a court of law cannot assess, and the question whether or not it would be in the interests of commerce and the public generally is, in my view, much better left for the legislature… This aspect is more fully developed in the speech to be delivered by my noble and learned friend Lord Brandon of Oakbrook, with whose views on the matter I respectfully agree.

My Lords, for the reasons which I have given, I would concur in the dismissal of the appeal.

13.3.9 LORD ROSKILL: Since it was accepted in the courts below and in argument before your Lordships' House that there was no relevant difference between the Scots law of delict and the English law of negligence, it follows that this appeal equally raises a question of fundamental importance in the development of the latter law… The appellants contended that there was no averment in the pursuers' pleadings relevant to found an action against the defenders in delict, and that therefore the action should be dismissed as irrelevant. The respondents, on the other hand, contended that proof before answer should be allowed. Both courts below allowed proof before answer. The learned Lord Ordinary started his opinion by stating that there was no Scottish authority directly in point, and while in argument before your Lordships' House much Scottish, English and indeed Commonwealth authority was cited, it remains the fact that no decision in any court that was cited to your Lordships conclusively shows the correct route to be taken, though many may be said greatly to illuminate that route.

. . . . . .

13.3.10   The main contract was not exhibited in the courts below. Your Lordships were not told whether that contract included as between the main contractors and the respondents any relevant exceptions clause, nor whether if there were such an exceptions clause it might be available for the benefit of the appellants. Nor were your Lordships told why the respondents had chosen to proceed in delict against the appellants rather than against the main contractors in contract, nor indeed why the main contractors had not been joined as parties to these proceedings. This economy of fact is in stark contrast to the wealth of citation of authority of which your Lordships have had the benefit. Thus the bare point of law has to be decided upon an assumption of the truth of the facts pleaded. But I cannot but suspect that the truth regarding the supposed deficiencies of this flooring at Grangemouth has long since been either established or disproved. Of those matters, however, your Lordships know and have been told nothing. Half a century ago your Lordships' House decided *Donoghue* v. *Stevenson* upon a similar plea of irrelevancy.

. . . . . .

13.3.11   My Lords, there was much discussion before your Lordships' House as to the effect of the pleadings. I see no need to discuss them in detail. They seem to me clearly to contain no allegation that the flooring was in a dangerous state or that its condition was such as to cause danger to life or limb or to other property of other persons or that repairs were urgently or imminently required to avoid any such danger, or that any economic or financial loss had been, or would be, suffered save as would be consequential upon the ultimate replacement of the flooring, the necessity of which was averred in Condescendence VII. The essential feature of the respondents' pleadings was that it advanced a claim for the cost of remedying the alleged defects in the flooring itself by replacement together with resulting economic or financial loss consequential upon that replacement.

. . . . . .

13.3.12   It was strenuously argued for the appellants that for your Lordships' House now to hold that in those circumstances which I have just outlined the appellants were liable to the respondents would be to extend the duty of care owed by a manufacturer and others, to whom the principles first enunciated in *Donoghue* v. *Stevenson* have since been extended during the last half century, far beyond the limits to which the courts have hitherto extended them. The familiar "floodgates" argument was once again brought fully into play. My Lords, although it cannot be denied that policy considerations have from time to time been allowed to play their part in the last century and the present, either in limiting or in extending the scope of the tort of negligence since it first developed as it were in its own right in the course of the last century, yet today I think its scope is best determined by considerations of principle rather than of policy. The "floodgates" argument is very familiar. It still may on occasion have its proper place, but if principle suggests that the law should develop along a particular route and if the adoption of that particular route will accord a remedy where the remedy has hitherto been denied, I see no reason why, if it be just that law should henceforth accord that remedy, that remedy should be denied simply because it will, in consequence of this particular development become available to many rather than to few.

13.3.13 My Lords, I think there is no doubt that *Donoghue* v. *Stevenson* by its insistence upon proximity, in the sense in which Lord Atkin used that word, as the foundation of the duty of care which was there enunciated, marked a great development in the law of delict and of negligence alike. In passing it should be noted that Lord Atkin emphasised at p. 323 of the report that the laws of Scotland and of England were in that case, as is agreed in the present, identical. But that advance having been thus made in 1932, the doctrine then enunciated was at first confined by judicial decision within relatively narrow limits.

. . . . . .

13.3.14 In *Hedley Byrne & Co. Ltd.* v. *Heller & Partners Ltd.*, your Lordships' House made plain that the duty of care was not limited in the manner for which the respondents in that appeal had contended. Your Lordships' House held without doubt that economic loss was recoverable without physical damage having been suffered, provided that the relevant duty of care had existed and that that duty existed when the party to whom the allegedly negligent advice was given, relied upon the "judgment" or "skill" (I take those two words from the speech of Lord Morris of Borth-y-Gest at p. 503) of him who gave the advice. I draw attention without citation to a passage of Lord Hodson at p. 509 where he refers to the *Greystoke Castle Case*. Two passages in the speech of Lord Devlin at p. 529 however demand quotation in full. The noble and learned Lord said this.

"I have had the advantage of reading all the opinions prepared by your Lordships and of studying the terms which your Lordships have framed by way of definition of the sort of relationship which gives rise to responsibility towards those who act upon information or advice and so creates a duty of care towards them. I do not understand any of your Lordships to hold that it is a responsibility imposed by law upon certain types of persons or in certain sorts of situations. It is a responsibility that is voluntarily accepted or undertaken either generally where a general relationship, such as that of solicitor and client or banker and customer, is created, or specifically in relation to a particular transaction."

13.3.15 Later at p. 530 Lord Devlin said: "I shall therefore content myself with the proposition that wherever there is a relationship equivalent to contract, there is a duty of care. Such a relationship may be either general or particular... I regard this proposition as an application of the general conception of proximity. Cases may arise in the future in which a new and wider proposition, quite independent of any notion of contract, will be needed. There may, for example, be cases in which a statement is not supplied for the use of any particular person, any more than in *Donoghue* v. *Stevenson* the ginger beer was supplied for consumption by any particular person; and it will then be necessary to return to the general conception of proximity and to see whether there can be evolved from it, as was done in *Donoghue* v. *Stevenson*, a specific proposition to fit the case."

13.3.16 My Lords, it was, as I think, this development of the law which led Lord Reid in *Dorset Yacht Co. Ltd.* v. *Home Office* at pp. 1026–1027 to say: "In later years there has been a steady trend towards regarding the law of negligence as depending on principle so that, when a new point emerges, one should ask not whether it is covered by authority but whether recognised principles apply to it. *Donoghue* v. *Stevenson* may be regarded as a milestone, and the well-known passage in Lord Atkin's speech should I think be regarded as a statement of principle. It is not to be treated as if it were a statutory definition. It will require qualification in new circumstances. But I think that the time has come when we can and should say that it ought to apply unless there is some justification or vital explanation for its exclusion... But where negligence is involved the tendency has been to apply principles analogous to those stated by Lord Atkin."

13.3.17 Similarly, in *Anns* v. *Merton L.B.C.*, Lord Wilberforce approving the earlier decisions of the Court of Appeal in *Dutton* v. *Bognor Regis U.D.C.* and *Sparham-Souter* v. *Town and Country Developments (Essex) Ltd.*, said of the trilogy of cases *Donoghue* v. *Stevenson, Hedley Byrne*, and *Dorset Yacht* at pp. 751–752: "The position has now been reached that in order to establish that a duty of care arises in a particular situation, it is not necessary to bring the facts of that situation within those of previous situations in which a duty of care has been held to exist. Rather the question has to be approached in two stages. First one has to ask whether, as between the alleged wrongdoer and the person who has suffered damage there is a sufficient relationship of proximity or neighbourhood such that, in the reasonable contemplation of the former, carelessness on his part may be likely to cause damage to the latter — in which case a *prima facie* duty of care arises. Secondly, if the first question is answered affirmatively, it is necessary to consider whether there are any considerations which ought to negative, or to reduce or limit the scope of the duty or the class of person to whom it is owed or damages to which a breach of it may give rise."

13.3.18 Applying those statements of general principle as your Lordships have been enjoined to do both by Lord Reid and by Lord Wilberforce rather than to ask whether the particular situation which has arisen does or does not resemble some earlier and different situation where a duty of care has been held or has not been held to exist, I look for the reasons why, it being conceded that the appellants owed a duty of care to others not to construct the flooring so that those others were in peril of suffering loss or damage to their persons or their property, that duty of care should not be equally owed to the respondents who, though not in direct contractual relationship with the appellants, were as nominated sub-contractors in almost as close a commercial relationship with the appellants as it is possible to envisage short of privity of contract, so as not to expose the respondents to a possible liability to financial loss for repairing the flooring should it prove that that flooring had been negligently constructed. It is conceded that if the flooring had been so badly constructed that to avoid imminent danger the respondents had expended money upon renewing it, the respondents could have recovered the cost of so doing. It seems curious that if the appellants' work had been so bad that to avoid imminent danger expenditure had been incurred, the respondents could recover that expenditure, but that if the work was less badly done so that remedial work could be postponed they cannot do so. Yet this is seemingly the result of the appellants' contentions.

. . . . . .

13.3.19 I think today the proper control lies not in asking whether the proper remedy should lie in contract or instead in delict or tort, not in somewhat capricious judicial determination whether a particular case falls on one side of the line or the other, not in somewhat artificial distinctions between physical and economic or financial loss when the two sometimes go together and sometimes do not — it is sometimes overlooked that virtually all damage including physical damage is in one sense financial or economic for it is compensated by an award of damages — but in the first instance establishing the relevant principles and then in deciding whether the particular case falls within or without those principles. To state this is to do no more than to restate what Lord Reid said in the *Dorset Yacht* case and Lord Wilberforce in *Anns*. Lord Wilberforce in the passage I have already quoted enunciated the two tests which have to be satisfied. The first is "sufficient relationship of proximity", the second any considerations negativing, reducing or limiting the scope of the duty or the class of person to whom it is owed or the damages to which a breach of the duty may give rise. My Lords, it is I think in the application of those two principles that the ability to control the extent of liability in delict or in negligence lies. The history of the development of the law in the last 50 years shows that fears aroused by the "floodgates" argument have been unfounded. Cooke J. in *Bowen* (p. 472) described the "floodgates" argument as specious and the argument against allowing a cause of action such as was alleged in *Dutton, Anns* and *Bowen* as "*in terrorem* or doctrinaire".

13.3.20 Turning back to the present appeal, I therefore ask first whether there was the requisite degree of proximity so as to give rise to the relevant duty of care relied on by the respondents. I regard the following facts as of crucial importance in requiring an affirmative answer to that question.

(1) The appellants were nominated sub-contractors.

(2) The appellants were specialists in flooring.

(3) The appellants knew what products were required by the respondents and their main contractors and specialised in the production of those products.

(4) The appellants alone were responsible for the composition and construction of the flooring.

(5) The respondents relied upon the appellants' skill and experience.

(6) The appellants as nominated sub-contractors must have known that the respondents relied upon their skill and experience.

(7) The relationship between the parties was as close as it could be short of actual privity of contract.

(8) The appellants must be taken to have known that if they did the work negligently (as it must be assumed that they did), the resulting defects would at some time require remedying by the respondents expending money upon the remedial measures as a consequence of which the respondents would suffer financial or economic loss.

My Lords, reverting to Lord Devlin's speech in *Hedley Byrne*, it seems to me that all the conditions existed which give rise to the relevant duty of care owned by the appellants to the respondents.

13.3.21 I then turn to Lord Wilberforce's second proposition. On the facts I have just stated, I see nothing whatever to restrict the duty of care arising from the proximity of which I have spoken. During the argument it was asked what the position would be in a case where there was a relevant exclusion clause in the main contract. My Lords, that question does not arise for decision in the instant appeal, but in principle I would venture the view that such a clause according to the manner in which it was worded might in some circumstances limit the duty of care, just as in the *Hedley Byrne* case the plaintiffs were ultimately defeated by the defendant's disclaimer of responsibility.

13.3.22 LORD BRANDON OF OAKBROOK (dissenting): My Lords, it appears to me clear beyond doubt that, there being no contractual relationship between the pursuers and the defenders in the present case, the foundation, and the only foundation for the existence of a duty of care owed by the defenders to the pursuers, is the principle laid down in the decision of your Lordship's House in *Donoghue* v. *Stevenson*. The actual decision in that case related only to the duty owed by a manufacturer of goods to their ultimate user or consumer, and can be summarised in this way: a person who manufactures goods which he intends to be used or consumed by others, is under a duty to exercise such reasonable care in their manufacture as to ensure that they can be used or consumed in the manner intended without causing physical damage to persons or their property.

13.3.23 While that was the actual decision in *Donoghue* v. *Stevenson*, it was based on a much wider principle embodied in passages in the speech of Lord Atkin, which have been quoted so often that I do not find it necessary to quote them again here. Put shortly, that wider principle is that, when a person can or ought to appreciate that a careless act or omission on his part may result in physical injury to other persons or their property, he owes a duty to all such persons to exercise reasonable care to avoid such careless act or omission.

It is, however, of fundamental importance to observe that the duty of care laid down in *Donoghue* v. *Stevenson* was based on the existence of a danger of physical injury to persons or their property.

. . . . . .

13.3.24 The averments contained in the condescendence in the present case do not include any averment that the defects in the flooring complained of by the pursuer either constitute presently, or might reasonably be expected to constitute in the future, a danger of physical damage to persons or their property, other than the flooring itself. In the absence of any averment of that kind, I am of opinion that the averments contained in the condescendence disclose no cause of action in delict and are accordingly irrelevant.

13.3.25 My Lords, a good deal of the argument presented to your Lordships during the hearing of the appeal was directed to the question whether a person can recover, in an action founded on delict alone, purely pecuniary loss which is independent of any physical damage to persons or their property. If that were the question to be decided in the present case, I should have no hesitation in holding that, in principle and depending on the facts of a particular case, purely pecuniary loss may be recoverable in an action founded on delict alone. Two examples can be given of such cases. First, there is the type of case where a person suffers purely pecuniary loss as a result of relying on another person's negligent misstatements: *Hedley*

Byrne & Co. Ltd. v. *Heller & Partners Ltd.* Secondly, there may be a type of case where a person, who has a cause of action based on *Donoghue* v. *Stevenson*, reasonably incurs pecuniary loss in order to prevent or mitigate imminent danger of damage to the persons or property exposed to that danger; see the dissenting judgment of Laskin J. in the Canadian Supreme Court case of *Rivtow Marine Ltd.* v. *Washington Iron Works*, referred to with approval in the speech of Lord Wilberforce in *Anns* v. *Merton L.B.C.* at p. 760.

. . . . . .

13.3.26 My Lords, in support of their contentions the pursuers placed reliance on the broad statements relating to liability in negligence contained in the speech of Lord Wilberforce in *Anns* v. *Merton L.B.C.* at pp. 751–752. [Lord Brandon then quoted the same passage as Lord Roskill at para. 13.3.17]... Applying that general statement of principle to the present case, it is as I indicated earlier common ground that the first question which Lord Wilberforce said one should ask oneself, namely, whether there is sufficient proximity between the parties to give rise to the existence of a duty of care owed by the one to the other, falls to be answered in the affirmative. Indeed it is difficult to imagine a greater degree of proximity in the absence of a direct contractual relationship, than that which, under the modern type of building contract, exists between a building owner and a sub-contractor nominated by him or his architect.

13.3.27 That first question having been answered in the affirmative, however, it is necessary, according to the views expressed by Lord Wilberforce in the passage from his speech in *Anns* v. *Merton L.B.C.* quoted above, to ask oneself a second question, namely, whether there are any considerations which ought, *inter alia*, to limit the scope of the duty which exists.

To that second question I would answer that there are two important considerations which ought to limit the scope of the duty of care which it is common ground was owed by the defenders to the pursuers on the assumed facts of the present case.

13.3.28 The first consideration is that, in *Donoghue* v. *Stevenson* itself and in all the numerous cases in which the principle of that decision has been applied to different but analogous factual situations, it has always been either stated expressly, or taken for granted, that an essential ingredient in the cause of action relied on was the existence of danger, or the threat of danger, of physical damage to persons or their property excluding for this purpose the very piece of property from the defective condition of which such danger, or the threat of danger, arises. To dispense with that essential ingredient in a cause of action of the kind concerned in the present case would, in my view, involve a radical departure from long-established authority.

13.3.29 The second consideration is that there is no sound policy for substituting the wider scope of the duty of care put forward for the pursuers for the more restricted scope of such duty put forward by the defenders. The effect of accepting the pursuers' contention with regard to the scope of the duty of care involved would be in substance to create as between two persons who are not in any contractual relationship with each other, obligations of one of these two persons to the other which are only really appropriate as between persons who do have such a relationship between them.

In the case of a manufacturer or distributor of goods, the position would be that he warranted to the ultimate user or consumer of such goods that they were as well designed, as merchantable and as fit for their contemplated purpose as the exercise of reasonable care could make them.

In the case of sub-contractors such as those concerned in the present case, the position would be that they warranted to the building owner that the flooring, when laid, would be as well designed, as free from defects of any kind and as fit for its contemplated purpose as the exercise of reasonable care could make it.

In my view, the imposition of warranties of this kind on one person in favour of another, when there is no contractual relationship between them, is contrary to any sound policy requirement.

13.3.30 It is, I think, just worth while to consider the difficulties which would arise if the wider scope of the duty of care put forward by the pursuers were accepted. In any case where complaint was made by an ultimate consumer that a product made by some persons with whom he himself had no contract was defective, by what standard or standards of quality would the question of defectiveness fall to be decided? In the case of goods bought from a retailer, it could hardly be the standard prescribed by the contract between the retailer and the wholesaler, or between the wholesaler and the distributor, or between the distributor and the manufacturer, for the terms of such contracts would not even be known to the ultimate buyer. In the case of sub-contractors such as the defenders in the present case, it could hardly be the standard prescribed by the contract between the sub-contractors and the main contractors, for, although the building owner would probably be aware of those terms, he could not, since he was not a party to such contract, rely on any standard or standards prescribed in it. It follows that the question by what standard or standards alleged defects in a product complained of by its ultimate user or consumer are to be judged remains entirely at large and cannot be given any just or satisfactory answer.

If, contrary to the views expressed above, the relevant contract or contracts can be regarded in order to establish the standard or standards of quality by which the question of defectiveness falls to be judged, and if such contract or contracts happen to include provisions excluding or limiting liability for defective products or defective work, or for negligence generally, it seems that the party sued in delict should in justice be entitled to rely on such provisions. This illustrates with special force the inherent difficulty of seeking to impose what are really contractual obligations by unprecedented and, as I think, wholly undesirable extensions of the existing law of delict.'

COMMENT

13.4.1 Decided: July 15, 1982.
May 19: Sophia Loren jailed for tax evasion.
June 8: Argentines bombed *Sir Galahad* and *Sir Tristram.*
June 9: 20p coin introduced.
July 12: Hostilities in Falklands declared at an end by the U.K.

13.4.2 There have been considerable developments in respect of this case. Academics and judges have suggested that it is at the very best a very special case. The following extract shows the frosty reception that the case had. As shall be seen, it has not been overruled and is still good law in its context.

13.4.3 It is important to pay attention to Lord Brandon's dissent, as that speech is beginning to gather ever more support. The most important point in these cases is perhaps the question of the measure of the duty where there is something limiting liability in the defenders' contract with the vanishing third party. It would seem grossly unfair to hold someone liable to a greater extent under delict than they would have been had the contract (which has been a crucial factor in establishing their delictual liability) been enforceable at the instance of the pursuer. Perhaps if that were laid down as a general rule under the principle, the principle would not be so generally regarded with suspicion.

13.4.4 Marcel Proust is generally regarded as writing the longest sentences in modern literature — his longest is about 400 words long. Lord Roskill, though, makes a bid in para. 13.3.18, managing about 150 words. Whether it can be said of Lord Roskill, as it was of Proust, that: "The whole sentence bursts forth, rocks backwards and forwards and then sinks away by fits and starts, in order to use its long accumulated energy to make a brutal attack and grasp us by the heart," must remain for the reader to judge. The true standard for a judge seeking to achieve lucidity must still be that of the author of "*Old Herbert Bundy, the defendant, was a farmer there*". (See *Lloyds Bank v. Bundy* [1974] 3 W.L.R. 501 at p. 504.)

53. Logie, "The Final Demise of Junior Books?"
1989 J.R. 5

13.5.1 'There can be few cases in recent years which have attracted as much comment and criticism as *Junior Books v. The Veitchi Co. Ltd.* The decision was not welcomed by English commentators, who regarded its implications as verging on the heretical. [The arguments are neatly summarised in B. S. Markensis, "An expanding Tort Law — The Price of a Rigid Contract Law" (1987) 103 L.Q.R. 354, and I. S. Stephenson, "Goodbye Junior Books" (1988) 138 N.L.J. 483.] Scots lawyers on the other hand welcomed it, albeit with some reservations.

Subsequent cases have treated it with some caution, but in a trilogy of recent cases, the House of Lords and Court of Appeal have made what appears to be a concerted attempt to kill off any attempts to widen its application.

. . . . . .

13.5.2 The treatment accorded to *Junior Books* in later cases [this discussion draws largely on the judgment of Bingham L.J. in *Simaan Construction Co. v. Pilkington Glass Ltd.* (No. 2) [1988] 2 W.L.R. 761, where a more detailed discussion of the cases noted may be found] has been wholly restrictive. In *Tate & Lyle Foods and Distribution Ltd. v. Greater London Council* [1983] 2 A.C. 509 it was suggested that "in *Junior Books* the plaintiff suffered personal injury or damage to his property." In *Muirhead v. Industrial Tank Specialities* [1986] Q.B. 507 Robert Goff L.J. considered at length the difficulties arising from the judgments of the House of Lords and concluded that: "it is, I think, safest for this court to treat *Junior Books* as a case in which, on its particular facts, there was considered to be such a very close relationship between the parties that the defenders could, if the facts as pleaded were proved, be held liable to the pursuers." Two decisions of the House of Lords then gave further indication that *Junior Books* had not made a significant breakthrough in relation to the recovery of economic loss, at least in relation to contracts which were rendered less profitable or unprofitable or in relation to persons with no legal or possessory interest in goods which had been damaged (*Candlewood Navigation Corporation Ltd. v. Mitsui O.S.K. Lines Ltd.* [1986] A.C. 1; *Leigh and Sillivan Ltd. v. Aliakmon Shipping Co. Ltd.* [1986] A.C. 785). But perhaps the most stinging criticism of the decision came in *Maloco v. Littlewoods Organisation Ltd.*, 1987 S.L.T. 425 [Ext. 50] (curiously, not a case concerned with economic loss), in which Lord Goff stated that "in *Junior Books...* some members of your Lordships' House succumbed, perhaps too easily, to the temptations to adopt a solution based simply on proximity."

. . . . . .

13.5.3 *Simaan General Contracting Co. v. Pilkington Glass Ltd. (No. 2)* [1988] 2 W.L.R. 761 — In *Simaan*, the plaintiffs were the main contractors for a building in Abu Dhabi. The contract specifically provided for double-glazed, green glass units manufactured by the defendants to be installed in the curtain walling of the building. The erection of the curtain walling was sub-contracted by the plaintiffs and the sub-contractors (who were not parties to the action) purchased the specified units from the defendants. The architect, however, rejected the units: instead of being a uniform shade of green, they were variable shades and some were even red. They were considered to be unpleasant in appearance, contrary to specification and not in accordance with the sample supplied. The discrepancy was regarded as being of particular significance as green is the colour of peace in the Islamic world. The sub-contractors were instructed to replace the units, but at the time of the action this had not taken place. In addition, the building owner had not paid the plaintiffs, who in turn had not paid the sub-contractors. The plaintiffs accordingly raised an action in negligence against the defendants alleging that by reason of the defects in the glass units they had suffered economic loss in that money which they would otherwise have received had been withheld. The official referee held that the defendants owed the plaintiffs a duty of care to avoid defects in the units which would cause the plaintiffs economic loss.

13.5.4   The Court of Appeal, however, reversed this decision. Lord Justice Bingham, delivering the leading judgment, reviewed the authorities on the question of economic loss... However, there was no sense in which the plaintiffs could be said to have relied on the defendants; nor was there any basis on which it could be said that the defendants had assumed a direct responsibility to the plaintiffs. Although he doubted whether *Junior Books* was a case of physical damage as had been suggested in *Tate & Lyle*, there was no physical damage in this case; "—what we have here are not, in my view, defects but failures to comply with Sale of Goods Act conditions of correspondence with description or sample, merchantability or (perhaps) fitness for purpose. It would, I think, be abuse of language to describe these units as damaged. The contrast with the floor in the *Junior Books* case is obvious."

   ... In any case, it was not just and reasonable to impose a duty of care to prevent economic loss on the defendants "because there is no reason why claims beginning with the Sheikh [the building owner] should not be pursued down the contractual chain, subject to any short-cut which may be agreed upon, ending with a contractual claim against the defendants."

13.5.5   *Greater Nottingham Co-operative Society Ltd.* v. *Cementation Piling and Foundations Ltd.* [1988] 3 W.L.R. 396 — The plaintiffs engaged contractors to their premises at Skegness. The piling work required for the work was sub-contracted to the defendants by the main contractors. However, in addition to the contract between the contractors and the sub-contractors, the plaintiffs entered into a separate agreement with the sub-contractors which provided *inter alia* that the sub-contractors would exercise all reasonable skill and care in the design of the sub-contract works and the selections of materials and goods. It also provided that the sub-contractors would perform the contract so that the contractors would not become entitled to an extension of time in which to perform the main contract. Piling operations commenced, but owing to the negligent operation of drilling equipment, damage was caused to an adjoining restaurant and work was suspended while the cause of the damage and how the work should proceed were ascertained. A prolonged dispute between the architect, the contractors, the sub-contractors and the plaintiffs then ensued, with the result that the piling operations were redesigned and the completion date was extended.

13.5.6 The plaintiffs sued the defendents in negligence for, *inter alia,* the additional costs under the main contract as a result of executing the revised piling scheme, additional expenses paid to the main contractors in respect of losses and expenses arising during the delay and the employers' consequential loss due to the delayed completion. The official referee found for the plaintiffs. The Court of Appeal once more reversed. Purchas L.J. applied the "checklist" found in the judgment of Lord Roskill in *Junior Books* [see para 13.3.20], and noted that in the present case there was actual privity of contract between the parties, a factor which had not been present in the earlier case. Although there could be concurrent liability in contract and tort, it was relevant to bear in mind two factors in determining whether the tortious liability could be more extensive than the contractual, namely: the parties had an actual opportunity to define their relationship by means of contract and took it; and the general contractual structure as between the employers, the main contractors and the sub-contractors provided a channel of claim which was open to the employers. The contract provided for liability for failure to use reasonable skill and care in the design of and the selection of materials in the pile-driving operation, but the contract was "significantly silent" as to the liability for the manner in which the contract was executed.

. . . . . .

13.5.7 *D & F Estates Ltd.* v. *Church Commissioners for England* [1988] 3 W.L.R. 368 — Between 1963 and 1965 a block of flats was built on land owned by the first defendants. The third defendants were the main contractors. Plasterwork was carried out by sub-contractors (who were the second defendants in the action) and the first defendants subsequently granted a lease of a flat to the plaintiff company. In 1980 it was discovered that some of the plasterwork was defective and some of it fell down. Remedial work of stripping off the defective plaster and replastering was carried out. The plaintiffs sued the defendants in negligence for, *inter alia,* the cost of the remedial work, the cost of cleaning the carpets and other possessions damaged or dirtied by the falling plaster, loss of rent while remedial work was carried out and disturbance. The judge at first instance held that the plaster had been defective because it had been incorrectly applied by the sub-contractors and that the third defendants ought to have known that that was the case. He awarded the plaintiffs damages. The Court of Appeal allowed an appeal by the plaintiffs, the House of Lords affirmed the judgment of the latter court. It held that the loss sustained in renewing the plaster was purely economic loss, which was not recoverable under the principle in *Donoghue* v. *Stevenson*. Furthermore, a main contractor did not in general assume a duty of care to any person who might be injured by a dangerous defect caused by the negligence of an apparently competent sub-contractor and there was nothing in the present case to displace that general rule.

Lord Bridge gave *Junior Books* short shrift: "The consensus of judicial opinion, with which I concur, seems to be that the decision of the majority is so far dependent upon the unique, albeit non-contractual, relationship between the pursuer and the defender in that case and the unique scope of the duty of care owed by the defender to the pursuer arising from that relationship that the decision cannot be regarded as laying down any principle of general application in the law of tort or delict." He went on to lend his support to the dissenting judgment given by Lord Brandon in *Junior Books*.

. . . . . .

13.5.8   *Comment*— It is perhaps somewhat surprising to find a Court of Appeal judge opining that it is difficult to see that "future citation from the *Junior Books* case can ever serve any useful purpose" less than six years after the original decision. Nonetheless, as far as English law is concerned, the statement is probably valid. The effect of these decisions is to confirm that in English law, *Junior Books* is confined to its "unique" facts and certainly did not open the doors to a general principle of recoverability of economic loss in tort... However, certain aspects of the manner in which the courts have closed the door on *Junior Books* deserve comment.

13.5.9   First of all, it is clear that one of the underlying reasons behind the decisions given in the cases above is the preservation of the distinction between the law of contract and the law of tort, and an ending of the use of the latter to supplement and extend the former... However, this "old simplistic narrow-mindedness" fails to take account of the fact that the need for tortious remedies in some circumstances arises principally because of the rigidity of the doctrine of privity of contract. In addition, it is now clear that the distinction between contract and tort is not absolutely rigid. It would be difficult to accept (unless you are a Court of Appeal judge!) that in circumstances like those in *Junior Books, Simaan* and *Greater Nottingham Co-operative Society* the appropriate remedy was for the owner of the property to sue the main contractor, who in turn would sue the sub-contractor, who in turn would sue the seller or another sub-contractor and so on rather than allowing the party who had suffered loss to sue the party which had caused it. If the remedy is to take this form, it is left largely in the hands of the owner or main contractor, who, for a variety of legitimate reasons, may not start the chain of legal action, leaving a party who had suffered loss without redress.

. . . . . .

13.5.10 Secondly, these cases mark a partial resuscitation of the "floodgates" argument: "—there is no precedent for the application of strict logic in treading the path leading from the basic principle established in *Donoghue* v. *Stevenson*... towards the Pandora's Box of unbridled damages at the end of the path of foreseeability." Although exposing the defendants to "liability in an indeterminate amount for an indeterminate time to an indeterminate class" is clearly a factor which courts can and do take into account in determining the question of liability, it is simply not relevant in many — if not most — economic loss cases. There is not an indeterminate amount of damages (the cost of remedial work in the cases above provided a ready measure of damages); there is not an indeterminate time involved (*Simaan* and *Greater Nottingham Co-operative Society* were originally raised three years after the loss had been suffered); and there is not an indeterminate class of potential plaintiffs (in *Simaan* and *Greater Nottingham Co-operative Society* there were only two — the main contractor who could have sued in contract and the principal employer who could attempt to raise a suit in tort). The injustice in giving the floodgates argument no weight in appropriate cases is more than balanced by the injustice of giving it too much weight in cases where it is not applicable.

13.5.11 Thirdly, the cases result in clear anomalies... Indeed, the result in [*Greater Nottingham Co-operative Society*] could, if taken to its logical extreme, give a new and unforeseen impact to guarantees issued by the manufacturer to the consumer if that guarantee creates contractual rights for limited purposes on the consumer. Similarly, the result in the *D. & F. Estates* case gives rise to the possibility that if someone is physically injured by the negligent work of a builder, he can recover damages. However, if he discovers the defects and puts them right before they cause any such damage or injury, he can recover nothing. In addition, it is by no means clear from the policy considerations advanced in these cases why bankers, for example, should be liable for the economic loss resulting from negligent statements made by them, while builders should be free of liability for economic loss resulting from their negligent acts. (See *Hedley Byrne* v. *Heller* [1964] A.C. 465.)

13.5.12 However, perhaps the most important issue from a Scottish perspective is the extent to which these cases are applicable in Scotland. It is difficult to see a Scottish judge laying so much emphasis on privity of contract or the need to restrict the delictual duty of care in the cases where the parties are in a contractual relationship. It has long been accepted that the fact that parties are in a contractual relationship does not prevent duties in delict arising, and despite the cautious approach taken to *Junior Books*, in England, the most recent treatment in Scotland suggests a more favourable attitude. In *Norwich Union Life Insurance Society* v. *Covell Matthews Partnership*, 1987 S.L.T. 452, Lord McCluskey rejected the approach taken in the later English cases and preferred to examine the problem presented to him in terms of basic principles derived from *Donoghue* v. *Stevenson*. Indeed, he seems to go even further than *Junior Books* at some stages in his judgment by suggesting that although reliance may be of critical importance in some cases of economic loss, it was not an essential ingredient without which economic loss could not be recovered. Rather than examine the question of reliance, he instead preferred to look at whether the test of proximity had been met and whether the economic loss was a foreseeable consequence of negligence on the part of the defenders. Having concluded that both questions should be answered in the affirmative, he held the case against the defender to be relevant.

Although this approach is clearly in line with Scottish authority and principle, it is by no means clear if it will withstand the assault on economic loss in *Simaan*, *Greater Nottingham Co-operative Society* and *D. & F. Estates*. But it may be too early yet to dance on the Scottish grave of *Junior Books*.'

COMMENT

13.6.1 Mr Logie's summary of the law and conclusion were substantially judicially adopted in the *Scott Lithgow v. G.E.C. Electrical Products*, 1992 S.L.T. 244, putting it beyond reasonable doubt, it is submitted, that *Junior Books* is the Lazarus of the Law Reports.

13.6.2 In *Scott Lithgow* Lord Clyde said: "It seems to me correct to see the decision in *Junior Books Ltd v. Veitchi Co. Ltd* as depending critically on the close proximity which was found there to exist between the parties. This was the consideration which Lord Fraser (at p. 265) and Lord Roskill (at pp. 277–278) both saw as distinguishing the case from that of the producer of goods to be offered for sale to the general public and so provided an answer to the 'floodgates' argument. It is that aspect which serves to distinguish the general observations on the law expounded by Lord Brandon in his dissenting speech in *Junior Books* and adopted with approval in *D & F Estates Ltd* [1989] A.C. 177. After making the comment about the *Junior Books* case which I have already quoted, Lord Bridge went on to say: 'The dissenting speech of Lord Brandon of Oakbrook on the other hand enunciates with cogency and clarity principles of fundamental importance which are clearly applicable to determine the scope of the duty of care owed by one party to another in the absence, as in the instant case, of either any contractual relationship or any such uniquely proximate relationship as that on which the decision of the majority in *Junior Books* was founded.' I note that his Lordship expressly refers to the uniquely proximate relationship as an exception from the application of the general rule expounded by Lord Brandon. Senior counsel for the pursuers accepted Lord Brandon's observations as properly presenting the general rule, but he submitted that they were not applicable to the circumstances of the *Junior Books* case where the particular relevant degree of proximity existed.

13.6.3 "Furthermore, I am not persuaded that the pursuers' proposed principle is sufficiently precise to represent what the legal position is or indeed might be. Merely to require that the delinquent was doing something specially for an ascertained person or persons does not seem to me to be sufficient. The test endeavours to distinguish the case where a person buys a suit made to measure as opposed to one off the peg. In the course of the discussion the purchaser of a wedding cake was compared with the purchaser of an ordinary loaf of bread and the purchase of a specially-built limousine with the purchase of a standard mass-produced motor car. But it is not evident that the distinction proposed sufficiently isolates the situation of the particularly proximate relationship which lies behind the duty of care. Certainly I have not been able to draw from the authorities to which I was referred a general proposition of the kind which counsel for the pursuers proposed. The question appears to defy any more general principle than the existence of a proximate relationship and thereafter the matter is one to be resolved in the circumstances of the case."

13.6.4 The position of *Junior Books* now seems secure. In *Murphy v. Brentwood* [1990] 3 W.L.R. 414, in which a court of seven Law Lords reconsidered much of the law of negligence, it was appreciated that *Junior Books* falls within the reasoning of *Hedley Byrne* and is not polluted in any way by the difficulties inherent in *Anns* from which the House of Lords departed in *Murphy*. In addition to bringing *Junior Books* within the *Hedley Byrne* mainstream of economic loss recovery cases, no doubt was cast upon it. (See Lord Keith at p. 427, Lord Bridge at p. 441; it is probably also comprehended within Lord Oliver's remarks at p. 446A.) Not everyone agrees. Duncan Wallace Q.C. does not: see "Negligence and Economic Loss" [1993] Tort L.Rev. 152.

The most significant point about *Murphy* relates to the categorisation of damage as being economic as opposed to physical. While *Anns*, following *Dutton* (now overruled), treated mistakes which made a building likely to be a danger to health if not repaired as causing physical damage, it has now been laid down that such a loss is economic. The person in the house must repair it or sell it and in carrying out each of these actions has lost money and not through damage to another's property as in secondary economic loss cases. The loss is therefore an economic loss and a primary economic loss. See paras. 13.3.18 and 13.3.25. In the particular circumstances of building cases, it will usually be the case that there will be insufficient proximity, special relationship or fairness and reasonableness to establish *Hedley Byrne*-type liability. However the facts must always be scrutinised: see *King v. North Cornwall D.C.* (February 8, 1995, unreported); *Stevenson v. A. & J. Stephen (Builders)*, 1996 S.L.T. 140. In *British Telecommunications plc v. James Thomson & Sons (Engineers) Ltd*, 1996 G.W.D. 14–802 decided by Lord Rodger in his brief spell in the Outer House, the employers right to sue sub-contractors for negligence allegedly causing damage by fire to BT's switching station was in dispute. The sub-contractors accepted that there was proximity but that *Marc Rich & Co. v. Bishop Rock Ltd* [1995] 3 W.L.R. 227 meant that an imposition of a duty of care had to be fair just and reasonable. It was held that because the employer imposed liability on the contractor for the negligence of sub-contractors like the defenders, the contractor was protected by an obligation on the employers (the pursuers) to insure against fire. Thus the defenders would not expect to be pursued for this claim and would not have built the cost of insurance into their tender. For a helpful note see Convery, J., "Subcontractors and the Contractual Matrix" 1996 Rep.B. 9–10. She quite rightly asks whether the fair just and reasonable test was meant to be applied to cases of damage to the pursuers' property as it can be *argued* that *Marc Rich* did. Can this case be explained as one where there *is* a duty but its *scope* is reduced by the obligations assumed by the defenders under their contract? On appeal (1996 G.W.D. 14–802) a majority upheld the dismissal of the case and generally ignored arguments from *Murphy*. The full report, will in due course, repay scrutiny.

Secondary Economic Loss

54. Dynamco (Appellants) v. Holland & Hannen & Cubitts (Scotland) Ltd
1971 S.C. 257 (I.H.)

13.7.1 'LORD MIGDALE: The point raised in each of these reclaiming motions is the same, so I propose to deal only with the first case. The pursuers, who are now the reclaimers, have a factory at East Mains Industrial Estate, Broxburn. They produced articles by means of machinery powered by electricity. At 2.50 p.m. on February 24, 1969, the electricity supply failed and it was not restored until 6.26 a.m. on February 25. For about 15 ½ hours their production stopped. The cause of the stoppage was that a J.B.C. (*sic*) excavator, operated by a servant of the defenders, came into contact with and damaged an underground electric supply cable which had been laid by and was the property of the South of Scotland Electricity Board. The pursuers claim damages from the defenders on the ground that they failed to ascertain the routes of such cables before using the excavator. The place where the cable was damaged was some 500 yards from the pursuers' property. The pursuers' premises, plant and material were not damaged. Their claim is in respect of financial loss resulting from loss of production during the 15 ½ hours for which their plant was idle and is made up of (a) wages and overhead costs, £335; and (b) loss of profits on lost products, £480 — a total of £815.

13.7.2 As the pursuers' case is a claim for reparation flowing from a breach of duty, they will have to show that the defenders owed them a duty and were in breach of that duty. The defenders deny that they owed any duty to the pursuers in the circumstances of this case. They also deny they were in breach of a duty owed to the pursuers, the damage which they claim to have sustained is not recognised as reparable by the law of Scotland. They contend that there are certain losses in respect of which that law will not sustain a claim. In particular, it will not recognise a claim for financial loss which does not stem from damage to the claimants' property.

13.7.3 The pursuers, on the other hand, contend that they have relevantly averred that the defenders owed them a duty to take reasonable care not to damage the electricity supply cable, that the defenders were in breach of that duty because they failed to ascertain the route of the cable and damaged it through the use of their excavator, and that their financial loss was a reasonably foreseeable consequence of the cutting-off of electricity. Accordingly the defenders should have had that event in contemplation. Counsel for the pursuers conceded that liability for consequences, even if foreseeable, does not extend to all events which can be causally traced back to the breach of duty, but contended that in this case the pursuers are liable.

13.7.4 While I recognise that it may be difficult to lay down a rule which can be of general application, it is not necessary to do so in this case. The law of Scotland has for over 100 years refused to accept that a claim for financial loss which does not arise directly from damage to the claimant's property can give rise to a legal claim for damages founded on negligence. That is the conclusion at which the Lord Ordinary has arrived, and I agree with him.

This proposition is supported by three cases. [His Lordship mentioned *Allan v. Barclay* (1864) 2 M. 873, Ext. 48.] The case of *Simpson & Co.* v. *Thomson* (1877) 5 R. (H.L.) 40 concerned a claim by underwriters against the owner of two vessels belonging to the same person, one of which was insured with them. The House of Lords held that the underwriters could have no greater right of action than the owner had, and, as the owner of the insured vessel was also the owner of and responsible for the negligent navigation of the wrongdoing vessel, neither he nor the underwriters could sue. In the course of his speech Lord Penzance, dealing with a contention for the pursuer, said (at p. 46): "The principle involved seems to me to be this, that where damage is done by a wrongdoer to a chattel, not only the owner of that chattel, but all those who by contract with the owner have bound themselves to obligations which are rendered more onerous, or have secured to themselves advantages which are rendered less beneficial, by the damage done to the chattel, have a right of action against the wrongdoer, although they have no immediate or reversionary property in the chattel, and no possessory right by reason of any contract attaching to the chattel itself, such as by lien or hypothecation." After giving some illustrations he went on to say (at pp. 45–47): "But the ground upon which I will ask your Lordships to reject this contention… is this, that… no precedent or authority has been found or produced to the House for an action against the wrongdoer, except in the name, and therefore in point of law on the part of one who had either some property in or possession of the chattel insured." Lord Blackburn agreed.

13.7.5 The third is *Reavis* v. *Clan Line Steamers*, 1925 S.C. 725. Mrs Reavis and her orchestra were involved in a collision between two vessels in which the *Rowan* sank. Some members of the orchestra were drowned and others were injured. Mrs Reavis claimed, as damages, a sum as compensation for personal injuries and loss of effects; a sum representing loss of profits on the orchestra from the date of the collision to the disbanding of the orchestra; and a sum representing loss of profits through the break-up of the orchestra which could not continue after losing so many of its members. The only dispute

concerned her claims for loss of profits due to the loss of service
through death or injuries of some of the members of the orchestra
and its consequent disbandment. These claims were disallowed. Lord
Constable in the Outer House referred to the passage by Lord Kinloch
in *Allan* v. *Barclay*, and he also referred to the speech of Lord Penzance
in *Simpson & Co* v. *Thomson* from which I have quoted. He draws the
conclusion that the sole right of action for injuries to property belongs
to those who have legal right therein. Mrs Reavis could claim for loss
of musical scores and for loss or diminution of her own earning power,
but not for financial loss because she had been deprived of the service
of persons who were useful to her. He accordingly dismissed this claim.
In the Inner House their Lordships of the First Division took the same
view. Lord President Clyde, after referring to *Allan* v. *Barclay* and a
passage in Lord Fraser's work on *Master and Servant* (3rd ed., p. 311),
said (at p. 740): 'In the law of Scotland... a person claiming reparation
for injury by another person's fault cannot go beyond the effect of
such injury on his own person, his own health, his own business or
other capabilities, and his own property.' His Lordship then referred
to the passage from the speech of Lord Penzance and finally reverted
to and accepted the passage by Lord Kinloch on the grand rule on the
subject of damages — 'none can be claimed except such as naturally
and directly arise out of the wrong done.' Lord Cullen pointed out —
(at p. 741) that since 1864 — the date of the decision in *Allan* v. *Barclay*
— no instance of an action in respect of a loss of services had emerged
in the law of Scotland. I think this line of authority covers the present
case. The pursuers cannot recover for loss of profits unless that loss
arises from damage to their plant or materials. They could not recover
for financial loss if the wrongful act of the defenders had deprived
them of the valuable services of an employee, and I see no difference
in principle between that financial loss and the financial loss they have
sustained because the wrongful act of the defenders has deprived them
of a supply of electricity. It was not their electricity. The damage was
done outside their premises and before the cable and no part of their
property was damaged.

13.7.6   Mr Cameron, for the pursuers, contended that the authorities
I have referred to were before the decision in *Donoghue* v. *Stevenson*
was pronounced. Lord Atkin said (at p. 44): 'Who, then, in law is my
neighbour? The answer seems to be — persons who are so closely
and directly affected by my act that I ought reasonably to have them
in contemplation as being so affected when I am directing my mind
to the acts or omissions which are called in question.' Counsel
contended that since that decision the range of liability had been
extended and that in the present case the defenders ought to have
had in contemplation the consequences to the pursuers (and other
users of electricity) if the supply was cut off. These consequences
embraced a stoppage of productions followed by a loss of profits. The

defenders not only owed a duty to the pursuer but were liable to recompense them for the loss arising from breach of duty. I do not think the case of *Donoghue* v. *Stevenson,* which dealt with persons to whom a wrongdoer owed a duty, has altered Scots law on the measure of damages.

. . . . . .

13.7.7   The Lord Ordinary has considered a number of English cases, including *S.C.M. Ltd.* v. *W. J. Whittall* [1971] 1 Q.B. 337. I prefer to decide the present case according to the law of Scotland, but nowhere among the English cases can I find the authority for the proposition that a person can recover damages for financial loss which does not arise directly from damage to his property. On the contrary, not only are dicta of Lord Denning M.R. at p. 344 and Winn L.J. at p. 348 in that case against that proposition, but so are the decisions in a number of the other cases referred to, including *Weller & Co.* v. *Foot and Mouth Disease Research Institute* [1966] 1 Q.B. 569.

In my opinion the Lord Ordinary arrived at the right decision and I would refuse the reclaiming motion and dismiss the action

13.7.8   LORD CAMERON: But in the law of Scotland the obligation to avoid acts or omissions which in fact result in loss or injury to another, and to take reasonable care to avoid such injury and to insure against it, arises only if that risk is a reasonable and probable consequence of the act or omission. Unless that can be affirmed, the act or omission cannot be branded as negligence. Further, it is not all consequences of negligent acts or omissions which are to be taken into account as qualifying for an award of damages: they may be too remote and remoteness may be determined by considerations of practical expediency or even of public policy.

13.7.9   It might be that a reasonable man in the defenders' situation might have contemplated physical damage to a cable consequent upon operations by mechanical tools in the ground if some care were not taken to ascertain its position horizontally and vertically, but that it is not this case. What the reclaimers are saying is that this type of loss, purely economic and not in any way associated with physical damage to their property, is one which should have been foreseen as reasonable and probable by the defenders as a consequence of their failure in the only matters condescended upon. How far is this to go? Is it to extend to every person or premise served by this cable, however far away from the site of rupture? The reclaimers do not limit the range of the duty geographically. Is it to be anticipated that fracture of one cable at a particular time of day is a reasonable and probable consequence of a failure to take action to ascertain the position and laid depth of cables which will in turn lead to a breakdown of production in this or any other factory or workshop within the range of supply? The reclaimers do not suggest that they are the only concern drawing supplies of electricity from this cable or that the defenders had reason to think that in the area where they were to work supply cables to factories were likely to be laid. No doubt a reasonable man might with some reason surmise that, if a cable were fractured, this might lead to industrial dislocation or even financial loss, but equally it might not. I am far from accepting the proposition put in wide general terms in the reclaimers' pleadings that this duty on which they found was owed to them, and to each and every other person or concern on the line of supply, wherever they might be. There may well be a duty owed to the electricity board, but that is another matter. Further, this is said to be a duty which is of general application, as Winn L.J. noted in the case of *S.C.M. Ltd.*, and, as he observed in that case, the consequences of acceptance would be enormous. There is no authority in the law of Scotland which directly supports a proposition so wide as this, or so momentous and onerous in its application as the reclaimers present it.'

COMMENT

13.8.1   Decided: July 15, 1971.
  May 12: Mick Jagger married Bianca.
  June 17: Dom Mintoff won election in Malta.
  July 6: Louis Armstrong died.

55. **North Scottish Helicopters Ltd v. United Technologies Corp. Inc.** 1988 S.L.T. 77

13.9.1   '[From the report.] A finance company leased a helicopter to the second pursuers. The terms of the lease placed all responsibility for keeping the helicopter operational upon the lessees. The finance company, although owners, were essentially financiers. In accordance with the provisions of the lease, the second pursuers permitted the first pursuers, their subsidiary, to use the helicopter. The pursuers had unrestricted use of the helicopter and were bound by the lease to comply with statutory maintenance and safety requirements and to indemnify the finance company against destruction of or damage to the helicopter. The helicopter caught fire and was damaged. Both pursuers sued the designers and manufacturers of the helicopter and the manufacturers of a component for damages for negligence. The defenders contended that neither pursuer had title to sue. The parties agreed to that issue being disposed of by preliminary proof.

13.9.2   LORD DAVIDSON: Although ownership of the helicopter remained with Scamba, the lease imposed various onerous obligations upon the second pursuers. The second pursuers were not entitled to any abatement of rental in respect of any period during which the helicopter was unserviceable and during any such period Scamba was not obliged to provide a replacement helicopter. The second pursuers undertook at their own expense to maintain the helicopter and keep it in first-class working order. Scamba, being financiers, employed no personnel capable of operating or of maintaining the helicopter. The second pursuers, on the other hand, employed qualified air crew and ground staff through whom they were able to secure compliance with the statutory provisions regulating the maintenance, repair and operation of helicopters... The lease also obliged the second pursuers not to bring any action against Scamba in respect of any defect which might at any time appear in the helicopter. They agreed to indemnify Scamba from and against destruction of or damage to the helicopter. The second pursuers accepted that they had selected the helicopter and had placed no reliance whatever on Scamba regarding its quality... The first defenders are sued as the designers and manufacturers of Sikorsky helicopters. The second defenders are sued on the ground that they manufactured a motor brake unit for the helicopter which, according to the pursuers, was defective and so caused the fire. The averments of fault made against each of the defenders are based on delict... Since resolution of the issue of title to sue could be of decisive importance to the outcome of the action, and since the relevant facts are in comparatively small compass, parties agreed to have it disposed of at a preliminary proof.

. . . . . .

13.9.3   The pursuers' position on title to sue can be simply stated. At the time when the fire occurred the first pursuers were in possession of the helicopter. They were its main users, and their possession of the helicopter was justified by the provisions of the lease and by correspondence referred to above. The correct legal category of the first pursuers' possession was commodate, or loan. The loan was a loan at will, and therefore qualified as *precarium.* Reference was made to Bell, *Prin.*, paras. 194 to 199; Erskine, *Inst.*, II, i, 20–25. The second pursuers had a right to possession of the helicopter under the lease with Scamba. At the material time the second pursuers enjoyed that right in a manner contemplated and sanctioned in terms of the lease. The first pursuers had possession of the helicopter, but they were wholly under the control of the second pursuers. In that state of affairs the second pursuers' possession was not less than that of a bailee... Furthermore, the terms of the lease were such as to make the second pursuers' position analogous to that of a charterer of a vessel by demise. Scamba retained property in the helicopter for the reasons which have been explained. From the practical point of view, however, the second pursuers were in the strongest position that could be conceived of short of ownership.

. . . . . .

13.9.4 The main contention advanced by counsel for the defenders was to the following effect. In the light of recent decisions of high authority it was clearly the policy of the law that a person whose link with a moveable was solely contractual could not sue an alleged wrongdoer for damage to that moveable by reason of the fact that the pursuers' contractual relations with the moveable were adversely affected by the alleged wrong and that performance of the pursuers' contractual obligation was made more onerous. The speech of Lord Fraser of Tullybelton in *Candlewood Navigation Corpn. Ltd.* v. *Mitsui O.S.K. Lines Ltd.* [1986] A.C. 1, at p. 19, also indicated a reluctance on the part of the courts to countenance a multiplicity of claimants suing a wrongdoer in respect of damage to a moveable. Any pursuer claiming a right to sue must be either the owner of the moveable, or a person deriving right from the owner, or a person who could instruct a right implied by law. Reference was made to *Fleming* v. *Gemmill* (1907) 15 S.L.T. 691. If, as the pursuer sought in the present case, a non-owner was to be allowed to sue for damage to the helicopter, he must be able to point to a right to claim openly conferred by the owner or, alternatively, he must rely upon a right implied by law.

. . . . . .

13.9.5 Under the common law of Scotland and, it would appear, of England too, the hirer of a moveable was not an insurer of that moveable. He was not bound to repair or replace a hired article if the loss or damage was caused not by his fault. In the present case the second pursuers, for reasons of their own, had entered into a contract under which they accepted unqualified liability to repair or replace the helicopter in the event of loss or damage occurring. The second pursuers' right to sue, if they had one, depended upon the terms of the lease. Had the second pursuers not undertaken that onerous provision, they would not have been bound to repair the helicopter. Counsel founded on the dictum of Lord Penzance in *Simpson & Co.* v. *Thomson* at p. 46, which had recently been endorsed once again by the House of Lords in *Candelwood* (*supra*): "The principle involved seems to me to be this, that where damage is done by a wrongdoer to a chattel, not only the owner of that chattel, but all those who by contract with the owner have bound themselves to obligations which are rendered more onerous, or have secured to themselves advantages which are rendered less beneficial, by the damage done to the chattel, have a right of action against the wrongdoer, although they have no immediate or reversionary property in the chattel, and no possessory right by reason of any contract attaching to the chattel itself, such as by lien or hypothecation." Counsel submitted that in the present case neither of the pursuers had a possessory right by reason of a contract attaching to the helicopter itself. Mere possession under a contract did not qualify as a possessory right by reason of a contract attaching to the helicopter itself. The difficulty facing the pursuers was that their loss arose solely out of the terms of the contract. The examples given by Lord Penzance of lien and hypothecation emphasised the pursuers' difficulties. A lien holder had a direct interest in the integrity of the moveable concerned.

13.9.6 The main argument for the defenders was developed under reference to the recent decision in *Nacap Ltd.* v. *Moffat Plant Ltd.*, 1987 S.L.T. 221. In that case a contractor had a physical possession of pipes which he had contracted to lay for the British Gas Corporation. Nevertheless the contractor failed to recover damages negligently caused to the pipes by a third party (*sic*). In the opinion of the court any possession of the pipes enjoyed by the pursuer was for a limited purpose only. That possession was much less than that enjoyed by an owner or a person with a possessory right or title recognised by the law. The terms of the contract between the pursuer and the British Gas Corporation made it clear that the pursuer was given possession of the site, not to enable him to enjoy any broad right of possession, but so that he might perform on the site duties which were laid on him under the contract. In their Lordships' view it was wholly inaccurate to describe the pursuers' right in that case as "a possessory right or title". The true description was that these were contractual rights. Counsel for the defenders then proceeded to examine the legal position of the two pursuers in the present action in the light of these dicta. So far as the first pursuers were concerned, he submitted that the decision in *Nacap* was indistinguishable. The decision in *Nacap* also excluded the second pursuers' claim, because they possessed the helicopter for a limited purpose and in the present case their claim was based on not possession but upon the contractual obligation to repair. Furthermore, even at the worst for the defenders, the claims of the pursuers were mutually exclusive. Only one of the pursuers could have possessed the helicopter at the material time. The claim of the second pursuers, who were not in possession, should therefore be dismissed.

. . . . . .

13.9.7 "[It] has ... in their Lordships' opinion, been established, by authority of long standing, that where one person, A, who has or is entitled to have the possession of goods, is deprived of such possession by the tortious conduct of another person, B, whether such conduct consists in the (*sic*) conversion or negligence, the proper measure in law of the damages recoverable by A from B is the full market value of the goods at the time when and the place where possession of them should have been given. For this purpose it is irrelevant whether A has a general property in the goods as the outright owner of them, or only a special property in them as pledgee, or only possession or a right to possession of them as a bailee. Furthermore the circumstance that, if A recovers the full market value of the goods from B, he may be liable to account for the whole or part of what he has recovered to a third party, C, is also irrelevant, as being *res inter alios acta*" (*The Jag Shakti*, *per* Lord Brandon of Oakbrook at p. 345). That statement of law made in a Privy Council appeal from Singapore was concurred in by Lord Keith of Kinkel and Lord Mackay of Clashfern... I see no inconsistency between Lord Brandon's statement of law in *The Jag Shakti* and any principle of the law of Scotland. I refer to Walker, *Civil Remedies*, at p. 638: the article on "Hiring" by Mr J. G. McIntyre (as he then was) in Green's *Encyclopaedia*, Vol. 7... In my opinion Lord Brandon's statement of law is in point and confirms that each of the pursuers has title to sue. I consider that the words "or only possession or a right to possession of them as a bailee" are apt to cover respectively the first and second pursuers on the day of the fires. In addition I find no inconsistency between Lord Brandon's statement and other dicta of the House of Lords and Privy Council relied upon by the defenders. I refer to *Leigh and Sillivan Ltd.* v. *Aliakmon Shipping Co. Ltd.* [1986] A.C. 785, *per* Lord Brandon at p. 809.

. . . . . .

13.9.8 In my opinion each of the pursuers had a possessory title to the helicopter at the time of the fire. The first pursuer had physical possession derived from the second pursuers in accordance with an arrangement which had the approval of Scamba. The second pursuers had been put in possession of the helicopter by Scamba under a lease which required them to comply with statutory safety requirements. Beyond that condition Scamba placed no restriction upon the use which the second pursuers could make of the helicopter during the currency of the lease. Similarly under the contractual arrangements which affected them, the first pursuers were not restricted in the use which they could make of the helicopter while it was in their possession. The line of authority quoted by Lord Brandon in *Leigh and Sillivan* emphasises the crucial importance of legal ownership of, or possessory title to, the property concerned. In none of the cases cited did the claimant maintain that he had possession of the property in question at the material time.

. . . . . .

13.9.9 If one adopts the test of "a possessory title to the property concerned" from Lord Brandon's speech in *Leigh and Sillivan*, the pursuers in my view are in no difficulty. I consider that by virtue of the lease the second pursuers had a possessory title to the helicopter and that the first pursuers' actual possession was based on a possessory title. Furthermore, I am not persuaded that in *Simpson & Co.* v. *Thomson* Lord Penzance imposed a more restrictive test. Counsel for the defenders founded on the words: "although they have no immediate or reversionary property in the chattel, and no possessory right by reason of any contract attaching to the chattel itself, such as by lien or hypothecation" ... The additional words "such as by lien or hypothecation" illustrate, but, in my view, do not restrict, the generality of the preceding words. I think it would be surprising if they did, because for the most part a lien confers no more than a limited right for a limited purpose. I see no indication that Lord Penzance purported to include limited possession by virtue of lien but to exclude unrestricted possession under a contract of lease or hire.

. . . . . .

13.9.10 Secondly, I regard it as significant that, in *Candlewood* and *Leigh and Sillivan*, bailment cases including *The Okehampton* [1913] P. 173, and *The Winkfield* [1902] P. 42, were cited in argument and distinguished on the ground that in these cases the bailee had sufficient interest to sue by virtue of possession... In *Nacap* at p. 223 the court explained the principle laid down in the authorities already cited as follows: "In our opinion, in the context within which these expressions appear, it is clear that the distinction which is being drawn is between ownership or a right of possession similar to that of an owner on the one hand and, on the other hand, mere contractual rights to have the use or services of the chattel for certain limited purposes." In future cases I anticipate that it may prove difficult to reconcile in all respects that formulation in *Nacap* with other authoritative statements of the principle. I am, however, of the opinion that the *Nacap* formulation creates no difficulty for either of the pursuers in this action. Agreeing on this point with Mr May, I think that the effect of the lease was to put the second pursuers in the position of being owners of the helicopter in substance if not in legal title. I also agree with the submission of the Dean of Faculty on behalf of the pursuers that the possession and control of the helicopter which the second pursuers enjoyed was analogous to that of a character of a vessel by demise.'

COMMENT

13.10.1 Decided: February 17, 1987.
Dec. 29, 1986: Harold Macmillan died.
Jan. 21, 1987: Prince Edward resigned from the Royal Marines.
Feb. 4: Liberace died.

13.10.2 Lord Davidson repelled the pleas of no title to sue. The question of title to sue runs into the question of the existence of a duty. The basis of his decision, at least on the face of it, was that the relationship created by this particular contract was sufficient to fall within the usual exclusionary rule in relation to recovery of secondary economic loss emphasised just prior to this case by the House of Lords in *Aliakmon* and the Inner House in *Nacap*. The outcome of this case could not have been forecast with any degree of certainty. The sheriff court case of *Blackburn v. Sinclair*, 1984 S.L.T. 368, which was a case of a hire-purchaser seeking to sue, must now be subject to reconsideration. The problem with this case is that lien and hypothec, while often created by contract, are property rights in a way different from the right of the hirer of moveables. Should *The Jag Shakti* be considered as turning on questions of bailment? If so, how far is bailment recognised or represented by an analogous concept in Scotland?

13.10.3   Borrow a compass and consider Wilson, W., "Mapping Economic Loss" in *Obligations in Context* (1990), p. 141.

13.10.4   See also *Mull Shellfish Ltd v. Golden Lea Produce Ltd*, 1992 S.L.T. 703 and the discussion in *Delict*, 5.26–5.30. *North Pacific Steamship Co. Ltd v. Canadian National Railways* discussed there has since been reported at [1992] 91 D.L.R. (4th) 289. See the analysis in Fleming, J.J. (1993) Tort L.Rev. 68. This case is probably the source of the terminology "contractual relational loss". See also Waddams, S.M., "Further Reflections on Economic Loss: a Canadian perspective" (1994) Tort L.Rev. 116. Consider also the Scottish case *Coleridge v. Miller Construction,* August 27, 1996, unreported. The contractors cut a power cable belonging to the electricity company and it was alleged that caused damage to a glass furnace and consequent damage. Is such a case an economic loss case at all?

CHAPTER 14

LIABILITY OF PUBLIC BODIES

The reception of the public body liability of Dorset Yacht Co. Ltd v. Home Office [1970] A.C. 1004

56. Bonthrone v. Secretary of State for Scotland
1987 S.L.T. 34

14.1.1 '[*From the summary*] John Bonthrone and his wife, Mrs Iris E. Bonthrone, raised an action of damages against (1) the Secretary of State for Scotland, representing the Scottish Home and Health Department, (2) Fife Health Board, (3) Dr C. H. Barton, a general practitioner in Fife, and (4) Mrs M. Albiston, a health visitor attached to Dr Barton's group practice. They sought damages both as joint guardians of their pupil child Richard Bonthrone and for themselves as individuals. The case came before the Lord Ordinary (Grieve) in procedure roll.

14.1.2 LORD GRIEVE: This case, which was debated before me on procedure roll, arises out of a tragic story. The first two pursuers are the parents of a young boy called Richard who is now nearly six years old, having been born on October 4, 1975. On February 25, Richard underwent the first vaccination in a course of vaccinations designed to give immunity from whooping cough, diphtheria and tetanus. This initial vaccination did not give immunity from whooping cough, nor was it designed to do so. In order to give such immunity a second vaccination had to be administered three months later, and, according to the first defender, a third vaccination some four to six months after the second. The second vaccination was administered to Richard on May 5, 1976. Shortly thereafter Richard began to have convulsions and after two visits to Dunfermline and West Fife Hospital, was eventually admitted to Victoria Hospital, Kirkcaldy where, according to the pursuers, he was found to be suffering from two types of epilepsy. The fact that after the second vaccination Richard had convulsions and was admitted to Dunfermline and West Fife Hospital is not the subject of dispute, but none of the defenders admit the pursuer's assertion that as a result of the second vaccination, and because of it, Richard sustained severe and irreversible brain damage which has left him severely and permanently handicapped.

. . . . . .

14.1.3   The first defender is the Secretary of State who is sued as the person having legal responsibility for the administration and management of the Scottish Home and Health Department, and the person entitled to exercise certain statutory powers to make arrangements for the vaccination of persons against any disease and for the dissemination of information *inter alia* for the prevention of disease. The second defenders are the Fife Health Board, a statutory body set up under the National Health Service (Scotland) Act 1972, who have certain functions in connection with the employment of doctors and health visitors within their area. The third defender is the general practitioner in whose surgery the second vaccination to Richard was administered, and the pursuers aver that the third defender administered it. The fourth defender is a health visitor attached to the third defender's group practice, who was employed by the second defenders, and who is alleged to have visited Richard's home after he had the first injection and been present in the third defender's surgery when the second vaccination was given to Richard.

14.1.4   The pursuers' case against the first defender is set out in art. 13 of the condescendence. I will have to consider that case in detail in the course of this opinion, but, in order to set the stage, so to speak, it can be briefly described as being based on an alleged failure by the Scottish Home and Health Department (for whom the Secretary of State is responsible) to exercise reasonable care in their policy of actively encouraging routine vaccination for infants against, *inter alia*, whooping cough, in pursuance of their statutory powers, as a result of which the pursuers were not made aware of the risks involved in such vaccinations. Had they been so aware, the pursuers aver that they would not have submitted Richard for vaccination.

14.1.5   The pursuers' case against the second defenders, the local health board, is set out in art. 14 of the condescendence in so far as the health board are blamed for their own actings, and, in brief, it is to the effect that they failed to institute and maintain a system whereby general practitioners, who were authorised to give whooping cough vaccinations, were advised to seek certain information from parents before giving such vaccinations. It is also averred that they failed to give proper instructions to their health visitors, and that, in regard to both the general practitioners and the health visitor, they failed to maintain a system whereby the risks inherent in the said vaccinations were made known to the parents of children who were to be vaccinated.

14.1.6   The case against the third defender is that he failed to exercise reasonable care in the administration of the vaccine to Richard as set out in art. 15 of the condescendence, in particular by not inquiring into Richard's medical history. He is also averred to have been responsible for making the health visitor aware of certain matters.

14.1.7   The case against the fourth defender is based on her alleged failure to familiarise herself with information regarding the administration of whooping cough vaccination, and to seek information from Richard's parents regarding his reaction to the first vaccination, and to report that information to, *inter alios,* the third defender. In art. 18 of the condescendence the pursuers aver that the second defenders are vicariously liable in respect of any loss caused to them by the actings of the fourth defender.

14.1.8   At the debate before me, counsel for the first defender maintained that the case against him was irrelevant and asked me to sustain his first plea in law. Counsel for the second and fourth defenders accepted that the averments of fault in arts. 17 and 18 of the condescendence, relative to the actings of the fourth defender, the health visitor, would have to be the subject of proof before answer. *Quoad ultra* counsel maintained that the case of direct fault against the second defenders should be dismissed as irrelevant and their second plea in law sustained to that extent. This submission also embraced a challenge of certain averments in which it was alleged the second defenders were vicariously liable for certain actings of the third defender.

Counsel for the third defender submitted that the averments at pp. 43E–44A, imputing responsibility to the third defender, should be deleted and that *quoad ultra* a proof before answer against the third defender should be allowed.

14.1.9   All the counsel for the several defenders challenged the competency of the pursuers' conclusions 1(b) and 1(c) whereby they sought damages for themselves as individuals. The third defender also challenged the relevancy of the averments in support of these conclusions. For the pursuers the Dean of Faculty conceded that, standing the decision of the First Division in the case of *Robertson* v. *Turnbull,* 1982 S.L.T. 96 at present the subject of an appeal to the House of Lords [see 1982 S.C.(H.L.) 1], the plea to the relevancy of these two conclusions would have to be upheld by me. In accordance with the opinions in *Robertson,* I agree that the correct challenge should be to the relevancy of the averments in support of the conclusion and accordingly I shall sustain the second plea in law for the third defender.

. . . . . .

The pursuers' case against the first defender and the challenge to the relevancy of the averments in support of it

14.1.10   In order to understand, and thereafter consider, the submissions made on behalf of the first defender, who is the Secretary of State for Scotland, it is necessary to look at the statutory background against which he is empowered to fulfil his functions under the National Health Service Acts and the statutory instruments made thereunder... Section 26 of the 1947 Act, which was repealed by s. 7 of the 1972 Act, enjoined the local health authorities to make arrangements with medical practitioners in their area for the vaccination of persons against smallpox and the immunisation of such persons against diphtheria, and empowered them, with the approval of the Secretary of State and, if directed by him, to make arrangements for vaccination or immunisation of persons against any other disease... One of the duties imposed by s. 1 of the 1947 Act is to promote a health service in Scotland "designed to secure... the prevention of illness" ... and under s. 2(1)(c) "medical, nursing and other services, whether in such accommodation or premises, in the home of the patient or elsewhere."

. . . . . .

14.1.11 In the exercise of the powers given to him by that section of the 1972 Act there was made the National Health Service (Functions of Health Boards) (Scotland) Order 1974 which came into operation on April 1, 1974. By para. 4 of that Order it is provided that [his Lordship quoted the terms of para. 4(*b*), (*g*) and (*k*) and continued:] These extracts from the relevant statutes and orders made thereunder contain the authority by which the Secretary of State was empowered to act in promoting, through the Scottish Home and Health Department (hereinafter referred to as "the department") measures for the prevention of illness, and in particular the illness of whooping cough. The pursuers' complaint against the Secretary of State can be shortly stated as being that, in the exercise of these powers, he failed to warn members of the public of the risks inherent in the triple vaccination designed to immunise children against diphtheria, tetanus and whooping cough, and by so doing, failed to exercise the degree of care which it was incumbent upon him to exercise.

. . . . . .

14.1.12 In art. 8 of the condescendence the pursuers aver that since 1957 the department actively encouraged the second defenders and their predecessors to make whooping cough vaccine generally available at public expense, and to promote such vaccination in infancy as a routine measure of preventative medicine. They go on to aver that the department did so by circularising doctors, such as the third defender, to that effect, and by an advertising campaign directed to the public at large. They then go on to aver that in 1963, and in later years, such persons and authorities were advised by booklet of the risks inherent in such vaccinations, particularly to babies who had manifested an adverse reaction to the first injection. In such an event the booklet advised that only the vaccine for diphtheria and tetanus should be administered and not that for whooping cough. They then refer to a booklet published in 1972, and another in 1974, both of which stressed the need for observance of contra-indications and adverse reactions to the vaccine and mentioning the risk of the developments of encephalopathy.

14.1.13 These warnings, however, according to the pursuers, were only issued to medical practitioners and health authorities, and in art. 9 the pursuers go on to aver that the public advertising campaign continued over the years and "only in 1976 for the first time was a leaflet issued for distribution to any members of the general public which made mention of possible side effects consequent upon some vaccines, and recommended that patients should discuss the matter, prior to vaccination with their doctors." In art. 9 of the condescendence the pursuers aver, *inter alia*, that had they been made aware by publication issued with the approval of, *inter alios*, the first defender that there was a risk of serious damage to Richard following on the administration of whooping cough vaccine they would not have had him vaccinated. The lack of such information denied them "any opportunity to exercise and form an opinion or decision".

14.1.14 In summary, then, the pursuers aver that the first defender, by the hand of the department from 1957 onwards, encouraged health authorities such as the second defenders (a) to make whooping cough vaccine generally available at public expense and (b) to promote such vaccination in infancy as a routine measure of preventative medicine.

. . . . . .

14.1.15 It is alleged that he did these things at least until 1976, without any warning of the risks of the encephalopathy, or any other side-effects, and without stressing the necessity of inquiring into the infant's history before administering the vaccine. It is further alleged that he limited the warning of the possible effects of the vaccine and the necessity of inquiring into the history of infants receiving it to medical practitioners and health authorities.

. . . . . .

14.1.16 The Dean of Faculty, who appeared on behalf of the pursuers, stated that the Secretary of State was exercising the powers conferred on him by s. 10 of the 1972 Act which I have quoted above and which deals with the dissemination of information relating to the maintenance of health and prevention of illness, and senior counsel for the first defender and the second and fourth defenders presented their submissions on that assumption. It was submitted by the learned Dean that in the exercise of that power the first defender owed a duty of care to the public which he did not comply with, because the information which he disseminated was incomplete and misleading. In so disseminating such information the first defender acted negligently and improperly exercised the powers given to him by the said s. 10.

. . . . . .

14.1.17 Counsel for the first defender submitted that, in the exercise of his powers, the first defender was exercising a discretion which could only be called in question if it was averred that in exercising it he had acted *in mala fide*, or *ultra vires*, or so unreasonably or irresponsibly as not to have exercised his discretion at all.

. . . . . .

14.1.18 On behalf of the pursuers it was submitted that in disseminating such information as he did to the public, information which did not make mention of the risks involved in the triple vaccination, the first defender had passed the stage of exercising his discretion. Before going on to consider the merits of these two competing submissions and the arguments in support of them, it is convenient to look at the three authorities which form the main basis for the parties' submissions.

I start with the case of *Home Office* v. *Dorset Yacht Co.* [1970] A.C. 1004. As appears from the headnote, that case was concerned with the alleged failure of the Home Office, through Borstal officers who were their servants, to take reasonable care to prevent some Borstal boys, who were working on an island under their control and supervision, escaping from the island and thereafter boarding, casting adrift, and damaging, the plaintiff's yacht which was moored offshore. The Home Office denied that they, or their servants, owed any such duty to the plaintiff... It was held that the Borstal officers were, in the circumstances, under the duty of care alleged by the plaintiff, and it was accepted by the respondents that, if they were, they would be vicariously liable for any negligence proved against the officers.

. . . . . .

14.1.19 It is to be noted, and can be seen from the speech of Lord Morris of Borth-y-Gest at p. 1036, that in that case no question arose as to the improper exercise of statutory powers by the governor or anyone else. It was not suggested that, by putting the officers in charge of these boys with instructions to keep them under supervision and control, the respondents, or anyone for whom they were responsible had failed to exercise statutory power in a reasonable way. The case was solely concerned with the question of whether the duty averred was owed to the plaintiff company by the officers, who had been put in charge of the boys, that duty being, in accordance with their instructions, to take reasonable care to see that the boys did not escape, it being reasonably foreseeable that, if they did, the company might suffer damage (Lord Reid at p. 1030 E–H). As Lord Reid put it at p. 1031B: "The present case does not raise that issue [*i.e.* the reasonable or unreasonable exercise of a discretionary power] because no discretion was given to the Borstal officers. They were given orders which they negligently failed to carry out." Accordingly this case as pled against the first defender is not akin to the *Dorset Yacht* case and anything said in it about the exercise by a minister or statutory powers is *obiter*... Nonetheless, while Lord Reid pointed out that in that case the question as to the reasonable or unreasonable exercise of a discretionary power did not arise, he did go on to deal with the circumstances in which a public authority might be liable to members of the public in the exercise of discretionary powers. At the top of p. 1031 his Lordship said: "Where Parliament confers a discretion the position is not the same. Then there may, and almost certainly will, be errors of judgment in exercising such a discretion and Parliament cannot have intended that members of the public should be entitled to sue in respect of such errors. But there must come a stage when the discretion is exercised so carelessly or unreasonably that there has been no real exercise of the discretion which Parliament has conferred. The person purporting to exercise his discretion has acted in abuse or excess of his power. Parliament cannot be supposed to have granted immunity to persons who do that. The present case does not raise this issue because no discretion was given to these Borstal officers. They were given orders which they negligently failed to carry out."

14.1.20 The second case was that of *Anns* v. *Merton L.B.C.* [1978] A.C. 728. The respondents in that case were lessees of maisonettes in Wimbledon, the foundations of which were inspected by the appellants' inspectors. It was averred in that case that structural damage had been caused by the negligence of the appellants in allowing the flats to be constructed on foundations which were only 2ft. 6 in. deep instead of 3 ft. It was alleged that this had happened due to the negligent inspection by the appellants' inspectors, the appellants having decided in their discretion that the foundations should be inspected. The question for their Lordships' decision was whether, in the circumstances, the appellants were under a duty of care to the respondents.

14.1.21 [Lord Salmon said] at p. 762 A–E ...: "Powers are undoubtedly conferred on the council in order to enable it to inspect the foundations and ensure that any defects which the inspection may reveal are remedied before the erection of the building begins. There is, however, nothing in the Act of 1936 nor in the bye-laws which explicitly provides how the council shall exercise these powers. This, in my view, is left to the council's discretion — but I do not think that this is an absolute discretion. It is a discretion which must be responsibly exercised." I pause to point out that his Lordship does not say: "It is a discretion which has to be exercised with reasonable care." Lord Salmon goes on: "The council could resolve to inspect the foundations of all buildings in its locality before they are covered, but certainly, in my view, it is under no obligation to do so. It could, *e.g.* resolve to inspect the foundations of a proportion of all buildings or of all buildings of certain types in its locality." [Lord Salmon] concludes by saying at p. 767 G–H: "The council is responsible only if it has exercised its powers to inspect; and the defects in the foundation would have been detected by an inspection carried out with reasonable care and skill." What his Lordship does not say is that in deciding whether or not to inspect, and if so how to do so, the council owed a duty to future tenants to exercise reasonable care, and would be liable in damages in the event of their failure to exercise such care in reaching that decision. That is evident from the passage quoted above at p. 762 and the last sentence in the first paragraph of it.

. . . . . .

14.1.22   It is clear that the exercise of reasonable care by the public authority is through their servants who carry out its policy or instructions. In my opinion there is no divergence of view between Lord Reid and Lord Salmon on the point as it was suggested there was. I respectfully agree with the propositions extracted from these cases by Lord Dunpark in the case of *Hallett* v. *Nicholson*, 1979 S.C. 1, and the third of the authorities founded on. The propositions extracted by Lord Dunpark were: "(1) Acts or omissions committed by a statutory authority in the proper exercise of its statutory duties or powers do not found a cause of civil action… (2) Acts or omissions which are committed by a statutory authority in the course of an improper exercise of its statutory duties or powers and which infringe the rights of third parties may be actionable at civil law. (3) For such an exercise to be improper it must be either (a) not authorised by statute or (b) not made *bona fide* in the interest of the public within the limits of any statutory discretion."

It was on (3) that the Dean relied, but I can find no suggestion in the averments to the effect that the information "disseminated" was not authorised by s. 10 or that it was disseminated *in mala fide*.

. . . . . .

14.1.23   To these three propositions I would venture to add a further in the following terms. When the exercise of a statutory power confers a discretion on the authority entitled to exercise it as to the manner in which, or the means by which it is to be exercised, then if the discretion is exercised within the ambit of the power, and *in bona fide*, albeit the exercise of it can be shown to display an error of judgment, a person who suffers loss as a result of the exercise of the power will not have an action of damages against the authority which exercised it. In my opinion the taking of reasonable care in arise until the discretionary stage of its exercise has ceased and the executive stage has begun.

. . . . . .

14.1.24   It also seems to me that the "information" to be disseminated must also be a matter for the Secretary of State's decision, save only that it must relate to the promotion and maintenance of health or the prevention of illness, or both... Once it is accepted, as it was, that there is a discretion given to the Secretary of State as to what information relative to the maintenance of health and the prevention of illness is to be disseminated it follows that there is a discretion as to the persons or authorities to whom that information is to be disseminated, and further, whether they are all to be provided with all the information... For the reasons which I have given I shall sustain the first plea in law for the first defender and dismiss the action so far as laid against him.

14.1.25   There is a secondary matter which was the subject of argument and which I shall deal with in case I am wrong in the opinion I have expressed on the relevancy of the pursuers' averments against the defender... Senior counsel for the first defender submitted that, if his first argument was held to be ill-founded, that is to say the argument which I have upheld, holding that the pursuers' case against the first defender is irrelevant, the pursuers had not relevantly averred that the first defender's failure to bring the inherent risks of the vaccinations to the notice of the public caused the injury to Richard. As averred in art. 2 of the condescendence, Richard entered on the course of vaccinations on the recommendation of the fourth defender, and not as a result of any advertisement issued by the department acting at the hand of the Secretary of State.

. . . . . .

14.1.26   The pursuers' averments, so far from demonstrating a breach of duty on the part of the second defenders, demonstrated that they had performed their duties by bringing to their notice the possible side-effects of vaccinations for whooping cough, and advising them to discuss the matter with their doctor, advice which they followed. Had I been in the position of having to decide on this argument whether the pursuers' case against the first defender should go to proof or not, I would have allowed a proof before answer. The pursuers' averments read as a whole and starting with the averment referring to the triple vaccination of their elder son, and the fact that at no time in connection with that vaccination were they warned about the risks about the said vaccination, paint a picture of encouragement to have children vaccinated without any mention of the risks involved.

. . . . . .

The relevancy of the case against the second defenders as being vicariously liable for the actings of the third defender

14.1.27   I now turn to consider the arguments as to whether the second defenders, the Health Board, can be vicariously liable for the actings of the third defender, the general practitioner who administered the second injection to Richard. It is accepted that the second defenders are vicariously liable for the actings of the fourth defender, the health visitor. The alleged failures in duty by the third defender are set out in art. 15 of the condescendence, and in art. 16 of the condescendence the second defenders are alleged to have been vicariously responsible for these alleged failures because they were committed in the course of the third defender's employment with them. It was accepted on behalf of the pursuers that, prior to the coming into force of the 1972 Act, it would not have been possible to maintain that a hospital board, the predecessor of the health board, was vicariously liable for the actings of a general medical practitioner, albeit it was so liable for the actings of a doctor employed in a hospital (*Macdonald* v. *Glasgow Western Hospitals Board,* 1954 S.L.T. 226). Has the 1972 Act altered the situation? Counsel for the pursuers maintained that it had done so.

. . . . . .

14.1.28   Reg. 9, under the heading "Service to patients", provides by subpara. (1): "A doctor is required to render to his patients all proper and necessary treatment." These and other regulations in the Schedule emphasise that the treatment of his patients is the responsibility of the doctor, and of no one else. Nowhere in the regulations can I find any suggestion that the doctor has to consult the health boards as to how he should treat any of his patients, nor any right by them to inquire how he does so. Before I go on to consider the submissions made by the Dean of Faculty on behalf of the pursuers on this point, it is convenient to refer again to the case of *Macdonald* which formed the basis for the learned Dean's argument. That case was concerned with the vicarious responsibility of a hospital board of management for their resident medical officers. The First Division held that the board were responsible for them and the *ratio* of their decision, after an exhaustive survey of the authorities, is to be found in the opinion of the Lord President at p. 235 where his Lordship said: "under the new Act and regulations the obligation on the State is in my view to *treat* the patient and not merely to make arrangements for his treatment by and at the sole responsibility of independent contractors" (emphasis added). That obligation clearly referred to the treatment of the patients in hospital... [The Dean of Faculty] also referred me to the National Health Service (Functions of Health Boards) (Scotland) Orders 1974 (S.I. 1974 No. 466) where para. 4 provides that [his Lordship quoted the terms of the regulation and continued:] These provisions and services are [his Lordship quoted the terms of s. 2(1)(*a*), (*b*) and (*c*), (3) and (4) of the Act of 1972 and continued:] The suggestion, as I understood it, was that medical practitioners were persons who provided services under the Act which it was the duty of the Secretary of State to provide and that he provided it through them in the same way as he provided hospital services... If that is a correct understanding of the argument, I consider with all respect that it is unsound. All that s. 2(4)(*a*) does is to give medical practitioners the right to use accommodation or premises provided by the Secretary of State for the purposes of their private practice. The fact is that if my interpretation of s. 2(3) of the 1972 Act is correct that Act does not change the position of general medical practitioners engaged in the National Health Service from what it was in 1947.

. . . . . .

14.1.29 In my opinion the law on the matter is correctly stated in Martin on *The Law Relating to Medical Practice* at p. 100 to the effect that, while the Secretary of State is responsible through his agents for the treatment of the National Health Service patients in hospital, he is not responsible for their treatment by general medical practitioners for whom arrangements have been made to provide general medical services under s. 34 of the Act of 1947. It follows that in my opinion art. 16 of the condescendence is irrelevant and cannot be remitted to probation.

The relevancy of the case made against the second defenders as being directly responsible to the pursuers for their loss

14.1.30 The second defenders are sued as having direct responsibility for the pursuers' alleged loss as well as vicarious responsibility for the actings of the third and fourth defenders... It is not said that the health board acting in *mala fide* or *ultra vires* in not doing what it is averred they ought to have done, nor can it be inferred, from what is said, that in any of their actings they had passed the stage of discretion and entered the sphere of execution... Without instructions from the department that [information as to possible risks] was, in some form or other, to be disseminated to health visitors, the board had a discretion whether to do so or not. If they decided to exercise that discretion by giving instructions as averred to health visitors, and the health visitors had failed to exercise reasonable care in carrying out these instructions, then the health board would be liable for any loss resulting from such negligence (*Dorset Yacht Co.*; *Anns*). It follows from what I have said that in my opinion the pursuers' averments in art. 14 of the condescendence are irrelevant and the second plea in law for the second and fourth defenders should be sustained to that extent.

14.1.31 If I am wrong in holding all the averments in art. 14 to be irrelevant on the ground indicated, I would certainly maintain that I am right in so far as the duties averred relate to medical practitioners. The institution and maintenance of a system of advising medical practitioners of an alleged proper practice and issuing of instructions to them regarding information they were to give to parents of children who were to be vaccinated, could only be a duty incumbent on the second defenders in the event of the medical practitioners in their area being their employees.

. . . . . .

Case against the third defender

14.1.32 Apart from the question of the relevancy of the pursuers' averments supporting conclusion 1(*b*) and 1(*c*), counsel for the third defender only challenged the relevancy of the pursuers' averments at pp. 43E–F and 44A, and *quoad ultra* accepted that so far as the case against the third defender was concerned there would require to be a proof before answer. The averments challenged are as follows: "It was his (the third defender's) duty to take reasonable care that health visitors, such as the fourth defender, who was attached to his practice were familiar therewith, and were aware also of the reasons for and the importance of, seeking information on, observing, reporting and advising on contra-indications and adverse reactions to such vaccination. In the exercise of reasonable care as aforesaid it was his duty prior to administering the second vaccination to Richard to seek information from the health visitor and from the pursuers or in any event from the second pursuer about Richard's medical history and in particular to ask them or her if there had been any unusual reaction following the first vaccination. In the fulfilment of each and all of the said duties incumbent on him, the third defender failed and by his failure caused said loss, injury and damage." The averments challenged by the third defender are those contained in the first sentence of that quotation. The attack on these averments is based on the submission that the health visitors are employees of the local health board and not of the doctor or doctors to whose practice they are attached. This is apparent from the pursuers' averments where the pursuers aver that the fourth defender is a health visitor in Dunfermline attached to the third defender's group practice, and is employed and paid in that capacity by the second defenders... I cannot see any link between the alleged failure by the third defender to satisfy himself as to the competence of the fourth defender and the injury complained of. Nowhere is it explained how the injury to Richard would have been obviated had the third defender done, *vis-à-vis* the fourth defender, what it is averred he should have done at pp. 43E–F and 44A. The red light as to the risk of administering the second vaccination would only have come on, on performance of the duty alleged at p. 44A–C. In any event it was for the second defenders to take reasonable care to see that their health visitors were competent before attaching them to the practice of medical practitioners in their area. I shall delete the averments at pp. 43E–F and 44A as irrelevant.'

COMMENT

14.2.1 Decided: October 10, 1981.
Oct. 6: Anwar Sadat assassinated.
Sept. 13: Guillotine abolished.
Sept. 6: Solidarity held first Congress.

14.2.2 This long extract illustrates a number of other points. It considers the standard of care (see Ext. 48) and vicarious liability (Chap. 22). *Anns v. Merton* [14.1.20] referred to in this extract has been departed from by the House of Lords in the case of *Murphy v. Brentwood* [1990] 3 W.L.R. 414. Lord Mackay explains that the proper view is that *Dorset Yacht*-type [14.1.18] liability remains and that the departure from *Anns* is in respect of a particular type of loss and a particular type of activity: "While of course I accept that duties at common law may arise in respect of the exercise of statutory powers or the discharge of statutory duties I find difficulty in reconciling a common law duty to take reasonable care that plans should conform with byelaws or regulations with the statute which has imposed on the local authority the duty not to pass plans unless they comply with the bye-laws or regulations and to pass them if they do. In these circumstances I have reached the clear conclusion that the proper exercise of the judicial function requires this House now to depart from *Anns* in so far as it affirmed a private law duty of care to avoid damage to property which causes present or imminent danger to the health and safety of owners, or occupiers, resting on local authorities in relation to their function of supervising compliance with building bye-laws or regulations, that *Dutton v. Bognor Regis United Building Co. Ltd* should be overruled and that all decisions subsequent to *Anns* which purported to follow it should be overruled. I accordingly reach the same conclusion as do my noble and learned friends.
I should make it clear that I express no opinion on the question whether, if personal injury were suffered by an occupier of defective premises as a result of a latent defect in those premises, liability in respect of that personal injury would attach to a local authority which had been charged with the public law duty of supervising compliance with the relevant building bye-laws or regulations in respect of a failure properly to carry out such duty." (at p. 419: see also Lord Keith at pp. 423, 426; Lord Oliver at p. 446). Lord Oliver's comments at p. 449 explain: "The only existing principle on which liability could be based was that propounded in the *Dorset Yacht* case [1970] A.C. 1004, that it is to say that the relationship which existed between the authority and the plaintiff was such as to give rise to a positive duty to prevent another person, the builder, from inflicting pecuniary injury. But in a series of decisions in subsequent cases, in particular *Curran v. Northern Ireland Co-ownership Housing Association Ltd* [1987] A.C. 718 and *Hill v. Chief Constable of West Yorkshire* [1989] A.C. 53, this House has been unable to find in the case of other regulatory agencies with powers as wide as or wider than those under the Public Health Acts such a relationship between the regulatory authority and members of the public for whose protection the statutory powers were conferred (see also *Yuen Kun-yeu v. Att.-Gen. of Hong Kong* [1988] A.C. 175). My Lords, I can see no reason why a local authority, by reason of its statutory powers under the Public Health Acts or its duties under the building regulations, should be in any different case. *Ex hypothesi* there is nothing in the terms or purpose of the statutory provisions

which support the creation of a private law right of action for breach of statutory duty.
There is equally nothing in the statutory provisions which even suggest that the purpose
of the statute was to protect owners of buildings from economic loss. Nor is there any
easily discernible reason why the existence of the statutory duties, in contradistinction
to those existing in the case of other regulatory agencies, should be held in the case of
a local authority to create a special relationship imposing a private law duty to members
of the public to prevent the conduct of another person which is not itself tortious."

14.2.3   There have been many English cases since *Murphy*. It is yet possible for duties
in private law to arise. The second stage of discredited *Anns* allowed exclusion of a duty
on the basis of public policy. That still remains and is likely to arise in these cases, see
Hill v. Chief Constable of West Yorkshire [1987] 1 All E.R. 1173. Even a flawed decision may
not be actionable: *X. v. Bedfordshire County Council* [1995] 3 All E.R. 353. (But see *E. v.
Dorset County Council*, [1994] 3 W.L.R. 853.) A power to negotiate does not of itself
create liability: *Yuen Kun-yen v. Att.-Gen. of Hong Kong* [1987] 2 All E.R. 705. Even a
failure to implement a decision actually taken is not sufficient: *Stovin v. Wise* [1996] 3
W.L.R. 388. That the defender although not an elected public body nor a branch of
government operates in the public interest may operate to prevent duty arising: *Marc
Rich & Co.v. Bishop Rock Ltd* [1996] 1 A.C. 211. The over-arching test of "new" duty, that
it be fair just and reasonable to do so, can be used in public body cases even where this
area of law has been considered in a number of Scottish cases. In *Johnstone v. Traffic
Commissioner*, 1990 S.L.T. 409, a case against the Traffic Commissioner for failing to
instruct a fuller specialist medical report and instead revoking a driver's PSV licence
on the basis of a hospital discharge summary, was dismissed. Reference was made to
the operational/policy decision. Lord Cameron, not unlike the Board in *Rowling*,
focused on the fact that there was a statutory review procedure. A proof before answer
was allowed against the Department of Transport in relation to the actual medical
examination. *Ross v. Secretary of State for Scotland*, 1990 S.L.T. 13, was a case involving
smallpox vaccine. It was held, after a consideration of *Bonthrone*, that the duties alleged
were within the area of discretion and in the absence of averments of bad faith, the
averments against the Secretary of State were refused probation. In *Wilson v. McCaffrey*,
1989 G.W.D. 1–37, *Bonthrone* was cited in dismissing a case against a local authority for
their failure to exercise a power under the Building (Scotland) Act 1959, s. 13(1)(*a*),
by requiring people to leave premises while compulsory building demolition was in
progress. It was held that the power was a discretionary one.

   In Scots law the public policy point is alive and effective: *Ward v. Chief Constable,
Strathclyde Police*, 1991 S.L.T. 292. In *Duff v. Highland and Islands Fire Board*, 1995 S.L.T.
1362 Lord McFadyen while assoilzing the defenders for lack of evidence accepted that
the *Hallett* facts did not apply when the brigade have actually gone into action. See the
English cases and the discussion of them in Convery, J., "Suing the Fire Brigade" 1996
Rep. B. 10–2. And see *Forbes v. City of Dundee Council*, 1997 G.W.D. 11–450, which contains
some comments on *Duff*.

14.2.4   This extract is an excellent example of the difference between a problem in
real life and in an examination paper. Note the need to keep all the possible defenders
in mind and the cases against each of them clear. Note the importance in Scots law of
the written pleadings.

14.2.5   Is there a causation point in this case?

14.2.6   Why do you think this case was "reported by request"?

14.2.7   The distinction between operational decisions and policy decisions used to be
urged as significant. Does the fact that in the mid-90s the Home Secretary said he
would not contemplate resignation over operational decisions in the prison service
but might over policy decisions rehabilitate it for private law?

CHAPTER 15

STATUTORY DUTY AND EUROREP.

57. McMullan v. Lochgelly Iron and Coal Co. (Appellants)
1933 S.C.(H.L.) 64

15.1.1 'LORD ATKIN: This is an appeal from the Second Division of the Court of Session, who, reversing the decision of the Lord Ordinary, held that the action was competent. The action is brought by the pursuer for damages, alleging that his son, a coal miner, while working in the employ of the defender was killed owing to the "fault and negligence" of the defenders in not making secure the roof of the place where the son was working. The objection made to the action is based on section 29 of the Workmen's Compensation Act 1925, which provides: "When the injury was caused by the personal negligence or wilful act of the employer or of some person for whose act or default the employer is responsible, nothing in this Act shall affect any civil liability of the employer... but the employer... shall not be liable to any proceedings independently of this Act, except in case of such personal negligence or wilful act as aforesaid." The question is whether, taking the allegations in the condescendence *pro veritate*, the proceedings allege injury caused by personal negligence or wilful act as aforesaid. It will be noticed that the provisions of the section are not directed to forms of action. They deal with substance; and whatever the form of action, if it is based upon the fact that injury was caused by personal negligence, &c., as aforesaid, it is not affected by the section.

15.1.2 Now, the pleading expressly alleges fault and negligence of the employer. The fault and negligence complained of is failure to observe the provisions of the Coal Mines Act. For this purpose it is unnecessary to determine whether the breach alleged is of section 49 or of section 52. They both involve an obligation to support the roof; and, if it were necessary to show that they are designed to secure the safety of persons employed in the mine, it is only necessary to refer to the terms of the sections themselves, and to the fact that they are contained in Part II of the Act which is entitled "Provisions as to Safety".

15.1.3 It is further beyond question that these provisions impose a special duty upon the employer towards those for whose safety they are designed; so that, unless section 29 intervenes, an action will lie against the employer by such a person if injured by a breach of such duty... And in an action founded on a breach of such a duty the doctrine of common employment has no application, for the duty is imposed upon the employer, and it is irrelevant whether his servants had disregarded his instructions or whether he knew or not of the breach.

15.1.4 Having reached these conclusions, I find the result to be that the employer is alleged to have committed a breach of a duty owed by him to his servant to take a particular precaution (*viz.*, support of the roof) for his servant's safety, whereby the servant was injured. In my opinion that state of facts constitutes negligence of the employer; and I am unable to conceive of any accurate definition of negligence which could exclude it. All that it is necessary to show is duty to take care to avoid injuring; and, if the particular care to be taken is prescribed by statute, and the duty to the injured person to take the care is likewise imposed by statute, and the breach is proved, all the essentials of negligence are present. I cannot think that the true position is, as appears to be suggested, that in such cases negligence only exists where the tribunal of fact agrees with the Legislature that the precaution is one that ought to be taken. The very object of the legislation is to put that particular precaution beyond controversy.

15.1.5 The next question that arises is whether the breach of duty alleged is personal negligence or wilful act of the employer or of some person for whose act or default the employer is responsible. It was contended that the employer could not be liable unless he himself was guilty of the act or omission complained of, or had ordered it or in some way was privy to it. I cannot so read the section. The words "personal negligence" apply both to employer and to the person, in order to make clear that in ordinary cases where the employer would only be vicariously liable for the negligence of his servants, but might be excused by the doctrine of common employment, he is to remain liable if it is he himself who was negligent and not merely his servants. Where the duty to take care is expressly imposed upon the employer and not discharged, then, in my opinion, the employer is guilty of negligence and of "personal" negligence.

15.1.6 But there is another view of the section which I do not find discussed in the judgments below, but which appears to make unnecessary even the imputation of negligence to the employer. If in violation of the statute the roof was not made secure, the failure to perform the statutory duty was negligence either of the employer or of his servants. No one can, I think, doubt that, if the obligation to observe statutory precautions is imposed upon a servant, the servant's breach is negligence. The servant would be liable to his fellow-servant for injuries caused by such breach — see *Lees* v. *Dunkerley Brothers* [1911] A.C. 5... It can therefore be affirmed that, in such a case as the present, the injury was caused by the negligence of some person for whom the employer is responsible, which is all that is necessary to defeat the operation of the latter part of section 29, subsection (1). Subject therefore to appropriate pleading, there is no difficulty in establishing the employer's liability in such a case.

15.1.7   No doubt an action upon a statute may have nothing to do with negligence; the first case cited in Comyn's Digest is an action for false imprisonment based, it is said, on a breach of Magna Carta. All that has to be shown is a breach of the statutory duty causing injury. But it does not follow that the duty imposed may not be a duty the breach of which does in fact constitute negligence. If so, the injury is caused by that negligence, and the section therefore applies. I am not impressed by the challenge to point out from what "proceedings independently of this Act" the employer is intended to be relieved by the latter words of the section.

. . . . . .

15.1.8   Lord Macmillan: The pursuer in this action claims damages from the defenders in respect of the death of his son, who was killed while at work in the defenders' employment in a coal mine at Cowdenbeath. He avers that the death of his son "was due to the fault and negligence of the defenders", and his first plea in law is that, "having suffered loss, injury, and damage through the fault of the defenders as condescended on", he "is entitled to reparation therefor". The particular fault on the part of the defenders which the pursuer alleges is that they failed to perform the duty imposed on them by section 49 of the Coal Mines Act 1911. Other failures in duty are mentioned, but it was agreed at your Lordships bar that the pursuer's case rested on the alleged breach of section 49. That section requires in absolute terms that "the roof and sides of every travelling road and working place shall be made secure". The pursuer avers that the roof of the place where his son was set to work was in point of fact not made secure, and that in consequence it fell on his son and killed him. All this seems straightforward enough. The action is a common-form action of damages for negligence, and the negligence alleged is failure on the part of the defenders to perform a duty imposed on them by statute in the interests of the safety of their workmen, of whom the deceased was one.

. . . . . .

15.1.9   The question thus comes to be whether the defenders are right in so characterising the pursuer's allegations. Their argument is that all that has been alleged is a breach of statutory obligation, and that such an allegation is not an allegation of negligence, or, at any rate, not of personal negligence. This argument is, in my opinion, untenable. It is plain, in the first place, that section 49 imposes an obligation on the defenders personally, for breach of which they are liable unless they can bring themselves within the protection of section 102, subsection (8). If the defenders do not comply with section 49, they are rendered by section 75 personally guilty of an offence against the Act, unless they establish the defence which the statute leaves open to them. In the next place, the duty to comply with section 49 is equally plainly imposed on the defenders in the interests of their workmen. The section occurs in Part II of the Act, the heading of which is "Provisions as to Safety", and the purpose of section 49 is to ensure the safety of the workmen employed in the mine.

15.1.10   Here then are the essential elements of a case of negligence. Where two persons stand in such a relation to each other that the law imposes on one of these persons a duty to take precautions for the safety of the other person, then, if the person on whom that duty is imposed fails to take the proper precautions and the other person is in consequence injured, a clear case of negligence arises. That is exactly the case here alleged. Such negligence is, in my opinion, "personal negligence" within the meaning of the Workmen's Compensation Act. It appears to me quite immaterial whether the duty to take care arises at common law or is imposed by statute. It is equally imperative in either case, and in either case it is a duty imposed by law. I am afraid I fail to understand the argument that an employer who is enjoined by statute to take particular precautions for the safety of his employees is not guilty of negligence, if one of his employees is injured through the employer's failure to take the precautions prescribed, merely because the duty to take those precautions has been imposed by statute, and does not, or may not, arise at common law. Such a doctrine is, in my opinion, no part of the law of Scotland. I accordingly agree with the learned judges of the Second Division of the Court of Session in holding that the defender's plea founded on section 29, subsection (1), of the Workmen's Compensation Act 1925, is not maintainable. So far as the English cases cited to your Lordships may countenance a contrary view, it would be perhaps enough to say that, in my opinion, they do not express the law of Scotland, but it is right that I should add that I find myself entirely in agreement with your Lordships' criticism of them.'

COMMENT

15.2.1   Decided: July 10, 1933.
    June 5: Toscanini refused to conduct at Bayreuth, as protest against Nazis.
    July 4: Gandhi sentenced to one year's imprisonment.
    July 16: New Deal legislation passed in USA.

15.2.2   There is a review of the applicable law by Lord Clyde in the Division in *Pullar v. Window Clean*, 1956 S.L.T. 17. The window cleaner who fell sought to make the owners liable for not having followed Dean of Guild legislation which was admittedly intended to make it easier to clean windows. Lord Clyde followed English cases like *Cutler v.*

Wandsworth Stadium Ltd [1948] 1 K.B. 291 and *Monk v. Warbey* [1935] 1 K.B. 75 as well as noting as important two Scottish cases, *Black v. Fife Coal Co.*, 1912 1 S.L.T. 20 and *Bett v. Dalmeny Oil Co.* (1905) 7F. 787. The window cleaner lost. The rules did not apply to *all* windows and so was unlikely to be part of a window cleaners charter. It was not clear that they contributed a protected *class* — ordinary householders cleaning windows might be encompassed. In any event the duty, if any there was, would be on whoever applied for the warrants, not a duty to maintain by the occupier. However where the class and purpose is clear local byelaws can establish liability: *Ghannan v. Glasgow Corp.*, 1950 S.L.T. 2.

15.2.3 The practical difference between this type of case and an ordinary case based on negligence is that the statute determines the existence of the duty, its content and its scope, thus often avoiding the difficulties of reasonable foreseeability and proximity. As the next extract shows, depending upon the terms of the statute, there may still be an inquiry into reasonableness, but only in relation to a duty framed in terms of reasonableness. (See also para. 5.1.11.)

The standard of duty

58. Nimmo (Appellant) v. Alexander Cowan & Sons Ltd
1967 S.L.T. 277 (H.L.)

15.3.1 'Lord Upjohn (in the majority): As a matter solely of construction of s. 29 taken by itself there can be no doubt that there is great force in the views expressed by the First Division, but I have reached the conclusion that this is too narrow a view to take of its true construction. My noble and learned friend, Lord Reid, in his speech has already drawn attention to the great variety of phraseology that has been employed in the drafting of the sections of the Factories Act and similar legislation... But this Act and its several predecessors are notoriously badly drafted, and in my opinion one must approach its true construction bearing in mind the object of the Act itself... It is not in doubt that the whole object of the Factories Act is to reinforce the common law obligation of the employer to take care for the safety of his workmen.

. . . . . .

15.3.2 I cannot believe that Parliament intended to impose upon the insured workman or, if dead, his widow or other personal representative the obligation to aver with the necessary particularity the manner in which the employer should have employed reasonably practicable means to make and keep the place safe for him. Although the pursuer can nowadays consult experts he is at a great disadvantage compared to the employer. He may have little recollection of the accident, or of course he may have been killed, and his widow be in an even worse state. [The employer] must know and be able to give the reasons why he considered it was impracticable for him to make the place safe. If he cannot explain that it can only be because he failed to give it proper consideration, in breach of his bounden duty to the safety of his workmen.

15.3.3 Although s. 29 is in different form [to certain mining regulations in another case] I think the same reasoning applies. I think that the section required the occupier to make it 100 per cent. safe (judged, of course, by a reasonable standard of care) if that is reasonably practicable and, if it is not, to make it as safe so far as is reasonably practicable to a lower percentage. It would, indeed, impose a very heavy burden upon the workman if he and his experts had to set out on such an investigation.

In my opinion Parliament intended to impose upon the occupier the obligation of averring and proving at the trial that it was not reasonably practicable to make and keep the place of work safe, so that the pursuer's averments cannot be dismissed as irrelevant.

I am supported in this view by the observations of judges in four English authorities in the Court of Appeal.

15.3.4 LORD REID (dissenting): A considerable number of statutes prescribe, or enable regulations to prescribe, what steps an employer or occupier must take to promote the safety of persons working in factories, mines and other premises where work is carried on. Sometimes the duty imposed is absolute: certain things must be done and it is no defence that it was impossible to prevent an accident because it was caused by a latent defect which could not have been discovered — still less it is a defence to prove that it was impracticable to carry out the statutory requirement.

15.3.5 But in many cases the statutory duty is qualified in one way or another so that no offence is committed if it is impracticable or not reasonably practicable to comply with the duty. Unfortunately there is great variety in the drafting of such provisions. Sometimes the duty is expressed in absolute terms in one section and in another section it is provided that it shall be a defence to prove that it was impracticable or reasonably practicable to comply with the duty. Sometimes the form adopted is that the occupier shall so far as reasonably practicable to do certain things. Sometimes it is that the occupier shall take all practicable steps to achieve or prevent a certain result. And there are other provisions which do not exactly fit into any of these classes. Often it is difficult to find any reason for these differences.

15.3.6 There has been much doubt where the onus rests in these cases. About the first class it may well be it is sufficient for the prosecutor or pursuer to aver and prove a breach of the duty set out in the one section, leaving it to the accused or defender to avail himself of the statutory defence if he can. But in the other cases there is much room for doubt. In the present case the pleadings have been deliberately drawn in such a way as to require a decision at least with regard to the section on which the pursuer relies.

The pursuer, the present appellant, avers that on May 18, 1964 he had, within a factory, to unload railway wagons filled with bales of pulp. In doing this he had to stand on some of the bales, and while he was standing on one of the bales it tipped up and caused him to fall and fracture his skull and three ribs. He founds on s. 29(1) of the Factories Act 1961 which is in these terms:

"There shall, so far as is reasonably practicable, be provided and maintained safe means of access to every place at which any person has at any time to work and every such place shall, so far as is reasonably practicable, be made and kept safe for any person working there."

He avers that the bales were insecurely placed in the wagons so that the place at which he had to work was not made and kept safe for his working there. He deliberately avoids averring that it was reasonably practicable for the respondents, his employers, to make that place safe. He says that he has averred a relevant case because under this section it is for the defender to aver and prove, if he can, that it was not reasonably practicable to make the place safe. The respondents, of course, had no control over the loading of the bales in the wagon: that no doubt was done by the seller who sold the pulp to them. They make averments to show that it was not reasonably practicable for them to make the place safe and they also plead that the pursuer's averments being irrelevant the action should be dismissed. This plea to the relevancy was sustained by the Lord Ordinary and the Second Division adhered to his interlocutor.

15.3.7   This matter is not a mere technicality. It has important practical consequences. If the respondents are right the pursuer must not only aver in general terms that it was reasonably practical to make the place safe — such an averment without more would be lacking in specification — he must also make sufficient positive averments to give notice to the defender of the method of making the place safe which he proposes to support by evidence. But if the appellant is right he can simply wait for the evidence which the respondent would have to lead to discharge the onus on him to show that it was not reasonably practicable to make the place safe, and then cross-examine the respondents' witnesses in any relevant way he chooses. He would only have to make positive averments if he intended to lead evidence that some particular method of making the place safe could have been adopted by the defender.

In my opinion this question should be approached by considering first what a prosecutor would have to allege and prove in order to obtain a conviction. For civil liability only arises if there has been a breach of the statutory duty, and I cannot see how a pursuer could succeed in civil action without averring and proving all the facts essential to establish the commission of an offence. It is true that the standard of proof is lower in a civil case, so that the pursuer only has to show that it is probable that an offence was committed. But that cannot mean that the onus of proof is different with regard to any of the essential elements of the offence.

15.3.8   I cannot see how a prosecutor or pursuer could frame a relevant complaint or condescendence by merely alleging that an explosion occurred, or that it spread, or that fumes were not removed, leaving it to the accused or the defender to show that no practicable steps could have been taken to avoid that. The offence here must be failure to take practicable steps and the prosecutor or pursuer must allege and prove such failure.

I get no assistance in this case from any general presumption that a person is not required to prove a negative or that a person is required to prove facts peculiarly within his own knowledge. I do not lay any stress on the facts that if the appellant is right the defender would have to prove a negative — that it was not reasonably practicable to make the place safe. And I do not think that the question whether this was reasonably practicable is a matter peculiarly within the knowledge of the defender — an expert witness for the pursuer should be as well able to deal with this as the defender.

I would dismiss this appeal.

15.3.9   LORD WILBERFORCE (dissenting): Parliament, when enacting safety legislation, has various choices open to it. It may impose an absolute duty to take precautions, or to produce a condition of safety, or it may impose a qualified duty. In this subsection of the Factories Act it has imposed a qualified duty — there is no dispute about this, only as to the nature of the qualification.

When a qualified duty is imposed, again there are alternatives. The qualification may be made an integral part of the definition: or the duty may be stated in unqualified terms followed by a proviso, exemption, or exception which, if satisfied or demonstrated, takes the case out of the section. In either case — and I shall return to this point — there is a qualification of the duty.

· · · · · ·

15.3.10   The language used in s. 29(1) of the Factories Act 1961, has been acutely analysed in the Inner House. Their Lordships, unanimously affirming the Lord Ordinary, found that the qualification of reasonable practicability is "woven into the verb". I find this analysis convincing and I shall not expand the argument. There is no need to, because no fault is found with it here. I only state why I am not persuaded by the arguments against following the linguistic signpost.

There is first the question of authority. Admittedly the question is open (see *Hall* v. *Fairfield Shipbuilding Co.*, 1964 S.L.T. 97), and if the trend of English decisions is in favour of the appellant, that in Scotland is indecisive ... Thirdly, an appeal is made to the policy of the Act which is said to be remedial — *i.e.* to prevent accidents. I agree with this, and this is the only argument which seems to me to have any weight against the natural meaning of s. 29(1). If I thought that Parliament's intention to add to the safety of working places could not be carried out or even would be less effectively implemented unless a particular (even though unnatural) construction were placed on the words it has used, I would endeavour to adopt that construction. But I am not satisfied that this is the case here, for the most that can be said is that in some unusual cases the employee or his personal representative may more easily prove the case if he is dispensed from averring what was reasonably practicable. This seems to me an insufficient basis for reading one set of words as if it were another. In my opinion the First Division came to a correct decision and I would dismiss the appeal.'

COMMENT

15.4.1 Decided: July 26, 1967.
April 3: Trial of publishers of *Last Exit to Brooklyn.*
May 25: Inter Milan lose European Cup Final
June 1: Sgt. Pepper's *Lonely Hearts Club Band* released.
June 6–10: Israel won Six Days' War against Egypt.
July 18: Britain withdrew from "East of Suez".

15.4.2 The issue is whether cases of statutory negligence have anything to do with the common law structure at all. (See *Delict*, 6.1.) The development of this liability seems to suggest that it is a liability related to the common law — the courts focusing on the question of duty can find that a duty arises from a statute as much as from proximity or a special relationship.

On the other hand, while it is accepted that liability for breach of statutory duty is a form of liability imposed by law for wrongdoing and is accordingly properly treated as delictual, another view is that it is a form of liability completely different from the imposition of liability at common law: "Firstly, it has to be borne in mind that neither in *Anns* nor in *Dutton v. Bognor Regis United Building Co. Ltd* ... which preceded it, was the liability of the local authority based on the proposition that the Public Health Act 1936 gave rise to an action by a private individual for breach of statutory duty of the type contemplated in *Cutler v. Wandsworth Stadium Ltd* [1949] 1 All E.R. 544, [1949] A.C. 398, a type of claim quite distinct from a claim in negligence (see *London Passenger Transport Board v. Upson* [1949] A.C. 155 at p. 168 *per* Lord Wright). The duty of the local authority was, as Lord Wilberforce stressed in the course of his speech in *Anns* [1978] AC 728 at 758, the ordinary common law duty to take reasonable care, no more and no less" (Lord Oliver in *Murphy v. Brentwood* [1990] 3 W.L.R. 414 at p. 443).

Cutler is an English case on the considerations involved in breach of statutory duty (*Delict*, 6.3).

15.4.3 Do you prefer the minority view in the above extract? If so, why? If not, why not? For another interesting Scottish examination of standard — see *Craigie v. North Scotland Hydro Board*, 1987 S.L.T. 178.

Europe

59. Fraser v. Greater Glasgow Health Board
1996 Rep. L.R. 58 (O.H.)

15.5.1 'STATUTORY PROVISIONS: The Manual Handling Operations Regulations 1992 provide: "4(1) — Each employer shall — (a) so far as is reasonably practicable, avoid the need for his employees to undertake any manual handling operations at work which involve a risk of their being injured; or (b) where it is not reasonably practicable to avoid the need for his employees to undertake any manual handling operations to work which involve a risk of their being injured — (i) make a suitable and sufficient assessment of all such manual handling operations to be undertaken by them, having regard to the factors which are specified in column 1 of Schedule 1 to these Regulations and considering the questions which are specified in the corresponding entry in column 2 of that Schedule, (ii) take appropriate steps to reduce the risk of injury to those employees arising out of their undertaking any such manual handling operations to the lowest level reasonably practicable, and (iii) take appropriate steps to provide any of those employees who are undertaking any such manual handling operations with general indications and, where it is reasonably practicable to do so, precise information on — (aa) the weight of each load, and (bb) the heaviest side of any load whose centre of gravity is not positioned centrally."

15.5.2   LORD MACLEAN: The pursuer... began working as an auxiliary nurse in April 1988 at Gartnavel Royal hospital where she is still employed as an auxiliary nurse. It is the only hospital she has ever worked at... In November 1992 when she was working in ward 15 she underwent two days' training on handling and lifting patients. It was conducted by Staff Nurses Murty and Sloan... By 9 p.m. on 15 April 1993 Staff Nurse Murty, who was the nurse in charge of the ward at that time, approached the pursuer and asked her if she could assist her to lift a patient called Jean Slater up the bed she had collapsed onto. Mrs Slater was a very elderly geriatric patient who was, at the time, very ill with a chest infection. She was also a very heavy patient, weighing just under 14 stones. She was classified as mobile, in the sense that at the time she could walk with some assistance... Mrs Slater was at the time in a four bedded side room. Miss Murty told the pursuer to go to Mrs Slater's left hand side. She herself went to the patient's right hand side. The pursuer understood that Miss Murty's intention was to lift the patient up the bed into a sitting position, by means of a shoulder or Australian lift, as she had been instructed with regard to that lift by Miss Murty at the training session she had received in November of the previous year. The bed was not adjusted. Miss Murty put a blue strap under the patient's buttocks and the pursuer with her left hand grasped her end of it. She placed her left shoulder under the patient's left armpit as Miss Murty put her right shoulder under the patient's right armpit. Both nurses were then facing towards the head of the bed. Miss Murty told the pursuer to put her left knee on the bed which she did, "not easily" she said. The pursuer put her right arm around the patient's back, copying what she thought her colleague was doing. She thought Miss Murty's arm was around the patient's lower back. Miss Murty asked the pursuer: "Are you ready?" When the pursuer said she was, Miss Murty said that they would lift on a count of three. She counted to three and then the two nurses attempted to lift the patient up the bed. It failed. The patient did not move because, in the pursuer's opinion, she was too heavy and a dead weight. She could not sit up by herself. At the point of attempting the lift the pursuer felt a sharp pain across the bottom of her back. As she walked away from the bed, the pain got worse. She told Staff Nurse Murty that her back had gone. Miss Murty went into the duty room of the ward to check the patient's care plan in order that she could check the patient's weight. In a passage of her evidence upon which she was not cross examined, the pursuer said that Miss Murty went to the duty room to check the patient's weight. She then said that they should not have used the lift they did. They should have used an ambulift (which is a mechanical lifting device) but they did not have a sling big enough for the patient. In fact, however, when the patient was moved, according to Staff Nurse Murty, it was realised that some other form of lifting was required and an ambulift was used which was then left at the foot of the patient's bed. I prefer Staff Nurse Murty's recollection about this, and reject the evidence of Mrs Mackay who said that four nurses using straps were engaged to move the patient that night.

. . . . . .

15.5.3   As the patient's medical records make clear — and Miss Murty made the relevant entries — an ambulift was thereafter used to lift the patient, probably with the assistance of Nurse Kerrigan. This involved using a medium sling which required to be placed through the patient's legs rather than under them. It was, in that respect, a somewhat undignified procedure for the patient. When she was asked why she had not initially used the ambulift, Staff Nurse Murty said that she had not made a conscious decision not to use it. It was a stressful situation because the patient had to be moved up the bed very quickly. But, as soon as she and the pursuer were unable to move the patient, she realised that some other form of lift would have to be used. There was no prior occasion when the patient had been lifted manually. The other form of lift, of course, was the ambulift which was thereafter left at the foot of the patient's bed. Indeed, in the course of that night, Staff Nurse Murty recalled, the patient twice had to be moved by means of the ambulift. She accepted that it was used because the patient was too heavy to lift by herself and another nurse. She also accepted that one should always consider a mechanical lift first. When that could not be done, a manual lift with an aid like a sling would have to be used. She agreed that using the Australian lift could give rise to a risk of injury for one or other nurse, whereas that risk would have been avoided if an ambulift had been used. While it was some distance from the patient's bed, it was available. If she had had time, she said, to make a proper assessment, she would not have used the Australian lift, but it was the quickest to use, especially as she was having to bear the weight of the patient and wanted to save her own back. She felt that she did not have sufficient time for the ambulift. It was not possible, she thought, to summon the other nurse to bring the ambulift to assist the pursuer and herself because she was in the sluice room in the cross gallery of the ward.

15.5.4 I turn now to deal with the evidence about the training the pursuer received with regard to the handling and lifting of patients… Her instructors were Staff Nurses Murty and Sloan. The pursuer thought that if a patient was over eight stones in weight, one or other of two mechanical aids should be used, depending upon whether the patient could stand or not. But if the patient had to be moved in bed without the use of a mechanical lift — that is, manually by means of the Australian lift — Staff Nurse Murty had taught her about that since she was the moving and handling instructor. The nurses would be on either side of the patient's bed, the height of which was adjusted. Each nurse would place her shoulder under the patient's armpit. The inner knee would be placed on the bed. For this purpose the bed might have to be adjusted. A blue strap was placed under the patient's buttocks and held by the nurses in their hands. The pursuer was clear that the nurses were instructed to put their free hands — that is, the hands that were not holding the blue strap — round the back of the patient, and not on the bed head or on the bed as seen in the RGN manual *The Handling of Patients* (1987 ed.), p. 27. The pursuer recalled Staff Nurse Murty teaching her that way and demonstrating the Australian lift along with Staff Nurse Sloan. Both staff nurses had their free hands round the back of the patient.

. . . . . .

15.5.5 Staff Nurse Murty gave evidence about her role as a manual handling instructor. She remembered teaching the two day course which the pursuer attended. With reference to the RGN manual at p. 29 she agreed that the order of the three questions there set out was important. They are: Can the patient manage alone? Is a lifting aid required? Or is manual lifting by nurses inescapable? A lifting aid would be a mechanical aid or a sling. With regard to what was said on p. 29, col. 2 of the manual, she appreciated that any patient over 65 kg (10 stones 4 lbs) should be regarded as potentially heavy. She taught nurses to put their free hands on the headboard or the bed itself when executing the Australian lift. What she taught was to be seen in the RGN manual at fig. 27. Normally only two persons would be involved in the lift, but a third might be used to lift the patient's legs in case of sores etc. If it were necessary to consider using a fourth nurse, a mechanical aid should be used. If a full body transfer were to be carried out, as when a patient was to be moved from chair to chair, she taught nurses to put their hands round the patient's back. Now, said Miss Murty, we put the free hand up the scapula of the patient. This was "the neuro-muscular approach". But the auxiliaries were confused if they thought that when moving a patient in bed the free hand was placed round the patient's back. Indeed, she had carried out an audit of those she had taught, to see what they remembered, and it was surprising what people had forgotten. She always corrected nurses' bad practice whenever she saw it. So far as the general principles of moving and handling were concerned, those nurses who had attended the training course, she thought, had given to them the handout which is no. 18/3 of process. It was definitely made available to nurses in the ward by Mr John Davidson.

. . . . . .

15.5.6 I thought that the pursuer, Mrs Furze and the two staff nurses were all genuinely attempting to recall what they had taught or been taught in relation to the Australian lift. Indeed, I found the pursuer a generally frank and open witness whom I accepted. I find it established that both the pursuer and Mrs Furze believed from the instruction they received that, when moving a patient up the bed, it was in accordance with proper practice to put their free hand round the patient's back. The two staff nurses gave conflicting evidence about what they had taught... If the two instructors were so much at odds about what they taught, it is not surprising to me that their pupils should have believed, as they did, that the free hand of the nurse engaged in lifting the patient up the bed should be round the patient's back... I am of opinion that the instructions she and Staff Nurse Sloan gave to nurses, including the pursuer and Mrs Furze, were so inadequate and insufficiently clear, that such nurses reasonably formed the view that that was the correct way of moving such a patient in bed.

15.5.7 The next question is what part, if any, the position of the pursuer's free hand played in the injury which she sustained. Here I turn to the evidence of Mr Christopher Hayne, a registered ergonomics practitioner who gave evidence on behalf of the pursuer. He was a member of the Institute of Occupational Safety and Health, and a member of the Institute of Risk and Safety Management. He was trained as a physiotherapist. After a brief period in the National Health Service he was an industrial physiotherapist for nine years. He returned to the National Health Service in 1978 where he served as a district superintendent physiotherapist until April 1995. Effectively since 1978 he had been concerned with "backs". Indeed, he had been involved in the implement of the manual handling legislation and regulations. He was mentioned in the acknowledgment to the first edition of the RGN handbook which in November 1992, he said, was the benchmark of good practice... In the witness's opinion it was an incorrect lift which was incorrectly performed, and it was not surprising that injury to the pursuer resulted.

15.5.8 Mr Hayne's evidence made perfect sense to me. It was not controverted and I accepted it, at least within the limits of his expertise. He was not, of course, an expert in nursing practice, and I gave no effect to any view he expressed about the choice which confronted Staff Nurse Murty as to how she should move the patient in the emergency which presented itself to her and the decision she in fact made. I find it proved that the position in which the pursuer placed her free hand on the patient's back in the course of the lift, gave rise to a foreseeable risk of injury to her back, and that it in fact caused that injury.

15.5.9 I turn now to consider the cases of fault averred against the defenders by the pursuer. In my opinion which I have already expressed, the pursuer received inadequate training as to how safely to lift and move patients. From the tuition she and Mrs Furze got, they both thought, with reasonable justification, that the proper and safe method of moving a patient in bed, involved the placing of their free hands across the patient's back. In these circumstances the defenders, who undoubtedly owed a duty of reasonable care to provide adequate and proper training for nurses like the pursuer, and to instruct them as to the proper and safe methods of lifting and moving patients, failed in the performance of that duty, and so caused the accident to the pursuer. I agree with counsel who appeared for the pursuer and who presented his case with coherence and clarity, that it would be wrong to fault Staff Nurse Murty for not using the ambulift which was available within the ward. She was faced with an emergency and only the pursuer was immediately available to give assistance. In normal course a mechanical aid should have been used or perhaps three nurses rather than two should have been engaged, if a manual lifting operation could not have been avoided. But, as a nurse of very considerable experience, Staff Nurse Murty reached the view on the spot that it was essential that the patient should be kept upright lest she drowned in her own chest fluid, and she did not have the strength to keep her upright by herself while the pursuer fetched the ambulift. Where, however, she was at fault in my opinion was in failing to check where the pursuer's free hand was. That was all the more important because she herself was using a method — the hand up the scapula — which she had just been taught. I thought counsel was well founded when he submitted that it could be inferred that the lifting method employed on that occasion was an improper method because there was no co-ordination between the two nurses on a critical aspect of the lift. It was not a properly co-ordinated Australian lift. The pursuer avers that it was the duty of Staff Nurse Murty to instruct the pursuer as to the proper method of lifting or moving the patient. I think that

that averment of duty is wide and flexible enough to cover the factual situation in which the pursuer placed her hand in one position and Staff Nurse Murty in another; and in which the staff nurse failed to determine in advance that they were carrying out the lift in the same way. The staff nurse was in breach of that duty. As a result, the lift was not co-ordinated; it was not in accordance with what was set out in the manual; and the method used was an improper method. In consequence, the lift failed and the pursuer's back was injured.

15.5.10 The pursuer also tables a case under reg. 4 of the Manual Handling Operations Regulations 1992 which came into force on 1 January 1993. Mr Miller submitted that in relation to reg. 4(1)(a) no relevant defence was stated. The onus was on the defenders to aver and prove that it was not reasonably practicable for them to avoid the need for their employees to undertake manual handling operations at work which involved a risk of their being injured, and that they had failed to do either. The difficulty I have with this is twofold. All the evidence is out and available for consideration. Further, Staff Nurse Murty was faced with an emergency situation in which, in her professional judgment, she deemed it necessary to move the patient by means of manual lifting. In the circumstances, as she saw them, it was not reasonably practicable to avoid the need to lift the patient manually. As for reg. 4(1)(b) I had the greatest difficulty seeing how this applies to the circumstances which occurred. This regulation seems to me to be applicable to manual handling operations which are regularly undertaken as a matter of course in the furtherance of an employer's business, and that it does not apply where a manual handling operation is undertaken in an emergency on the initiative of an employee. Besides, the defenders supplied mechanical assistance to avoid the need for a manual handling operation. It just was not sufficiently to hand to be used on the particular occasion. Lastly, if the defenders were in breach of either or both subparagraphs of reg. 4, I do not understand how such breach caused the accident.'

COMMENT

15.6.1   Decided: March 20, 1996.
  March 20: Stephen Dorrell announced link between BSE (mad cow disease) and CJD in humans.
  March 25: "Braveheart" wins best film at the Oscars.

60. Anderson v. Lothian Health Board
1996 Rep. L.R. 88

15.7.1   'An employee was injured while he was loading laundry into a commercial washing machine. The laundry to be washed was sorted in a room above the washing machines. It was then weighed and placed into a cylindrical canvas chute which conveyed it down to the vicinity of the washing machine. The bottom of the canvas chute was tied, thus retaining the load within the chute. The washing was then loaded into the washing machine by the employee pushing the free-hanging lower end of the chute close to the open washing machine door, untying the rope retaining the laundry, and transferring the laundry into the machine. It was necessary for the employee to push the latter part of the load into the washing machine with some force, and it was while doing this that the employee suffered a neck strain.

The employers had instituted a system which set a maximum weight of load for the washing machines, which was usually 40kg. They had also sought advice from an occupational health physician as to the steps which ought to be taken by them to avoid the risk of injury to employees in loading the machines. The evidence at the proof, however, was that the employees engaged in loading washing machines were not properly familiar with the maximum weights for the washing to be loaded into the machines. The pursuer submitted that there had been a breach of the regulations in that there had been a failure by the defenders to avoid the need for employees to undertake manual handling operations (reg. 4(1)(a)), and, alternatively, even if there had been no such failure, there had also been a failure to take steps to reduce the risk of injury involved in the manual handling operations (reg. 4(1)(b)(ii)).

. . . . . .

15.7.2 LORD MACFADYEN: On record the pursuer avers specifically that the defenders failed in their duties under these and certain other provisions of reg. 4, without distinguishing one duty from another. The defenders plead that Dr Agius's report and another departmental report (to which no reference was made in evidence) were suitable and sufficient assessments. The defenders do not in their pleadings say anything to put reasonable practicability in issue.

"In her submissions, counsel for the pursuer argued first that the defenders were in breach of their duty under reg. 4(1)(a), and secondly that, if that were not so, they were in breach of their duty under reg. 4(1)(b)(ii). In my opinion the first of these submissions is well founded. Further, if that were not so, I am of opinion that the alternative submission would be well founded.

15.7.3 In order to establish a breach of reg. 4(1)(a) the pursuer must in my view establish, first, that the operation which he was undertaking was a manual handling operation and, secondly, that that operation involved a risk of his being injured. In connection with the second of these factors, counsel for the defenders referred me to two authorities on s. 72 of the Factories Act 1961, which is concerned with the lifting of "any load so heavy as to be likely to cause injury" to the employee (*Bailey v Rolls Royce (1971) Ltd* [1984]

I.C.R. 688, and *Whitfield v H. & R. Johnson (Tiles) Ltd* [1990] 3 All E.R. 426). As counsel for the defenders accepted, these cases demonstrate that a risk of injury is something less than a likelihood of injury (*Bailey* at p. 699F; *Whitfield* at p. 434F). In my opinion for there to be a risk of injury, injury need be no more than a foreseeable possibility; it need not be a probability. On that basis I am satisfied in the present case both that the pursuer was undertaking a manual handling operation (which was not a matter of dispute), and that that operation was one that involved a risk of his being injured.

15.7.4 Once that stage is reached, the defenders are in my opinion obliged by the regulation to avoid the need for manual handling unless it would not have been reasonably practicable for them to do so. Counsel for the pursuer submitted, by analogy with the established law in relation to s. 29(1) of the Factories Act 1961, that the onus of proving that avoidance of the need for manual handling was not reasonably practicable was on the defenders. She cited *Nimmo v Alexander Cowan & Sons ltd*, 1967 S.C.(H.L.) 79; 1967 S.L.T. 277, especially per Lord Guest at pp. 102–103 (pp. 280–281), and *Mains v Uniroyal Englebert Tyres Ltd*, 1995 S.L.T. 1115. It was for the defenders, if so advised, to invoke and establish by evidence the reasonably practicability defence (*Mains*, per Lord Sutherland at p. 1123J). Counsel for the pursuer submitted that the defenders had neither invoked nor established that defence. It was therefore not available to them. Counsel for the defenders submitted that after proof it was open to him to invite me to come to a view on reasonable practicability on the evidence which had been led. He submitted that, bearing in mind that the laundry had been purpose built as recently as the early 1980s, it was fanciful to suggest that it was reasonably practicable to avoid manual handling in the loading of the washing machines. In my opinion, counsel for the pursuer's submission on this point is sound. On a sound construction of the Regulations it is in my view for the defenders to put the question of reasonably practicability in issue in their pleadings. It is unnecessary for me to go so far as to hold that defenders must, in all cases in which they have invoked the defence, lead positive evidence in support of it, since it may be that in some cases the defence could be held to be established by the evidence led by the pursuer. The defence fails in this case first because it has not been invoked, and secondly because I am not satisfied that it would be a sound view of the evidence to hold that it would not have been reasonably practicable to avoid manual handling. The defenders were therefore in my opinion in breach of reg. 4(1)(a) in not avoiding the need for the pursuer to undertake the manual handling of the load of laundry. The causal connection between that breach and the injury which the pursuer suffered is in my view clear. If the need for manual handling had been avoided, he would not have been injured. The pursuer's case under reg. 4(1)(a) therefore in my opinion succeeds.

15.7.5 In these circumstances the pursuer's case under reg. 4(1)(b) does not arise. It is appropriate, however, that I should indicate briefly the view which I would have taken of that case had it arisen. If it were held that avoidance of manual handling would not have been reasonably practicable, consideration would require to be given to the duties under reg. 4(1)(b). The first of these is the duty to make a suitable and sufficient assessment. Counsel for the defenders argued that the work undertaken by Dr Agius amounted to such an assessment. Counsel for the pursuer accepted that work done before the commencement of the 1992 Regulations could nevertheless be a suitable and sufficient assessment for the purpose of reg. 4(1)(b)(i), and, as I understood her, that what Dr Agius did could be regarded as constituting such an assessment. The matter does not, however, end there. As counsel for the pursuer submitted, the defenders' duty goes beyond making an assessment, and requires them to take appropriate steps to reduce the risk of injury to the lowest level reasonably practicable. Counsel for the defenders argued that the defenders fulfilled that duty by introducing the system of maximum loads. I am not persuaded, however, that the defenders did sufficient in that connection. Against the background of an assessment by Dr Agius which identified 40kg as the maximum load for the small machines, appropriate steps to reduce the risk of injury to the lowest level reasonably practicable would in my opinion have involved taking all reasonably practicable steps to secure that the maximum of 40kg was not in fact exceeded. That in turn would have involved not merely passing information about the maximum loads to the operators by word of mouth, as was done, but also putting up notices listing the maxima. The reasonable practicability of that step is demonstrated by the fact that it was done after the accident. There would thus, in my opinion, if the issue had arisen, have been at the time of the accident a contravention by the defenders of their duty under reg. 4(1)(b)(ii) in respect of their failure to take the reasonably practicable step of putting the system of maximum loads into effect by the more reliable and effective means of notices.

15.7.6 Had I been relying on a contravention of reg. 4(1)(b)(ii) as the ground for holding the defenders liable to the pursuer, it would have been necessary to consider whether there was a causal connection between that contravention and the accident. There are two aspects to that issue. The first is whether the use of such notices would have prevented the overloading which occurred on the occasion of the accident. Since, for the reasons set out above, I find that as a matter of balance of probabilities the overloading which continued to occur after the recalibration of the weighing machine and occurred on the occasion of the accident took place because of the inadequacy of the means adopted for securing that the operators at all times knew and remembered the various maxima, I would have held that that aspect of causation was established. The other aspect of the question of causation in connection with the reg. 4(1)(b)(ii) case is whether the accident which the pursuer suffered would have been prevented if the maximum of 40kg had not been exceeded. The defenders argued plausibly that it could not be shown that the extra 4kg made the difference between safety and injury. On balance, however, I take the view that, in light of the maximum set by the defenders' system, the evidence that the injury occurred at the last stage of the loading operation, and the evidence that the loading became progressively awkward and stressful towards the end, I am entitled to infer that the excess load caused the pursuer's injury. I would therefore have held that the defenders' breach of duty under reg. 4(1)(b)(ii) caused the pursuer's injury, had I not found for the pursuer under reg. 4(1)(a).'

COMMENT

15.8.1   Decided: June 12, 1996.
   June 15: IRA bomb Manchester towncentre.
   June15: Ella Fitzgerald dies.
   June 23: Archbishops Tutu retires.
   June 26: Gareth Southgate becomes Scottish football hero.

15.8.2   These cases are in a sense, simple. They are an attempt to establish a statutory duty based on regulations made under a statute. But the regulations are based on European legislation. Should they be interpreted at large, by reference to similar U.K. legislation or to achieve the aim of the European legislators? *Anderson* seems to take a U.K. approach. In *Divit v. British Telecommunications plc*, 1997 G.W.D. 12–530, counsel did argue from the European provenance of the regulations, and the Schedule to the regulations. On this basis, another regulations case, *Cullen v. North Lanarkshire Council*, 1996 Rep.L.R. 87, had considered the regulations narrowly. What if Parliament had not pushed the regulations — can the government be sued for the damages that could have been obtained? What if it has passed the legislation inadequately? A whole new area of law is considered in the next extract. See especially para. 15.9.34.

61. Upton, "Crown Liability in Damages under Community Law — 1"
1996 S.L.T. (News) 175

15.9.1   'On 5 March this year, the European Court of Justice ("ECJ") issued a judgment in joined cases C-46/93 and C-48/93, *Brasserie du Pêcheur SA v. Federal Republic of Germany* and *R v. Secretary of State for Transport, ex p. Factortame Ltd, The Times*, 7 March 1996. (In what follows, the two cases are referred to jointly as *Brasserie du Pêcheur*; where the second case is singled out for comment, it is referred to as *Factortame III*.) A few days later, there followed the judgment of the Court in case C-392/93, *R v. H.M. Treasury, ex p. British Telecommunications plc*.

The combined effect of the decisions is of comparable importance to that of the well known case of *Francovich* in 1991. Their practical significance arises not only from a further change in the relationship between Parliament and the courts, with the introduction of liability for wrongful legislation, but from the qualifications that they place on the implications that *Francovich* had — or was thought to have. To a limited extent, the two new decisions also serve to illustrate attitudes, both within and outwith the Court, to the way in which it undertakes its work.

The history of the *Factortame* litigation

15.9.2   The judgment of 5 March is the seventh decision in the case of *R v. Secretary of State for Transport, ex p. Factortame Ltd* to have been reported since it was brought into court on 16 December 1988: see [1989] 2 CMLR 353 (QBD and CA); [1990] 2 AC 85 (HL); [1991] 1 AC 603 (ECJ and HL); and [1991] ECR I-3905 (ECJ). That does not include the related decisions in case C-3/87, *R v. Ministry of Agriculture, Fisheries and Food, ex p. Agegate Ltd* [1990] 2 QB 151; case C-261/87, *R v. Ministry of Agriculture, Fisheries and Food, ex p. Jaderow Ltd* [1990] 2 QB 193; and case 246/89, *Commission v. United Kingdom* [1989] ECR 3125; [1991] ECR I-455.

15.9.3   *Factortame* is an application for judicial review brought by a number of companies who owned fishing vessels that were registered as British prior to the entry into force of Pt. II of the Merchant Shipping Act 1988 and the Merchant Shipping (Registration of Fishing Vessels) Regulations 1988. The directors and shareholders of the companies are Spaniards. The 1988 Act and Regulations prevented the registration of the vessels under the new registration régime, because they provided that vessels managed or controlled from another country, or by foreign nationals, or by companies a given proportion of the shares of which were owned by foreign nationals, were ineligible for registration in the new register that was thereby established. Fishing vessels ineligible for registration were deprived of the right to fish in British waters.

15.9.4   Five of the earlier decisions concerned an application for an interim order that the regulations and Pt. II of the Act be disapplied in respect of the applicants' vessels, pending a reference to the ECJ under art. 177 of the E.C. Treaty. The questions referred were, in effect, whether the Act and Regulations were compatible with Community law. The Divisional Court made an interim order in the terms sought. The subsequent appeals to the Court of Appeal and the House of Lords concerned the competence of orders disapplying an Act of Parliament, and of interim injunctions against the Crown. In that regard, a second reference was made to the ECJ. The decision of the ECJ, as it was thereafter applied by the House of Lords, was that where the applicant founded upon a right granted to him by Community law, the rules of English law rendering those remedies incompetent were overridden, and, in the circumstances, the interim orders sought should be granted. (The decisions up to that point are sometimes referred to as "*Factortame I*".)

15.9.5 The interim orders having been made, the cause itself required to be decided. To that end, the ECJ subsequently determined the *original* reference in July 1991, by holding that arts. 52 and 221 of the EC Treaty did not allow a member state to impose conditions such as those of which the applicants complained. (That decision is known as "*Factortame II*".) This in effect determined that the United Kingdom had acted in breach of Community law by enacting and enforcing the relevant provisions of the 1988 Act and Regulations. Consequent amendments to the 1988 Act were made by the Merchant Shipping Act 1988 (Amendment) Order 1989 (SI 1989/2006).

15.9.6 It hardly needs to be said *Factortame I* and *II* are now widely recognised as leading authorities on the relationship of national quotas under the Common Fisheries Policy to the EC rules prohibiting discrimination on the ground of nationality, on interim remedies in cases brought under Community law, and on the relationship of the European Communities Act 1972 to the principle of the sovereignty of Parliament.

The third reference to the ECJ

15.9.7 Not content with that mark on the law, and — more to the point — not having obtained reparation for the period during which they were allegedly prevented from fishing, the applicants have now gone on to obtain a decision on the circumstances under which a member state is obliged to pay damages to a person who has suffered loss as a result of that state's infringement of Community law.

15.9.8 From the outset the application for judicial review contained an application for damages. After the sundry procedure narrated above, the case went back to the Divisional Court, which on 18 November 1992 made a third reference to the ECJ. Two questions were referred. First, where national legislation infringed articles of the EC Treaty, were persons who had suffered losses as a result of those infringements of Community law entitled *as a matter of Community law* to compensation by that member state? Secondly, the Divisional Court sought guidance on the considerations (if any) that Community law required national courts to apply relative to claims in respect of, inter alia, loss of income, losses arising from forced sales of vessels, shares in vessels, and shares in companies owning vessels, and fines, bonds and legal expenses arising from criminal prosecutions, and to claims for exemplary damages.

Brasserie du Pêcheur

15.9.9   On reaching the ECJ *Factortame III* was conjoined with a case
that had been referred by the German Federal High Court, the
Bundesgerichtshof, viz. *Brasserie du Pêcheur SA v. Federal Republic of
Germany.* This was an action of reparation brought by a French
company that had allegedly been prevented from exporting to
Germany beer that did not comply with the Biersteuregesetz ("Law
on Beer Duty"). The German law had previously been found by the
ECJ to be inconsistent with art. 30 of the EC Treaty (case 178/84,
Commission v. Federal Republic of German [1987] ECR 1227). Thus in
both cases the pursuers were seeking damages for loss caused by
national legislation that infringed Community law.

Francovich

15.9.10   In the meantime, while *Factortame I* and *II* were proceeding,
the question of a right to damages from a member state for failing to
comply with Community law had come before the ECJ in joined cases
C-6/90 and C-9/90, *Francovich v. Italian Republic* [1991] ECR I-5357.
Signor Francovich had suffered loss because Italy had failed to
implement an EC directive. The absence of national legislation
implementing a directive does not necessarily entail that an individual
who would have benefited from such implementation cannot avail
himself of the directive; for if the terms of the directive are sufficiently
clear, precise and unconditional, then the ECJ has held that it gives
an individual a right of action against the state and other public bodies.
That is sometimes called "direct effect". The directive in question did
not give Signor Francovich such a right. Consequently, his only
recourse was to bring an action, not on the directive, but on art. 189
of the EC Treaty, which obliges member states to implement directives.

15.9.11   When his case was referred to the ECJ, the Court said that
"the principle whereby a state must be liable for loss and damage
caused to individuals as a result of breaches of Community law for
which the state can be held responsible is inherent in the system of
the Treaty ... [but] the conditions under which that liability gives rise
to a right to reparation depend on the nature of the breach of
Community law giving rise to loss and damage" (pp. 5414–5415, paras.
35 and 38). In the particular case of a failure to implement a directive,
the ECJ held that where (1) a directive entailed the grant of rights to
individuals; (2) the contents of which rights could be identified from
the directive; and (3) there was a causal link between the failure to
implement the directive and the injured party's loss, then by virtue of
Community law that party had a right to reparation. The Court said
that the presence of those three conditions alone was sufficient to
instruct liability. In the sense that liability does not depend on the

seriousness of the failure to implement the directive, or on establishing fault, liability under *Francovich* may be described as "strict".

15.9.12 *Francovich* left some questions unanswered. The case was concerned only with failure to implement a directive. It was not concerned with the question of an infringement of any provision of the Community Treaties other than art. 189, or of an EC regulation, or of any of the common law principles of Community law. It was subsequently interpreted in three different ways.

15.9.13 The narrowest interpretation was that the right to reparation was restricted to cases of failures to implement directives that did not have direct effect. A slightly broader interpretation was that it applied to a failure to implement any directive that sought to grant identifiable rights to individuals. The broadest interpretation was that it established a principle obliging a member state to pay damages for infringement of any rule of Community law, be its source a Treaty, a regulation, a directive, or be it a general principle of EC law. While a literal reading of the judgment clearly suggested that the third interpretation was the correct one, it left open the question of the conditions under which there would arise liability for infringements of Community law that did not consist in failing to implement a directive.

15.9.14 It can therefore be seen that *Francovich* on the one hand, and *Brasserie du Pêcheur* on the other, had this in common, that they both concerned failures to obtemper an article of the EC Treaty (arts. 189, and 30 and 52, respectively); and this difference, that *Francovich* concerned a wrongful omission to legislate, whereas the UK and Germany in *Brasserie du Pêcheur* had committed positive acts of wrongful legislation.

The decision of 5 March

15.9.15 In *Brasserie du Pêcheur*, the ECJ has now held, first, that it is a principle of Community law that member states are obliged to make reparation for loss caused to an individual by a breach of Community law that is attributable to that state. In doing so it explicitly rejected the narrowest, and approved the widest, of the three interpretations of the ratio of *Francovich*. Secondly, the Court held that that principle of liability applies even where the national legislature was responsible for the breach in question.

15.9.16 The decision goes into greater detail in setting out the precise conditions under which that obligation arises. Repeating what was said in *Francovich*, the Court observed that those conditions depended on the nature of the breach of Community law that was at issue. In particular, the Court said, they depended on the extent of the discretion that the member state had been entitled to exercise under Community law when it enacted the unlawful measure. In short, the wider range of legitimate choices open to the member state, the less readily Community law would penalise it for selecting an unlawful option.

15.9.17   From that starting point, the Court said that, "in the absence of Community harmonization", the German legislature had "had a wide discretion… in laying down rules on the quality of beer put on the market". Equally, in regulating the registration of fishing vessels, the UK Parliament had had a wide discretion, and, in relation to the regulation of fishing itself, at least "a margin of discretion" (judgment, paras. 48–49, pp. 12–13).

15.9.18   In those circumstances, the ECJ decided that there are three criteria for there to be an obligation to make reparation: (1) the rule of Community law that has been infringed must have been intended to confer rights on individuals; (2) the breach of that rule must be "sufficiently serious"; and (3) there must be a direct causal link between the breach of the obligation resting on the state and the pursuer's loss.

15.9.19   The presence of these conditions is both necessary and sufficient for liability under Community law, although national law may apply rules that are more favourable to the injured party.

15.9.20   The first criterion will seemingly be met wherever the Community law that has been broken has "direct effect" (in the sense in which that expression was defined above); in the cases before it, the Court said that it was met by the relevant articles of the EC Treaty, arts. 30 and 52.

15.9.21   On the second criterion, the Court said that a breach would be "sufficiently serious" if the member state had "manifestly and gravely disregarded the limits on its discretion" (para. 55, p. 13). This is probably the element of the test that will be fought over most fiercely in the future. The Court disavowed any intention of making negligence a necessary condition of liability. At the same time, the Court said that in deciding whether a breach was "manifest and grave", the factors that could be considered included (i) the clarity and precision of the rule that had been breached; (ii) the measure of discretion which that rule left to the national authorities; (iii) whether the infringement and the loss that it caused had been arrived at intentionally or involuntarily; (iv) whether any error of law was excusable or inexcusable; (v) any position taken by a Community institution that might have contributed towards the member state's so acting; and (vi) "the adoption or retention of national measures or practices contrary to Community law" (para. 56, p. 13).

15.9.22   The Court added that where the infringement postdated a judicial ruling that made it clear that the member state was in breach of Community law, that would be sufficient to fulfil the second criterion. Beyond that, the application of these tests was a matter for the national courts in each case. With regard to the liability of the UK to Factortame Ltd and their co-applicants, the Court did however draw a distinction between the conditions relative to nationality that Britain had imposed — which it said were "manifestly contrary to Community law" — and those relative to the residence and domicile of the owners and operators of fishing vessels — in relation to which the High Court would be entitled to take into account "the assessments of the state of certainty of Community law made by the national courts" at the time, and "the attitude of the Commission" (paras. 61 and 63, pp. 14–15). (The inclusion of the last factor is perhaps slightly odd, since outwith matters over which it has a quasi-judicial jurisdiction, the views of the Commission have as such no special legal authority.)

15.9.23 The third criterion, of causation, speaks for itself.

Quoad ultra, the Court pointed out, "the conditions for reparation of loss and damage laid down by national law must not be less favourable than those relating to similar domestic claims and must not be such as in practice to make it impossible or excessively difficult to obtain reparation" (para. 67, p. 15). Those are of course the two established principles that regulate national remedies and procedures in actions brought to enforce Community rights.

15.9.24 The measure of recoverable loss remains in principle a matter for national law. All that the Court said on that topic that is of relevance to Scots law was that the extent of loss recoverable should be such as to ensure effective protection for the rights of the injured party, and determined by rules not less favourable than those applicable to similar claims under national law; that there was nothing to prevent the principle of mitigation of loss being applied; and that loss of profit should not be excluded from the allowable heads of damage.

British Telecommunications

15.9.25 The Court explained in *Brasserie du Pêcheur* that in cases of failure to implement directives, such as *Francovich*, strict liability applied because EC law imposes upon the member state "obligations to achieve a particular result... which reduce its margin of discretion, sometimes to a considerable degree". However, it seems that Community law will not always characterise as "narrow" the degree of discretion that a member state exercises when implementing a directive. This is important, because it means that in an action of reparation in which the ground of action is a failure to implement a directive, the strict régime established by *Francovich* will not necessarily apply. For even since *Brasserie du Pêcheur* was decided, on 5 March, the law has moved on.

15.9.26 On 26 March, the ECJ issued its judgment in case C-392/ 93, *R v. H.M. Treasury, ex p. British Telecommunications plc.* This was a reference from the Queen's Bench Division in proceedings brought to reduce Sched. 2 to the Utilities Supply and Works Contracts Regulations 1992 (S.I. 1992/3279). The regulations had been made by two Lords Commissioners of H.M. Treasury in order to implement the EEC Council Directive 90/531 anent public procurement procedures. The directive applies in terms to a number of named undertakings including, inter alios, British Telecommunications plc ("BT"), but not to contracts awarded by them in order to provide telecommunication services "where other entities are free to offer the same services in the same geographical area and under substantially the same conditions". The directive established a procedure for companies such as BT to notify the Commission when they were availing themselves of that exemption, and obliged them to keep records sufficient to enable them to justify the claim that the exemption applied. Schedule 2 to the UK regulations proceeded to define the services provided by BT to which the exemption did and did not apply. BT's complaint was that the directive had intended that it should be left to them to claim an exemption in the case of a given contract. The regulations identified a priori the cases to which the exemption applied. BT had thus been deprived of the discretion which the directive had intended should be conferred upon them.

15.9.27 The ECJ agreed with BT that, in that regard, the regulations did not correctly implement the directive. The question then arose of whether the UK was obliged to make reparation to BT for loss caused through the erroneous implementation of the directive. The Court's response was to refer to the decision in *Brasserie du Pêcheur*, and in particular to the rule that "with regard to a breach of Community law for which a Member State, acting in a field in which it has a wide discretion in taking legislative decisions, can be held responsible", liability depends on the presence of the three conditions laid down in *Brasserie du Pêcheur*. "Those same conditions" the Court continued, "must be applicable to the situation… in which a Member State incorrectly transposes a Community directive into national law. A restrictive approach to state liability is justified in such a situation" (paras. 39–40, p. 10). In the instant case, the Court said that the national court could only conclude that the Lords Commissioners' error had not been a "manifest and grave" breach of EC law, largely because the relevant article of the directive was "imprecisely worded and was reasonably capable of bearing, as well as the construction applied to it by the Court in this judgment, the interpretation given to it by the United Kingdom in good faith and on the basis of arguments which are not entirely devoid of substance" (para. 43, p. 11).

Francovich **today**

15.9.28   The decision in *British Telecommunications* appears to be of considerable significance for most of the cases in which, after *Francovich*, the UK may have been thought to face a possible obligation in reparation. Whether an error in implementing a directive is "manifest and grave" will of course always depend on the facts of the case. What is important for future cases, however, is that *British Telecommunications* appears to state that, as a general rule in a question of whether reparation is owed, the implementation of a directive falls within an area of legislative activity in which a member state has a wide discretion. It would follow that in such a case the pursuer who seeks damages will always have to meet the test of a "manifest and grave" breach of Community law. That is significantly different from the position under *Francovich*, where no such test applied.

15.9.29   *Francovich* concerned a total failure to take any steps to implement a directive. *British Telecommunications* applies in a case of "incorrect transposition" of a directive. It seems unlikely that the Court intended the latter phrase to embrace a case like *Francovich*. If that is so, then strict liability applies to member states who take no steps to implement a directive, but on the other hand, a state which makes the attempt but gets it wrong is protected, inasmuch as unless its error is "manifest and grave", it will not have to pay damages.

15.9.30   It might be thought that, taken together, *Brasserie du Pêcheur* and *British Telecommunications* create a situation in which a person injured by a total failure to implement a directive is in a significantly stronger position than someone whose loss flows either from a flawed attempt to do so, or from a breach of Community law unconnected with the implementation of any directive. However, it must be very doubtful whether the contrast between the two different tests will lead to results that differ from those that would obtain if the criterion of a "manifest and grave breach" applied also to a total failure to implement a directive — for the simple reason that a total failure to implement must almost inevitably constitute a "manifest and grave" breach of Community law.

15.9.31   It follows that it is academic that nothing in the latest decisions has expressly overruled *Francovich* by extending the "manifest and grave" test to such a case. However, a more substantial issue that may need to be resolved is which test applies to a case like *Wagner Miret*... C-334/92, *Wagner Miret v. Fondo de Garantia Salarial* [1995] 2 CMLR 49 (decided on 16 December 1993).

. . . . . .

Assessment of *Brasserie du Pêcheur and British Telecommunications*

15.9.32   The decision in *British Telecommunications* three weeks after *Brasserie du Pêcheur* confirms the impression that, compared with *Francovich*, the Court has now framed rules of liability for cases other than total failures to attempt to implement directives, in a manner that is considerably more favourable to the member state than to the pursuer. As we said above, the fact that the Court has not overruled *Francovich* seems in effect to be academic. What is significant is that the Court did not extend the strict régime of *Francovich* to the facts of *Brasserie du Pêcheur* and *British Telecommunications*. To that extent, the decision in *Brasserie du Pêcheur* is not in the terms for which counsel for Factortame Ltd and their fellow applicants contended, at least primarily, viz that the rule should be one of strict liability, as with *Francovich*. Indeed, the decision adopts criteria of liability that are comparable to those urged on the court by counsel for HM Government.

15.9.33   A difficulty with extending the rule of strict liability adumbrated by *Francovich*, was its apparent inconsistency with the case law on art. 215 of the EC Treaty. Article 215 governs the delictual liability of Community institutions such as the Council and the Commission. Where those institutions make a law that is later found to be unlawful, the ECJ has held that art. 215 means that, for there to be a duty to pay damages for consequent loss, the illegality must arise from a superior rule of law intended to protect the individual, and that the breach must be manifest and grave (case 5/71, *Zuckerfabrik Schöppenstedt v. Council* [1971] ECR 975). In the decision of the Court of Appeal in *Bourgoin SA v. Ministry of Agriculture, Fisheries and Food* [1986] 1 QB 716, Parker LJ had been only one of many commentators to remark upon the odd contrast that "the *Schöppenstedt* formula" would make with a rule that member states, unlike Community institutions, were subject to strict liability. What the ECJ has now done is attempt to square the circle, by expressly equating the conditions of liability in *Brasserie du Pêcheur* with those in *Schöppenstedt*, on the basis that both are concerned with authorities exercising a wide discretion, and to leave *Francovich* as the exceptional case of strict liability.

15.9.34   The recent decisions may therefore be thought to suggest the development of an inchoate principle of "judicial protection" of the taxpayer. For a member state such as the UK which has a very good record for implementing directives, but which faces a number of arguments that the terms of certain implementing measures do not comply with the true meaning of the relevant directives, the adoption of the same test in *British Telecommunications* is clearly good news. Is it to be expected that the defence that any error was not "manifest or grave" will be explored in, for example, the disputes over the former exclusion of employees of non-commercial undertakings from the scope of the Transfer of Undertakings

(Protection of Employment) Regulations 1981 (S.I. 1981/1794), and over the test of "reasonable practicability" in measures implementing the Health and Safety Directives.

. . . . . .

15.9.35 *Francovich, Brasserie du Pêcheur* and *British Telecommunications* are concerned only with the liabilities of *the state*. One obvious area in which to watch out for developments is that of the liability in private law of one individual to make reparation to another for loss caused as a result of a breach of a duty in Community law (cf. *Garden Cottage Foods Ltd v. Milk Marketing Board* [1984] AC 130; case C-128/92, *H. F. Banks & Co. Ltd v. British Coal Corporation* [1994] ECR I–1209; W. van Gerven, "Non-contractual Liability of Member States, Community Institutions and Individuals for Breaches of Community Law with a view to a Common Law of Europe", MJECL 1 (1994) 6).

The context of Scots and English law

15.9.36 How novel are the rules that *Francovich, Brasserie du Pêcheur* and *British Telecommunications* have introduced into Scots and English law?

In some respects, the approach that a national court must now adopt in assessing the liability of the Crown is not as new to Scots administrative law as one might at first think. Thus when *Brasserie du Pêcheur* directs attention to the "excusability" of legislating in breach of a Community law, the Scottish courts have in fact already had some experience of determining whether reparation is owed by a public authority in the light of the question of whether a mistake of law was or was not a pardonable error: see e.g. *Edwards v. Parochial Board of Kinross* (1891) 18 R. 867 per Lord McLaren at p. 869, and *Ballantyne v. City of Glasgow District Licensing Board*, 1987 S.L.T. 745, per Lord Jauncey at pp. 747–748.

15.9.37 However, what *is* novel is the application of such criteria to legislation. "Wrongful legislation" is an unfamiliar concept in the Scots law of delict because, unless it infringes the European Communities Act 1972, an Act of Parliament cannot be unlawful (unless, possibly, it infringes certain provisions of the Act of Union). In the case of persons other than Parliament who have the power to make measures that can be described as legislation (chief amongst whom are the General Assembly, Her Majesty in Council, Ministers of the Crown, the Court of Session, the High Court of Justiciary, local authorities, universities, and various statutory undertakers), the rules that they make *may* in principle be unlawful, either because they are ultra vires, or because of a procedural irregularity, or because they are unreasonable to the point of perversity. However, so far as the writer is aware, no one in Scotland has ever recovered damages for wrongful subordinate legislation. From first principles it can be said that in such a case there would be no entitlement to damages unless the legislator had acted in the knowledge that his conduct could injure the pursuer, and in bad faith; that is to say, either with malice or some other improper consideration as his motive, or in the knowledge that the legislation was unlawful. That is what is called in England "misfeasance in public office" (cf. *Micosta v. Shetland Islands Council*, 1986 S.L.T. 193, per Lord Ross at pp. 198–199).

. . . . . .

15.9.38 *Brasserie du Pêcheur* has been described above as favourable to defenders. However, if it is compared with Scots and English common law, the position at which Community law has now arrived is obviously vastly more favourable to pursuers, by obviating the former criteria for liability, while at the same time creating for the first time the possibility of reparation for loss caused by an Act of Parliament.'

Chapter 16

OCCUPIERS' LIABILITY

62. Occupiers' Liability (Scotland) Act 1960
(8 & 9 Eliz. 2, c. 30)

16.1.1 '2.—(1) The care which an occupier of premises is required, by reason of his occupation or control of the premises, to show towards a person entering thereon in respect of dangers which are due to the state of the premises or to anything done or omitted to be done on them and for which the occupier is in law responsible shall, except in so far as he is entitled to and does extend, restrict, modify or exclude by agreement his obligations towards that person, be such care as in all the circumstances of the case is reasonable to see that that person will not suffer injury or damage by reason of any such danger.

. . . . . .

(3) Nothing in the foregoing provisions of this Act shall be held to impose on an occupier any obligation to a person entering on his premises in respect of risks which that person has willingly accepted as his; and any question whether a risk was so accepted shall be decided on the same principles as in other cases which one person owes to another a duty to show care.

16.1.2 3.—(1) Where premises are occupied or used by virtue of a tenancy under which the landlord is responsible for the maintenance or repair of the premises, it shall be the duty of the landlord to show towards any persons who or whose property may from time to time be on the premises the same care in respect of dangers arising from any failure on his part in carrying out his responsibility aforesaid as is required by virtue of the foregoing provisions of this Act to be shown by an occupier of premises towards persons entering on them.

16.1.3 This Act shall bind the Crown ...'

COMMENT

16.2.1 The Occupiers' Liability (Scotland) Act 1960 was passed to free Scotland of a régime applying to such cases which was that of the law of England, applied by the House of Lords in *Dumbreck*. Prior to that case the matter had been dealt with simply by applying the common law of negligence. The law between these dates depended upon whether the injured person was an invitee, licensee or trespasser. An "occupier of premises" is defined by section 1(i) as "a person occupying or having control of land or other premises". Control is determined by the common law: "It must be such control as entitles the person having it to take steps desiderated to make the premises safe ... Unless a person is in a position to do or refrain from doing whatever is statutorily requisite in relation to the state of the premises, I do not consider that he can properly be regarded as having control relevant to the Act." Per Lord Dervaird, *Feely v. Co-operative Wholesale Society Ltd*, 1990 S.L.T. 547. Curiously *Telfer v. Glasgow District Council*, 1974 S.L.T. (Notes) 51 was not cited to the court (see *Delict*, 7.4) despite it involving the same two defenders on a similar question of interpretation.

16.2.2 It has been held that despite the positive language of this section, the Act does not impose an evidential onus on the occupier. In *Wallace v. City of Glasgow D.C.*, 1985 S.L.T. 23, the Inner House considered the point. Counsel for the pursuer indicated that the pleadings had been drafted deliberately to enable the pursuer to do no more than aver that a danger existed on the premises over which the defenders had control and that as a result of that danger the accident had occurred. This was admittedly a result which was contrary to the common law position. Interestingly, the pursuer argued by analogy from the interpretation in *Nimmo* (Ext. 58), of the Factories Act 1961. The Inner House required that: "the pursuer has to aver and prove that the danger was one of which the occupier knew or ought to have been aware, and why, and what steps were open to the occupier but not taken by him to remove the danger before the accident occurred." If a state of affair exists which is eloquent of sustained negligent and lack of care, it is not essential to establish a failure in a scheme of inspection: *Scott v. Glasgow District Council*, 1994 G.W.D. 28–1715.

16.2.3 The English law has been changed not once but twice! The Occupiers' Liability Act 1957 abolished the distinction then prevailing between invitees and licensees and substituted a single common duty of care to "visitors". The Occupiers' Liability Act 1984 gave protection to persons other than visitors, mostly trespassers, to a slightly lesser extent than the common duty of care. (See Winfield and Jolowicz, pp. 206–227.)

16.2.4 There is an interesting question as to whether the Act applies to roads and streets. On the face of the Act it would seem it should. Gloag and Henderson say that it does not (para. 32–17). That view is supported by *Lamont v. Monklands District Council*, 1992 S.L.T. 428. Brian J. Gill in Vol. 15 of the *Stair Encyclopaedia* points out the matter was conceded, that there was no argument on the point and so it should not be treated as deciding the point. At common law reasonable care must be taken but again the onus is on the pursuer to specify the fault — thus it is not the case that a person who trips in a hole in the pavement will recover damages. Much depends on where it is and whether it was brought to the attention of the authority. It is also often necessary to state what inspections or precautions a reasonable authority ought to take. It is not possible to simply state what seems as a matter of common sense to be a reasonable rate of inspection because of the decision in *Gibson v. Strathclyde Regional Council*, 1993 S.L.T. 1243. That case overruled an unreported decision of the sheriff principal discussed in the report. Can you support the sheriff principal's reasoning?

It is of course also the case that *some* street or road cases might raise the whole issue of whether the authority are under any duty at all. See *Stovin v. Wise and Norfolk County Council* [1996] 3 W.L.R. 388.

Finally slipping, tripping and falling cases are the bread and butter of some members of the profession. The crystal clarity of the law becomes a morass of specification. See Douglas Kinloch's articles at 1995 Civil Practice B. 1–9 and 1995 Rep. B. 4–7.

63. McGlone (Appellant) v. British Railways Board
1966 S.L.T. 2

16.3.1 'LORD REID: In this case the appellant sues under the Occupiers' Liability (Scotland) Act 1960 for damages in respect of injuries suffered by his pupil son on premises occupied by the respondent... The First Division held that the respondent was not liable and granted decree of absolvitor... At the point where the accident occurred there is a vertical wall rising some 8 ft. on the south side of the line, and above that there is a steeply sloping bank running up to a public footpath. The fence which divides the respondent's property from this footpath was in bad repair, and it is not disputed that children from a neighbouring housing estate were in the habit of playing on this bank. Some months before the accident the line was electrified and the booster transformer was erected on a concrete platform at the foot of this bank near the top of the vertical wall. It consisted of a structure about 20 ft. high; at a height of about 9 ft. one live wire was attached to this structure and another was attached to it at a point several feet higher up. The voltage was 2,500. The respondent surrounded this structure and platform on three sides by a strongly-constructed meshed fence at least 9 ft. high but there was no fence on the side nearest the railway line... The sides of the meshed fence running down towards the line did not reach the vertical wall and there were gaps on each side of about 4 or 5 ft. between the ends of the fence and the vertical wall. These gaps were each closed by five strands of barbed wire running fanwise from a point on the ground at the top of the wall to various points at the ends of the meshed fence. There were small notices attached to the fence bearing the words: "Danger — Overhead Live Wires".

On June 16, 1962, the appellant's son, aged 12, and another boy of about the same age were playing on the bank near the transformer and the appellant's son decided to climb the transformer structure. It is not clear how he got through the barbed wire, but that could easily be done by an active boy. He climbed upwards past the first live wire but somehow his arm came into contact with the uppermost live wire and he sustained severe burning from electric shock.

16.3.2 The question is whether the steps which the respondent took to fence this transformer were adequate to discharge their duty which is now statutory... I do not think it necessary or helpful in this case to discuss the state of the law before this Act was passed. One thing, however, is clear. This section renders the decision of this House in *Dumbreck* v. *Addie & Sons (Collieries)*, 1929 S.C.(H.L.) 51 no longer authoritative. It abolishes the categories of invitee, licensee and trespasser and it imposes on occupiers a higher liability to trespassers than that laid down in Dumbreck's case. But I do not intend to consider whether or not this section conferred on tresspasses greater rights than they were thought to have had before that decision. The wealth of authority discussed in the Court of Session in that case (1928 S.C. 547) shows that the law was then far from clear and I have not attempted to form any view as to how this case would have been treated before *Dumbreck's* case was decided.

The section applies both to trespassers and to persons entering property by invitation or licence, express or implied. But that does not mean that the occupier must always show equal care for the safety of all such persons. The care required is such care as is reasonable, and it may be reasonable to require a greater degree of care in one such case than in another. In deciding what degree of care is required, in my view regard must be had both to the position of the occupier and to the position of the person entering his premises, and it may often be reasonable to hold that an occupier must do more to protect a person whom he permits to be on his property than he need do to protect a person who enters his property without permission. Trespassers on the steep bank were so frequent that I would be prepared, if necessary, to hold that licence to play on the bank could be implied. Certainly the respondent ought to have expected that boys would play on it near this transformer and the respondent's witness admitted that, when such apparatus is erected at places open to the public, means are taken to warn people against climbing transformers. The question here is whether the means which were taken were sufficient to discharge the statutory duty.

The appellant pleaded that it was the respondent's duty to surround the transformer by a fence adequate to prevent children from doing what this boy did. But that would mean that whenever an occupier brings a highly dangerous object on to his land where children are accustomed to be, he must surround it by an impenetrable and unclimbable fence.

16.3.3 I do not think that the respondent was at fault in closing the gaps with barbed wire instead of prolonging the fence. The live wires were only a danger to a boy old enough to climb up this structure, and I think that the respondent could properly assume that such a boy would understand that the barbed wire was intended to keep him out and that there would or might be danger if he forced his way into this small enclosure. This is not a case of danger to a child too young to understand such things. The evidence shows that the boy knew quite well that the barbed wire was intended to keep him out and that to climb the transformer was dangerous. But he knew little or nothing about electricity and he did not know about live wires. So even if he had read the notices he would have learned little from them.

In a case like this an occupier does in my view act reasonably if he erects an obstacle which a boy must take some trouble to overcome before he can reach the dangerous apparatus.

16.3.4 The Lord Ordinary attached importance to the fact that the meshed fence could easily have been extended. As this matter came into the case at so late a stage, we do not know whether there would have been any practical difficulty in doing this. But even if this would have involved no substantial difficulty or expense, I do not think that an occupier is bound to do more than fulfil the statutory duty. It would put occupiers in an impossible position if, having provided adequate protection, they then had to weigh possible further reduction of risk of accidents against the trouble and expense of taking further precautions. An occupier must do what he is bound to do, but he is not in fault in failing to do more, however easy it might have been to do that.

Finally the respondent relied on section 2(3) of the Act. That subsection merely puts in words the principle *volenti non fit injuria*, and it is a sufficient answer to the application of that principle to this case and that this boy did not have a proper appreciation of the risk from live wires.

I would therefore dismiss this appeal.'

COMMENT

16.4.1   Decided: October 27, 1965.
Aug. 8: Kim Philby's OBE cancelled.
Sept. 30: First woman High Court judge appointed.
Oct. 26: The Beatles received MBEs.

16.4.2   In the case Lord Reid commented that if a notice was to be effective it would have to have been "more prominent, larger and clearer than the notices which the respondent displayed."

16.4.3   See the next case (Ext. 64) for a more mature pursuer and discussion of the *volenti non fit injuria* point.

16.4.4   Children are always getting into trouble — even in playgrounds — see *Sinclair v. Falkirk D.C.*, 1995 G.W.D. 40–2099 where despite mankind being able to put men on the moon, swing parks prove much more dangerous.

64. **Titchiner (Appellant) v. British Railways Board**
1984 S.L.T. 192

16.5.1   'LORD FRASER OF TULLYBELTON: On February 23, 1974 about 11 p.m. the appellant, who was then aged 15, was struck by a train on the respondents' railway line, between Shettleston and Carntyne stations in Glasgow. She was in the company of a young man, named John Grimes, aged 16, who was also struck by the train. John Grimes was killed, and the appellant suffered very serious injuries, some of which will leave permanent effects upon her. In this action, the appellant sues the respondents for damages under the Occupiers' Liability (Scotland) Act 1960. Her case is that the accident was caused by the negligence of the respondents in failing to maintain the fence along their railway in a reasonable state of repair. The respondents deny that they owed a duty to the appellant to maintain the fence in good condition. They also deny liability on other grounds to which I shall return, and they pleaded that the appellant's averments were irrelevant. A proof before answer was heard by the Lord Ordinary (Lord Ross), who assoilzied the defenders... The appellant has now appealed to this house.

. . . . . .

16.5.2 For a person walking northwards in Earnside Street, towards the railway bridge, there was a fence, for which the respondents had not responsibility, on the right-hand side. At right-angles to that fence there was another fence, for which the respondents were responsible, running along the south side of the railway both east and west of the bridge. The latter fence was made of sleepers standing upright in the ground, but at the time of the accident, and apparently for some years before that, there were gaps in it. In particular there was a gap between the sleeper fence to the east of the bridge and the fence along the east side of Earnside Street, the gap being wide enough for a person to pass through it without difficulty. In order to reach the gap from Earnside Street a person would have to climb a slope up to the embankment on which the railway ran. There was a rough path up the slope leading to the gap in the fence. Having passed through the gap a person could either cross the railway lines, and go through any of the several gaps in the fence on the north side of the railway, or he could walk along the line in either direction. The route across the line was used to some extent as a short cut to a housing area further to the north. It was also used as a short cut to a brickworks which lay immediately to the north of the railway line, and to the east of the bridge. This brickworks was a popular resort for courting couples. There was no necessity to walk across the line in order to reach the housing estate or the brickworks; the proper way was to continue along Earnside Street and under the railway bridge, but that route was apparently rather longer than the short cut and was also liable to flooding. The Lord Ordinary concluded after careful review of the evidence that "there was a certain amount of passage across the railway line... on both the east and west sides of the bridge". He also concluded that the respondents "must have been aware that people from time to time did cross the line in the vicinity of the bridge".

The appellant... gave evidence, apparently very frankly, about having crossed the railway line with John Grimes on the way to and from the brickworks, on several previous occasions. There were no eye-witnesses to the accident, but several witnesses gave evidence of having seen the appellant and John Grimes together earlier in the evening up until about 10 p.m.

. . . . . .

16.5.3 I did not understand counsel for either party to criticise the Lord Ordinary's findings of fact as being erroneous, but counsel for the respondents submitted to the Division, and more briefly to this

House, that they did not go far enough to entitle him to hold that the appellant had proved her case as averred on record… In my opinion, with all respect to Lord Hunter and Lord Grieve, it would not be reasonable to reach a decision adverse to the appellant merely on the ground that she had not precisely proved her case as averred. The respondents had ample notice that the case against them was based on the fact that the accident occurred at a part of the line in the vicinity of the bridge where, to their knowledge, people were in the habit of walking across it, after getting through gaps in the fence. Nothing turned upon the exact spot where the appellant was struck, and it is of no consequence whether it was on the east or the west side of the bridge. The respondents were in at least as good a position as the appellant to identify the point of impact, as the appellant herself has no recollection of the accident. The railway police appear to have been at the locus soon after the accident, although none of them was called as a witness. I have no hesitation in rejecting the argument for the respondents on what I may call the pleading point.

16.5.4   The duty of care owed by an occupier of premises towards a person entering thereon is now stated in the Occupiers' Liability (Scotland) Act 1960. [His Lordship quoted s. 2(1) and (3) — see para. 16.1.1 — and continued:] These two subsections are intimately related, but I shall as far as possible consider them separately. I shall consider first whether the respondents as occupiers owed to the appellant as a person entering on their premises in respect of dangers due to something done on the premises (namely the running of trains) a duty to maintain the fence in better condition than it was at the time of the accident. Let me repeat that the fence had gaps through which persons like the appellant could easily pass, and that the respondents knew that persons did pass through the gaps and walk across the line.

The duty under s. 2(1) was considered by your Lordships' House in *McGlone v. British Railways Board* where Lord Guest said (1966 S.L.T. at p. 11): "The duty is not to ensure the entrant's safety but only to show reasonable care. What is reasonable care must depend on all the circumstances of the case." One of the circumstances is the age and intelligence of the entrant. That appears from the provision in s. 2(1) that the duty is to show "such care as in all the circumstances of the case is reasonable to see that *that person* will not suffer injury" (emphasis added). The question in each case relates to the particular person who has entered upon the premises. The submission of counsel for the respondents was that they did more than enough to discharge their obligations to this appellant because the fences along the north and south sides of the line, notwithstanding that they had gaps, gave her warning that if she went on she would be entering upon railway premises. She was well aware, as she admitted, of the danger of walking across or along the line, and she said that when doing so she normally kept a look-out for trains. By giving her that warning, the respondents were, said counsel, doing more than they were obliged to do, because this appellant already knew that the railway was there, and therefore needed no warning. Counsel accepted that the logical conclusion of this argument was that, as the appellant had no need of warning, the respondents could have left their premises near the bridge completely unfenced without being in breach of any duty towards her. *A fortiori* they had no duty to do more than they did.

. . . . . .

16.5.5 I must emphasise that the question in this appeal is not whether the respondents, and other operators of railways if any there be, have as a general rule a duty to the public to maintain fences beside their lines in good condition or at all. The existence and extent of a duty to fence will depend on the circumstances of the case including the age and intelligence of the particular person entering upon the premises; the duty will tend to be higher in a question with a very young or a very old person than in the question with a normally active and intelligent adult or adolescent. The nature of the locus and the obviousness or otherwise of the railway may also be relevant. In the circumstances of this case, and in a question with this appellant, I have reached the opinion that the Lord Ordinary was well entitled to hold, as he did, that the respondents owed no duty to her to do more than they in fact did to maintain the fence along the line. I reached that view primarily because the appellant admitted that she was fully aware that the line existed, that there was danger in walking across it or along it, that she ought to have kept a look-out for trains, and that she had done so when crossing the line on previous occasions… Accordingly she could not possibly have strayed on to the line unawares. Enough of the fence remained to give her further warning, if that were necessary, that she would be going on to railway premises where (as she knew) there was danger from the trains.

. . . . . .

16.5.6 Taking all these circumstances together I consider that the respondents did not owe the appellant a duty to maintain the fence in better condition than it was. If it were necessary to do so, I would hold that they owed her no duty to provide any fence at all. If I am right so far, that would be enough to dispose of this appeal in favour of the respondents. But the Lord Ordinary and the Division based their decisions also on other grounds and I ought briefly to consider those additional grounds.

16.5.7 In the first place the Lord Ordinary held that, even if the respondents were at fault in failing to maintain the fence and to repair the gaps in it, the appellant had failed to prove, as a matter of probability, that if the respondents had performed their duty in those respects, the accident would have been prevented. The Lord Ordinary expressed himself strongly on this point and concluded that the appellant and her companion would not have been stopped by anything short of an impenetrable barrier. No doubt he reached that conclusion mainly because of the appellant's evidence in cross-examination, that the respondents should have put up an impenetrable barrier which would have been "impossible to get through"... But the appellant also said that even an ordinary post and wire fence would have been enough to prevent her from crossing the line because she could not have climbed over it. This was at least partly because she was wearing platform shoes. The Lord Ordinary disbelieved her evidence on this point, but counsel submitted that, in the absence of any other evidence, he had not been entitled to do so. In my opinion the Lord Ordinary was in no way bound to accept the appellant's evidence on this point, even though it was uncontradicted. Having regard to the fact that the appellant, helped perhaps by her boyfriend, was apparently able to climb up the embankment and walk across the line, platform shoes and all, I consider that the Lord Ordinary was fully entitled to conclude that she had failed to satisfy him that a post and wire fence would have deterred her.

. . . . . .

16.5.8 Secondly the Lord Ordinary held that the respondents had established a defence under s. 2(3) of the 1960 Act by proving that the appellant had willingly accepted the risk of walking across the line. As Lord Reid said in *McGlone*, s. 2(3) merely puts in words the principle *volenti non fit injuria*. That principle is perhaps less often relied upon in industrial accident cases at the present time than formerly, but so far as cases under the 1960 Act are concerned, the principle is expressly stated in s. 2(3) and there is no room for an argument that it is out of date or discredited. If the Lord Ordinary was entitled to sustain this defence, the result would be that, whether the respondents would otherwise have been in breach of their duty to the appellant or not, the appellant had exempted them from any obligation towards her... On this matter I am of opinion, in agreement with Lord Hunter, that the Lord Ordinary was well founded in sustaining this defence. The reasons for doing so are in the main the same as the reasons for holding that the respondents were not in breach of their duty. The appellant admitted that she was fully aware that this was a line along which trains ran, and that it would be dangerous to cross the line because of the presence of the trains. She said in cross-examination "it was just a chance I took", and the Lord Ordinary evidently accepted that she understood what she was saying. She was in a different position from the boy in *McGlone*, 1966 S.L.T. 2 (Ext. 63), who did not have a proper appreciation of the danger from live wires — see Lord Reid at p. 10 and Lord Pearce at p. 12. As I said already the appellant did not suggest the train which injured her had been operated in an improper or unusual way. The importance of that is that the chance which she took was no doubt limited to the danger from a train operated properly, in the "ordinary and accustomed way" — see *Slater* v. *Clay Cross Co. Ltd.* (1956) 2 Q.B. at p. 271, *per* Denning L.J.... In my opinion therefore the defence under s. 2(3) is established.'

COMMENT

16.6.1 Decided: November 24, 1983.
Sept. 1: Ian McGregor took over at National Coal Board.
Sept. 29: Australia won Americas Cup for first time.
Oct. 14: Cecil Parkinson resigned over Sara Keays affair.

16.6.2 It is interesting to read the Lord Chancellor, Lord Hailsham of St Marleybone's, comments. They do not add anything to Lord Fraser's legal analysis, but they are a strong condemnation of the defenders for allowing the fence to remain unrepaired. He mentioned the danger to children and animals and passengers on trains. He had a good point. Delict is supposed to be hortatory, *i.e.* it is supposed to encourage people to behave properly. Is a potential defender entitled to weigh up the cost of paying off claims for dead people against the cost of providing expensive fencing (expensive in the sense of requiring to be repaired all the time) and decide that the dead people are cheaper? Would it help if it were possible to award punitive damages when a child was squashed by a train?

16.6.3 This case perplexed Mr Jaffey, and there is no disputing that his article at 1985 C.L.J. 87 is an interesting examination of the problem. It does, with respect, seem to be predicated on some elements of English law, notably the difficulty with consideration.

16.6.4 Railways are still so dangerous that English transport police run "Q-trains" full of police officers which stop and arrest trespassing children. They are then cautioned in front of their parents.

CHAPTER 17

PRODUCT LIABILITY

65. Consumer Protection Act 1987
(1987 c. 43)

17.1.1 '1... (2) In this Part, exce pt in so far as the context otherwise requires —

. . . . . .

17.1.2 "Producer", in relation to a product, means,

(*a*) the person who manufactured it;

(*b*) in the case of a substance which has not been manufactured but has been won or abstracted, the person who won or abstracted it;

(*c*) in the case of a product which has not been manufactured, won or abstracted but essential characteristics of which are attributable to an industrial or other process having been carried out (for example, in relation to agricultural produce), the person who carried out that process;

"product" means any goods or electricity and (subject to subsection (3) below) includes a product which is comprised in another product, whether by virtue of being a component part or raw material or otherwise; and

. . . . . .

17.1.3 (3) For the purposes of this Part a person who supplies any product in which products are comprised, whether by virtue of being component parts or raw materials or otherwise, shall not be treated by reason only of his supply of that product as supplying any of the products so comprised.

17.1.4 2.—(1) Subject to the following provisions of this Part, where any damage is caused wholly or partly by a defect in a product, every person to whom subsection (2) below applies shall be liable for the damage.

(2) This subsection applies to —

(*a*) the producer of the product;

(*b*) any person who, by putting his name on the product or using a trade mark or other distinguishing mark in relation to the product, has held himself out to be the producer of the product;

(*c*) any person who has imported the product into a member State from a place outside the member States in order, in the course of any business of his, to supply it to another.

(3) Subject as aforesaid, where any damage is caused wholly or partly by a defect in a product, any person who supplied the product (whether to the person who suffered the damage, to the producer of any product in which the product in question is comprised or to any other person) shall be liable for the damage if —

(*a*) the person who suffered the damage requests the supplier to identify one or more of the persons (whether still in existence or not) to whom subsection (2) above applies in relation to the product;

(*b*) that request is made within a reasonable period after the damage occurs and at a time when it is not reasonably practicable for the person making the request to identify all those persons; and

(*c*) the supplier fails, within a reasonable period after receiving the request, either to comply with the request or to identify the person who supplies the product to him.

(4) Neither subsection (2) nor subsection (3) above shall apply to a person in respect of any defect in any game or agricultural produce if the only supply of the game or produce by that person to another was at a time when it had not undergone an industrial process.

(5) Where two or more persons are liable by virtue of this Part for the same damage, their liability shall be joint and several.

(6) This section shall be without prejudice to any liability arising otherwise than by virtue of this Part.

17.1.5   3.—(1) Subject to the following provisions of this section, there is a defect in a product for the purposes of this part if the safety of the product is not such as persons generally are entitled to expect; and for those purposes "safety", in relation to a product, shall include safety with respect to products comprised in that product and safety in the context of risks of damage to property, as well as in the context of risks of death or personal injury.

(2) In determining for the purpose of subsection (1) above what persons generally are entitled to expect in relation to a product all the circumstances shall be taken into account, including —

(*a*) the manner in which, and purposes for which, the product has been marketed, its get-up, the use of any mark in relation to the product and any instructions for, or warnings with respect to, doing or refraining from doing anything with or in relation to the product;

(*b*) what might reasonably be expected to be done with or in relation to the product; and

(*c*) the time when the product was supplied by its producer to another;

and nothing in this section shall require a defect to be inferred from the fact alone that the safety of a product which is supplied after that time is greater than the safety of the product in question.

17.1.6   4.—(1) In any civil proceedings by virtue of this Part against any person ("the person proceeded against") in respect of a defect in a product it shall be a defence for him to show —

(*a*) that the defect is attributable to compliance with any requirements imposed by or under any enactment or with any Community obligation; or

(*b*) that the person proceeded against did not at any time supply the product to another; or

(*c*) that the following conditions are satisfied, that is to say —

    (i) that the only supply of the product to another by the person proceeded against was otherwise than in the course of a business of that person's; and

    (ii) that section 2(2) above does not apply to that person or applies to him by virtue only of things done otherwise than with a view to profit; or

(*d*) that the defect did not exist in the product at the relevant times; or

(*e*) that the state of scientific and technical knowledge at the relevant time was not such that a producer of products of the same description as the product in question might be expected to have discovered the defect if it had existed in his products while they were under his control; or

(*f*) that the defect —

    (i) constituted a defect in a product ("the subsequent product") in which the product in question had been comprised; and

    (ii) was wholly attributable to the design of the subsequent product or to compliance by the producer of the product in question with instructions given by the producer of the subsequent product.

. . . . . .

17.1.7   5... (2) A person shall not be liable under section 2 above in respect of any defect in a product for the loss of or any damage to the product itself or for the loss of or any damage to the whole or any part of any product which has been supplied with the product in question comprised in it.

(3) A person shall not be liable under section 2 above for any loss of or damage to any property which, at the time it is lost or damaged, is not

(*a*) of a description of property ordinarily intended for private use, occupation or consumption; and

(*b*) intended by the person suffering the loss or damage mainly for his own private use, occupation or consumption.

(4) No damages shall be awarded to any person by virtue of this Part in respect of any loss of or damage to any property if the amount which would fall to be awarded to that person apart from this subsection and any liability for interest, does not exceed £275.

. . . . . .

17.1.8   6... (3) Section 1 of the Congenital Disabilities (Civil Liability) Act 1976 shall have effect for the purpose of this Part as if —

(*a*) a person were answerable to a child in respect of an occurrence caused wholly or partly by a defect in a product if he is or has been liable under section 2 above in respect of any effect of the occurrence on a parent of the child, or would be so liable if the occurrence caused a parent of the child to suffer damage;

(*b*) the provisions of this Part relating to liability under section 2 above applied in relation to liability by virtue of paragraph (*a*) above under the said section 1; and

(*c*) subsection (6) of the said section 1 (exclusion of liability) were omitted.

(4) Where any damage is caused partly by a defect in a product and partly by the fault of the person suffering the damage, the Law Reform (Contributory Negligence) Act 1945 and section 5 of the Fatal Accidents Act 1976 (contributory negligence) shall have effect as if the defence were the fault of every person liable by virtue of this Part for the damage caused by the defect.

. . . . . .

7. The liability of a person by virtue of this Part to a person who has suffered damage caused wholly or partly by a defect in a product, or to a dependant or relative of such a person, shall not be limited or excluded by any contract term, by any notice or by any other provision.

. . . . . .

17.1.9   9.—(1) Subject to subsection (2) below, this Part shall bind the Crown.'

COMMENT

17.2.1   This Act, a piece of U.K. legislation, was promulgated as a result of action by the EEC, namely Directive 85/374. This was ironic in that there had been considerable pressure for change in the U.K. (see *Delict*, 7.15–7.16 and also Clark (1981) 26 J.L.S. 398; (1985) 48 M.L.R. 325; 1987 S.L.T. (News) 257; Blaikie (1987) 32 J.L.S. 325). The Act does not repeal the common law of negligence and merely supplements it but to considerable effect. Accordingly the common law as stated in *Donoghue* is still the law, see para. 8.1.10.

17.2.2   Further, it is possible under the common law to prove *Donoghue*-type liability with the assistance of the maxim *res ipsa loquitur*, leading to a form of liability not all that far removed from strict liability in its effect in appropriate cases. The common law will still apply where actions are raised where the defective goods were not for consumption; where the damage caused is non-personal injury below £275; where the product in question falls outwith the definition of "defective" or of "product"; where the defender is not a producer as defined; or otherwise where the Act just does not in its terms apply, another example being goods supplied before the Act came into force on March 1, 1988.

17.2.3   There was some doubt as to whether the U.K. has properly implemented the Directive. Directives, unlike E.C. Regulations, are brought into effect in national law by the member State in its own way. However, the national legislation must achieve the same effect. Thus compare para. 17.1.6 with the following (Article 7): "The producer shall not be liable as a result of this Directive if he proves ... (*e*) that the state of scientific and technical knowledge at the time when he put the product into circulation was not such as to enable the existence of the defect to be discovered." If it does not would an uncompensated pursuer be able to sue the government? — see Euro rep. in Chapter 15.

17.2.4 The common law was difficult in relation to importers: *Thomson v. Sinclair*, 1992 G.W.D. 8–439. The common law could deal with "installation" cases on the basis of fault: *McNeill Estates v. Faulds of Girvan*, 1992 G.W.D. 1–42.

17.2.5 The European Commission has reviewed the implementation of optional provision in the directive — see Table 1, at the end of this chapter.

66. **Alistair M. Clark: "Conclusions"**
(From *Product Liability* (1989), Chap. 8)

17.3.1 'It was always clear that the introduction of a statutory scheme covering a major area such as product liability would necessarily involve the exclusion of certain persons from the scope of reparation. The drawing of the required boundaries is done by a new set of concepts, in particular, "defect", "product", "damage" and the development risks defence. Each of these concepts carries with it uncertainties and ambiguities which are capable of being resolved only after litigation. Perhaps the least clear of these concepts is the elusive notion of "defect". The Act gives no readily ascertainable objective standard against which products can be measured. A major policy aim of the reformers was the encouragement of higher safety standards, but a manufacturer must have a clear understanding of the type of deficiency which could expose him to litigation. The lack of clarity evident in the Act's definition will minimise its hortatory function.

17.3.2 Replacing the doctrine of reasonable care with a criterion which focuses upon the product introduces so many variables into the inquiry that the ability of courts rationally to adjudicate upon product design can be called into question. Seeking refuge from the *ad hoc* nature of a simple consumer expectation test, many American courts, urged on by academic commentators, have devised often quite complex risk-benefit indicators — so-called "decisional models". It is not to be expected that courts in the United Kingdom will follow this example. However, some flesh requires to be put on to the rather bare criterion in the Act, at least in order that legal advisers can advise their clients with some degree of certainty. Some form of risk-benefit model may achieve this aim.

17.3.3 As far as the concept of "product" and the chain of liability is concerned, the scheme in the Act strikes a fair balance... Again however, the new concept creates some shadows of ambiguity, for example as regards the treatment of information products.

Important questions will also arise in regard to the use of warnings and instructions attached to products. The Act is likely to create an increase in the use of such information, but it is doubtful whether the criteria for strict liability in warnings cases have advanced much beyond that of the law of negligence.

. . . . . .

17.3.4 The Act is quite definite on the matter of recoverable loss, although as the general American experience demonstrates there is significant room for improvement upon the rather unsubtle approach typified by decisions such as the *East River* case [*East River Steamship Corpn. v. Transamerica Delaval Inc.* (1986) 106 S.Ct. 2295].

. . . . . .

17.3.5 In general the defences available under the Act are reasonable, with some minor difficulties of interpretation, and with the exception of development risks.

These criticisms would perhaps have been rather insubstantial on their own and the uncertainties inherent in the new scheme may have been tolerable in a properly-constructed régime of strict liability. The new rules, while in places opaque and requiring of judicial interpretation, would have comprised a worthwhile step forward for the law. These new concepts should eventually, in some cases after litigation, provide more certainty than the open-textured language of the common law. With certainty will come shorter judgments, speedier justice and less expensive litigation... For defects caused by the manufacturing process there will, admittedly, be no real change — such defects would trigger liability under negligence as well as under the new rules. Similarly, for defects which could not feasibly have been discovered the development risks defence returns us to a position close to that in the law of negligence. However, in the key area of design defects, the major impact of the changes brought about by the Act may be felt. The new rules will provide the courts with more opportunities to stigmatise a design as defective than under the law of negligence.

. . . . . .

17.3.6 As originally mooted, with no development risks defence, the scheme of strict liability represented a balanced whole, albeit with some inherent uncertainties. That balance has been upset by the inclusion of a development risks defence, which goes even further than permitted by the Directive.'

COMMENT

17.4.1 In *East River Steamship Corpn. v. Transamerica Delaval Inc.*, the U.S. Supreme Court rejected a claim based upon damage to a product itself. Four oil-transporting supertankers were constructed by a shipbuilding company, which contracted with Delaval to design, manufacture and supervise the installation of the turbines. These turbines, which cost $1.4 million each, were to be the main propulsion units for the vessels. Charterers of the ships sued, in tort, for the cost of repairing the ships and for income lost while the ships were out of service, arguing that design and manufacturing defects in the turbines caused the supertankers to malfunction while the vessels were operating. Claims based upon contractual warranty were untenable as the limitation period had elapsed.

The court noted that the traditional claim in respect of property damage involved damage to "other property", and that in the present case there was no such damage: the chief allegations were that each supertanker's defectively-designed turbine components damaged only the turbine itself. The Supreme Court held that damage to the product itself was purely economic loss which was not recoverable in tort.

The court took the view that, where the product itself is damaged, the injury suffered — the failure of the product to function properly — is the essence of a warranty action, through which a contracting party can seek to recoup the benefit of its bargain. Damage to a product itself means simply that the product has not met the customer's expectations.

17.4.2   The whole question of actionable damage in relation to a defective product was considered in some detail in *Murphy v. Brentwood* [1990] 3 W.L.R. 414, which itself was principally concerned with damage to heritable property. Certain principles emerge which may well be applicable to moveables — indeed it could be argued that the restrictive approach in that case is partly engendered by a fear that liberality in cases involving houses would imperil the law relating to defective (as opposed to dangerous) moveables (*anglice* chattels). The current attitude of the law can, it is submitted, be appreciated from the following passage from Lord Keith's speech: "It is difficult to draw a distinction in principle between an article which is useless or valueless and one which suffers from a defect which would render it dangerous in use but which is discovered by the purchaser in time to avert any possibility of injury. The purchaser may incur expense in putting right the defect, or, more probably, discard the article. In either case the loss is purely economic" (at p. 426).

Lord Keith explained further: "On analysis, the nature of the duty held by *Anns* to be incumbent on the local authority went very much further than a duty to take reasonable care to prevent injury to safety or health. The duty held to exist may be formulated as one to take reasonable care to avoid putting a future inhabitant owner of a house in a position in which he is threatened, by reason of a defect in the house, with avoidable physical injury to person or health and is obliged, in order to continue to occupy the house without suffering such injury, to expend money for the purpose of rectifying the defect. The existence of a duty of that nature should not, in my opinion, be affirmed without a careful examination of the implications of such affirmation. To start with, if such a duty is incumbent on the local authority, a similar duty must necessarily be incumbent also on the builder of the house. If the builder of the house is to be so subject, there can be no grounds in logic or in principle for not extending liability on like grounds to the manufacturer of a chattel. That would open on an exceedingly wide field of claims, involving the introduction of something in the nature of a transmissible warranty of quality. The purchaser of an article who discovered that it suffered from a dangerous defect before that defect had caused any damage would be entitled to recover from the manufacturer the cost of rectifying the defect, and, presumably, if the article was not capable of economic repair, the amount of loss sustained through discarding it. Then it would be open to question whether there should not also be a right to recovery where the defect renders the article not dangerous but merely useless. The economic loss in either case would be the same. There would also be a problem where the defect causes the destruction of the article itself, without causing any personal injury or damage to other property. A similar problem could arise, if the *Anns* principle is to be treated as confined to real property, where a building collapses when unoccupied. In America the courts have developed the view that in the case of chattels damage to the chattel itself resulting from careless manufacture does not give a cause of action in negligence or in product liability. Thus in *East River Steamship Corpn. v. Transamerica Delaval Inc.* (1986) 476 US 858, charterers of a supertanker were denied recovery on either of these grounds, against the manufacturers of turbines which had suffered damage through design or manufacturing defect and which had had to be replaced. Blackmun J., delivering the judgment of the Supreme Court, expressed the opinion (at 870–873) that a claim of this character fell properly into the sphere of warranty under contract law. This judgment was followed by the United States Court of Appeals, Third Circuit, in *Aloe Coal Co.* v. *Clark Equipment Co.* (1987) 816 F. 2d. 110, where recovery in negligence was refused in respect of damage to a tractor shovel which caught fire and was destroyed, allegedly due to careless manufacture. The view of these courts is in line with the dissenting judgment of Lord Brandon in *Junior Books Ltd.* v. *Veitchi Co. Ltd.* ... These American cases would appear to destroy the authority of the earlier decision in *Quackenbush* v. *Ford Motor Co.* (1915) 167 App. Div. 433, founded on by the New Zealand Court of Appeal in *Bowen* v. *Paramount Builders (Hamilton) Ltd.* [1977] 1 N.Z.L.R. 394, from which Lord Wilberforce in *Anns* v. *Merton L.B.C.* [1978] A.C. 728 at pp. 759–760 said that he had derived assistance. He referred similarly to the dissenting judgment of Laskin J. in the Canadian Supreme Court case of *Rivtow Marine Ltd.* v. *Washington Iron Works* [1974] S.C.R. 1189 at pp. 1220–1221. That was a case where a crane installed on the plaintiffs' barge was revealed as being dangerously defective as a result of a similar crane having collapsed and killed a man while being operated elsewhere. The manufacturers and the suppliers were aware of this occurrence but delayed considerably in warning the plaintiffs, so that they were placed under the necessity of taking the crane out of service for rectification at the height of the logging season instead of in the slack season. The majority of the Supreme Court held the manufacturers and suppliers liable for the loss of profit sustained by the plaintiffs through not having been given earlier warning of the defect. This was on the *Hedley Byrne* principle. They did not allow the electric wiring had been installed by a sub-contractor and due to a defect caused by lack of care a fire occurred which destroyed the building, it might not be stretching ordinary principles too far to hold the electrical sub-contractor liable for the damage. If in the *East River* case the defective turbine had caused the loss of the ship the manufacturer of it could consistently with normal principles, I would think, properly have been held liable for that loss. But, even if Lord Bridge's theory were to be held acceptable, it would not seem to extend to the founding of liability on a local authority, considering that the purposes of the 1936 Act are concerned with averting danger to health and safety, not danger or damage to property. Further, it would not cover the situation which might arise through discovery, before any damage had occurred, of a defect likely to give rise to damage in the future. Liability under the *Anns* decision is postulated on the existence of a present or imminent danger to health or safety. But, considering that the loss involved in incurring expenditure to avert the danger is pure economic loss, there would seem to be no logic in confining the remedy to cases where such danger exists. There is likewise no logic in confining it to cases where some damage (perhaps comparatively slight) has been caused to the building, but refusing it where the existence of the danger has come to light in some other way, for example through a structural survey which happens to have been carried out, or where the danger inherent in some particular component or material has been revealed through failure in some other building. Then there is the question whether the remedy is available where the defect is rectified, not in order to avert danger to an inhabitant occupier himself, but in order to enable an occupier, who may be a corporation, to continue to occupy the building through its employees without putting those employees at risk."

17.4.3 *Murphy* is also significant in its rejection of the complex structure theory associated with Lord Bridge and mentioned in the foregoing passage from Lord Keith's speech. As can be seen, the theory potentially applies to heritage or moveables: "In my speech in the *D & F Estates* case [1989] A.C. 177 at 206–207 I mooted the possibility that in complex structures or complex chattels one part of a structure or chattel might, when it caused damage to another part of the same structure or chattel, be regarded in the law of tort as having caused damage to 'other property' for the purpose of the application of *Donoghue* v. *Stevenson* principles. I expressed no opinion as to the validity of this theory, but put it forward for consideration as a possible ground on which the facts considered in *Anns* might be distinguishable from the facts which had to be considered in *D & F Estates* itself. I shall call this for convenience 'the complex structure theory' and it is, so far as I can see, only if and to the extent that this theory can be affirmed and applied that there can be any escape from the conclusions I have indicated above under the rubric 'Dangerous defects and defects of quality'." (at p. 436).

The following is an illustration of his rejection of the complex structure theory in product liability: "If I buy a secondhand car and find it to be faulty, it can make no difference to the manufacturer's liability in tort whether the fault is in the brakes or in the engine, *i.e.* whether the car will not stop or will not start. In either case the car is useless until repaired. The manufacturer is no more liable in tort for the cost of the repairs in the one case than in the other" (at p. 437).

However, Lord Bridge explains what is left of the complex structure theory and it is an explanation, which with respect, raises more questions than it answers: "The reality is that the structural elements in any building form a single indivisible unit of which the different parts are essentially interdependent. To the extent that there is any defect in one part of the structure it must to a greater or lesser degree necessarily affect all other parts of the structure. Therefore any defect in the structure is a defect in the quality of the whole and it is quite artificial, in order to impose a legal liability which the law would not otherwise impose, to treat a defect in an integral structure, so far as it weakens the structure, as a dangerous defect liable to cause damage to 'other property'.

"A critical distinction must be drawn here between some part of a complex structure which is said to be a 'danger' only because it does not perform its proper function in sustaining the other parts and some distinct item incorporated in the structure which positively malfunctions so as to inflict positive damage on the structure in which it is incorporated. Thus, if a defective central heating boiler explodes and damages a house or a defective electrical installation malfunctions and sets the house on fire, I see no reason to doubt that the owner of the house, if he can prove that the damage was due to the negligence of the boiler manufacturer in the one case or the electrical contractor in the other, can recover damages in tort on *Donoghue* v. *Stevenson* principles. But the position in law is entirely different where, by reason of the inadequacy of the foundations of the building to support the weight of the superstructure, differential settlement and consequent cracking occur. Here, once the first cracks appear, the structure as a whole is seen to be defective and the nature of the defect is known. Even if, contrary to any view, the initial damage could be regarded as damage to other property caused by a latent defect, once the defect is known the situation of the building owner is analogous to that of the car owner who discovers that the car has faulty brakes. He may have a house which, until repairs are effected, is unfit for habitation, but, subject to the reservation I have expressed with respect to ruinous buildings at or near the boundary of the owner's property, the building no longer represents a source of danger and as it deteriorates will only damage itself. For these reasons the complex structure theory offers no escape from the conclusion that damage to a house itself which is attributable to a defect in the structure of the house is not recoverable in tort on *Donoghue* v. *Stevenson* principles, but represents purely economic loss which is only recoverable in contract or in tort by reason of some special relationship of proximity which imposes on the tortfeasor a duty of care to protect against economic loss."

One obvious problem with the reasoning above is the existence, even in England, of occupier's liability to trespassers. Take a defective building which looks alright. I discover a defect but, because it does not immediately pose a danger, I cannot recover. It deteriorates. I cannot afford to repair but must sell at a loss. I obtain other premises and take up occupation, say with a relative. Prior to sale a family of squatters enter and are crushed when the wall collapses. Is the entry of the squatters so unlikely that I cannot bring my otherwise economic loss into the category of preventative other-person protection?

In *Stevenson v. A. J. Stephen (Builders) Ltd*, 1995 G.W.D. 20–1145 Lord Osborne accepted *Murphy* as the law of Scotland. The pursuer sued the defender for failing to build in a firm stop which it was alleged would have materially delayed the fire. It was in the plans but wasn't built. The defenders claimed *Murphy* as an immunity — it was a defective building. In allowing a proof before answer Lord Osborne considered the loss not to be attributable to a defect but to a fire which would not have caused serious damage without the defect. This is very much an application of Lord Bridge's dictum in *Murphy* quoted in the section above.

17.4.4 A further point that might need to be reconsidered in the light of *Murphy* is the importance of intermediate examination: "However, an essential feature of the species of liability in negligence established by *Donoghue* v. *Stevenson* was that the carelessly-manufactured product should be intended to reach the injured consumer in the same state as that in which it was put up with no reasonable prospect of intermediate examination (see [1932] A.C. 562 at p. 599, *per* Lord Atkin; also *Grant* v. *Australian Knitting Mills Ltd.* [1936] A.C. 85 at pp. 103–105, *per* Lord Wright). It is the latency of the defect which constitutes the mischief. There may be room for disputation whether the likelihood of intermediate examination and consequent actual discovery of the defect has the effect of negativing a duty of care or of breaking the chain of causation (compare *Farr* v. *Butters Bros. & Co.* [1932] 2 K.B. 606, with *Denny* v. *Supplies and Transport Co. Ltd.* [1950] 2 K.B. 374). But there can be no doubts that, whatever the *rationale*, a person who is injured through consuming or using a product of the defective nature of which he is well aware has no remedy against the manufacturer."

17.4.5 See Powles, D. "Product Liability — A Novel Dimension in Scotland" in *Obligation in Context* (1990).

Christopher Hodges, "The European Commissions 1995 Review of the Product Liability Directive" [1996] JPIL 135

Table 1. Implementation of Optional Provisions in the Directive 85/374/EEC.

	Date on which implementing legislation came into force	Unprocessed primary agricultural products and game included in definition of "product" (Art. 2)	"Development risks" defence (Art. 7(e))	Limitation of total liability to at least 70 million ECU, (Art. 16)
Austria	July 1, 1988	excluded	included	no
Belgium	April 1, 1991	excluded	included	no
Denmark	June 10, 1989	excluded	included	no[1]
Finland	September 1, 1991	excluded	excluded	no[2]
France	not implemented	included[3]	included[4]	no
Germany	January 1, 1990	excluded	included[5]	yes
Greece	July 30, 1988	excluded	included[6]	yes[7]
Ireland	December 16, 1991	excluded	included	no
Italy	May 24, 1988	excluded	included	no
Luxembourg	May 2, 1991	included	excluded	no
The Netherlands	November 1, 1990	excluded	included	no
Norway	January 1, 1989	excluded[8]	excluded	no[9]
Portugal	November 11, 1989	excluded	included	yes
Spain	July 1995	excluded	included[10]	yes
Sweden	January 1, 1994	included	included	no
Switzerland	January 1, 1994	excluded	included	no
United Kingdom	March 1, 1988	excluded	included	no

Notes
[1]   Subject to regulation by another statute.
[2]   Subject to regulations by another statute; and except for medicines.
[3]   In draft form.
[4]   In draft form.
[5]   Except for medicines.
[6]   Though modified.
[7]   Though modified.
[8]   Though modified.
[9]   Except for medicines.
[10] Except for medical products, foodstuffs or food products aimed at human consumption.

Chapter 18

ANIMALS

The common law of negligence

67. Henderson v. John Stuart (Farms) Ltd
1963 S.C. 245 (O.H.)

18.1.1 A farm worker was killed when he was gored by a bull as he was cleaning its loose-box.

'Lord Hunter: If this case were to be considered against the background of the modern law of Scotland relating to the duty of care owed by the employers to employees, uncomplicated by authorities on the subject of liability of owners for injury caused by their animals, I do not think that its decision would present any serious difficulty. One example of the employer's duty to take reasonable care for the safety of the employee is his duty to take reasonable care to provide and maintain a safe system of work. It is on breach by the defenders of such a duty that the pursuers found the present action.

· · · · · ·

18.1.2 It was common ground between the parties in argument, and it is obvious from the pleadings, that there is no averment by the pursuer that the bull, which gored and crushed the deceased, had on any previous occasion, to the knowledge of the defenders, exhibited a dangerous propensity. It is indeed admitted by the pursuers that the deceased had experience in tending cattle, that for about two years he had regularly tended this bull by feeding it and cleaning out its loose-box without accident, and that it was the regular practice for the bull to remain untethered while the deceased was engaged in cleaning out the loose-box. What the pursuers do offer to prove, however, is that the bull was a Friesian dairy bull which had not been dehorned, and that it was allowed, in accordance with the defenders' normal practice, to remain untethered in its loose-box, which was not fitted with any escape gaps or baffles, while the loose-box was being cleaned out by the deceased, who had to enter the loose-box to do so. The pursuers also offer to prove that bulls kept in a loose-box are potentially dangerous to persons who necessarily disturb them by entering the box, and may at any time become potential killers of such persons, whom they might crush or gore; that Friesian dairy bulls are particularly dangerous in this respect; and that the defenders were or ought to have been aware of this generally recognised propensity of all such bulls, *i.e.* bulls kept in a loose-box, and of Friesian dairy bulls in particular. Upon the foregoing basis, the pursuers aver that it was the defenders' duty to institute and maintain a system of working whereby the bull was removed from the loose-box, or in any event was securely tethered in it, before anyone entered the loose-box to clean it, particularly having regard to the fact that the loose-box was not fitted with any escape gaps or baffles. The pursuers further aver that these precautions are in accordance with normal practice and in any event, were obviously necessary.

18.1.3 Regarding the matter as one of principle in the law of master and servant, and assuming that the duty of care owned to their employees by employers in agriculture is not lower than that owed to their employees by employers in other industries, I must confess it would never have occurred to me that the pursuers' averments which I have just summarised were not relevant for inquiry. Moreover, if it is open to me to apply in the present case the broad principles of the law of negligence as understood in Scotland, I would conclude that the pursuers have relevantly averred a breach by the defenders of the duty to take care, as that duty was defined, for example, by Lord Thankerton and Lord Macmillan in *Bourhill* v. *Young*, 1942 S.C.(H.L.) 78, at pp. 83 and 88 respectively. The defenders maintained, however, that I was precluded by authority from allowing any inquiry, and that the action ought to be dismissed.

. . . . . .

18.1.4 But before examining the authorities it is necessary to consider what the present action is, and, equally important, what it is not. Beginning with the negative proposition, the present action is not what would be called in England a *scienter* action, nor is it the Scottish equivalent of such an action, assuming for the moment that such a Scottish equivalent exists. The positive proposition is that the present action is an action on the ground of negligence, and the particular ground is failure by the defenders to take reasonable care for the safety of the deceased, who was their employee. It is, I think, important to bear these propositions in mind when considering the authorities both Scottish and English. Moreover, in view of the emphasis which was placed on the English authorities by counsel for the defenders, it is essential to understand that principle which lies behind the English action which came to be known as the *scienter* action. That principle is the primitive principle of strict liability, and its origin lies in what has been called the "coarse and impolitic idea" that a man acts always at his peril. Cattle-trespass is another example of the application of the primitive rule, and the doctrine of

Rylands v. *Fletcher* (1868) L.R. 3 H.L. 330, which now operates in England in a well-defined and limited field, appears to spring from similar origins. The general movement in the law of England now appears to be away from the primitive rule, and there is a tendency to regard cases of strict liability as isolated exceptions to the general rule applied in the law of negligence, which was of much later development than forms of action such as cattle-trespass and *scienter*.

. . . . . .

18.1.5   It cannot be too often repeated that the principle that a man acts always at his peril has never been part of the law of Scotland, and I refer in this connection to the opinion of Lord President Cooper in *McLaughlan* v. *Craig*, 1948 S.C. 599 at pp. 610–611, in which Lord Carmont concurred. This is not to say that the law of Scotland might not in certain circumstances reach the same result as the law of England, on the ground, as Lord Cooper put it, that "the facts raise a presumption of negligence so compelling as to be practically incapable of being displaced." ... If a man were to keep a tiger and failed to confine it effectually with the result that it devoured a passing pedestrian, the inference of *culpa* would, in most circumstances, be practically irrebuttable. Nevertheless under the law of Scotland, I would not think that a pursuer would necessarily succeed in proving *culpa* even in such a case, if it were established, for example, that the animal had escaped as a result of an act of God or of the Queen's enemies, or through the wrongful act of a third party, or if the effective cause of the accident was the meddling and rash act of the injured person himself. Here again the law of England may reach broadly similar results, but by a different route, namely, the recognition of certain limited and well-defined defences to the *scienter* action, which, although the authorities have wavered, apparently have some similarity to the defences recognised as being open in cases where the doctrine of *Rylands* v. *Fletcher* applies.

. . . . . .

18.1.6   In Scotland the doctrine of *culpa* is, in my opinion, wide enough to cover both the duty to confine effectually and the duty to take reasonable care.

In many Scottish authorities the *fons et origo* of liability for animals has been found in Stair, *Inst.*, I,ix,5, and, through Stair, in the Book of Exodus, XXI, 28 *et seq*. The law of England has, on the whole been less enthusiastic in seeking a biblical inspiration... By contrast Stair, in the passage cited, is engaged in stating a principle, and refers to the primitive rule in Exodus merely as an illustration of that principle. For the purposes of the present case it is a very useful illustration, since it demonstrates that Stair was dealing not with the duty to take care, but with the duty to confine effectually. This, indeed, is clear from the language used in the passage from Stair itself. The principle being dealt with is anterior accession to delinquence, of which one example is failure by a master who has foreknowledge to restrain outrageous and pernicious servants or beasts kept by him. Such failure renders the master who keeps such servants or beasts liable in reparation, on the ground, in my opinion, of *culpa*; but the fault consists not in failure to take reasonable care, but in failure to restrain or confine. Similarly, the rough justice meted out in the Law of Moses to the owner of the pushing ox is based on failure by the owner who has knowledge of the vice to keep the ox in, that is, to confine it.

. . . . . .

18.1.7 In fact the passage from Exodus, which has been so often referred to, is itself an illustration of the coarse and impolitic idea that a man acts always at his peril, and that in its crudest and most primitive form: "Eye for eye, tooth for tooth." This indeed is one of the strictest forms of liability ever codified, and, if it had been incorporated in its entirety as part of the law of Scotland, there would have been little practical need for the introduction of absolute liability under Factories Acts and Coal Mines Acts. In my opinion, if, as a result of the passage from Stair, Exodus XXI, 28 and 29 have been made part of the law of Scotland, as Lord Guthrie seems to suggest in *Milligan* v. *Henderson*, 1915 S.C. 1030 at p. 1046, it is for a very limited and special purpose, namely to create liability in certain well-defined circumstances without independent proof of negligence, and I consider that the basis of that liability is failure to confine the ox effectually. "But if the ox were wont to push with his horn in time past, and it hath been testified to his owner, and he hath not kept him in, but that he hath killed a man or a woman; the ox shall be stoned, and his owner also shall be put to death." The words speak for themselves.

. . . . . .

18.1.8 The modern law of Scotland relating to liability for injury caused by bulls is unlikely to be enshrined in two verses of the Book of the Covenant, or in a single passage from Stair, written and published long before our law of negligence as between employer and employee had begun to achieve its main development... Upon the view which I have taken of the present case it is unnecessary to consider what would have been the result had the pursuer not been a servant of the defenders. Indeed the circumstances are not of a sort likely to arise in the case of a stranger and, if they did arise, the considerations might be very different. Amongst other things the stranger might have to explain his presence beside the bull confined in its loose-box, and questions of the provision of a defective system of work would not arise. There may, in the case of a stranger suing on the ground of failure to confine, be something to be said for providing a remedy on a rather arbitrary basis... but the existence of a remedy on a somewhat strict or even arbitrary basis for breach of the duty to confine an animal does not, in my opinion, deprive a stranger of his right to sue an action on the ground of failure to take reasonable care. That an action on the ground of negligence in respect of injury caused by an animal is available to a stranger under the law of Scotland is, in my opinion, well vouched by authority... Considering the Scottish authorities cited to me as a whole, and bearing in mind the subject-matter with which they were concerned, I would not shrink from the proposition that averments such as the pursuer makes in the present case would, in appropriate circumstances, be relevant even in the mouth of a stranger.'

COMMENT

18.2.1   Decided: November 9, 1962.
Oct. 15: Amnesty International founded.
Oct. 22: William Vassall jailed for 18 years for spying for USSR.
Oct. 28: Khrushchev agreed to remove missiles from Cuba.
Nov. 2: KGB snatched Greville Wynne as alleged spy.

18.2.2   What do you think the result would be if the person injured were an amateur bullfighter?

18.2.3   A bull is not a dangerous wild animal under the 1987 Act, but probably belongs to a species whose members generally are, by virtue of their physical attributes or habits likely (unless controlled or restrained) to injure severely or kill persons or animals, or damage property to a material extent: although perhaps the species as a whole, including as it does many docile cattle, should not be considered as falling within this definition.

18.2.4   See Carey-Miller, D.L., "The Scottish Institutional Writers on Animal Liability", 1974 J.R. 1. *Henderson* is considered in one of the first cases on the Animals (Scotland) Act 1987, *Fairlie v. Carruthers*, an extract of which follows the following extract from the Act.

68. The Animals (Scotland) Act 1987
(1987 c. 9)

18.3.1   '1.—(1)... a person shall be liable for any injury or damage caused by an animal if —
(*a*) at the time of the injury or damage complained of, he was a keeper of the animal;
(*b*) the animal belongs to a species whose members generally are by virtue of their physical attributes or habits likely (unless controlled or restrained) to injure severely or kill persons or animals, or damage property to a material extent; and
(*c*) the injury or damage complained of is directly referable to such physical attributes or habits.

. . . . . .

18.3.2   (3) For the purpose of subsection (1) (*b*) above—

(*a*) dogs, and dangerous wild animals within the meaning of section 7(4) of the Dangerous Wild Animals Act 1976, shall be deemed to be likely (unless controlled or restrained) to injure severely or kill persons or animals by biting or otherwise savaging, attacking or harrying; and

(*b*) any of the following animals in the course of foraging, namely — cattle, horses, asses, mules, hinnies, sheep, pigs, goats and deer, shall be deemed to be likely (unless controlled or restrained) to damage to a material extent land or the produce of land, whether harvested or not.

(4) Subsection (1) above shall not apply to any injury caused by an animal where the injury consists of disease transmitted by means which are unlikely to cause severe injury other than disease.

(5) Subsection (1) above shall not apply to injury or damage caused by the mere fact that an animal is present on a road or in any other place.

(6) For the purposes of the Law Reform (Contributory Negligence) Act 1945, any injury or damage for which a person is liable under this section shall be treated as due to his fault as defined in that Act.

. . . . . .

18.3.3   2.—(1) A person shall not be liable under section 1(1) of this Act if —

(*a*) the injury or damage was due wholly to the fault of
  (i) the person sustaining it; or
  (ii) in the case of injury sustained by an animal, a keeper of the animal;

(*b*) the person sustaining the injury or damage or a keeper of the animal sustaining the injury willingly accepted the risk of it as his; or

(*c*) subject to subsection (2) below, the injury or damage was sustained on, or in consequence of the person or animal sustaining the injury or damage coming on to, land which was occupied by a person who was a keeper, or by another person who authorised the presence on the land, of the animal which caused the injury or damage; and either —
  (i) the person sustaining the injury or damage was not authorised or entitled to be on that land; or (as the case may be)
  (ii) no keeper of the animal sustaining the injury was authorised or entitled to have the animal present on that land.

(2) A person shall not be exempt from liability by virtue of subsection (1) (*c*) above if the animal causing the injury or damage was kept on the land wholly or partly for the purpose of protecting persons or property, unless the keeping of the animal there, and the use made of the animal, for that purpose was reasonable, and if the animal was a guard dog within the meaning of the Guard

Dogs Act 1975, unless there was compliance with section 1 of that Act.

. . . . . .

18.3.4   5.—(1) Subject to subsection (2) below, for the purposes of this Act a person is a keeper of an animal if —

(*a*) he owns the animal or has possession of it; or

(*b*) he has actual care and control of a child under the age of 16 who owns the animal or has possession of it.

(2) For the purposes of this section —

(*a*) a person shall not be regarded as having possession of an animal by reason only that he is detaining it under section 3 of this Act or is otherwise temporarily detaining it for the purpose of protecting it or any person or other animal or of restoring it as soon as is reasonably practicable to its owner or a possessor of it;

(*b*) if an animal has been abandoned or has escaped, a person who at the time of the abandonment or escape was the owner of it or had it in his possession shall remain its owner or shall be regarded as continuing to have possession of it; and

(*c*) the Crown shall not acquire ownership of an animal on its abandonment.'

COMMENT

18.4.1 What happens if you catch a disease from a rabid dog which licks your hand?

18.4.2   What is the law if you are bitten by a sheep or your crops are trampled by baboon? There is strict liability for dog bites: *O'Neil v. Coyle*, 1995 G.W.D. 21–1185

18.4.3 The English have a similar Act, The Animals Act 1971. It is, however, different in many important respects.

18.4.4   See generally Carey Miller, "A Statutory Substitute for Scienter", 1973 J.R. 61, and the same author's commentary on the Scottish Act; Blackie, J. "The Provoking Dogs Problem 2", 1993 J.L.S. — a translation of the South African case *Da Silva v. Otto,* 1986 (3) S.A. 538 (T) — and "The Provoking Dogs Problem 2", 1993 J.L.S. 148.

18.4.5   The Parts of the Act dealing with animals *as property* rather than as a source of liability are set out in Chapter 6.

69. Fairlie v. Carruthers
1996 S.L.T. (Sh. Ct.) 56

18.5.1   'SHERIFF A. M. BELL: This is an action of damages at the instance of Mrs Margaret Fairlie against John Carruthers in respect of personal injuries sustained on 4 December 1990.

On that date the pursuer was exercising her dog in a field in Roslin. She was with a friend named Mrs Audrey Fairley who is not related to her. The defender was in the field with his dog. The defender's dog ran up to the pursuer, knocked against her and knocked her down.

Evidence was given by the pursuer, Mrs Audrey Fairley and the defender.

The accident occurred just after 8 a.m. on 4 December 1990 in this field which was regularly used by the two ladies for exercising their dogs. The pursuer had not noticed the defender's dog approaching her, although she knew the defender and the dog. She said the dog was very full of life and rather frisky. The pursuer, however, did not see the dog approaching her on this occasion and knew nothing about it until she found herself knocked to the ground. The pursuer said that she could not even remember anything bumping into her. She said the whole thing happened so suddenly. However, she found she could not get off the ground and was taken to hospital. Although the pursuer herself did not see what caused her to fall to the ground, there is no doubt that she fell as a result of the defender's dog knocking into her... The pursuer was asked what she knew about the defender's dog and said "she wasn't very biddable but then she was young". She also said "retrievers are inclined to be boisterous". However, although she had had dogs for nearly 50 years she had never had a golden retriever. Her own dog was a bearded collie who was nine at the time. She spoke to an incident when she rescued the defender's dog from the road. This had been some months before the accident to her. The dog had run across the road towards her. This was the main road into Roslin. The dog had not been on a lead and had run across to see the pursuer's dog. The pursuer accepted that the field was regularly used by dog owners and that dogs regularly ran round this field off the lead. She accepted in cross examination that the defender's dog came to him when called just as hers did. All the circumstances that morning, up till the moment of her accident, were perfectly normal. She accepted that the fall was not as a result of any vicious conduct by the dog and she also accepted that it was not as a result of the dog attacking her and indeed in her own answer to that question replied "No, it was an accident". Mrs Audrey Fairley was with the pursuer at the time of the accident. She had seen the defender and his dog. She said "I hoped the dog wouldn't see us because it always bounded towards us". In answer to a leading question as to whether the dog tended to get over excited, she replied "It was a young dog". She said it did not always go back when it was called. She was asked another leading question as to whether she had experience of the dog failing to obey commands and appeared to assent to this, in a somewhat half hearted manner. She said on the morning in question the dog raced across the field. She thought the defender called on it but it didn't stop. She said "It just came towards us like an express train and instead of slowing down it just banged into" the pursuer and knocked her over. She said she did not consider the dog had been properly trained, because, in her opinion, a dog should respond to a command. She accepted that everything was as normal that morning apart from the unfortunate accident. She was asked what the dog did after the pursuer was knocked down and said it just stayed beside them and the defender came over. She said the dog hit the pursuer on the leg and knocked her down. She thought the accident could have been avoided if the dog had gone back when it was called.

18.5.2   The defender also gave evidence. He said it was half light and misty and he had not seen either of the ladies in the field. He met the pursuer's dog about 30 yards from his own dog. At that point his dog left him and joined the pursuer and her dog. The defender said he then called his dog back and his dog did come back. He was in the process of attaching the lead to her when he looked over and saw the pursuer sitting on the ground. He then ran down with his dog to see what had happened. The pursuer told him that his dog had knocked her over. He helped her to hospital. He said that at the time of the accident his dog was 13 months old. He had had her since she was eight weeks old. This was his first golden retriever. He had taken the dog to training classes from when she was about 16 weeks old from February to June at a class in Peebles and from June onwards to a class at Dalkeith. He thought the training had been successful because the dog had been promoted from the beginners' class to the advanced class. He said the dog was extremely biddable. He had not seen the accident occurring. He thought it was an unfortunate accident which could have happened with any of the dogs. He did not believe his dog had run like an express train. However, he had not seen his dog running across to the pursuer. He said his dog was not a particularly fast dog. He accepted his dog was lively, but did not accept she was boisterous. He remembered the incident when the dog ran across the main road in Roslin. The incident had alarmed him. The road was quiet at the time. He was just about to put the dog on the lead when his dog spotted the pursuer's dog and ran across the road. The dog had been a pup at the time. He accepted on that occasion he had been a bit slow in grabbing hold of it. He said he was not on the main road but approaching it. He thought this had happened when the dog was about 16–18 weeks old. There was no traffic about. The defender himself said there had been one incident when he had had to go across to get his dog because she was reluctant to come back to him and he was in a hurry.

. . . . . .

18.5.3   The evidence therefore was not really in dispute, but what was in dispute was the question of whether liability arose in the light of that evidence. The pursuer has two cases. The first relies on a breach of s. 1(1) of the Animals (Scotland) Act 1987. The allegation is that the pursuer sustained injury and damage caused by the defender's dog and that the defender is liable for such injury and damage because it is directly referable to physical attributes or habits of dogs which are likely to injure severely or kill persons or animals or damage property to a material extent. This is a short reading of s. 1(1) of the 1987 Act, which goes on to provide by s. 1(3) that for the purposes of s. 1(1) dogs shall be deemed to be likely (unless controlled or restrained) to injure severely or kill persons or animals by biting or otherwise savaging, attacking or harrying. Both agents accepted that that the effect of these provisions is that the defender is strictly liable for injury or damage directly referable to the dog biting or otherwise savaging, attacking or harrying the pursuer. I think that is a correct interpretation of the somewhat tortuously expressed provisions of s. 1 of the 1987 Act. The pursuer also has an alternative claim based on the ordinary principles of negligence.

. . . . . .

18.5.4 I deal first with the question of liability under the Animals (Scotland) Act 1987. Neither agent who addressed me referred me to any authority and I have been unable to find any reported case on the application of this Act. It may well be that there is no reported case on the application of this Act. This Act introduced a new form of strict liability to replace the former common law strict liability for animals, which depended, in the case of animals mansuetae naturae, on proof of knowledge on the part of the owner that the particular animal had previously shown a dangerous or vicious tendency of the kind complained of. There is no doubt that the defender was the keeper at the time. That was not disputed and indeed could not be. Section 1 provides by subs. (3)(a) that dogs are deemed likely to cause harm, to humans or other animals, by biting or otherwise savaging, attacking or harrying. In the first place, it is accepted that there was no question in this case of the dog biting or otherwise savaging. That is clearly correct. The agent for the pursuer sought to persuade me that there had been "attacking or harrying". A commonsense meaning must be given to these words. It is clear that the extended meaning of "harry" in s. 7 which says that it "includes chase in such a way as may be likely to cause injury or suffering", does not assist in this case. What then is the normal meaning of the word "harry"? The definition in *Chambers 20th Century Dictionary* is "to plunder; to ravage; to destroy; to harass". To me the word "harry" has a connotation of continual harassing or worrying. Conquering hordes harry a country which they have invaded. They raid it and ravage it and overrun it. People and animals may also of course be harried and indeed the word would seem quite appropriate to describe a dog, for instance, chasing sheep. However, it appears to me to be a misuse of language to describe what this dog did to the pursuer as "harrying" her. On the evidence, it ran into her once, knocked her down and did nothing more. However that may be described, it cannot be called "harrying". That leaves the question of whether what the dog did could be described as attacking the pursuer. This appears to me to be more difficult.

18.5.5 Although I was not referred to it by either of the agents, there is an English case, *Cresswell* v. *Sirl* [1948] 1 KB 241; [1947] 2 All E.R. 730 in which the English Court of Appeal discuss whether certain conduct by dogs constitutes an "attack" for the purposes of the English common law. It was held in that case that chasing by dogs which caused any real and present danger of serious harm to animals chased constituted an "attack" which entitled the owner to take effective measures of prevention. This was not a matter of statutory interpretation, as it appears that the English common law entitles an owner of animals to take effective measures of prevention against a dog "attacking" the animals. I have mentioned this case in case it might be thought that it had been overlooked, but nothing in the judgment of the court helps me in deciding whether what the dog did in this case amounted to "attacking". The answer to that question has caused me some difficulty. *Chambers 20th Century Dictionary* defines attack as "to fall upon violently: to assault: to assail". The answer may simply be that supplied by the pursuer herself in cross examination when she was asked "So your fall... it's not as a result of any dog attack or anything like that?", and replied "No, it was an accident." It is significant that when the question of an attack was put to the pursuer her immediate response was to say "No, it was merely an accident." This appears to me to be the commonsense view of what happened. In any event, I am certainly not persuaded that the pursuer has established on the evidence that the dog attacked her. The concept of an assault by a dog is a difficult one, but the use of the word "attack" seems to me to imply some form of intent, just as an assault cannot happen accidentally, but must at the very least amount to a deliberate act. I appreciate, of course, that on the question of intent, juries are frequently told that they cannot look into anyone's mind, and a fortiori I would not wish to attempt the task of looking into a dog's mind. What I have to do is to decide this by looking at what actually happened and deciding whether what the dog did could properly be described as an attack. Taking all these matters into account, I have come to the view that the pursuer has not established to my satisfaction that she was attacked by the dog. Once again, it would be more consistent with an attack if the dog, having knocked her down, had proceeded to take further action against her. The fact that she was merely knocked over and the dog did nothing more tends, if anything, to indicate that this was not an attack, but merely a playful or accidental push against her, perhaps when the dog was attempting to get near the other dogs. I do not think I need to come to a concluded view on this and it is sufficient if I say that the pursuer has not established to my satisfaction that what happened was an attack on her by the dog.

That appears to me to dispose of the pursuer's case under the Act, and I turn to deal with the common law case.

18.5.6   There is no doubt that an alternative claim based upon the ordinary principles of negligence remains open to the pursuer. The new form of strict liability under the 1987 Act merely replaces the common law rule imposing liability on the basis of proof that an animal is dangerous or harmful. It was recognised in *Henderson* v. *John Stuart (Farms) Ltd.*, 1963 S.C. 245; 1963 S.L.T. 22 that a claim based on negligence was always open, but in a common law claim the knowledge of the defender as to any dangerous propensity would be an important factor. That is because the duty under the common law cannot be any higher than a duty to take reasonable care and, if the pursuer is to establish that the defender failed to take reasonable care, facts would have to be established from which the defender could be held to have known, or ought to have known, that he should not have allowed his dog to run free, because that is essentially the failure which is relied on. The only facts which are relied on to show that it might be dangerous to allow his dog to run free were two incidents. The first was an incident when the dog admittedly ran across the road to see the pursuer's dog. That appears to me to be a perfectly natural thing for a dog to do, and it has not been established to the contrary. Further, the fact that the dog might have been inclined to have run away when it was a mere puppy to see another dog does not appear to me to indicate that the defender should have anticipated that it might have knocked over a human being in a field at a time when all dogs were running free. At best, that might tend to indicate that the dog, like I would suspect most other dogs, would be happy to run away if it saw a dog it wished to meet. That, however, is hardly the point. The dogs were all running loose in the field and presumably it was anticipated by all concerned that they might run up to each other. There is nothing in that incident which tends to indicate to me that the defender should have been on his guard against his dog acting dangerously and knocking down a human being. The other incident is of even less significance in my opinion and in fact I have some doubts as to whether I should take that into account at all. It was not pled or spoken to in evidence by the pursuer or her witness and it only came out in the evidence of the defender himself. In any event, it appears a matter of very little significance indeed. On the defender's evidence, and there is no other evidence about this incident, on one occasion he had to go over and pull his dog away from the other dogs and put her on the lead in order to take her away. Whether looked at separately or together, these incidents cannot in my opinion mean that the defender had knowledge of the likelihood of his dog behaving in a dangerous manner and knocking down a person such as the pursuer.

. . . . . .

18.5.7   There is a plea of contributory negligence, but it was not argued and I can see no way in which any blame for the accident could be attributed to the pursuer.'

COMMENT

18.6.1   Decided: May 26, 1995.
   May 28: Jean Muir died.
   June 5: Scrabble player sues, having been allowed insufficient toilet time.
   June 17: Harry Webb becomes Sir Cliff.

Chapter 19

EMPLOYERS' LIABILITY

70. English v. Wilsons and Clyde Coal Co. (Appellants)
1937 S.C.(H.L.) 46

19.1.1 'Lord Thankerton: The respondent, who is an oncost workman in one of the appellants' coal mines, claims damages at common law from the appellants in respect of personal injuries sustained by him on March 27, 1933, while employed at the appellants' Glencraig Colliery... The respondent, on the date in question, was employed underground on the work of repairing an airway leading off the Mine Jigger Brae, one of the main haulage roads. When he was proceeding at the end of the day shift, between 1.30 and 2 p.m. to the pit bottom by way of the Mine Jigger Brae, the haulage plant was put in motion, and, before he could reach one of the manholes provided, he was caught by a rake of hutches and crushed between it and the side of the road. The respondent's case was that the time fixed by the appellants for raising the day-shift men up the pit was between 1.30 and 2 p.m. and that it was a necessary part of a safe system of working that the haulage should be stopped on the main haulage roads during this period, and that this was in accordance with usual and recognised mining practice in Scotland.

. . . . . .

19.1.2 The questions put to the jury and their answers were as follows:
"*Ques*. 1. Was a reasonably safe system of working provided for the men on day shift in the Butter's Section of the Glencraig Colliery returning to the pit bottom at the end of the shift? — *Ans*. No.

Ques. 2. Did (1) the defender's Board of Directors or (2) the agent know of the said system of working in operation in the said section? — *Ans*. (1) No. (2) Yes.

Ques. 3. Did (1) the defender's Board of Directors or (2) the agent know of any defect in the said system? — *Ans*. (1) No. (2) Yes.

Ques. 4. Was the provision of the said system of working part of the technical management of the Colliery? — *Ans*. Yes.

Ques. 5. Was the accident to the pursuer caused by failure to provide a reasonably safe system of working in the said section? — *Ans*. Yes.

Ques. 6. Did the pursuer fail to take reasonable care for his own safety? *Ans*. No.

Ques. 7. If so, did he cause or materially contribute to the accident? *Ans.* No.

Ques. 8. Was the pursuer in breach of (1) section 43(1), or (2) section 74 of the Coal Mines Act 1911? *Ans.* (1) No. (2) No.

Ques. 9. On the assumption that the pursuer is entitled to damages, at what figure do you assess the damages? — *Ans.* £500."

The question in the appeal arises on the first five questions and the answers of the jury.

. . . . . .

19.1.3   Counsel for the appellants admitted that primarily the master has a duty to take care to provide and maintain a reasonably safe system of working in the mine, and he stated the question in the appeal as being whether a master, who has delegated the duty of taking due care in the provision of a reasonably safe system of working to a competent servant is responsible for a defect in the system of which he had no knowledge... It seems to me that the fallacy in the appellants' argument lies in the view that the master, being under a duty to take care in the provision of a reasonably safe system of working, is absolved from that duty by the appointment for a competent person to perform the duty. In my opinion the master cannot "delegate" his duty in this sense, although he may appoint someone as his agent in the discharge of the duty for whom he will remain responsible under the maxim *respondeat superior*. It therefore becomes necessary to examine the nature and limits of the doctrine of common employment.

19.1.4   It appears clear then that, when the workman contracts to do the work, he is not to be held as having agreed to hold the master immune from the latter's liability for want of due care in the provision of a reasonably safe system of working. But the appellants maintain that the master absolves himself from the discharge of that duty if he appoints a competent servant to discharge the duty... The workman, under his contract of employment is not to be held impliedly to have taken the risk of want of due care in the provision of a reasonably safe system of working, and the master cannot transfer the duty on to the shoulders of a subordinate. If he appoints a servant to attend to the discharge of such duty, such servant, in this respect, is merely the agent or hand of the master, and the maxim *qui facit per alium facit per se* renders the master liable for such servant's negligence, as being in the view of the law, the master's own negligence. The same servant may have other duties relative to the working or operation of the mine, as to which the doctrine of common employment might apply; but that doctrine is not applicable to the provision of reasonably safe conditions under which the working or operation of the mine is to be carried on... I agree with the Lord President that the principle of vicarious liability of the master has been uniformly applied to defective plant and defective premises, and is equally applicable in the case of defective systems.

. . . . . .

19.1.5   There remains the recent case of *Bain* v. *Fife Coal Co.*, 1935 S.C. 681, in which *Fanton's* case [1932] 2 K.B. 309 came under the consideration of the Second Division of the Court of Session. I agree with comments of the Lord Justice-Clerk (at p. 693) on *Fanton's* case and will repeat them and adopt them, if I may: "This appears to me to be a startling whittling down of the duties which the law has hitherto recognised, at any rate in Scotland, as attaching to a master towards his servant. It ignores what has always been regarded as a fundamental doctrine of the law of master and servant — *viz.*, that there are certain duties owed by a master to his servant so imperative and vital to safety that the master cannot divest himself of responsibility by entrusting their performance to others, so as to avoid liability in the event of injury arising to the servant through neglect of any of these duties. The master's liability as for breach of these paramount duties is unaffected by the doctrine of fellow servant, for in the eye of the law they are duties that cannot be delegated. If, in fact, they are entrusted by the master to others, the maxim applies *qui facit per alium facit per se*. The duty may not be absolute, and may be only a duty to exercise due care, but, if in fact the master entrusts the duty to someone else instead of performing it himself, he is liable for injury caused through the want of care of that someone else, as being, in the eye of the law, his own negligence." That admirable statement of the law, which, in my opinion, applies also in England, involves the rejection of the appellants' contentions, except the special contention that their exclusion from interference in the technical management by section 2(4) of the Coal Mines Act, 1911, relieves them from responsibility in view of the fourth answer of the jury. I agree with the opinion expressed by the five learned judges in the Court of Session who rejected this contention: neither of the learned judges who dissented appears to have expressed an opinion on this point. I agree with the Lord President's statement [1936 S.C. at p. 902]: "There is no reason in principle that a compulsory delegation should displace the vicarious responsibility of the employer, if a *de facto* delegation, which is often unavoidable, has not the same effect. I hold that the responsibility is the same whether the employer is himself qualified to act as manager or not, and whether, if qualified, he chooses to act himself or to delegate to a qualified servant as manager. In all these cases he is answerable either directly for his own negligence or vicariously for his servant's negligence, if the negligent affects the provision of a safe system of working."

19.1.6   LORD MACMILLAN: In this appeal your Lordships have to consider and accommodate the spheres of operation in the law of master and servant of two competing doctrines, the doctrine of vicarious liability and the doctrine of common employment. According to the former, a master is responsible for the negligence of his servant acting within the scope of his employment; according to the latter a master is not responsible for negligence of his servant causing injury to a fellow servant. Both doctrines are well established in the law. It is obvious that they may come into conflict. If a servant is injured by the negligence of a fellow servant acting within the scope of their common employment, the former doctrine would impose liability on the master, while the latter doctrine would exculpate him. The question is, which of these two principles is applicable to the present case?

. . . . . .

19.1.7   But then it is said that, if the person injured in consequence of the non-performance of the owner's duty by the owner's agent is an employee of the owner, there is no redress, because the agent is engaged in a common employment with the injured party and the latter took the risk of the negligence of his fellow employees. To this the conclusive answer is that the agent engaged in discharging the owner's duty of providing a safe system of working in the mine is not engaged in a common employment with the ordinary workmen in the mine. He is not collaborating with them; he is performing the duty of the owner, not the duty of an employee. The doctrine of common employment implies that the employment must be common employment with the miners who work in the colliery, and the agent carrying out the obligations of the owner is not collaborating with the workmen in the mine. Consequently the defence of common employment is not available to the mine owner where an accident occurs to an employee in the mine through the negligent performance of the owner's duty by the person appointed by the owner to perform that duty for him, for such agent of the owner and the injured workman are not in this respect engaged in a common employment... I should like to associate myself with Lord Thankerton's appreciation of the admirable opinions delivered by the Lord President in the present case and by Lord Justice-Clerk Aitchison in the case of *Bain v. Fife Coal Co.*

19.1.8   LORD WRIGHT: ... The extent of the employer's obligation has several times been stated by this House. Thus in *Wilson* v. *Merry & Cuninghame* (1868) 6 M. (H.L.) 84 at p. 89, Lord Cairns said: "What the master is, in my opinion, bound to his servant to do, in the event of his not personally superintending and directing the work, is to select proper and competent persons to do so, and to furnish them with adequate materials and resources for the work." To this must be added a third head — namely, to provide a proper system of working (see *per* Lord Colonsay in *Merry's* case). By this is meant, not a warranty, but a duty to exercise (by himself and his servants and agents) all reasonable care.

. . . . . .

19.1.9 I think the whole course of authority consistently recognises a duty, which rests on the employer and which is personal to the employer, to take reasonable care for the safety of his workman, whether the employer be an individual, a firm, or a company, and whether or not the employer takes any share in the conduct of the operations. The obligation is threefold, as I have explained. Thus the obligation to provide and maintain a proper plant and appliances is a continuing obligation. It is not, however, broken by a mere misuse or failure to use proper plant and appliances due to the negligence of a fellow servant or a merely temporary failure to keep in order or adjust plant and appliances, or a casual departure from the system of working, if these matters can be regarded as the casual negligence of the managers, foremen, or other employees.'

COMMENT

19.2.1 Decided: July 16, 1937.
 May 6: *Hindenburg* exploded at New Jersey.
 May 12: Coronation of George VI.
 June 3: Duke of Windsor married Wallis Simpson.
 July 2: Amelia Earhart vanished on round-the-world flight.
 July 11: George Gershwin died.

19.2.2 Under the doctrine of common employment — abolished in both Scotland and England by the Law Reform (Personal Injuries) Act 1948 — an employer was not vicariously liable (see Chapter 22) for the negligence of an injured workman's fellow employee (see Ingman, 1978 J.R. 106). The rule did not apply to a personal duty upon the employer.
 This helps explain the cautious exposition of the employer's primary duty as being threefold. Since the doctrine of common employment has gone, the ordinary law of negligence applies and an employer can be held liable outwith the threefold duty. See *Longworth v. Coppas International (U.K.) Ltd*, 1985 S.L.T. 111. On the other hand when pleading cases the known heads are best used if possible and appropriate facts averred.

Statutory liability

71. **Hunter (Appellant) v. British Steel Corporation**
1980 S.L.T. 31 (I.H.)

19.3.1 '[From the report] The Factories Act 1961, s. 29(1) provides: "There shall, so far as is reasonably practicable, be provided and maintained safe means of access to every place at which any person has at any time to work, and every such place shall, so far as is reasonably practicable, be made and kept safe for any person working there."

. . . . . .

19.3.2 OPINION OF THE COURT: The factual basis of the pursuer's case on his pleadings was, briefly, that in the course of his employment with the defenders as a labourer in their factory he had sustained burning injuries when he stumbled and came in contact with an electric heater while he was cleaning a room. The defenders, on the other hand, averred that the pursuer, who was prone to blackouts, had sat on the heater when he suffered a blackout. The legal basis of his case was common law fault and breach of statutory duty. The former was twofold. Fault was averred on the defenders' employee who had not switched off the heater and on the defenders who, if the accident had occurred as they averred and in the knowledge that the pursuer suffered from blackouts, were at fault in exposing him to the risk of contact with the heater when it was switched on. The case on breach of statutory duty was based on a breach of s. 29(1) of the Factories Act 1961 which relates to the safety of places of work in factories. The sheriff, *inter alia*, found that the cause of the pursuer falling on and remaining for a short time on the heater was that he had suffered a blackout. He assoilzied the defenders from the cases at common law, but held that they were in breach of statutory duty and awarded damages.

. . . . . .

19.3.3 The appeal was limited to the case on breach of statutory duty, pursuer's counsel having accepted that the decisions of the sheriff and the sheriff principal on the common law cases could not be successfully attacked... The issue between the parties was further narrowed by the agreement between counsel that the question of whether there had been a breach of s. 29(1) of the Act of 1961 depended on the test of reasonable foreseeability. Following *Keenan* v. *Rolls-Royce*, 1970 S.L.T. 90 and the other cases quoted there, it was agreed that the test was whether the place of work was safe against any reasonably foreseeable cause of injury to any person acting in any way in which a human being may reasonably be expected to act in the circumstances which may reasonably be expected to occur. It was not disputed that the sheriff principal had applied that test but the argument for the pursuer was that he had reached the wrong conclusion.

. . . . . .

19.3.4 The reasonable foreseeability of a stumble or fall is, in our opinion, an essential prerequisite of a breach of s. 29(1) in this case. On the pursuer's argument any working place would be unsafe if an employee there stumbled and fell on to or into something which injured him, for example, an open fire or even a table edge. There would, on this argument, be a breach of s. 29(1) simply because a person stumbled, fell and injured himself by falling. There must, in our view, be more than a possibility to bring in s. 29(1) that is, there must be something which makes it reasonably foreseeable that there might be a fall. On the evidence there was nothing to suggest that there was any more likelihood of a stumble or fall in this place than in any other place. The heater was not the cause of the fall. The facts that the heater was small, was on the floor and was unguarded and not glowing although switched on cannot, in our opinion, support the pursuer's case on breach of s. 29(1), when the fall was not reasonably foreseeable.

We are of the opinion that the sheriff principal reached the correct decision and we refuse the appeal.'

COMMENT

19.4.1 Decided: October 19, 1979.
Aug. 17: Lord Mountbatten, his boatman and his grandson "executed" by IRA.
Sept. 2: Yorkshire Ripper killed his 12th victim.
Oct. 11: Houdsfield wins Nobel Prize for CAT scanner.

72. **Rose v. Colville's Ltd**
1950 S.L.T. (Notes) 72

19.5.1 '[From the note] Section 26(1) of the Factories Act 1937 enacts: "There shall, so far as is reasonably practicable, be provided and maintained safe means of access to every place at which any person has at any time to work." A labourer who was engaged in clearing the casting bay of a smelting shop in a steel foundry had occasion to go to the lavatory. In order to reach it he had to pass between a bogie full of hot slag and a wagon loaded with red-hot ingots. As he passed the slag bogie a loose piece of hot slag fell from it, pinned him to the ground and inflicted serious injuries upon him. He brought an action of damages against his employers on the ground of their negligence at common law and also of their breach of section 26(1) of the Factories Act 1937. The defenders conceded that the pursuer had stated a relevant case at common law, but they challenged the relevancy of the case averred on breach of statute. After hearing counsel in the procedure roll the Lord Ordinary (Blades) sustained the defenders' plea to the relevancy of the pursuer's case under statute on the ground that while section 26(1) imposed upon employers the duty of providing and maintaining a safe means of access to every place at which a person had to work, the route taken by the pursuer when he was injured was a "means of access" to the lavatory and not a "means of access" to a "place" at which he had "at any time to work."'

COMMENT

19.6.1   Decided: November 3, 1950.
Nov. 2: George Bernard Shaw died aged 94.
July 15: Princess Anne born.

19.6.2   It is of course possible to sue both under the statute and at common law — the last extract being a good example. The reasoning of Lord Blades was recently rejected in Dundee Sheriff Court (36 years offers no protection from criticism in the law!). In *Cavanagh v. Godfreys of Dundee*, February 28, 1996, unreported, a workman tripped going to his locker to get his tools — the *Rose* point was taken but rejected. A proof before answer was allowed. Do you think we can expect the same sophistry in considering the new regulations which apply to traffic routes in workplaces? See also *Scott v. EDL Pipeworks*, 1995 S.L.T. 561 to answer the question — is a place where you are not to go a place at which a person has to work?

19.6.3   The last two cases illustrate how the principles illustrated in Chapter 15 apply in relation to one particular statute. (See *Delict*, Chap. 6.) Naturally students should be familiar with the commonly-used sections. It being a U.K. statute, English cases on interpretation are, of course, very influential: the same way on both sides of the border. In practice cases are often brought based on regulations made under the principal Act.

19.6.4   Even though the law is generally favourable to employees, a perusal of *Greens Weekly Digest* will show that they are often unsuccessful — why might this be?

CHAPTER 20

DEFENCES

73. Tennent (Appellant) v. Earl of Glasgow
(1864) 2 M.(H.L.) 22

20.1.1 'LORD CHANCELLOR: My Lords, the points in this case are, I think, too clear to leave any doubt upon your Lordships' minds, and therefore I apprehend that your Lordships will feel it your duty not to call upon the respondents... The facts of the case are these: The noble defender is the owner of a piece of land of considerable extent, which is bounded upon one side by a public road, and upon another side by a parish road — the parish road entering at right angles, or nearly so, into the public road. The land slopes with a considerable declivity towards the public road, and at some distance upwards from the public road. Along the scope of the land runs an ancient burn or brook, which finds its way... along the slope of the noble defender's land, and then enters the parish road. Previously to the erection of the wall by the noble defender, both the parish road, and also the public road, were fenced off, and the land was bounded by a thorn hedge. But from the point where the burn entered the parish road it was conducted by a conduit beneath the parish road. The defender thought proper to enclose his land, as he had a perfect right to do, by a wall running along the parish road, and also the public road — the wall of course having an opening to admit of the burn passing under it into the conduit.

20.1.2 My lords, it might have been a very material thing in this case, if the injury, or the wrong as I should rather call it, sustained by the appellant could have been shewn to be caused by a state of circumstances directly occasioned by the building of the wall by the noble defender over the conduit, and along the parish road, because it is clear that the natural course of the stream was down the parish road and that the conduit provided a means of carrying the water beneath the parish road. If by reason of the taking away of the thorn hedge by the side of the parish road, and the substituting a wall for it without proper apertures, it had been shewn that the flood which occurred had been pent up by means of that substitute wall, and consequently the water kept in and precipitated down the declivity against the wall that bounded the public road, the state of things before your Lordships might have admitted of a different result. But, on the contrary, it is found distinctly in this case, and necessarily results from the facts stated in the interlocutor, that the portion of the wall bounding the public road which gave way and furnished a vent to the water by which it invaded the appellant's grounds and house, so gave way under the pressure of water which had accumulated — not water which had overflowed at the conduit — not an accumulation which was in any manner occasioned by the erection of the wall bounding the parish road but an accumulation arising from another circumstance, namely that the descent of the water down the channel of the brook to the point where the channel makes a natural elbow or bend was so great in consequence of a fall of rain found to have been unprecedented, that the volume or rush of water at that spot overpowered the banks of the burn, and consequently a great volume of water descended directly down to the wall bounding the public road, escaping from the point of that elbow where the rush of water had burst the natural banks. This occurrence, therefore, was a natural occurrence and not in the smallest degree occasioned or augmented by reason of anything which had been done, or had been omitted to be done by the noble defender. It was a thing of which, so far as the facts found warrant an inference of the kind, there had been no example before; nor was it likely from anything that had occurred, that any such occurrence could have been anticipated...

20.1.3   My Lords, it is further material to observe with reference to the argument, that it is not found in this interlocutor, nor is it a conclusion to be drawn from any of the findings in this interlocutor, that the water had ever been in the habit of descending down a hill from the channel of the burn, and finding its escape into the public road through the thorn hedge. No such fact is established. And that is a material circumstance, because if it had been a common occurrence, either a daily occurrence or an occurrence happening at intervals, that water, escaped from the burn, descended directly down the land, and found an exit through the hedge into the public road, the possibility of such an occurrence might possibly have thrown upon the noble defender the obligation of guarding against that contingency. But, as I have observed, no such thing is found. And, on the contrary, that it might have been reasonably expected, is a conclusion which is altogether precluded and prevented from being implied by the facts that are distinctly found, namely, that the bursting of the burn at the elbow was the result of the great pressure of an extraordinary quantity of water which had unexpectedly accumulated by reason of an unprecedented fall of rain.

. . . . . .

20.1.4   My Lords, this case differs very much from those which have been cited and relied upon at the bar. If anything be done by an individual which interferes with natural occurrences such as, for example, in *Lord Orkney's* case, throwing a dam across the course of a stream, it is undoubtedly the duty of that individual so to construct the work as to provide in an efficient manner, not only against usual occurrences and ordinary state of things, but also to provide against things which were unusual and extraordinary. And, therefore, the decision of the court, in the *Earl of Orkney's* case (20 D. 299), where a dam gave way, was properly referable to that circumstance.

. . . . . .

20.1.5 Under these circumstances, my Lords, what has occurred is one of those things which do not involve any legal liability — what are denominated in the law of Scotland *damnum fatale* occurrences — circumstances which no human foresight can provide against, and of which human prudence is not bound to recognise the possibility, and which when they do occur, therefore, are calamities that do not involve the obligation of paying for the consequences that may result from them.

Under these circumstances, my Lords, I think you will agree with me in the conclusion that this appeal ought to be dismissed, and that it must be dismissed with costs.

20.1.6 LORD CRANWORTH: My Lords, I think if your Lordships should come to any other conclusion than that which my noble and learned friend has indicated, you would be laying down doctrines which would be quite startling to mankind. For the proposition contended for by the appellants, that this nobleman having built a wall where no water had ever been in the habit of flowing, and which was at a distance of a third of a mile, or rather more than a third of a mile, I think, from a stream running parallel to the wall which he erected, is legally responsible, because after an "unprecedented fall" of water (which, even if the word be taken in a figurative sense must mean a fall of water such as no living memory could find a parallel to) had happened, the river burst the natural protection of its banks and that which naturally shut it in, and the water escaping from it in a direction in which it had never escaped before, came down to this wall and knocked it down, whereby the injury in question was occasioned... Now, if a person is to be responsible for damage so occasioned, no man can know what he can do with safety.

. . . . . .

20.1.7 LORD CHELMSFORD: My Lords, I agree with my noble and learned friends that this interlocutor appealed from ought to be affirmed. I think that the pursuer was not entitled to recover against the defender without shewing some negligence or default upon his part which occasioned the injury. It is not at all like the case of *May and Burdett* [(1846) 9 Q.B. 101] with regard to the monkey, because there the monkey was described to be a mischievous and ferocious animal — an animal which was dangerous to keep, and could only be kept upon condition of its doing no injury to any person.

. . . . . .

20.1.8   This case is not at all like the case of *Lord Orkney* — that is, the case with respect to the dam, because there, as I have already intimated, the stream before the erection of the dam flowed harmlessly to the pursuer's mill. Lord Orkney erected a dam, by which he obstructed and headed up the course of the water. He was bound, therefore, under those circumstances — interfering with the stream, and another person's right over the stream, to provide against every contingency. And although it was an extraordinary flood in that case which occasioned the bursting of the dam, it was one which he ought to have provided against. He ought to have made the dam capable of resisting any force which might be directed against it... Under these circumstances, therefore, I agree entirely with my nobled learned friends that the interlocutor appealed from ought to be affirmed.'

COMMENT

20.2.1   Decided: March 3, 1864.
   —English *materiel* seized at Jutland in the Dano-German War.

20.2.2   Lord Cranworth's second sentence consists of 152 words (20.1.6).

20.2.3   This case should be read against the materials contained in Chapter 5.

20.2.4   Although this is certainly a defence to almost all known forms of delictual liability, it may now be of considerably less significance. Referring back to Extract 21, it can be seen that the law of Scotland seems to be fully committing itself, on a doctrinal basis, to liability based on fault. A *damnum fatale* excludes fault, but its main function has been as a defence to strict liability. There may of course still be cases where liability is strict. If liability is strict, or even if *culpa* is likely to be inferred from the happening of an event, *damnum fatale* is likely to constitute a defence. This is because, by definition, it is an event outside the bounds of human foresight and accordingly suggests an absence of fault. The defence probably operates differently in the context of the delict (see *Mustard*, Ext. 30).

Contributory negligence

74. Law Reform (Contributory Negligence) Act 1945
(8 & 9 Geo. 6, c. 28)

20.3.1   '**1.**—(1) Where any person suffers damage as the result partly of his own fault and partly of the fault of any other person or persons, a claim in respect of that damage shall not be defeated by reason of the fault of the person suffering the damage, but the damages recoverable in respect thereof shall be reduced to such extent as the court thinks just and equitable having regard to the claimant's share in the responsibility for the damage:

Provided that—

    (*a*) this subsection shall not operate to defeat any defence arising under a contract;

    (*b*) where any contract or enactment providing for the limitation of liability is applicable to the claim, the amount of damages recoverable by the claimant by virtue of this subsection shall not exceed the maximum limit so applicable.

20.3.2   (2) Where damages are recoverable by any person by virtue of the foregoing subsection subject to such reduction as is therein mentioned, the court shall find and record the total damages which would have been recoverable if the claimant had not been at fault...

20.3.3   (4) Where any person dies as the result partly of his own fault and partly of the fault of any other person or persons, a claim by any dependant of the first mentioned person for damages or solatium in respect of that person's death shall not be defeated by reason of his fault, but the damages or solatium recoverable shall be reduced to such extent as the court thinks just and equitable having regard to the share of the said person in the responsibility for his death.

20.3.4   (5) Where, in any case to which subsection (1) of this section applies, one of the persons at fault avoids liability to any other such person or his personal representative by pleading the Limitation Act 1939, or any other enactment limiting the time within which proceedings may be taken, he shall not be entitled to recover any damages or contributions from that other person or representative by virtue of the said subsection.

20.3.5   (6) Where any case to which subsection (1) of this section applies is tried with a jury, the jury shall determine the total damages which would have been recoverable if the claimant had not been at fault and the extent to which those damages are to be reduced...

20.3.6   **3.**—(1) This Act shall not apply to any claim to which section 1 of the Maritime Conventions Act 1911 applies and the Act shall have effect as if this Act had not passed.

20.3.7   (2) This Act shall not apply to any case where the acts or omissions giving rise to the claim occurred before that passing of this Act.

20.3.8   **4.** The following expressions have the meanings hereby respectively assigned to them, that is to say—

    "court" means, in relation to any claim, the court or arbitrator by or before whom the claim falls to be determined;

    "damage" includes loss of life and personal injury;

    "fault" means negligence, breach of statutory duty or other act or omission which gives rise to a liability in tort or would, apart from this Act, give rise to the defence of contributory negligence.

20.3.9 **5.** In the application of this Act to Scotland—

(*a*) the expression "dependant" means, in relation to any person, any person who would in the event of such first mentioned person's death through the fault of a third party be entitled to sue that third party for damages or solatium; and the expression "fault" means wrongful act, breach of statutory duty or negligent act or omission which gives rise to liability in damages, or would, apart from this Act, give rise to the defence of contributory negligence;

(*b*) section 3 of the Law Reform (Miscellaneous Provisions) (Scotland) Act 1940 (contribution among joint wrongdoers) shall apply in any case where two or more persons are liable, or would if they had all been sued be liable, by virtue of section 1(1) of this Act in respect of the damage suffered by any person.'

75. **Mackay v. Borthwick**
1982 S.L.T. 265

20.4.1 'LORD ROSS: Whether or not it is negligent for a pursuer not to wear a seat belt must depend upon the circumstances of the particular case, and as with all allegations of contributory negligence, the onus of proving that there was a duty to wear a seat belt and that wearing a seat belt would have lessened the injuries, rests upon the defenders.

20.4.2 In the instant case, I am of opinion that the defenders have failed to discharge that onus. In the first place, the pursuer explained that she did not wear a seat belt because she found it uncomfortable to wear because she suffered from a hiatus hernia, and on this particular make of car the seat belt ran across her chest and thus caused discomfort. In cross-examination, she explained that she did wear a seat belt in a smaller car and for long journeys, but that it was not her practice to wear it on short journeys.

I am prepared to accept that, save in exceptional cases, it is the duty of every driver and front-seat passenger to take reasonable precautions for his own safety by wearing a seat belt at all times (*Froom* v. *Butcher* [1976] Q.B. 286). However, I regard the instant case as an exceptional one. The pursuer suffered from hiatus hernia which made it uncomfortable for her to wear a seat belt, and although she was prepared to tolerate such discomfort on long journeys, I do not feel that there was negligence in failing to wear the seat belt on shorter journeys such as the one which she was making at the time of the accident.

20.4.3 In the second place, even if I am not well-founded in concluding that the pursuer's case was exceptional because of the medical condition from which she suffered, I am of opinion that there was no acceptable evidence to indicate that the pursuer's injures would have been lessened if she had been wearing a seat belt at the time of the accident. Counsel for the defender contended that it was obvious that she would not have suffered the facial injuries if she had been wearing the seat belt. There was no evidence about this, but it is certainly possible that a seat belt which ran across her chest near the site of the hernia might have caused her severe injuries... For all I know, the injuries sustained by the pursuer might have been more severe if she had been wearing a seat belt.

. . . . . .

20.4.4 In the third place, even if contrary to my opinion it could be held that the pursuer would not have sustained the facial injuries if she had been wearing a seat belt, there was no material placed before me to enable me to assess what proportion of the blame should be attached to the pursuer. She would still have sustained most of the injuries which she in fact suffered. On the evidence, I feel that any proportion of blame which could properly be attributed to the pursuer would in this case be minimal.'

COMMENT

20.5.1 Decided: Nov. 13, 1981.
   Sept. 14: Seventeen-year-old who fired blanks at Queen sentenced to five years' imprisonment.
   Sept. 18: President Mitterand abolished guillotine.
   Oct. 15: Norman Tebbit made his bicycle speech.
   Nov. 12: Church of England voted to allow women to become deacons.

20.5.2 This case was decided before the legislature made the wearing of seat belts in cars compulsory (S.I. 1982 No. 1203). That regulation permits persons not to wear seat belts if they hold a medical certificate stating that it is inadvisable on medical grounds to wear a belt. How would *McKay* be decided today if the pursuer did not have a medical certificate and did not wear a belt? Consider *Hanlon v. Cuthbertson*, 1981 S.L.T. (Notes) 57 in which a lady did not wear a belt because it was floury and made her dress dirty.
   Do you think a person who sits in with a driver with a provisional licence should be held to be contributorily negligent — see *Buchanan v. Allan*, 1994 G.W.D. 35–2088. Consider *Hughes* (Ext. 41)? Do you think there could have been contribution by the child in that case (Lord Ordinary thought not)? There are many cases involving children. See, *e.g. Banner's Tutor v. Kennedy's Trs.*, 1978 S.L.T. (Notes) 83. Can a defender have contributed by 100 per cent and lose his claim? The lawyer's immediate answer would be yes because prior to the 1945 legislation one per cent of contribution meant zero damages. However, the precise wording of the Act does admit of doubt. See also *Harris v. Abbey National plc*, Sh. Craik, Edin. Sh. Ct., August 28, 1996, allowing the doctrine to apply to damages for the loss of property.

Volenti non fit injuria

76. **Winnick v. Dick (Appellant)**
1984 S.L.T. 185

20.6.1 '[From the report] Eric Anderson raised an action for damages in the Sheriff Court at Edinburgh for damages of £2,000 against Kenneth Dick, junior. On June 16, 1980, the sheriff decerned against the defender for payment to the pursuer of the sum of £375.

The defender appealed to the sheriff principal who, on March 6, 1981 affirmed the interlocutor of the sheriff. The defender appealed to the Court of Session. The case was heard before the Second Division. The circumstances of the case are set out in the opinion of the Lord Justice-Clerk.

The Road Traffic Act 1972 provides:

"148.—... (3) Where a person uses a motor vehicle in circumstances such that under section 143 of this Act there is required to be in force in relation to his use of it such a policy of insurance or security as is mentioned in subsection (1) of that section, then, if any other person is carried in or upon the vehicle while the user is so using it, any antecedent agreement or understanding between them (whether intended to be legally binding or not) shall be of no effect so far as it purports or might be held — (a) to negative or restrict any such liability of the user in respect of persons carried in or upon the vehicle as is required by section 145, of this Act to be covered by a policy of insurance; or (b) to impose any conditions with respect to the enforcement of any such liability of the user; and the fact that a person so carried has willingly accepted as his the risk of negligence on the part of the user shall not be treated as negativing any such liability of the user. For the purposes of this subsection references to a person being carried in or upon a vehicle include references to a person entering or getting on to, or alighting from, the vehicle, and the reference to an antecedent agreement is to one made at any time before the liability arose."

20.6.2 THE LORD JUSTICE-CLERK (Lord Wheatley): On June 30, 1978 the pursuer was a passenger in a motor car driven by the defender which was involved in an accident resulting in certain injuries to the pursuer... The pleadings in the case contain averments normally found in a reparation action arising out of a motor accident, but they had in addition two additional features. In the first place the defender has a plea-in-law, supported by averments, of *volenti non fit injuria*, and when the case was before the sheriff principal the defender added, by way of amendment, a new plea-in-law maintaining that the pursuer was not entitled to recover damages by reason of public policy. The sheriff found that the defender had been guilty of negligence which caused loss, injury and damage to the pursuer, but he also found that the pursuer had been guilty of negligence by reason of (a) his embarking on the motor car's journey when he knew that the driver, *i.e.* the defender, was under the influence of alcohol at the time, and (b) his failure to use a seat belt. The sheriff assessed liability on a 50-50 basis and reduced his computation of damages accordingly. None of these elements in his decision has been challenged by the parties.

20.6.3 The sheriff found that the defender's plea of *volenti non fit injuria* had been established at common law, but he further found that by virtue of the provisions of s. 148(3) of the Road Traffic Act 1972 the fact that the pursuer willingly accepted the risk of negligence on the part of the defender did not negative the liability of the defender. The sheriff principal adhered to the sheriff's decision on these matters, but had to deal with a new matter which was introduced before him but which had not been advanced to the sheriff. This argument was to the effect that public policy should preclude the recovery of damages where the parties are engaged in a common criminal enterprise which was the situation here. There was no record for such an argument; but the defender was allowed to amend his record, without objection, to incorporate a new plea in law to cover it.

20.6.4 It should be noted that no additional averments were made to support that plea-in-law. In the result, however, the sheriff principal rejected this argument, holding that it was a misuse of language to say that the pursuer, because he was being driven by one with excess of alcohol in his blood, was engaged in a criminal enterprise. He pointed out that the defender had been convicted of contraventions of ss. 3 and 6(1) of the Road Traffic Act 1972, but that the pursuer was not charged with acting art and part in the commission of these statutory offences. Nor was there any finding that he was acting art and part, and the sheriff principal was not prepared to proceed on the assumption that he was.

20.6.5 Before this court similar general stances were taken… It seems to me logical to consider first of all whether the pursuer's attack on the sheriff's findings on *volenti* was well founded. If it was, then the defender's arguments do not get off the ground. In considering this — and indeed the other arguments — it has to be remembered that the sheriff's findings-in-fact, which were not challenged by either party, constitute the factual basis against which the legal issues have to be determined. The argument presented by counsel for the pursuer, that the findings-in-fact did not warrant the sheriff's decision on the point, was based on a submission that there was nothing in the findings to show that the accident was caused by reason of the defender's consumption of alcohol. There was accordingly no causal connection between the condition to which the pursuer consented and the accident.

20.6.6 In my opinion this argument can be disposed of shortly. It is true that there is no findings-in-fact to the effect that there was such a causal connection. Pursuer's counsel fastened on the fact that finding no. 14 simply says: "The accident was caused by the fault of the defender." But if the findings are read as a whole, a picture is presented which fills in the bare bones of that finding. In my view this argument has to be rejected.

20.6.7   The case for the appellant took three forms. In the first place it was submitted that there must be a duty to take care before any liability can be incurred, and since *volenti* had been established it meant the pursuer had *ab ante* absolved the defender from taking reasonable care so far as he was concerned. That meant that there was no duty on the defender's part, and accordingly no liability to which the provisions of s. 148(3) could relate. In the second place it was argued that on a proper construction of s. 148(3) the terms thereof did not apply to circumstances such as were present in this case. Finally it was submitted that it would be contrary to public policy to allow one party to a joint criminal enterprise to recover damages from another party in that enterprise in respect of the latter's negligence while engaged in that enterprise.

. . . . . .

20.6.8   On a purely technical basis I find it difficult to entertain an argument which seems to run contrary to the defender's own pleadings. In the circumstances of the accident the pursuer in cond. 3 averred various duties of care which the defender owed to him. Far from asserting that the defender owed no duties of care to the pursuer in the circumstances, the defender opened his averments in ans. 3 with the words: "Admitted that certain duties of care were incumbent of the defender... *quoad ultra* not known and not admitted." He then ascribed certain duties of care which were incumbent upon the pursuer which he followed up with the averment: "The pursuer voluntarily assumed the risk of harm to himself by accepting a lift from the defender when he knew him to be so drunk as to be unable to drive the car safely or exercise reasonable care." There is no plea-in-law which specifically asserts that the defender owed the pursuer no duty to take care in the circumstances.

20.6.9   This argument of the defender seems to be based on an observation of Asquith J. in *Dann* v. *Hamilton* [1939] 1 K.B. 509 where his Lordship said at p. 512: "As a matter of strict pleading it seems that the plea *volenti* is a denial of any duty at all, and, therefore, of any breach of duty, and an admission of negligence cannot strictly be combined with the plea." I pause to observe that the same might be said about an admission of duty. In *Bankhead* v. *McCarthy*, 1936 S.L.T. 144, Lord Walker expressed an *obiter* view to the effect that he was not at all clear that the plea of *volenti* in England operates in the same way as it does in Scotland, and quoted the above passage in the opinion of Asquith J. as illustrative of the English view. He went on to say that in Scotland the plea of *volenti* has never been regarded as being a denial of the duty, but rather as a consent to accept the consequences of a breach of duty. For my part I am content to examine the Scottish view on the matter for the decision in this case. Although in the case of *McCaig* v. *Langan*, 1964 S.L.T. 121, Lord Kilbrandon disagreed with Lord Walker's judgment in *Bankhead* v. *McCarthy*, this was in relation to the decision on contributory negligence and not on what Lord Walker said about *volenti*.

. . . . . .

20.6.10 Finally, in *Fowler* v. *Tierney*, 1974 S.L.T. (Notes) 23, Lord Maxwell said (at p. 23): "In the normal *volenti* case there is required, I think, proof that the pursuer had knowingly submitted himself to some special or exceptional risk in such circumstances that the court can infer from the whole facts that he is consenting to run the risk of the other party's negligence at his own expense or, to put the matter in another way, that he is consenting to lack of reasonable care on the part of the other party."

From these expressions of view as to what is involved in the maxim so far as the law of Scotland is concerned, I can find no support for, but rather refutation of, the contention that its effect here is to establish that on this journey there never was any duty on the defender as the driver of the car to take reasonable care *quoad* the pursuer; that consequently there could never be any liability on the defender at all; and that consequently there could be no liability which fell within the view of s. 148(3) of the Road Traffic Act 1972. In my opinion the effect of the maxim was not to relieve the defender from any duty to take care *quoad* his passengers. On the contrary the maxim proceeds on the basis that there is a duty to take care and not be negligent, but the successful establishment of the maxim means that the pursuer has accepted the risk of the defender's negligence in the exercise of his legal duties and has absolved the defender from the consequences arising from the negligence. So even apart from the technical difficulty of accepting it at all, to which I referred earlier, I am of the opinion that the defender's first argument fails.

20.6.11 I now consider the second submission in relation to the meaning and effect of s. 148(3) aforesaid. Counsel for the defender maintained that the provisions of that subsection had no bearing on a *volenti* case. As I understood the argument, it was that the references to ss. 143 and 145 of the Act in the subsection meant that "liability" therein related throughout to the liability of the user of the car to indemnify third parties entitled to indemnity under a policy of insurance, and not in the three lines following (*b*) to his liability to a passenger in respect of a breach of a legal duty in the use of the car. In my opinion that latter liability in the subsection means the liability in law owed by the user of the vehicle to persons carried therein in respect of whom an insurance policy under s. 145 has been issued. The words used seem to me clearly to relate to the maxim by their very terms. I accordingly reject this argument.

20.6.12   This brings me to the "public policy" argument. This was an argument conjured up by counsel for the defender during the debate before the sheriff principal. It was not addressed to the sheriff, for very obvious reasons. There was neither averment nor plea on the record to warrant it. There was accordingly no evidence led in support of it to ascertain *inter alia* the nature and degree of the crime in which the pursuer and defender were alleged to be engaged jointly. Even the insertion of the new plea-in-law during the debate before the sheriff principal made not the slightest difference to the position so far as averment was concerned and the plea itself, standing in unsplendid isolation, is so vague as to be meaningless. In my opinion it should never have been allowed. It was argued before us that the ingredients of the ground on which the plea is based can be found in the findings-in-fact. I disagree. Defender's counsel were in doubt as to the "crime" in which the pursuer and defender were jointly engaged by way of a common criminal enterprise, and suggested for instance that it was a contravention of the Road Traffic Act 1972 with which neither the defender nor the pursuer had been charged. In view of all these considerations I do not regard a refusal to entertain this ground of appeal as simply a technical decision. The defence which counsel sought to erect is one which could have far-reaching effects, and is one which could give rise to delicate decisions on what is embraced in "crime" in this context. It would be very unfortunate if such matters had to be decided on barren pleadings and the absence of evidence which exist here. I am accordingly of the opinion that this defence should not be entertained in the circumstances here present, and in that situation it seems to me to be inadvisable to express any views on the law on the subject.'

COMMENT

20.7.1   Decided: November 22, 1983.
   Oct. 5: Lech Walesa awarded Nobel Prize.
   Nov. 4: 39 Israeli soldiers killed by kamikaze Arab lorry bomber.

20.7.2   *Volenti* is a very difficult defence to locate in the structure of the modern law. Its roots are said to lie in the philosophy of Aristotle and in the Roman law. (See generally, Ingman, 1981 J.R. 1.) A freeman could not be treated as a slave, so some unscrupulous enterprising Romans would sell one another into slavery, pocket the money and then arrange to have the freeman liberated the next day. To prevent this the doctrine of *volenti non fit injuria* was applied, and the confidence trickster treated as a slave. In Roman law it may have been what we would now describe as an estoppel or personal bar or even a waiver. It has generally been treated as a defence in its own right. It is sometimes called a principle, sometimes a doctrine and sometimes a maxim. It is difficult to distinguish it from (1) another defence called consent; (2) a finding that there is no duty owed to the defender in the circumstances; (3) a finding of 100 per cent contributory negligence; or (4) that the pursuer was the sole cause of his injuries.

20.7.3   The House of Lords gave the defence some support in the case of *Titchiner v. B.R.B.* (Ext. 64) to which the reader is referred especially at 16.5.8.

20.7.4   In England the relationship between the existence of a duty of care and the defence of *volenti* has been perceived. Consider the views of Diplock L.J. in *Wooldridge v. Sumner* [1963] 2 Q.B. 43: "The spectator takes the risk because such an act involves no breach of the duty of care owed by the participant to him. He does not take the risk by virtue of the doctrine expressed or obscured by the maxim *volenti non fit injuria*. That maxim states a principle of estoppel applicable originally to a Roman citizen who consented to being sold as a slave ... In my view, the maxim in the absence of expressed contract has no application to negligence *simpliciter* where the duty of care is based solely upon proximity or 'neighbourship' in the Atkinian sense ... With the development of the law of negligence in the last 20 years a more consistent explanation of this type of case is that the test of liability on the part of the person creating the dangerous physical condition is whether it was reasonably foreseeable by him that the plaintiff would so act in relation to it as to endanger himself" (at p. 69). This seems to be a sound statement of the law and consistent with the Scottish distinction between intentional and unintentional harm. See the English Court of Appeal decision in relation to this dictum in *Morris v. Murray*, 1990 N.L.J. 1459 at 1460, in which it appears the maxim was applied in a case of negligence *Simpliciter*.

Ex turpi causa non oritur actio

77. **Weir v. Wyper**
1992 S.L.T. 579

20.8.1   'A passenger in a car was seriously injured when the car, which she alleged was being driven in a negligent manner, left the road and overturned. The passenger was then 16 years of age. The driver held only a provisional driving licence and was later convicted of careless driving and driving without being supervised by a qualified driver. The passenger raised an action of damages against the driver of the car. The driver admitted the accident and subsequent conviction but averred that the passenger knew at the relevant time that he was not being supervised, and nonetheless asked him to drive her home. The driver further averred that he and his passenger were therefore engaged in a common criminal activity. The passenger admitted that she knew that the driver had only a provisional licence but averred that when she started the journey, there was a supervising driver present, who got out of the car with another person in a country lane. When they did not return, the passenger became anxious at being where she was late on a December evening and asked to be taken home. The accident then occurred. The driver argued that the maxim *ex turpi causa non oritur actio* applied.

20.8.2   LORD COULSFIELD: In my opinion, the Scottish authorities, far from supporting the contention of counsel for the defender that Scots law has adopted a firm rule that participation in any type of criminal conduct, however minor, disables an injured party from recovering damages, indicate that the matter is one of the particular facts.

20.8.3   That view is also, in my opinion, consistent with the Australian and English cases to which I was referred. In *Jackson v. Harrison* [(1978)

138 C.L.R. 438] the High Court of Australia held, by a majority of four to one, that where a passenger was injured through the negligent driving of a person who was disqualified from holding a driver's licence, to the passenger's knowledge, the passenger was not disabled from recovering damages. Three of the judges in the majority held that illegality did not bear on the standard of care reasonably to be expected of the driver and the fourth held that the relevant statutory provisions did not require recovery of damages to be denied and the driver exempted from liability. Much of the discussion in the case concerned a previous decision of the High Court, *Smith* v. *Jenkins* [(1970) 117 C.L.R. 397], in which recovery was denied in a case where the driver and the injured party were concerned in taking a car without the owner's consent. It is, I think, clear that the judges of the majority regarded the rule which denies recovery to the injured person as an application of public policy and that none of them was prepared to accept that there were sufficient grounds of public policy for the imposition of the rule in the case of any joint criminal enterprise irrespective of the nature or seriousness of it or its relevance to the standard of care. The judges expressed their views in somewhat different ways, but the general approach taken can, I think, be seen in the following passage from the judgment of Mason J. (at p. 453): "The elimination of civil liability between the participants in a joint criminal enterprise cannot be sustained on the ground that it is a deterrent against criminal activity; it might with equal force be put forward as an inducement to such activity. Even if punishment of illegal conduct is not a matter for the exclusive attention of the criminal law, as I think it should be, a policy of deterrence directed against the participants in a joint criminal enterprise but not against the individual criminal makes very little sense. In point of policy the application of the ex turpi causa doctrine would be less susceptible to criticism.

"A rule so absolute in its terms as to preclude the bringing of an action by a passenger in a motor vehicle who is injured through the negligence of a driver when the passenger knows that the driver is committing a breach of the law in driving the vehicle because he is unlicensed or because the vehicle's equipment does not comply in all respects with motor traffic requirements is too draconian to command acceptance. There is nothing inherent in the character of an unlicensed driver which is inconsistent with his owing a duty of care to other road users and to his passengers who happen to be engaged in unlawful activity."

20.8.4 Barwick C.J., who dissented, was prepared to apply a rule which would deny recovery to a participant in a criminal course of conduct irrespective of the nature or seriousness of the conduct in question, but even he was prepared to concede that there were some statutory offences to which the principle would not apply (see at p. 451).

20.8.5 The Court of Appeal decision is *Pitts* v. *Hunt* [[1991] 1 Q.B. 24], a case in which the plaintiff and a friend spent the evening drinking at a disco before setting off on the friend's motorcycle. The plaintiff was aware that the motorcyclist was neither licensed to ride a motorcycle nor insured. Nevertheless, on the journey, the plaintiff encouraged the cyclist to ride the cycle in a fast, reckless and hazardous manner, deliberately designed to frighten members of the public. This conduct eventually led to a collision with an oncoming car in which the plaintiff was severely injured. As I read the judgments, none of the judges was prepared to lay down a strict or absolute role…

20.8.6 Balcombe L.J. quoted and approved a passage from the judgment of Mason J. in *Jackson* v. *Harrison* and based his conclusion on the view that the circumstances of the particular case were such as to preclude the court from finding that the deceased owed a duty of care to the plaintiff. Dillon L.J. also quoted from the judgments in *Jackson* v. *Harrison* and observed that for relief to be denied on the ground of the illegality, the circumstances of the joint illegal venture in the course of which the accident which caused the plaintiff's injuries occurred must be such as to negate, as between the parties, any ordinary standard of care.

20.8.7 It therefore appears to me that the only judge who has been prepared to adopt the absolute rule contended for by counsel for the defender in the present case is Barwick C.J. in *Jackson* v. *Harrison* and, as I have observed, even he did so with qualifications. It follows, in my view, that these two authorities support the view that the proper course is to examine the whole facts and circumstances before attempting to arrive at a conclusion.

20.8.8 I would add that it is, in my view, easy to envisage circumstances in which the denial of a right to recover damages to a person driven by an unqualified driver would be plainly wrong: take, for example, the case of an unqualified driver conveying a nurse who is not herself a qualified driver, to attend to a person who is seriously ill. In the present case, the pursuer, a 16 year old girl, found herself alone with the defender late at night on a country road. She may not have been prudent in allowing herself to be placed in that situation but that is not the issue. I find it hard to see that, given this situation, it could be said that in allowing, or even asking, the defender to drive her home she was participating in any significant criminal activity or that any reasonable application of public policy would deny her a right to recover damages for injuries caused by negligent driving on the part of the defender. Nevertheless, for the reasons I have indicated, the question is, in my view, one depending on the particular facts and circumstances and the proper course is to allow a proof before answer.'

COMMENT

20.9.1 Decided March 25, 1992.
  March 25: Punch magazine ceased publication.
  April 10: IRA blow up Baltic Exchange in London, killing three people.
  April 12: Euro-Disney opens in Paris.

20.9.2 See *Clunis v. Camden Health Authority* [1996] T.L.R. 752 for an English case treating the defence as "flexible" and not strictly applicable in tort cases. See para. 20.6.12 for a wise refusal to consider the topic without full agreement.

Prescription

78. Renfrew Golf Club v. Ravenstone Securities Ltd
1984 S.L.T. 170

20.10.1 'A golf club raised an action against a property development company and against a building company. The case against the development company was based upon an alleged failure to provide what had been contracted for, a new golf course properly designed and constructed, and upon their negligence in making that provision. The case against the builders was a case in negligence for failing properly to construct the golf course. Both defenders pleaded that any right of action had prescribed, the golf club having been aware of damage more than five years before the raising of the action.

20.10.2 LORD ALLANBRIDGE: [After dealing with certain matters not reported his Lordship continued:] Having heard the argument of counsel, the main question for me to answer at this stage of the action is when did the injuria and damnum concur so as to give the pursuers a right of action. The sections of the Prescription and Limitation (Scotland) Act 1973 which have primarily to be considered in determining this issue are s. 6(1) and s. 11(1). As was stated by Lord Justice-Clerk Wheatley in *Dunlop* v. *McGowans* (1979 S.L.T. at p. 37): "The crucial subsection is 11(1), which provides that for the purposes of s. 6 the obligation shall be regarded as having become enforceable on the date when the loss, injury or damage occurred. This determines the point from which the prescriptive period starts to run. 'Enforceable' means that there has been created a legal right which can be enforced through the processes of the law. That means that a point has to be reached when there is a concurrence of injuria and damnum. The key question thereby becomes: 'what is *damnum?*'" Now, whilst the case of *Dunlop v. McGowans* was concerned with whether separate items of loss which continued to arise after the initial loss could be held to constitute separate and distinct causes of action and the Second Division answered that question in the negative, the key question in the present case is also "what is *damnum?*" On that matter, and in the context of this case, I find the very recent observations of

Lord Fraser in the English case of *Pirelli General Cable Works Ltd.* v. *Oscar Faber & Partners* [[1983] 2 A.C. 1] to be of great assistance. Lord Fraser said: "I think, with all respect to Geoffrey Lane L.J., that there is an element of confusion between *damage* to the plaintiff's body and latent defect in the foundations of a building. Unless the defect is very gross, it may never lead to any damage at all to the building. It would be analogous to a predisposition or natural weakness in the human body which may never develop into disease or injury. The plaintiff's cause of action will not accrue until *damage* occurs, which will commonly consist of cracks coming into existence as a result of the defect even though the cracks or the defect may be undiscovered and undiscoverable". It is to be noted that Lord Fraser went on to explain that he did not find the distinction between personal injuries and damage to property drawn in the case of *Sparham-Souter* v. *Town and Country Developments (Essex) Ltd.* [[1976] 2 All E.R. 65] (referred to by counsel for the third defenders in this case) convincing and observed that in the later case of *Dennis v. Charnwood Borough Council* [[1983] Q.B. 409] (also referred to by counsel for the third defenders) the Court of Appeal had found the distinction surprising. Be that as it may, it is quite clear that Lord Fraser's clear distinction between defect and damage arising in cases of damage to property, is of high authority. It was concurred in by all the other judges in the House of Lords. Whilst the result in *Pirelli* was primarily concerned with the question of when the damage was discovered or was discoverable, a problem which does not arise in Scotland due to the terms of s. 11 (3), the distinction between defect and actual damage to a building or other property is of vital importance and must be applied by me in this case. Thus in the case of a golf course any defect in design or workmanship will not give rise to damnum until actual damage is caused to the course. Such damage could be manifested in many ways but water lying on the greens and not draining away is a clear indication of underlying defects which are causing damage and interference on the playing surface.

20.10.3 With that reference to the law, as I understand it, applicable to this case I turn to the facts of this case and the arguments of counsel. The facts can briefly be summarised as far as the question of prescription is concerned. In 1969 and 1970 the first defenders as a development company wished to acquire the pursuers' original golf course and offered to construct a new golf course for them. The first defenders and the third defenders agreed in April 1971 that the third defenders would be the main contractors. It is noteworthy that nothing is said in the pleadings on record as to any finishing date for the construction of the new course or any specific date of entry being given to the pursuers. Whilst the golf course was in the course of construction and before it was handed over to them, the pursuers became aware the greens were flooding and considered that considerable work would be required to remedy this situation and wrote to the first defenders in December 1971 to this effect. The first defenders obtained a report in early 1972 from John R. Stutt Ltd. and between 1972 and 1973 further works were carried out on the course by John R. Stutt Ltd. During the period from 1973 until 1977 there were no further complaints regarding the greens as there was no cause for complaint. In May 1973, before the remedial work was completed, the golf course was handed over to the pursuers and that remedial work was completed by September 1973 when the course was officially opened. In late 1976 the greens had for the first time to be closed after even moderate amounts of rain and in May 1977, the Sports Turf Research Institute referred for the first time to drainage problems first emerging. On 29 December 1980 the pursuers raised the present action against the first defenders and brought in the third defenders as defenders on 26 February 1981.

20.10.4 Turning to the arguments of all six counsel which were clearly put forward it was interesting that as the debate continued the first date founded on as the terminus a quo by the first and third defenders, namely, the date of the letter in December 1971, became more difficult to argue. This was because there was no apparent date agreed for the handing over of the new golf course and as at December 1971, the course was still in the course of construction. That being so it was difficult, if not impossible, to argue that the pursuers had then suffered any loss because they were not then the owners of the golf course. They had a contract to receive a new golf course from the first defenders but it had not then been given to them. For that reason I am of the opinion that the pursuers had suffered no damnum and had no cause of action in December 1971. Counsel for the third defenders, in the fifth speech, tried to argue that the pursuers had incurred expense in obtaining a technical report and legal advice and therefore had a claim against the third defenders as at December 1971. On this matter I agree with counsel for the pursuers that, as the pursuers had merely sought advice in mid-contract, which they had no legal right (sic) to do as they could have awaited the handing over of a completed golf course, they could not have sued anyone for such expenses incurred before the contract was completed and the golf course handed over. By the time the course was handed over it appeared that the damage to the golf course in respect of flooded greens had been corrected by the remedial work.

20.10.5 The next terminus a quo argued for by both defenders was May 1973 when the golf course was handed over to the pursuers, albeit remedial work was not then finished. The problem regarding this date for both defenders is that by this time there was no damnum, as the matter was explained by Lord Fraser in *Pirelli*. By May 1973 some remedial work had been carried out and as at that date there was then no damage, according to the pursuers' averments, to the playing surface of the golf course. Whether or not there were then underlying defects in the golf course which had not been corrected or eradicated by the remedial work is not conclusive when considering whether or not there was damnum as at that date. What is conclusive and what matters is whether there was actual damage to the playing surface of the golf course or, in any event, in terms of s. 11(3) of the Act, actual damage of which the pursuers were aware or ought with reasonable diligence to have been aware. On the present pleadings in this case I am clearly of the opinion that I cannot at this stage of the case on procedure roll, be satisfied that as at May 1973, injuria and damnum had then occurred so as to give the pursuers an "enforceable obligation" in terms of s. 11(1) of the Act against either the first or third defenders. In fact on the pleadings it would appear that the earliest date they could have had such an obligation would have been in late 1976 when the playing surface of the course was such that the greens had to be closed after even moderate amounts of rain. Thus the five-year period would not have expired earlier than late 1981, and the present action against both defenders was raised before that date and it is therefore not time-barred.

20.10.6 In this situation I am not prepared to dismiss the action at this stage on the grounds of prescription.'

COMMENT

20.11.1 Decided: October 28, 1983.

20.11.2 Although *Dunlop* is the weightier case this one is with short compass and shows how such cases are argued with parties taking a view on the possible starting and finishing dates. See the Act which is Appendix, Ext. 10, and *Delict*, 11.37. For a full treatment see Walker (5th ed. 1996). See the Scottish Law Commission Report on Prescription and Limitation of Actions (Latent Damage and Other Related Issues) S.L.C. No. 122. See Stewart, W.J., "Reparation — Prescription and Limitation", 1994 J.L.S. 374. MacQueen, H., "Latent Defects, Collateral Warranties and Time Bar", 1991 S.L.T. (News) 77, 91, 99.

Limitation

79. **Elliot v. J. & C. Finney**
1989 S.L.T. 208 (O.H.); 1989 S.L.T. 605 (I.H.)

20.12.1 'LORD SUTHERLAND: The pursuer sustained injury in a motor accident on 23 March 1983. The pursuer's car was struck by an articulated lorry owned by the defenders and driven by one of their employees. The defenders' driver was subsequently convicted of a contravention of s. 3 of the Road Traffic Act 1972. Although averments are made in the pleadings to the effect that the accident was partly caused by fault on the part of the pursuer, it should be said that throughout the negotiations for settlement it was never suggested by the defenders' insurers that liability should be repudiated in whole or in part and a similar concession was made by counsel for the defenders at this proof.

20.12.2 After the accident the pursuer was taken to Dundee Royal Infirmary where he was found to be suffering from multiple injuries including a fracture of the frontal bone of the skull, fracture of the nasal bones, fractured ribs and a fractured ankle. That evening an operation was performed on the skull and the nasal fractures and a box frame splint was applied to his head. It is likely that for a short period after the accident the pursuer was unconscious but he was conscious when taken by ambulance to the Infirmary and on admission to the ward he was said to be "alert, co-operative and fully orientated". Neurological observations were taken because of the nature of the injury but at no stage did he show any abnormal neurological state. On 25 March 1983 the pursuer was visited in hospital by P.C. Mackie who was the police officer in charge of the inquiry into the accident. The pursuer in evidence recollected his visit, remembered that he had asked the officer whether he was in any way to blame for the accident and was reassured by the officer that he was in no way to blame. The pursuer accepted that he could have asked the officer for the name and address of the driver of the lorry but said that at that stage it was of no interest to him to find out these details. The evidence of P.C. Mackie was to the effect that before visiting the pursuer he had obtained permission from the ward sister. By the time he visited the pursuer he had virtually completed his inquiries and was satisfied that the accident was not caused to any extent by fault on the part of the pursuer. He had already charged the driver of the lorry with careless driving. His purpose in visiting the pursuer was to take a short formal statement from him, which he did. Had the pursuer asked the identity of the driver of the lorry the officer would have given him this information. I am quite satisfied on the evidence led before me that if the pursuer had wished to find out on 25 March the particulars of the defenders and of their driver he would have been able to do so from P.C. Mackie. I accept that the pursuer was at that time in considerable discomfort and no doubt he was much more concerned about his recovery and to be satisfied that he was not in any way to blame for the accident rather than trying to find out the precise details of the driver of the lorry. While this is perfectly understandable it must be made clear that there was in my opinion no medical reason whatever why the pursuer should not have asked these questions had he so wished.

20.12.3 Shortly after the pursuer's release from hospital on 2 April 1983 his solicitor, with whom he was in contact in connection with other matters, advised him that a claim for compensation would be appropriate. Steps were then taken by his solicitor to obtain the necessary information from the police and on 13 May 1983 a claim was intimated to the defenders at their head office in Manchester. On 19 May the defenders replied from that office intimating that the claim had been passed to their insurers and the letter heading disclosed that the defenders had an address in Glasgow. Thereafter negotiations were carried out between the pursuer's solicitor and the defenders' insurers initially in Manchester and subsequently from their Glasgow office. While the claim was a straightforward one on the merits the matter of damages gave rise to considerable problems. The pursuer had been employed as a consultant psychiatrist and after the accident was off work until about July 1983. He then tried to return to work but found that his concentration was impaired and he was only able to work part time. Ultimately in May 1984 he felt that he could no longer continue his work and felt obliged to resign. Not surprisingly the defenders' insurers wished to be satisfied that his decision was justified on medical grounds and a number of medical reports were thereafter obtained. There were also problems relating to the pursuer's pension entitlement position. The pursuer's solicitor ultimately obtained sufficient information to put before counsel and counsel's opinion on the value of the claim was obtained in about October 1985. Eventually on 28 January 1986 the pursuer's solicitor intimated to the insurance company that the claim was valued at £140,000 and that unless proposals from the insurers were made within 10 days for settlement the pursuer would proceed to instruct court proceedings. No reply was received to this letter and I should say that I do not blame the insurers in any way for that in that the pursuer's solicitor's letter enclosed 26 pages of documentation in connection with the claim but without showing in any way how the figure of £140,000 was made up.

20.12.4 Because no reply was received the pursuer's solicitor instructed Edinburgh agents to raise an action by letter dated 11 February 1986. Certain additional papers were required and these were received by the Edinburgh agents on 14 February 1986. Counsel was duly instructed and a draft summons was received by the solicitors sometime before 6 March 1986. The draft summons stated the address for the defenders as being their Glasgow address, this information being obtained from the defenders' letter of May 1983. The summons was signeted on 6 March 1986. The court partner in the firm of Edinburgh solicitors, Mr Ritchie, decided that because of the proximity of the expiry of the triennium the appropriate course of action would be to have the defenders cited personally at their Scottish premises by messengers at arms. Mr Ritchie was out of the office on 7 March and as far as he can recollect may have also been out of the office on some days at least in the following week. He was married on 14 March and was away from the office until 24 March. On 13 March he instructed a second year trainee to transmit the summons to messengers at arms for personal service on the defenders. His evidence was that the trainee was well aware that the triennium was due to expire on 23 March and his instructions to the trainee were to make this clear to the messengers at arms. On 14 March the trainee dictated instructions to the messengers at arms but the letter did not contain any reference to the expiry of the triennium. Mr Ritchie accepted that the trainee had not carried out his instructions in specific terms. Although the letter was dictated on 14 March 1986 there were difficulties in getting the letters typed and it appears that partly because the trainee did not have sufficient influence in the office the letter did not get typed until 19 March. The letter and the summons for service were sent to the messengers at arms on that day. The messengers at arms acknowledged receipt of the summons on 20 March and wrote that the instructions would be carried out timeously. On 20 March the messengers attempted to find the defenders' address but ascertained that the whole site had been cleared to make way for the Glasgow Garden Festival. The messengers had not noticed that the triennium was due to expire on 23 March and accordingly made inquiries to try to find the defenders at another address in Glasgow. These inquires were fruitless but delayed matters until 26 March on which date they contacted Mr Ritchie to inform him of the position. Mr Ritchie immediately telephoned the defenders at their Manchester address and was told that they no longer had an address in Scotland. He accordingly served the summons postally upon them on 27 March. It is a matter of agreement that the summons was received on 29 March by the defenders and that that is the date upon which service was effected upon them.

20.12.5 The defenders' first plea in law is that the pursuer's action not having been raised until more than three years after the date of the accident it is barred by lapse of time. The pursuer's third plea in law is to the effect that the pursuer was not aware and it was not reasonably practicable for him to have been aware that the defenders were persons to whose act or omission his injuries were attributable until at least 2 April 1983 and that accordingly the action is not barred by lapse of time. I assume that this date has been chosen because it was the date on which the pursuer was released from hospital. The pursuer's fourth plea in law is that separatim in the circumstances it is equitable that the court permit the pursuer to proceed with the action in terms of s. 19A of the Prescription and Limitation (Scotland) Act 1973. The case appeared on procedure roll when a preliminary proof was allowed. The defenders reclaimed against this interlocutor but the reclaiming motion was refused. The proof which I heard was the preliminary proof relating to matters of time bar.

20.12.6 I deal first with the pursuer's contention that the triennium had not in fact expired by 29 March 1986. Section 17(2) of the Prescription and Limitation (Scotland) Act 1973 provides as follows: [his Lordship quoted the terms of the subsection set out supra, and continued:] It was conceded by counsel for the pursuer that at least by 25 March 1983 the pursuer was aware that his injuries were sufficiently serious to justify his bringing an action of damages and that his injuries were attributable in whole or in part to an act or omission on the part of the lorry driver. The contention was that it was not reasonably practicable for him to become aware as at that date of the identity of the person to whose act or omission the injuries were attributable. Counsel stressed that in terms of the section it was necessary to be reasonably practicable for the pursuer himself to acquire the necessary knowledge. Accordingly his state of mind at the material time is of the utmost materiality. If for example the pursuer was in a coma it would not be possible let alone reasonably practicable for him to acquire the necessary knowledge. While counsel accepted that it would have been practicable within the normal meaning of that word for the pursuer to ask P.C. Mackie for the name and address of the offending lorry driver it was not reasonably practicable for him to do so because of his state of mind at the material time. The evidence of Mr Jacobson, a consultant neurosurgeon, and of the ward sister indicated that patients suffering from severe injuries following upon accidents do not normally inquire as to the particulars of the other party involved. It was therefore not reasonable to expect the pursuer to make these inquiries on 25 March whereas it would be reasonable to expect him to make the inquiries as at 2 April when he was released from hospital.

20.12.7 In my opinion this argument cannot succeed. There is no doubt that the pursuer at the time when he saw P.C. Mackie was perfectly capable of asking a number of questions relating to the accident and would have been perfectly capable of asking for the particulars of the lorry driver. While it may be, although I do not need to decide this matter, that a pursuer who was in a coma might be in a different position, that does not assist the present pursuer in any way. I note that in s. 17(3) it is provided that in the computation of time there shall be disregarded any time during which the pursuer who sustained the injuries was under legal disability by reason of nonage or unsoundness of mind. It could at least be argued that a person in a coma was not at the material time of sound mind and accordingly that s. 17(3) would cover the situation of a pursuer in a coma. The question that has to be decided is not whether the pursuer had a reasonable excuse for not asking the material questions but whether it would have been reasonably practicable for him to do so. In my opinion it would be reasonably practicable for a pursuer to become aware of necessary information if he would be able to do so without excessive expenditure of time, effort or money. I do not consider that the mere fact that he did not feel like asking these questions can in any way render the acquiring of the information not reasonably practicable. In my view it would have been reasonably practicable for him to obtain the necessary information from P.C. Mackie on 25 March 1983 and accordingly on any view the triennium expired on 25 March 1986. That is all that it is necessary for me to decide for the purposes of this case. I would not wish it to be thought however that I am necessarily deciding that the triennium could not commence at a date prior to 25 March 1983. I shall accordingly repel the pursuer's third plea in law.

20.12.8   The pursuer's alternative contention was that the court should in the exercise of its discretion allow the pursuer to proceed with the present action. Section 19A has been the subject of many decisions and the principles to be adopted in deciding whether or not to apply the discretion contained therein are fully set out in three Inner House cases, *Donald* v. *Rutherford* [1984 S.L.T. 70], *Forsyth* v. *A. F. Stoddard & Co. Ltd.* [1985 S.L.T. 51] and *Anderson* v. *City of Glasgow District Council* [1987 S.L.T. 279]. It is clear that the onus is on the pursuer to persuade the court that it is equitable to exercise discretion in his favour. The exercise of discretion is unfettered, the basic principle being that the interests of the parties should be balanced and a decision taken on an equitable basis. There are a number of factors which are relevant and perhaps two of the important ones are in the first place that the exercise of discretion in the pursuer's favour will inevitably prejudice the defenders in that they lose the statutory protection conferred upon them by s. 17 of the Act, and in the second place that if the pursuer has an alternative remedy the discretion should not so freely be exercised in his favour. Other considerations are the behaviour of the parties and their advisers, and also the extent of the delay judged against the background of the circumstances in which the triennium came to be exceeded.

20.12.9   In the present case the conduct of the pursuer as an individual and of the defenders and their insurers is not in question. It was not suggested that the defenders would suffer any prejudice over and above the clearly important prejudice that they would lose their right of protection under s. 17. Counsel for the defenders founded strongly upon the fact that the pursuer would have a good right of action against the Edinburgh solicitors. Evidence was given on behalf of the defenders by Mr Gibb, an experienced solicitor in litigation matters. His view was that there was negligence in failing to communicate to the messengers at arms the fact that the triennium was due to expire on 23 March. He also considered that it was very difficult to justify the delay between 6 March when the summons was signeted and 13 March when Mr Ritchie got round to instructing that the summons should be served, and the delay between 14 March and 19 March in actually sending the service copy to the messengers at arms appeared to be negligent. It would not be appropriate for me in this action to decide positively whether or not the Edinburgh solicitors were negligent. It is sufficient to say that it seems to me that they would have very grave difficulties in trying to persuade any court that they were not negligent in the whole circumstances of this case.

20.12.10 That however is not an end of the matter. Mr Gibb also gave evidence to the effect that the action against the Edinburgh solicitors would not be entirely straightforward. If he was acting for the insurers of the Edinburgh solicitors he would do his best to try to find some ground upon which the messengers at arms could be brought into the action as third parties. Because of the size of the pursuer's claim even a 10 per cent contribution from the messengers at arms or their insurers would be of value. There would also be the possibility that the solicitors' insurers would be tempted to try to bring in the local agents, on the view that they had delayed excessively in sending the papers to their Edinburgh correspondents. Mr Gibb's view on that matter however was that there was no question of negligence on the part of the local agents as the sending of papers to Edinburgh correspondents five weeks before the expiry of the triennium was in his experience if anything on the generous side. In my view it is unlikely that any statable case could be made against the local agents and I therefore disregard that possibility. As far as the messengers at arms are concerned, evidence was given by Mr Carrera, a partner in the firm of Abernethy McIntyre, the messengers at arms concerned. He was aware that time bar could be a problem in actions of reparation but said that he only looked at the summons to ascertain the date of expiry of a triennium if this matter had been drawn to his attention by the solicitors' letter of instruction. It was not the practice of his firm to read the summons to ascertain dates although if by any chance he was aware of the date of expiry of a triennium he would treat the matter with particular urgency. As things stand therefore, I cannot say that any ground of fault on the part of the messengers at arms has been established in this proof. This does not however exclude the possibility that the solicitors' insurers might be able to obtain evidence as to practice of other messengers of arms when dealing with reparation summonses. As Mr Gibb said, it would be tempting to bring them in as third parties in the hope of getting a contribution.

20.12.11 While therefore I am satisfied that there is a very strong likelihood of the pursuer succeeding in an action of professional negligence against the Edinburgh solicitors, it does not follow that this action could be brought to a conclusion in a short period of time. If the messengers at arms were brought in as third parties and the case was fought, it could take up to two years before the pursuer would obtain his compensation. The pursuer does not have the benefit of legal aid in this case because of his financial circumstances. It follows that if this action is dismissed he will be liable in the whole expenses of the action to the defenders and this amount will be immediately payable. He would then require to fund the next action against his solicitors. It is perfectly true that assuming he succeeds against his solicitors at the end of the day he will recover from them the whole expense to which he has been put and will also receive interest on any payments which he has made. I do regard it however as being of importance that not only may he be delayed some considerable time in receiving any compensation at all but he will require to find not insubstantial sums in the interim period. Counsel for the defenders stressed that the prejudice to the defenders in having to meet a substantial claim would be a real and permanent one whereas the prejudice to the pursuer in having to sue his solicitors would be a temporary one. In considering this factor I bear this criticism in mind. Counsel for the pursuer founded upon certain other matters as being relevant. In the first place the Edinburgh solicitors had the fullest information on quantification of the claim including the benefit of counsel's opinion and they might be in possession of information which would reduce the value of the claim to the pursuer. This however is wholly speculative and I do not take this factor into account. Counsel then founded on the fact that there was no delay in dealing with the matter initially and there was no delay in serving the summons as soon as it was realised that the triennium had expired. The failure to serve the summons timeously arose out of a chapter of accidents. There was therefore no gross negligence on the part of the solicitors for which the pursuer must be held responsible. I accept that this is not a case of wilful negligence on the part of the solicitors and there is no doubt that the delay in effecting service is at the most six days. Finally it was argued by counsel for the pursuer that the defenders were in no way prejudiced in their investigation of the claim and were in fact in a position on receipt of the local agents' letter of 10 January 1986 to make a final proper quantification of the pursuer's claim. I accept that this also is a factor to be put in the balance although perhaps not too much weight in the circumstances of this case should be attached to it.

20.12.12 Having weighed all the relevant factors as best I can, I have come to be of opinion that in the particular circumstances of this case it would be equitable to allow the present action to proceed. I reach this conclusion after balancing the likely prejudice to the pursuer against the undoubted prejudice to the defenders if the action proceeds, bearing in mind the explanation for the action not having been brought timeously and the fact that the delay is one of only six days. In these circumstances I shall repel the first and second pleas in law for the defenders and sustain the fourth plea in law for the pursuer.'

. . . . . .

80. And on appeal—
1989 S.L.T. 605 (I.H.)

20.12.13 'LORD DUNPARK: In my opinion there is no substance in the defenders' criticism of the Lord Ordinary's approach. He did not take into account the irrelevant factors or omit to consider relevant ones. All the factors that he considered were relevant circumstances and it was for him to assess their weight seriatim and cumulatively. I find the Lord Ordinary's opinion and conclusion to be entirely satisfactory. The circumstances of this case, in my opinion, exactly fit the objective of s. 19A. This is not a stale claim case. The defenders' driver who caused the pursuer's injuries was subsequently convicted of careless driving. It has never been suggested that the pursuer was in any way to blame for the accident and, as the Lord Ordinary notes, the defenders' insurers have never suggested that they could escape full liability for the pursuer's injuries. But for "the chapter of accidents" which prevented the summons from being served timeously, the defenders' insurers would have by now reimbursed the pursuer in full. I am sure that, if this action had been dismissed, Lord Diplock would have regarded the exclusion of the defenders' liability to the pursuer "as being in the nature of a windfall" (see *Thompson* v. *Brown* [1981] 1 W.L.R. at p. 750).

20.12.14 While it may be that the pursuer would eventually recover full reparation from his solicitors' insurers, I consider that the Lord Ordinary gave due weight to the factors of delay and the financial burdens which would rest upon the pursuer if this case were to be dismissed and came to the correct conclusion that it was equitable in all the circumstances for this action to proceed.

. . . . . .

20.12.15 I therefore agree that this reclaiming motion should be refused, that we should adhere to the Lord Ordinary's interlocutors dated 24 June and 1 July 1988 and remit the cause to the Lord Ordinary to proceed as accords.'

COMMENT

20.13.1 Decided: June 24, 1988.
June 30: Archbishop Lefevre severs all links with Rome, installing four bishops himself.
July 4: Boris Becker beaten by Stefan Edberg at Wimbledon.
July 6: Piper Alpha oil rig blows up. Litigation continues as this edition goes to press.

20.13.2   One day reader, you might be that trainee! It is a lesson both for the trainee *and* the employer to have a system of prioritisation in an office. My own system is of red, amber and green letters. The partners secretary must type a trainee's red in priority to a partner's ambers and greens. Of course, a trainee who cried "red" with every letter would be eaten by the wolves. Phone the sheriff officers if there is an urgent coming. Even doing all that there is always the thing you have not thought of to worry about!

20.13.3   There are very many cases on the separate issues of the starting date and the discretion. Many are digested in Stewart, W. J., "Reparation — Prescription and Limitation", 1994 J.L.S. 374. For a close examination of a specific difficult and practical problem — see Wade, P., "Time Bar in Disease cases", 1995 Rep. B. 6–2.

CHAPTER 21

VERBAL INJURIES

DEFAMATION

Communication

81. **Ramsay v. MacLay & Co. (Appellants)**
(1890) 18 R. 130

21.1.1 'The Lord Ordinary (Kinnear) approved this issue:—
"Whether the defenders wrote and sent, or caused to be written and sent to the pursuer a letter in the terms contained in the schedule hereto annexed [*i.e.* the letter of February 20, 1890], and whether the said letter is of and concerning the pursuer, and falsely and calumniously represents that he had dishonestly appropriated moneys belonging to the defenders, to the loss, injury, and damage of the pursuer?

"NOTE.—The words of which the pursuer complains are not in themselves actionable; but the innuendo which he proposes is not inconsistent with their natural meaning. The case of *Mackay* v. *McCankie*, 10 R. 537, appears to me to be in point."

The defenders reclaimed and argued:— There was no dispute that a letter addressed to a person might found an action of damages at his instance, but to found an action for damages in respect of slander there must be an averment that the charges were false.

. . . . . .

21.1.2 LORD JUSTICE-CLERK: The question is whether the issue, with the accompanying innuendo which has been lodged for the pursuer, is to be allowed.

The case is rare in this respect, that the pursuer is complaining not of a slander uttered in public, but of a slander contained in a letter addressed to himself, which would not have obtained publicity unless he himself gave it publicity. Such an action is not known in England, but it is settled law that in this country the aggrieved party is entitled to sue for damages in respect of the injury done to his feelings.

Now, undoubtedly the defenders had good grounds for writing to inquire about the sum of money, for it had plainly been collected by the pursuer, and had not been accounted for to the defenders; it is not said to have been accounted for yet. But the question is whether the sting which they put into their letter is not such as to entitle the pursuer to an issue.

The letter certainly suggests very distinctly that if the pursuer did not take a particular course, the matter might be delivered over to the public authorities, with consequences which would be very unpleasant to the pursuer. That would not be actionable without the innuendo, but then I think that the innuendo can fairly be put as an interpretation on the language of that letter. It is for a jury to say whether, the letter being proved, the innuendo is "not inconsistent with" the natural meaning of the letter. That being so, I think the case ought to go to a jury.

21.1.3 LORD YOUNG [dissenting]: I am disposed to regard this as a case of first-rate importance. The dispute is a trifling one, but the letter which is complained of as a slander does not contain a single slanderous expression; it is a letter written by a clerk of the defenders in the ordinary course of business, demanding payment of a debt which is due. Is that to found an action of damages?

. . . . . .

21.1.4 Now, the state of facts here is this: Accounts due to the defenders had been uplifted and received by the pursuer or his cashier. It is admitted that both the accounts in question were due to the defenders, and to no one else. There was a question whether the pursuer by himself or cashier was entitled to receive the sums due under these accounts. That he had no title in a question with the defenders is certain. That his receipt to the debtor is good is equally certain, for he had been in use to collect such accounts, and the debtor had received no notice that his authority to do so had been recalled.

The case then is a case of good discharge by a person who had himself no right to the debt. But the money had been uplifted, and when the true creditor asks the debtor for payment, the debtor exhibits receipts form the pursuer's cashier. The defenders then demanded payment from the pursuer, exhibiting these receipts from his own cashier, and liability is repudiated. The defenders then wrote the letter complained of.

Now, there is not a word in it which is not true: the money was uplifted, and was not paid over or accounted for... Now, no doubt the letter takes an unfavourable view of the conduct of the pursuer. But there is no misrepresentation of fact, and it is not slanderous to express an opinion that the matter is one for the consideration of the fiscal.

. . . . . .

21.1.5 LORD RUTHERFURD CLARK: I agree with your Lordship in the chair. I do not think that we can withhold this case from a jury.'

COMMENT

21.2.1 Decided: November 18, 1890.
Marcel Proust enrols in Faculté de Droit, Paris.

21.2.2 The majority thought there was no need to put malice in the issue — Lord Young thought that if the case was to proceed, malice should be put in.

21.2.3 Would abusive party/party communications be best left to statutory offences?

Defamatory

82. Cuthbert v. Linklater (Appellant)
1935 S.L.T. 94

21.3.1 'THE LORD JUSTICE-CLERK (Aitcheson): I have no doubt that the Lord Ordinary was right in allowing an inquiry in this case.

The pursuer, who is publicly known by the name of "Wendy Wood" and is chairman of an organisation called the Democratic Scottish Self-Government Organisation, complains of a passage in a book which was written by the defender Mr Linklater and published by the defenders Jonathan Cape Ltd. The passage is set out in the issue and is in these terms: "Magnus" — that is the hero of the book — "found himself buttonholed by the young woman who looked like Joan of Arc. She introduced herself as Beaty Bracken. Magnus had heard a good deal about her and he was interested to meet her, for she had recently achieved fame by removing a Union Jack from the Castle and placing it in a public urinal."

21.3.2 Now it has been conceded that, on the pursuer's averments and for purposes of relevancy, the young woman "Beaty Bracken", whose conduct is described in the passage I have just read, might be identified with the pursuer, who had achieved some notoriety by removing a Union Jack from Stirling Castle. Accordingly we do not need to consider any questions as to whether or not the passage complained of points to the pursuer, or may point to her if she succeeds in proving her averments.

21.3.3 The only question we have to consider is whether the passage complained of is defamatory, with or without innuendo. For myself, I would have been prepared to hold the passage defamatory without an innuendo. I think it contains an imputation of indelicacy of a gross kind against a woman, and that, in my view, plainly amounts to an actionable wrong. I do not think we have anything whatever to do with the views, political or economic, the pursuer may hold. Whatever her views may be, they do not, and ought not to, deprive her of her right to the protection of the courts of law in this country if she is subjected to an attack upon her modesty or her propriety according to ordinarily accepted standards of conduct. I think the law on this matter is put very succinctly in a sentence in the opinion of Lord McLaren in the case of *Macfarlane* v. *Black & Co.* (1887) 14 R. 870 at p. 873, to which we were referred and which is in these terms: "It is not necessary, in order that the statement should be calumnious, that it should impute a crime; a statement may amount to a libel if it accuses a person of what is universally considered to be an immoral act, or if it imputes conduct which is contrary to the generally accepted standard of honour or propriety amongst gentlemen — amongst the class of persons to which the individual aggrieved belongs." Now that seems to me to express exactly the law in this case if one substitutes the word "women" for the word "gentlemen". I think, therefore, that there must be an issue.

21.3.4 As regards the issue proposed, it is an issue with an innuendo, and at the end of the day the criticism upon the innuendo proposed resolved itself into two points. First it was said that the passage complained of could not be taken to mean that the urinal, which the pursuer is said to have entered, was a urinal for men. Well, I do not think it necessary to say that this is the only meaning of the words "public urinal", but if the words are capable of being read in that sense by ordinary members of the public who may read them, that is enough to justify the pursuer putting that innuendo into the issue. The other criticism was this — that the statement that the pursuer had "placed" a Union Jack in a public urinal could not be reasonably innuended as meaning that she had entered a public urinal. There again, I think, if the word "placed" is capable of more than one meaning, it is enough that ordinary readers might have attached to the words complained of the meaning set out in the innuendo by the pursuer. I think the criticisms upon the form of issue fail.

. . . . . .

21.3.5 LORD ANDERSON: ... I do not differ from your Lordships, because it may well be that it is for the jury to solve these doubts and not for the courts.

I should not have been sorry, I would like to add, if we had been able to dispose of this action at this stage, because it is one with which I have not the slightest sympathy, and my own personal opinion is that it should never have been brought.'

COMMENTS

21.4.1 Decided: November 14, 1934.
　　　Sept. 28: Brigitte Bardot born.
　　　Oct. 5: Uprising in Catalonia.
　　　Oct. 21: Mao began his long march.

21.4.2 This case raises the matter of innuendo. What do you think the issue in the case actually said? (For the answer see 1935 S.L.T. 95.)

21.4.3 The case was decided in 1934. Do you think it would be decided differently today if perhaps it was suggested a spice girl went into a mens lavatory?

21.4.4 Try reading *Magnus Merriman*. The episode concerned is, in the present writer's view, nothing other than a bit of colour — it could have been left out without affecting the artistic merit of the book. However, one could also say that Mozart could have left out some of his notes!?

21.4.5 Clearly the decision as to what words are or are not actionable relates closely to the individual's freedom of expression as balanced against the individual's right not to be harmed. The word "defamation" describes the battle-zone of interests. The foregoing case is particularly interesting as being very close to the border of what ought to be allowed. To extend or go further than this might unduly restrict artistic freedom. Further study of the circumstances of this case show (i) how unpredictable the law was so far as the author was concerned; (ii) how the threat of such proceedings can affect a litigant.

Mr Linklater must have had in mind the possibility of some form of action — some of his characters were based on living and prominent people. The book when published, and before any question of legal action, had the following "Admonition" inserted at the start:

"When I wrote my first novel I was so foolish as to make the hero a medical student. As I myself had been a medical student, certain misguided readers assumed that *White Mana's saga* was autobiographical. To be saddled with this romantic reputation was very embarrassing.

"When I wrote *Juan in America* I was so unwise as to let it be known that I, as well as Juan, had recently spent some time in the United States. Certain misguided readers assumed that Juan's adventures had originally been mine, and many people begged me to tell them what Olympias was really like. To be saddled with this romantic reputation was embarrassing in many ways.

"Now, in *Magnus Merriman*, I have been so indiscrete as to let my hero contest a parliamentary by-election when I myself have but recently recovered from such an experience. And in view of previous misunderstandings I desire to state that Merriman's adventure in Kinluce is not an actual replica of mine in an actual constituency: that my election agent did not behave in the regrettable manner of Captain Smellie: that Merriman is one person and I, thank heaven, am quite a different person: that Merriman's friends, acquaintances, and enemies are his own and not mine. I have written a novel: I have not filled a photograph album or published confessions of a misspent life.

"It is true that I have taken an occasional backcloth from reality, and it is true that I have borrowed from a very good friend a snuff-box, an eyelid and a generous disposition: but unlike Meiklejohn, my friend of the eyelid, the snuff-box and the generosity has never misconducted himself in the Tarascon Restaurant, nor been in prison, nor even deserved to be. A Roman nose does not make a Roman portrait, nor does a scarlet cloak demand the existence of a Red Ridinghood. And though I have created a political situation with some resemblance to actuality it will readily be seen that I have not endeavoured to make a truthful record of the events of 1931: because it did not suit my purpose to do so.

"Magnus Merriman, then, is neither photography nor history but a novel. And the material of a novel is fiction."

It would have been difficult to put the matter more plainly. Indeed it is somewhat ironic that the admonition might have been written to deflect action by another individual. Mr Parnell, Mr Linklater's biographer, has kindly allowed the reproduction of the following correspondence which he was able to locate. Particularly relevant is this letter to Lesley Storm (Jan. 14, 1934): "I told Cape to send you a copy of *Magnus*, which I hoped you liked, and if you didn't, well, you ought to. If you think you discover a tiny hint of a portrait of a mutual friend of ours — well, read the Admonition again." One of the characters bears a very close relation to Christopher Grieve (Hugh McDiarmid).

Finally, it is clear that the whole episode of the litigation caused one of the finest Scottish writers of this century some considerable anxiety. Mr Parnell in *Eric Linklater: A Critical Biography* (1984) sets out the general position at p. 157 and also goes on to deal with the relationship of the book to life.

From Mr Linklater's letters (kindly supplied by Mr Parnell and whose reproduction has been authorised), a fuller picture appears of course of the litigation. It is an example of what goes on in the mind of a litigant.

On March 15, 1934 he wrote to Compton Mackenzie: "the egregious Wendy Wood is suing me for libel because, in *Magnus*, one Becky Brocker is said to have pinched a Union Jack from the castle and put it in a urinal. This she says, is defamatory and slanderous and contrary to morality. My reply is (a) that Becky is not Wendy ... (Becky raids Edinburgh Castle, Wendy raided Stirling Castle), and (b) that the onus is on her to prove that it is immoral to put a flag in a lavatory. What I am chiefly worried about is that I might be required to go home this or next month — and I can't leave Marjorie, and it's too late for her to travel. She's amazingly fit and full of spirits and I grow more ridiculously in love with her all the time. So I may have to defy the arm of the law and evade capture in Florence — though I hope my solicitors, if they don't settle the matter out of court, will at least be able to secure a postponement of the case."

The same day he writes to his solicitor Douglas Walker: "One tiny point, about the suggested immorality of the flag-carrying: there is no suggestion that Becky Brocker took the flag into a men's lavatory: there are — thank God — public conveniences for women as well. This, I think, will make their attempt to prove the manoeuvre immoral a little more difficult."

The subsequent correspondence is a useful indication of the pressures both on litigants and agents in the course of a litigation. On May 7, 1934 Linklater wrote to Walker: "It's rather a nuisance that Wendy has bobbed up again, but it can't be helped now. Your suggestion about offering the lady a small sum of money does not suit well with my parsimonious disposition: it would have to be a very small sum to suit me: and the payment of even a minute sum might be an unfortunate precedent and predispose others to attempt similar blackmail ... Wendy's claim to be the head of the democratic Scottish Self-Government Organisation I cannot dispute, for I have never heard of it: though I was aware she claimed to be head of some party or other. But 2000 strong? Even counting heads, tails and both hands, I doubt it. And to the best of my knowledge it has no connection with the National Party or the Scottish Party ..."

The matter's conclusion can be seen in a letter to Rupert Hart-Davis of his publishers (Feb. 7, 1935): "[The case is] being settled on precisely the terms I offered a year ago: that is, an apology for *inadvertently* hurting the lady's feelings, and an agreement to remove the offending passage from any further editions: that is, the words "and placed it in a public urinal". But owing to a year's argy-bargying it will now cost me something over £200. This, I am told, is less than my costs would be if it went to trial, even if I won all along the line. What I think would happen in a trial, would be an award to Wendy of nominal damages: but I would have to pay her costs as well as mine, and that would be a hell of a lot more than £200. So I'm cutting my losses, and sacrificing nothing to the position I took up a year ago. The apology I have submitted for approval is quite a dignified one, and refers to this original offer. I do not do a public crawl before her."

The position is so bad that John Braine, a modern novelist, suggested that writers should choose the names of their characters from gazetteers and then check them all against the leading professional directories. Taking into account the problems experienced by Salman Rushdaie it might be useful also to check them against the Koran!

83. **Wragg v. D. C. Thomson & Co. Ltd (Appellants)**
1909 2 S.L.T. 315 and 409

21.5.1 '(In the First Division) The Lord President said that in view of the recent decision of the House of Lords in the case of *Jones* v.

Hulton & Co. [1909] 2 K.B. 444, aff. (H.L.) 6th Dec., 1909) the Court was not prepared to withhold an issue.

21.5.2 (From the report of the first instance decision of the Lord Ordinary): "This was an action for slander brought by George Wragg, music-hall artiste and comedian, known professionally as George Reeves, against the proprietors of the *Weekly News* newspaper printed and published in Dundee, and circulating in Glasgow, as well as over Scotland generally. The pursuer averred (Cond. 3) that on February 13, 1909, while the pursuer was performing at the Palace Theatre, Glasgow, the defenders printed and published a paragraph in the following terms:

> "GEORGE REEVES SHOOTS WIFE TWICE
> THEN ENDS HIS OWN LIFE.
>
> X-RAYS SAVE WOMAN.

Bare-headed, her breast penetrated by a bullet and her left arm shattered by another, Mrs George Reeves staggered from her home, tottered along the street to the house of Dr Fred C. Hecket, and collapsing at the door just as the doctor appeared, managed to say, 'My husband shot me'. The surgeon took her into the office, ripped off her cloak, placed her on a couch and telephoned to the hospital for an ambulance. Then he put into operation his X-ray apparatus, and before the ambulance arrived he located one of the bullets between the fourth and fifth ribs. The other bullet had gone through the arm.

> FIRED AT HER WITH REVOLVER.

During a lucid interval Mrs Reeves said her husband had been drinking heavily for a month, and that she remonstrated with him, whereupon he pulled a revolver and fired twice at her, each shot taking effect. 'Then I ran to the street,' she said, 'and he fired twice after me.' I had just sense enough to go to the doctor's house." A few minutes after the shooting neighbours who had heard the shots ran out of the house and meeting a policeman shouted, 'Reeves is shooting in the basement, and his wife is in danger.' They had not seen the woman leave, but pedestrians had, and told the policeman of the strange scene on the street. The policeman got into the first floor and leaned over the balustrade on the stairs to reconnoitre, knowing the culprit had a revolver. He saw Reeves, and Reeves saw him. The policeman made a bound down to the landing, pistol in hand. Reeves was too quick for him, and with a cry of 'Alice' — his wife's Christian name — sprang into the kitchen, slammed the door and gained a bedroom, the door of which he also closed. As the policeman opened the door a few inches a shot sounded, and Reeves fell against the door on the inside. The policeman forced the door open and found that Reeves had fired a bullet into his brain. As the policeman and neighbours were carrying Reeves to the street the ambulance containing his wife approached, and the two were taken together to the hospital. Reeves will die."

21.5.3 In Answer 3 the defenders explained that [they] took said paragraph practically *verbatim* from an American newspaper. It appeared in the defenders' newspaper immediately after a paragraph reporting a series of occurrences in America. Accordingly, and because of its journalistic style, it obviously referred to an incident of American life, and had no application to the pursuer.

. . . . . .

21.5.4 From the defenders' Answer 3 it seems possible, if not indeed probable, that the notice complained of contained in the American papers, from which it is said to have been copied or adapted, particulars of locality and other details which would have naturally prevented such mistake and injury as is here alleged and complained of. If excision of such details by the defenders were averred by the pursuer, it seems to be clear that it would be for a jury to say whether the excision of such details by the defenders (whether done unwittingly, or designed to benefit their circulation by causing curiosity or anxiety among all friends of all persons called George Reeves residing in places where the paper circulated was not a reckless neglect of an ordinary and reasonable caution which they were bound to employ to prevent their paper containing libellous statements. But no such averment is made. For aught said by the pursuer, the defenders' notice may have been a verbatim reproduction of a paragraph in an American newspaper.

Taking it then, on that hypothesis I have come to the conclusion, although with hesitation, that the defenders' conduct might reasonably be held to involve slander of the pursuer, and that it might reasonably be held that such slander was due in law to the defenders' fault.

21.5.5 Whether the notice was of and concerning the pursuer would be for the jury to say. On the question of whether it is necessary to aver and prove that the defenders actually intended to refer to the pursuer, or whether it is not enough that they acted so as to lead people reasonably to believe that they referred to the pursuer, I concur with the majority of the Court of King's Bench in *Jones* v. *Hulton & Co.* [1909] 2 K.B. 471) presently under appeal to the House of Lords. No doubt, if it was clear that no one could reasonably conclude that the paragraph referred to the pursuer, then the case ought not to be allowed to proceed. The defenders argued that there was sufficient in the article, even cursorily read to show that the occurrence could not have happened in Great Britain. There is force in the defenders' criticisms, but I am bound to say that when I read the article for the first time these points escaped me, although I noticed them when I read the article carefully a second time with the view of seeing whether such points were not in the article. The defenders also maintained that, even if the article did not obviously exclude the pursuer, there was nothing to identify him with the George Reeves mentioned in the article except the name… The London Directory for 1909 only contains two instances and there are none in either the Edinburgh or Glasgow Directories.'

COMMENT

21.6.1   Decided: December 8, 1909.
Early December: typescript of first part of *Le Temps Perdu* delivered to *Le Figaro*.

21.6.2   What if both actor and suicide had been called John Macdonald?

21.6.3   Obviously the House of Lords had set its face against *culpa* as a determinant or *sine qua non* of liability in such cases. The mention of the decision in *Hulton* makes it clear that they decided the appeal largely on the strength of it. The provisions of the Defamation Act 1952 make it clear that Parliament has assumed that *culpa* is unnecessary for liability.

21.6.4   If, since *R.H.M. Bakeries*, a man clearly does not act at his peril, is it fair that he speaks at his peril? Read App., Ext. 17, and para. 21.14.7, and decide whether the 1996 Act would make any difference in a case such as this.

VERBAL INJURY/CONVICIUM

84. **Paterson v. Welch (Appellant)**
(1893) 20 R. 744

21.7.1   The defender made comments in public to the effect that the pursuer had made earlier comments that to admit poor children to the schools for which he was, as a governor, partly responsible. The pursuer was provost of the burgh and as a result of the defender repeating, it was said, falsely, the comments of the pursuer about poor children, the pursuer's party did badly at the elections. The pursuer sued for slander and for damages on the basis that the statements and representations made by the defender were false and were made maliciously causing injury.

21.7.2   'THE LORD PRESIDENT (Robertson): The fact complained of is that on two occasions the defender publicly ascribed to the pursuer words which he never used, those words being to the effect that the pupils from the board schools of St Andrews would contaminate the scholars at the Madras College if the two sets of children were educated together in certain classes... Now, in the first place, I do not think that to say of B that he on a specified occasion used slanderous words of C is the same thing as calling B a slanderer, and there are decisions as to accusations of falsehood which point the difference. But secondly, I do not agree that an injurious charge against a class of the community, and particularly a large class of the community, has the same legal quality as the same charge directed against an individual or individuals... My opinion is therefore that the pursuer has not a good ground of action on the head of slander. In this view it is not necessary to consider whether on both or either of these occasions when the defender spoke he was privileged, even on the shewing of the pursuer.

21.7.3 But assuming, as I now do, that the words sued on do not found a claim of damages on the head of slander, it by no means follows that they are not actionable. The true case of the pursuer is this — he says to the defender, "You publicly asserted that I said certain things; your assertion was false; it was made with design to injure me, and I have been injured." In my opinion that is a good claim in damages. In judging of the relevancy of such a claim, it is of course necessary that the words ascribed to the pursuer should be such as reasonably support the essential averments, that the attributing them to him was done with an intention to injure, and with the result of injuring. But subject to this observation, it seems to me that when speech is ascribed to A by B, A will have an action if (1) the statement of B is false; (2) the statement was made with design to injure; and (3) injury has resulted. The pursuer's case complies with these conditions. He begins by saying that he never used the words ascribed to him. These words are invidious words, to utter which may well be supposed to bring down on him, who was alleged to have used them, the hatred of his neighbours. The pursuer goes on to say that the defender ascribed these words to him, because the defender calculated their effect, and desired to inflict that injury on him. He ends by saying that the falsehood did its work; that he has become an object of public hatred; that the people have tried to burn him in effigy at his own door; that his personal comfort and public influence have been impaired; and all this through the falsehood of the defender.

The case thus presented is, in my opinion, one of legal wrong, which it proved, will entitle the pursuer to damages.'

COMMENT

21.8.1   Decided: May 31, 1893.
   Jan. 13: Independent Labour Party met for the first time.
   March 27: First long-distance telephone call made.
   May 24: *New World Symphony* completed.

85. **McLaren v. Ritchie**
July 8, 1856, unreported

21.9.1   'DUNCAN M'LAREN, merchant, Edinburgh, brought an action of damages against the proprietor and the editor of the *Scotsman* and *Daily Scotsman* newspapers published there. A Parliamentary election for the city of Edinburgh was pending, in which the pursuer was one of the candidates, and the defenders were supporting his opponent. The defenders attacked the pursuer in a series of articles spread over eleven numbers, from 30th January to 11th February, and these contained the alleged defamation for which the action was brought.

Lord Benholme reported the case to the Second Division on the adjustment of issues.

Penney and *A. S. Logan* for the defenders pleaded that the articles did not refer to the pursuer's private character, for which, as well as for his character in many respects as a public man, the defenders had uniformly expressed the highest esteem, and that they were written with the view of promoting the interests of the candidate of whom Mr M'Laren was an opponent, and referred to the pursuer solely as a public man. At any rate, the pursuer was not entitled to succeed merely by proving that the language was false, as it was figurative and could not be taken for literally true, but he would have to show that it was used for the purpose of holding him up to public contempt and ridicule. *Walker* v. *Robertson*, 5th June, 1821 (Macfarlane on Issues, 69); *Mackay* v. *Campbell*, 11 S. 1031; *Waddell* v. *Forsyth*, 22nd June, 1836 (Macfarlane, 43); *Macfarlane* v. *M'Kechnie*, 16th January 1834, (*ibid.* 42); *Sheriff* v. *Wilson*, 17 D. 528 (1855).

Dean of Faculty Inglis and *Young* for pursuer, after maintaining that there was a case of slander on record, departed from that and consented to taking an issue of holding up to contempt and ridicule. It was argued that it was not only aspersion on moral character that was actionable, but that intention to injure the feelings "by the uttering of words, which are calculated to injure the character of a man, or to render it little or contemptible," entitled the man to redress by damages. (Erskine, Institutes, Book IV., Tit. iv., 80.)

Passages, some of them of considerable length, from seven different articles were quoted in the issues, of which the following are fair specimens:—

"Every class of creature known in the political world was there represented — Mammalia, aves, pisces, and reptilia. It might be impolite to suggest that any one appeared for the *quadrumanae*, or even that there were any odd specimens of the *pisces*, but, as for the *viperidae*, what could be a more delightful object of Christian contemplation than Sir William Johnstone and Mr Duncan M'Laren lovingly intertwining the folds of their affections, no longer with anything 'cold' between them... . We cannot trust ourselves to comment on such a speech — old principles cast to the wind, old friends traduced, their lives scoffed at, and their death predicted, venom in every word and a dagger in every sentence."

"There is no man, of whom, though we would it had been otherwise, we have had to say harder things than of Duncan M'Laren. At this moment, not insidiously, but to his teeth, we charge him with deserting principles, and traducing friends, and deceiving enemies, and acting for his own purposes, and especially his own malignities."

"THE UNHOLY ALLIANCE."

"A viper met with an anti-viper,
    'How do you do?' says he;
'Shall we give that fellow Black a wiper?'
    'Yes, we'll both agree.'

"A viper met a 'calumniator,'
    'How do you?' says he;
'Of Black I'm a strong though a sneaking hater,'
    'You the man shall be.'"

There were also verses of a similar character under the heading of "Miss Biddy (Qy. B.D.?) and the Eden-boro Snake," in which the pursuer was referred to as a snake.

The publication was admitted and the issue as finally adjusted concluded — Whether the said articles, passages, verses, and fictitious advertisement, or any parts thereof, are of and concerning the pursuer, and whether the pursuer is thereby calumniously and injuriously held up to public hatred, contempt, and ridicule to his loss and damage? Damages claimed £1000.

21.9.2   LORD JUSTICE-CLERK (HOPE) said: "Everybody mixing in election matters from the time of the Athenians downwards, must lay his account to being subjected to a certain amount of ridicule and censure. It just comes to be a question if these articles exceed the kind of censure to which such an individual necessarily exposes himself by coming forward publicly to take part in an election. It is just like a criticism of a book. You are not under the disguise of a criticism of a man's work, to slander him or improperly hold him up to contempt. The question is whether these articles do exceed that kind of liberty or license which is expected in such a case, and whether they are written expressly for the purpose of holding him up to contempt and ridicule. It was clearly not for any moral defamation contained in these articles, but with the view to that this issue is sought. Somebody has reason to complain of the defenders because they allege that this term 'snake' originated with some particular individual. He is unnamed here, but he has good reason to complain of this allusion.

I think we may strike out the word false, it is not a case of falsehood at all."

21.9.3 In his charge to the jury the Lord Justice-Clerk said: "It is a mistake to say that everything may be said of a man's public character and conduct in whatever terms, provided it does not enter into his private affairs or private character. There is no such distinction in law. It is said that the defenders went into an excess of language in their attacks on the pursuer, and that while entitled to make remarks on his conduct in not supporting his former friend Mr Black, and not going along with that party, yet he (pursuer) says that they plunged from that feeling of resentment into invectives that were calumnious and injurious to him. Now it is not enough in answer to that to say — we advert merely to your public acts, writings, and conduct. I think it rather a strong thing to ask that in the phrase acting only for his own purposes and specially his own malignities, we should be asked to put in a word and read political malignities. The pursuer, it is said, was only alluded to with reference to his malignity against the Whig party, and that that is the fair interpretation of that passage. You will keep in view the fact that malignity means a quality of the mind, and that if political enmity is what is intended, it should have been so expressed as to prevent this construction. No doubt the passage goes on to say 'we speak only of Mr M'Laren's public character,' but you will judge whether this takes the edge off the statement that he has traduced his friends. That is an act directly against a private individual, and you will judge whether it takes off the effect of that to say that the writer is only referring to public conduct. You will judge especially whether in using the word malignities, it ought to have been so qualified as to take off that which appears to be the impression which you probably would otherwise form from the passage as it stands."

COMMENT

21.10.1 This case is reported only in the Appendix to Glegg on *Reparation* (2nd ed., 1905), p. 611. The case is cited in most books and so it is reproduced here for the benefit of students and teachers. It is one of the few cases where Falsity was not an issue. Norrie comments that this case, *Sheriff v. Wilson* (1855) 17 D. 528 and *Cunningham v. Phillips* (1868) 6 M. 926 "must be regarded as, at the very least, superseded by later developments", Norrie, *Defamation and Related Actions in Scots Law* (1995), p. 41.

86. Crotty v. McFarlane
January 27, 1891, unreported

21.11.1 'Crotty, or Burns, a female operatic singer, raised an action of damages against the *Scottish Leader* newspaper on account of two articles criticising her appearance in two different operas, "Marguerite" in Faust, and "Violetta" in La Traviata. She alleged that she had played these parts for twelve years with brilliant success, and that all the musical and dramatic authorities throughout the United Kingdom had testified to the talented and successful manner in which she had always interpreted and executed said parts. She was the acknowledged "Marguerite" of the British stage, and was completely equal to all operatic parts demanding brilliancy of execution and dramatic instinct and power. With the exception founded on, the whole press comments and criticisms had been entirely favourable. The passages in the articles complained of were:

"In spite of all that has been said, however, those who heard Miss Ella Russell two years ago in the part of 'Violetta' must have felt that a great artist could almost triumph over all the inherent difficulties in creating an illusion of power and artistic fitness. Unfortunately the performance by the Carl Rosa Company last night, with all its merits, was awanting in this element of success. Madame Georgina Burns is a singer of very considerable gifts, and has many of the arts of an accomplished actress, but it is not within her capacity to portray the varying moods and experiences of the unhappy woman who, with all her errors, is found capable of true affection for her lover, and of noble sacrifice of his love, and his good opinion of herself, when this seems demanded of her in his interest. Madame Burns' brilliant and incisive tones are not well adapted to the rendering of pathos, and the dying scene failed accordingly to make anything like its full impression. But it is only fair to add, that in several of the airs, such as *Ah fors e lui*, and in the execution of the gymnastic passages, which are plentifully and inappropriately dispersed throughout the part, she acquitted herself to the satisfaction of the audience, and received considerable applause. In the scene with Alfred's father also, she was successful both in acting and singing. Signor Runcio did not make so good an appearance in the character of Alfred as he did two years ago, perhaps because the inspiration from the heroine was lacking." And,

"The cast last night was on the whole a strong one. It cannot indeed be said that Madame Burns had made an ideal 'Marguerite'; her figure, her style, her voice, are all naturally unsuited to the part of the simple maiden, who loved not wisely but too well, and suffered cruelly for her sin. Her whole aim and method are too artificial, too sophisticated, too self-conscious, to realise either the innocent *naiveté* of the earlier passages, or the passionate emotion of the later scenes; and her voice, with all its excellent qualities, is fatally lacking in just that sympathetic timbre which above all is demanded by the character. It says a great deal for Madame Burns' abilities, however, that with all these natural disadvantages, she yet made a decided favourable impression in many of the scenes, and, indeed, sang and acted throughout with an acceptance beyond what might reasonably have been expected."

The pursuer alleged that these statements were false, calumnious, and malicious. Further, they were intended to create, and they did create, in the public mind, and to the said company, the impression that the pursuer in the pursuit of her profession was unworthy of the high position of *prima donna* which she held, and in which she had been placed by the said company, that was naturally unsuited and unfitted for, and incapable of performing the said parts of "Violetta" and "Marguerite", and that through her incapacity she was the cause of Signor Runcio, another member of the company, not performing the part allotted to him in said opera of "La Traviata" as he otherwise ought to have done, or would have done.

Pursuer further averred that through these statements her position and reputation in the theatrical and musical world, and also before the public, had been much impaired. She had suffered injury in her feelings, and the receipts for each second production of "Faust" and "La Traviata" had, in consequence of the statements, been reduced by a very large sum.

Defender pleaded that there was no relevant case, and that the articles were within the limits of fair criticism.

The pursuer proposed the following issues, publication of the articles (schedules) being admitted:

1. Whether the said paragraphs, or one or other of them, were falsely and calumniously intended and calculated to, and did, hold the pursuer up to public ridicule, and to represent, and did represent, falsely and calumniously, that it is not within her capacity to portray the character of "Violetta" in Verdi's opera "La Traviata", to the loss, injury, and damage of the pursuer.

2. Whether the said paragraphs, or one or other of them, falsely and calumniously represented that the pursuer, in the pursuit of her profession, is unworthy of the high position of *prima donna* which she holds, and that she is naturally and physically unsuited and unfitted for, and incapable of performing the parts of "Violetta" in Verdi's opera "La Traviata", and of "Marguerite" in the opera of "Faust", and other parts allotted to her, and undertaken by her upon the stage, to the loss, injury, and damage of the pursuer.

21.11.2 LORD STORMONTH-DARLING: This is an action of damages for alleged libel, at the instance of Madame Georgina Burns, who is a leading member of the Carl Rosa Opera Company, against the proprietor of the *Scottish Leader* newspaper, founded upon two paragraphs which appeared in that paper on 26th and 28th November respectively, criticising the performance by the pursuer of the parts of "Violetta" in the opera of "La Traviata", and of "Marguerite" in the opera of "Faust". There is a plea by the defender as to the relevancy of the action, and another to the effect that the paragraphs in question are within the limits of fair criticism. It was thought better that the issues proposed by the pursuer should be lodged before discussing these pleas, and accordingly the first question which arises is whether the condescendence discloses any issuable matter at all. I am of opinion that it does not. It was urged for the pursuer that wherever the alleged libel is contained in a newspaper article, and the true question between the parties is whether or not the article exceeds the bounds of fair criticism, the case ought to go before a jury as the proper judges of that question. I cannot assent to so general and sweeping a proposition. A jury are the proper judges of whether a publication is in point of fact false and calumnious, but their arbitrament is invoked only if the Court in the first instance are of opinion that the publication is capable of a libellous construction. I do not know of any authority for saying that a defence of fair criticism displaces the duty, which attaches to the Court in all other cases of libel, of inquiring whether there is issuable matter. The pursuer referred to the case of *Merivale* against *Carson*, 1887, Queen's Bench Division, which undoubtedly contains some "dicta" of the Court of Appeal in England, to the effect that a question of fair criticism ought always to be left to the jury. But these "dicta" must be taken in connection with English rules of procedure, which are, as I understand, much more favourable than ours to letting all sorts of questions go before a jury. The course followed by the First Division in the recent case of *Godfrey* against *Thomson*, 10th July, 1890, shows conclusively that in dealing with newspaper articles as with all other vehicles of alleged libel, it is the duty of the Court before allowing an issue, to examine the article for themselves, and to see whether it is capable of bearing the libellous construction attached to it by the pursuer. Now, the plea of fair criticism seems to me to affect the question of libel or no libel in this way. Every member of the public has the right, and newspapers have no higher right in this matter than ordinary citizens, to criticise any kind of public performer — using the term in its widest sense — favourably or unfavourably, wisely or foolishly, justly or unjustly, so long as the criticism is fair — that is so long as it is criticism, and not mere abuse or invective under the guise of criticism, and so long as it is an expression of opinion, which, however erroneous, an ordinary man might reasonably entertain. If it is kept within these limits, there is no libel, if it exceeds them, it becomes libel for this reason, that libel implies malice proved or presumed, and in the case supposed there is either such extravagance of language as to indicate actual malice, or such reckless disregard of the feelings and interests of the person attacked, as amounts in law to constructive malice. I hope I am not presumptuous in attempting these definitions, but it seems to me that something of the kind would have to be laid down to the jury if an issue were allowed. It may be said that in charging a jury the judge would be in a better position to define fair criticism, because he would then have the advantage of having heard the evidence. But I am willing, as I am bound at this stage, to assume all the facts in favour of the pursuer. I will assume that, as stated in Condescendence 2, "all the musical and dramatic authorities throughout the United Kingdom have testified to the talented and successful manner in which she has always interpreted and executed the parts of 'Violetta' and 'Marguerite'." I will assume also that "she is completely equal to all operatic parts demanding brilliancy of execution and dramatic instinct and power"; I will assume, further, as stated in Condescendence 5, that the articles in question have impaired her position and reputation in the theatrical and musical world, and before the public — in other words, I will assume that the defender's comments are altogether unjust. But still, the question would remain, Are the articles within the limits of fair criticism? And it seems to me that the question would stand in exactly the same position at the end of the evidence as it does at this moment. There being no allegation of actual or private malevolence, the words of the articles would have to be scanned then as now in order to see whether they express honest opinions, however unjust, or whether they are couched in language so reckless and exaggerated that no reasonable man could possibly have entertained the opinion or used the language. I do not think that any one can hesitate as to which of these two descriptions is correct. The articles are hostile, it may be, in the main, but they are not couched in the language of indiscriminate censure. On the contrary they acknowledge that the pursuer "is a singer of very considerable gifts and has many of the arts of an accomplished actress," and they admit that she was successful in many of the scenes of both operas. At its worst the criticism is that she is naturally unsuited to the two parts as a whole. But although that may be unjust — even it may be grossly unjust — I cannot say that it is not an expression of opinion, and an expression of opinion which a dramatic critic might honestly entertain, unless it is to be held that so soon as a lady has attained to the position of a leading member in the Carl Rosa Opera Company, all criticism of an adverse character is to be hushed. I do not see that the articles could be met by anything but counter expressions of opinion, and if so it seems to me that the jury would have to be told that it was impossible for them to find a verdict for the pursuer. In such circumstances it is more in accordance with our practice to find at this stage that there is nothing on which to go to a jury at all. I will only add that in my opinion the articles do not warrant the innuendo in the second issue, that the pursuer "is unworthy of the high position of *prima donna* which she holds," or that she is naturally unsuited for "other parts" than those of "Violetta" or "Marguerite". Neither do I think that a grave and serious criticism like this can fairly be said to "hold the pursuer up to public ridicule". The interlocutor therefore will be — "Find that the summons does not disclose any issuable matter, therefore disallows the issues proposed by the pursuer, sustains the defences, dismisses the action, and finds the defender entitled to expenses."'

COMMENT

21.12.1   This case is reported only in the appendix of Glegg on *Reparation*. As Norrie correctly states (*Defamation*, p. 146) that "the definition of 'fair' in this context has been given little consideration in Scotland", this additional authority is quite valuable (see Norrie, *Defamation*, p. 148). Note the contrast with *Merivale v. Carson*.

87. Steele v. Scottish Daily Record and Sunday Mail Ltd
1970 S.L.T. 53

21.13.1   'G. H. Steele, a motor dealer, raised an action in the Sheriff Court of Lanarkshire at Glasgow, in which he craved the court to grant decree against Scottish Daily Record and Sunday Mail Ltd for payment of £5,000.

· · · · · ·

The article in respect of which damages were sought, was in the following terms:

"The young man mentioned below has been landed with a car he didn't ask for, doesn't want and can't use … All because a big car dealer, Mr G. H. Steele, shop owner and financier of St George's Road, Glasgow, stuck to the law.

"He's 23-year-old Davie McLeod, of 37 St Peter's Street, St George's Cross. And while Mr Steele and his firm have the law on their side, Mr McLeod wishes he had luck on his.

"If he had, he wouldn't be in the mess he is in today.

"Life looked rosy and bright for young David two months ago. He had scrimped and saved to buy a small flat. He was getting married. And he planned to buy a good second-hand ice-cream van to replace the old one from which he made a living.

"He saw the van he wanted in Steele's shop in St George's Road, and days before he married his young English girl-friend, Christine, he put £20 part-deposit on the vehicle. The full deposit was to be £100.

New venture

"'As soon as we were married,' David told me yesterday, 'we set about getting this money to improve my little business. At the same time we gathered up enough cigarettes, sweets, etc., to stock the van.'

"Last week the young couple's hard work paid off. They had enough to give Mr Steele's firm the full deposit.

"An agreement was signed for purchase of the mobile shop … £100 down, leaving a balance of £450, which included about £100 interest charges. And with the near-£60-worth of stock they had gathered, David McLeod was ready to set his new venture going.

Then tragedy struck

"Their ground floor flat was burgled and they lost most of their valuables — including the stock for the new van.

"'They took our clothes, emptied our gas and electric meters ... even took my shaver,' David told me. 'They left us with £1 between us until our next pay day.'

"David contacted Steele's to tell them his bad news, and asked if they could cancel the deal for the new van. 'I just cant afford to continue with the purchase after this disaster,' he told me.

"But he was turned down. 'I was told,' says David, 'that if I didn't continue with the purchase of the van I could be sued for breach of contract.'

Civil court

"'That put me in a real panic. I just didn't know what to do. Then they suggested I take the Morris Minor instead.

"'It cost £110 which meant I had to pay another £10. As it would save me from being sued I thought it worth it. But I don't need or want a car. It's the last thing I want at this time.'

"When I contacted Mr Steele he told me that he considered his firm had been 'very lenient' with Mr McLeod.

"'He could have lost what he paid us for the length of time we kept the vehicle for him. Instead of that we gave him a vehicle.'

"Well, there's no need to tell me the law, Mr Steele. I know you could have hauled young Mr McLeod into a civil court.

Tough times

"I know it would have been easy for you to win a breach of contract case which would probably have meant Mr McLeod losing his entire deposit.

"But fair's fair — Did your firm have to make him take a car he didn't want? A car he can't even afford to run? A car that he's going to find very hard to sell with the coming of winter.

"You're in the big time, Mr Steele. Probably you didn't know the tough times young Mr McLeod was going through.

"Come on ... let's show us that the big time has a big heart too."

. . . . . .

21.13.2 LORD WHEATLEY: This is an appeal from the sheriff court in an unusual type of action which has had an unusual and somewhat chequered history. The facts are fully set forth in the sheriff-substitute's findings and with one or two exceptions these have been accepted by both parties ... The action was originally presented as one of defamation. The sheriff-substitute dismissed the action as irrelevant and the pursuer appealed to the sheriff. Before the appeal was heard the pursuer made amendments to his pleadings with the avowed intention of translating it into an action of *convicium*. The learned sheriff dealt with the case as one of *convicium* although there appears to have been at that stage a certain amount of interplay between *convicium* and verbal injury. This is perhaps not surprising in view of the mixed opinions which have been expressed about the constituents of these two types of actions and of defamation down through the years. In the result the learned sheriff allowed a proof before answer and a proof duly took place before the sheriff-substitute. The latter in the event granted decree of absolvitor to the defenders but he decided the issue on the basis of relevancy. It is against his interlocutor granting absolvitor that the pursuer now appeals. It is perhaps worthy of note that counsel then appearing for the pursuer presented his case as one of *convicium*, while the counsel for the defenders maintained that it could only be one of verbal injury. The sheriff-substitute *prima facie* appears to have dealt with the case as one of *convicium*, although at times he seems to be trying to ride both horses in the different situation with which he was presented.

21.13.3   Throughout the appeal in this court, counsel for both parties treated this simply as a case of verbal injury and invited the court to deal with it as such. In the light of the foregoing history it may be fortunate for the pursuer if the amendments made to convert a case of defamation into one of *convicium* are liable to support a case of verbal injury.

We had an interesting perambulation throughout the developing history of defamation, *convicium* and verbal injury and the different elements which are said to be required to support each of these different types of action, and while we are indebted to counsel for their painstaking research and admirable presentation, I do not propose to follow them into the labyrinth. When both parties are now agreed that this action has to be treated as one of verbal injury and nothing else, then it seems appropriate to confine consideration to that narrow field.

21.13.4   In its modern concept an action for verbal injury is based on the dictum of Lord President Robertson in *Paterson* v. *Welch* (1893) 20 R. 744 at p. 749... How then should the matter be approached? The competing views of counsel in this case turned not on a challenge of the Lord President's three conditions which had to be satisfied, but on how they should be interpreted. The conditions stated are: (1) that the statement was false; (2) that the statement was made with a design to injure; and (3) that injury resulted. In *Paterson* v. *Welch* the injury was said to be one of holding the pursuer up to public hatred, and the action was restricted accordingly to a claim for solatium. This explains the terms of the issue allowed. But in applying these qualifying conditions to an individual case, it seems to me that the second and third require to be expanded, so that the pursuer has to aver that the false statement was designed to injure him in a particular way, and in fact did injure him in that way. Merely to refer to injury *in vacuo* does not seem to me to be enough. Such a further specification as I have desiderated would disclose the real basis of the pursuer's complaint and ground of action. It would indicate for instance whether the complaint was that the conduct alleged injured his character or public esteem or affected him in business dealings or both. Counsel for the defenders maintained that an allegation against character or credit which inferred that the pursuer was guilty of conduct of a dishonourable or immoral kind (to quote the phrase used by Lord President Robertson in *Paterson* v. *Welch*) was slanderous and accordingly excluded an action for verbal injury. It was accepted that the words used here were not slanderous and so they could not be said to impute dishonourable conduct to the pursuer. As I understood his argument, counsel for the defenders distinguished between slander and verbal injury in this way. An ordinary action of slander relates to a suggestion that the pursuer has some defect in character or credit in the eyes of right-thinking men. An action for verbal injury would lie if the statement made did not reflect dishonourable or immoral conduct on the part of the pursuer but was designed to bring him into public hatred and contempt, and did so. By the same token a false statement which did not reflect on the pursuer's business credit but was designed to do harm to his business and did so (for example to say that he was giving up business) would justify an action for verbal injury.

21.13.5   Counsel for the pursuer sought to qualify his analysis of the law under reference to Lord President Robertson's three conditions by saying that while false allegations of character or credit which imputed crime, immorality, dishonourable conduct or insolvency and the like, would instruct an action for slander, statements falling short of this affecting character or credit would justify an action of verbal injury if the other conditions were satisfied.

21.13.6   As I see the position, it is this. If the words used are slanderous or can be innuendoed as slanderous, the proper form of action is one of slander. In that situation the courts have refused to allow an issue of verbal injury to stand alongside an issue of slander arising out of the same *species facti*. If it is conceded (as here) that the words used are not slanderous, then what is required to establish a case of verbal injury? I interject a reminder that counsel for the defenders accepted that there was no difference between false attribution to the pursuer of unpopular statements and a false attribution of unpopular acts.

. . . . . .

21.13.7 In the present case the pursuer asks the court to award him damages under two heads. One could spend a long time in a discussion on semantics, but basically these two heads are (a) solatium for injury to his feelings through him being held up to public hatred and contempt, and (b) damages for the injury done to his business. Each of these has to be examined separately. Under the first head the pursuer has to aver and prove (1) that the article, though not slanderous, was false at least in some material respect; (2) that the falsity was intended to bring him into public hatred and contempt; and (3) that it did so. Under the second head the pursuer has to aver and prove (1) the falsity of the article as above; (2) that the falsity was intended to injure him in his business; and (3) that it did so... In my opinion the averments of condescendence 3 of the pursuer's pleadings only support a case of bringing him into public hatred and contempt and do not lay any basis for a case of injury to business.

. . . . . .

21.13.8 The statements in the article are said to have been made falsely and maliciously and to be calculated to bring him into public hatred and contempt... The sheriff-substitute has found that the article is inaccurate in a number of respects but particularly in one of materiality and great importance to the pursuer's case. He finds that it was not the pursuer or anyone on his behalf who suggested that McLeod might have a second-hand car in lieu of the deposit he had paid on the travelling shop, but McLeod himself. This finding was not attacked by defender's counsel and it provides the pursuer with the starting-point, namely a false statement on a material matter. This, in effect, is the crux of the pursuer's complaint about the article, because it is on this mis-statement that the other obnoxious passages are hinged, particularly those which suggest that the pursuer (or his firm) "had landed McLeod with a car he didn't ask for, doesn't want and can't use."

The threat by the writer of the article to the pursuer in advance of publication that he would "expose" the pursuer if he did not let McLeod have his money back is sufficient in itself to establish intent. It is also relevant in considering the pursuer's averment of malice, although the latter does not rest on that alone. The sheriff-substitute, rightly, in my view, has described the article as unfair, one-sided and inaccurate.

. . . . . .

21.13.9 Even if the writer wrote the article with the self-expressed purpose of "exposing" the pursuer to the public, and the article was calculated to bring him into public hatred and contempt, he did not commit an actionable wrong if, in fact, the article cannot reasonably be read as bringing the pursuer into public hatred and contempt in the legal sense of the term… It might be argued that the test of public hatred and contempt is the same both in slander and verbal injury, the difference being that it might be easier to establish if the statements were slanderous. If, however, the test is the one applied by Lord McLaren in *McLaughlin* v. *Orr Pollock & Co.* (1894) 22 R. 38, at p. 43 (wrongly ascribed by the sheriff-substitute to Lord Young in *Macfarlane* v. *Black & Co.* (1887) 14 R. 870) that an issue of holding up to public hatred, ridicule and contempt ought not to be granted except where the libel imputes moral depravity of some kind, or is capable of being read as containing such an imputation. I cannot see how the tests can be equiparated. *McLaughlin supra* was a defamation action based on an alleged libel of a man in public life, and if the imputation is one of moral depravity it is defamation, which verbal injury is not.

21.13.10   In this very unusual type of action, namely verbal injury, I agree that the words complained of must produce something more than public disapproval, adverse comment or criticism. I do not consider, however, that people would have to "hate" the complainer in the full sense of that word. In my opinion, something of the order of condemn or despise is the proper test. This I would regard as something stronger than the test laid down in England by Lord Atkin in *Sim* v. *Stretch* (1936) 52 T.L.R. 669, namely "tending to lower the plaintiff in the estimation of right thinking members of society."… Even applying a less rigorous test than the one applied by the sheriff-substitute I have come to the conclusion that he was entitled to hold that fairly read both in content and in presentation the article cannot be said to bring the pursuer into public hatred and contempt in the legal sense of the term. I have reached this conclusion with some regret, because in my opinion, the article was irresponsible, biased and inaccurate. It would be strange indeed if it did not give the pursuer offence, and it may well have had an effect on his business, as the sheriff-substitute has in fact found. If, however, the article has constituted no legal wrong in the action as pleaded, the pursuer has no legal redress.

. . . . . .

21.13.11   LORD MILLIGAN: … In my opinion the submission of the defenders to the effect that in a case of verbal injury a pursuer must aver and prove in what particular way the words or article complained of were designed to injure him is well-founded. In a case of slander intention to injure is presumed, but in a case of verbal injury a pursuer has to aver and prove that the words complained of were intended to produce the effect which the words are said to have had (*Cunningham* v. *Phillips* (1868) 6 M. 926, *per* Lord President Inglis, at p. 927). A bare averment that the words or article were designed "to injure the pursuer" is not sufficient… I am unable to find in the pursuer's averments any averment to the effect that the article was designed to injure the pursuer in his business ... Merely to say, moreover, that the article was calculated to bring the pursuer into public hatred and contempt is not sufficient unless it can be said that the article was of such a nature that it could reasonably have this result. "Public hatred and contempt" are strong words and mean more than causing the person referred to be looked on with disapproval or even disgust. They connote, in my opinion, something akin to popular revulsion.

. . . . . .

21.13.12   In the present case the pursuer does not hold any public position, and the latitude which may be allowed in the case of a person in a public position will not be allowed in his case, but nevertheless the expression "public hatred" has still got to be satisfied. In *McLaughlin* v. *Orr Pollock & Co.* (1894) 22 R. 38, admittedly a public-position case, Lord McLaren, with whom the other members of the court concurred said that, in his view, the expression "public hatred" was the most important and significant part of the issue On this issue of relevancy the question that has to be asked is whether the article could be capable of bringing the pursuer into public hatred and contempt. On the issue I have reached the conclusion that the article cannot reasonably be said to have possibly had that effect... It might also cause his friends and members of the public to think considerably less of him as a business man and as an individual, but I cannot think that he would be "publicly hated" or held "in contempt" by those who read the article. The article does not say that he used any illegitimate means of holding McLeod to his bargain. On the contrary it indicates that he tried to help McLeod in his difficulties. The offer of the car was not an unreasonable offer and it was made in circumstances in which the pursuer was under no obligation to make any offer at all.

. . . . . .

21.13.13   LORD FRASER: Counsel on both sides accepted that words which were not defamatory might nevertheless be actionable, and that the usual description (at least in modern usage) of the delict committed by one who utters such actionable words was verbal injury. The action for verbal injury is comparatively rare, and counsel were not entirely agreed as to its scope, but in the argument before us, although evidently not before the sheriff-substitute and the sheriff, counsel on both sides treated the present action as being one for verbal injury.

In the light of the authorities to which we were referred, and particularly *Paterson* v. *Welch* (1893) 20 R. 744, and *Waddell* v. *Roxburgh* (1894) 21 R. 883, I am of opinion that the pursuer in the present action cannot succeed unless he has relevantly averred, and also proved, each of the following three elements, *viz.* (1) that the article of which he complains was false in a material respect; (2) that it was written with the intention of injuring him; (3) that it did in fact injure him. I note in passing that the second of these elements constitutes one of the main distinctions between an action for verbal injury and one for defamation — see *Waugh* v. *Ayrshire Post Ltd.* (1894) 21 R. 326, *per* Lord Adam at p. 329.'

COMMENT

21.14.1   Decided: July 2, 1969.
  April 17: Alexander Dubcek removed as leader of Czechoslovakian Communist Party.
  May 1: Major Chichester-Clark becomes Prime Minister of Northern Ireland.
  July 2: Brian Jones found drowned in swimming pool.

21.14.2   See Professor Walker's note at 1970 J.R. 157.

21.14.3   The wider context of verbal injury and its relationship to other interests in personality can be found in Blom-Cooper, "The Right to be Let Alone" [1989] J.L.S. 402. Many of the points made in the text are relevant, particularly to the press. He begins by quoting a seminal article, Warren and Brandeis, "The Right of Privacy" [1890] Harv.L.R. 193: "The press is overstepping in every direction the obvious bounds of propriety and decency. Gossip is no longer the resource of the idle and the vicious, but has become a trade, which is pursued with industry as well as effrontery." Do you agree with footnote 1 to Blom-Cooper's article?: "On the subject of privacy there is a fundamental difference between the common law of England and that of Scotland. By contrast with England, Scottish authorities assert that even though there is no conclusive judicial precedent, there is no reason why a Scottish court should not give a remedy for an infringement of privacy *simpliciter*. By the law of Scotland (unlike the law of England) it is not necessary for conduct, in order that it should qualify as an actionable wrong, to be assignable to any particular legal category; and in any event, certain invasions of privacy would support an *actio injuriarum* or an action for *convicium* (a form of action akin to defamation but not defeated by proof that the words complained of were true)." There is considerable doubt as to the accuracy of this statement which broadly follows Professor Walker. [See Norrie, *Defamation* (1995), and Clive, Watt and McKain, *Scots Law for Journalists* (5th ed., 1988), p. 204.] It is interesting that Blom-Cooper finally suggests a tort which is an amalgam of defamation and privacy, a tort of protection of the person: "Any unauthorised use or disclosure of personal information calculated or intended to cause or which did cause distress, annoyance or embarrassment, or damage the reputation of another, is actionable, unless otherwise justified on the grounds of the nature of the personal information and the legitimate public interest (if any) of such information." If such an amalgamation were undertaken it would be relevant to consider also the place of confidentiality, breach of which can be constituted by an "unauthorised use or disclosure of personal information". See Chapter 3.

21.14.4   The written constitution in the United States has *helped* the law of privacy to develop (although the English case of *Albert v. Strange* (1849) 1 De G. & Sm 652 was influential). It is an open question whether the European Convention on Human Rights may have a similar effect. The U.K. government does pay attention to decisions of the Commission and so lawyers must always consider the relevant provisions — Articles 8 and 10. See generally, Wallace, *International Law* (2nd ed. 1992), pp. 206–214.

21.14.5   The debate concerning privacy has not stopped. There were two reports (U.K. wide) by the Calcutt Committee. (See Carey Miller, D. L., and Hardy, H., "Calcutt II: Comments from a Scots Perspective", 1993 S.L.T. (News) 199. Various views have been expressed on the topic. See Bonnington, A.J., "Privacy: Letting the Right Alone", 1992 S.L.T. (News) 289; Hogg, M. A., "Privacy: a valuable and protected interest in Scots Law", 1992, S.L.T. (News) 349; Laurie, G. T., "Privacy, Paucity and the Press", 1993 S.L.T. (News) 285.

A very wide-ranging and thoughtful overview of the whole issue concerning Scots law in particular (and bringing up some unusual cases) is Martin Hogg's essay "The very private life of the Right of Privacy" in the Hume Paper (Vol. 2, No. 3) in *Privacy and Property* (1994).

21.14.6   For an interesting review of Scots damages awards in defamation cases see McFadden, J. "Why Scots awards for defamation don't rival English damages," *Glasgow Herald*, October 17, 1990 and "£350,000 Libel Damages for Elton John: why it could not happen in Scotland", 1994 J.L.S. 24.

21.14.7   Despite all of the exciting proposals for change, nothing all that outstanding was brought about by the Defamation Act 1996. Anyone who transmits a defamatory statement is liable for it. *Hayforth v. Forrester-Paton* 1927 S.C. 740, *Morrison v. Ritchie and Co.*(1902) 4 F. 645. Section 1 of the Act provides a limited defence for innocent dissemination but not for authors, editors or publishers. The practical effect of an offer of amends (provided by s. 4 of the 1952 Act) is that, the respondent who refuses the offer having to show that the wrongdoer did not innocently defame. It is no longer essential that the offer be made as soon as is practicable. Section 12 of the Act amended s. 12 of the Law Reform (Miscellaneous Provisions) (Scotland) Act 1968 (see App. Ext. 7). A last minute addition to the Act (s. 13), allows M.P.s to sue for defamation where it would have been unfair as the defence of *veritas* would have infringed parliamentary privilege. Sadly the M.P. who made use of it abandoned his action before it was concluded. S. 14 as can be seen clarifies a grey area in Scots law providing for absolute privilege for fair and accurate reports of court proceedings. It has to be made contemporaneously and it has to be a U.K. court or the ECJ (actually on the basis that all courts are Euro-Courts within European law, there is an argument that at least in respect of proceedings with a "Euro" dimension, the same rule should apply). [See for non-contemporaneous reports of a foreign court.] The categories of statutory privilege are extended by the new "schedule" categories. See Wade, G., "The Defamation Act 1996", 1996 Rep. B. 9–2 and Norrie, K., "The Defamation Act 1996", 1996 S.L.T. (News) 311. Not all issues have been resolved. See Styles, S. C., "Two flaws in the Law of Defamation", 1991 S.L.T. (News) 31.

21.14.8   Finally Professor Norrie's book *Defamation and related actions in Scots Law* (1995), deals with many of the topics discussed in this chapter and is a *critical* reappraisal of much received wisdom.

CHAPTER 22

VICARIOUS LIABILITY AND SOME SPECIAL PARTIES

88. Williams v. A. & W. Hemphill Ltd (Appellants)
1966 S.C.(H.L.) 31

22.1.1 'LORD STRACHAN (in the Inner House narrating the facts): The pursuer was returning to Glasgow from a Boys' Brigade camp at Benderloch, Argyll, in a lorry which had been hired from the defenders for the purpose of transporting camp equipment, baggage, and a baggage party. At the time the pursuer was not quite 14 years of age. The lorry had been hired by the Boys' Brigade company, of which the pursuer was a member. It was being driven by the defenders' servant, John McKechnie Ross. On the same day a company of the Girls' Guildry who had also been camping at Benderloch, were returning to Dollar by train. The shortest route from Benderloch to Glasgow was by Loch Lomond, but at the request of some of the boys on the defenders' lorry Ross drove the lorry to Connell station and then to Stirling station in order that the boys from the Boys' Brigade might meet the girls from the Girls' Guildry at those places. At Stirling, in response to a further request from the boys, Ross agreed to drive the lorry to Dollar in order that the boys might again meet the girls on their arrival at Dollar. At a bend in the road near Dollar the lorry swerved off the road and crashed into an adjacent field.

. . . . . .

22.1.2 LORD PEARCE (in the House of Lords): The defenders' servant was employed by them as a driver and he had been ordered to drive the boys and their baggage to Glasgow. His duty was, by implication, to drive by the most direct route. When the accident happened, he had not yet completed his overall duty of driving the boys and baggage to Glasgow, but he was on a part of the road where he would not have been if he had carried out his orders. He should not have gone anywhere near the place of the accident, and his employers, had they been asked, would certainly not have permitted him to go there. Was he still acting within the scope of his employment so as to make his employers vicariously liable for his negligence? The leading Scottish case which deals in general terms with vicarious liability for a servant is *Kirby* v. *National Coal Board*, 1958 S.C. 514. There the Lord President, following *Goh Choon Seng* v. *Lee Kim Soo* [1925] A.C. 550 and

Canadian Pacific Ry. Co. v. *Lockhart* [1942] A.C. 591 said (at p. 532): "Vicarious responsibility for the act of a servant will only attach to the master if the act of the servant is done within the scope of the employment. It is probably not possible, and it is certainly inadvisable, to endeavour to lay down an exhaustive definition of what falls within the scope of the employment. Each case must depend to a considerable extent on its particular facts. But, in the decisions, four different types of situation have been envisaged as guides to the solution of this problem. In the first place, if the master actually authorised the particular act, he is clearly liable for it. Secondly, where the workman does some work which he is appointed to do, but does it in a way which his master has not authorised, and would not have authorised had he known of it, the master is nevertheless still responsible, for the servant's act is still within the scope of his employment. On the other hand, in the third place, if the servant is employed only to do a particular work or a particular class of work, and he does something outside the scope of that work, the master is not responsible." "The master is exempt only when the servant was exclusively on his own business," says Salmond on *Torts* (13th ed., p. 133). And Professor Fleming writes (2nd ed., p. 336): "The question is whether the activity was reasonably incidental to the performance of his authorised duties or involved so substantial a departure that the servant must *pro hac vice* be regarded as a stranger *vis-à-vis* his master."

22.1.3   The particular problem which is presented by deviation from an authorised route has been considered in three English cases in which injury was done to persons who were not passengers in the vehicle driven by the servant — *Joel* v. *Morison* (1834) 6 C. & P. 501, *Mitchell* v. *Crassweller* (1853) 13 C.B. 237 and *Storey* v. *Ashton* (1869) L.R., 4 Q.B. 476. It is a question of fact and degree in each case whether the deviation is sufficiently detached from the master's business, to constitute a frolic of the servant unconnected with the enterprise for which he was employed.

Through each of the three English cases cited runs the idea of a new journey entirely unconnected with the master's business as opposed to a mere detour for the servant's selfish purposes. "If he was going out of his way, against his master's implied commands, when driving on his master's business, he will make his master liable; but if he was going on a frolic of his own, without being at all on his master's business, the master will not be liable," said Parke, B., in the leading case of *Joel* v. *Morison.*

22.1.4   Had the driver in the present case been driving a lorry which was empty or contained nothing of real importance, I think that so substantial a deviation might well have constituted a frolic of his own. The presence of passengers, however, whom the servant is charged *qua* servant to drive to their ultimate destination, makes it impossible (at all events, provided that they are not all parties to the plans for deviation) to say that the deviation is entirely for the servant's purposes. Their presence and transport is a dominant purpose of the authorised journey, and, although they are transported deviously, continues to play an essential part. It was said in argument that there must be some limits to that contention and that one could not hold that, if the driver had gone to Inverness, he would still be acting on his master's business. No doubt there are such limits to the argument as common sense may set on the facts of each case. But when there are passengers whom the servant on his master's behalf has taken aboard for a transport to Glasgow, their transport and safety does not cease at a certain stage of the journey to be the master's business, or part of his enterprise, merely because the servant has for his own purposes chosen some route which is contrary to his instructions.

21.1.5 The more dominant are the current obligations of the master's business in connection with the lorry, the less weight is to be attached to disobedient navigational extravagances of the servant … In the present case the defenders remained liable, in spite of the deviation, for their driver's negligence. It is unnecessary, therefore, to consider how far the pursuer could rely on the defender's duty to him *qua* passenger or base his claim on further arguments not available to a mere pedestrian. The Lord Ordinary did not deal with it on that basis and no case was pleaded in contract. I would dismiss the appeal.'

COMMENT

22.2.1 Decided: June 22, 1966.
    April 10: Evelyn Waugh died.
    May 6: Moors murderers jailed.
    June 11: Mary Quant and Peter Sellers awarded M.B.E.

22.2.2 What is your view on the question left unanswered — that is, what would have been the position if it had been one of the girl-guide-seeking brigadiers who had been injured? What if (a) the driver was pulling into a lay-by to relieve himself; (b) the driver made a detour to pick up some medication; (c) the deviation was to a place which did not lie between the points of departure and destination?

22.2.3 Extract 3 discusses the case and Lord President Inglis' dictum in *Kirby* further. See para. 2.3.3. for a mention of vicarious liability by Erskine, and para. 2.5.4. for Bell. See Lord Avonside in *Angus v. Glasgow Corporation*, 1977 S.L.T. 206 for a conventionally deferential reception of this House of Lords decision.

Vicarious liability outwith employment

89. Scobie v. Steele & Wilson Ltd
1963 S.L.T. (Notes) 45

22.3.1 'A pedestrian was injured when he was in collision with a motor vehicle owned by a limited company which, at the time of the accident, was being driven by one of the directors of the company.

The pedestrian brought an action claiming damages against the company. The company contended that the pursuer had not made a relevant case of vicarious liability inasmuch as the doctrine of vicarious liability applied only in the case of an employee or servant of a company, and a director not being a servant of a company, could not therefore involve the company in vicarious liability.

22.3.2   Counsel for the pursuer, on the other hand, maintained that the fact that the driver was a director was irrelevant to the issue of the company's liability if the vehicle was owned by the company and was being driven on the company's business and on the company's authority. He referred to the case of *Ormrod* v. *Crosville Motor Services* [1953] 1 W.L.R. 1120, for authority for the general proposition that service or agency are the bases on which vicarious liability for negligent driving of a vehicle is rested. In his submissions it was relevantly averred that the driver was acting as agent for the defenders at the time, and the fact that he was a director was irrelevant.

22.3.3   Lord Cameron said: "The point is a short one and not covered by any direct authority so far as the researches of counsel disclosed. I do not think that the authority founded upon by counsel for the defenders advances his case, as it was concerned with a wholly different problem. If he is correct, then in no case, even of a small private company with directors taking part in the everyday operations of the business, can the company be made liable vicariously for injury caused by their negligence. This appears to me to be an extravagant proposition, but one which is an inevitable corollary of counsel for the defenders' contention.

22.3.4   In my opinion, if it is relevantly averred that a company director is driving a company vehicle with the knowledge and on the authority of the company upon company business, and through his negligent driving is involved in an accident, the company may be made vicariously liable for that negligence. That seems to me common sense and sound law."'

COMMENT

22.4.1   Decided: March 20, 1963.
    Katanga gave up attempt to secede from Belgian Congo.
    First kidney transplant.

22.4.2   The case mentioned, *Ormrod*, is authority for a head of vicarious liability which does not depend upon the existence of a contract between the parties, certainly not a particular contract of agency or employment. As a result of the efforts of the House of Lords in *Launchbury v. Morgans* [1973] A.C. 127, the effect of *Ormrod* is to make the owner of a vehicle liable if he expressly or by implication instructs someone to drive the car for his (the owner's) purposes. Consider such a case from a Scottish perspective. Would the existence of an implied contract of mandate explain the decision? Consider Dr Rodger's concluding remarks on the passage from Alfenus Varrus (1988 C.L.P. 1) in this context. *Launchbury* made it clear that this doctrine would not apply to a car used as a family car in the absence of the driver carrying out a task for the owner. Simple permission to drive does not establish vicarious liability. Insurance lies behind these decisions, the hope being that an insured defender can be found. Another solution to that problem has been found in England, and that is to utilise the concept of statutory liability in conjunction with the Road Traffic Act. The Act provides that it is an offence to permit someone to drive one's car if there is no third-party insurance in effect in respect of that person. Accordingly the failure to comply with the statutory duty materially contributes to the pursuer suffering what is in effect a financial loss. (See *Monk v. Warbey* [1935] 1 K.B. 75. Note the problems caused by this Act in relation to *volenti non fit injuria*: see Ext. 76.)

It has recently been held in England that a director of a one man company can be personally liable for a negligent misrepresentation (2–1 in the Court of Appeal): *Williams v. Natural Life Health Foods*, January 9, 1997, unreported.

Vicarious liability: multiple employers

90. **Park v. Tractor Shovels**
1980 S.L.T. 94 (O.H.)

22.5.1   'LORD COWIE: In April 1974 the pursuer was employed by the first defender as a plant fitter on a site at Ravenscraig Steel Works, Motherwell. The first defenders were engaged in clearing top soil on this 50 acre site in preparation for the erection of buildings and the laying of railway lines to form a marshalling yard. In my opinion the overall work upon which the first defenders were engaged fell within the definition of works of engineering construction. The equipment which they were using to carry out this work consisted of about six large earth-moving vehicles described as TS 24s. In order to service these vehicles and keep them in working condition the first defenders employed welders and plant fitters who were based at their workshops at Wellwood Yard, Dunfermline, but in the case of the pursuer he was permanently based on the site of the operations and had a Transit van there, containing spare parts and other equipment to enable him to carry out his job. He was the only plant fitter on the site who was employed by the first defenders and on occasions required the assistance of other men when the job was too heavy for him to do himself, or specialised work was needed, such as welding.

22.5.2   In addition to the vehicles owned by the first defenders, there were a number of other vehicles on site which were on hire to them by other firms. In particular there were three TS 24s belonging to the second defender and at least one vehicle, an RH4 belonging to a firm called Tractor Shovels (Fife) Ltd. Each of these vehicles had their own operators and in addition the second defender had, on site, a plant fitter who was responsible for servicing and maintaining the second defender's vehicles. The second defender's plant fitter in April 1974 at Ravenscraig Steel Works was a man called Hatten. He was the second defender's senior representative on the site; furthermore he was in a special position *vis-à-vis* his employer, because it was his responsibility to keep his employer's vehicles in working condition, to keep the time-sheets on the basis of which his employer was paid, and he even had a measure of authority over the drivers of his employer's vehicles in the sense that they would have to inform him if they were not available for work at any time. His duties were not strictly defined and, broadly, the evidence indicated that as the second defender's senior representative on the site, he was expected to further the second defender's interests in any way he could.

22.5.3   The main task which Hatten had was to keep his employer's vehicles working to the limit of their capacity, and this was no easy task since they were not new vehicles and required a good deal of attention. In his efforts to fulfil his responsibilities Hatten very often had to have assistance, and while he was entitled to call on the driver of the vehicle which was being repaired to help him and other specialised assistance, he also sought and received from time to time help from the first defender's employees and in particular from their resident plant fitter, the pursuer. The evidence in the case showed a very good spirit of co-operation between the employees of the firms on the site and this co-operation manifested itself not only at Ravenscraig Steel Works but also at a previous site where the same firms had been working, namely Westfield Open Cast Mining Site. There is no doubt in my mind that this spirit of co-operation must have been known to the employers of various workmen involved and was to their great advantage particularly in the case of the second defender, since he was the main beneficiary of the assistance provided by others, due to the greater amount of work required on his vehicles.

22.5.4   In his turn Hatten from time to time provided assistance to the first defender's plant fitter when it was required, and this was only to be expected in return for the help he received, and must, in my opinion, have been reasonably within the contemplation of the second defender in the light of the spirit of co-operation which existed both at Ravenscraig Steel Works and Westfield Open Cast Mining Site. In any event Hatten, as the second defender's senior representative at Ravenscraig, had a wide discretion in the amount of co-operation which he could give to the employees of other firms working on the site.

. . . . . .

22.5.5   Against that general background it is now necessary to consider the events of Saturday, April 20, 1974. On that day the pursuer had to change the differential of one of the TS 24s belonging to his employers, the first defender. The vehicle was lying at a part of the main site set aside for carrying out of repairs and adjacent to the

Transit van in which the pursuer kept his spare parts and equipment…
The first task which the pursuer had to perform was to detach the old
differential from the vehicle, let it drop to the ground underneath
and then move the vehicle away so that it was clear of the old
differential. The differential having been removed the next thing the
pursuer had to do was to remove the drive coupling from it so that it
could be fitted to the new differential.

· · · · · ·

22.5.6   Thereafter and probably during the dinner break, Hatten,
the second defender's plant fitter, discovered that the wrong size of
gasket had been delivered to the pursuer by Yeoman and informed
him that he had a spare gasket for a TS 24 in his car. He went and got
it and then in accordance with the spirit of co-operation referred to,
offered to help the pursuer lift the differential into place by operating
the lifting mechanism of a vehicle known as RH4 which was parked
up near the TS 24 awaiting minor repair. This vehicle, which was not
described in detail in the evidence, had a hydraulic arm or jib to
which could be fitted a hammer for breaking rocks … In any event
this RH4, which was the only one on the site, belonged to neither the
first defenders nor the second defender, but a firm called Tractor
Shovels (Fife) Ltd., and was on hire to the first defenders along with
its own operator. Up to this point, what I have narrated was not
seriously in dispute and where hereafter I propose to make findings-
in-fact without comment, I do so on the evidence which I have accepted
as credible and reliable.

· · · · · ·

22.5.7   It was clear that in order to fit the differential to the TS 24 a
lifting device of some sort would be required because of its weight,
and when Hatten offered to operate the RH4 for that purpose the
pursuer accepted. Plant fitters do not normally operate machines of
this sort to do the job the machines are designed to do, but they work
on them for the purpose of repair and maintenance and become
familiar with the controls while testing them. In the case of Hatten,
however, while he was generally familiar with the controls of
hydraulically-operated machinery, he had never operated the controls
of an RH4 previously or indeed any other lifting appliance, and he
certainly had never been trained in their use. Having said that, two
things should be made clear. The first is that although Hatten had
never operated an RH4 before for lifting purposes, he had driven it
over the ground the previous day and he clearly knew which lever
operated the raising, lowering and slowing of the hydraulic arm.
Furthermore because of his experience in repairing and testing
hydraulic machinery he was confident of his ability to operate this
machine as a lifting device. The second thing is that the pursuer had

no reason to suppose that Hatten had not operated the lifting device on the RH4 before, and indeed as a skilled plant fitter there was no reason why Hatten should not have been capable of mastering the controls very easily.

On receiving the proper gasket for the TS 24 and the offer by Hatten to operate the lifting device of the RH4 for the purpose of fitting the new differential, the pursuer decided to accept Hatten's offer of assistance and to finish the job that day instead of waiting to do it another day. Accordingly he moved the TS 24 until it was positioned over the new differential and then put a wire sling on to it. The end of the sling was led upwards to the top of the bonnet of the TS 24 and the pursuer climbed up there with the intention of attaching the sling to the arm of the RH4 when it was brought over him.

. . . . . .

22.5.8 Meanwhile Hatten had started up the RH4 and brought it over to the TS 24. He stopped it in a position which was convenient for bringing the arm of the vehicle over the point where the pursuer was crouching. At a signal from the pursuer Hatten operated the control lever and slewed the arm of the RH4 to the left. In doing so the arm passed about six inches above the head of the pursuer and continued until it struck the air breather stack near the point where the metal stays are attached to it.

. . . . . .

22.5.9 The pursuer's account of the accident... was that after Hatten swung the arm of the RH4 to the left and struck the air breather stack, the arm came downwards and struck pursuer on the back, crushing him to some extent against the bonnet of the TS 24 and knocking him off the vehicle.

I have no hesitation in accepting the account given by the pursuer, partly because I found him a credible and reliable witness, but also because I found his account to be a much more likely explanation for this accident.

. . . . . .

22.5.10 That brings me to the fourth case which the pursuer makes, and it is directed against the second defender in respect of the negligence of his employee, James Hatten, for whose actings in the course of his employment the pursuer says the second defender is responsible.

The response to this case which the second defender makes is twofold. First, the pursuer has not established negligence on the part of James Hatten in respect of the pursuer's accident; and second, in any event the second defender is not liable for any negligence on the part of Hatten because at the time of the accident to the pursuer he was acting outwith the scope of his employment with the second defender... Although I consider the question to be a narrow one, I have come to the conclusion on the evidence, that Hatten failed to exercise reasonable care in the operation of the arm of the RH4, and that his failure to do so caused the accident to the pursuer.

......

22.5.11 Having reached the decision, the next question is whether the second defender is vicariously liable for the negligence of his servant Hatten. It is quite obvious that the second defender can only be so liable if at the time of this accident Hatten was acting within the scope of his employment with him. For the second defender senior counsel argued, forcefully and succinctly, that in the circumstances of this case, Hatten was clearly acting outwith the scope of his employment because his employment with the second defender in April 1974 was that of a plant fitter, whereas, when this accident occurred, he had arrogated to himself the duties of a crane operator. He pointed out that both jobs required skill, and that what Hatten had done was to exchange one in which he had skill, for another in which he had none.

......

22.5.12 The Dean of Faculty pointed out that although Hatten's principal duties were in connection with the repair and maintenance of his employer's machines, he also had to keep time-sheets for him and his drivers would inform him if for any reason they had to be absent from work, although Hatten's actual consent for their absence was not required. The Dean of Faculty submitted that the evidence showed that Hatten was more like a general foreman than a mere plant fitter... In these circumstances what Hatten was doing at the time of the pursuer's accident, even if it was not specifically authorised by his employer, and even might not have been authorised by him, was so connected with acts which he was authorised to do as to be rightly regarded as a mode although an improper mode of doing them (*cf.* Salmond on *Torts* (17th ed.), at p. 465).

22.5.13 It is trite law that an employer is vicariously liable for the negligence of his servant when the latter is acting within the scope of his employment. Furthermore the test to be applied for the purpose of discovering whether a particular act is within or outwith the scope of the servant's employment is relatively clear. The difficulty which the court often has is to apply that test to the particular circumstances of the individual case.

This has often been said, and in particular Lord President Clyde in *Kirby* v. *National Coal Board*, 1959 S.L.T. 7, endeavoured to indicate the four types of situation which had been envisaged in the decided cases as a guide to the solution of this problem [his Lordship then cited substantially the same passage as set out at 22.1.2]. This passage was quoted with approval by Lord Pearce in *Williams* v. *A. & W. Hemphill Ltd.*, 1966 S.L.T. at p. 260, Ext 67 and provides the basis upon which I must approach the present case.

22.5.14 Another test which provides a useful guide to deciding this difficult question in the circumstances of any particular case is put forward in Fleming's *Law of Torts* (5th ed.) at p. 368, where the learned author states that: "The question is whether the activity was reasonably incidental to the performance of his authorised duties or involved so substantial a departure that the servant must *pro hac vice* be regarded as a stranger *vis-à-vis* his master."

. . . . . .

22.5.15 [Senior counsel for the second defenders argued that Hatten] was employed to do the work of a plant fitter, and he took on the skilled work of a crane driver. Accordingly, senior counsel argued he had taken himself out of the scope of his employment with the second defender... He reinforced his argument by submitting that in any event that was no evidence in this case to show that what Hatten was doing at the time of the accident to the pursuer, was incidental to the performance of his authorised duties, and so, as a matter of law, he could not be held to have been acting within the scope of his employment.

22.5.16 While I have great sympathy for the clear and impressive arguments presented by senior counsel for the second defender, I am not prepared to accept them.

In the first place, I am not prepared to hold that there is no evidence to support the view that what Hatten was doing at the time of the accident was incidental to his employment as a plant fitter. I accept that Hatten had never operated a lifting appliance for the purpose of repairing other vehicles, but there was evidence that such appliances did have to be used occasionally to repair the type of vehicle which the defenders were operating on this site and at the previous site at Westfield, and in these circumstances the use of a lifting appliance could be said to be an accepted part of the work of repairing and maintaining these vehicles.

22.5.17 In the second place, I am not prepared to take such a strict view of Hatten's actings as the court did in the cases of *McAulay* v. *Dunlop*, 1926 S.L.T. 341, and *Alford* v. *National Coal Board*, 1951 S.L.T. 163... In my opinion he was doing something during his working hours and on his employer's premises and although what he was doing was directly in furtherance of the interests of the first defenders, it was indirectly in the interests of the second defender also, because it furthered the spirit of co-operation on the site which benefited his own employer to a substantial degree. In addition, as I have already indicated, his actings seemed to me to have a close connection with his work of repairing and maintaining these heavy vehicles. If I had to equiparate the circumstances of this case with any of the decided cases to which I was referred, I would be inclined to choose the case of *Kay* v. *I.T.W. Ltd.* [1968] 1 Q.B. 140 rather than the cases referred to by counsel for the second defender.

. . . . . .

22.5.18 As I have already said, although Hatten was not directly furthering his own employer's interests, he was doing so indirectly, and in the words of Fleming in *The Law of Torts* his actings did not in my opinion involve "so substantial a departure that [Hatten] must *pro hac vice* be regarded as a stranger *vis-à-vis* his master"... It would seem to follow therefore that the second defender is liable for the loss, injury and damage sustained by the pursuer, but for one circumstance. In addition to the other cases which the pursuer makes, he avers that the first defenders are vicariously liable for the negligence of Hatten, on the basis that they accepted him as a volunteer and by doing so took him into their employment. In that situation it is at least in theory possible that although Hatten was acting within the scope of his employment with the second defender, he was at the time of this accident in the temporary employment of the first defenders. Having stated that possible argument, I have no hesitation in rejecting it. In the present case, in the light of my decision that Hatten was acting within the scope of his employment with the second defender when this accident occurred, he was in my opinion in the same category as a crane driver operating his crane in connection with work being done by the first defenders; that being so the burden of proof of showing that responsibility for his actings shifted from the second defender to the first defenders falls on the pursuer. It is a heavy burden and can only be charged in quite exceptional circumstances (*John Young & Co., (Kelvinhaugh) Ltd.* v. *O'Donnell and Ors.*, 1958 S.L.T. (Notes) 46 and *Mersey Docks and Harbour Board* v. *Coggins and Griffith (Liverpool) Ltd.* [1947] A.C. 1. It is quite clear on the facts of the present case that that burden has not been discharged and accordingly in my opinion the responsibility for Hatten's actings remains with the second defender as his general employer... Having reached that decision it seems to me that that disposes of any question of joint liability on the part of the defenders based on vicarious responsibility. In my opinion it is not merely a tenet of the Christian faith that a man cannot serve two masters, but applies also to the legal doctrine of vicarious liability.

. . . . . .

22.5.19 On the question of contributory negligence the only point which was put forward by the defender was that the pursuer was at fault because he allowed the RH4 to be used without its authorised usual operator... In these circumstances I am not prepared to hold that the pursuer was at fault in allowing Hatten, whom he knew to be an experienced plant fitter, to use the RH4 to assist him in lifting the new differential into position. The pursuer was in my opinion entitled to assume that as a plant fitter Hatten would be reasonably familiar with the controls of the machine and would not have volunteered to operate it had he not considered himself competent to do so.'

COMMENT

22.6.1   Decided: November 30, 1978.
Sept. 8: Shah of Iran imposed martial law in face of unrest.
Oct. 16: Karol Wojtyla became first non-Italian pope in modern times.
Nov. 29: 913 people committed suicide in Revd. Jim Jones' Jonestown, Guyana.

22.6.2   Is it necessarily the case that a man cannot serve two masters? If he can, might it not be possible, in an appropriate case, to have joint liability?

22.6.3   Lord Caplan found *pro hac vice* employment established in a claim by a canteen worker against the catering company who were responsible for the catering in her own usual employer's canteen. The basis of her case was that the spilled food upon which she slipped had been dropped either by the catering company's own employees or those of her own employer who were *pro hac vice* employees of the catering company. Decree was granted with contributory negligence assessed at 25 per cent (*Sime v. Sutcliffe Catering (Scotland) Ltd*, 1990 S.L.T. 687). See also *McGregor v. J. S. Duthie and Sons*, 1966 S.L.T.; *Moir v. Wide Arc Services*, 1987 S.L.T. 495.

22.6.4   *Marshall v. William Sharp & Sons*, 1991 S.L.T. 114 is notable for Lord Dunpark's defence of a passage he inserted in Gloag and Henderson in 1968: "There is no general rule that an employer is not liable for breach of his personal duties to an employee injured through the negligent work of an independent contractor employed by the employer." With respect I find that statement difficult and the actual decision does not seem correct either. It remains in the tenth edition, 1995. See *Baxter v. Pritchard*, 1992 G.W.D. 24–1385 for a case where a case averring vicarious liability for an independent contractor which was dismissed and this was upheld by the sheriff principal.

PARTIES

Mental abnormality

91. Waugh (Appellant) v. James K. Allan Ltd
1964 S.C.(H.L.) 102

22.7.1   'The following narrative of the facts is taken from the speech of Lord Reid:
"While walking on the pavement of a street in Edinburgh, the appellant was struck and seriously injured by a heavy lorry belonging to the respondents and being driven by their servant, Robert Gemmell. The immediate cause of the accident was that Gemmell was suddenly disabled by an attack of coronary thrombosis. The lorry had been properly driven at a normal speed. Then it appeared to draw in to its

near side: it did not slacken speed, mounted the pavement, knocked down a lamp standard and struck the appellant. Then it returned to the roadway, collided with one or two vehicles, and finally came to rest on the other side of the road in contact with another vehicle. While out of control it travelled some 85 yards. Before it came to rest, Gemmell was seen to be slumped over the steering wheel. He was still breathing when it came to rest, but died immediately after. So the respondents plead inevitable accident. But the appellant maintains that, by reason of his physical condition, Gemmell ought to have realised that he was unfit to drive at the time of the accident, and that is the issue in this case.

"Gemmel was a big, powerful man aged 44. His doctor gave evidence for the appellant, and from him we learn that Gemmell suffered attacks of gastritis from time to time, but was an impatient man who would not give in. Otherwise, he appears to have enjoyed good health, as his doctor had no suspicion that he might suffer from thrombosis or any other cause of sudden collapse.

"On the day of the accident Gemmell, after making another call, took his lorry sometime before 11 a.m. to Gorgie Mills… When loading started, Cox's men put each bag on the lorry and then Gemmell put it in its proper place. Apparently he found no difficulty in lifting these heavy bags. But after six tons had been properly stowed on the lorry he 'turned badly' according to one of the men in the squad. Another says he 'got a fit of coughing', while loading bags of bone dust. The men offered to finish the job for him, and he jumped down off the lorry and went to a booth some distance away for a drink of water. When he came back, he vomited water, and the men noticed that sweat was pouring from him and he looked very ill and pale. The men offered Gemmell tea and suggested that he should rest, but he refused. So they left him leaning against the lorry, and it is clear that, at that moment, he could not have driven the lorry.

"But a minute or two later, he was sitting in his driving seat in the cab when the foreman came up and told him he must wait to sign for the load. He merely indicated that he understood. The foreman says he did not look ill, only flushed, but it would seem that he paid little attention to Gemmell: he did not know he had been ill… He drove off immediately. The dispatch clerk saw that he was sweating heavily and belching, but did not think he was ill or on the point of collapse: but he also did not know that Gemmell had been ill, and he did not take much notice of him… But he only drove about a quarter of a mile before he collapsed. A witness, in a car following his lorry at that point, saw nothing wrong with his driving until the lorry began to draw into its near side without slackening speed: then she realised that there was something wrong, but fortunately was able to avoid colliding with the lorry."

. . . . . .

22.7.2 Lord Reid: The issue is not whether Gemmell was in fact unfit to drive when he left the glue works. It is whether, as a reasonable man, he ought to have realised that he was unfit. He had no reason to suspect thrombosis, even his doctor had never suspected it. But were his symptoms such that an ordinary layman would have taken them as a warning that it was hazardous to drive off immediately?... [Gemmell's doctor] thought that, in fact, the illness in the glue works was connected with the thrombosis, but that, unless there was acute pain, Gemmell would assume that this was another attack of gastritis. Apart from pain, the symptoms were similar. He agreed that nausea could be brought on by a bad smell.

. . . . . .

22.7.3 I am therefore of opinion that the appellant has failed to prove that Gemmell acted rashly or negligently in driving off so soon after his illness, and no other fault can be imputed to him. One must have great sympathy with the appellant who has suffered so severely through no fault of his own, but I find it impossible to blame Gemmell.

22.7.4 Viscount Radcliffe: I confess that, if left to myself, I would have been disposed to allow this appeal. Even after studying the opinions in the Court of Session and those of your Lordships, which I have been able to read in advance, I cannot altogether rid my mind of the impression that Gemmell failed in proper care in taking his lorry out into Gorgie Road so soon after his bad and rather mysterious attack of vomiting. What weighs with me is that he had no power to diagnose himself or to relate his illness with any certainty to his previous gastric disorder. In that situation, I think that anyone responsible for him would have told him that he must not drive until much more time had elapsed without further trouble or a doctor had been able to advise him. There was not one on the spot to be responsible for him, and I think that he ought to have so advised himself.

But this is only a matter of judgment, and I do not want to set my own tentative view against the clear conclusion which has been reached by my colleagues. In those circumstances, I must agree that the appeal ought to be dismissed.'

Comment

22.8.1 Decided: June 4, 1964.
March 27: First guilty verdicts in Great Train Robbery trials.
April 20: Nelson Mandela's trial begins.
June 4: Ian Smith threatens to declare UDI in Rhodesia.

22.8.2 Although not deciding the point, it seems to be clear that the court accepted that a person out of his mind would not be liable in delict, unless he ought to have suspected that there was something wrong beforehand. He might then be held liable for this anterior neglect. This is even more clearly the English approach for, in

Roberts v. Ramsbottom [1980] 1 All E.R. 7, a man who suffered an attack and was said to be in a state of automatism, was held liable, but on the basis that after the first warnings he had continued to drive. Motoring cases, where the drivers are insured, are less likely to encourage a rigorous examination because the court knows that there are insurers in the background simply waiting to pay. The issue would be clearly focused if the action were against a person uninsured in respect of the incident, who was at the time of the proof restored to his right mind. Professor Walker's view that there should be no such liability, supported by reference to Dig. IX, 2.5.2 would seem perfectly reasonable. In cases, though, where fault is not at issue, if any be left, then it is more difficult to tender any view. Probably there should be no liability in such cases — perhaps on the view that a sudden attack by a wasp or a heart attack is *damnum fatale*. On the other hand, to classify such events as *damnum fatale* might allow insurers to avoid indemnity on the basis of Act of God clauses in the policy of insurance.

Children

92. Hamilton v. Fife Health Board
1993 S.L.T. 624

22.9.1   In 1976 a mother gave birth to a baby boy who died three days after he was born. The child's parents raised an action against the health board for loss of society in respect of the death of their child. According to the parents' averments, the child died as a result of negligent acts carried out by doctors before the child was born. The defenders argued that the claim for loss of society was irrelevant as a person only came into existence on birth and therefore there was no person alive at the time that the injuries were sustained. The Lord Ordinary held that the words "personal injuries" did not cover injury sustained by a child not yet born as there was no person at that stage and dismissed the action so far as relating to the conclusions for loss of society. The pursuers reclaimed.

· · · · · ·

22.9.2   Lord MacLuskey: In my opinion, the only issue which it is necessary to decide is as to the meaning and application of s. 1 (1) of the Damages (Scotland) Act 1976. What that section does is to make a wrongdoer ("the responsible person") liable to pay damages to a "relative" (as defined in the Schedule) of a person who has died. The death of that person must have been in consequence of personal injuries sustained by that person as a result of an act or omission giving rise to liability (in the responsible person) to pay damages to the injured person or his executor. As the act or omission must be one giving rise to liability to pay damages, there can be no liability until both damnum and injuria concur. There can be no liability to pay damages until there is a person in respect of whose loss the claim to damages arises. An unborn person, a foetus, is not a person in the eyes of the law — at least in relation to the law of civil remedies — and there can be no liability to pay damages to a foetus, even although the foetus has sustained injuries resulting from a negligent act or omission constituting a breach of duty owed.

22.9.3 There is no difficulty whatsoever in Scots law in holding that doctors engaged in the delivery of a foetus owe a duty of care to avoid injury to that foetus: that is trite. But once the foetus ceases on birth to be a foetus and becomes a person there is a concurrence of injuria and damnum and the newly born child has a right to sue the person whose breach of duty has resulted in the child's loss. The coming into existence òf that right to sue does not depend upon the application of any fiction. It depends upon the neighbourhood doctrine of *Donoghue* v. *Stevenson* [1932 S.C.(H.L.) 31]. The doctors engaged in the medical work of assisting in the delivery of a child can obviously foresee that a failure to exercise due care and skill by them may result in injuries to the foetus, being injuries which will cause the child to suffer loss: if the loss to the living child is the foreseeable, direct and probable consequence of the failure to exercise due care and skill at an earlier stage, there is a breach of duty owed, in the law of negligence, to the child and that breach occurs when the child is born. If the injuries with which he is born are injuries to his organs or skeleton or tissues then they are properly and sensibly described as "personal injuries" even although when they were inflicted he did not enjoy legal personality; they are injuries to his person although not to his legal persona. They are to him an impairment of his physical condition. To suppose that only one who enjoys legal personality can sustain "personal injuries" is to attach an artificial meaning to the adjective "personal" in s. 1 (1). Legal personality is a construct of the law and merely relates to a basket of rights and responsibilities recognised by the law as effeiring to certain specified creatures, including man-made creatures: there are many examples in history of adult, sentient human beings being denied human status and legal personality and of limited liability companies and even of non-human animals being accorded rights and responsibilities normally appropriate only to human beings.

22.9.4 In the circumstances, I see no reason to restrict "personal" in the phrase "personal injuries" so that it means injuries suffered by one on whom the law has conferred legal personality for certain purposes. In my view, it is equally clear that the whole phrase "personal injuries sustained by him" in this context is perfectly apt to include injuries inflicted to the person of a child immediately before his birth and continuing to have their effects on him by impairing his physical condition at and after the time of his birth. Whether or not the phrase would be apt to cover some form of trauma to a foetus in the early days of pregnancy it is not necessary to decide; different legal systems for different purposes have to decide such issues relating to the legal status and rights of a foetus in their context as best they can when they arise: cf. *Roe* v. *Wade* [410 US 113 (1973)], I am not persuaded that the use of the personal pronoun "him" in the phrase "sustained by him" was intended by Parliament to have the bizarre result that there was no one to injure or to sustain injuries in the few days before the child was born. It is perfectly common in ordinary speech to refer to the child in utero as "he", "she", "him" or "her" and I do not feel driven by the use of such ordinary parlance in this section to the view which the Lord Ordinary accepted, that "Parliament envisaged a person sustaining injuries", meaning a person enjoying legal personality. It was this child who sustained injuries to his person and who died in consequence of personal injuries sustained by him. That appears to me to be enough to require me to hold that the responsible person became liable, on the child's birth, to pay damages to him. There being no dispute that the child was a person who died in consequence of the injuries inflicted on him immediately before his birth, it follows, in my opinion, that the responsible person is also liable to pay damages to the pursuers and reclaimers under s. 1 (1). It will thus be seen that I prefer the approach of the reclaimer which I have endeavoured to summarise at an earlier stage and that I have simply reformulated the four question test which was promulgated in the reclaimers' submissions.

· · · · · ·

22.9.5 LORD CAPLAN: In my view the rule of law relating to a child in utero to the effect that it is not a living being (which on one view itself is a fiction) cannot apply in both directions. If the foetus is not a living being then it is mere organic matter — a fuse or conduit which if affected by the negligence of a defender can lead (because it is a feature in the chain of causation) to the emergence of personal injuries when the child is born. In *de Martell* [*v. Merton and Sutton Health Authority* [1992] 3 W.L.R. 637] at p. 650 Phillips J. aptly refers to comments of Holmes J. in *Dietrich* v. *Northampton* [(1884) 138 Mass. 14], Holmes J. stated at p. 16 of the report: "that, on general principles, an injury transmitted from the actor to a person through his own organic substance, or through his mother, before he became a person, stands on the same footing as an injury transmitted to an existing person through other intervening substances outside him".

The implication of the point I have been making is that even if I am wrong in attributing to "sustained", as the word is used in s. 1(1), a meaning such as "borne" or "experienced", then personal injuries were not "sustained" until the infant was born. Certainly damage was done at an earlier stage to the foetus but it is only at birth that for the first time one could say "here is a living being who has sustained personal injuries". As Phillips J. puts it (at p. 650 of *de Martell*): "In law and in logic no damage can have been caused to the plaintiff before the plaintiff existed. The damage was suffered by the plaintiff at the moment that, in law, the plaintiff achieved personality and inherited the damaged body for which the health authority (on the assumed facts) was responsible."

22.9.6 The defenders attack the applicability to Scotland of *de Martell* and *Burton* [*v. Islington Health Authority* [1992] 3 W.L.R. 637]. These cases were both concerned with ante-natal injuries to a child suffered before the passage of the Congenital Disabilities (Civil Liability) Act 1976. Thus the court was concerned with determining the relevant English common law as it existed before the 1976 statute. It appears to me that the reasoning I have set out above, although supported by English and foreign authority, is based on principles which are also applicable to Scots law. The respondents' senior counsel contended that it was not necessary for the court to erect an elaborate argument such as (it is said) happened in *Burton* because in Scotland the matter should be determined by the applicability of the civil law fiction. I see no need for fiction at all in relation to the right of a deceased child to raise an action based on what happened to it before birth. The civil law fiction is clearly necessary for the resolution of certain categories of case. I do not think it can be disputed that it is needed to create a right of succession in relation to a posthumous child. It may also be needed in a reparation context in a case such as *Cohen* v. *Shaw* [1992 S.L.T. 1022] because it is certainly arguable that without the fiction the posthumous child was not a "relative" at the time of the father's death. However in the present case it seems to me that the child would have had a perfectly clear right to sue on the basis of established common law principles. It should be noted that in England the common law recognises a principle equivalent to our civil law fiction. This point is brought out in the judgment of Dillon L.J. in *Burton* at pp. 655 and 656. His Lordship then states: "For my part, I think it would be open to the English courts to apply the civil law maxim directly to the situations we have in these two appeals, and treat the two plaintiffs as lives in being at the times of the events which injured them as they were later born alive, but it is not necessary to do so".

22.9.7 I would agree with that view in relation to the suggested need to apply the civil law fiction in an equivalent situation in Scotland. I consider that parents who otherwise qualify would have had a right of action for damages prior to 1976 in respect of a child who had died because of ante-natal damage. That is because the child itself would have had a right of action independent of the limiting features of the civil law fiction. That being so, I am confirmed in my view that it was not the intention of the legislature to innovate upon the existing law in respect of the relevant matter. Indeed innovation within the context of the 1976 Act would have been surprising and would have required clear statement.'

COMMENT

22.10.1   Decided March 24, 1993.
    April 3: Grand National void after false start.
    April 30: Steffi Graf "fan" stabs Monica Seles.
    May 4: Asil Nadir jumps bail.

22.10.2   There are related issues, see *Delict*, 9.3. The case of parents suing for wrongful birth has become controversial. See *Jones v. Lanarkshire Health Authority*, 1990 S.L.T. 19. And there is wrongful life too — see *McFarlane v. Tayside Health Board*, 1996 Rep.L.R. 159 (under appeal). The *Hamilton* case was quietly dismissed as having been effected by limitation: 1995 G.W.D. 9–516.

Relatives

See Appendix, Extract 10.

Partnerships

See Appendix, Extract 1: Partnership Act 1890.

The Crown

See Appendix, Extract 3: Crown Proceedings Act 1947.

Spouses

See Appendix, Extract 13: Law Reform (Husband and Wife) Act 1984.
See generally *Delict*, Chapters 9 and 10.

CHAPTER 23

PRIVATE INTERNATIONAL LAW — JURISDICTION AND CHOICE OF LAW IN DELICT

Jurisdiction

93. Davenport v. Corinthian Motor Policies at Lloyds
1991 S.L.T. 774

23.1.1 'In September 1983 an individual was knocked down in a road traffic accident. In 1986 she raised an action in Glasgow Sheriff Court against the driver of the vehicle involved and, the action being undefended, obtained decree against him for the principal sum with interest and expenses. She obtained no payment from the defender and in 1989 raised an action in Glasgow Sheriff Court against his insurers in terms of s. 151 of the Road Traffic Act 1988. The insurers were domiciled in England. The insurers argued that Glasgow Sheriff Court had no jurisdiction as they were not domiciled there and the pursuer had failed to aver any circumstances to show that that court had jurisdiction. The pursuer sought to found jurisdiction on art. 5(3). The sheriff repelled the defenders' plea of no jurisdiction but the sheriff principal sustained it and dismissed the action. The pursuer appealed. In the Inner House the pursuer also made a formal submission that Glasgow Sheriff Court had jurisdiction under art. 5(4) of Sched. 4.

23.1.2 LORD PROSSER: There is however a prior question as to jurisdiction. The sheriff held that there was jurisdiction. On appeal, the sheriff principal held that there was no jurisdiction. The present appeal by the pursuer is against that decision.

23.1.3 The question of jurisdiction turns on the provisions of the Civil Jurisdiction and Judgments Act 1982... The questions which arise in the present case turn upon words found in Sched. 4 which also appear in the unmodified version of the Convention found in Sched. 1. Such modifications (by way of omission, addition or substitution) as are introduced by Sched. 4 have in my opinion no material bearing on the interpretation of the relevant words.

23.1.4 Title II of the Convention, as set out in its modified form in Sched. 4 to the Act, provides by art. 2 that subject to the provisions of the Title, "persons domiciled in a part of the United Kingdom shall ... be sued in the courts of that part". That provision would provide jurisdiction against the present defenders in England, but not in Scotland. Article 3 provides that persons domiciled in a part of the United Kingdom may be sued in the courts of another part of the United Kingdom "only by virtue of the rules set out in Sections 2, 4, 5 and 6 of this Title". Section 2 of the Title is headed "Special Jurisdiction". It contains a number of articles, but of these, only art. 5 is directly in point in the present proceedings.

. . . . . .

23.1.5 Of the various heads, only head (8) [of Art. 5] is not to be found in the unmodified Convention, and only the final words of head (3) ("or in the case of a threatened wrong is likely to occur") reflect any substantive alteration to the other heads. The various heads cover a wide range of matters, but their specific provisions are not in point, and the ground of jurisdiction relied upon by the pursuer is that contained in head (3). The defenders, being domiciled in England, may be sued in Scotland "in matters relating to tort, delict or quasi-delict, in the courts for the place where the harmful event occurred".

23.1.6 In the present proceedings, are the defenders being sued "in matters relating to delict"? If so, I do not understand it to be disputed that Glasgow Sheriff Court would be a court "for the place where the harmful event occurred". The pursuer's claim against Mr Dunlop arose out of a motor accident which she attributes to his negligence. That accident was within the jurisdiction of Glasgow Sheriff Court and we are concerned with no other harmful event or delict. But are the present defenders, in the present proceedings, the legal basis of which is a statutory obligation created by s. 151 of the 1988 Act, being sued in a matter relating to delict?

23.1.7 Plainly, the defenders are not being sued "in delict", nor could this be described as an "action of delict". Nor, in my view, is it an action which could be described as based upon, or founded upon delict, or as an action the ground of which is delict. The pursuer does not seek to establish any delict or delictual liability on the part of the defenders. If head (3) of art. 5 had provided that a party domiciled in England could be sued in Scotland in delict, or in actions of delict, or in actions based or founded upon delict, or in actions the ground of which was delict, it does not seem to me that an action such as this, based upon the s. 151 obligation to pay, could be said to fall within the scope of the provision. But I did not understand the pursuer to contend that the present action would comply with descriptive phrases of the kind I have mentioned.

23.1.8 The contention for the pursuer was that the language employed in head (3) of art. 5 is wider and looser, and should be interpreted accordingly as having a wider scope than actions which are themselves based or founded upon assertions of delictual liability. It provides for a person being sued in "matters relating" to delict. Each of these two words is very wide and inspecific, when a narrow intention could perfectly well have been expressed in various narrow ways. This showed that narrowness was not intended, and that jurisdiction was being conferred not merely where there was an actual action founded upon alleged delict, but over a wider field of matters which merely related to delict in some less direct way. The same two words occurring in head (1) ("matters relating to a contract") would afford jurisdiction even when no contractual liability was asserted, and when alleged contract was not the basis, or even the subject matter of the action. So also under head (3), there would be jurisdiction when a person was sued in matters which related to delict in some ordinary sense, notwithstanding that the precise legal basis of the action might be some right arising from some source other than delict.

23.1.9 Having regard to the imprecise words in question, and the ease with which a more precise terminology could have been adopted, I find these arguments quite persuasive. Moreover, when one turns to the terminology of s. 151, it is not difficult to regard the obligation there imposed upon an insurer as being related to delict, although not, of course, itself an obligation ex delicto. The starting point is a judgment in respect of a liability of the insured. On the facts of the present case, that means a decree in respect of Mr Dunlop's liability in respect of bodily injury to the pursuer, in an action founded upon his delict. What the insurer has to pay is the sum payable under that decree. One can thus reasonably say that what the present action seeks is payment of a sum of damages for a delictual wrong, although obviously the delict was Mr Dunlop's and not the insurers'. The payment which is sought in the present action would on that basis be a payment of damages for that delictual wrong, and would be reparation to the pursuer for that wrong. That being the nature of the remedy which the present action seeks, is not suing the defenders for that remedy properly to be regarded as suing them in a matter relating to delict?

23.1.10 In contending for an affirmative answer to this question, counsel for the pursuer and appellant maintained that the crucial words should be given an ordinary or "literal" interpretation. However, counsel for the defenders and respondents contended that a strict or narrow interpretation of these words was appropriate. This contention was founded upon the cases of *Kalfelis* v. *Bankhaus Schröder* [(189/87); [1988] E.C.R. 5565] and *Six Constructions Ltd.* v. *Humbert* [(32/88); [1989] E.C.R. 341]. In each of these cases, the European Court treated the "special jurisdictions" set out in arts. 5 and 6 of the Convention as "derogations" from the "principle" that jurisdiction is vested in the courts of the state where the defendant is domiciled, and held that as such they must be interpreted restrictively. In dealing with Sched. 4 to the 1982 Act, one is not concerned with different states, but I am satisfied that if a restrictive meaning is to be given to particular words in the Convention itself, as set out in Sched. 1, that same meaning is to be given to those same words in Sched. 4, in the absence of any modification which alters their context and, in consequence, their interpretation.

23.1.11 I am not at all sure that I understand why the general jurisdiction based on domicile is seen as a "principle", from which the special jurisdictions are seen as "derogations". I should have thought it possible to see jurisdiction based on domicile as a useful general catch all, with the list of special jurisdictions representing obviously useful (and often more sensible) criteria for jurisdiction, affording a choice rather than derogating from a principle. However, having regard to the requirements of s. 3 of the 1982 Act, any question as to the meaning or effect of any provision of the Convention has to be determined in accordance with the principles laid down by and any relevant decision of the European Court. It is furthermore provided that judicial notice shall be taken of any decision of, or expression of opinion by, the European Court on any such question. On that basis, I feel obliged to proceed upon the basis that the special jurisdictions are to be regarded as derogations, and are to be interpreted restrictively. That being so in relation to the Convention itself as set out in Sched. 1 to the 1982 Act, I can see no justification for a different interpretation of the same words in the same article in its modified form in Sched. 4, notwithstanding the fact that the Sched. 4 version is concerned with allocation of jurisdiction within the United Kingdom, where it might be easier to regard jurisdiction based on domicile as less a matter of principle, and the "special" jurisdictions not as derogations from any such principle and in that sense "odd", but as being, in each specific category, an obviously sensible (and perhaps the obviously sensible) basis for jurisdiction.

23.1.12 Accepting that a "restrictive" approach is appropriate, what does this entail? *Six Constructions Ltd.* v. *Humbert* does not appear to me to afford any real help, on the facts of the present case. *Kalfelis* v. *Bankhaus Schröder* is largely concerned, in the discussion of art. 5(3), with determining that the expression "matters relating to tort, delict or quasi-delict" must be regarded as an independent concept: it would plainly be unacceptable if the relationship to tort, delict or quasi-delict was one which was recognised in, and perhaps resulted from legal principles special to, one member state and not another. In excluding such particular relationships from the interpretation of the phrase, a "restrictive" interpretation is adopted. It cuts out any such special meanings, but it leaves the phrase open to a natural or "literal" interpretation otherwise. This breadth of possible interpretation is perhaps reflected in the indication in *Kalfelis* that this independent concept would cover "all actions which seek to establish the liability of a defendant and which are not related to a 'contract' within the meaning of Article 5(1)". That very wide definition (which was naturally founded upon by the pursuer and appellant) must in my view be read in context, and cannot be taken as making art. 5(3) an almost universal ground of jurisdiction, omitting only those matters within art. 5(1). But I think it is important to note that the restriction of the concept to a general Community interpretation, omitting relationships created or recognised under individual systems of law, leaves open the possibility of a very wide scope for the words in art. 5(3).

23.1.13 The more specific restriction recognised by the court in *Kalfelis* was to the effect that a court which has jurisdiction under art. 5(3) over an action in so far as it is based on tort or delict, does not have a jurisdiction over that same action in so far as it is not so based. That proposition results partly from the decision that the phrase is an independent concept: particular legal systems may allow one to sue in contract, or on the basis of unjust enrichment, in a particular action, if there is also a claim founded upon delict, with a ground of jurisdiction appropriate to delict. That type of "relationship", when the other bases of claim have no delictual element in themselves, is excluded. Thus far, the restriction adopted by the court does not appear to me to turn upon the view that the special jurisdictions are derogations from the general jurisdiction based upon domicile. At least in relation to contract, the decision appears to turn more upon the view that heads (1) and (3) appear to be mutually exclusive. That again would be a particular form of "restrictiveness" which does not seem to me to entail any generally narrow meaning of the vital phrase in head 5(3). Moreover, it does not appear that there is a similar need for mutual exclusivity between either of these two heads and some of the others.

23.1.14 Nonetheless, the requirement of a restrictive interpretation is expressed in general terms, and it is clear that if art. 5(3) is to be so interpreted that it makes the minimum inroads on the general jurisdiction based on domicile, the expression "matters relating to" must not be so interpreted as to cover all manner of loose or indirect relationships between the matter in hand and the concept of delict. What types of relationship will be covered and what types will not, does not seem to me to receive any general clarification in *Kalfelis*, although it illustrates certain relationships which will not suffice.

23.1.15 While the word "matters" is in a sense loose and wide, I find it reasonably clear that in this context it refers to the particular action, and its subject matter. As I have indicated, in the present case the action and its subject matter are not themselves, and are not argued to be, matters of delict. It is rather the expression "relating to" which is said to extend the scope of head (3) beyond cases which are themselves a matter of delict. I have indicated the way in which the actual subject matter of this case has, inherent in it, a relationship with the prior delictual claim against Mr Dunlop, and can indeed be seen as seeking a delictual remedy. In my view, that makes this a much stronger case than *Kalfelis* for the contention that the relationship is truly a relationship covered by head (3). There is, I think, on any view, a relationship of a kind between this action and delict.

23.1.16 In the end of the day, however, I have come to the view that even upon a literal or ordinary reading of the section, that kind of relationship is not one which would naturally lead one to describe this case or its subject matter as a "matter relating to delict". It is essentially a matter relating to the vindication of a statutory right, and while of course it has relationships with various other factual and legal situations and concepts, and a relatively close relationship with a particular delict and the provision of remedies for that delict, I am not persuaded that in ordinary language that suffices to make it a matter relating to delict at the same time as being a matter of vindicating a statutory right. The expression "relating to" may often indicate quite loose relationships, particularly when the phrase is used in contradistinction to some more precise expression which indicates a direct relationship or connection. I would not wish to hold that in the context of art. 5(3), the expression may not cover something rather wider than actual actions founded upon delict. But interpretation comes to be a matter of impression at borderlines, and even in terms of ordinary or literal language, I am not satisfied that the phrase in question covers the situation in question.

23.1.17 The requirement to be restrictive does not therefore seem to me in this particular case to make any difference. If I had reached the opposite view on the ordinary meaning of head (3), the requirement to be restrictive would nonetheless have driven me to the conclusion which I have reached without that requirement.'

Comment

23.2.1 Decided: May 24, 1991.

23.2.2 It is essential to consider the European interpretation of the convention to interpret this U.K. statute — just in the way Lord Prosser at the court did above. Some other relevant cases are as follows: *Biev v. Mires de Potasse d'Alsace* (21/76) [1976] E.C.R. 1735; 1984 S.L.T. (News) A6 (called the *Reinwater* case) was a case by Dutch pursuers in the Netherlands whose agricultural work was allegedly damaged by a French company polluting the Rhine in France before it reached the Netherlands. It is clear that the draftsmen intended to leave this issue to the courts, namely whether the pursuers could sue in the Netherlands even though the wrongful act was in France. It was decided that the defender can be sued at the option of the pursuer either in the courts for the place where the damage occurred or in the courts for the place of the event which gives rise to and is at the origin of that damage. However the decision must be taken in the context of the circumstances and against the idea that domicile *is* the general rule. In *Dumez France au Tracoba v. Hessiche Lands bank (Helalsa)*, 1992 S.L.T. (News) A2 the *Biev* approach was explained as above and certainly as exclusively indirect claim — the plaintiffs sued in respect of the insolvency of their subsidiaries. The *Biev* rules applied only where the event giving rise to the event directly produced its harmful effects upon the person who is the immediate victim of that event. Consider too our domestic considerations of the issue — these are to an extent still relevant as showing how a domestic Scottish court characterises the question posed by the Act. *Russell v. F.W. Woolworth and Co. Ltd*, 1982 S.L.T. 428; *Kirkcaldy District Council v. Household Manufacturing Ltd*, 1987 S.L.T. 617. These cases were decided under previous local legislation. An attempt to use *Biev* to interpret it was, correctly, unsuccessful. See generally Anton and Beaumont, "Civil Jurisdiction in Scotland" (2nd ed., 1995).

NOTE

23.3.1 Jurisdiction seeks to determine which court(s) can hear the case at all. The law is set out in the Civil Jurisdiction and Judgments Act 1982, discussed in the foregoing extract. But there are some cases excluded. The "general rule" is that the defender be sued in the court of his domicile. (See Mennie, A., "Domicile: the new rules", 1987 S.L.T. (News) 321, 329.) There are rules allowing concurrent jurisdiction in another court.

Choice of law

94. **Private International Law (Miscellaneous Provisions) Act 1995**
(1995 c. 42)

An Act to make provision about interest on judgment debts and arbitral awards expressed in a currency other than sterling; to make further provision as to marriages entered into by unmarried persons under a law which permits polygamy; to make provision for choice of law rules in tort and delict; and for connected purposes.   [8th November 1995]

[1]PART III

NOTE
[1]Effective May 1, 1996: S.I. 1996 No. 995.

CHOICE OF LAW IN TORT AND DELICT

Purpose of Part III
9.—(1) The rules in this Part apply for choosing the law (in this Part referred to as "the applicable law") to be used for determining

issues relating to tort or (for the purposes of the law of Scotland) delict.

(2) The characterisation for the purposes of private international law of issues arising in a claim as issues relating to tort or delict is a matter for the courts of the forum.

(3) The rules in this Part do not apply in relation to issues arising in any claim excluded from the operation of this Part by section 13 below.

(4) The applicable law shall be used for determining the issues arising in a claim, including in particular the question whether an actionable tort or delict has occurred.

(5) The applicable law to be used for determining the issues arising in a claim shall exclude any choice of law rules forming part of the law of the country or countries concerned.

(6) For the avoidance of doubt (and without prejudice to the operation of section 14 below) this Part applies in relation to events occurring in the forum as it applies in relation to events occurring in any other country.

(7) In this Part as it extends to any country within the United Kingdom, "the forum" means England and Wales, Scotland or Northern Ireland, as the case may be.

(8) In this Part "delict" includes quasi-delict.

Abolition of certain common law rules

10. The rules of the common law, in so far as they—

(a) require actionability under both the law of the forum and the law of another country for the purpose of determining whether a tort or delict is actionable; or

(b) allow (as an exception from the rules falling within paragraph (a) above) for the law of a single country to be applied for the purpose of determining the issues, or any of the issues, arising in the case in question,

are hereby abolished so far as they apply to any claim in tort or delict which is not excluded from the operation of this Part by section 13 below.

Choice of applicable law: the general rule

11.—(1) The general rule is that the applicable law is the law of the country in which the events constituting the tort or delict in question occur.

(2) Where elements of those events occur in different countries, the applicable law under the general rule is to be taken as being—

(a) for a cause of action in respect of personal injury caused to an individual or death resulting from personal injury, the law of the country where the individual was when he sustained the injury;

(b) for a cause of action in respect of damage to property, the law of the country where the property was when it was damaged; and

(c) in any other case, the law of the country in which the most significant element or elements of those events occurred.

(3) In this section "personal injury includes disease or any impairment of physical or mental condition.

Choice of applicable law: displacement of general rule

12.—(1) If it appears, in all the circumstances, from a comparison of—

(a) the significance of the factors which connect a tort or delict with the country whose law would be the applicable law under the general rule; and

(b) the significance of any factors connecting the tort or delict with another country,

that it is substantially more appropriate for the applicable law for determining the issues arising in the case, or any of those issues, to be the law of the other country, the general rule is displaced and the applicable law for determining those issues or that issue (as the case may be) is the law of that other country.

The factors that may be taken into account as connecting a tort or delict with a country for the purposes of this section include, in particular, factors relating to the parties, to any of the events which constitute the tort or delict in question or to any of the circumstances or consequences of those events.

Exclusion of defamation claims from Part III

13.—(1) Nothing in this Part applies to affect the determination of issues arising in any defamation claim.

(2) For the purposes of this section "defamation claim" means—

(a) any claim under the law of any part of the United Kingdom for libel or slander or for slander of title, slander of goods or other malicious falsehood and any claim under the law of Scotland for verbal injury; and

(b) any claim under the law of any other country corresponding to or otherwise in the nature of a claim mentioned in paragraph (a) above.

Transitional provision and savings

14.—(1) Nothing in this Part applies to acts or omissions giving rise to a claim which occur before the commencement of this Part.

(2) Nothing in this Part affects any rules of law (including rules of private international law) except those abolished by section 10 above

(3) Without prejudice to the generality of subsection (2) above, nothing in this Part—

(a) authorises the application of the law of a country outside the forum as the applicable law for determining issues arising in any claim in so far as to do so—

(i) would conflict with principles of public policy; or

(ii) would give effect to such a penal, revenue or other public law as would not otherwise be enforceable under the law of the forum;

or

(*b*) affects any rules of evidence, pleading or practice or authorises questions of procedure in any proceedings to be determined otherwise than in accordance with the law of the forum.

(4) This Part has effect without prejudice to the operation of any rule of law which either has effect notwithstanding the rules of private international law applicable in the particular circumstances or modifies the rules of private international law that would otherwise be so applicable.

Crown application

15.—(1)This Part applies in relation to claims by or against the Crown as it applies in relation to claims to which the Crown is not a party.

(2) In subsection (1) above a reference to the Crown does not include a reference to Her Majesty in Her private capacity or to Her Majesty in right of Her Duchy of Lancaster or to the Duke of Cornwall.

(3) Without prejudice to the generality of section 14(2) above, nothing in this section affects any rule of law as to whether proceedings of any description may be brought against the Crown.

COMMENT

23.5.1 The basic common law rule in Scotland was (and is) to the extent the Act does not apply is that there is a double delict rule — the case must be actionable both by Scots law and the foreign law (which may be English law). See *McElroy v. McAllister*, 1949 S.C. 110; *Mitchell v. McCulloch*, 1976 S.C. 1; *James Burrough Distilleries plc v. Speymalt Whisky Distributors*, 1979 G.W.D. 186. The rule was often criticised. See Black, R., 1968 J.R. 40; Thomson, J. M. (1976) 25 ICCQ 873. The old rules still apply to defamation. For a full commentary see Rodger, B. J., "The Halley: Holed and now sunk", 1996 SLPQ 397 and see William, J.M. and Mead, P., "Abolition of the Double Accountability Rule — Question's still to be answered", 1996 J.P.I.C. 112.

NOTE

23.6.1 Private international law is taught as a separate subject in the Scottish universities. It is not essential for those who want to be solicitors but is for advocates. Understandably the topic is not treated in the other undergraduate classes (usually). If solicitors who subsequently practice delict as reparation litigators then they will not be sensitised to a few important points that they sometimes need, at least to diagnose for further reference to a specialist at the bar.

CHAPTER 24

PROOF

Res ipsa loquitur

95. Devine v. Colvilles (Appellants)
1969 S.L.T. 154

24.1.1 'LORD GUEST: The respondent was injured at the appellant's Ravenscraig steel works when he jumped from a platform about 15 feet above ground. His action was the result of his having been put in a state of fear for his own safety occasioned by a very violent explosion which occurred some 75 yards away in proximity to a converter plant. This plant was used for the manufacture of steel and the explosion took place following on a fire in a flexible hose which was used for conveying oxygen from an inlet pipe to a lance used for injecting oxygen into the converter containing about 100 tons of molten metal. The process by which was used for the purpose of a more rapid heating of the metal to the desired temperature was an Austrian improvement on the more traditional method. The oxygen originated from the British Oxygen Co.'s works and entered the appellant's premises by means of a pipe extending to about one mile in length. There is no dispute that the respondent's action in jumping off the platform was in consequence of the violent explosion, and no question therefore arises as to the liability of the appellants for the accident if negligence against them is established.

. . . . . .

24.1.2 The respondent accepts that his only case against the appellants is on the basis of the maxim *res ipsa loquitur*. The doctrine emanates from the well-known passage of Erle C.J. in *Scott v. London & St Katherine Docks Co.* (1865) 3 H. & C. 596 at p. 601 which is to the following effect: "There must be reasonable evidence of negligence. But where the thing is shown to be under the management of the defendant or his servants and the accident is such as in the ordinary course of things does not happen if those who have the management use proper care, it affords reasonable evidence, in the absence of explanation by the defendants, that the accident arose from want of care."

The Lord Justice-Clerk has examined very carefully the applicability of the doctrine and has reached the conclusion that it does apply to the circumstances of this case. While I agree with the Lord Justice-Clerk that the maxim is of limited ambit, I am not satisfied that any of the criticisms made by the appellants' counsel have any validity. I agree with the conclusion of the Lord Justice-Clerk with which Lord Wheatley and Lord Milligan concurred. Lord Walker who dissented and did not think the maxim applicable, did so upon the view that he was not satisfied upon the evidence that oxygen hoses do not burst in the ordinary course of things if those who have the management of them use proper care. The *res* which is said to speak for itself was the explosion. I must say that, without evidence to the contrary, I should have thought it self-evident that an explosion of such violence that causes fear of imminent danger to the workers does not occur in the ordinary course of things in a steel works if those who have the management use proper care.

24.1.3   If the brocard does apply it becomes necessary to consider whether the appellants can escape liability. They are absolved if they can give a reasonable explanation of the accident and show that this explanation was consistent with no lack of care on their part. In my view, the Lord Ordinary has imposed too heavy a burden on the appellants. The most probable explanation on the evidence is that the fire which caused the burning of the hose resulted from the particles in the oxygen stream being ignited by friction. The Lord Ordinary describes this explanation as "speculation", but in my opinion, it goes further than that and amounts at any rate to a "plausible explanation"… No other more probable explanation is put forward by any of the witnesses. In this respect I agree with the Lord Justice-Clerk. It is not necessary that there should be positive proof of the existence of the particles in the oxygen stream to establish the appellants' explanation.

24.1.4   But this explanation only carries the appellants half-way to success. The explanation to be available as a defence must be consistent with no negligence on their part… The appellants sought to prove a system of inspection of the hose and I agree with the Lord Ordinary that this system was not adequately established. But if the cause of the ignition was particles inside the hose, no external examination of the hose could have revealed the presence of particles and no internal examination was, in the nature of things, practicable.

If the particles were not in the hose *ab initio* they must have been introduced with the stream of oxygen coming from the British Oxygen Co.'s works. Questions by the Lord Ordinary at the conclusion of Flanagan's evidence revealed that there were filters for the oxygen on the appellants' premises. No evidence was forthcoming from the appellants as to any inspection of the filters being made by them.

What the inspection would have revealed I do not know. But if the appellants have to show that they exercised due diligence to avoid the accident, they cannot escape by saying that oxygen came from the British Oxygen Co. They knew that particles might cause fire. A filter is presumably for the purpose of preventing the access of impurities. They led no evidence to suggest that any inspection of the filters was ever made to see if they were working properly. In those circumstances I agree with the Lord Justice-Clerk that they have not discharged the onus on them. I would dismiss the appeal.'

COMMENT

24.2.1 Decided: March 11, 1969.
  Feb. 3: Yasser Arafat appointed leader of PLO.
  March 5: Kray Brothers sentenced to life imprisonment.
  March 10: James Earl Ray pled guilty to murder of Martin Luther King: sentenced to 99 years' imprisonment.

24.2.2 Obviously *res ipsa loquitur* has to be kept within its proper confines particularly by insisting upon the defender's control, otherwise the substantive law could be undermined. On the other hand to be excessively strict about proving legal requirements could in itself cause injustices. The law of evidence, it has to be remembered, is quite uniform in its application in the civil law whether relating to delict, contract, trust or conveyancing. Accordingly, there is little prospect of it adjusting to suit peculiarities of the law of delict, although prior to the Civil Evidence (Scotland) Act a special exception had been made for personal injuries cases to be proved in the absence of a corroborating witness, if none were available. However, in a delict case, courts can use the law of evidence to achieve an appropriate balance, which mirrors the spirit of the substantive law, between who must prove what and what evidence must be adduced. The courts do this generally and in the law of delict by a judicious use of the logical exercise known as inference. The next case explains how this is carried out in the context of the law of delict.

Inferrence

96. **Inglis v. London, Midland and Scottish Railway Co. (Appellants)**
1941 S.C. 551

24.3.1 'LORD PRESIDENT (Normand): The decision in this case, as the argument showed, depends on one simple issue of fact, whether the railway carriage door on the offside of the train through which the deceased boy fell was opened by his inadvertent pressure on the handle when he was in the act of throwing out of the window silver paper which he had removed from a piece of chocolate. There was no suggestion that he had opened the door deliberately, or that the door had been opened by the act, deliberate or not, of anyone else in the railway carriage. The pursuer's counsel relied on the evidence of the boy's mother and of three other women in the carriage, who were accompanying their children on the same journey, that the boy had not interfered with the handle. The defenders relied on the guard's evidence that he had inspected the outside handles of the door before the train left St Enoch's Station and found them all in the closed or horizontal position; on the evidence of a more casual inspection by another railway servant at the same station; on the evidence of their technical witnesses that the door and its hinges and lock were found after the accident to be in good order, and that if the door, when the train left St Enoch's, was improperly closed so that the tongue of the lock was on the outer side of the safety catch, it must have swung open at a very early stage of the journey and long before the train had travelled 26 miles, as it did before the accident occurred. On that evidence they maintained that it was impossible for the door to open where it did without interference by someone in the carriage. The defender's counsel also criticised the evidence of the four witnesses who were in the compartment. Their evidence was, it was said, merely negative — that they had not seen the boy touch the handle and one of them in her cross-examination said that on the journey and before the accident the inside handle was in the vertical position, from which it would necessarily follow that the door was properly closed with the tongue of the lock in the slot.

. . . . . .

24.3.2 The learned sheriff... leaves us in no doubt about the impression which [the witnesses] made on him, for I find this emphatic passage in his note: "I am bound to say that their whole demeanour in the witness-box impressed me greatly. I felt convinced that they were witnesses whose credit I could place reliance on. I am satisfied that they were telling the truth when they all stated that neither the pursuer's boy nor anyone else in that compartment touched or interfered with the inside handle of the door which opened, from the moment of their entering the compartment until the happening of the accident. The result of that is that I am bound to hold that no one in that compartment was responsible for the door swinging open when it did. In reaching this conclusion I took into account discrepancies in the evidence of the pursuer's witnesses."

. . . . . .

24.3.3 In considering these points, and also the value of the evidence that a proper inspection had been made of the door handles on the offside of the train at St Enoch's, the court is bound to bear in mind that railway carriage doors have been known to open, as indeed the reported cases show, although they were equipped with locking arrangements which generally worked well, and although the usual inspection had been made before the train left the platform. A railway company has a difficult task when it attempts to prove that an accident of this kind must be held to have been caused by the interference of someone in the train merely by evidence that its equipment and systems of inspection are so near perfection as to make such an accident well-nigh impossible, unless there is interference by a passenger.

. . . . . .

24.3.4   The evidence is not wholly negative in character. It is positive to the extent that each witness describes the boy as using both hands, the right hand holding the paper which he was throwing and the other holding the chocolate. I find it difficult to think that a boy of eight, so occupied, could open the carriage door by inadvertent pressure on the handle. The handle was on his left, and in the fully closed position it would itself incline a little towards the left. Pressure directly towards the right and then downwards would have no effect; there must be a pull downwards, and this pull must be equivalent to a force of some 11 pounds.

. . . . . .

24.3.5   On the simple issue of fact, I do not find in the evidence anything which satisfies me that the learned sheriff-substitute arrived at a wrong conclusion. He had the advantage, denied to us, of seeing the witnesses and of judging of their truthfulness and accuracy, and I accept his decision without reluctance or hesitation, although the issue is debatable and certainty is impossible.

It is now settled by authority that the opening of a railway carriage door when the train is running and without the interference of passengers, is *prima facie* evidence that the railway company's servant failed to take due care to see that the door was securely fastened when the train left a previous station: *Gee* v. *Metropolitan Railway Co.* (1873) 8 Q.B. 161; *Richards* v. *Great Eastern Railway* (1873) 28 L.T. 711; *Burns* v. *North British Railway Co.*, 1914 S.C. 754. In the present case we are concerned with the door on the offside of the train, and the only probable way in which the accident can be explained is that the inspection at St Enoch's failed to discover that the external door handle was in the open position, or that, after the inspection, the door was used by one of the company's servants who failed to close it properly. The *prima facie* evidence of negligence is not met by any counter evidence from the defenders of interference by third parties. The consequence is that we must hold the defenders' negligence to have been the cause of the accident.

24.3.6   The learned sheriff-substitute in his note refers at considerable length to the cases in which the maxim *res ipsa loquitur* is expounded. In my opinion that maxim does not properly apply. I have in a recent case [*O'Hara* v. *Central S.M.T. Co.*, 1941 S.C. 754] expressed my opinion on the scope and usefulness of the maxim, and I do not propose to repeat what I then said. I will only say that, in my view, this maxim has a certain utility when an accident occurs at a moment when the thing which causes the injury is outside immediate human control. When that condition is not present, it is better to avoid the expression *res ipsa loquitur*, and to consider whether the facts and circumstances proved are *prima facie* evidence of negligence and affect the onus of proof. It may be that this is merely a matter of phraseology, but the truth is that the words *res ipsa loquitur* are sometimes used as if they possessed a magical power to solve difficult questions of negligence. The learned sheriff-substitute has not erred in substance but I think that, if he had relied less on the Latin maxim, he would have seen the necessity of an express finding of negligence in that the defenders had failed to close and properly fasten the door or to see that it was properly closed and fastened before the train left St Enoch's Station as it was their duty to do. That finding is clearly implied by the sheriff's note and it should find a place in the interlocutor... With these alterations I think that we should affirm the findings.

24.3.7 LORD MONCRIEFF: In a case such as the present, in which the defenders ceased to be in control of the door before the commencement of the journey, the unexplained opening of the door, while still relevant *prima facie* to infer negligence, is thus in no way relevant even *prima facie* to infer negligence for which the defenders are responsible. The *res*, or if it be preferred the *res ipsa*, is thus unavailing to transfer the onus of proof; the doctrine or maxim does not apply; and the pursuer must, as in other cases, undertake the whole burden of proving his case. In discharging that burden he may, however, rely as part of his proof on the opening of the door as affording *prima facie* evidence of negligence and may complete his proof, and either bring that negligence directly home to the defenders or in turn charge them to acquit themselves of negligence by having resort to the familiar method of exclusion. It is this method which the pursuer has followed in this case, and I agree with the learned sheriff-substitute and with your Lordships in finding that he has followed it with success. I thus suggest a difference from the opinion of the learned sheriff-substitute, but only on a point of form, and am fully in agreement with the substance of his opinion.'

COMMENT

24.4.1   Decided: July 3, 1941.
  May 10: Man landing near Glasgow from Messerschmitt found to be Rudolph Hess.
  May 24: Bob Dylan born.
  May 27: Unsinkable battleship *Bismarck* sunk.
  June 30: Hitler invaded Russia.
  July 21: London première of Coward's *Blithe Spirit*.

24.4.2　How useful a source of empirical evidence do you consider the law reports to be? (See para. 24.3.3.)

24.4.3　Note how the court approached discrepancies in evidence. Every day in the courts, it is found that there are discrepancies in the evidence of witnesses. Two explanations are usually given in support of such discrepant evidence by the experienced advocate: (1) it has been a long time since the incident; (2) the discrepancies (which it will be suggested relate only to minor matters) prove that the witness is telling the truth, otherwise in making up a story the witness could have easily avoided discrepancies. In other words, it is up to the judge to decide the effect of the discrepancies in the evidence — they may be neutral, they may destroy the credibility and/or the reliability of the witness or they may support his credibility and perhaps to a lesser extent his reliability. What a judge cannot do is make up the gaps in evidence from his own research — as if the court in this case had gone off after argument to read train safety manuals. (See para. 10.1.4.) What would be the advantages of allowing judges to do this? What would be the disadvantages?

97. O'Donnell (Appellant) v. Murdoch McKenzie & Co.
1967 S.C.(H.L.) 63

24.5.1　'LORD UPJOHN: The defenders called no evidence, and in such cases, as was established in your Lordships' House in *Ross* v. *Associated Portland Cement Manufacturers* [1964] 1 W.L.R. 768 only the most favourable inferences should be drawn from the pursuer's evidence. If my summary of the effect of the evidence as to the pursuer's movements between the scaffold and sill is correct, then, in my opinion, it is not right to draw the inference that on the balance of probabilities he would at the time of the accident have left the safety of the scaffold even to square the corners. The pursuer himself said he could have finished the work from a proper scaffold, and his evidence is not, in my opinion, effectively contradicted by his other witnesses. In my opinion it does not lie in the mouth of the defenders, who were in breach of their obligations and called no evidence, to point to the very vague evidence of McGarvie and McGinley and invite the court to draw inference that he would have done so.

. . . . . .

24.5.2　So, reluctant as an appellate court must be to differ from the judge who has heard the witness on questions of fact, yet when it comes to questions of the inference as to what the pursuer would have done had proper provisions been made for his safety (as it was not) and the judge does not appear to have addressed his mind to the proper question, I think it is the duty of the appellate court to express its own views. As I have already said, I think that on the balance of probabilities the pursuer would not have left the safety of a scaffold at the time of his accident had the respondents performed their obligations. In my opinion the pursuer establishes all three necessary ingredients of his action.

24.5.3　LORD WILBERFORCE: In order for the appellant to succeed in his appeal it is necessary for him to show (1) that the work he was required to do could not safely be done on or from the ground or from part of a building or other permanent structure; (2) that no suitable scaffold was provided; and (3) that the failure to provide a suitable scaffold caused the accident by which he was injured. These requirements are derived from the Construction (General Provisions) Regulations 1961.

On points (1) and (2) the appellant has a decision in his favour of the Second Division, as to (1) by unanimity and as to (2) by a majority. I agree with these findings for the reasons given below and find no need to add to them. On point (3) the appellant failed both before the Lord Ordinary and the Inner House.

24.5.4 It was for the appellant to prove a causal connection between his employers' breach of statutory duty and the injury, so that, with the decisions of two courts against him, his task might now appear formidable. But, as against this, he can claim the benefit of certain legal considerations before the evidence is examined. He has proved a breach of statutory duty to establish which involved a finding that the work could not safely have been done from the ground or from the building or permanent structure, so that a scaffolding was necessary; thus we start from a presumption that he could not safely have done this work from the wall. This being so, and an accident having occurred while he was in fact working from the wall, it does not require much in the way of evidence to connect the accident with the breach of duty. The burden on him must be further diminished when it is recollected that he was working with an unsuitable tool, which from its awkwardness and weight must have increased the risk of working from an unsuitable place. No evidence was called by the respondents, and we have the warrant of observations in this House in *Ross v. Associated Portland Cement Manufactures Ltd.* for the proposition that in such circumstances, if inferences are to be drawn from the pursuer's evidence, they should be those favourable to him.

. . . . . .

24.5.5 The difficulty of working from the platform was increased by the nature of the tool supplied by the employers. The proper tool with which to do this work was a pugger, but no tool of this kind was made available by the employers, so use had to be made of a jack hammer, a heavier and more cumbrous tool, like a pneumatic drill, which was three feet long and weighed 90 pounds... The evidence showed that the tool was liable to become jammed between the reinforcing rods of the concrete and was then difficult to dislodge. One way to dislodge it was to rock it from side to side until it became free. It was after it had become so jammed, and while the appellant, with Aird's help was trying to dislodge it, that the accident occurred.

. . . . . .

24.5.6 The case against him was that, whether a scaffolding had been provided or not, he would still have been working at the position in which he was, rather than on the scaffold, so that the scaffold, had it existed, would not have saved him. This would mean that the accident was not caused by the failure to provide the scaffold. In order to test this line of argument it is important to state with some precision the question which has to be asked. One question, which is that to which, in the main, the courts below addressed themselves, is whether, in order to complete the squaring of the aperture, the appellant would not have stood in the aperture, if a proper scaffolding had been there.

. . . . . .

24.5.7 [A] further question remains, namely, when the tool jammed, and it was necessary, with Aird's help, to free it, would the appellant have been where he was (*i.e.* so far inside the aperture) had there been a proper scaffolding on the outer side? It is because I do not find this distinction fully perceived in the courts below that I feel bound, notwithstanding their findings, to endeavour to make my own assessment of the evidence.

. . . . . .

24.5.8 No case of negligence was made out against the pursuer. He starts with the advantage that he was provided with an unsuitable and unwieldly tool, and that his employers failed to provide a scaffolding which, in the interests of safe working, they were obliged to provide. An accident occurs, which, though perhaps usual (but so are many industrial accidents), is precisely of the kind which the safety regulation is designed to prevent. And so far from drawing from the evidence the conclusion that this accident would have happened anyway, even if there had been a proper tubular scaffolding with a guard-rail, I feel obliged to draw the opposite conclusion. The appellant would indeed, in my opinion, succeed with less than he has been able to show.'

COMMENT

24.6.1 Decided: July 26, 1967.
  May 8: Muhammed Ali, boxer, indicted for draft evasion.
  June 10: Spencer Tracy died.
  June 29: Jagger and Richards sentenced to imprisonment for drugs offences.
  July 14: Third reading of Abortion Bill.

24.6.2 The facts are set out towards the end of the extract. Read them again and ponder what you would have decided had you not read the judicial analysis first. For a recent application of the Doctrine see *Laing v. Tayside Health Board*, 1996 Rep. L.R. 51 (extracted below for a different point).

24.6.3 So, although from reading the chapters on negligence it might seem very difficult to establish a case in negligence, this is not the whole picture. Remember that the reported cases, and the cases that go to court but are unreported, are the tip of an iceberg. Many cases are won on paper by communication with insurers by the claimant setting out the facts and the evidence. Very many cases that are contested are contested on the substantial matters of fact involved — *e.g.* that the lock was broken. On the other hand there are many who, while subscribing still to the fault system, might prefer inferences to be used more enthusiastically for pursuers. The courts — quite rightly, in the present writer's view — do not agree with this as the current status of *McGhee* indicates. The best course for the pursuer-orientated campaigner is probably to give up on the common law fault system and try to have piecemeal statutory strict-liability régimes introduced.

Evidence

98. **Laing v. Tayside Health Board**
1996 Rep. L.R. 51

24.7.1 'A nursing auxiliary was injured when she was lifting an elderly patient from his bed. She had not been provided with any assistance in moving the patient. She raised an action of damages in which she averred that as she was moving the patient his bed moved, and she was left supporting his entire weight. She averred that two nurses should have been provided to lift the patient. The pursuer led evidence at proof that two nurses were required to lift a patient if the patient was not able to help himself or to bear his weight. The pursuer also gave evidence that she had never been given any training in lifting patients without assistance.

. . . . . .

24.7.2 LORD RODGER: The pursuer is a lady aged 46. She seeks damages in respect of an injury which she alleges she suffered on 3 August 1990 during her employment as an auxiliary nurse with the second defenders, the Tayside Health Board.

24.7.3 It is in the light of that assessment of the pursuer's evidence that the first submissions of counsel for the defenders fail to be considered. He argued that, even if I accepted the pursuer's evidence as to what happened, I should not hold it proved that an incident had occurred on 3 August 1990 in the home of Mr William Bennett because his wife had been present at the time of the incident and she had not been called as a witness. He referred to s. 1(1) of the Civil Evidence (Scotland) Act 1988 and to *Morrison* v. *J. Kelly & Sons Ltd.* [1970 S.L.T. 198]; *McGowan* v. *Lord Advocate* [1972 S.L.T. 188]; and *Gordon* v. *Grampian Health Board* [1991 S.C.L.R. 213]. The decisions in *Morrison* and *Gordon* are decisions of the First Division. They concern a provision in earlier legislation which was similar to, but not identical with, s. 1(1) of the 1988 Act. Both decisions are, however, distinguishable.

24.7.4   In *Morrison* the pursuer's account was contradicted by a "solid body of testimony" and the Lord Ordinary did not wholly accept the pursuer's evidence, while in *McGowan* there were three other eyewitnesses to the accident whom the pursuer might have led, but in fact he led only one of them and that witness contradicted the pursuer's version of the events. In this case, by contrast, I am satisfied that the pursuer is a credible and reliable witness and her evidence is not contradicted. Moreover, it is not clear to me that Mrs Bennett would necessarily have been available to give evidence for the pursuer. The incident occurred five years ago and, according to the pursuer, at that time Mrs Bennett was a lady in her sixties. I do not know whether she is still alive or, if she is, whether she is fit to give evidence or can now remember the incident. None of these matters was explored in evidence. In that situation I consider that, having regard to the terms of s. 1(1) of the 1988 Act, I am entitled to find any fact proved if I am satisfied that it has been established by the pursuer's evidence, even though her evidence is not corroborated.'

COMMENT

24.8.1   Decided: January 26, 1996.

24.8.2   The Act was when pommulgated thought to be an extension of the pursuer's right to prove a case on his own testimony. However as can be seen restrictive interpretations of similar prior legislation are argued to apply to the new Act. In addition to the cases in the opinion read *M'Laren v. Caldwell's Paper Mill Co. Ltd*, 1973 S.L.T. 158; 1986 Scot Law Com. Report No. 100 para. 2.8; Field, D., "Civil Evidence: a quantum leap", 1988 S.L.T. (News) 349; "Going it alone", 1989 S.L.T. (News) 216. Read Lord Stott's comments in his *Judge's Diary* (1995), p. 241, where he calls *Morrison* "a silly case". Thus his comments on M'Laren (which he calls M'Lean) are instructive. Despite his dissent the case never made it to the House of Lords. Against that background this is a welcome decision and correct. For a short practical treatment of proof in a common type case see, Kinloch, D., "Slippery Substances", 1995 Rep. B. 4–7.

DELICT STATUTES

NOTE: This appendix, primarily for the use of students studying the law of delict, was prepared from the *Parliament House Book* available to the author at the time (release 41).

Extract   *Page*

1. Partnership Act 1890 456
    (53 & 54 Vict. c. 39)
2. Law Reform (Contributory Negligence) Act 1945 459
    (8 & 9 Geo. 6, c. 28)
3. Crown Proceedings Act 1947 461
    (10 & 11 Geo. 6, c. 44)
4. Law Reform (Personal Injuries) Act 1948 472
    (11 & 12 Geo. 6, c. 41)
5. Defamation Act 1952 474
    (15 & 16 Geo. 6 and 1 Eliz. 2, c. 66)
6. Interest on Damages (Scotland) Act 1958 477
    (6 & 7 Eliz. 2, c. 61)
7. Law Reform (Husband and Wife) Act 1962 478
    (10 & 11 Eliz. 2, c. 48)
8. Law Reform (Miscellaneous Provisions) (Scotland) Act ... 479
    1968 (1968 c. 70)
9. Employer's Liability (Defective Equipment) Act 1969 482
    (1969 c. 37)
10. Prescription and Limitation (Scotland) Act 1973 484
    (1973 c. 52)
11. Damages (Scotland) Act 1976 505
    (1976 c. 13)
12. Unfair Contract Terms Act 1977 512
    (1977 c. 50)
13. Administration of Justice Act 1982 518
    (1982 c. 53)
14. Law Reform (Husband and Wife) (Scotland) Act 1984 .. 523
    (1984 c. 15)
15. Civil Evidence (Scotland) Act 1988 526
    (1988 c. 32)
16. Damages (Scotland) Act 1993... 530
    (1993 c. 5)

17.　Defamation Act 1996 532
　　　　(1996 c. 31)
18.　Damages Act 1996.. 543
　　　　(1996 c. 48)

1. [1]Partnership Act 1890
(53 & 54 Vict. c. 39)

An Act to declare and amend the law of partnership.

[14th August 1890]

NOTE

[1]Extended by the Limited Partnerships Act 1907, s. 7.

Definition of partnership

1.—(1) Partnership is the relation which subsists between persons carrying on a business in common with a view of profit.

(2) But the relation between members of any company or association which is —

  (*a*)　Registered as a company under the Companies Act 1862, or any other Act of Parliament or the time being in force and relating to the registration of joint stock companies; or

  (*b*)　Formed or incorporated by or in pursuance of any other Act of Parliament or letter patent, or Royal Charter; or

  (*c*)　A company engaged in working mines within and subject to the jurisdiction of the Stannaries:

is not a partnership within the meaning of this Act.

. . . . . .

Relations of Partners to persons dealing with them.

Power of partner to bind the firm

5. Every partner is an agent of the firm and his other partners for the purpose of the business of the partnership; and the acts of every partner who does any act for carrying on in the usual way business of the kind carried on by the firm of which he is a member bind the firm and his partners, unless the partner so acting has in fact no authority to act for the firm in the particular matter, and the person with whom he is dealing either knows that he has no authority, or does not know or believe him to be a partner.

Partners bound by acts on behalf of firm

6. An act or instrument relating to the business of the firm done or executed in the firm-name, or in any other manner showing an intention to bind the firm, by any person thereto authorised, whether a partner or not, is binding on the firm and all the partners.

Provided that this section shall not affect any general rule of law relating to the execution of deeds or negotiable instruments.

Partner using credit of firm for private purposes

7. Where one partner pledges the credit of the firm for a purpose apparently not connected with the firm's ordinary course of business, the firm is not bound, unless he is in fact specially authorised by the other partners; but this section does not affect any personal liability incurred by an individual partner.

Effect of notice that firm will not be bound by acts of partner

8. If it has been agreed between the partners that any restriction shall be placed on the power of any one or more of them to bind the firm, no act done in contravention of the agreement is binding on the firm with respect to persons having notice of the agreement.

Liability of partners

[1]**9.** Every partner in a firm is liable jointly with the other partners, and in Scotland severally also, for all debts and obligations of the firm incurred while he is a partner: and after his death his estate is also severally liable in a due course of administration for such debts and obligations, so far as they remain unsatisfied, but subject in England or Ireland to the prior payment of his separate debts.

NOTE
[1]See the Value Added Tax Act 1983 (c. 55), s. 30(5).

Liability of the firm for wrongs

10. Where, by any wrongful act or omission of any partner acting in the ordinary course of the business of the firm, or with the authority of his co-partners, loss or injury is caused to any person not being a partner in the firm, or any penalty is incurred, the firm is liable therefor to the same extent as the partner so acting or omitting to act.

Misapplication of money or property received for or in custody of the firm

11. In the following cases; namely—

(a) Where one partner acting within the scope of his apparent authority receives the money or property of a third person and misapplies it; and

(b) Where a firm in the course of its business receives money or property of a third person, and the money or property so received is misapplied by one or more of the partners while it is in the custody of the firm;

the firm is liable to make good the loss.

Liability for wrongs joint and several

12. Every partner is liable jointly with his co-partners and also severally for everything for which the firm while he is a partner therein becomes liable under either of the two last preceding sections.

Improper employment of trust-property for partnership purposes

13. If a partner, being a trustee, improperly employs trust-property in the business or on the account of the partnership, no other partner is liable for the trust-property to the persons beneficially interested therein:

Provided as follows:—

(1) This section shall not affect any liability incurred by any partner by reason of his having notice of a breach of trust; and

(2) Nothing in this section shall prevent trust-money from being followed and recovered from the firm if still in its possession or under its control.

Persons liable by "holding out"

14.—(1) Every one who by words spoken or written or by conduct represents himself, or who knowingly suffers himself to be represented, as a partner in a particular firm, is liable as a partner to any one who has on the faith of any such representation given credit to the firm, whether the representation has or has not been made or communicated to the person so giving credit by or with the knowledge of the apparent partner making the representation or suffering it to be made.

(2) Provided that where after a partner's death the partnership business is continued in the old firm-name, the continued use of that name or of the deceased partner's name as part thereof shall not of itself make his executors or administrators estate or effects liable for any partnership debts contracted after his death.

Admissions and representations of partners

15. An admission or representation made by any partner concerning the partnership affairs, and in the ordinary course of its business, is evidence against the firm.

Notice to acting partner to be notice to the firm

16. Notice to any partner who habitually acts in the partnership business of any matter relating to partnership affairs operates as notice to the firm, except in the case of a fraud on the firm committed by or with the consent of that partner.

Liabilities of incoming and outgoing partners

17.—(1) A person who is admitted as a partner into an existing firm does not thereby become liable to the creditors of the firm for anything done before he became a partner.

(2) A partner who retires from a firm does not thereby cease to be liable for partnership debts or obligations incurred before his retirement.

(3) A retiring partner may be discharged from any existing liabilities, by an agreement to that effect between himself and the members of the firm as newly constituted and the creditors, and this agreement may be either express or inferred as a fact from the course of dealing between the creditors and the firm as newly constituted.

Revocation of continuing guaranty by change in firm

18. A continuing guaranty or cautionary obligation given either to a firm or to a third person in respect of the transactions of a firm is, in the absence of agreement to the contrary, revoked as to future transactions by any change in the constitution of the firm to which, or of the firm in respect of the transactions of which, the guaranty or obligation was given.

. . . . . .

2. Law Reform (Contributory Negligence) Act 1945
(8 & 9 Geo. 6, c. 28)

[1]An Act to amend the law relating to contributory negligence and for purposes connected therewith. [15th June 1945]

NOTE
[1]Applied to the Crown by the Crown Proceedings Act 1947 (c. 44), s. 4(3). Extended by the Merchant Shipping Oil Pollution Act 1971 (c. 59), s. 1, and the Deposit of Poisonous Waste Act 1972 (c. 21), s. 2(4). Applied by the Animals (Scotland) Act 1987 (c. 9), s. 1(6).

Apportionment of liability in case of contributory negligence

[1]**1.**—(1) Where any person suffers damage as the result partly of his own fault and partly of the fault of any other person or persons, a claim in respect of that damage shall not be defeated by reason of the fault of the person suffering the damage, but the damages recoverable in respect thereof shall be reduced to such extent as the court thinks just and equitable having regard to the claimant's share in the responsibility for the damage:
Provided that—
(a) this subsection shall not operate to defeat any defence arising under a contract;
(b) where any contract or enactment providing for the limitation of liability is applicable to the claim, the amount of damages recoverable by the claimant by virtue of this subsection shall not exceed the maximum limit so applicable.

(2) Where damages are recoverable by any person by virtue of the foregoing subsection subject to such reduction as is therein mentioned, the court shall find and record the total damages which would have been recoverable if the claimant had not been at fault.

(3) [Repealed by the Civil Liability (Contribution) Act 1978 (c. 47), Sched. 2.]

[1](4) Where any person dies as the result partly of his own fault and partly of the fault of any other person or persons, a claim by way dependant of the first mentioned person for damages or

solatium in respect of that person's death shall not be defeated by reason of his fault, but the damages or solatium recoverable shall be reduced to such extent as the court thinks just and equitable having regard to the share of the said person in the responsibility for his death.

(5) Where, in any case to which subsection (1) of this section applies, one of the persons at fault avoids liability to any other such person or his personal representative by pleading the Limitation Act 1939, or any other enactment limiting the time within which proceedings may be taken, he shall not be entitled to recover any damages or contributions from that other person or representative by virtue of the said subsection.

(6) Where any case to which subsection (1) of this section applies is tried with a jury, the jury shall determine the total damages which would have been recoverable if the claimant had not been at fault and the extent to which those damages are to be reduced.

(7) [Repealed by the Carriage by Air Act 1961 (c. 27), Sched. 2.]

NOTES
[1]Modified by the Control of Pollution Act 1974 (c. 40), s. 88(4).
[2]As applicable to Scotland by s. 5(*c*).

2. [Repealed by the National Insurance (Industrial Injuries) Act 1946 (c. 62), Sched. 9.]

Saving for Maritime Conventions Act 1911, and past cases
3.—(1) This Act shall not apply to any claim to which section 1 of the Maritime Conventions Act 1911 applies and that Act shall have effect as if this Act had not passed.

(2) This Act shall not apply to any case where the acts or omissions giving rise to the claim occurred before the passing of this Act.

Interpretation
[1]**4.** The following expressions have the meanings hereby respectively assigned to them, that is to say —

"court" means, in relation to any claim, the court or arbitrator by or before whom the claim falls to be determined;
"damage" includes loss of life and personal injury;
"fault" means negligence, breach of statutory duty or other act or omission which gives rise to a liability in tort or would, apart from this Act, give rise to the defence of contributory negligence.

NOTE
[1]As amended by the National Insurance (Industrial Injuries) Act 1946 (c. 62), Sched. 9, and the Fatal Accidents Act 1976 (c. 30), Sched. 2.

Application to Scotland
5. In the application of this Act to Scotland —

(*a*) the expression "dependant" means, in relation to any person, any person who would in the event of such first mentioned person's death through the fault of a third party be entitled to sue that third party for damages or solatium; and the expression "fault" means wrongful act, breach of statutory duty or negligent act or omission which gives rise to liability in damages, or would, apart from this Act, give rise to the defence of contributory negligence;

[1](*b*) section 3 of the Law Reform (Miscellaneous Provisions) (Scotland) Act 1940 (contribution among joint wrongdoers) shall apply in any case where two or more persons are liable, or would if they had all been sued be liable, by virtue of section 1(1) of this Act in respect of the damage suffered by any person.

NOTE
[1]Substituted by the Civil Liability (Contribution) Act 1978 (c. 47), Sched. 1.

. . . . . .

Short title and extent
7. This Act may be cited as the Law Reform (Contributory Negligence) Act 1945.

. . . . . .

3. [1]Crown Proceedings Act 1947
(10 & 11 Geo. 6, c. 44)

An Act to amend the law relating to the civil liabilities and rights of the Crown and to civil proceedings by and against the Crown, to amend the law relating to the civil liabilities of persons other than the Crown in certain cases involving the affairs or property of the Crown, and for purposes connected with the matters aforesaid.
[31st July 1947]

NOTE
[1]Applied by the Employment Protection Act 1975 (c. 71), Sched. 1, and the Occupiers' Liability (Scotland) Act 1960 (c. 30), s. 4.

[1]Part I.—Substantive Law

NOTE
[1]Extended by the Plant Varieties and Seeds Act 1964 (c. 14), s. 14.

. . . . . .

Liability of the Crown in tort
2.—(1) Subject to the provisions of this Act, the Crown shall be subject to all those liabilities in tort to which, if it were a private person

of full age and capacity, it would be subject:—
  (*a*) in respect of torts committed by its servants or agents;
  (*b*) in respect of any breach of those duties which a person owes
         to his servants or agents at common law by reason of being
         their employer; and
  (*c*) in respect of any breach of the duties attaching at common law
         to the ownership, occupation, possession or control of property:
Provided that no proceedings shall lie against the Crown by virtue
of paragraph (*a*) of this subsection in respect of any act or omission
of a servant or agent of the Crown unless the act or omission would
apart from the provisions of this Act have given rise to a cause of
action in tort against that servant or agent or his estate.

(2) Where the Crown is bound by a statutory duty which is binding
also upon persons other than the Crown and its officers, then, subject to
the provisions of this Act, the Crown shall, in respect of a failure to comply
with that duty, be subject to all those liabilities in tort (if any) to which it
would be so subject if it were a private person of full age and capacity.

(3) Where any functions are conferred or imposed upon an officer
of the Crown as such either by any rule of the common law or by
statute, and that officer commits a tort while performing or purporting
to perform those functions, the liabilities of the Crown in respect of
the tort shall be such as they would have been if those functions had
been conferred or imposed solely by virtue of instructions lawfully
given by the Crown.

(4) Any enactment which negatives or limits the amount of the
liability of any Government department or officer of the Crown in
respect of any tort committed by that department or officer shall, in
the case of proceedings against the Crown under this section in respect
of a tort committed by that department or officer, apply in relation to
the Crown as it would have applied in relation to that department or
officer if the proceedings against the Crown had been proceedings
against that department or officer.

(5) No proceedings shall lie against the Crown by virtue of this
section in respect of anything done or omitted to be done by any
person while discharging or purporting to discharge any
responsibilities of a judicial nature vested in him, or any responsibilities
which he has in connection with the execution of judicial process.

[1](6) No proceedings shall lie against the Crown by virtue of this
section in respect of any act, neglect or default or any officer of the
Crown, unless that officer has been directly or indirectly appointed
by the Crown and was at the material time paid in respect of his duties
as an officer of the Crown wholly out of the Consolidated Fund of the
United Kingdom, moneys provided by Parliament, or any Fund
certified by the Treasury for the purposes of this subsection or was at
the material time holding an office in respect of which the Treasury
certify that the holder thereof would normally be so paid.

NOTE
[1]As amended by the Statute Law (Repeals) Act 1981 (c. 19).

Infringement of intellectual property rights
[1]**3.**—(1) Civil proceedings lie against the Crown for an infringement committed by a servant or agent of the Crown, with the authority of the Crown, of—

    (*a*) a patent,

    [2](*b*) a registered trade mark,

    (*c*) the right in a registered design,

    (*d*) design right, or

    (*e*) copyright;

but save as provided by this subsection no proceedings lie against the Crown by virtue of this Act in respect of an infringement of any of those rights.

(2) Nothing in this section, or any other provision of this Act, shall be construed as affecting—

    (*a*) the rights of a government department under section 55 of the Patents Act 1977, Schedule 1 to the Registered Designs Act 1949 or section 240 of the Copyright, Designs and Patents Act 1988 (Crown use of patents and designs), or

    (*b*) the rights of the Secretary of State under section 22 of the Patents Act 1977 or section 5 of the Registered Designs Act 1949 (security of information prejudicial to defence or public safety).

NOTES
[1]Substituted by the Copyright, Designs and Patents Act 1988 (c. 48), Sched. 7, para. 4(1). Para. 4(2) provides:

"(2) In the application of sub-paragraph (1) to Northern Ireland—

    (*a*) the reference to the Crown Proceedings Act 1947 is to that Act as it applies to the Crown in right of Her Majesty's Government in Northern Ireland, as well as to the Crown in right of Her Majesty's Government in the United Kingdom, and

    (*b*) in the substituted section 3 as it applies in relation to the Crown in right of Her Majesty's Government in Northern Ireland, subsection (2)(*b*) shall be omitted."

[2]As amended by the Trade Marks Act 1994 (c. 26), Sched. 5 (effective October 31, 1994: S.I. 1994 No. 2550). See *ibid.*, Sched. 4, para. 1.

Application of law as to indemnity, contribution, joint and several tortfeasors, and contributory negligence
4.—(1) Where the Crown is subject to any liability by virtue of this Part of this Act, the law relating to indemnity and contribution shall be enforceable by or against the Crown in respect of the liability to which it is so subject as if the Crown were a private person of full age and capacity.

(2) Without prejudice to the effect of the preceding subsection. Part II of the Law Reform (Married Women and Tortfeasors) Act 1935 (which relates to proceedings against, and contribution between, joint and several tortfeasors), shall bind the Crown.

(3) Without prejudice to the general effect of section one of this Act, the Law Reform (Contributory Negligence) Act 1945 (which amends the law relating to contributory negligence), shall bind the Crown.

. . . . . .

Provisions relating to the armed forces

[1]**10.**—(1) Nothing done or omitted to be done by a member of the armed forces of the Crown while on duty as such shall subject either him or the Crown to liability in tort for causing the death of another person, or for causing personal injury to another person, in so far as the death or personal injury is due to anything suffered by that other person while he is a member of the armed forces of the Crown if—

(a) at the time when that thing is suffered by that other person, he is either on duty as a member of the armed forces of the Crown or is, though not on duty as such, on any land, premises, ship, aircraft or vehicle for the time being used for the purposes of the armed forces of the Crown; and

(b) the Secretary of State certifies that his suffering that thing has been or will be treated as attributable to service for the purposes of entitlement to an award under the Royal Warrant, Order in Council or Order of His Majesty relating to the disablement or death of members of the force of which he is a member:

Provided that this subsection shall not exempt a member of the said forces from liability in tort in any case in which the court is satisfied that the act or omission was not connected with the execution of his duties as a member of those forces.

(2) No proceedings in tort shall lie against the Crown for death or personal injury due to anything suffered by a member of the armed forces of the Crown if—

(a) that thing is suffered by him in consequence of the nature or condition of any such land, premises, ship, aircraft or vehicle as aforesaid, or in consequence of the nature or condition of any equipment or supplies used for the purposes of those forces; and

(b) the Secretary of State certifies as mentioned in the preceding subsection;

nor shall any act or omission of an officer of the Crown subject him to liability in tort for death or personal injury, in so far as the death or personal injury is due to anything suffered by a member of the armed forces of the Crown being a thing as to which the conditions aforesaid are satisfied.

(3) A Secretary of State, if satisfied that it is the fact:—

(a) that a person was or was not on any particular occasion on duty as a member of the armed forces of the Crown; or

(b) that at any particular time any land, premises, ship, aircraft, vehicle, equipment or supplies was or was not, or were or were not, used for the purposes of the said forces;

may issue a certificate certifying that to be the fact; and any such certificate shall, for the purposes of this section, be conclusive as to the fact which it certifies.

NOTE
[1]As amended by S.I. 1953 No. 1198, S.I. 1964 No. 488, Ministry of Social Security Act 1966, s. 2(3), and S.I. 1968 No. 1699; extended by the Civil Defence (Armed Forces) Act 1954 (c. 66), s. 1(3); extended to hovercraft by S.I. 1972 No. 971. Repealed in respect of acts or omissions on or after 15th May 1987 by the Crown Proceedings (Armed Forces) Act 1987 (c. 25), subject to provision for its revival by order.

Saving in respect of acts done under prerogative and statutory powers
11.—(1) Nothing in Part I of this Act shall extinguish or abridge any powers or authorities which, if this Act had not been passed, would have been exercisable by virtue of the prerogative of the Crown, or any powers or authorities conferred on the Crown by any statute, and, in particular, nothing in the said Part I shall extinguish or abridge any powers or authorities exercisable by the Crown, whether in time of peace or of war, for the purpose of the defence of the realm or of training, or maintaining the efficiency of, any of the armed forces of the Crown.

[1](2) Where in any proceedings under this Act it is material to determine whether anything was properly done or omitted to be done in the exercise of the prerogative of the Crown, a Secretary of State may, if satisfied that the act or omission was necessary for any such purpose as is mentioned in the last preceding subsection, issue a certificate to the effect that the act or omission was necessary for that purpose; and the certificate shall, in those proceedings, be conclusive as to the matter so certified.

NOTE
[1]As amended by S.I. 1964 No. 488.

. . . . . .

[1]Part II.—Jurisdiction and Procedure

NOTE
[1]Extended by the Taxes Management Act 1970 (c. 9), s. 100(3), and the Finance Act 1975 (c. 7), Sched. 4.

The High Court

Civil proceedings in the High Court
13. Subject to the provisions of this Act, all such civil proceedings by or against the Crown as are mentioned in the First Schedule to this Act are hereby abolished, and all civil proceedings by or against the Crown in the High Court shall be instituted and proceeded with in accordance with rules of court and not otherwise.

In this section the expression "rules of court" means, in relation to any claim against the Crown in the High Court which falls within the jurisdiction of that court as a prize court, rules of court made under section 3 of the Prize Courts Act 1894.

14–20. [Not applicable to Scotland.]

Nature of relief

21.—(1) In any civil proceedings by or against the Crown the court shall, subject to the provisions of this Act, have power to make all such orders as it has power to make in proceedings between subjects, and otherwise to give such appropriate relief as the case may require: Provided that:—

(a) where in any proceedings against the Crown any such relief is sought as might in proceedings between subjects be granted by way of injunction or specific performance, the court shall not grant an injunction or make an order for specific performance, but may in lieu thereof make an order declaratory of the rights of the parties; and

(b) in any proceedings against the Crown for the recovery of land or other property the court shall not make an order for the recovery of the land or the delivery of the property, but may in lieu thereof make an order declaring that the plaintiff is entitled as against the Crown to the land or property or to the possession thereof.

(2) The court shall not in any civil proceedings grant any injunction or make any order against an officer of the Crown if the effect of granting the injunction or making the order would be to give any relief against the Crown which could not have been obtained in proceedings against the Crown.

. . . . . .

[1]PART III.—JUDGMENTS AND EXECUTION

NOTE
[1]Applied by the Finance Act 1975 (c. 7), Sched. 4.

24–25. [Not applicable to Scotland.]

Execution by the Crown

26.—[1](1) Subject to the provisions of this Act, any order made in favour of the Crown against any person in any civil proceedings to which the Crown is a party may be enforced in the same manner as an order made in an action between subjects, and not otherwise.

[2](2) The exception in respect of taxes contained in section 4 of the Debtors (Scotland) Act 1880, from the enactment therein contained abolishing imprisonment for debt shall apply only in respect of death duties.

(3) Nothing in this section shall affect any procedure which immediately before the commencement of this Act was available for enforcing an order made in favour of the Crown in proceedings brought by the Crown for the recovery of any fine or penalty, or the

forfeiture or condemnation of any goods, or the forfeiture of any ship or any share in a ship.

NOTES

¹As amended by the Statute Law (Repeals) Act 1993 (c. 50), Sched. 1, Pt. I (effective November 5, 1993).

²As applicable to Scotland by s. 49. As amended by the Finance Act 1972 (c. 4), Sched. 28, Pt. II.

27. [Not applicable to Scotland.]

PART IV.—MISCELLANEOUS AND SUPPLEMENTAL

Miscellaneous

. . . . . .

Limitation of actions

30. [Repealed by the Merchant Shipping Act 1995 (c. 21), Sched. 12 (effective January 1, 1996: s. 316(2)).]

Application to the Crown of certain statutory provisions

31.—(1) This Act shall not prejudice the right of the Crown to take advantage of the provisions of an Act of Parliament although not named therein; and it is hereby declared that in any civil proceedings against the Crown the provisions of any Act of Parliament which could, if the proceedings were between subjects, be relied upon by the defendant as a defence to the proceedings, whether in whole or in part, or otherwise, may, subject to any express provision to the contrary, be so relied upon by the Crown.

(2) Section 6 of the Debtors Act 1869 (which empowers the court in certain circumstances to order the arrest of a defendant about to quit England), shall, with any necessary modifications, apply to civil proceedings in the High Court by the Crown.

. . . . . .

Interpretation

38.—(1) Any reference in this Act to the provisions of this Act shall, unless the context otherwise requires, include a reference to rules of court or county court rules made for the purposes of this Act.

(2) In this Act, except in so far as the context otherwise requires or it is otherwise expressly provided, the following expressions have the meanings hereby respectively assigned to them, that is to say:—

"Agent", when used in relation to the Crown, includes an independent contractor employed by the Crown;

"Civil proceedings" includes proceedings in the High Court or the county court for the recovery of fines or penalties, but does not include proceedings on the Crown side of the King's Bench Division;

"His Majesty's aircraft" does not include aircraft belonging to His Majesty otherwise than in right of His Government in the United Kingdom;

[1]"His Majesty's ships" means ships of which the beneficial interest is vested in His Majesty of which are registered as Government ships for the purposes of the Merchant Shipping Act 1995, or which are for the time being demised or subdemised to or in the exclusive possession of the Crown, except that the said expression does not include any ship in which His Majesty is interested otherwise than in right of His Government in the United Kingdom unless that ship is for the time being demised or subdemised to His Majesty in right of His said Government or in the exclusive possession of His Majesty in that right;

"Officer", in relation to the Crown, includes any servant of His Majesty, and accordingly (but without prejudice to the generality of the foregoing provisions) includes a Minister of the Crown;

"Order" includes a judgment, decree, rule, award or declaration;

"Prescribed" means prescribed by rules of court or county court rules, as the case may be;

"Proceedings against the Crown" includes a claim by way of set-off or counter-claim raised in proceedings by the Crown;

[1]"Ship" has the same meaning as in the Merchant Shipping Act 1995;

"Statutory duty" means any duty imposed by or under any Act of Parliament.

[2](3) Any reference in this Act to His Majesty in His private capacity shall be construed as including a reference to His Majesty in right of His Duchy of Lancaster and to the Duke of Cornwall.

[3](4) Any reference in Parts III, IV [or V] of this Act to civil proceedings by or against the Crown, or to civil proceedings to which the Crown is a party, shall be construed as including a reference to civil proceedings to which the [Lord Advocate], or any Government department, or any officer of the Crown as such is a party;

(5) [Repealed by the Armed Forces Act 1981 (c. 55), Sched. 5.]

(6) References in this Act to any enactment shall be construed as references to that enactment as amended by or under any other enactment, including this Act.

NOTES

[1]As amended by the Merchant Shipping Act 1955 (c. 21), Sched. 13, para. 21 (effective January 1, 1996: s. 316(2)).

[2]Extended by the Animals Act 1971 (c. 22), s. 12(2), and the Health and Safety at Work, etc., Act 1974 (c. 37), s. 48(6).

[3]As applicable to Scotland by s. 51.

. . . . . .

Savings

40.—(1) Nothing in this Act shall apply to proceedings by or against, or authorise proceedings in tort to be brought against His Majesty in his private capacity.

(2) Except as therein otherwise expressly provided, nothing in this Act shall:—

(a) affect the law relating to prize salvage, or apply to proceedings in causes or matters within the jurisdiction of the High Court as a prize court or to any criminal proceedings; or

(b) authorise proceedings to be taken against the Crown under or in accordance with this Act in respect of any alleged liability of the Crown arising otherwise than in respect of His Majesty's Government in the United Kingdom, or affect proceedings against the Crown in respect of any such alleged liability as aforesaid; or

(c) affect any proceedings by the Crown otherwise than in right of His Majesty's Government in the United Kingdom; or

(d) subject the Crown to any greater liabilities in respect of the acts or omissions of any independent contractor employed by the Crown than those to which the Crown would be subject in respect of such acts or omissions if it were a private person; or

(e) subject the Crown, in its capacity as a highway authority, to any greater liability than that to which a local authority is subject in that capacity; or

(f) affect any rules of evidence or any presumption relating to the extent to which the Crown is bound by any Act of Parliament; or

(g) affect any right of the Crown to demand a trial at bar or to control or otherwise intervene in proceedings affecting its rights, property to profits; or

(h) affect any liability imposed on the public trustee or on the Consolidated Fund of the United Kingdom by the Public Trustee Act 1906;

and, without prejudice to the general effect of the foregoing provisions, Part III of this Act shall not apply to the Crown except in right of His Majesty's Government in the United Kingdom.

(3) A certificate of a Secretary of State:—

(a) to the effect that any alleged liability of the Crown arises otherwise than in respect of His Majesty's Government in the United Kingdom;

(b) to the effect that any proceedings by the Crown are proceedings otherwise than in right of His Majesty's Government in the United Kingdom;

shall, for the purposes of this Act, be conclusive as to the matter so certified.

(4) Where any property vests in the Crown by virtue of any rule of law which operates independently of the acts or the intentions of the Crown, the Crown shall not by virtue of this Act be subject to any liabilities in tort by reason only of the property being so vested; but the provisions of this subsection shall be without prejudice to the liabilities of the Crown under this Act in respect of any period after the Crown or any person acting for the Crown has in fact taken possession or control of any such property, or entered into occupation thereof.

(5) This Act shall not operate to limit the discretion of the court to grant relief by way of mandamus in cases in which such relief might have been granted before the commencement of this Act, notwithstanding that by reason of the provisions of this Act some other and further remedy is available.

[1]PART V.—APPLICATION TO SCOTLAND

NOTE
[1]Applied by the Sex Discrimination Act 1975, s. 85(9), and the Race Relations Act 1976, s. 75(7).

Application of Act to Scotland
41.—The provisions of this Part of this Act shall have effect for the purpose of the application of this Act to Scotland.

Exclusion of certain provisions
42. Section 1, Part II (except section 13 so far as relating to proceedings mentioned in the First Schedule) [*sic*] and section 21, Part III (except section 26) and section 28 of this Act shall not apply to Scotland.

Interpretation for purposes of application to Scotland
43. In the application of this Act to Scotland:—
  (*a*) for any reference to the High Court (except a reference to that court as a prize court) there shall be substituted a reference to the Court of Session; for any reference to the county court there shall be substituted a reference to the sheriff court; the expression "plaintiff" means pursuer; the expression "defendant" means defender; the expression "county court rules" means Act of Sederunt applying to the sheriff court; and the expression "injunction" means interdict;
  (*b*) the expression "tort" means any wrongful or negligent act or omission giving rise to liability in reparation, and any reference to liability or right or action or proceedings in tort shall be construed accordingly; and for any reference to Part II of the Law Reform (Married Woman and Tortfeasors) Act 1935 there shall be substituted a reference to section 3 of the Law Reform (Miscellaneous Provisions) (Scotland) Act 1940.

Proceedings against the Crown in the sheriff court

[1]**44.** Subject to the provisions of this Act and to any enactment limiting the jurisdiction of the sheriff court (whether by reference to the subject-matter of the proceedings or otherwise) civil proceedings against the Crown may be instituted in the sheriff court in like manner as if the proceedings were against a subject:

Provided that where in any proceedings against the Crown in the sheriff court a certificate by the Lord Advocate is produced to the effect that the proceedings may involve an important question of law, or may be decisive of other cases, or are for other reasons more fit for trial in the Court of Session, the proceedings shall be remitted to the Court of Session, and where any proceedings have been so remitted to the Court of Session, and it appears to that court that the remit has occasioned additional expense to the pursuer, the court shall take account of the additional expense so occasioned in deciding any question as to expenses.

NOTE

[1]Proviso excluded by the Sex Discrimination Act 1975, s. 85(9) and the Race Relations Act 1976, s. 75(7).

Satisfaction of orders granted against the Crown in Scotland

[1]**45.**—(1) Where in any civil proceedings by or against the Crown or to which the Crown has been made a party, any order (including an award of expenses) is made by any court in favour of any person against the Crown or against a Government department or against an officer of the Crown as such, the clerk of court shall, on an application in that behalf made by or on behalf of that person at any time after the expiration of 21 days from the date of the order, or, in a case where there is an award of expenses and the expenses require to be taxed, at any time after taxation whichever is the later, issue to that person a certified copy of the order of the court.

(2) A copy of any such order may be served by the person in whose favour the order is made upon the person for the time being named in the record as the solicitor, or the person acting as solicitor, for the Crown or for the Government department or officer concerned.

(3) If the order decerns for the payment of any money by way of damages or otherwise or of any expenses, the appropriate Government department shall, subject as hereinafter provided, pay to the person entitled or to his solicitor the amount appearing from the order to be due to him together with the interest, if any, lawfully due thereon:

Provided that the court by which any such order as aforesaid is made or any court to which an appeal against the order lies may direct that, pending an appeal or otherwise, payment of the whole of any amount so payable, or any part thereon, shall be suspended.

(4) No such order as aforesaid shall warrant any diligence or execution against any person to enforce payment of any such money or expenses as

aforesaid, and no person shall be individually liable under any order for the payment by the Crown, or any Government department or any officer of the Crown as such, of any such money or expenses.

NOTE
[1]See the Debtors (Scotland) Act 1987, ss. 79(5) and 105.

Provisions as to arrestment

46. Arrestment in the hands of the Crown or of a Government department or of any officer of the Crown as such shall be competent in any case where arrestment in the hands of a subject would have been competent:

Provided that nothing in the foregoing provisions shall warrant the arrestment of:—

(*a*) [Repealed by the Debtors (Scotland) Act 1987, Sched. 8.]

(*b*) any money which is subject to the provisions of any enactment prohibiting or restricting assignation or charging or taking in execution;

(*c*) [Repealed by the Law Reform (Miscellaneous Provisions) (Scotland) Act 1985, s. 49(*b*) and Sched. 4, with effect from December 30, 1985.]

Recovery of documents in possession of Crown

[1]**47.** Subject to and in accordance with Acts of Sederunt applying to the Court of Session and the sheriff court, commission and diligence for the recovery of documents in the possession of the Crown may be granted in any action whether or not the Crown is a party thereto, in like manner in all respects as if the documents were in the possession of a subject:

Provided that—

(i) this subsection shall be without prejudice to any rule of law which authorises or requires the withholding of any document on the ground that its disclosure would be injurious to the public interest; and

(ii) the existence of a document shall not be disclosed if, in the opinion of a Minister of the Crown, it would be injurious to the public interest to disclose the existence thereof.

NOTE
[1]Applied by the Administration of Justice (Scotland) Act 1972, s. 1(4).

. . . . . .

4. Law Reform (Personal Injuries) Act 1948
(11 & 12 Geo. 6, c. 41)

An Act to abolish the defence of common employment, to amend the law relating to the measure of damages for personal injury or death, and for purposes connected therewith.

[30th June 1948]

Common employment

1.—(1) It shall not be a defence to an employer who is sued in respect of personal injuries caused by the negligence of a person employed by him, that that person was at the time the injuries were caused in common employment with the person injured.

(2) Accordingly the Employers' Liability Act 1880 shall cease to have effect, and is hereby repealed.

(3) Any provision contained in a contract of service or apprenticeship, or in an agreement collateral thereto (including a contract or agreement entered into before the commencement of this Act), shall be void in so far as it would have the effect of excluding or limiting any liability of the employer in respect of personal injuries caused to the person employed or apprenticed by the negligence or persons in common employment with him.

Measure of damages

[1]**2.**—(1) In an action of damages for personal injuries (including any such action arising out of a contract), where this section applies there shall in assessing those damages be taken into account, against them, one half of the value of any rights which have accrued or probably will accrue to the injured person from the injuries in respect of—

[2](*a*) any of the relevant benefits, within the meaning of section 81 of the Social Security Administration Act 1992, or

(*b*) any corresponding benefits payable in Northern Ireland,

for the five years beginning with the time when the cause of action accrued.

[2,3](1A) This section applies in any case where the amount of the damages that would have been awarded apart from any reduction under subsection (1) above is less than the sum for the time being prescribed under section 85(1) of the Social Security Administration Act 1992 (recoupment of benefit: exception for small payments).

(2) [Repealed with effect from 3rd September 1990 by the Social Security Act 1989, Sched. 4, para. 22(3).]

(3) The reference in subsection (1) of this section to assessing the damages for personal injuries shall, in cases where the damages otherwise recoverable are subject to reduction under the law relating to contributory negligence or are limited by or under any Act or by contract, be taken as referring to the total damages which would have been recoverable apart from the reduction or limitation.

(4) In an action for damages for personal injuries (including any such action arising out of a contract), there shall be disregarded, in determining the reasonableness of any expenses, the possibility of avoiding those expenses or part of them by taking advantage of facilities available under the National Health Service Act 1977, or the National Health Service (Scotland) Act 1978, or of any corresponding facilities in Northern Ireland.

(5) [Repealed by the Fatal Accidents Act 1959, Sched.]

(5A) [Repealed by the Damages (Scotland) Act 1976, Sched. 2.]
[4](6) For the purposes of this section disablement benefit in the form of a gratuity is to be treated as benefit for the period taken into account by the assessment of the extent of the disablement in respect of which it is payable.

NOTES
[1]As amended by the National Insurance Act 1971, Sched. 5, para. 1, the Social Security (Consequential Provisions) Act 1975, Sched. 2, the Social Security Pensions Act 1975, Sched. 4, the National Health Service Act 1977, Sched. 15, the National Health Service (Scotland) Act 1978, Sched. 16, the Health and Social Security Act 1984, Sched. 4, para. 1, the Social Security Act 1990, Sched. 1, para. 7, with effect from 13th July 1990, and by the Social Security Act 1989, Sched. 4, para. 22, with effect from 3rd September 1990.
[2]As amended by the Social Security (Consequential Provisions) Act 1992 (c. 6), Sched. 2, para. 2 (effective 1st July 1992; s. 7(2)).
[3]Inserted with effect from 3rd September 1990 by the Social Security Act 1989, Sched. 4, para. 22(2).
[4]As substituted by the Social Security (Consequential Provisions) Act 1975, Sched. 2.

Definition of "personal injury"
3. In this Act the expression "personal injury" includes any disease and any impairment of a person's physical or mental condition, and the expression "injured" shall be construed accordingly.

Application to Crown
4. This Act shall bind the Crown.

. . . . . .

5. Defamation Act 1952
(15 & 16 Geo. 6 and 1 Eliz. 2, c. 66)

[1]An Act to amend the law relating to libel and slander and other malicious falsehoods.   [30th October 1952]

NOTE
[1]See general Scottish application provisions in s. 14(*d*), *infra*.

1, 2. [Not applicable to Scotland.]

Actions for verbal injury
[3]**3.** In any action for verbal injury it shall not be necessary for the pursuer to aver or prove special damage if the words on which the action is founded are calculated to cause pecuniary damage to the pursuer.

NOTE
[1]As substituted for Scotland by s. 14(*b*).

4. [Repealed by the Defamation Act 1996 (c. 31), Sched. 2, effective September 4, 1996, s. 19(2).]

Justification

5. In an action for libel or slander in respect of words containing two or more distinct charges against the plaintiff, a defence of justification shall not fail by reason only that the truth of every charge is not proved if the words not proved to be true do not materially injure the plaintiff's reputation having regard to the truth of the remaining charges.

Fair comment

6. In an action for libel or slander in respect of words consisting partly of allegations of fact and partly of expression of opinion, a defence of fair comment shall not fail by reason only that the truth of every allegation of fact is not proved if the expression of opinion is fair comment having regard to such of the facts alleged or referred to in the words complained of as are proved.

7–8. [Repealed by the Defamation Act 1996 (c. 31), Sched. 2, effective September 4, 1996, s. 19(2).]

Extension of certain defences to broadcasting

9.—(1) Section 3 of the Parliamentary Papers Act 1840 (which confers protection in respect of proceedings for printing extracts from or abstracts of parliamentary papers) shall have effect as if the reference to printing included a reference by broadcasting by means of wireless telegraphy.

(2)–(3) [Repealed by the Defamation Act 1996 (c. 31), Sched. 2, effective September 4, 1996, s. 19(2).]

Limitation on privilege at elections

10. A defamatory statement published by or on behalf of a candidate in any election to a local government authority or to Parliament shall not be deemed to be published on a privileged occasion on the ground that it is material to a question in issue in the election, whether or not the person by whom it is published is qualified to vote at the election.

Agreements for indemnity

11. An agreement for indemnifying any person against civil liability for libel in respect of the publication of any matter shall not be unlawful unless at the time of the publication that person knows that the matter is defamatory, and does not reasonably believe there is a good defence on any action brought upon it.

Evidence of other damages recovered by plaintiff

12. In any action for libel or slander the defendant may give evidence in mitigation of damages that the plaintiff has recovered damages, or has brought actions for damages, for libel or slander in respect of the publication of words to the same effect as the words on which the action is founded, or has received or agreed to receive compensation in respect of any such publication.

13. [Not applicable to Scotland.]

Application of Act to Scotland

14. This Act shall apply to Scotland subject to the following modifications, that is to say:—

(*a*) sections 1, 2, 8 and 13 shall be omitted;

(*b*) for section 3 there shall be substituted the following section — [see *supra*, s. 3];

(*c*) subsection (2) of section 4 shall have effect as if at the end thereof there were added the words [see *supra*, s. 4(2)];

(*d*) for any reference to libel, or to libel or slander, there shall be substituted a reference to defamation; the expression "plaintiff" means pursuer; the expression "defendant" means defender; for any reference to an affidavit made by any person there shall be substituted a reference to a written declaration signed by that person; for any reference to the High Court there shall be substituted a reference to the Court of Session or, if an action of defamation is depending in the sheriff court in respect of the publication in question, the sheriff[1]; the expression "costs" means expenses; and for any reference to a defence of justification there shall be substituted a reference to a defence of *veritas*.

NOTE

[1]For interpretation of the term "sheriff" see the Sheriff Courts (Scotland) Act 1971 (c. 58), s. 4, and the Interpretation Act 1978 (c. 30), Sched. 1.

. . . . . .

Interpretation

[1]**16.**—(1) Any reference in this Act to words shall be construed as including a reference to pictures, visual images, gestures and other methods of signifying meaning.

(2)–(3) [Repealed by the Defamation Act 1996 (c. 31), Sched. 2, effective September 4, 1996, s. 19(2).]

(4) [Repealed by the Cable and Broadcasting Act 1984 c. 46), Sched. 6.]

Proceedings affected and saving

17.—(1) This Act applies for the purposes of any proceedings begun after the commencement of this Act, whenever the cause of action arose, but does not affect any proceedings begun before the commencement of this Act.

(2) Nothing in this Act affects the law relating to criminal libel.

Short title, commencement, extent and repeals

[1]**18.**—(1) This Act may be cited as the Defamation Act 1952, and shall come into operation one month after the passing of this Act.

(2) This Act shall not extend to Northern Ireland.

NOTE

[1]As amended by the Northern Ireland Constitution Act 1973 (c. 36), Sched. 6.

. . . . . .

6. Interest on Damages (Scotland) Act 1958
(6 & 7 Eliz. 2, c. 61)

An Act to amend the law of Scotland relating to the power of the courts to order payment of interest on damages.

[1st August 1958]

Power of courts to grant interest on damages

1.—[1](1) Where a court pronounces in interlocutor decerning for payment by any person of a sum of money as damages, the interlocutor may include decree for payment by that person of interest, at such rate or rates as may be specified in the interlocutor, on the whole or any part of that sum for the whole or any part of any period between the date when the right of action arose and the date of the interlocutor.

[1](1A) Where a court pronounces an interlocutor decerning for payment of a sum which consists of or includes damages or solatium in respect of personal injuries sustained by the pursuer or any other person, then (without prejudice to the exercise of the power conferred by subsection (1) of this section in relation to any part of that sum which does not represent such damages or solatium) the court shall exercise that power so as to include in that sum interest on those damages and on that solatium or on such part of each as the court considers appropriate, unless the court is satisfied that there are reasons special to the case why no interest should be given in respect thereof.

[1](1B) For the avoidance of doubt, it is hereby declared that where, in any action in which it is competent for the court to award interest under this Act, a tender is made in the course of the action, the tender shall, unless otherwise stated therein, be in full satisfaction of any claim to interest thereunder by any person in whose favour the tender is made; and in considering in any such action whether an award is equal to or greater than an amount tendered in the action, the court shall take account of the amount of any interest awarded under this Act, or such part of that interest as the court considers appropriate.

(2) Nothing in this section shall—

(*a*)   authorise the granting of interest upon interest, or

(*b*)   prejudice any other power of the court as to the granting of interest, or

(*c*)   affect the running of any interest which apart from this section would run by virtue of any enactment or rule of law.

NOTE
[1]Substituted for subs. (1) by the Interest on Damages (Scotland) Act 1971, s. 1.

2. [Repealed with saving by the Law Reform (Miscellaneous Provisions) (Scotland) Act 1980, s. 11 (2) (*d*) and Sched. 3.]

Citation, interpretation, extent and commencement

3.—(1) This Act may be cited as the Interest on Damages (Scotland) Act 1958.

[1](2) In this Act, "personal injuries" includes any disease and any impairment of a person's physical or mental condition.

(3) This Act shall extend to Scotland only, and shall not apply to any action commenced against any person before the passing of this Act.

NOTE

[1]Substituted by the Interest on Damages (Scotland) Act 1971, s. 1.

. . . . . .

7. Law Reform (Husband and Wife) Act 1962
(10 & 11 Eliz. 2, c. 48)

An Act to amend the law with respect to civil proceedings between husband and wife.   [1st August 1962]

. . . . . .

Proceedings between husband and wife in respect of delict

2.—(1) Subject to the provisions of this section, each of the parties to a marriage shall have the like right to bring proceedings against the other in respect of a wrongful or negligent act or omission, or for the prevention of a wrongful act, as if they were not married.

[1](2) Where any such proceedings are brought by one of the parties to a marriage against the other during the subsistence of the marriage, the court may dismiss the proceedings if it appears that no substantial benefit would accrue to either party from the continuation thereof; and it shall be the duty of the court to consider at any early stage of the proceedings whether the power to dismiss the proceedings under this subsection should or should not be exercised.

(3) This section extends to Scotland only.

NOTE

[1]By s. 21 of the Matrimonial Homes (Family Protection) (Scotland) Act 1981, this subsection does not apply to any proceedings brought before the court in pursuance of any provision of that Act.

Short title, repeal, interpretation, saving and extent

3.—(1) This Act may be cited as the Law Reform (Husband and Wife) Act 1962.

(2) [Repealed by the Statute Law (Repeals) Act 1974.]

(3) The references in subsection (1) of section 1 and subsection (1) of section 2 of this Act to the parties to a marriage include references to the persons who were parties to a marriage which has been dissolved.

(4) This Act does not apply to any case of action which arose, or would but for the subsistence of a marriage have arisen, before the commencement of this Act.

(5) This Act does not extend to Northern Ireland.

. . . . . .

8. Law Reform (Miscellaneous Provisions) (Scotland) Act 1968
(1968 c. 70)

An Act to ... amend the law of evidence in civil proceedings in Scotland
...   [25th October 1968]

. . . . . .

PART III

AMENDMENT OF THE LAW OF EVIDENCE IN CIVIL PROCEEDINGS

. . . . . .

Convictions, etc., as evidence in civil proceedings

Convictions as evidence in civil proceedings
[1]**10.**—(1) In any civil proceedings the fact that a person has been convicted of an offence by or before any court in the United Kingdom or by a court-martial there or elsewhere shall (subject to subsection (3) of this section) be admissible in evidence for the purpose of proving, where to do so is relevant to any issue in those proceedings, that he committed that offence, whether he was so convicted upon a plea of guilty or otherwise and whether or not he is party to the civil proceedings; but no conviction other than a subsisting one shall be admissible in evidence by virtue of this section.

(2) In any civil proceedings in which by virtue of this section a person is proved to have been convicted of an offence by or before any court in the United Kingdom or by a court-martial there or elsewhere—

(*a*) he shall be taken to have committed that offence unless the contrary is proved, and

(*b*) without prejudice to the reception of any other admissible evidence for the purpose of identifying the facts which constituted that offence, the contents of any document which is admissible as evidence of the conviction, and the contents of the complaint, information, indictment or charge-sheet on which the person in question was convicted, shall be admissible in evidence for that purpose.

(3) Nothing in this section shall affect the operation of section 12 of this Act or any other enactment whereby a conviction or a finding of fact in any criminal proceedings is for the purposes of any other proceedings made conclusive evidence of any fact.

(4) Where in any civil proceedings the contents of any document are admissible in evidence by virtue of subsection (2) of this section, a copy of that document, or of the material part thereof, purporting to be certified or otherwise authenticated by or on behalf of the court or authority having custody of that document, shall be admissible in evidence and shall be taken to be a true copy of that document or part unless the contrary is shown.

[2](5) Nothing in any of the following enactments, that is to say—
  (a) section 13 of the Powers of Criminal Courts Act 1973 (under which a conviction leading to probation or discharge is to be disregarded except as therein mentioned);
  (b) section 191 of the Criminal Procedure (Scotland) Act 1975 (which makes similar provision in respect of convictions on indictment in Scotland);
  (c) section 8 of the Probation Act (Northern Ireland) 1950 (which corresponds to the said section 12) or any corresponding enactment of the Parliament of Northern Ireland for the time being in force,
shall affect the operation of this section; and for the purposes of this section any order made by a court of summary jurisdiction under section 383 of the said Act of 1975 shall be treated as a conviction.

(6) In this section "court-martial" means a court-martial constituted under the Army Act 1955, the Air Force Act 1955 or the Naval Discipline Act 1957 or a disciplinary court constituted under section 50 of the said Act of 1957, and in relation to a court-martial "conviction", as regards a court-martial constituted under either of the said Acts of 1955, means a finding of guilty which is, or falls to be treated as, a finding of the court duly confirmed and, as regards a court-martial or disciplinary court constituted under the said Act of 1957, means a finding of guilty which is, or falls to be treated as, the finding of the court, and "convicted" shall be construed accordingly.

NOTES
[1]Extended: see the Fair Trading Act 1973, s. 36(1).
[2]As amended by the Powers of Criminal Courts Act 1973, Sched. 5, para. 32, and as read with the Interpretation Act 1978, s. 17(2).

Findings of adultery and paternity as evidence in civil proceedings
[1]**11.**—(1) In any civil proceedings—
  (a) the fact that a person has been found guilty of adultery in any matrimonial proceedings,
shall (subject to subsection (3) of this section) be admissible in evidence for the purpose of proving, where to do so is relevant to any issue in those civil proceedings, that he committed the adultery to

which the finding relates, whether or not he offered any defence to the allegations of adultery and whether or not he is party to the civil proceedings; but no finding other than a subsisting one shall be admissible in evidence by virtue of this section.

(2) In any civil proceedings in which by virtue of this section a person is proved to have been found guilty of adultery as mentioned in subsection (1)(a) of this section —

(a) he shall be taken to have committed the adultery to which the finding relates, unless the contrary is proved; and

(b) without prejudice to the reception of any other admissible evidence for the purpose of identifying the facts on which the finding was based, the contents of any document which was before the court, or which contains any pronouncement of the court, in the matrimonial proceedings in question shall be admissible in evidence for that purpose.

(3) Nothing in this section shall affect the operation of any enactment whereby a finding of fact in any matrimonial proceedings is for the purposes of any other proceedings made conclusive evidence of any fact.

[2](4) Nothing in this section shall entitle the Court of Session to pronounce a decree of divorce without receiving evidence from the pursuer.

(5) Subsection (4) of section 10 of this Act shall apply for the purposes of this section as if the reference therein to subsection (2) were a reference to subsection (2) of this section.

(6) In this section—

(a) "matrimonial proceedings" means any consistorial action, any matrimonial cause in the High Court or a county court in England and Wales or in the High Court in Northern Ireland, or any appeal arising out of any such action or cause.

NOTES
[1]As amended by the Law Reform (Parent and Child) (Scotland) Act 1986, Sched. 2, with effect from 8th December 1986.
[2]As amended by the Divorce (Scotland) Act 1976 (c. 39), Sched. 1, para. 4.

Conclusiveness of convictions for purposes of defamation actions

12.—[1](1) In an action for defamation in which the question whether the pursuer did or did not commit a criminal offence is relevant to an issue arising in the action, proof that, at the time when that issue falls to be determined, he stands convicted of that offence shall be conclusive evidence that he committed that offence; and his conviction thereof shall be admissible in evidence accordingly.

[2](2) In any such action as aforesaid in which by virtue of this section the pursuer is proved to have been convicted of an offence, the contents of any document which is admissible as evidence of the conviction, and the contents of the complaint, information, indictment, or charge-sheet on which he was convicted shall,

without prejudice to the reception of any other admissible evidence for the purpose of identifying the facts which constituted that offence, be admissible in evidence for the purpose of identifying those facts.

[3](2A) In the case of an action for defamation in which there is more than one pursuer—

    (*a*)   the references in subsections (1) and (2) above to the pursuer shall be construed as references to any of the pursuers, and

    (*b*)   proof that any of the pursuers stands convicted of an offence shall be conclusive evidence that he committed that offence so far as the fact is relevant to any issue arising in relation to his cause of action or that of any other pursuer.

(3) For the purposes of this section a person shall be taken to stand convicted of an offence if but only if there subsists against him a conviction of that offence by or before a court in the United Kingdom or by a court-martial there or elsewhere.

(4) Subsections (4) to (6) of section 10 of this Act shall apply for the purposes of this section as they apply for the purposes of that section, but as if in the said subsection (4) the reference to subsection (2) were a reference to subsection (2) of this section.

(5) The foregoing provisions of this section shall apply for the purposes of any action begun after the coming into operation of this section, whenever the cause of action arose, but shall not apply for the purposes of any action begun before such commencement or any appeal or other proceedings arising out of any such action.

NOTES

  [1]As amended by the Defamation Act 1996 (c. 31), s. 12(2), effective September 4, 1996, s. 19(2).

  [2]As amended by the Defamation Act 1996 (c. 31), s. 12(2), effective September 4, 1996, s. 19(2).

  [3]Inserted by the Defamation Act 1996 (c. 31), s. 12(2), effective September 4, 1996, s. 19(2).

. . . . . .

9. Employer's Liability (Defective Equipment) Act 1969

(1969 c. 37)

An Act to make further provision with respect to the liability of an employer for injury to his employee which is attributable to any defect in equipment provided by the employer for the purposes of the employer's business; and for purposes connected with the matter aforesaid. [25th July 1969]

Extension of employer's liability for defective equipment

    1.—(1) Where after the commencement of this Act—

(*a*) an employee suffers personal injury in the course of his employment in consequence of a defect in equipment provided by his employer for the purposes of the employer's business; and

(*b*) the defect is attributable wholly or partly to the fault of a third party (whether identified or not),

the injury shall be deemed to be also attributable to negligence on the part of the employer (whether or not he is liable in respect of the injury apart from this subsection), but without prejudice to the law relating to contributory negligence and to any remedy by way of contribution or in contract or otherwise which is available to the employer in respect of the injury.

(2) In so far as any agreement purports to exclude or limit any liability of an employer arising under subsection (1) of this section, the agreement shall be void.

(3) In this section—

"business" includes the activities carried on by any public body;

"employee" means a person who is employed by another person under a contract of service or apprenticeship and is so employed for the purposes of a business carried on by that other person, and "employer" shall be construed accordingly;

"equipment" includes any plant and machinery, vehicle, aircraft and clothing;

"fault" means negligence, breach of statutory duty or other act or omission which gives rise to liability in tort in England and Wales or which is wrongful and gives rise to liability in damages in Scotland; and

"personal injury" includes loss of life, any impairment of a person's physical or mental condition and any disease.

(4) This section binds the Crown and persons in the service of the Crown shall accordingly be treated for the purposes of this section as employees of the Crown if they would not be so treated apart from this subsection.

Short title, commencement and extent

[1]**2.**—(1) This Act may be cited as the Employer's Liability (Defective Equipment) Act 1969.

(2) This Act shall come into force on the expiration of the period of three months beginning with the date on which it is passed.

. . . . . .

(4) This Act does not extend to Northern Ireland.

NOTE
[1]As amended by the Northern Ireland Constitution Act 1973, Sched. 6.

. . . . . .

10. **Prescription and Limitation (Scotland) Act 1973**
(1973 c. 52)

An Act to replace the Prescription Acts of 1469, 1474 and 1617 and make new provision in the law of Scotland with respect to the establishment and definition by positive prescription of title to interests in land and of positive servitudes and public rights of way, and with respect to the extinction of rights and obligations by negative prescription; to repeal certain enactments relating to limitation of proof; to re-enact with modifications certain enactments relating to the time-limits for bringing legal proceedings where damages are claimed which consist of or include damages or solatium in respect of personal injuries or in respect of a person's death and the time-limit for claiming contribution between wrongdoers; and for purposes connected with the matters aforesaid.   [25th July 1973]

PART I

PRESCRIPTION

Positive prescription

Interests in land: general
  ¹**1.**—(1) If in the case of an interest in particular land, being an interest to which this section applies,—
   (*a*) the interest has been possessed by any person, or by any person and his successors, for a continuous period of ten years openly, peaceably and without any judicial interruption, and
   (*b*) the possession was founded on, and followed (i) the recording of a deed which is sufficient in respect of its terms to constitute in favour of that person a title to that interest in the particular land, or in land of a description habile to include the particular land, or (ii) registration of that interest in favour of that person in the Land Register of Scotland, subject to an exclusion of indemnity under section 12(2) of the Land Registration (Scotland) Act 1979,
then, as from the expiration of the said period, the validity of the title so far as relating to the said interest in the particular land shall be exempt from challenge.
  (1A) Subsection (1) above shall not apply where—
   (*a*) possession was founded on the recording of a deed which is invalid *ex facie* or was forged; or
   (*b*) possession was founded on registration in respect of an interest in land in the Land Register of Scotland proceeding on a

forged deed and the person appearing from the Register to be entitled to the interest was aware of the forgery at the time of registration in his favour.

(2) This section applies to any interest in land the title to which can competently be recorded or which is registrable in the Land Register of Scotland.

(3) In the computation of a prescriptive period for the purposes of this section in a case where the deed in question is a decree of adjudication for debt, any period before the expiry of the legal shall be disregarded.

(4) Where in any question involving an interest in any foreshore or in any salmon fishings this section is pled against the Crown as owner of the regalia, subsection (1) above shall have effect as if for the words "ten years" there were substituted the words "twenty years".

(5) This section is without prejudice to the operation of section 2 of this Act.

NOTE

[1]As amended by the Land Registration (Scotland) Act 1979 (c. 33), s. 10. Excluded by the Coal Industry Act 1994 (c. 21), s. 10(2)(b) (effective October 31, 1994; s. 68(2) and S.I. 1994 No. 2553).

Interests in land: special cases

[1]**2.**—(1) If in the case of an interest in particular land, being an interest to which this section applies,—

   (a)   the interest has been possessed by any person, or by any person and his successors, for a continuous period of twenty years openly, peaceably and without any judicial interruption, and

   (b)   the possession was founded on, and followed the execution of, a deed (whether recorded or not) which is sufficient in respect of its terms to constitute in favour of that person a title to that interest in the particular land, or in land of a description habile to include the particular land,

then, as from the expiration of the said period, the validity of the title so far as relating to the said interest in the particular land shall be exempt from challenge except on the ground that the deed is invalid *ex facie* or was forged.

(2) This section applies—

   (a)   to the interest in land of the lessee under a lease;

   (b)   to any interest in allodial land;

   (c)   to any other interest in land the title to which is of a kind which, under the law in force immediately before the commencement of this Part of this Act, was sufficient to form a foundation for positive prescription without the deed constituting the title having been recorded.

(3) This section is without prejudice to the operation of section 1 of this Act.

NOTE
[1]See the Registration of Leases (Scotland) Act 1857 (c. 26), s. 16(2), and the Land Tenure Reform (Scotland) Act 1974 (c. 38), s. 18 and Sched., 6, para. 3. Excluded by the Coal Industry Act 1994 (c. 21), s. 10(2)(*b*) (effective October 31, 1994; s. 68(2) and S.I. 1994 No. 2553).

Positive servitudes and public rights of way

3.—(1) If in the case of a positive servitude over land—
   (*a*)   the servitude has been possessed for a continuous period of twenty years openly, peaceably and without any judicial interruption, and
   (*b*)   the possession was founded on, and followed the execution of, a deed which is sufficient in respect of its terms (whether expressly or by implication) to constitute the servitude,
then, as from the expiration of the said period, the validity of the servitude as so constituted, shall be exempt from challenge except on the ground that the deed is invalid *ex facie* or was forged.

(2) If a positive servitude over land has been possessed for a continuous period of twenty years openly, peaceably and without judicial interruption, then, as from the expiration of that period, the existence of the servitude as so possessed shall be exempt from challenge.

(3) If a public right of way over land has been possessed by the public for a continuous period of twenty years openly, peaceably and without judicial interruption, then, as from the expiration of that period, the existence of the right of way as so possessed shall be exempt from challenge.

(4) References in subsections (1) and (2) of this section to possession of a servitude are references to possession of the servitude by any person in possession of the relative dominant tenement.

(5) This section is without prejudice to the operation of section 7 of this Act.

Judicial interruption of periods of possession for purposes of sections 1, 2 and 3

4.—(1) In sections 1, 2 and 3 of this Act references to a judicial interruption, in relation to possession, are references to the making in appropriate proceedings, by any person having a proper interest to do so, of a claim which challenges the possession in question.

(2) In this section "appropriate proceedings" means—
   (*a*)   any proceedings in a court of competent jurisdiction in Scotland or elsewhere, except proceedings in the Court of Session initiated by a summons which is not subsequently called;
   (*b*)   any arbitration in Scotland;
   (*c*)   any arbitration in a country other than Scotland, being an arbitration an award in which would be enforceable in Scotland.

(3) The date of a judicial interruption shall be taken to be—
   (*a*)   where the claim has been made in an arbitration and the nature of the claim has been stated in a preliminary notice

relating to that arbitration, the date when the preliminary notice was served;

(*b*) in any other case, the date when the claim was made.

(4) In the foregoing subsection "preliminary notice" in relation to an arbitration means a notice served by one party to the arbitration on the other party or parties requiring him or them to appoint an arbiter or to agree to the appointment of an arbiter, or, where the arbitration agreement or any relevant enactment provides that the reference shall be to a person therein named or designated, a notice requiring him or them to submit the dispute to the person so named or designated.

Further provisions supplementary to sections 1, 2 and 3

5.—(1) In sections 1, 2 and 3 of this Act "deed" includes a judicial decree; and for the purposes of the said sections any of the following, namely an instrument of sasine, a notarial instrument and a notice of title, which narrates or declares that a person has a title to an interest in land shall be treated as a deed sufficient to constitute that title in favour of that person.

(2) [Repealed by the Requirements of Writing (Scotland) Act 1995) (c. 7), Sched. 5 (effective August 1, 1995).]

Extinction of obligations by prescriptive periods of five years

6.—(1) If, after the appropriate date, an obligation to which this section applies has subsisted for a continuous period of five years—

(*a*) without any relevant claim having been made in relation to the obligation, and

(*b*) without the subsistence of the obligation having been relevantly acknowledged,

then as from the expiration of that period the obligation shall be extinguished:

Provided that in its application to an obligation under a bill of exchange or a promissory note this subsection shall have effect as if paragraph (*b*) thereof were omitted.

(2) Schedule 1 to this Act shall have effect for defining the obligations to which this section applies.

(3) In subsection (1) above the reference to the appropriate date, in relation to an obligation of any kind specified in Schedule 2 to this Act is a reference to the date specified in that Schedule in relation to obligations of that kind, and in relation to an obligation of any other kind is a reference to the date when the obligation became enforceable.

[1](4) In the computation of a prescriptive period in relation to any obligation for the purposes of this section—

(*a*) any period during which by reason of—

(i) fraud on the part of the debtor or any person acting on his behalf, or

(ii)   error induced by words or conduct of the debtor or any person acting on his behalf,

the creditor was induced to refrain from making a relevant claim in relation to the obligation, and

[1](b)   any period during which the original creditor (while he is the creditor) was under legal disability,

shall not be reckoned as, or as part of, the prescriptive period:

Provided that any period such as is mentioned in paragraph (a) of this subsection shall not include any time occurring after the creditor could with reasonable diligence have discovered the fraud or error, as the case may be, referred to in that paragraph.

(5) Any period such as is mentioned in paragraph (a) or (b) of subsection (4) of this section shall not be regarded as separating the time immediately before it from the time immediately after it.

NOTES

[1]Applied by the Merchant Shipping (Liner Conferences) Act 1982 (c. 37), s. 8(3).
[2]See the Age of Legal Capacity (Scotland) Act 1991 (c. 50), s. 8.

Extinction of obligations by prescriptive periods of twenty years

7.—(1) If, after the date when any obligation to which this section applies has become enforceable, the obligation has subsisted for a continuous period of twenty years—

(a)   without any relevant claim having been made in relation to the obligation, and

(b)   without the subsistence of the obligation having been relevantly acknowledged,

then as from the expiration ot period the obligation shall be extinguished:

Provided that in its application to an obligation under a bill of exchange or a promissory note this subsection shall have effect as if paragraph (b) thereof were omitted.

[1](2) This section applies to an obligation of any kind (including an obligation to which section 6 of this Act applies), not being an obligation to which section 22A of this Act applies or an obligation specified in Schedule 3 to this Act as an imprescriptible obligation or an obligation to make reparation in respect of personal injuries within the meaning of Part II of this Act or in respect of the death of any person as a result of such injuries.

NOTE

[1]As amended by the Prescription and Limitation (Scotland) Act 1984 (c. 45), Sched. 1, para. 2, as regards any obligation not extinguished before September 26, 1984; *ibid.* s. 5(3), and by the Consumer Protection Act 1987 (c. 41), Sched. 1, para. 8.

Extinction of other rights relating to property by prescriptive periods of twenty years

8.—(1) If, after the date when any right to which this section applies has become exercisable or enforceable, the right has subsisted for a continuous period of twenty years unexercised or unenforced, and without any relevant claim in relation to it having been made, then as from the expiration of that period the right shall be extinguished.

(2) This section applies to any right relating to property, whether heritable or moveable, not being a right specified in Schedule 3 to this Act as an imprescriptible right or falling within section 6 or 7 of this Act as being a right correlative to an obligation to which either of those sections applies.

Extinction of obligations to make contributions between wrongdoers

[1]**8A.**—(1) If any obligation to make a contribution by virtue of section 3(2) of the Law Reform (Miscellaneous Provisions) (Scotland) Act 1940 in respect of any damages or expenses has subsisted for a continuous period of two years after the date on which the right to recover the contribution became enforceable by the creditor in the obligation—

    (a)   without any relevant claim having been made in relation to the obligation; and

    (b)   without the subsistence of the obligation having been relevantly acknowledged;

then as from the expiration of that period the obligation shall be extinguished.

(2) Subsections (4) and (5) of section 6 of this Act shall apply for the purposes of this section as they apply for the purposes of that section.

NOTE
[1]Inserted by the Prescription and Limitation (Scotland) Act 1984, s. 1.

Definition of "relevant claim" for purposes of sections 6, 7 and 8

[1]**9.**—[2](1) In sections 6, 7 and 8A of this Act the expression "relevant claim", in relation to an obligation, means a claim by or on behalf of the creditor for implement or part-implement of the obligation, being a claim made—

    (a)   in appropriate proceedings; or

    [3](b)   by the presentation of, or the concurring in, a petition for sequestration or by the submission of a claim under section 22 or 48 of the Bankruptcy (Scotland) Act 1985; or

    (c)   by a creditor to the trustee acting under a trust deed as defined in section 5(2)(c) of the Bankruptcy (Scotland) Act 1985;

    [4](d)   by the presentation of, or the concurring in, a petition for the winding up of a company or by the submission of a claim in a liquidation in accordance with rules made under section 411 of the Insolvency Act 1986;

and for the purposes of said sections 6, 7 and 8A the execution by or on behalf of the creditor in an obligation of any form of diligence directed to the enforcement of the obligation shall be deemed to be a relevant claim in relation to the obligation.

(2) In section 8 of this Act the expression "relevant claim", in relation to a right, means a claim made in appropriate proceedings by or on behalf of the creditor to establish the right or to contest any claim to a right inconsistent therewith.

(3) Where a claim which, in accordance with the foregoing provisions of this section, is a relevant claim for the purposes of section 6, 7, 8 or 8A of this Act is made in an arbitration, and the nature of the claim has been stated in a preliminary notice relating to that arbitration, the date when the notice was served shall be taken for those purposes to be the date of the making of the claim.

(4) In this section the expression "appropriate proceedings" and, in relation to an arbitration, the expression "preliminary notice" have the same meanings as in section 4 of this Act.

NOTES
[1]As amended by the Prescription and Limitation (Scotland) Act 1984, Sched. 1, para. 3.
[2]As amended by the Bankruptcy (Scotland) Act 1985, Sched. 7, para. 11, with effect from April 1, 1986.
[3]As amended by the Prescription (Scotland) Act 1987, s. 1(2).
[4]Inserted by the Prescription (Scotland) Act 1987, s. 1(1). By section 1(3) of the same Act: "The said section 9 as amended by subsection (1) above shall have effect as regards any claim (whenever submitted) in a liquidation in respect of which the winding up commenced on or after December 29, 1986."

Relevant acknowledgment for purposes of sections 6, 7 and 8A
[1]**10.**—(1) The subsistence of an obligation shall be regarded for the purposes of sections 6, 7 and 8A of this Act as having been relevantly acknowledged if, and only if, either of the following conditions is satisfied, namely—
  (a) that there has been such performance by or on behalf of the debtor towards implement of the obligation as clearly indicates that the obligation still subsists;
  (b) that there has been made by or on behalf of the debtor to the creditor or his agent an unequivocal written admission clearly acknowledging that the obligation still subsists.

(2) Subject to subsection (3) below, where two or more persons are bound jointly by an obligation so that each is liable for the whole, and the subsistence of the obligation has been relevantly acknowledged by or on behalf of one of those persons then—
  (a) if the acknowledgment is made in the manner specified in paragraph (a) of the foregoing subsection it shall have effect for the purposes of the said sections 6, 7 and 8A as respects the liability of each of those persons, and
  (b) if it is made in the manner specified in paragraph (b) of that subsection it shall have effect for those purposes only as respects the liability of the person who makes it.

(3) Where the subsistence of an obligation affecting a trust estate has been relevantly acknowledged by or on behalf of one of two or

more co-trustees in the manner specified in paragraph (*a*) or (*b*) of subsection (1) of this section, the acknowledgment shall have effect for the purposes of the said sections 6, 7 and 8A as respects the liability of the trust estate and any liability of each of the trustees.

(4) In this section references to performance in relation to an obligation include, where the nature of the obligation so requires, references to refraining from doing something and to permitting or suffering something to be done or maintained.

NOTE
[1]As amended by the Prescription and Limitation (Scotland) Act 1984, Sched. 1, para. 4.

Obligations to make reparation
11.—(1) Subject to subsections (2) and (3) below, any obligation (whether arising from any enactment, or from any rule of law or from, or by reason of any breach of, a contract or promise) to make reparation for loss, injury or damage caused by an act, neglect or default shall be regarded for the purposes of section 6 of this Act as having become enforceable on the date when the loss, injury or damage occurred.

(2) Where as a result of a continuing act, neglect or default loss, injury or damage has occurred before the cessation of the act, neglect or default the loss, injury or damage shall be deemed for the purposes of subsection (1) above to have occurred on the date when the act, neglect or default ceased.

(3) In relation to a case where on the date referred to in subsection (1) above (or, as the case may be, that subsection as modified by subsection (2) above) the creditor was not aware, and could not with reasonable diligence have been aware, that loss, injury or damage caused as aforesaid had occurred, the said subsection (1) shall have effect as if for the reference therein to that date there were substituted a reference to the date when the creditor first became, or could with reasonable diligence have become, so aware.

[1](4) Subsections (1) and (2) above (with the omission of any reference therein to subsection (3) above) shall have effect for the purposes of section 7 of this Act as they have effect for the purposes of section 6 of this Act.

NOTE
[1]As amended by the Prescription and Limitation (Scotland) Act 1984, Sched. 2.

Savings
12.—(1) Where by virtue of any enactment passed or made before the passing of this Act a claim to establish a right or enforce implement of an obligation may be made only within a period of limitation specified in or determined under the enactment, and, by the expiration of a prescriptive period determined under section 6, 7 or 8 of this Act the right or obligation would, apart from this subsection,

be extinguished before the expiration of the period of limitation, the said section shall have effect as if the relevant prescriptive period were extended so that it expires—

    (*a*)   on the date when the period of limitation expires, or

    (*b*)   if on that date any such claim made within that period has not been finally disposed of, on the date when the claim is so disposed of.

(2) Nothing in section 6, 7 or 8 of this Act shall be construed so as to exempt any deed from challenge at any time on the ground that it is invalid *ex facie* or was forged.

Prohibition of contracting out

[1]**13.** Any provision in any agreement purporting to provide in relation to any right or obligation that section 6, 7, 8 or 8A of this Act shall not have effect shall be null.

NOTE

[1]As amended by the Prescription and Limitation (Scotland) Act 1984, Sched. 1, para. 5.

General

Computation of prescriptive period

    14.—(1) In the computation of a prescriptive period for the purposes of any provision of this Part of this Act—

    (*a*)   time occurring before the commencement of this Part of this Act shall be reckonable towards the prescriptive period in like manner as time occurring thereafter, but subject to the restriction that any time reckoned under this paragraph shall be less than the prescriptive period;

    [1](*b*)   any time during which any person against whom the provision is pled was under legal disability shall (except so far as otherwise provided by subsection (4) of section 6 of this Act including that subsection as applied by section 8A of this Act) be reckoned as if the person were free from that disability;

    (*c*)   if the commencement of the prescriptive period would, apart from this paragraph, fall at a time in any day other than the beginning of the day, the period shall be deemed to have commenced at the beginning of the next following day;

    (*d*)   if the last day of the prescriptive period would, apart from this paragraph, be a holiday, the period shall, notwithstanding anything in the said provision, be extended to include any immediately succeeding day which is a holiday, any further immediately succeeding days which are holidays, and the next succeeding day which is not a holiday;

    (*e*)   save as otherwise provided in this Part of this Act regard shall be had to the like principles as immediately before the commencement of this Part of this Act were applicable to the computation of periods of prescription for the purposes of the Prescription Act 1617.

(2) In this section "holiday" means a day of any of the following descriptions, namely, a Saturday, a Sunday and a day which, in Scotland, is a bank holiday under the Banking and Financial Dealings Act 1971.

NOTE
[1]As amended by the Prescription and Limitation (Scotland) Act 1984, Sched. 1, para. 6.

Interpretation of Part I

15.—(1) In this Part of this Act, unless the context otherwise requires, the following expressions have the meanings hereby assigned to them, namely—

"bill of exchange" has the same meaning as it has for the purposes of the Bills of Exchange Act 1882;

"date of execution", in relation to a deed executed on several dates, means the last of those dates;

"enactment" includes an order, regulation, rule or other instrument having effect by virtue of an Act;

"holiday" has the meaning assigned to it by section 14 of this Act;

"interest in land" does not include a servitude;

"land" includes heritable property of any description;

"lease" includes a sub-lease;

"legal disability" means legal disability by reason of nonage or unsoundness of mind;

"possession" includes civil possession, and "possessed" shall be construed accordingly;

[1]"prescriptive period" means a period required for the operation of section 1, 2, 3, 6, 7, 8 or 8A of this Act;

"promissory note" has the same meaning as it has for the purposes of the Bills of Exchange Act 1882;

"trustee" includes any person holding property in a fiduciary capacity for another and, without prejudice to that generality, includes a trustee within the meaning of the Trusts (Scotland) Act 1921; and "trust" shall be construed accordingly;

and references to the recording of a deed are references to the recording thereof in the General Register of Sasines.

(2) In this Part of this Act, unless the context otherwise requires, any reference to an obligation or to a right includes a reference to the right or, as the case may be, to the obligation (if any), correlative thereto.

(3) In this Part of this Act any reference to an enactment shall, unless the context otherwise requires, be construed as a reference to that enactment as amended or extended, and as including a reference thereto as applied, by or under any other enactment.

NOTE
[1]As amended by the Prescription and Limitation (Scotland) Act 1984, Sched. 1, para. 7.

Amendments and repeals related to Part I
16.—(1) The enactment specified in Part I of Schedule 4 to this Act shall have effect subject to the amendment there specified, being an amendment related to this Part of this Act.

(2) Subject to the next following subsection, the enactments specified in Part I of Schedule 5 to this Act (which includes certain enactments relating to the limitation of proof) are hereby repealed to the extent specified in column 3 of that Schedule.

[1](3) Where by virtue of any Act repealed by this section the subsistence of an obligation in force at the date of the commencement of this Part of this Act was immediately before that date, by reason of the passage of time, provable only by the writ or oath of the debtor the subsistence of the obligation shall (notwithstanding anything in sections 16(1) and 17(2)(a) of the Interpretation Act 1978, which relates to the effect of repeals) as from that date be provable as if the said repealed Act had not passed.

NOTE
[1]As amended by the Interpretation Act 1978, s. 25(2).

[1]Part II

Limitation of Actions

NOTE
[1]Saved by the Administration of Justice Act 1982, s. 73(5).

Part II not to extend to product liability
[1]**16A.** This Part of this Act does not apply to any action to which section 22B or 22C of this Act applies.

NOTE
[1]Inserted by the Consumer Protection Act 1987, Sched. 1, para. 9.

Actions in respect of personal injuries not resulting in death
[1]**17.**—(1) This section applies to an action of damages where the damages claimed consist of or include damages in respect of personal injuries, being an action (other than an action to which section 18 of this Act applies) brought by the person who sustained the injuries or any other person.

(2) Subject to subsection (3) below and section 19A of this Act, no action to which this section applies shall be brought unless it is commenced within a period of three years after—

    (a)   the date on which the injuries were sustained or, where the act or omission to which the injuries were attributable was a continuing one, that date or the date on which the act or omission ceased, whichever is the later; or

    (b)   the date (if later than any date mentioned in paragraph (a) above) on which the pursuer in the action became, or on which, in the opinion of the court, it would have been reasonably practicable for him in all the circumstances to become aware of all the following facts—

(i) that the injuries in question were sufficiently serious to justify his bringing an action of damages on the assumption that the person against whom the action was brought did not dispute liability and was able to satisfy a decree;

(ii) that the injuries were attributable in whole or in part to an act or omission; and

(iii) that the defender was a person to whose act or omission the injuries were attributable in whole or in part or the employer or principal of such a person.

[2](3) In the computation of the period specified in subsection (2) above there shall be disregarded any time during which the person who sustained the injuries was under legal disability by reason of nonage or unsoundness of mind.

NOTES

[1]Substituted by the Prescription and Limitation (Scotland) Act 1984, s. 2, as regards rights of action accruing both before and after the commencement of that Act; *ibid.* s. 5(1).

[2]See the Age of Legal Capacity (Scotland) Act 1991, s. 8.

Actions where death has resulted from personal injuries

[1]**18.**—(1) This section applies to any action in which, following the death of any person from personal injuries, damages are claimed in respect of the injuries or the death.

(2) Subject to subsections (3) and (4) below and section 19A of this Act, no action to which this section applies shall be brought unless it is commenced within a period of three years after—

(*a*) the date of death of the deceased; or

(*b*) the date (if later than the date of death) on which the pursuer in the action became, or on which, in the opinion of the court, it would have been reasonably practicable for him in all the circumstances to become, aware of both of the following facts—

(i) that the injuries of the deceased were attributable in whole or in part to an act or omission; and

(ii) that the defender was a person to whose act or omission the injuries were attributable in whole or in part or the employer or principal of such a person.

[2](3) Where the pursuer is a relative of the deceased, there shall be disregarded in the computation of the period specified in subsection (2) above any time during which the relative was under legal disability by reason of nonage or unsoundness of mind.

(4) Subject to section 19A of this Act, where an action of damages has not been brought by or on behalf of a person who has sustained personal injuries within the period specified in section 17(2) of this

Act and that person subsequently dies in consequence of those injuries, no action to which this section applies shall be brought in respect of those injuries or the death from those injuries.

(5) In this section "relative" has the same meaning as in Schedule 1 to the Damages (Scotland) Act 1976.

NOTES

[1] Substituted by the Prescription and Limitation (Scotland) Act 1984, s. 2, as regards rights of action accruing both before and after the commencement of that Act: *ibid.*, s. 5(1).

[2] See the Age of Legal Capacity (Scotland) Act 1991, s. 8.

Limitation of defamation and other actions

[1]**18A.**—(1) Subject to subsections (2) and (3) below and section 19A of this Act, no action for defamation shall be brought unless it is commenced within a period of three years after the date when the right of action accrued.

[2](2) In the computation of the period specified in subsection (1) above there shall be disregarded any time during which the person alleged to have been defamed was under legal disability by reason of nonage or unsoundness of mind.

(3) Nothing in this section shall affect any right of action which accrued before the commencement of this section.

(4) In this section—

(a) "defamation" includes *convicium* and malicious falsehood, and "defamed" shall be construed accordingly; and

(b) references to the date when a right of action accrued shall be construed as references to the date when the publication or communication in respect of which the action for defamation is to be brought first came to the notice of the pursuer.

NOTES

[1] Inserted by the Law Reform (Miscellaneous Provisions) (Scotland) Act 1985, s. 12(2).

[2] See the Age of Legal Capacity (Scotland) Act 1991, s. 8.

19. [Repealed by the Prescription and Limitation (Scotland) Act 1984, s. 2.]

Power of court to override time-limits, etc.

[1]**19A.**—[2](1) Where a person would be entitled, but for any of the provisions of section 17 or section 18 and 18A of this Act, to bring an action, the court may, if it seems to it equitable to do so, allow him to bring the action notwithstanding that provision.

(2) The provisions of subsection (1) above shall have effect not only as regards rights of action accruing after the commencement of this section but also as regards those, in respect of which a final judgment has not been pronounced, accruing before such commencement.

(3) In subsection (2) above, the expression "final judgment" means an interlocutor of a court of first instance which, by itself, or taken along with previous interlocutors, disposes of the subject matter of a cause notwithstanding that judgment may not have been pronounced on every question raised or that the expenses found due may not have been modified, taxed or decerned for; but the expression does not include an interlocutory dismissing a cause by reason only of a provision mentioned in subsection (1) above.

[3](4) An action which could not be entertained but for this section shall not be tried by jury.

NOTES
[1]Inserted by the Law Reform (Miscellaneous Provisions) (Scotland) Act 1980, s. 23(a).
[2]As amended by the Prescription and Limitation (Scotland) Act 1984, Sched. 1, para. 8(a) and by the Law Reform (Misellaneous Provisions) (Scotland) Act 1985, s. 12(3)
[3]Added by the Prescription and Limitation (Scotland) Act 1984, Sched. 1, para. 8(b).

20, 21. [Repealed by the Prescription and Limitation (Scotland) Act 1984, Sched. 2.]

Interpretation of Part II and supplementary provisions
[1]**22.**—(1) In this Part of this Act—
"the court" means the Court of Session or the sheriff court; and
"personal injuries" includes any disease and any impairment of a person's physical or mental condition.

[2](2) Where the pursuer in an action to which section 17, 18 or 18A of this Act applies is pursuing the action by virtue of the assignation of a right of action, the reference in subsection (2)(b) of the said section 17 or of the said section 18 or, as the case may be, subsection (4)(b) of the said section 18A to the pursuer in the action shall be construed as a reference to the assignor of the right of action.

(3) For the purposes of the said subsection (2)(b) knowledge that any act or omission was or was not, as a matter of law, actionable, is irrelevant.

(4) An action which would not be entertained but for the said subsection (2)(b) shall not be tried by jury.

NOTES
[1]Substituted by the Prescription and Limitation (Scotland) Act 1984, s. 3.
[2]As amended by the Law Reform (Miscellaneous Provisions) (Scotland) Act 1985, s. 12(4).

[1]Part IIA

Prescription of Obligations and Limitation of Actions under Part I of the Consumer Protection Act 1987

NOTE
[1]Inserted by the Consumer Protection Act 1987, Sched. 1, para. 10.

Prescription of Obligations

Ten years' prescription of obligations

22A.—(1) An obligation arising from liability under section 2 of the 1987 Act (to make reparation of damage caused wholly or partly by a defect in a product) shall be extinguished if a period of 10 years has expired from the relevant time, unless a relevant claim was made within that period and has not been finally disposed of, and no such obligation shall come into existence after the expiration of the said period.

(2) If, at the expiration of the period of 10 years mentioned in subsection (1) above, a relevant claim has been made but has not been finally disposed of, the obligation to which the claim relates shall be extinguished when the claim is finally disposed of.

(3) In this section a claim is finally disposed of when—

(*a*) a decision disposing of the claim has been made against which no appeal is competent;

(*b*) an appeal against such a decision is competent with leave, and the time limit for leave has expired and no application has been made or leave has been refused;

(*c*) leave to appeal against such a decision is granted or is not required, and no appeal is made within the time limit for appeal; or

(*d*) the claim is abandoned;

"relevant claim" in relation to an obligation means a claim made by or on behalf of the creditor for implement or part implement of the obligation, being a claim made—

(*a*) in appropriate proceedings within the meaning of section 4(2) of this Act; or

(*b*) by the presentation of, or the concurring in, a petition for sequestration or by the submission of a claim under section 22 or 48 of the Bankruptcy (Scotland) Act 1985; or

(*c*) by the presentation of, or the concurring in, a petition for the winding up of a company or by the submission of a claim in a liquidation in accordance with the rules made under section 411 of the Insolvency Act 1986;

"relevant time" has the meaning given in section 4(2) of the 1987 Act.

(4) Where a relevant claim is made in an arbitration, and the nature of the claim has been stated in a preliminary notice (within the meaning of section 4(4) of this Act) relating to that arbitration, the date when the notice is served shall be taken for those purposes to be the date of the making of the claim.

Limitation of Actions

Three year limitation of actions

22B.—(1) This section shall apply to an action to enforce an obligation arising from liability under section 2 of the 1987 Act (to make reparation for damage caused wholly or partly by a defect in a product), except where section 22C of this Act applies.

(2) Subject to subsection (4) below, an action to which this section applies shall not be competent unless it is commenced within the period of three years after the earliest date on which the person seeking to bring (or a person who could at an earlier date have brought) the action was aware, or on which, in the opinion of the court, it was reasonably practicable for him in all the circumstances to become aware, of all the facts mentioned in subsection (3) below.

(3) The facts referred to in subsection (2) above are—

(a) that there was a defect in a product;

(b) that the damage was caused or partly caused by the defect;

(c) that the damage was sufficiently serious to justify the pursuer (or other person referred to in subsection (2) above) in bringing an action to which this section applies on the assumption that the defender did not dispute liability and was able to satisfy a decree;

(d) that the defender was a person liable for the damage under the said section 2.

(4) In the computation of the period of three years mentioned in subsection (2) above, there shall be disregarded any period during which the person seeking to bring the action was under legal disability by reason of nonage or unsoundness of mind.

(5) The facts mentioned in subsection (3) above do not include knowledge of whether particular facts and circumstances would or would not, as a matter of law, result in liability for damage under the said section 2.

(6) Where a person would be entitled, but for this section, to bring an action for reparation other than one in which the damages claimed are confined to damages for loss of or damage to property, the court may, if it seems to it equitable to do so, allow him to bring the action notwithstanding this section.

Actions under the 1987 Act where death has resulted from personal injuries

22C.—(1) This section shall apply to an action to enforce an obligation arising from liability under section 2 of the 1987 Act (to make reparation for damage caused wholly or partly by a defect in a product) where a person has died from personal injuries and the damages claimed include damages for those personal injuries or that death.

(2) Subject to subsection (4) below, an action to which this section applies shall not be competent unless it is commenced within the period of three years after the later of—

(a) the date of death of the injured person;

(b) the earliest date on which the person seeking to make (or a person who could at an earlier date have made) the claim was aware, or on which, in the opinion of the court, it was reasonably practicable for him in all the circumstances to become aware—

(i) that there was a defect in the product;

(ii) that the injuries of the deceased were caused (or partly caused) by the defect; and

(iii) that the defender was a person liable for the damage under the said section 2.

(3) Where the person seeking to make the claim is a relative of the deceased, there shall be disregarded in the computation of the period mentioned in subsection (2) above any period during which that relative was under legal disability by reason of nonage or unsoundness of mind.

(4) Where an action to which section 22B of this Act applies has not been brought within the period mentioned in subsection (2) of that section and the person subsequently dies in consequence of his injuries, an action to which this section applies shall not be competent in respect of those injuries or that death.

(5) Where a person would be entitled, but for this section, to bring an action for reparation other than one in which the damages claimed are confined to damages for loss of or damage to property, the court may, if it seems to it equitable to do so, allow him to bring the action notwithstanding this section.

(6) In this section "relative" has the same meaning as in the Damages (Scotland) Act 1976.

(7) For the purposes of subsection (2)(*b*) above there shall be disregarded knowledge of whether particular facts and circumstances would or would not, as a matter of law, result in liability for damage under the said section 2.

Supplementary

Interpretation of this Part

22D.—(1) Expressions used in this Part and in Part I of the 1987 Act shall have the same meanings in this Part as in the said Part I.

(2) For the purposes of section 1(1) of the 1987 Act, this Part shall have effect and be construed as if it were contained in Part I of that Act.

(3) In this Part, "the 1987 Act" means the Consumer Protection Act 1987.

Amendments and repeals related to Part II

23. [Repealed by the Consumer Protection Act 1987, Sched. 1, para. 11.]

[1]PART III

SUPPLEMENTAL

NOTE
[1]Saved by the Administration of Justice Act 1982, s. 73(5).

Private international law application

[1]**23A.**—(1) Where the substantive law of a country other than Scotland falls to be applied by a Scottish court as the law governing an obligation, the court shall apply any relevant rules of law of that country relating to the extinction of the obligation or the limitation of time within which proceedings may be brought to enforce the obligation to the exclusion of any corresponding rule of Scots law.

(2) This section shall not apply where it appears to the court that the application of the relevant foreign rule of law would be incompatible with the principles of public policy applied by the court.

(3) This section shall not apply in any case where the application of the corresponding rule of Scots law has extinguished the obligation, or barred the bringing of proceedings prior to the coming into force of the Prescription and Limitation (Scotland) Act 1984.

NOTE
[1]Inserted by the Prescription and Limitation (Scotland) Act 1984, s. 4, as regards proceedings commenced on or after 26th September 1984; *ibid.* s. 5(2).

The Crown
24. This Act binds the Crown.

Short title, commencement and extent
25.—(1) This Act may be cited as the Prescription and Limitation (Scotland) Act 1973.

[1](2) This Act shall come into operation, as follows:—
(*a*) Parts II and III of this Act, Part II of Schedule 4 to this Act and Part II of Schedule 5 to this Act shall come into operation on the date on which this Act is passed;
(*b*) except as aforesaid this Act shall come into operation on the expiration of three years from the said date.

(3) [Repealed by the Prescription and Limitation (Scotland) Act 1984, Sched. 2.]

(4) This Act extends to Scotland only.

NOTE
[1]As amended by the Prescription and Limitation (Scotland) Act 1984, Sched. 2.

SCHEDULES

SCHEDULE 1

OBLIGATIONS AFFECTED BY PRESCRIPTIVE PERIODS OF FIVE YEARS UNDER SECTION 6

1. Subject to paragraph 2 below, section 6 of this Act applies—
(*a*) to any obligation to pay a sum of money due in respect of a particular period—
(i) by way of interest;

(ii)   by way of an instalment of an annuity;

(iii)   by way of feuduty or other periodical payment under a feu grant;

(iv)   by way of ground annual or other periodical payment under a contract of ground annual;

(v)   by way of rent or other periodical payment under lease;

(vi)   by way of a periodical payment in respect of the occupancy or use of land, not being an obligation falling within any other provision of this sub-paragraph;

(vii)   by way of a periodical payment under a land obligation, not being an obligation falling within any other provision of this sub-paragraph;

(*b*)   to any obligation based on redress of unjustified enrichment, including without prejudice to that generality any obligation of restitution, repetition or recompense;

(*c*)   to any obligation arising from *negotiorum gestio*;

(*d*)   to any obligation arising from liability (whether arising from any enactment or from any rule of law) to make reparation;

(*e*)   to any obligation under a bill of exchange or a promissory note;

(*f*)   to any obligation of accounting, other than accounting for trust funds;

(*g*)   to any obligation arising from, or by reason of any breach of, a contract or promise, not being an obligation falling within any other provision of this paragraph.

2. Notwithstanding anything in the foregoing paragraph, section 6 of this Act does not apply—

(*a*)   to any obligation to recognise or obtemper a decree of court, an arbitration award or an order of a tribunal or authority exercising jurisdiction under any enactment;

(*b*)   to any obligation arising from the issue of a bank note;

(*c*)   [Repeated by the Requirements of Writing (Scotland) Act 1995 (c. 7), Sched. 5 (effective 1st August 1995).]

(*d*)   to any obligation under a contract of partnership or of agency, not being an obligation remaining, or becoming, prestable on or after the termination of the relationship between the parties under the contract;

(*e*)   except as provided in paragraph 1(*a*) of this Schedule, to any obligation relating to land (including an obligation to recognise a servitude);

(*f*)   to any obligation to satisfy any claim to terce, courtesy, legitim, *jus relicti* or *jus relictae*, or to any prior right of a surviving spouse under section 8 or 9 of the Succession (Scotland) Act 1964;

(*g*)   to any obligation to make reparation in respect of personal injuries within the meaning of Part II of this Act or in respect of the death of any person as a result of such injuries;

[1](*gg*)   to any obligation to make reparation or otherwise make good in respect of defamation within the meaning of section 18A of this Act;

[2](*ggg*) to any obligation arising from liability under section 2 of the Consumer Protection Act 1987 (to make reparation for damage caused wholly or partly by a defect in a product);

(*h*)   to any obligation specified in Schedule 3 to this Act as an imprescriptible obligation.

NOTES

[1]Inserted by the Law Reform (Miscellaneous Provisions) (Scotland) Act 1985 (c. 73), s. 12(5).

[2]Inserted by the Consumer Protection Act 1987 (c. 41), Sched. 1, para. 12.

3. [Repealed by the Requirements of Writing (Scotland) Act 1995 (c. 7), Sched. 5 (effective August 1, 1995).]

4. In this Schedule—

(*a*)   "land obligation" has the same meaning as it has for the purposes of the Conveyancing and Feudal Reform (Scotland) Act 1970;

(*b*) [Repealed by the Requirements of Writing (Scotland) Act 1995 (c. 7), Sched. 5 (effective August 1, 1995).]

SCHEDULE 2

Appropriate Dates for Certain Obligations for Purposes of Section 6

1.—(1) This paragraph applies to any obligation, not being part of a banking transaction, to pay money in respect of—
(*a*)   goods supplied on sale or hire, or
(*b*)   services rendered,
in a series of transactions between the same parties (whether under a single contract or under several contracts) and charged on continuing account.
(2) In the foregoing sub-paragraph—
(*a*)   any reference to the supply of goods on sale includes a reference to the supply of goods under a hire-purchase agreement, a credit-sale agreement or a conditional sale agreement as defined (in each case) by section 1 of the Hire-Purchase (Scotland) Act 1965; and
(*b*)   any reference to services rendered does not include the work of keeping the account in question.
(3) Where there is a series of transactions between a partnership and another party, the series shall be regarded for the purposes of this paragraph as terminated (without prejudice to any other mode of termination) if the partnership or any partner therein becomes bankrupt; but, subject to that, if the partnership (in the further provisions of this sub-paragraph referred to as "the old partnership") is dissolved and is replaced by a single new partnership having among its partners any person who was a partner in the old partnership, then, for the purposes of this paragraph, the new partnership shall be regarded as if it were identical with the old partnership.
(4) The appropriate date in relation to an obligation to which this paragraph applies is the date on which payment for the goods last supplied, or, as the case may be, the services last rendered, became due.
2.—(1) This paragraph applies to any obligation to repay the whole, or any part of, a sum of money lent to, or deposited with, the debtor under a contract or loan or, as the case may be, deposit.
(2) The appropriate date in relation to an obligation to which this paragraph applies is—
(*a*)   if the contract contains a stipulation which makes provision with respect to the date on or before which repayment of the sum or, as the case may be, the part thereof is to be made, the date on or before which, in terms of that stipulation, the sum or part thereof is to be repaid; and
(*b*)   if the contract contains no such stipulation, but a written demand for repayment of the sum, or, as the case may be, the part thereof, is made by or on behalf of the creditor or the debtor, the date when such demand is made or first made.
3.—(1) This paragraph applies to any obligation under a contract of partnership or of agency, being an obligation remaining, or becoming, prestable on or after the termination of the relationship between the parties under the contract.
(2) The appropriate date in relation to an obligation to which this paragraph applies is—
(*a*)   if the contract contains a stipulation which makes provision with respect to the date on or before which performance of the obligation is to be due, the date on or before which, in terms of that stipulation, the obligation is to be performed; and
(*b*)   in any other case the date when the said relationship terminated.
4.—(1) This paragraph applies to any obligation—
(*a*)   to pay an instalment of a sum of money payable by instalments, or
(*b*)   to execute any instalment of work due to be executed by instalments, not being an obligation to which any of the foregoing paragraphs applies.

(2) The appropriate date in relation to an obligation to which this paragraph applies is the date on which the last of the instalments is due to be paid or, as the case may be, to be executed.

SCHEDULE 3

RIGHTS AND OBLIGATIONS WHICH ARE IMPRESCRIPTIBLE FOR THE PURPOSES OF SECTIONS 7 AND 8 AND SCHEDULE 1

The following are imprescriptible rights and obligations for the purposes of sections 7(2) and 8(2) of, and paragraph 2(*h*) of Schedule 1 to, this Act, namely—

(*a*)   any real right of ownership in land;

(*b*)   the right in land of the lessee under a recorded lease;

(*c*)   any right exercisable as a *res merae facultatis*;

(*d*)   any right to recover property *extra commercium*;

(*e*)   any obligation of a trustee—

    (i)   to produce accounts of the trustee's intromissions with any property of the trust;

    (ii)   to make reparation or restitution in respect of any fraudulent breach of trust to which the trustee was a party or was privy;

    (iii) to make furthcoming to any person entitled thereto any trust property, or the proceeds of any such property, in the possession of the trustee, or to make good the value of any such property previously received by the trustee and appropriated to his own use;

(*f*)   any obligation of a third party to make furthcoming to any person entitled thereto any trust property received by the third party otherwise than in good faith and in his possession;

(*g*)   any right to recover stolen property from the person by whom it was stolen or from any person privy to the stealing thereof;

(*h*)   any right to be served as heir to an ancestor or to take any steps necessary for making up or completing title to any interest in land.

SCHEDULE 4

ENACTMENTS AMENDED

PART I

AMENDMENT TAKING EFFECT ON EXPIRATION OF THREE YEARS FROM PASSING OF THIS ACT

The Limitation (Enemies and War Prisoners) Act 1945

In subsection (1) of section 1, as substituted for Scotland by paragraph (*a*) of section 4, in the list of enactments appended to the subsection for the entries relating to the Acts of the Parliament of Scotland 1579 cap. 21, 1669 cap. 14 and 1695 cap. 7, and to section 37 of the Bills of Exchange (Scotland) Act 1772, there shall be substituted the words "section 6 of the Prescription and Limitation (Scotland) Act 1973".

[1]PART II

AMENDMENTS TAKING EFFECT ON PASSING OF THIS ACT

NOTE

[1]As amended by the Prescription and Limitation (Scotland) Act 1984, Sched. 2.

The Carriage by Air Act 1961

In section 11(*c*), for the words "section six of the Law Reform (Limitation of Actions, &c.) Act 1954" there shall be substituted the words "section 17 of the Prescription and Limitation (Scotland) Act 1973".

The Law Reform (Miscellaneous Provisions) Act 1971

In section 4(2), for the words "section 6 of the Law Reform (Limitation of Actions, &c.) Act 1954" there shall be substituted the words "section 22(1) of the Prescription and Limitation (Scotland) Act 1973".

11. **Damages (Scotland) Act 1976**
(1976 c. 13)

An Act to amend the law of Scotland relating to the damages recoverable in respect of deaths caused by personal injuries; to define the rights to damages in respect of personal injuries and death which are transmitted to an executor; to abolish rights to assythment; to make provision relating to the damages due to a pursuer for patrimonial loss caused by personal injuries whereby his expectation of life is diminished; and for purposes connected with the matters aforesaid. [13th April 1976]

NOTES
[1]Applied by the Merchant Shipping Act 1995 (c. 21), Sched. 8, Pt. II, para. 6(2) (effective 1st January 1996; s. 316(2)). See the Consumer Protection Act 1986 (c. 43), s. 6(2), and the Income and Corporation Taxes Act 1988 (c. 1), s. 329A (inserted by the Finance Act 1995 (c. 4), s. 142) (structured settlements: sums received after May 1, 1995).

Rights of relatives of a deceased person

[0]1.—(1) Where a person dies in consequence of personal injuries sustained by him as a result of an act or omission of another person, being an act or omission giving rise to liability to pay damages to the injured person or his executor, then, subject to the following provisions of this Act, the person liable to pay those damages (in this section referred to as "the responsible person") shall also be liable to pay damages in accordance with this section to any relative of the deceased, being a relative within the meaning of Schedule 1 to this Act.

(2) No liability shall arise under this section if the liability to the deceased or his executor in respect of the act or omission has been excluded or discharged (whether by antecedent agreement or otherwise) by the deceased before his death, or is excluded by virtue of any enactment.

[1](3) The damages which the responsible person shall be liable to pay to a relative of a deceased under this section shall (subject to the provisions of this Act) be such as will compensate the relative for any loss of support suffered by him since the date of the deceased's death

or likely to be suffered by him as a result of the act or omission in question, together with any reasonable expense incurred by him in connection with the deceased's funeral.

[2](4) If the relative is a member of the deceased's immediate family (within the meaning of section 10(2) of this Act) there shall be awarded, without prejudice to any claim under subsection (3) above, such sum of damages, if any, as the court thinks just by way of compensation for all or any of the following—

    (a)   distress and anxiety endured by the relative in contemplation of the suffering of the deceased before his death;

    (b)   grief and sorrow of the relative caused by the deceased's death;

    (c)   the loss of such non-patrimonial benefit as the relative might have been expected to derive from the deceased's society and guidance if the deceased had not died,

and the court in making an award under this subsection shall not be required to ascribe specifically any part of the award to any of paragraphs (a), (b) and (c) above.

[3](5) Subject to subsection (5A) below, in assessing for the purposes of this section the amount of any loss of support suffered by a relative of a deceased no account shall be taken of—

    (a)   any patrimonial gain or advantage which has accrued or will or may accrue to the relative from the deceased or from any other person by way of succession or settlement;

    (b)   any insurance money, benefit, pension or gratuity which has been, or will be or may be, paid as a result of the deceased's death;

and in this subsection—

"benefit" means benefit under the Social Security Act 1975 or the Social Security (Northern Ireland) Act 1975, and any payment by a friendly society or trade union for the relief or maintenance of a member's dependants;

"insurance money" includes a return of premiums; and

"pension" includes a return of contributions and any payment of a lump sum in respect of a person's employment.

(5A) Where a deceased has been awarded a provisional award of damages under section 12(2) of the Administration of Justice Act 1982, the making of that award does not prevent liability from arising under this section but in assessing for the purposes of this section the amount of any loss of support suffered by a relative of the deceased the court shall take into account such part of the provisional award relating to future patrimonial loss as was intended to compensate the deceased for a period beyond the date on which he died.

(6) In order to establish loss of support for the purposes of this section it shall not be essential for a claimant to show that the deceased was, or might have become, subject to a duty in law to provide or contribute to the support of the claimant; but if any such fact is established it may be taken into account in determining whether, and

if so to what extent, the deceased, if he had not died, would have been likely to provide or contribute to such support.

[4](7) Except as provided in this section or in Part II of the Administration of Justice Act 1982 or under section 1 of the International Transport Conventions Act 1983 no person shall be entitled by reason of relationship to damages (including damages by way of solatium) in respect of the death of another person.

NOTES
[0]As amended by the Damages (Scotland) Act 1993 (c. 5), s. 1 (effective 18th April 1993; s. 8(3)). See the Consumer Protection Act 1987 (c. 43), s. 6(1)(c). Extended (*prosp.*): see the Antarctic Minerals Act 1989 (c. 21), s. 13(1). Excluded by the Social Security Act 1989, s. 22(4)(d) and the Social Security Administration Act 1992 (c. 5), s. 81(3)(d) (effective July 1, 1992; s. 192(4)). See also s. 92.
[1]Extended: see the Administration of Justice Act 1982 (c. 14), s. 9(2).
[2]Saved by the International Transport Conventions Act 1983 (c. 14), Sched. 1, para. 1.
[3]Applied by the International Transport Conventions Act 1983 (c. 14), Sched. 1, para. 2.
[4]As amended by the Administration of Justice Act 1982 (c. 53), s. 14(1), and the International Transport Conventions Act 1983 (c. 14), Sched. 1, para. 4(a).

Transmissibility to executor of rights of deceased relative
[1]**1A.** Any right to damages under any provision of section 1 of this Act which is vested in the relative concerned immediately before his death shall be transmitted to the relative's executor; but, in determining the amount of damages payable to an executor by virtue of this section, the court shall have regard only to the period ending immediately before the relative's death.

NOTE
[1]Inserted by the Damages (Scotland) Act 1993 (c. 5), s. 2 (effective April 18, 1993; s. 8(3)).

Rights transmitted to executor in respect of deceased person's injuries
[1]**2.**—(1) Subject to the following provisions of this section, there shall be transmitted to the executor of a deceased person the like rights to damages in respect of personal injuries (including a right to damages by way of solatium) sustained by the deceased as were vested in him immediately before his death.

(2) There shall not be transmitted to the executor under this section a right to damages by way of compensation or patrimonial loss attributable to any period after the deceased's death.

(3) In determining the amount of damages by way of solatium payable to an executor by virtue of this section, the court shall have regard only to the period ending immediately before the deceased's death.

(4) In so far as a right to damages vested in the deceased comprised a right to damages (other than for patrimonial loss) in respect of injury resulting from defamation or any other verbal injury or other injury to reputation sustained by the deceased, that right shall be

transmitted to the deceased's executor only if an action to enforce that right had been brought by the deceased before his death and had not been concluded by then within the meaning of section 2A(2) of this Act.

NOTE

[1]As substituted by the Damages (Scotland) Act 1993 (c. 5), s. 3 (effective April 18, 1993; s. 8(3)).

Enforcement by executor of rights transmitted to him.

[1]**2A.**—(1) For the purpose of enforcing any right transmitted to an executor under section 1A or 2 of this Act the executor shall be entitled—

(*a*) to bring an action; or

(*b*) if an action for that purpose has been brought by the deceased but had not been concluded before his death, to be sisted as pursuer in that action.

(2) For the purpose of subsection (1) above, an action shall not be taken to be concluded while any appeal is competent or before any appeal taken has been disposed of.

NOTE

[1]As inserted by the Damages (Scotland) Act 1993 (c. 5), s. 4 (effective April 18, 1993; s. 8(3)).

Certain rights arising on death of another not transmissible

3. [Repealed by the Damages (Scotland) Act 1993 (c. 5), s. 7(3) (effective April 18, 1993; s. 8(3)).]

Executor's claim not to be excluded by relatives' claims: and vice versa

[1]**4.** A claim by the executor of a deceased person for damages under section 2 of this act is not excluded by the making of a claim by a relative of the deceased for damages under section 1 of this Act; or by a deceased relative's executor under section 1A of this Act; nor is a claim by a relative of a deceased person or by a deceased relative's executor for damages under the said section 1 or (as the case may be) the said section 1A excluded by the making of a claim by the deceased's executor for damages under the said section 2.

NOTE

[1]As amended by the Administration of Justice Act 1982 (c. 53), s. 14(2)(*a*), and the Damages (Scotland) Act 1993 (c. 5), Sched., para. 1 (effective 18th April 1993; s. 8(3)).

5. [Repealed by the Administration of Justice Act 1983 (c. 53), s. 14(2).]

Limitation of total amount of liability

[1]**6.**—[2](1) Where in any action to which this section applies, so far as directed against any defender, it is shown that by antecedent agreement, compromise or otherwise, the liability arising in relation to that defender from the personal injuries in question

had, before the deceased's death, been limited to damages of a specified or ascertainable amount, or where that liability is so limited by virtue of any enactment, nothing in this Act shall make the defender liable to pay damages exceeding that amount; and accordingly where in such an action there are two or more pursuers any damages to which they would respectively be entitled under this Act apart from the said limitation shall, if necessary, be reduced *pro rata.*

(2) Where two or more such actions are conjoined, the conjoined actions shall be treated for the purposes of this section as if they were a single action.

³(3) This section applies to any action in which, following the death of any person from personal injuries, damages are claimed—

(*a*) by the executor of the deceased, in respect of the injuries from which the deceased died;

⁴(*b*) in respect of the death of the deceased, by any relative of his, or, if the relative has died, by the relative's executor.

NOTES

¹Excluded by the International Transport Convention Act 1983 (c. 14), Sched. 1, para. 2.

²As amended by the Administration of Justice Act 1982 (c. 53), s. 14(2)(*b*)(i).

³Added by the Administration of Justice Act 1982 (c. 53), s. 14(2)(*b*)(ii).

⁴As amended by the Damages (Scotland) Act 1993 (c. 5), Sched., para. 2 (effective April 18, 1993; s. 8(3)).

Amendment of references in other Acts

7. In any Act passed before this Act, unless the context otherwise requires, any reference to solatium in respect of the death of any person (however expressed) shall be construed as a reference to a loss of society award within the meaning of section 1 of this Act; and any reference to a dependant of a deceased person, in relation to an action claiming damages in respect of the deceased person's death, shall be construed as including a reference to a relative of the deceased person within the meaning of this Act.

Abolition of right of assythment

8. After the commencement of this Act no person shall in any circumstances have a right to assythment, and accordingly any action claiming that remedy shall (to the extent that it does so) be incompetent.

Damages due to injured person for patrimonial loss caused by personal injuries whereby expectation of life is diminished

9.—(1) This section applies to any action for damages in respect of personal injuries sustained by the pursuer where his expected date of death is earlier than it would have been if he had not sustained the injuries.

(2) In assessing, in any action to which this section applies, the amount of any patrimonial loss in respect of the period after the date of decree—

(*a*) it shall be assumed that the pursuer will live until the date when he would have been expected to die if he had not sustained the injuries (hereinafter referred to as the "notional date of death");

(*b*) the court may have regard to any amount, whether or not it is an amount related to earnings by the pursuer's own labour or other gainful activity, which in its opinion the pursuer, if he had not sustained the injuries in question, would have received in the period up to his notional date of death by way of benefits in money or money's worth, being benefits derived from sources other than the pursuer's own estate;

(*c*) the court shall have regard to any diminution of any such amount as aforesaid by virtue of expenses which in the opinion of the court the pursuer, if he had not sustained the injuries in question, would reasonably have incurred in the said period by way of living expenses.

Solatium for loss of expectation of life

[1]**9A.**—(1) In assessing, in an action for damages in respect of personal injuries, the amount of damages by way of solatium, the court shall, if—

(*a*) the injured person's expectation of life has been reduced by the injuries; and

(*b*) the injured person is, was at any time or is likely to become, aware of that reduction,

have regard to the extent that, in consequence of that awareness, he has suffered or is likely to suffer.

(2) Subject to subsection (1) above, no damages by way of solatium shall be recoverable in respect of loss of expectation of life.

(3) The court in making an award of damages by way of solatium shall not be required to ascribe specifically any part of the award to loss of expectation of life.

NOTE
[1]As inserted by the Damages (Scotland) Act 1993 (c. 5), s. 5 (effective April 18, 1993; s. 8(3)).

Interpretation

10.—[0](1) In this Act, unless the context otherwise requires—

"personal injuries" includes any disease or any impairment of a person's physical or mental condition and injury resulting from defamation or any other verbal injury or injury to reputation;

"relative", in relation to a deceased person, has the meaning assigned to it by Schedule 1 to this Act.

[2](2) References in this Act to a member of a deceased person's immediate family are references to any relative of his who falls within subparagraph (*a*) (*aa*) (*b*) or (*c*) of paragraph 1 of Schedule 1 to this Act.

(3) References in this Act to any other Act are references to that Act as amended, extended or applied by any other enactment, including this Act.

NOTE
[0]As amended by the Damages (Scotland) Act 1993 (c. 5), s. 7(3) (effective 18th April 1993; s. 8(3)).
[1]As amended by the Damages (Scotland) Act 1993 (c. 5), Sched., para. 3 (effective April 18, 1993; s. 8(3)).
[2]As amended by the Administration of Justice Act 1982 (c. 53), s. 14(4).

Repeals

11. [Repealed by the Damages (Scotland) Act 1993, s. 7(3).]

Citation, application to Crown, commencement and extent
12.—(1) This Act may be cited as the Damages (Scotland) Act 1976.
(2) This Act binds the Crown.
(3), (4) [Repealed by the Damages (Scotland) Act 1993, s. 7(3).]
(5) This Act extends to Scotland only.

SCHEDULES

Section 1   SCHEDULE 1

DEFINITION OF "RELATIVE"

1. In this Act "relative" in relation to a deceased person includes—
    (a)   any person who immediately before the deceased's death was the spouse of the deceased;
    [1](aa)   any person, not being the spouse of the deceased, who was, immediately before the deceased's death, living with the deceased as husband or wife;
    (b)   any person who was a parent of child of the deceased;
    (c)   any person not falling within paragraph (b) above who was accepted by the deceased as a child of his family;
    (d)   any person who was an ascendant or descendant (other than a parent or child) of the deceased;
    (e)   any person who was, or was the issue of, a brother, sister, uncle or aunt of the deceased; and
    (f)   any person who, having been a spouse of the deceased, had ceased to be so by virtue of a divorce;
but does not include any other person.

NOTE
[1]Inserted by the Administration of Justice Act 1982, s. 14(4).

2. In deducing any relationship to the purposes of the foregoing paragraph—
    (a)   any relationship by affinity shall be treated as relationship by consanguinity; any relationship of the half blood shall be treated as a relationship of the whole blood; and the stepchild of any person shall be treated as his child; and
    [1](b)   section 1(1) of the Law Reform (Parent and Child) (Scotland) Act 1986 shall apply; and any reference (however expressed) in this Act to a relative shall be construed accordingly.

NOTE
[1]As amended by the Law Reform (Parent and Child) (Scotland) Act 1986, Sched. 1, para. 15, with effect from December 18, 1986.

12. **Unfair Contract Terms Act 1977**
(1977 c. 50)

An Act to impose further limits on the extent to which under the law of England and Wales and Northern Ireland civil liability for breach of contract, or for negligence or other breach of duty, can be avoided by means of contract terms and otherwise, and under the law of Scotland civil liability can be avoided by means of contract terms.   [26th October 1977]

. . . . . .

PART II

AMENDMENT OF LAW FOR SCOTLAND

Scope of Part II
15.—(1) This Part of this Act is subject to Part III of this Act and does not affect the validity of any discharge or indemnity given by a person in consideration of the receipt by him of compensation in settlement of any claim which he has.

(2) Subject to subsection (3) below, sections 16 to 18 of this Act apply to any contract only to the extent that the contract—
  (*a*) relates to the transfer of the ownership or possession of goods from one person to another (with or without work having been done on them);
  (*b*) constitutes a contract of service or apprenticeship;
  (*c*) relates to services of whatever kind, including (without prejudice to the foregoing generality) carriage, deposit and pledge, care and custody, mandate, agency, loan and services relating to the use of land;
  (*d*) relates to the liability of an occupier of land to persons entering upon or using that land;
  (*e*) relates to a grant of any right or permission to enter upon or use land not amounting to an estate or interest in the land.

(3) Notwithstanding anything in subsection (2) above, sections 16 to 18—
  (*a*) do not apply to any contract to the extent that the contract—
      (i)   is a contract of insurance (including a contract to pay an annuity on human life);
      (ii) relates to the formation, constitution or dissolution of any body corporate or unincorporated association or partnership;

(*b*) apply to—
a contract of marine salvage or towage;
a charger party of a ship or hovercraft;
a contract for the carriage of goods by ship or hovercraft; or,
a contract to which subsection (4) below relates,
only to the extent that—
   (i) both parties deal or hold themselves out as dealing in the course of a business (and then only in so far as the contract purports to exclude or restrict liability for breach of duty in respect of death or personal injury); or
   (ii) the contract is a consumer contract (and then only in favour of the consumer).

(4) This subsection relates to a contract in pursuance of which goods are carried by ship or hovercraft and which either—
   (*a*) specifies ship or hovercraft as the means of carriage over part of the journey to be covered; or
   (*b*) makes no provision as to the means of carriage and does not exclude ship or hovercraft as that means.
in so far as the contract operates for and in relation to the carriage of the goods by that means.

NOTE
[1]As amended by the Law Reform (Miscellaneous Provisions) (Scotland) Act 1990, s. 68(2) and Sched. 9, in relation to liability for any loss of damage which is suffered on or after April 1, 1991 (*ibid.*, s. 68(6); S.I. 1991 No. 330).

Liability for breach of duty
[1]**16.**—(1) Subject to subsection (1A) below where a term of a contract or a provision of a notice given to persons generally or to particular persons purports to exclude or restrict liability for breach of duty arising in the course of any business or from the occupation of any premises used for business purposes of the occupier, that term or provision—
   (*a*) shall be void in any case where such exclusion or restriction is in respect of death or personal injury;
   (*b*) shall, in any other case, have no effect if it was not fair and reasonable to incorporate the term in the contract or, as the case may be, if it is not fair and reasonable to allow reliance on the provision.

(1A) Nothing in paragraph (*b*) of subsection (1) above shall be taken as implying that a provision of a notice has effect in circumstances where, apart from that paragraph, it would not have effect.

(2) Subsection (1)(*a*) above does not affect the validity of any discharge and indemnity given by a person, on or in connection with an award to him of compensation for pneumoconiosis attributable to employment in the coal industry, in respect of any further claim arising from his contracting that disease.

(3) Where under subsection (1) above a term of a contract or a provision of a notice is void or has no effect, the fact that a person agreed to, or was aware of, the term of provision shall not of itself be sufficient evidence that he knowingly and voluntarily assumed any risk.

NOTE

[1] As amended by the Law Reform (Miscellaneous Provisions) (Scotland) Act 1990, s. 68(3)(*a*), (*b*) and (*c*), in relation to liability for any loss or damage which is suffered on or after April 1, 1991 (*ibid.*, s. 68(6)).

Control of unreasonable exemptions in consumer or standard form contracts

17.—(1) Any term of a contract which is a consumer contract or a standard form contract shall have no effect for the purpose of enabling a party to the contract—

(*a*) who is in breach of a contractual obligation, to exclude or restrict any liability of his to the consumer or customer in respect of the breach;

(*b*) in respect of a contractual obligation, to render no performance, or to render a performance substantially different from that which the consumer or customer reasonably expected from the contract;

if it was not fair and reasonable to incorporate the term in the contract.

(2) In this section "customer" means a party to a standard form contract who deals on the basis of written standard terms of business of the other party to the contract who himself deals in the course of a business.

Unreasonable indemnity clauses in consumer contracts

18.—(1) Any term of a contract which is a consumer contract shall have no effect for the purpose of making the consumer indemnify another person (whether a party to the contract or not) in respect of liability which that other person may incur as a result of breach of duty or breach of contract, if it was not fair and reasonable to incorporate the term in the contract.

(2) In this section "liability" means liability arising in the course of any business or from the occupation of any premises used for business purposes of the occupier.

"Guarantee" of consumer goods

19.—(1) This section applies to a guarantee—

(*a*) in relation to goods which are of a type ordinarily supplied for private use or consumption; and

(*b*) which is not a guarantee given by one party to the other party to a contract under or in pursuance of which the ownership or possession of the goods to which the guarantee relates is transferred.

(2) A term of a guarantee to which this section applies shall be void in so far as it purports to exclude or restrict liability for loss or damage (including death or personal injury)—

(*a*) arising from the goods proving defective while—
    (i)   in use otherwise an exclusively for the purposes of a business; or
    (ii) in the possession of a person for such use; and
(*b*) resulting from the breach of duty of a person concerned in the manufacture or distribution of the goods.

(3) For the purposes of this section, any document is a guarantee if it contains or purports to contain some promise or assurance (however worded or presented) that defects will be made good by complete or partial replacement, or by repair, monetary compensation or otherwise.

. . . . . .

Evasion by means of secondary contract

23. Any term of any contract shall be void which purports to exclude or restrict, or has the effect of excluding or restricting—
(*a*) the exercise, by a party to any other contract, of any right or remedy which arises in respect of that other contract in consequence of breach of duty, or of obligation, liability for which could not by virtue of the provisions of this Part of this Act be excluded or restricted by a term of that other contract;
(*b*) the application of the provisions of this Part of this Act in respect of that or any other contract.

The "reasonableness" test

[1]**24.**—(1) In determining for the purposes of this Part of this Act whether it was fair and reasonable to incorporate a term in a contract, regard shall be had only to the circumstances which were, or ought reasonably to have been, known to or in the contemplation of the parties to the contract at the time the contract was made.

(2) In determining for the purposes of section 20 or 21 of this Act whether it was fair and reasonable to incorporate a term in a contract, regard shall be had in particular to the matters specified in Schedule 2 to this Act; but this subsection shall not prevent a court or arbiter from holding, in accordance with any rule of law, that a term which purports to exclude or restrict any relevant liability is not a term of the contract.

(2A) In determining for the purposes of this Part of this Act whether it is fair and reasonable to allow reliance on a provision of a notice (not being a notice having contractual effect), regard shall be had to all the circumstances obtaining when the liability arose or (but for the provision) would have arisen.

(3) Where a term in a contract or a provision of a notice purports to restrict liability to a specified sum of money, and the question arises for the purposes of this Part of this Act whether it was fair and reasonable to incorporate the term in the contract or whether it is fair and reasonable to allow reliance on the provision, then, without

prejudice to subsection (2) above in the case of a term in a contract, regard shall be had in particular to—
  (a)   the resources which the party seeking to rely on that term or provision could expect to be available to him for the purpose of meeting the liability should it arise;
  (b)   how far it was open to that party to cover himself by insurance.
  (4) The onus of proving that it was fair and reasonable to incorporate a term in a contract or that it is fair and reasonable to allow reliance on a provision of a notice shall lie on the party so contending.

NOTE
  [1]As amended by the Law Reform (Miscellaneous Provisions) (Scotland) Act 1990 (c. 40), s. 68(4)(a), (b) and (c), in relation to liability for any loss or damage suffered on or after April 1, 1991 (ibid., s. 68(6); S.I. 1991 No. 330).

Interpretation of Part II
  25.—(1) In this Part of this Act—
  "breach of duty" means the breach—
  (a)   of any obligation, arising from the express or implied terms of a contract, to take reasonable care or exercise reasonable skill in the performance of the contract;
  (b)   of any common law duty to take reasonable care or exercise reasonable skill;
  (c)   of the duty of reasonable care imposed by section 2(1) of the Occupiers' Liability (Scotland) Act 1960;
  "business" includes a profession and the activities of any government department or local or public authority;
  "consumer" has the meaning assigned to that expression in the definition in this section of "consumer contract";
  "consumer contract" means a contract (not being a contract of sale by auction or competitive tender) in which—
  (a)   one party to the contract deals, and the other party to the contract ("the consumer") does not deal or hold himself out as dealing, in the course of a business, and
  (b)   in the case of a contract such as is mentioned in section 15(2)(a) of this Act, the goods are of a type ordinarily supplied for private use or consumption;
  and for the purposes of this Part of this Act the onus of proving that a contract is not to be regarded as a consumer contract shall lie on the party so contending;
  [1]"goods" has the same meaning as in the Sale of Goods Act 1979;
  "hire-purchase agreement" has the same meaning as in section 189(1) of the Consumer Credit Act 1974;
  [2]"notice" includes an announcement, whether or not in writing, and any other communication or pretended communication;
  "personal injury" includes any disease and any impairment of physical or mental condition.

(2) In relation to any breach of duty or obligation, it is immaterial for any purpose of this Part of this Act whether the act or omission giving rise to that breach was inadvertent or intentional, or whether liability for it arises directly or vicariously.

[3](3) In this Part of this Act, any reference to excluding or restricting any liability includes—

    (*a*)   making the liability or its enforcement subject to any restrictive or onerous conditions;

    (*b*)   excluding or restricting any right or remedy in respect of this liability, or subjecting a person to any prejudice in consequence of his pursuing any such right or remedy;

    (*c*)   excluding or restricting any rule of evidence or procedure;

but does not include an agreement to submit any question to arbitration.

(4) [Repealed by the Law Reform (Miscellaneous Provisions) (Scotland) Act 1990, s. 68(5)(*b*) and Sched. 9.]

(5) In sections 15 and 16 and 19 to 21 of this Act, any reference to excluding or restricting liability for breach of an obligation or duty shall include a reference to excluding or restricting the obligation or duty itself.

NOTES

[1]As amended by the Sale of Goods Act 1979, Sched. 2, para. 22.

[2]Inserted by the Law Reform (Miscellaneous Provisions) (Scotland) Act 1990, s. 68(5)(*a*); applies only in relation to liability for any loss or damage suffered on or after April 1, 1991 (*ibid.*, s. 68(6)).

[3]As amended by the Law Reform (Miscellaneous Provisions) (Scotland) Act 1990, s. 68(5)(*b*) and Sched. 9, in relation to liability for any loss or damage suffered on or after April 1, 1991 (*ibid.*, s. 68(6)).

Part III

Provisions applying to whole of United Kingdom

Miscellaneous

International supply contracts

26.—(1) The limits imposed by this Act on the extent to which a person may exclude or restrict liability by reference to a contract term do not apply to liability arising under such a contract as is described in subsection (3) below.

(2) The terms of such a contract are not subject to any requirements of reasonableness under section 3 or 4; and nothing in Part II of this Act shall require the incorporation of the terms of such a contract to be fair and reasonable for them to have effect.

(3) Subject to subsection (4), that description of contract is one whose characteristics are the following—

    (*a*)   either it is a contract of sale of goods or it is one under or in pursuance of which the possession of ownership of goods passes; and (*b*)   it is made by parties whose places of business (or, if they have none, habitual residences) are in the territories of different States (the Channel Islands and the Isle of Man being treated for this purpose as different States from the United Kingdom).

(4) A contract falls within subsection (3) above only if either—

(*a*)   the goods in question are, at the time of the conclusion of the contract, in the course of carriage, or will be carried, from the territory of one State to the territory of another; or

(*b*)   the acts constituting the offer and acceptance have been done in the territories of different States; or

(*c*)   the contract provides for the goods to be delivered to the territory of a State other than that within whose territory those acts were done.

. . . . . .

13. **Administration of Justice Act 1982**
(1982 c. 53)

An Act to make further provision with respect to the administration of justice and matters connected therewith; to amend the law relating to actions for damages for personal injuries, including injuries resulting in death, and to abolish certain actions for loss of services; ...   [28th October 1982]

. . . . . .

[1]PART II

DAMAGES FOR PERSONAL INJURIES ETC. — SCOTLAND

NOTE
    [1]In force 1st January 1983, except for ss. 12 and 14(2), which came into force on September 1, 1984; s. 76(3), (4) and (11) and S.I. 1984 No. 1287. See the Consumer Protection Act 1987, s. 6(1)(*d*).

Damages in respect of services
    7. Where a person (in this Part of this Act referred to as "the injured person")—

(*a*)   has sustained personal injuries, or

(*b*)   has died in consequence of personal injuries sustained,

as a result of an act or omission of another person giving rise to liability in any person (in this Part of this Act referred to as "the responsible person") to pay damages, the responsible person shall also be liable to pay damages in accordance with the provisions of sections 8 and 9 of this Act.

Services rendered to injured person

8.—(1) Where necessary services have been rendered to the injured person by a relative in consequence of the injuries in question, then, unless the relative has expressly agreed in the knowledge that an action for damages has been raised or is in contemplation that no payment should be made in respect of those services, the responsible person shall be liable to pay to the injured person by way of damages such sum as represents reasonable remuneration for those services and repayment of reasonable expenses incurred in connection therewith.

[1](2) The injured person shall be under an obligation to account to the relative for any damages recovered from the responsible person under subsection (1) above.

[1](3) Where, at the date of an award of damages in favour of the injured person, it is likely that necessary services will, after that date, be rendered to him by a relative in consequence of the injuries in question, then, unless the relative has expressly agreed that no payment shall be made in respect of those services, the responsible person shall be liable to pay to the injured person by way of damages such sum as represents—

(*a*) reasonable remuneration for those services; and

(*b*) reasonable expenses which are likely to be incurred in connection therewith.

[1](4) The relative shall have no direct right of action in delict against the responsible person in respect of any services or expenses referred to in this section.

NOTE

[1]As substituted for former subs. (2) by the Law Reform (Miscellaneous Provisions) (Scotland) Act 1990, s. 69(1). S. 69(2) provides:

"Without prejudice to Parts II and III of the Prescription and Limitation (Scotland) Act 1973, this section shall apply to rights accruing both before and after the date appointed for its coming into force [March 1, 1991], but shall not affect any proceedings commenced before that date."

Services to injured person's relative

9.—(1) The responsible person shall be liable to pay to the injured person a reasonable sum by way of damages in respect of the inability to render the personal services referred to in subsection (3) below.

(2) Where the injured person has died, any relative of his entitled to damages in respect of loss of support under section 1(3) of the Damages (Scotland) Act 1976 shall be entitled to include as a head of damage under that section a reasonable sum in respect of the loss to him of the personal services mentioned in subsection (3) below.

(3) The personal services referred to in subsections (1) and (2) above are personal services—

(*a*) which were or might have been expected to have been rendered by the injured person before the occurrence of the act or omission giving rise to liability.

(b) of a kind which, when rendered by a person other than a relative, would ordinarily be obtainable on payment, and

(c) which the injured person but for the injuries in question might have been expected to render gratuitously to a relative.

(4) Subject to subsection (2) above, the relative shall have no direct right of action in delict against the responsible person in respect of the personal services mentioned in subsection (3) above.

Assessment of damages for personal injuries

10. Subject to any agreement to the contrary, in assessing the amount of damages payable to the injured person in respect of personal injuries there shall not be taken into account so as to reduce that amount—

(a) any contractual pension or benefit (including any payment by a friendly society or trade union);

(b) any pension or retirement benefit payable from public funds other than any pension or benefit to which section 2(1) of the Law Reform (Personal Injuries) Act 1948 applies;

(c) any benefit payable from public funds, in respect of any period after the date of the award of damages, designed to secure to the injured person or any relative of his a minimum level of subsistence;

(d) any redundancy payment under the Employment Protection (Consolidation) Act 1978, or any payment made in circumstances corresponding to those in which a right to a redundancy payment would have accrued if section 81 of that Act had applied;

(e) any payment made to the injured person or to any relative of his by the injured person's employer following upon the injuries in question where the recipient is under an obligation to reimburse the employer in the event of damages being recovered in respect of those injuries;

(f) subject to paragraph (iv) below, any payment of a benevolent character made to the injured person or to any relative of his by any person following upon the injuries in question;

but there shall be taken into account —

(i) any remuneration or earnings from employment;

[1](ii) any unemployment benefit;

(iii) any benefit referred to in paragraph (c) above payable in respect of any period prior to the date of the award of damages;

(iv) any payment of a benevolent character made to the injured person or to any relative of his by the responsible person following on the injuries in question, where such a payment is made directly and not through a trust or other fund from which the injured person or his relatives have benefited or may benefit.

NOTE
[1]Prospectively amended by the Jobseekers Act 1995 (c. 18), Sched. 2, para. 6, to substitute contribution-based jobseekers' allowance payable under that Act.

Maintenance at public expense to be taken into account in assessment of damages: Scotland

11. In an action for damages for personal injuries (including any such action arising out of a contract) any saving to the injured person which is attributable to his maintenance wholly or partly at public expense in a hospital, nursing home or other institution shall be set off against any income lost by him as a result of the injuries.

Award of provisional damages for personal injuries: Scotland

12.—(1) This section applies to an action for damages for personal injuries in which—

  (a) there is proved or admitted to be a risk that at some definite or indefinite time in the future the injured person will, as a result of the act or omission which gave rise to the cause of the action, develop some serious disease or suffer some serious deterioration in his physical or mental condition; and

  (b) the responsible person was, at the time of the act or omission giving rise to the cause of the action.

      (i)   a public authority or public corporation; or

      (ii) insured or otherwise indemnified in respect of the claim.

(2) In any case to which this section applies, the court may, on the application of the injured person, order—

  (a) that the damages referred to in subsection (4)(a) below be awarded to the injured person; and

  (b) that the injured person may apply for the further award of damages referred to in subsection (4)(b) below,

and the court may, if it considers it appropriate, order that an application under paragraph (b) above may be made only within a specified period.

(3) Where an injured person in respect of whom an award has been made under subsection (2)(a) above applies to the court for an award under subsection (2)(b) above, the court may award to the injured person the further damages referred to in subsection (4)(b) below.

(4) The damages referred to in subsections (2) and (3) above are—

  (a) damages assessed on the assumption that the injured person will not develop the disease or suffer the deterioration in his condition; and

  (b) further damages if he develops the disease or suffers the deterioration.

(5) Nothing in this section shall be construed—

(a)   as affecting the exercise of any power relating to expenses including a power to make rules of court relating to expenses; or

(b)   as prejudicing any duty of the court under any enactment or rule of law to reduce or limit the total damages which would have been recoverable apart from any such duty.

(6) The Secretary of State may, by order, provide that categories of defenders shall, for the purposes of paragraph (b) of subsection (1) above, become or cease to be responsible persons, and may make such modifications of that paragraph as appear to him to be necessary for the purpose.

And an order under this subsection shall be made by statutory instrument subject to annulment in pursuance of a resolution of either House of Parliament.

Supplementary

13.—(1) In this Part of this Act, unless the context otherwise requires —

"personal injuries" includes any disease or any impairment of a person's physical or mental condition and injury resulting from defamation or any other verbal injury or other injury to reputation.

"relative", in relation to the injured person, means—

(a)   the spouse or divorced spouse;

(b)   any person, not being the spouse of the injured person, who was, at the time of the act or omission giving rise to liability in the responsible person, living with the injured person as husband or wife;

(c)   any ascendant or descendant;

(d)   any brother, sister, uncle or aunt; or any issue of any such person;

(e)   any person accepted by the injured person as a child of his family.

In deciding any relationship for the purposes of the foregoing definition—

(a)   any relationship by affinity shall be treated as a relationship by consanguinity; any relationship of the half blood shall be treated as a relationship of the whole blood; and the stepchild of any person shall be treated as his child; and

[2](b)   section 1(1) of the Law Reform (Parent and Child) (Scotland) Act 1986 shall apply; and any reference (howsoever expressed) in this Part of this Act to a relative shall be construed accordingly.

(2) Any reference in this Part of this Act to a payment, benefit or pension shall be construed as a reference to any such payment, benefit or pension whether in cash or in kind.

(3) This Part of this Act binds the Crown.

NOTE

[1]As amended by the Damages (Scotland) Act 1993 (c. 5), Sched., para. 4 (effective April 18, 1993; s. 8(3)).

[2]As amended by the Law Reform (Parent and Child) (Scotland) Act 1986 (c. 9),
Sched. 1, para. 19.

Amendment and repeal of enactments
   14.—(1), (2), (4) [Amendments to the Damages (Scotland) Act
1976, sections 1(7), 4, 5 (repealed), 6, 10(2) and Sched. 1, para. 1,
are incorporated in the print of that Act, *supra*.]
   (3) Notwithstanding section 73(5) of this Act, where an action to
which section 5 of that Act applies has been raised and has not, prior
to the commencement of subsection (2) above, been disposed of, the
court shall not dismiss the action on the ground only that the pursuer
has failed to serve notice of the action as required by subsection (6)
of the said section 5.

· · · · · ·

PART IX

GENERAL AND SUPPLEMENTARY

Transitional provisions and savings
   73...
   (5) Without prejudice to the provisions of Parts II and III of the
Prescription and Limitation (Scotland) Act 1973, Part II of this Act shall
apply to rights of action which accrued before, as well as rights of action
which accrue after, the coming into operation of that Part of this Act; but
nothing in Part II of this Act other than the repeal of section 5 of the
Damages (Scotland) Act 1976 shall affect any proceedings commenced
before that Part of this Act comes into operation.

· · · · · ·

Extent
   77...
   (3) Part II of this Act and section 26 above extend to Scotland only ...

· · · · · ·

Citation
   78. This Act may be cited as the Administration of Justice Act 1982.

· · · · · ·

14. **Law Reform (Husband and Wife) (Scotland) Act 1984**
(1984 c. 15)

An Act to amend the law relating to husband and wife and breach of
   promise of marriage and for connected purposes.
                                              [24th May 1984]

Abolition of actions of breach of promise of marriage, adherence and enticement

Promise of marriage not an enforceable obligation

1.—(1) No promise of marriage or agreement between two persons to marry one another shall have effect under the law of Scotland to create any rights or obligations; and no action for breach of any such promise or agreement may be brought in any court in Scotland, whatever the law applicable to the promise or agreement.

(2) This section shall have effect in relation to any promise made or agreement entered into before it comes into force, but shall not affect any action commenced before it comes into force.

Actions of adherence and enticement abolished

2.—(1) No spouse shall be entitled to apply for a decree from any court in Scotland ordaining the other spouse to adhere.

(2) No person shall be liable in delict to any person by reason only of having induced the spouse of that person to leave or to remain apart from that person.

(3) This section shall not affect any action commenced before this Act comes into force.

Abolition of miscellaneous rules relating to husband and wife

Curatory after marriage

3.—(1) No marriage person shall, by reason only of minority, be subject to the curatory of his parent or of any person appointed by his parent.

[1](2) No wife shall, by reason only of minority, be subject to the curatory of her husband.

(3) Section 2 of the Married Women's Property (Scotland) Act 1920 (husband to be curator to his wife during her minority) is repealed.

NOTE

[1]Prospectively repealed by the Children (Scotland) Act 1995 (c. 30), Sched. 5, *infra.*

Abolition of husband's right to choose matrimonial home

4. Any rule of law entitling the husband, as between husband and wife, to determine where the matrimonial home is to be, shall cease to have effect.

Abolition of certain rules relating to ante-nuptial marriage contracts

5.—(1) In relation to an ante-nuptial contract of marriage entered into after this Act comes into force—

  (*a*)   any rule of law enabling a woman to create an alimentary right in her own favour in respect of any property provided by her shall cease to have effect;

  (*b*)   any rule of law whereby the marriage is onerous consideration for any provision of the contract, shall cease to have effect.

(2) Nothing in paragraph (*b*) of subsection (1) above shall affect the operation of any enactment relating to gifts in consideration of marriage.

Abolition of husband's remaining liability for wife's debts incurred before marriage

6.—(1) A husband shall not be liable, by reason only of being her husband, for any debts incurred by his wife before marriage.

(2) Subsection (1) above shall have effect in relation to any such debts, whether incurred before or after this Act comes into force.

(3) Section 4 of the Married Women's Property (Scotland) Act 1877 (liability of husband for wife's ante-nuptial debts limited to amount of property received through her) is repealed.

Abolition of Praepositura

7.—(1) For the purpose of determining a husband's liability for any obligation incurred by his wife after this Act comes into force, a married woman shall not be presumed as a matter of law to have been placed by her husband in charge of his domestic affairs, and any rule of law to the contrary shall cease to have effect.

(2) No warrant of inhibition or inhibition in whatever form may be granted at the instance of a husband for the purpose of cancelling his wife's authority to incur any obligation on his behalf.

(3) No such inhibition granted before the date this Act comes into force shall be registered on or after that date, and any such inhibition registered before that date shall be treated as discharged on that date.

Abolition of husband's liability for wife's judicial expenses when neither a party nor dominus litis

8. Any rule of law whereby a husband—

(*a*) who is not a party to an action between his wife and a third party, and

(*b*) who is not, in relation to that action, *dominus litis,*

may nevertheless be found to that action, shall cease to have effect.

General

Consequential amendments and repeals

9.—(1) The enactments specified in Schedule 1 shall have effect subject to the amendments specified in that Schedule, being amendments consequential to the provisions of this Act.

(2) The enactments specified in Schedule 2 are repealed to the extent specified in the third column of that Schedule.

Citation etc.

10.—(1) This Act may be cited as the Law Reform (Husband and Wife) (Scotland) Act 1984.

(2) This Act shall come into force at the end of the period of two months beginning with the day on which it is passed.

(3) This Act extends to Scotland only.

. . . . . .

15. Civil Evidence (Scotland) Act 1988
(1988 c. 32)

An Act to make fresh provision in relation to civil proceedings in Scotland regarding corroboration of evidence and the admissibility of hearsay and other evidence; and for connected purposes.   [29th July 1988]

Rule requiring corroboration abolished

1.—(1) In any civil proceedings the court or, as the case may be, the jury, if satisfied that any fact has been established by evidence in those proceedings, shall be entitled to find that fact proved by that evidence notwithstanding that the evidence is not corroborated.

(2) Any rule of law whereby any evidence may be taken to be corroborated by a false denial shall cease to have effect.

Admissibility of hearsay

2.—(1) In any civil proceedings—

(*a*)   evidence shall not be excluded solely on the ground that it is hearsay;

(*b*)   a statement made by a person otherwise than in the course of the proof shall be admissible as evidence of any matter contained in the statement of which direct oral evidence by that person would be admissible; and

(*c*)   the court, or as the case may be the jury, if satisfied that any fact has been established by evidence in those proceedings, shall be entitled to find that fact proved by the evidence notwithstanding that the evidence is hearsay.

(2) Nothing in this section shall affect the admissibility of any statement as evidence of the fact that the statement was made.

(3) In paragraph (*e*) of section 5 of the Court of Session Act 1988 (power to make provision as regards the Court of Session for admission of written statements etc. in lieu of parole evidence), for the words "the admission in lieu of parole evidence of written statements (including affidavits) and reports, on such conditions as may be prescribed" there shall be substituted the words "written statements (including affidavits) and reports, admissible under section 2(1)(*b*) of the Civil Evidence (Scotland) Act 1988, to be received in evidence, on such conditions as may be prescribed without being spoken to by a witness".

(4) [The substituted s. 32(1)(*e*) of the Sheriff Courts (Scotland) Act 1971 is shown in the print of that Act.]

Statement as evidence as to credibility

3. In any civil proceedings a statement made otherwise than in the course of the proof by a person who at the proof is examined as to the statement shall be admissible as evidence in so far as it tends to reflect favourably or unfavourably on that person's credibility.

Leading of additional evidence

4.—(1) For the purposes of section 2 or 3 above, any person may at the proof, with leave of the court, at any time before the commencement of closing submissions—

(*a*) be recalled as a witness whether or not he has been present in court since giving evidence initially; or

(*b*) be called as an additional witness whether or not he has been present in court during the proof (or during any other part of the proceedings).

(2) Nothing in section 3 of the Evidence (Scotland) Act 1840 (presence in court not to disqualify witnesses in certain cases) shall apply as respects a witness called or recalled under subsection (1) above.

Document as part of business records

¹**5.**—(1) Unless the court otherwise directs, a document may in any civil proceedings be taken to form part of the records of a business or undertaking if it is certified as such by a docquet purporting to be signed by an officer of the business or undertaking to which the records belong; and a statement contained in any document certified as aforesaid may be received in evidence without being spoken to by a witness.

(2) For the purpose of this section, facsimile of a signature shall be treated as a signature.

NOTE
¹Saved by the Finance Act 1994 (c. 9), s. 22(2)(c).

Production of copy document

¹**6.**—(1) For the purposes of any civil proceedings, a copy of a document, purporting to be authenticated by a person responsible for the making of the copy, shall, unless the court otherwise directs, be—

(*a*) deemed a true copy; and

(*b*) treated for evidential purposes as if it were the document itself.

(2) In subsection (1) above, "copy" includes a transcript or reproduction.

(3) Sections 3 to 5 of the Bankers' Books Evidence Act 1879 (mode of proof of entries in bankers' books, proof that book is a bankers' book and verification of copy of entry in such a book) shall not apply to civil proceedings.

NOTES
¹Saved by the Finance Act 1994 (c. 9), s. 22(2)(*c*).
²Saved by the Merchant Shipping Act 1995 (c. 21), s. 288(8) (effective January 1, 1996 s. 316(2)).

Statement not contained in business records

7.—(1) In any civil proceedings, the evidence of an officer of a business or undertaking that any particular statement is not contained in the records of the business or undertaking shall be admissible as evidence of that fact whether or not the whole or any part of the records have been produced in the proceedings.

(2) The evidence referred to in subsection (1) above may, unless the court otherwise directs, be given by means of the affidavit of the officer.

(3) In section 6 of the Bankers' Books Evidence Act 1879 (case in which banker not compellable to produce book), after the word "Act" there shall be inserted the words "or under the Civil Evidence (Scotland) Act 1988".

Evidence in actions concerning family relationships, etc.

8.—(1) In any action to which this subsection applies (whether or not appearance has been entered for the defender), no decree or judgment in favour of the pursuer shall be pronounced until the grounds of action have been established by evidence.

(2) Subsection (1) above applies to actions for divorce, separation or declarator of marriage, nullity of marriage, legitimacy, legitimation, illegitimacy, parentage or non-parentage.

(3) Subject to subsection (4) below, in any action for divorce, separation or declarator of marriage or nullity of marriage, the evidence referred to in subsection (1) above shall consist of or include evidence other than that of a party to the marriage (or alleged or purported marriage).

[1](4) The Lord Advocate may by order made by statutory instrument provide that subsection (3) above shall not apply, or shall apply subject to such modifications as may be specified in the order, in respect of such class or classes of action as may be so specified.

(5) No order shall be made under this section unless a draft of the order has been laid before Parliament and has been approved by resolution of each House.

NOTE
[1]See S.I. 1989 No. 582.

Interpretation

9. In this Act, unless the context otherwise requires—

"business" includes trade or profession;

"civil proceedings" includes, in addition to such proceedings in any of the ordinary courts of law—

[1](a) any hearing by the sheriff under section 42 of the Social Work (Scotland) Act 1968 of an application for a finding as to whether grounds for the referral of a child's case to a children's hearing are established, except in so far as the application relates to a ground mentioned in section 32(2)(g) of that Act (commission by the child of an offence);

(b) any arbitration, whether or not under an enactment, except in so far as, in relation to the conduct of the arbitration, specific provision has been made as regards the rules of evidence which are to apply;

(c) any proceedings before a tribunal or inquiry, except in so far as, in relation to the conduct of proceedings before the tribunal or inquiry, specific provision has been made as regards the rules of evidence which are to apply; and

(d) any other proceedings conducted wholly or mainly in accordance with rules of procedure agreed between the parties themselves (or as respects which it would have been open to them to agree such rules had they wished to do so) except in so far as any such agreement makes specific provision as regards the rules of evidence which are to apply;

"court" shall be construed in accordance with the definition of "civil proceedings";

"document" includes, in addition to a document in writing,—

(a) any map, plan, graph or drawing;

(b) any photograph;

(c) any disc, tape, sound track or other device in which sounds or other data (not being visual images) are recorded so as to be capable (with or without the aid of some other equipment) of being reproduced therefrom; and

(d) any film, negative, tape or other device in which one or more visual images are recorded so as to be capable (as aforesaid) of being reproduced therefrom;

"film" includes a microfilm;

"hearsay" includes hearsay of whatever degree;

"made" includes "allegedly made";

"proof" includes trial or other hearing of evidence, proof on commission and any continued proof;

"records" means records in whatever form;

"statement" includes any representation (however made or expressed) of fact or opinion but does not include a statement in a precognition; and

"undertaking" includes any public or statutory undertaking, any local authority and any government department.

NOTE
[1]Prospectively amended by the Children (Scotland) Act 1995 (c. 36), Sched. 4, para. 44.

Repeals and application
10.—(1) The enactments specified in columns 1 and 2 of the Schedule to this Act are hereby repealed to the extent specified in column 3 of the Schedule.

(2) This Act shall apply to proceedings whether commenced before or after the date of its coming into force (but not to proceedings in which proof commenced before that date).

(3) Nothing in this Act shall affect the operation of the following enactments—

   (*a*)   section 2 of the Documentary Evidence Act 1868 (mode of proving certain documents);

   (*b*)   section 2 of the Documentary Evidence Act 1882 (documents printed under superintendence of Stationery Office);

   (*c*)   section 1 of the Evidence (Colonial Statutes) Act 1907 (proof of statutes of certain legislatures);

   (*d*)   section 1 of the Evidence (Foreign, Dominion and Colonial Documents) Act 1933 (proof and effect of registers and official certificates of certain countries); and

   (*e*)   section 5 of the Oaths and Evidence (Overseas Authorities and Countries) Act 1963 (provision in respect of public registers of other countries).

Citation, commencement and extent

11.—(1) This Act may be cited as the Civil Evidence (Scotland) Act 1988.

[1](2) This Act shall come into force on such a day as the Lord Advocate may by order made by statutory instrument appoint.

(3) This Act shall extend to Scotland only.

NOTE

[1]S.I. 1989 No. 556 provides for the provision of this Act to come into force on April 3, 1989.

. . . . . .

16. **Damages (Scotland) Scotland Act 1993**
(1993 c. 5)

An Act to clarify and amend the law of Scotland concerning the right of certain relatives of a deceased person, and the right of executors, to claim damages in respect of the death of the deceased from personal injuries; to make provision regarding solatium where personal injuries result in loss of expectation of life; and for connected purposes.   [18th February 1993]

. . . . . .

Transitional and retrospective provisions

6.—(1) Section 1A of the 1976 Act (as substituted by section 2 of this Act) shall have effect as if it expressly provided that the reference to a right to damages under section 1 of the 1976 Act included a reference to a right under that section as it existed at the time when the right vested, and section 2A shall have effect accordingly.

(2) Section 1A of the 1976 Act shall also have effect as if it provided that the reference to a right to damages under section 1 of the 1976 Act included a reference to a right to damages by way of solatium in respect of the death of a person under the law in force before 13th May 1976, and section 2A shall have effect accordingly.

(3) Section 9A of the 1976 Act shall not affect any proceedings commenced before this Act comes into operation.

(4) Subject to the following provisions of this section, this Act shall have effect only in relation to deaths occurring on or after its commencement.

(5) Notwithstanding section 3 of the 1976 Act, section 1A of that Act shall have effect, subject to subsection (8) below, in the case of the death on or after 16 July 1992 of the relative concerned.

(6) Notwithstanding section 2 of the 1976 Act as it existed prior to the commencement of this Act, that section as substituted by section 3 of this Act shall have effect, subject to subsections (7) and (8) below, in the case of the death on or after 16 July 1992 of a person in whom was vested immediately before his death a right to damages in respect of personal injuries.

(7) Subsection (6) above shall not apply in the case of a death before the commencement of this Act in so far as it would enable an executor to recover damages (other than for patrimonial loss) in respect of injury resulting from defamation or any other verbal injury or other injury to reputation sustained by the deceased.

(8) Neither subsection (5) nor (6) above shall apply where the rights to damages which transmitted to the deceased's executor under section 1 or 2 of the 1976 Act prior to the commencement of this Act have been subject to—

(a)   a full and final settlement; or

(b)   determination by a court in a final judgment within the meaning of section 19A(3) of the Prescription and Limitation (Scotland) Act 1973,

before commencement of this Act.

(9) In calculating whether a claim made by an executor by virtue of subsection (5) or (6) above is unenforceable by virtue of the provisions of Part II of the Prescription and Limitation (Scotland) Act 1973, the period starting with the date of death and ending with the commencement of this Act shall not be taken into account.

Interpretation, minor and consequential amendments and repeals

7.—(1) In any enactment passed or made before this Act, unless the context otherwise requires, any reference to a loss of society award shall be construed as a reference to an award under section 1(4) of the 1976 Act as amended by section 1 of this Act.

(2) The enactments mentioned in the Schedule to this Act shall have effect subject to the minor and consequential amendments respectively specified in that Schedule.

(3) [Repeal of ss. 3, 10(1) (definition of loss of society award), 11, 12(3) and (4) of and Sched. 2 to the Damages (Scotland) Act 1976 (c. 13), is shown in the print of that Act.]

Short title, application to Crown, commencement and extent

8.—(1) This Act may be cited as the Damages (Scotland) Act 1993.

(2) This Act binds the Crown.

(3) This Act shall come into force at the end of the period of 2 months beginning with the day on which it is passed.

(4) This Act extends to Scotland only.

. . . . . .

17. Defamation Act 1996
(1996 c. 31)

An Act to amend the law of defamation and to amend the law of limitation with respect to actions for defamation or malicious falsehood. [4th July 1996]

Responsibility for publication

Responsibility for publication

1.—(1) In defamation proceedings a person has a defence if he shows that—

(*a*) he was not the author, editor, or publisher of the statement complained of,

(*b*) he took reasonable care in relation to its publication, and

(*c*) he did not know, and had no reason to believe, that what he did caused or contributed to the publication of a defamatory statement.

(2) For this purpose "author", "editor" and "publisher" have the following meanings, which are further explained in subsection (3)—

"author" means the originator of the statement, but does not include a person who did not intend that his statement be published at all;

"editor" means a person having editorial or equivalent responsibility for the content of the statement or the decision to publish it; and

"publisher" means a commercial publisher, that is, a person whose business is issuing material to the public, or a section of the public, who issues material containing the statement in the course of that business

(3) A person shall not be considered the author, editor or publisher of a statement if he is only involved—

(*a*) in printing, producing, distributing or selling printed material containing the statement;

(*b*) in processing, making copies of, distributing, exhibiting or selling a film or sound recording (as defined in Part I of the Copyright, Designs and Patents Act 1988) containing the statement;

(*c*) in processing, making copies of, distributing or selling any electronic medium in or on which the statement is recorded, or in operating or providing any equipment, system or service by means of which the statement is retrieved, copied, distributed or made available in electronic form;

(*d*) as the broadcaster of a live programme containing the statement in circumstances in which he has no effective control over the maker of the statement;

(*e*) as the operator of or provider of access to a communications system by means of which the statement is transmitted, or made available, by a person over whom he has no effective control.

In a case not within paragraphs (*a*) to (*e*) the court may have regard to those provisions by way of analogy in deciding whether a person is to be considered the author, editor or publisher of a statement.

(4) Employees or agents of an author, editor or publisher are in the same position as their employer or principal to the extent that they are responsible for the content of the statement or the decision to publish it.

(5) In determining for the purposes of this section whether a person took reasonable care, or had reason to believe that what he did caused or contributed to the publication of a defamatory statement, regard shall be had to—

(*a*) the extent of his responsibility for the content of the statement or the decision to publish it,

(*b*) the nature or circumstances of the publication, and

(*c*) the previous conduct or character of the author, editor or publisher.

(6) This section does not apply to any cause of action which arose before the section came into force.

Offer to make amends

Offer to make amends

2.—(1) A person who has published a statement alleged to be defamatory of another may offer to make amends under this section.

(2) The offer may be in relation to the statement generally or in relation to a specific defamatory meaning which the person making the offer accepts that the statement conveys ("a qualified offer").

(3) An offer to make amends—

(*a*)   must be in writing,

(*b*)   must be expressed to be an offer to make amends under section 2 of the Defamation Act 1996, and

(*c*)   must state whether it is a qualified offer and, if so, set out the defamatory meaning in relation to which it is made.

(4) A offer to make amends under this section is an offer—

(*a*)   to make a suitable correction of the statement complained of and a sufficient apology to the aggrieved party,

(*b*)   to publish the correction and apology in a manner that is reasonable and practicable in the circumstances, and

(*c*)   to pay to the aggrieved party such compensation (if any), and such costs, as may be agreed or determined to be payable.

The fact that the offer is accompanied by an offer to take specific steps does not affect the fact that an offer to make amends under this section is an offer to do all the things mentioned in paragraphs (*a*) to (*c*).

(5) An offer to make amends under this section may not be made by a person after serving a defence in defamation proceedings brought against him by the aggrieved party in respect of the publication in question.

(6) An offer to make amends under this section may be withdrawn before it is accepted; and a renewal of an offer which has been withdrawn shall be treated as a new offer.

Accepting an offer to make amends

3.—(1) If an offer to make amends under section 2 is accepted by the aggrieved party, the following provisions apply.

(2) The party accepting the offer may not bring or continue defamation proceedings in respect of the publication concerned against the person making the offer, but he is entitled to enforce the offer to make amends, as follows.

(3) If the parties agree on the steps to be taken in fulfilment of the offer, the aggrieved party may apply to the court for an order that the other party fulfil his offer by taking the steps agreed.

(4) If the parties do not agree on the steps to be taken by way of correction, apology and publication, the party who made the offer may take such steps as he thinks appropriate, and may in particular—

(*a*)   make the correction and apology by a statement in open court in terms approved by the court, and

(*b*)   give an undertaking to the court as to the manner of their publication.

(5) If the parties do not agree on the amount to be paid by way of compensation, it shall be determined by the court on the same principles as damages in defamation proceedings.

The court shall take account of any steps taken in fulfilment of the offer and (so far as not agreed between the parties) of the suitability of the correction, the sufficiency of the apology and whether the manner of their publication was reasonable in the circumstances, and may reduce or increase the amount of compensation accordingly.

(6) If the parties do not agree on the amount to be paid by way of costs, it shall be determined by the court on the same principles as costs awarded in court proceedings.

(7) The acceptance of an offer by one person to make amends does not affect any cause of action against another person in respect of the same publication, subject as follows.

(8) [Does not apply to Scotland.]

(9) In Scotland—

(a) subsection (2) of section 3 of the Law Reform (Miscellaneous Provisions) (Scotland) Act 1940 (right of one joint wrongdoer as respects another to recover contribution towards damages) applies in relation to compensation paid under an offer to make amends as it applies in relation to damages in an action to which that section applies; and

(b) where another person is liable in respect of the same damage (whether jointly or otherwise), the person whose offer to make amends was accepted is not required to pay by virtue of any contribution under section 3(2) of that Act a greater amount than the amount of compensation payable in pursuance of the offer.

(10) Proceedings under this section shall be heard and determined without a jury.

Failure to accept offer to make amends

4.—(1) If an offer to make amends under section 2, duly made and not withdrawn, is not accepted by the aggrieved party, the following provisions apply.

(2) The fact that the offer was made is a defence (subject to subsection (3)) to defamation proceedings in respect of the publication in question by that party against the person making the offer.

A qualified offer is only a defence in respect of the meaning to which the offer related.

(3) There is no such defence if the person by whom the offer was made knew or had reason to believe that the statement complained of—

(a) referred to the aggrieved party or was likely to be understood as referring to him, and

(b) was both false and defamatory of that party;

but it shall be presumed until the contrary is shown that he did not know and had no reason to believe that was the case.

(4) The person who made the offer need not rely on it by way of defence, but if he does he may not rely on any other defence.

If the offer was a qualified offer, this applies only in respect of the meaning to which the offer related.

(5) The offer may be relied on in mitigation of damages whether or not it was relied on as a defence.

. . . . . .

Evidence of convictions

Evidence of convictions

12.—(1) [Does not apply to Scotland.]

(2) In section 12 of the Law Reform (Miscellaneous Provisions) (Scotland) Act 1968 (conclusiveness of convictions for purposes of defamation actions), in subsections (1) and (2) for "a person" substitute "the pursuer" and for "that person" substitute "he"; and after subsection (2) insert—

"(2A) In the case of an action for defamation in which there is more than one pursuer—

(*a*)   the references in subsections (1) and (2) above to the pursuer shall be construed as references to any of the pursuers, and

(*b*)   proof that any of the pursuers stands convicted of an offence shall be conclusive evidence that he committed that offence so far as that fact is relevant to any issue arising in relation to his cause of action or that of any other pursuer."

The amendments made by this subsection apply only for the purposes of an action begun after this section comes into force, whenever the cause of action arose.

(3) [Does not apply to Scotland.]

Evidence concerning proceedings in Parliament

Evidence concerning proceedings in Parliament

13.—(1) Where the conduct of a person in or in relation to proceedings in Parliament is in issue in defamation proceedings, he may waive for the purposes of those proceedings, so far as concerns him, the protection of any enactment or rule of law which prevents proceedings in Parliament being impeached or questioned in any court or place out of Parliament.

(2) Where a person waives that protection—

(*a*)   any such enactment or rule of law shall not apply to prevent evidence being given, questions being asked or statements, submissions, comments or findings being made about his conduct, and

(*b*)   none of those things shall be regarded as infringing the privilege of either House of Parliament.

(3) The waiver by one person of that protection does not affect its operation in relation to another person who has not waived it.

(4) Nothing in this section affects any enactment or rule of law so far as it protects a person (including a person who has waived the

protection referred to above) from legal liability for words spoken or things done in the course of, or for the purposes of or incidental to, any proceedings in Parliament.

(5) Without prejudice to the generality of subsection (4), that subsection applies to—

(*a*) the giving of evidence before either House or a committee;

(*b*) the presentation or submission of a document to either House or a committee;

(*c*) the preparation of a document for the purposes of or incidental to the transacting of any such business;

(*d*) the formulation, making or publication of a document, including a report, by or pursuant to an order of either House or a committee; and

(*e*) any communication with the Parliamentary Commissioner for Standards or any person having functions in connection with the registration of members' interests.

In this subsection "a committee" means a committee of either House or a joint committee of both Houses of Parliament.

Statutory privilege

Reports of court proceedings absolutely privileged

14.—(1) A fair and accurate report of proceedings in public before a court to which this section applies, if published contemporaneously with the proceedings, is absolutely privileged.

(2) A report of proceedings which by an order of the court, or as a consequence of any statutory provision, is required to be postponed shall be treated as published contemporaneously if it is published as soon as practicable after publication is permitted.

(3) This section applies to—

(*a*) any court in the United Kingdom,

(*b*) the European Court of Justice or any court attached to that court,

(*c*) the European Court of Human Rights, and

(*d*) any international criminal tribunal established by the Security Council of the United Nations or by an international agreement to which the United Kingdom is a party.

In paragraph (*a*) "court" includes any tribunal or body exercising the judicial power of the State.

(4) In section 8(6) of the Rehabilitation of Offenders Act 1974 and in Article 9(6) of the Rehabilitation of Offenders (Northern Ireland) Order 1978 (defamation actions: reports of court proceedings), for "section 3 of the Law of Libel Amendment Act 1888" substitute "section 14 of the Defamation Act 1996".

Reports, &c. protected by qualified privilege

15.—(1) The publication of any report or other statement mentioned in Schedule 1 to this Act is privileged unless the publication is shown to be made with malice, subject as follows.

(2) In defamation proceedings in respect of the publication of a report or other statement mentioned in Part II of that Schedule, there is no defence under this section if the plaintiff shows that the defendant—

(*a*) was requested by him to publish in a suitable manner a reasonable letter or statement by way of explanation or contradiction, and

(*b*) refused or neglected to do so.

For this purpose "in a suitable manner" means in the same manner as the publication complained of or in a manner that is adequate and reasonable in the circumstances.

(3) This section does not apply to the publication to the public, or a section of the public, of matter which is not of public concern and the publication of which is not for public benefit.

(4) Nothing in this section shall be construed—

(*a*) as protecting the publication of matter the publication of which is prohibited by law, or

(*b*) as limiting or abridging any privilege subsisting apart from this section.

Supplementary provisions

Repeals
16. The enactments specified in Schedule 2 are repealed to the extent specified.

Interpretation
17.—(1) In this Act—

"publication" and "publish", in relation to a statement, have the meaning they have for the purposes of the law of defamation generally, but "publisher" is specially defined for the purposes of section 1;

"statement" mean words, pictures, visual images, gestures or any other method of signifying meaning; and

"statutory provision" means—

(*a*) a provision contained in an Act or in subordinate legislation within the meaning of the Interpretation Act 1978, or

(*b*) a statutory provision within the meaning given by section 1(*f*) of the Interpretation Act (Northern Ireland) 1954.

(2) In this Act as it applies to proceedings in Scotland—
"costs" means expenses; and
"plaintiff" and "defendant" mean pursuer and defender.

General provisions

18.—(1) The following provisions of this Act extend to England and Wales—

section 1 (responsibility for publication),
sections 2 to 4 (offer to make amends), except section 3(9),
section 5 (time limit for actions for defamation or malicious falsehood),
section 7 (ruling on the meaning of a statement),
sections 8 to 10 (summary disposal of claim),
section 12(1) (evidence of convictions),
section 13 (evidence concerning proceedings in Parliament),
sections 14 and 15 and Schedule 1 (statutory privilege),
section 16 and Schedule 2 (repeals) so far as relating to enactments extending to England and Wales,
section 17(1) (interpretation),
this subsection.
section 19 (commencement) so far as relating to provisions which extend to England and Wales, and
section 20 (short title and saving).
—(2) The following provisions of this Act extend to Scotland—
section 1 (responsibility for publication),
section 2 to 4 (offer to make amends), except section 3(8),
section 12(2) (evidence of convictions),
section 13 (evidence concerning proceedings in Parliament),
sections 14 and 15 and Schedule 1 (statutory privilege),
section 16 and Schedule 2 (repeals) so far as relating to enactments extending to Scotland,
section 17 (interpretation),
this subsection,
section 19 (commencement) so far as relating to provisions which extend to Scotland, and
section 20 (short title and saving).
(3) The following provisions of this Act extend to Northern Ireland—
section 1 (responsibility for publication),
sections 2 to 4 (offer to make amends), except section 3(9),
section 6 (time limit for actions for defamation or malicious falsehood),
section 7 (ruling on the meaning of a statement),
sections 8 to 11 (summary disposal of claim),
section 12(3) (evidence of convictions),
section 13 (evidence concerning proceedings in Parliament),
sections 14 and 15 and Schedule 1 (statutory privilege),
section 16 and Schedule 2 (repeals) so far as relating to enactments extending to Northern Ireland,
section 17(1) (interpretation),
this subsection,
section 19 (commencement) so far as relating to provisions which extend to Northern Ireland, and
section 20 (short title and saving).

Commencement

19.—(1) Sections 18 to 20 (extent, commencement and other general provisions) come into force on Royal Assent.

(2) The following provisions of this Act come into force at the end of the period of two months beginning with the day on which this Act is passed—

section 1 (responsibility for publication),

sections 5 and 6 (time limit for actions for defamation or malicious falsehood),

section 12 (evidence of convictions),

section 13 (evidence concerning proceedings in Parliament),

section 16 and the repeals in Schedule 2, so far as consequential on the above provisions, and

section 17 (interpretation), so far as relating to the above provisions.

(3) The provisions of this Act otherwise come into force on such day as may be appointed—

(*a*)   for England and Wales or Northern Ireland, by order of the Lord Chancellor, or

(*b*)   for Scotland, by order of the Secretary of State,

and different days may be appointed for different purposes.

(4) Any such order shall be made by statutory instrument and may contain such transitional provisions as appear to the Lord Chancellor or Secretary of State to be appropriate.

Short title and saving

20.—(1) This Act may be cited as the Defamation Act 1996.

(2) Nothing in this Act affects the law relating to criminal libel.

SCHEDULES

Section 15   *SCHEDULE 1*

QUALIFIED PRIVILEGE

PART I

STATEMENTS HAVING QUALIFIED PRIVILEGE WITHOUT EXPLANATION OR CONTRADICTION

1. A fair and accurate report of proceedings in public of a legislature anywhere in the world.

2. A fair and accurate report of proceedings in public before a court anywhere in the world.

3. A fair and accurate report of proceedings in public of a person appointed to hold a public inquiry by a government or legislature anywhere in the world.

4. A fair and accurate report of proceedings in public anywhere in the world of an international organisation or an international conference.

5. A fair and accurate copy of or extract from any register or other document required by law to be open to public inspection.

6. A notice or advertisement published by or on the authority of a court, or of a judge or office of a court, anywhere in the world.

7. A fair and accurate copy of or extract from matter published by or on the authority of a government or legislature anywhere in the world.

8. A fair and accurate copy of or extract from matter published anywhere in the world by an international organisation or an international conference.

PART II

STATEMENTS PRIVILEGED SUBJECT TO EXPLANATION OR CONTRADICTION

9.—(1) A fair and accurate copy of or extract from a notice or other matter issued for the information of the public by or on behalf of—
 (a)   a legislature in any member State or the European Parliament;
 (b)   the government of any member State, or any authority performing governmental functions in any member State or part of a member State, or the European Commission;
 (c)   an international organisation or international conference.
(2) In this paragraph "governmental functions" includes police functions.

10. A fair and accurate copy of or extract from a document made available by a court in any member State or the European Court of Justice (or any court attached to that court), or by a judge or officer of any such court.

11.—(1) A fair and accurate report of proceedings at any public meeting or sitting in the United Kingdom of—
 (a)   a local authority or local authority committee;
 (b)   a justice or justices of the peace acting otherwise than as a court exercising judicial authority;
 (c)   a commission, tribunal, committee or person appointed for the purposes of any inquiry by any statutory provision, by Her Majesty or by a Minister of the Crown or a Northern Ireland Department;
 (d)   a person appointed by a local authority to hold a local inquiry in pursuance of any statutory provision;
 (e)   any other tribunal, board, committee or body constituted by or under, and exercising functions under, any statutory provision.
(2) In sub-paragraph (1)(a)—
"local authority" means—
 (a)   in relation to England and Wales, a principal council within the meaning of the Local Government Act 1972, any body falling within any paragraph of section 100J(1) of that Act or an authority or body to which the Public Bodies (Admission to Meetings) Act 1960 applies,
 (b)   in relation to Scotland, a council constituted under section 2 of the Local Government etc. (Scotland) Act 1994 or an authority or body to which the Public Bodies (Admission to Meetings) Act 1960 applies,
 (c)   in relation to Northern Ireland, any authority or body to which sections 23 to 27 of the Local Government Act (Northern Ireland) 1972 apply; and
   "local authority committee" means any committee of a local authority or of local authorities, and includes—

(a)   any committee or sub-committee in relation to which sections 100A to 100D of the Local Government Act 1972 apply by virtue of section 100E of that Act (whether or not also by virtue of section 100J of that Act), and

(b)   any committee or sub-committee in relation to which sections 50A to 50D of the Local Government (Scotland) Act 1973 apply by virtue of section 50E of that Act.

(3) A fair and accurate report of any corresponding proceedings in any of the Channel Islands or the Isle of Man or in another member State.

12.—(1) A fair and accurate report of proceedings at any public meeting held in a member State.

(2) In this paragraph a "public meeting" means a meeting bona fide and lawfully held for a lawful purpose and for the furtherance or discussion of a matter of public concern, whether admission to the meeting is general or restricted.

13.—(1) A fair and accurate report of proceedings at a general meeting of a UK public company.

(2) A fair and accurate copy of or extract from any document circulated to members of a UK public company—

(a)   by or with the authority of the board of directors of the company,

(b)   by the auditors of the company, or

(c)   by any member of the company in pursuance of a right conferred by any statutory provision.

(3) A fair and accurate copy of or extract from any document, circulated to members of a UK public company which relates to the appointment, resignation, retirement or dismissal of directors of the company.

(4) In this paragraph "UK public company" means—

(a)   a public company within the meaning of section 1(3) of the Companies Act 1985 or Article 12(3) of the Companies (Northern Ireland) Order 1986, or

(b)   a body corporate incorporated by or registered under any other statutory provision, or by Royal Charter, or formed in pursuance of letters patent.

(5) A fair and accurate report of proceedings at any corresponding meeting of, or copy of or extract from any corresponding document circulated to members of, a public company formed under the law of any of the Channel Islands or the Isle of Man or of another member State.

14. A fair and accurate report of any finding or decision of any of the following descriptions of association, formed in the United Kingdom or another member State, or of any committee or governing body of such an association—

(a)   an association formed for the purpose of promoting or encouraging the exercise of or interest in any art, science, religion or learning, and empowered by its constitution to exercise control over or adjudicate on matters of interest or concern to the association, or the actions or conduct of any person subject to such control or adjudication;

(b)   an association formed for the purpose of promoting or safeguarding the interests of any trade, business, industry or profession, or of the persons carrying on or engaged in any trade, business, industry or profession, and empowered by its constitution to exercise control over or adjudicate upon matters connected with that trade, business, industry or profession, or the actions or conduct of those persons;

(c)   an association formed for the purpose of promoting or safeguarding the interests of a game, sport or pastime to the playing or exercise of which members of the public are invited or admitted, and empowered by its constitution to exercise control over or adjudicate upon persons connected with or taking part in the game, sport or pastime;

(d)   an association formed for the purpose of promoting charitable objects or other objects beneficial to the community and empowered by its constitution to exercise control over or to adjudicate on matters of interest or concern to the association, or the actions or conduct of any person subject to such control or adjudication.

15.—(1) A fair and accurate report of, or copy of or extract from, any adjudication, report, statement or notice issued by a body, officer or other person designated for the purposes of this paragraph—

(*a*)   for England and Wales or Northern Ireland, by order of the Lord Chancellor, and

(*b*)   for Scotland, by order of the Secretary of State.

(2) An order under this paragraph shall be made by statutory instrument which shall be subject to annulment in pursuance of a resolution of either House of Parliament.

PART III

SUPPLEMENTARY PROVISIONS

16.—(1) In this Schedule—

"court" includes any tribunal or body exercising the judicial power of the State;

"international conference" means a conference attended by representatives of two or more governments;

"international organisation" means an organisation of which two or more governments are members, and includes any committee or other subordinate body of such an organisation; and

"legislature" includes a local legislature.

(2) References in this Schedule to a member State include any European dependent territory of a member State.

(3) In paragraphs 2 and 6 "court" includes—

(*a*)   the European Court of Justice (or any court attached to that court) and the Court of Auditors of the European Communities,

(*b*)   the European Court of Human Rights,

(*c*)   any international criminal tribunal established by the Security Council of the United Nations or by an international agreement to which the United Kingdom is a party, and

(*d*)   the International Court of Justice and any other judicial or arbitral tribunal deciding matters in dispute between States.

(4) In paragraphs 1, 3 and 7 "legislature" includes the European Parliament.

17.—(1) Provision may be made by order identifying—

(*a*)   for the purposes of paragraph 11, the corresponding proceedings referred to in sub-paragraph (3);

(*b*)   for the purposes of paragraph 13, the corresponding meetings and documents referred to in sub-paragraph (5).

(2) An order under this paragraph may be made—

(*a*)   for England and Wales or Northern Ireland, by the Lord Chancellor, and

(*b*)   for Scotland, by the Secretary of State.

(3) An order under this paragraph shall be made by statutory instrument which shall be subject to annulment in pursuance of a resolution of either House of Parliament.

. . . . . .

18. **Damages Act 1996**
(1996 c. 48)

An Act to make new provision in relation to damages for personal injury, including injury resulting in death.   [24th July 1996]

Assumed rate of return on investment of damages

1.—(1) In determining the return to be expected from the investment of a sum awarded as damages for future pecuniary loss in an action for personal injury the court shall, subject to and in accordance with rules of court made for the purposes of this section, take into account such rate of return (if any) as may from time to time be prescribed by an order made by the Lord Chancellor.

(2) Subsection (1) above shall not however prevent the court taking a different rate of return into account if any part to the proceedings shows that it is more appropriate in the case in question.

(3) An order under subsection (1) above may prescribe different rates of return for different classes of case.

(4) Before making an order under subsection (1) above the Lord Chancellor shall consult the Government Actuary and the Treasury; and any order under that subsection shall be made by statutory instrument subject to annulment in pursuance of a resolution of either House of Parliament.

(5) In the application of this section to Scotland for references to the Lord Chancellor there shall be substituted references to the Secretary of State.

Consent orders for periodical payments

2.—(1) A court awarding damages in an action for personal injury may, with the consent of the parties, make an order under which the damages are wholly or partly to take the form of periodical payments.

(2) In this section "damages" includes an interim payment which the court, by virtue of rules of court in that behalf, orders the defendant to make to the plaintiff (or, in the application of this section to Scotland, the defender to make to the pursuer).

(3) This section is without prejudice to any powers exercisable apart from this section.

3. [Does not apply to Scotland.]

Enhanced protection for structured settlement annuitants

4.—(1) In relation to an annuity purchased for a person pursuant to a structured settlement from an authorised insurance company within the meaning of the Policyholders Protection Act 1975 (and in respect of which that person as annuitant is accordingly the policyholder for the purposes of that Act) sections 10 and 11 of that Act (protection in the event of liquidation of the insurer) shall have effect as if any reference to ninety per cent of the amount of the liability, of any future benefit or of the value attributed to the policy were a reference to the full amount of the liability, benefit or value.

(2) Those sections shall also have effect as mentioned in subsection (1) above in relation to an annuity purchased from an authorised insurance company within the meaning of the 1975 Act pursuant to any order incorporating terms corresponding to those of a structured

settlement which a court makes when awarding damages for personal injury.

(3) Those sections shall also have effect as mentioned in subsection (1) above in relation to an annuity purchased from or otherwise provided by an authorised insurance company within the meaning of the 1975 Act pursuant to terms corresponding to those of a structured settlement contained in an agreement made by—

    (*a*) the Motor Insurers' Bureau; or

    (*b*) a Domestic Regulations Insurer,

in respect of damages for personal injury which the Bureau or Insurer undertakes to pay in satisfaction of a claim or action against an uninsured driver.

(4) In subsection (3) above "the Motor Insurers' Bureau" means the company of that name incorporated on 14th June 1946 under the Companies Act 1929 and "a Domestic Regulations Insurer" has the meaning given in the Bureau's Domestic Regulations.

(5) This section applies if the liquidation of the authorised insurance company begins (within the meaning of the 1975 Act) after the coming into force of this section irrespective of when the annuity was purchased or provided.

Meaning of structured settlement

5.—(1) In section 4 above a "structured settlement" means an agreement settling a claim or action for damages for personal injury on terms whereby—

    (*a*) the damages are to consist wholly or partly of periodical payments; and

    (*b*) the person to whom the payments are to be made is to receive them as the annuitant under one or more annuities purchased for him by the person against whom the claim or action is brought or, if he is insured against the claim, by his insurer.

(2) The periodical payments may be for the life of the claimant, for a specified period or of a specified number or minimum number or include payments of more than one of those descriptions.

(3) The amounts of the periodical payments (which need not be at a uniform rate or payable at uniform intervals) may be—

    (*a*) specified in the agreement, with or without provision for increases of specified amounts or percentages; or

    (*b*) subject to adjustment in a specified manner so as to preserve their real value; or

    (*c*) partly specified as mentioned in paragraph (*a*) above and partly subject to adjustment as mentioned in paragraph (*b*) above.

(4) The annuity or annuities must be such as to provide the annuitant with sums which as to amount and time of payment correspond to the periodical payments described in the agreement.

(5) Payments in respect of the annuity or annuities may be received on behalf of the annuitant by another person or received and held

on trust for his benefit under a trust of which he is, during his lifetime, the sole beneficiary.

(6) The Lord Chancellor may by an order made by statutory instrument provide that there shall for the purposes of this section be treated as an insurer any body specified in the order, being a body which, though not an insurer, appears to him to fulfil corresponding functions in relation to damages for personal injury claimed or awarded against persons of any class or description, and the reference in subsection (1)(*b*) above to a person being insured against the claim and his insurer shall be construed accordingly.

(7) In the application of subsection (6) above to Scotland for the reference to the Lord Chancellor there shall be substituted a reference to the Secretary of State.

(8) Where—

(*a*)   an agreement is made settling a claim or action for damages for personal injury on terms whereby the damages are to consist wholly or partly of periodical payments;

(*b*)   the person against whom the claim or action is brought (or, if he is insured against the claim, his insurer) purchases one or more annuities; and

(*c*)   a subsequent agreement is made under which the annuity is, or the annuities are, assigned in favour of the person entitled to the payments (so as to secure that from a future date he receives the payments as the annuitant under the annuity or annuities),

then, for the purposes of section 4 above, the agreement settling the claim or action shall be treated as a structured settlement and any such annuity assigned in favour of that person shall be treated as an annuity purchased for him pursuant to the settlement.

(9) Subsections (2) to (7) above shall apply to an agreement to which subsection (8) above applies as they apply to structured settlement as defined in subsection (1) above (the reference in subsection (6) to subsection (1)(*b*) being read as a reference to subsection (8)(*b*).

Guarantees for public sector settlements

6.—(1) This section applies where—

(*a*)   a claim or action for damages for personal injury is settled on terms corresponding to those of a structured settlement as defined in section 5 above except that the person to whom the payments are to be made is not to receive them as mentioned in subsection (1)(*b*) of that section; or

(*b*)   a court awarding damages for personal injury makes an order incorporating such terms.

(2) If it appears to a Minister of the Crown that the payments are to be made by a body in relation to which he has, by virtue of this section, power to do so, he may guarantee the payments to be made under the agreement or order.

(3) The bodies in relation to which a Minister may give such a guarantee shall, subject to subsection (4) below, be such bodies as are designated in relation to the relevant government department by guidelines agreed upon between the department and the Treasury.

(4) A guarantee purporting to be given by a Minister under this section shall not be invalidated by any failure on his part to act in accordance with such guidelines as are mentioned in subsection (3) above.

(5) A guarantee under this section shall be given on such terms as the Minister concerned may determine but those terms shall in every case require the body in question to reimburse the Minister, with interest, for any sums paid by him in fulfilment of the guarantee.

(6) Any sums required by a Minister for fulfilling a guarantee under this section shall be defrayed out of money provided by Parliament and any sums received by him by way of reimbursement or interest shall be paid into the Consolidated Fund.

(7) A Minister who has given one or more guarantees under this section shall, as soon as possible after the end of each financial year, lay before each House of Parliament a statement showing what liabilities are outstanding in respect of the guarantees in that year, what sums have been paid in that year in fulfilment of the guarantees and what sums (including interest) have been recovered in that year in respect of the guarantees or are still owing.

(8) In this section "government department" means any department of Her Majesty's government in the United Kingdom and for the purposes of this section a government department is a relevant department in relation to a Minister if he has responsibilities in respect of that department.

(9) The Schedule to this Act has effect for conferring corresponding powers on Northern Ireland departments.

Interpretation

7.—(1) Subject to subsection (2) below, in this Act "personal injury" includes any disease and any impairment of a person's physical or mental condition and references to a claim or action for personal injury include references to such a claim or action brought by virtue of the Law Reform (Miscellaneous Provisions) Act 1934 and to a claim or action brought by virtue of the Fatal Accidents Act 1976.

(2) In the application of this Act to Scotland "personal injury" has the meaning given by section 10(1) of the Damages (Scotland) Act 1976.

(3) In the application of subsection (1) above to Northern Ireland for the references to the Law Reform (Miscellaneous Provisions) Act 1934 and to the Fatal Accidents Act 1976 there shall be substituted respectively references to the Law Reform (Miscellaneous Provisions) Act (Northern Ireland) 1937 and the Fatal Accidents (Northern Ireland) Order 1977.

Short title, extent and commencement
  8.—(1) This Act may be cited as the Damages Act 1996.
  (2) Section 3 does not extend to Scotland but, subject to that, this Act extends to the whole of the United Kingdom.
  (3) This Act comes into force at the end of the period of two months beginning with the day on which it is passed.

SELECTED BIBLIOGRAPHY

I have tried to include most Scottish articles (Scottish in the sense of being written from the perspective of Scots law) written after the publication of the second edition of Walker's *Delict* in 1981. I have included some others earlier than that as being very helpful or particularly important. I have included a selection from the vast literature in the English journals where they deal with topics that are of relevance to Scots law—mostly relating to negligence but in this edition also articles relating to the work the student will do if (s)he goes on to practice. It should be of some assistance to all students but I hope those studying honours level will find it particularly so. Practitioners looking for arguments or guidance will find many helpful articles.

BOOKS

Allen, D. (Bourne and Holyoak, eds.), *Accident Compensation after Pearson* (1979).
Allen, D., *Misrepresentation* (1988).
Atiyah, P. S., *Accidents Compensation and the Law* (4th ed., 1987).

Baker, C. D., *Tort* (6th ed., 1996).
Black, R., An Introduction to Written Pleading (1982).
Boberg, P., *Law of Delict: Actio Injuriarum* (1988).
Boberg, P., *The Law of Delict: Aquilian Liability* (1984).
Buckley, R., *The Modern Law of Negligence* (1988).

Calabresi, G., *The Cost of Accidents* (1970).
Charlesworth, J., *The Law of Negligence* (8th ed., Percy, R. A., 1990).
Clark, A., *Product Liability* (1989).
Clerk, J. F. and Lindsell, W. H. B., *Law of Torts* (17th ed., 1995).
Curran, P., *Personal Injury Pleadings* (1995).

Dias, R. W. M. and Markesinis, B. S., *Tort Law* (2nd ed., 1989).
Dugdale, A. M. and Stanton, K. M., *Professional Negligence* (3rd ed., 1996).

Erskine, J., An Institute of the Law of Scotland (8th ed., Nicholson, 1870).
Evans, H., *Lawyer's Liabilities* (1996)
Ewing, K. D. and Finnie, W., Civil Liberties in Scotland—Cases and Materials (2nd ed., 1988).

Fleming, J., *Law of Torts* (8th ed., 1993).

Glegg, A. T., The Law of Reparation in Scotland (4th ed., Duncan, J.L., 1955).
Gloag, W. M. and Henderson, R.C., Introduction to the Law of Scotland (10th ed., Wilson and Forte, 1995).
Gurry, F., *Breach of Confidence* (1984).

Harlow, C., *Compensation and Government Torts* (1982).
Harlow, C., *Understanding Tort Law* (1987).
Hart, H.L.A. and Honoré, T., *Causation in the Law* (2nd ed., 1985).
Hepple, B. A. and Mathews, M. H., *Tort Cases and Materials* (3rd ed., 1985).

Heydon, J. D., *Economic Torts* (2nd ed., 1978).
Holyoak, J. and Allen, D., *Civil Liability for Defective Premises* (1982).

Jackson and Powell, *Professional Negligence* (3rd ed., 1992).
Jones, M., *Textbook on Torts* (5th ed., 1996).

Kearney, B., An Introduction to Ordinary Civil Procedure in the Sheriff Court (1982).
Kidner, R., *Casebook on Torts* (4th ed., 1996).
Kolbert, C. (Trans.), *The Digest: Theft, Rapine, Damage and Insult* (1979).

Lawson, F. H., *Negligence in the Civil Law* (1950).

McKain, B. and Bonnington, A., *Scots Law for Journalists* (6th ed., 1995).
McEwan, V. and Paton, A., Damages in Scotland (2nd ed., 1989).
McQueen, H. L., Copyright, Competition and Industrial Design (1989).

Norrie, K. McK., *Defamation and Related Actions in Scots Law* (1995).
North, P. M., *Occupiers Liability* (1972).

Prosser, W. L. and Keeton, *Handbook of the Law of Torts* (5th ed., 1984).

Salmond, J. and Heuston, R. F. V., *The Law of Torts* (21st ed., 1996).
Smith, T. B., A Short Commentary on the Law of Scotland (1962).
Stair, The Institutions of the Law of Scotland (6th ed., Walker, 1981).
Stanton, D. M., *Breach of Statutory Duty* (1986).
Stewart, W. J., Delict (2nd ed., 1993).
Stewart, W. J., The Law of Restitution in Scotland (1992, Supp. 1995).
Street, H., *On Torts* (8th ed., Brazier, 1988).

Thomson, J. M., *Delictual Liability* (1994).

Wacks, R. I., *Privacy and the Law* (1989).
Wadlaw, C., The Law of Passing-off (2nd ed., 1994).
Walker, D. M., The Law of Civil Remedies in Scotland (1974).
Walker, D. M., The Law of Delict in Scotland (2nd ed., 1981).
Walker, D. M., The Law of Prescription and Limitation of Actions (4th ed., 1990).
Walker, D. M., Principles of Scottish Private Law (4th ed., 1988).
Weir, T., *A Casebook on Tort* (Sweet & Maxwell) (8th ed., 1996).
Williams, G. L., *Liability for Animals* (1951).
Winfield, P. H. and Jolowicz, J. A., *Tort* (14th ed., 1994).

CHAPTERS IN BOOKS

Black, R., *et al.*, Obligations (*Stair Encyclopaedia*, Vol. 15).

McBryde, W. W., "Donoghue v. Stevenson: The Story of the 'Snail in the Bottle' Case" in Obligations in Context (1990).
McKechnie, H., Delict and Quasi-delict (*Stair Encyclopaedia*, Vol. 20).

Powles, D. G., "Product Liability—A Novel Dimension in Scotland" in Obligations in Context (1990).

Whitty, N. R., Nuisance (*Stair Encyclopaedia*, Vol. 14).
Wilson, W. A., "The analysis of negligence" in Introductory Essays on the Law of Scotland (2nd ed., 1984).
Wilson, W. A., "Mapping Economic Loss" in Obligations in Context (1990).

ARTICLES

Abel, R. L. A., "A Critique of Torts" (1994) 1 Tort L. Rev. 99
Adams, J., "Is there a tort of unfair competition?" 1985 J.B.L. 26.
Adams, J. and Brownsword, R., "The Aliakmon' and the Hague rules," 1990 J.B.L. 23.
Allison, J. R. J., "Limitation of actions in Child abuse cases" [1996] J.P.I.L. 19.
Allen, D., "Local authority liability for defective premises" (1985) 274 E.G. 657.
Amin, S. H., "Extending the neighbourhood" 1982 S.L.T. (News) 61.
Anderson, P., "Making Insurers Pay for Joyriders" [1996] J.P.I.L. 29.
Andrews, N. H., "'Occidere' and the 'Lex Aquila'", 1987 C.L.J. 315.
Armstrong, N., "ADR and the Public Interest in Personal Injury" [1994] J.P.I.L. 178.
Armstrong, N. and Tucker, A., "Class Struggles" [1996] J.P.I.L. 94.
Arnott, J. M., "Defects in building and pure economic loss" (1989) 34 J.L.S. 183.
Ashcroft, S., "Law Commision Paper No. 224: Structured Settlements and Interim and
    Provisional Damages — A practitioners review" [1995] J.P.I.L. 3.
Ashworth, A., "Punishment and compensation: Victims, offenders and the state" (1986)
    6 O.J.L.S. 86.

Bailey, S. H. and Bowman, M. J., "The policy/operational dichotomy—a cuckoo in the
    next" 1986 C.L.J. 430.
Balen, P., "Multi-party Actions and the Legal Aid Board" [1996] J.P.I.L. 231.
Bates, F., "What must be foreseen?" 1970 S.L.T. (News) 97.
Beaumont, P. R., "Jurisdiction in delict in Scotland" (1983) 28 J.L.S. 528.
Bennett, S., "Loss of society awards: quid juris?" 1982 S.L.T. (News) 101.
Black, J. and Todd, S., "Accident Compensation and the Barring of Actions for Damages"
    (1993) 1 Tort L. Rev. 197.
Black, R., "Delict and the conflict of laws" 1968 J.R. 40.
Black, R., "A historical survey or delictual liability in Scotland for personal injuries and
    death" (1975) 8 C.I.L.J.S.A. 46, 189, 316; (1976) 9 C.I.L.J.S.A. 57.
Black, R., "Styles for averring jurisdiction under the 1982 Act" 1987 S.L.T. (News) 1.
Blackie, J., "Enrichment and Wrongs in Scots Law" 1992 Acta Juridicta 23.
Blackie, J., "Liability as Occupier to User of a Right of Way" 1994 S.L.T. (News) 349.
Blaikie, J., "Product liability" (1987) 32 J.L.S. 325.
Blaikie, J., "Negligent solicitors and disappointed beneficiaries" 1989 S.L.T. (News)
    317.
Blaikie, J., "Provisional Damages: A progress report" 1991 J.L.S. 109.
Blaikie, J., "Injured Workers and the Consumer Protection Act 1987" 1993 S.L.T. (News)
    153.
Blaikie, J., "Personal Injuries Claims: Damages in foreign currency" 1993 S.L.T. (News)
    184.
Blaikie, J., "The Dilatory Solicitor and the Disappointed Legatee" 1993 S.L.T. (News)
    329.
Blaikie, J. "Personal Injury Claims: the valuation of services" 1994 S.L.T. (News) 167.
Blaikie, J., "Nervous Shock: Traumatised fellow workers and bystanders" 1994 S.L.T.
    (News) 297.
Blaikie, J., "Assessment of Pension Rights in Personal Injuries Claims" 1995 J.R. 40.
Blaikie, J., "Foreign Torts and Choice of Law Flexibility" 1995 S.L.T. (News) 23.
Blaikie, J., "Professional Negligence: the dilatory solicitor and the disappointed legatee"
    1996 S.L.P.Q. 245.
Blom-Cooper, L., "The right to be let alone" (1989) 34 J.L.S. 402.
Boch, C. and Lane, R., "A New Remedy in Scots Law: Damages from the Crown for
    breach of Community Law (News) 1992 S.L.T." 145.
Bolton, R., "Other Approaches to Valuing Loss of Pension Benefits" [1995] J.P.I.L.
    216.
Bonnington, A. J., "Privacy: Letting the right alone" 1992 S.L.T. (News) 289.
Bonnington, A. J., "The Defamation Bill" (1996) 41 J.L.S. 102.
Brodie, D., "Pursuing the Police" 1995 J.R. 292.

Brodie, D., "Primary and Secondary Nervous Shock" 1995 Rep. L.B. 5–2.
Brodie, D., "Public Authorities and the Duty of Care" 1996 J.R. 127.
Brodie, D., "Undermining Murphy" 1996 Rep. L.B. 8–3.
Brodie, D., "Subsidiarity and Subsidence" 1996 Rep. L.B. 9–3.
Buckley, R., "Liability in tort for breach of statutory duty" (1984) 100 L.Q.R. 204.

Cameron, J. T., "Intimidation and the right to strike" 1964 S.L.T. (News) 81.
Campbell, E., "The Uninsured Driver, the MIB and the Insurance Disk System" (1994) 39 J.L.S. 170.
Cane, P., "Economic loss in tort: is the pendulum out of control?" 1989 M.L.R. 200.
Cane, P., "Does No-fault have a Future?" [1994] J.P.I.L. 302.
Cane, P., "Tortious Interference with Contractual Remedies" (1995) 111 L.Q.R. (Note) 400.
Capper, D., "Damages for Breach of the Equitable Duty of Confidence" 1994 L.S. 313.
Carey Miller, D.L., "A Statutory Substitute for Scienter" 1973 J.R. 61.
Carey Miller, D. L., "The Scottish institutional writers on animal liability" 1974 J.R. 1.
Carey Miller, D. L., "The use of Roman law in Scotland: A reply" 1975 J.R. 64.
Carey Miller, D. L., "Defamation by a judge" 1980 J.R. 88.
Carey Miller, D. L., "Privacy: Interception of communications: Could Scots law have a remedy" 1980 S.L.T. 209.
Carey Miller, D. L. and Lardy, H., "Calcutt II: Comments from a Scots perspective" 1993 S.L.T. (News) 199.
Carling, C., "Damages for Pain Suffering and Loss of Amenity" [1994] J.P.I.L. 108.
Carty, H., "Intentional violation of economic interests: the limits of common law liability" (1988) 104 L.Q.R. 242.
Cassimatis, A. E., "Defamation — The Constitutional public officer defence" (1996) Tort L. Rev. 27.
Cheer, U., "New Zealand Court of Appeal Rejects the "Murphy" Approach to Tort Liability for Defective Buildings" (1995) Tort L. Rev. 90.
Clark, A., "Liability for defective products" (1981) 26 J.L.S. 398.
Clark, A., "U.S. product liability" (1982) 27 J.L.S. 514.
Clark, A., "Conceptual basis of product liability" (1985) 48 M.L.R. 325.
Clark, A., "Product liability: The new rules" 1987 S.L.T. (News) 257.
Clarke, H., "Civil ability of public authorities" (1986) 136 N.L.J. 435, 495.
Clifford, P. and Sharp, C., "Negligence, Duty, Economic Loss and Policy" (Note) (1995) Tort L. Rev. 169.
Clive, E. M., "The action for passing-off" 1963 J.R. 117.
Colbey, R., "Personal Injury Claims arising out of Food Poisoning" [1994] J.P.I.L. 294.
Collins, R., "Striking out for want of Prosecution: The end of acquiescence estoppel?" [1994] J.P.I.L. 97.
Convery, J., "Subcontractors and the Contractual Matrix" 1996 Rep. L.B. 9–10.
Craig, P. P., "Negligence in the exercise of a statutory power" (1978) 94 L.Q.R. 428.
Cross, G., "Does only the Careless Polluter Pay?" (1995) 111 L.Q.R. 445.
Cullen, W.D., "The Liability of the Good Samaritan" 1995 J.R. 20.

Davidson, F. P., "Insurers—Duty of disclosure and duty of care" 1988 S.L.T. (News) 73.
Davies, I., "Wrongful Dispositions of Motor Vehicles — A Legal Quagmire" [1995] J.B.L. 36.
Davies, M., "The road from Morocco: Polemis, Donoghue, No-fault" (1982) 45 M.L.R. 534.
Davies, M., "The end of the Affair: Duty of care and liability insurance" 1989 L.S. 67.
Desmond, A., "Surgery Through the Keyhole" [1996] J.P.I.L. 135.
Devereux, J. A., "Actions for Wrongful Birth" (1996) Tort L. Rev. 107.
Dickinson, I., "Still no Interdicts against the Crown" 1994 S.L.T. (News) 217.
Downie, G. H., "New Right to Damages in Community Law" (1992) 37 J.L.S. 424.
Doyle, J. J., "The Liability of Public Authorities" (1994) 1 Tort L. Rev. 189.
Duff, A., "Civil Actions and Sporting Injuries sustained Professional Footballers" 1994 S.L.T. (News) 175.

Duff, P., "Criminal Injuries Compensation, Nervous Shock and Secondary Victims" 1992 S.L.T. (News) 311.

Duff, P., "The 1996 Criminal Injuries Compensation Scheme" 1996 S.L.T. 221, 239.

Dugdale, A. M., "Public Authority Liability: To what standard?" (1994) 1 Tort L. Rev. 143.

Duncan Wallace, I.N., "Negligence and defective buildings: confusion confounded?" (1989) 105 L.Q.R. 46.

Duncan Wallace, I. N., "No Somersault after Murphy: New Zealand follows Canada" (1995) 111 L.Q.R. 285.

Dwyer, J. A., "Comedy of Errors (Comment on White v. Jones and a similar Australian case now heard on appeal by the High Court there)" (1996) Tort L. Rev. 77.

Dwyer, J. L., "Solicitors Duties in Tort to Persons other than their Clients" (1994) 1 Tort L. Rev. 29.

Eden, S., "Structured Settlements" 1996 Rev. L. B. 11–3.

Elliot, R. C., "Recent Developments in English Law: Negligence: The tide turns" 1993 S.L.T. (News) 141.

Elliot, R. C., "Recent Developments in English Law: Libel: Free speech, privacy and reputation" 1993 S.L.T. (News) 223.

Elliot, W. A., "What is culpa?" (1954) 66 J.R. 6.

Elliot, W. A., "Reparation and the English tort of negligence" (1952) 64 J.R. 1.

Epp, J. and Stone, P. R. "Selected Aspects of Bystander Recovery Law in Texas and England" [1996] J.P.I.L. 203.

Ervine, W. C. H., "Product liability and Part 1 of the Consumer Protection Act 1987" 1988 ScoLAG Bul. 21.

Ervine, W. C. H., "Multi-party Actions" 1995 S.L.T. (News) 207.

Ewing, K., "Interdicts in labour law" 1980 S.L.T. (News) 121.

Feenan, D. K., "Medical Negligence (Hunter v. Hanley 35 years on: A reply)" 1991 S.L.T. 321.

Fennell, S., "Access to Justice for Personal Injury Litigants" [1994] J.P.I.L. 30.

Fergusson, P. R., "Pharmaceutical Products Liability" 1992 J.R. 226.

Fergusson, P.R., "Compensation for alleged Vaccine Injury" (1994) 39 J.L.S. 80.

Fergusson, P. W., "Liability in negligence for trespassing criminals" 1987 S.L.T. (News) 233.

Field, D., "Negligent Misrepresentation: A suitable case for treatment" 1980 S.L.T. 173.

Field, D., "Civil evidence: A quantum leap" 1988 S.L.T. (News) 349.

Field, D., "Going it alone" 1989 S.L.T. (News) 216.

Fleming, "Products Liability" Paisley Papers.

Fleming, J. G., "Economic Loss in Canada" (1993) 1 Tort L. Rev. 68.

Fleming, J. G., "Once More: Tort liability for structural defects" (1995) 111 L.Q.R. 362.

Fleming, J. G., "Tort in a Contractual Matrix" (1995) 3 Tort L. Rev. 12.

Fleming, J. G., "The Fall of the Crippled Giant (Rylands v. Fletcher)" (1995) 3 Tort L. Rev. 56.

Forte, A., "Disclaiming liability for negligent property surveys" 1986 S.L.T. (News) 293.

Forte, A., "Negligent misrepresentations" (1988) 33 J.L.S. 93.

Fridman, G.H.L., "Interference with Trade or Business" (1993) 1 Tort L. Rev. 19, 99.

Gardiner, D., "Market Value of Needed Services as the Fair and Reasonable Value" (1993) 1 Tort L. Rev. 233.

Garrett, G, "Speculative Actions Insurance" (1996) 41 J.L.S. 423.

Gething, M., "The action in unjust enrichment to recover the proceeds of a tort" (1995) Tort L. Rev. 123.

Giles, M. and Szyszczak, E., "Negligence and Defective Buildings: Demolishing the foundations of Anns?" 1991 L.S. 85.

Goddard, C., "European Law: New origins for health and safety regulation" 1994 J.P.I.L. 5.

Gordon, M., "The Epidemiological Trap" (1996) 41 J.L.S. 397.

Gordon, W. M., "Householders' liabilities" (1982) 27 J.L.S. 253.
Gore, A., "Meeting the Challanges of Expert Evidence" [1996] J.P.I.L. 247.
Gow, J. J., "Delict and private international law" (1949) 65 L.Q.R. 313.
Gow, J. J., "Is culpa amoral?" (1953) 65 J.R. 17.
Graham, A., "Economic Heirs: Concurrent Liability" 1995 Rep. L. B. 4–4 (5–3).
Grainger, C. J., "Wrongful Life: A wrong without a remedy" (1994) 1 Tort L. Rev. 164.
Gregor, S. and Mays, R., "Health and Safety — the employer's common law duty of care redefined" 1995 S.L.T. (News) 323.
Greive, E. E. M., "Chronic Multi-site Arm Pain Reports" [1996] J.P.I.L. 135.
Gretton, G. L., "Breach of Arrestment" 1991 J.R. 96.
Griffiths, J. R. "Medical Negligence" 1995 S.L.P.Q. 25.
Grubb, A., "Contraceptive advice and doctors—a law unto themselves?" 1988 C.L.J. 12.

Haberman, P., "The Changing World of Multipliers" [1996] J.P.I.L. 41.
Hadden, J., "Contract tort and crime: the forms of legal thought" (1971) 87 L.Q.R. 240.
Hedley, S., "Group Personal Injury Litigation and Public Opinion" 1994 L.S. 70.
Heuston, "Overview of the Law of Negligence" Paisley Papers.
Hogg, K., "Relational loss, the exclusory rule and the High Court of Australia" (1995) 3 Tort L. Rev. 26.
Hogg, Martin A., "Privacy: A valuable and Protected Interest in Scots Law" 1992 S.L.T. 349.
Hill, J., "Litigation and negligence" (1986) 6 O.J.L.S. 183.
Holyoak, J., "Accountancy and negligence" 1986 J.B.L. 120.
Holyoak, J., "Economic loss in product and premises liability cases" 1988 J.B.L. 139.
Holyoak, J. "Raising the Standard of Care" 1990 L.S. 201.
Holyoak, J. and Mazzocchetti, F., "The legal Protection of Economic Interests" (1993) 1 Tort L. Rev. 185.
Honoré, T., "*Hedley Byrne & Co. Ltd.* v. *Heller & Partners*" (1965) 8 J.S.P.T.L. 284.
Hoyano, L. C. H., "The Dutiful Tortfeasor in the House of Lords" (1995) 3 Tort L. Rev. 63.
Howarth, D., "My Brother's Keeper? Liability for Acts of Third Parties" 1994 L.S. 88.
Hudson, A. H., "Crime, tort and reparation — what solution?" 1984 S.L.T. (News) 321.
Hudson, A. H., "Crime, Tort and Reparation: A common solution" 1992 S.L.T. (News) 203.

Ingman, T., "Rise and fall of the doctrine of common employment" 1978 J.R. 106.
Ingman, T., "A history of the defence of volenti non fit injuria" 1981 J.R. 1.

Jackson, B. S., "Liability for animals in Scottish legal literature" 1977 J.R. 139.
Jaffey, A. E., "*Volenti non fit injuria*" 1985 C.L.J. 87.
James, M. F., "Professional negligence and the reasonableness test" 1987 J.B.L. 286.

Kamba, W. J., "Concept of duty of care and aquilian liability in Roman Dutch law" 1975 J.R. 252.
Kidner, R., "Resiling from the *Anns* principle: the variable nature of proximity in negligence" (1987) 7 L.S. 319.
Kidner, R., "Remoteness of Damage: the duty interest theory and the re-interpretation of the Wagon Mound" 1989 L.S. 1.
Kidner, R., "The Variable Standard of Care, Contributory Negligence and Volenti" 1991 L.S. 1.
Kilbrandon, Lord, "The Law of Privacy in Scotland" (1971) 2 Camb. L.R. 35.
Kinloch, D., "Slippery Substances" 1995 Rep. L. B. 4–7.
Kostal, R. W., "Currents in the Counter-reformation: Illegality and the duty of care in Canada and Australia" (1995) Tort L. Rev. 100.

Langstaff, B., "Upper Limb Disorders: Work related or unrelated?" [1994] J.P.I.L. 14.
Laurie, G. T., "Damages, Duty and Hamilton v. Fife Health Board" 1994 J.R. 110.
Laurie, G. T., "Privacy, Paucity and the Press" 1993 S.L.T. (News) 285.
Lazarowicz, M., "Health and Safety at Work" (1996) 41 J.L.S. 104.

Lewis, R., "Insurers Agreements not to Enforce Strict Legal Rights" 1985 48 M.L.R. 275.

Logie, J. G., "Proof of causation in medical negligence cases" 1988 S.L.T. (News) 25.

Logie, J. G., "Rethinking negligence" 1988 S.L.T. (News) 185.

Logie, J. G., "Special relationships, reasonable foreseeability and distinct possibilities" 1988 J.R. 77.

Logie, J. G., "Affirmative action in the law of tort: the case of the duty to warn" 1989 C.L.J. 115.

Logie, J. G., "The final demise of Junior Books?" 1989 J.R. 5.

Logie, J.G., "Liability in Negligence of Company Accountants and Auditors" 1991 S.L.T. (News) 169.

McBryde, W. W., "The advantages of fault" 1975 J.R. 32.

McBryde, N. J. and Hughes, A., "Hedley Byrne in the House of Lords" 1995 L.S. 376.

MacCormack, G., "Culpa tenet suos auctores: The application of a principle" 1973 J.R. 159.

MacCormack, G., "Culpa in the Scots law of reparation" 1974 J.R. 13.

McEvoy, S. A., "When You have no Right to Remain Silent: Tort liability for sexually-transmitted diseases" (1994) 1 Tort L. Rev. 175.

McEwan, V., "Playing the game: Negligence in sport" (1986) 130 S.J. 581.

McGrade, T., "Actions against The Police: Some Practical Points" 1995 Rep. L.B. 6–4.

McGrath, M., "The recovery of pure economic loss" (1985) 3 O.J.L.S. 350.

McGuire, F., "The Damages (Scotland) Act 1993" 1993 S.L.T. (News) 245.

Mackay, R. E., "The Resuscitation of Assythment?" 1992 J.R. 242.

McKendrick, E., "Pirelli Re-examined" 1991 L.S. 326.

Mackenzie S., "Liability of common carriers" (1926) 38 J.R. 205.

Mackintosh, J., "The edict nautae caupones stabularii" (1891) 3 J.R. 306.

MacKintosh, J., "Wee McGlen and the action of passing-off" 1982 S.L.T. (News) 225.

McLaren, J. P. S., "Nuisance law and the industrial revolution" (1983) 3 O.J.L.S. 155.

McLean, A. W. D., "When Stress Fractures" 1996 Rep. L. B. 12–3.

McLean, S. A., "Compensation and medical injury" (1981) 63 ScoLAG Bul. 361.

McManus, F., "The Duty of Care and Alcohol Abuse" 1995 J.R. 313.

McManus, F., "Bye-bye Rylands — Again!" 1995 J.R. (Note) 394.

McManus, F., "Culpa and the law of Nuisance" 1995 J.R. (Note) 462.

McManus, F., "Nervous Shock — Back to square one?" 1996 J.R. 159.

McMillan, A., "Scotland — Last colony of empire?" 1996 S.L.T. (News) 19.

MacQueen, H. L., "The Wee McGlen case: representations of Scottishness—passing-off and unfair trading" (1983) v. E.I.P.R. 18.

MacQueen, H. L., "Latent Defects, Collateral Warranties and Time Bar" 1991 S.L.T. (News) 77, 91, 99.

Malcolm, A. C. (The Hon David K.), "The High Court and Informed Consent: The Bolam principle abandoned" (1994) 1 Tort L. Rev. 81.

Markesinis, B. S., "An expanding tort law—the price of a rigid contract law" (1987) 103 L.Q.R. 354.

Markesinis, B. S., "Negligence, nuisance and affirmative duties of action" (1989) 105 L.Q.R. 104.

Markesinis, B. S., "The not-so-dissimilar tort and delict" (1977) 93 L.Q.R. 78.

Mayou, R., "Psychological, Quality of Life and Legal Consequences of Road Traffic injury" [1995] J.P.I.L. 277.

Meakin, T., "The Role of "Knowledge" under the Limitation Act 1980 etc." [1996] J.P.I.L. 12.

Middleton, K. W. B. "Liability without fault" 1960 J.R. 72.

Mildred, M., "Group Actions Present and Future" (1994) J.P.I.L. 276.

Mildred, M., "The use of the Brussels Convention in Group Actions" [1996] J.P.I.L. 121.

Miller, K., "Nuisance and reasonable care" (1985) 16 J.S.P.L.P. 79.

Milligan, R., "Approaching Future Wage Loss" 1995 S.L.T. (News) 173.

Milligan, R., "Civil Juries on Trial" 1995 Rep. L.B. 4–6.
Morris-Coole, C., "Epilepsy: Litigation considerations and the claim for general damages" [1996] J.P.I.L. 215.
Morrisson, J. M., "Pleading alternative cases" 1987 S.L.T. (News) 193.
Mullany, N. J. "Recovery for Psychiatric Injury by Report: Another small step forward" (1996) Tort L. Rev. 96.
Murphy, J., "Negligently Inflicted Psychiatric Harm: A reappraisal" 1995 L.S. 415.

Newdick, C., "The future of negligence in product liability" (1987) 103 L.Q.R. 288.
Newdick, C., "The development risk defence" 1988 C.L.J. 455.
Norrie, K., "Actionability of birth" 1983 S.L.T. (News) 121.
Norrie, K., "Common practice and the standard of care in medical negligence" 1985 J.R. 145.
Norrie, K., "Damages for birth of a child" 1985 S.L.T. (News) 69.
Norrie, K., "Hurts to character, honour and reputation" 1985 J.R. 163.
Norrie, K., "Informed consent and duty of care" 1985 S.L.T. (News) 289.
Norrie, K., "Liability for failed sterilisation" 1986 S.L.T. (News) 145.
Norrie, K., "Liability of solicitors to third parties" 1988 S.L.T. (News) 309; 317.
Norrie, K., "Wrongful life in Scots Law: No right, no remedy" 1990 J.R. 205.
Norrie, K., "Defamation, Negligence and Employers References" (1994) 39 J.L.S. 418.
Norrie, K., "The Defamation Act" 1996 S.L.T. (News) 311.

O'Brien, L. S., "The Validity of the Diagnosis of Post Traumatic Stress Disorder" 1994 J.P.I.L. 257.
O'Carroll, M., "Nervous Shock: Proposals for reform" (1995) 40 J.L.S. 231.
O'Donovan, M., "Risk Management and the Medical Profession" [1996] J.P.I.L. 51.
Olowofoyeku, A., "The Crumbling Citadel: Absolute judicial immunity derationalised" 1990 L.S. 271.
O'Neil, A., "Francovich Damages and the Working Time Directive" 1996 S.L.T. (News) 381.
Oughton, D., "Liability in tort for economic loss suffered by the consumer of defective goods" 1987 J.B.L. 370.

P.F., "Nuisance and negligence" 1986 J.R. 107.
Palmer, N., "Quasi-Bailment and Possessory Title" (1995) Tort L. Rev. 186.
Peysner, J., "Health Care Litigation: Examination, diagnosis and prognosis" [1995] J.P.I.L. 91.
Pheasant, S., "Repetitive Strain Injury — Towards a clarification of the points at issue" [1994] J.P.I.L. 223.
Phillips, A. F., "Further reflections on medical causation" 1988 S.L.T. (News) 325.
Phillips, A. F., "Medical negligence and no-fault compensation" (1989) 34 J.L.S. 239.
Phillips, A. F., "Lost Chances in Delict" 1995 J.R. 401.
Phillips, J. and Coleman, A., "Passing off and the common field of activity" (1985) 101 L.Q.R. 242.
Pickering, J. and Armstrong, N., "Taking Costs Seriously" [1995] J.P.I.L. 21.
Pollock, A. S., "Criminal Injuries Compensation: The tariff" (1996) 41 J.L.S. 93.
Pugh, C., "Poisoning and Civil Compensation" [1996] J.P.I.L. 192.

Redmond-Cooper, R., "Structured Settlements and Provisional Damages: Harmonisation perspectives" [1995] J.P.I.L. 12.
Reed, A., "Carer's Recompense held on Trust" [1994] J.P.I.L. 215.
Reed, A., "Professional Liability of Agents in Tort" (1996) Tort L. Rev. 62.
Reid, C. T., "Damages for deliberate abuse of power" 1988 S.L.T. (News) 121.
Rennie, R., "Negligence Instructions and the Lender's need to Know" (1994) 39 J.L.S. 135.
Reynolds, F. M. B., "Tort actions in contractual situations" (1985) 11 N.Z.L.R. 215.
Ritchie, A., "Smith v. Manchester Awards: How do courts assess loss of capacity on the labour market" [1994] J.P.I.L. 103.

Ritchie, A., "Medical Evidence in Whiplash Claims involving Soft Tissue Injuries to the Neck" [1995] J.P.I.L. 260.
Robertson, G., "Duty of Care and the Negligent Fireraiser" 1980 S.L.T. 13.
Rodger, A., "Spuilzie in the modern world" 1970 S.L.T. (News) 33.
Rodger, A., "Labeo, Proculus and the ones that got away" (1972) 88 L.Q.R. 402.
Rodger, A., "Antenatal injury" 1974 J.R. 83.
Rodger, A., "Mrs Donoghue and Alfenus Varrus" 1988 C.L.P. 1.
Rodger, B., "The Halley: Holed and now Sunk: Part III of the Private International law (Miscellaneous Provisions) Act 1995".
Rodger, B. L., "Bouygnes and the Scottish Choice of Law Rules in Delict" 1995 S.L.P.Q. 58.
Rowley, J. J., "A Guide to Pension Loss Calculation" [1995] J.P.I.L. 107.
Rowley, J. J., "An updated guide to Pension Loss Calculation" [1995] J.P.I.L. 212.
Russell, J. A., "Further observations—Pleading alternative cases" 1987 S.L.T. (News) 397.
Russell, P., "The commercial exploitation of fictitious names" (1980) 130 N.L.J. 256.

Sandison, D., "Medical Negligence Claims: The paucity of funding?" (1995) 40 J.L.S. 309.
Shaffer, N., "Volenti non fit injuria" 1965 S.L.T. (News) 133.
Shearer, A., "Delictual liability for economic loss" 1983 S.L.T. (News) 157.
Slater, C., "House valuations and surveys" (1988) 33 J.L.S. 89.
Slesenger, J., "Overseas Medical Reports" [1995] J.P.I.L. 33.
Slesenger, J., "Chronic Back Pain" [1996] J.P.I.L. 46.
Smith, J. C. and Burns, P., "Donoghue v. Stevenson—the not-so-golden anniversary" (1983) 46 M.L.R. 147.
Smith, T. B., "Damn injuria again" 1984 S.L.T. (News) 85.
Sopinka, Justice J., "The Liability of Public Authorities: Drawing the line" (1993) 1 Tort L. Rev. 123.
Spink, P., "Brasserie du Pecheur: Defining the boundaries of state liability for breach of community law" (1996) 41 J.L.S. 355.
Spink, P., "British Beer and Brussels" (1996) 41 J.L.S. 395.
Stanton, K. M., "Insurance, the Hedley Byrne Principle and Concurrent Liability (1995) Tort L. Rev. 85.
Stapleton, J., "Products liability reform—real or illusory" (1986) 6 O.J.L.S. 392.
Stapleton, J., "The gist of negligence" (1988) 104 L.Q.R. 213, 389.
Stapleton, J., "Duty of Care: Peripheral parties and alternative opportunities for detterrence" (1995) 111 L. Q. R. 301.
Steele, J., "Private Law and the Environment: Nuisance in context" 1995 L.S. 236.
Stein, P., "The actio de effusis vel dejectis and the concept of quasi-delict in Scots law" (1955) 4 I.C.L.Q. 356.
Stephenson, I. S., "Goodbye Junior Books" (1988) 138 N.L.J. 483.
Stevenson, D., "Repetitive Strain Injury" (1994) 39 J.L.S. 49.
Stewart, A., "Belated Acceptence of Judicial tender and Defender's expenses" 1994 S.L.T. (News) 159.
Stewart, A., "Damages for the Birth of a Child" (1995) 40 J.L.S. 298.
Stewart, A., "A Live Issue — Damages for wrongful birth" (1996) 41 J.L.S. 443.
Stewart, J. B., "Football: Civil aspects" 1981 S.L.T. (News) 157.
Stewart, Q., "The law of passing-off—a Scottish perspective" (1983) v. E.I.P.R. 64.
Stewart, W. J., "Economic loss from damage to others' property" 1987 S.L.T. (News) 145.
Stewart, W. J., "Lawburrows: Elegant remedy or absurd form" 1988 S.L.T. (News) 181.
Stewart, W. J., "A note on the liability of pupils in delict" 1989 S.L.T. (News) 404.
Stewart, W. J., "Ski-ing and the law: the first case" (1990) 35 J.L.S. 27.
Stewart, W. J., "Smith's Question Mark, Walker's Exhortation and Quasi-delict" 1990 J.R. 71.
Stewart, W. J., "Reparation — Road traffic accidents" (1994) 39 J.L.S. 211.
Stewart, W. J., "Reparation — Prescription and limitation" (1994) 39 J.L.S. 374.

Stewart, W. J., "Future Los and Employability Some preliminary thoughts" 1995 Rep. L.B. 1–5.

Stewart, W. J., "Personal Injuries and CRU" 1995 Rep. L. B. 6–5.

Stewart, W. J.., "Connected persons from the limitation buster" 1996 Rep. L. B. 16–9.

Stewart, W. J., "Smoking in the Courts: There may be trouble ahead." 1996 Rep. L.R. 11–4.

Stoppa, A, "The concept of defectiveness in the Consumer Protection Act 1987: a critical analysis" 1992 L.S 210.

Stuart, S., "Bad neighbours" 1984 S.L.T. (News) 45.

Stuart, S. L., "Widening the Scope of the Employment" 1980 S.L.T. (News) 241.

Stuart, S. L., "Title to sue in respect of damage to property" 1986 S.L.T. (News) 257.

Styles, S.C., "Two flaws in the law of Defamation" 1991 S.L.T. (News) 31.

Summers, A., "Assignation of Collateral Warranties" 1993 S.L.T. (News) 181.

Sutherland, L., "No fishing: Recovery of medical records pre-litigation" 1995 Rep. L. B. 1–3.

Sutherland, L., "The Brain Damaged Baby" 1995 Rep. L. B. 2–3.

Sutherland, L., "Failed Sterilisation" 1995 Rep. L. B. 3–4.

Sutherland, L., "Medical Negligence — A Relationship of Mutual Trust" 1995 Rep. B. 5–4.

Sutherland, L., "Medical Negligence — A Single Standard of Care" (1995) Rep. L. B. 6–11.

Sutherland, R. D., "Optional Procedure in the Court of Session" 1991 S.L.T. (News) 17.

Tan, C. G. S., "Volenti Non Fit Injuria: An alternative framework" (1995) Tort L. Rev. 208.

Taylor, N., "Limitation of Liability of Aircarriers to Aircrash victims — Has the Warsaw convention reached its retirement age?" [1994] J.P.I.L. 113.

Teff, H., "Liability for negligently inflicted nervous shock" (1983) 99 L.Q.R. 100.

Teff, H., "The Requirement of "Sudden Shock" in Liability for Negligently Inflicted Psychiatric Damage" (1996) Tort L. Rev. 44.

Tetley, W., "Choice of Law — Tort and Delict — Common Law/Civil Law/Maritime Law — Maritime Torts" (1993) 1 Tort L. Rev. 42.

Thomson, J., "Who could sue on the Lex Aquila?" (1975) 91 L.Q.R. 207.

Thomson, J., "Delictual Liability Between Parties to a Contract" 1994 S.L.T. (News) 29.

Thomson, J., "Delictual Liability for Pure Economic Loss: Recent developments" 1995 S.L.T. (News) 139.

Tippler, J. H. and Christensen, M. J., "The Possibility of Bringing a United States Lawsuit for Product Liability Damages Arising in the United Kingdom" [1995] J.P.I.L. 185.

Todd, S., "Negligence liability of public authorities: divergence in the common law" (1986) 102 L.Q.R. 370.

Todd, S., "Defective Property: The turn of the Privy Council" (1996) Tort L. Rev. 91.

Upton, M., "Crown Liability in Damages under Community Law" 1996 S.L.T. (News) 175, 211.

W. A. W. "The Product Liability Directive" 1980 S.L.T. (News) 1.

Wacks, R., "The poverty of privacy" (1980) 96 L.Q.R. 73.

Waddams, S. M., "Causation in Canada and Australia" (1993) 1 Tort L. Rev. 75.

Waddams, S. M., "Further Reflections on Economic Loss: A Canadian perspective" (1994) 1 Tort L. Rev 116.

Wade, G., "The Defamation Bill" 1996 Rep. L. B. 9–2.

Wade, P., "Sheriff Court Reparation — A nightmare" 1995 Rep. L.B. 2–2.

Wade, P., "High Valuations versus Bill Lending" 1995 Rep L. B. 4–2.

Wade, P., "Time Bar in Disease Cases" 1995 Rep. L. B. 6–2.

Walker, D. M., "The development of reparation" (1952) 64 J.R. 101.

Walker, D. M., "Remoteness of damage and Re Polemis" 1961 S.L.T. (News) 37.

Walker, D. M., "Spuilzie" 1949 S.L.T. (News) 136.

Walker, D. M., "Strict liability in Scotland" (1954) 66 J.R. 231.

Walker, D. M., "Verbal injury—Convicium or defamation?" 1970 J.R. 157.

Walker, E. D., "Reflections on a Leading Case: Hughes v. Lord Advocate" (1992) 37 J.L.S. 394.

Walker, I., "Criminal Injuries Compensation: A government betrayal" [1994] J.P.I.L. 47.

Wallace, I. N. D., "Negligence and Economic Loss: A view of the future" (1993) 1 Tort L. Rev. 152.

Wallace, I. N. D., "Murphy Rejected: The Bryan v. Maloney Landmark" (1995) Tort L. Rev. 231.

Watchman, P., "What the law says about burst pipes" 1987 Sco-LAG 10.

Wei, G., "Surreptitious Takings of Confidential Information" 1992 L.S. 302.

Weir, T., "A Damnosa Hereditas?" (Notes White v. Jones) 1995 (111) L.Q.R. 357.

Wheat, K., "Nervous Shock: proposals for reform" [1994] J.P.I.L. 207.

Wheeler, J. and Ross, M., "The Role of the Non-lawyer in Criminal Justice — Reparation and mediation" 1993 S.L.T. (News) 365.

Wilkinson, A. B. and Forte, A. M., "Pure Economic Loss–A Scottish Perspective" 1985 J.R. 1.

Williams, G., "The risk principle" (1961) 77 L.Q.R. 179.

Williams, J. M., "Bringing Proceedings in the U.S. for English Plaintiffs — the obstacle of Forum non-conveniens" [1996] J.P.I.L. 2.

Williams, J. M., and Mead, P., "Abolition of the Double Actionability Rule — Questions still to be answered" [1996] J.P.I.L. 112.

Wilton, G. W., "Reminiscences of the Scottish bar: Striking slander suits" (1944) 56 J.R. 11.

Woolman, S. E., "Defaming the dead" 1981 S.L.T. (News) 29.

Young, A. R. W., "Secondary Action: recent developments" 1991 S.L.T. (News) 367.

Young, A. R. W., "Rights of Relief" 1992 S.L.T. (News) 225.

Zeeman, (Hon. Justice) W. P. M., "Contributory Negligence — A defence limited to actions in Tort?" (1994) 1 Tort L. Rev. 16.

THE DELICT STUDENT AND INTERNET RESOURCES

This book being for students you might know more about the internet than many of your teachers. However, many lawyers and law teachers have, despite being older dogs, learned the new tricks. I have outlined resources as they have grown elsewhere (see "CyberPetronius" (1995) 40 J.L.S. 317; "CyberPetronius 2" (1996) 41 J.L.S.; "CyberPetronius 3" (1997) 42 J.L.S. 231). I have arranged to have as many World Wide Web links as might be of use to a Scots lawyer appear on the Scots Law Site — this might be the only URL you would have to type — after that you ought to be able to point and click your way through many interesting legal sites: http://www.scotnet.co.uk/als/scotslaw.htm. Most legal resources can be found there or more likely from there. Start by looking at the web pages of the Scottish law schools which are listed.

Merely by way of example of sites you can reach from there are the following. The Web Journal of Current Legal Issues offers the following delict/tort items:
http://www.ncl.ac.uk/~nlawwww/articles4/jones4.html — Liability for Psychiatric Illness More Principle, Less Subtlety?;

http://www.ncl.ac.uk/~nlawwww/articles2/wheat2.html — Law Commission Consultation Paper No 137 — Liability for Psychiatric Illness;
http://www.ncl.ac.uk/~nlawwww/articles1/hedley1.html — Recovering Lost Legacies: *White v. Jones* in the House of Lords;
http://www.ncl.ac.uk/~nlawwww/1996/issue2/mayss2.html — Statutory Reform of Choice of Law in Tort and Delict: A Bitter Pill or a Cure for the Ill?

House of Lords judgments appear immediately on the internet keeping you well ahead of printed sources. While writing this, for example, Lord Hope's speech in *Abnett v. British Airways Plc. (Scotland)* was available: http://www.parliament.the-stationery-office.co.uk/pa/ldl99697/ldjudgmt/jd961214/abnett01.htm. Very many delict/tort cases are available soon after they come out in the *Times Law Reports*: http://www.the-times.co.uk.

United States resources are ample but clearly a diversion for the ordinary student — perhaps not so for the honours student. Try http://oyez.at.nwu.edu/oyez.html for A Supreme Court WWW resource. There is even a site which allows you to hear the original tape recorded speeches of counsel in famous Supreme Court cases like *Roe v. Wade.*

It is not yet the case that the internet will allow you to do your delict course from your bed with the laptop plugged into the phone socket (although it is now possible to take a postgraduate degree this way at the University of Strathclyde), but it is very easy to combine recreation and some serious work. One of the great benefits for students of using these resources is that the tasks of photocopying and notetaking are dramatically eased. Subject always to the limited right you have as a student under the law of copyright it is easy to copy retain and organise citations or quotations for your studies — the mere click and drag of a mouse. While some students may consider the university computer laboratory "nerdy" it is not always so and if you still have the price of a pint of premium lager then it is possible to go to one of the cyber cafes in the main cities, buy a coffee and surf delict. I have only mentioned the World Wide Web because it is the easiest — E:mail and IRC Chat let you communicate with other students beyond your own campus; Usenet has discussion groups on legal topics but I have seldom come across anything worthwhile.

Finally, as you are already a student you could say quite a bit about what it is like to be a law student — find out what someone else thought http://legal-pad.com/dara.html. This is the diary of Dara — a first year law student.

I would be grateful if students and teachers could forward any relevant resources they discover.

INDEX

absolute liability, *see* **strict liability**
actio de effusis vel dejectis, 5.8.2, 5.9.1–4, 5.10.2
actio de positivis vel suspensis, 5.7.6, 5.8.2, 5.10.2
  England and Wales, 5.10.5
actio injuriarum, 2.7.1–5
  invasion of privacy, 21.14.3
actio quod metus causa, 7.12.1
acts of God, 5.1.5, 5.1.10, 22.8.2
aemulationem vicini, 5.11.1–3
alterum non laedere, 9.1.5
animals, *see also* **dogs**
  Animals (Scotland) Act 1987, 6.9.1–7, 18.3.1–4
  common law liability, 18.1.1–8, 18.5.6–7
  England and Wales, 18.4.3
  Exodus, 18.1.6–7
  goring by bulls, 18.1.1-8
  meaning of 'harrying', 18.5.4
  personal injuries, 18.5.1–7
  Stair's Institutions, 18.1.6
  statutory liability, 18.5.1–5
  strict liability, 5.2.3, 5.10.3, 18.5.4
aquae pluviae arcendae, 5.2.5
arrest, police powers, 2.11.2, 3.3.4, 3.3.6–8
arrestment, breach 2.1.12
asbestosis, 1.1.1–3
  compensation, 1.2.1–2
  insurance, 1.2.1
  level of awards, 1.4.16
  speculative actions, 1.11.6
  victims, 1.5.4, 1.6.1–3, 1.7.1–2, 1.8.1–5
assault,
  Bell's Principles, 3.1.3
  by dogs, 18.5.5
  differences with England, 3.1.4
  provocation, 3.1.1–5
assythment, 2.1.12
  abolition, 2.6.3
  decline, 2.7.3
automatism, 22.8.2
Bell's Principles, 2.5.1–4, 5.9.7
  assault, 3.1.3
  quasi-delict, 5.9.5
building control, duty of care, 13.2.6, 14.2.2, 17.4.2
building defects
  contractual standards, 13.2.6

  primary economic loss, 13.3.1–30
burden of proof
  breach of statutory duty, 15.3.7
  causation, 10.3.4
  culpa, 5.3.4
  occupiers liability, 16.2.2
  passing-off, 7.1.3–4
  reasonable practicality, 15.7.4
Calvin, *Lexicon Juridicon,* 5.9.6
careless driving, 20.8.1–8
  limitation of actions, 20.12.1–15
causation, 8.5.1–6, 10.1.1–8
  dermatitis, 10.5.1–7
  medical negligence, 10.6.4
  pneumoconiosis, 10.3.1–5
  reasonable conduct, 10.7.1–5
  statistical evidence, 10.6.4
children
  legal personality, 22.9.4
  unborn children, 22.9.1–7
  wrongful birth, 22.10.2
choice of law, 23.4.1
  defamation, 23.6.1
circumvention, 2.1.12
civil rights, 3.4.2
  arrest and detention, 3.3.1–14
  privacy, 21.14.4
Clydeside Action on Asbestos, 1.5.1, 1.7.2, 1.8.4, 1.8.5, 1.11.10
coal mining
  safe system of work, 19.1.1–9
  statutory duties, 15.1.1–10, 19.1.5
common criminal enterprise
  driving without proper licence, 20.8.1–8
  drunk driving, 20.6.3, 20.6.7, 20.6.12
common property, 5.11.1–6
communications, defamation 21.1.1–5
companies, vicarious liability of directors 22.3.1–4
compensation
  asbestosis, 1.2.1–2
  death, 1.2.1
  no-fault compensation, 1.11.11
competition, *aemulatio vicini,* 5.14.4
confidentiality, 4.1.1–2
  and public interest, 4.2.1
  breaches, 4.1.1–2, 21.1.4.3
  duty of secret intelligence services, 4.3.1–9

consent, defences, 20.7.2
conspiracy
 definition, 7.5.6
 economic embargoes, 7.5.1–23
 industrial disputes, 7.11.2
 intentions, 7.5.22, 7.5.11–13
 malice, 7.5.16, 7.5.18
consumer protection *see also* **product liability**
 1987 Act 17.1.1–9
 manufacturers' duty of care, 8.1.1–24
 Scottish and English laws, 8.1.3, 8.1.13, 8.1.15, 8.1.18, 8.1.21
 strict liability, 5.10.3
contract
 contractual relational loss, 13.10.4
 liability in delict or contract, 2.4.3, 2.11.2, 13.3.10, 13.3.19, 13.4.3, 13.5.4, 13.5.9
 wrongful inducement to breach of contract, 7.7.1–5, 7.9.5–7
contravention 2.1.12
contributory negligence 12.1.39, 22.5.19
 1945 Act, 20.3.1–9
 failure to wear a seatbelt, 20.4.1–4
 or *volenti non fit injuria*, 20.7.2
conversion, torts 6.1.7
convicium 2.7.4
 artistic criticism, 21.11.1–2
 invasion of privacy, 21.14.3
 or verbal injury, 21.13.2
 political opponents, 21.7.1–3, 21.9.1–3
corroboration, pursuers' evidence, 24.7.1–4
court proceedings, privileged reports, 21.14.7
Crown liability, damages under EU law, 15.9.1–38
culpa see **negligence**
customs, evidence of common law custom, 6.5.6
damages *see also* **loss of society; non-patrimonial loss; patrimonial loss; personal injuries; remoteness of damages**
 common criminal enterprise, 20.6.3, 20.6.7, 20.6.12
 Crown liability under EU law for wrongful legislation, 15.9.1–38
 Damages (Scotland) Bill 1992, 1.5.1–4, 1.7.1–2, 1.9.1–18, 1.10.1–20, 1.11.1–17
 defamation, 21.14.6
 distress, 1.3.34, 1.3.36
 economic or physical, 13.6.4
 grave breaches of EU law, 15.9.28
 injuries to unborn children, 22.9.4
 interest, 1.4.32–33

 provisional damages for asbestosis, 1.4.16, 1.10.3
 quantification, 13.2.4
 relatives' grief, 1.3.34, 1.3.36
 Stair Institutions, 2.1.4
 third-party damages, 12.1.1–44
damnum
 basis of English actions for reparation, 3.1.4
 founding jurisdiction, 2.10.2–4
damnum absque injuria, 7.5.9
damnum emergens, 2.1.5
damnum fatale, 5.1.5, 5.1.10, 20.1.5, 20.2.4, 22.8.2
damnum infectum, 5.8.2
dangerous things, 8.1.9, 8.1.11
 heritable property, 17.4.2, 17.4.3
 interference by trespassers, 12.1.33
 intrinsic danger, 9.1.10
deaths *see also* **loss of services; loss of society; loss of support**
 amount of damages for relatives, 1.3.33, 1.4.7–10
 compensation, 1.2.1
 consultation on legal damages, 1.3.41
 effect on personal injury claims, 1.3.13, 1.4.2, 1.4.6–10
 industrial diseases, 1.3.7
 relatives' claims, 1.3.14–16
 statistics of claims, 1.3.6–8
 tactical incentives to delay, 1.3.18, 1.3.24, 1.4.17, 1.4.39, 1.11.4
defamation *see also convicium*
 1996 Act changes, 21.14.7
 characters in novels, 21.3.1–5
 choice of law, 23.6.1
 communications, 21.1.1–5
 culpa, 21.5.1–5
 damages, 21.14.6
 identity of person defamed, 21.5.1–5
 or verbal injury, 21.13.4
 Stair's Institutions, 2.1.7
 transmissibility of claims after death, 1.4.54
defective goods, 17.4.2, 17.4.3
 economic loss, 17.4.2
 jurisdiction, 2.10.1–4
 title to sue for damages, 13.9.1–10
defects *see also* **defective goods**
 design defects, 17.3.5
 distinction between defect and damage, 20.10.2
 heritable property, 17.4.2
 latent defects, 17.4.4, 20.10.1–6
 meaning in Consumer Protection Act, 17.3.1

defences
  consent, 20.7.2
  contributory negligence, 20.3.1–9,
    20.4.1–4
  damnum fatale, 5.1.5, 5.1.10, 20.1.1–8,
    20.2.4, 22.8.2
  development risks, 17.3.1, 17.3.5,
    17.4.5
  ex turpi causa non obitur actio, 20.8.1–8
  fair criticism, 21.11.2
  limitation of actions, 20.12.1–15
  prescription, 20.10.1–6
  volenti non fit injuria, 16.3.4, 16.5.8,
    20.6.1–12, 20.7.2, 22.4.3
deforcement, 2.1.12
delay
  defenders' tactics, 1.3.1–5, 1.3.9–10
  tactical incentives in personal injury
    claims, 1.3.18, 1.3.24, 1.4.17, 1.4.39,
    1.11.4
delegation, duty of care 19.1.3
delict
  Erskine's Institutes, 2.3.1–3
  meaning, 2.5.2
  or breach of contract, 2.4.3, 2.11.2,
    13.3.10, 13.3.19, 13.4.3, 13.5.4,
    13.5.9
  separation from concept of punishment,
    2.5.4
  Stair's Institutions, 2.1.1–12
  terminology, 2.7.1–5
  use as safety net, 5.2.4
delinquence, 2.3.1, 5.9.1
  Stair's Institutions, 2.1.2, 2.1.5, 2.1.11
dermatitis, causation 10.5.1–7
designs, registered designs 7.1.3
detention, 2.11.2, 3.3.1–14
directives
  consumer protection, 17.2.1
  direct effect, 15.9.10, 15.9.20
  failure to implement, 15.9.11–14
  implementation of 85/374, 17.2.1,
    17.3.1
  incorrect implementation, 15.9.25–
    27
  strict liability for failure to implement,
    15.9.11, 15.9.25, 15.9.29, 15.9.33
directors, vicarious liability 22.3.1–4
disclaimers
  effect on duty of care, 13.1.6
  Unfair Contract Terms Act 1977,
    13.2.5
diseases
  death from industrial diseases, 1.3.7
  legal aid for industrial disease actions,
    1.11.8
  limitation of actions, 20.13.2

distress
  damages, 1.3.34
  statutory damages, 1.3.36
dogs, 18.4.2, 18.4.4
  causing personal injuries, 18.5.1–7
  meaning of attack, 18.5.5
  strict liability for dog bites, 18.4.2,
    18.5.3
dolus, 2.7.5, 5.9.6
domicile, 23.1.1
  defenders' domicile or place of delict,
    23.2.5
double delict rule, 23.6.1
drunk driving, 20.6.1–12
duty of care,
  accountants of public companies to
    members of the public, 13.2.6
  advisers, 13.1.4
  against third party damage, 12.1.1–44
  building authorities, 13.2.6, 14.2.2
  building society surveyors to house
    purchasers, 12.1.1–12
  checklist founded on proximity,
    13.3.20, 13.5.6
  delegation, 19.1.3
  drivers to persons on roads, 8.3.1–13
  finance companies to one another,
    6.3.9
  founded on proximity, 13.3.13, 13.3.17
  house builders to third parties, 13.2.6
  innkeepers, 6.5.2
  manufacturers to consumers, 8.1.1–24
  Secretary of State to the public in
    health matters, 14.1.16
  sub-contractors to occupiers, 13.3.1–30
  to unborn children, 22.9.3
economic loss *see also* **primary economic
    loss; secondary economic loss**
  bar, 6.2.2
  breaches of statutory duties, 14.2.2
  categories, 13.2.2
  defective and dangerous goods,
    17.4.2
  difficulty of proof, 6.1.7
  Erskine's Institutes, 2.3.2, 2.4.2
  foreseeability, 12.1.44, 13.2.3
  liability in contract or delict, 2.4.3,
    2.11.2, 13.3.10, 13.3.19, 13.4.3,
    13.5.4, 13.5.9
  United States, 17.4.1, 17.4.2
ejections, 2.1.12, 5.2.3
electricity, economic loss resulting from
    supply cut 13.7.1–7
employers liability *see also* **safe means of
    access; safe place of work; safe
    plant and equipment; safe system
    of work; vicarious liability**

actions under statute and common law, 19.6.2
common employment, 19.1.3, 19.1.6–7, 19.2.2
standard of care, 15.3.1–10, 15.5.1–10, 15.7.1–6
statutory duties, 19.3.1–4, 19.5.1

England and Wales
actio de positivis vel suspensis, 5.10.5
animals, 18.4.3
damages for loss of life expectancy, 1.4.64
damages for non-patrimonial loss, 1.3.35
disclaimers, 13.2.5
harmonisation with Scots law of damages for personal injuries, 1.4.47
inducement to breach of contract, 7.9.5, 7.10.2
innkeepers' duty of care, 6.5.4
interference with trade, 7.10.4
land use in *aemulationem vicini*, 5.12.3
medical negligence, 9.3.2
occupiers liability, 16.2.3
professional negligence, 13.2.3
scienter actions, 18.1.4
similarity of Scots law, 13.3.9
standards of negligence in medical cases, 9.3.2
strict liability, 18.1.4
thin skull rule, 11.3.6, 11.3.9
tort of conversion, 6.1.7
transmissibility of *solatium* after death, 1.3.28, 1.4.52
treatment of assault, 3.1.4
volenti non fit injuria, 20.7.4

Erskine's Institutes, 2.3.1–4
economic loss, 2.3.2, 2.4.2
Praetor's Edict, 6.5.7
spuilzie, 6.1.2

EU legislation *see also* **directives**
consumer protection, 17.2.1
damages for breaches, 15.9.28
manual handling operations, 15.5.1–10, 15.7.1–6
source of UK law, 19.6.5
wrongful implementation in national legislation, 15.9.1–38

European Convention on Human Rights, law of privacy, 21.14.4

evidence *see* **burden of proof; corroboration; inference; res ipsa loquitur**

ex turpi causa non obitur actio, 20.8.1-8

extortion, 2.1.12

factories, 19.3.1–4, 19.5.1

fair criticism, defences against *convicium* 21.11.2

feudal law, neighbours disputes 5.2.4

fire, damages by third parties 12.1.1–44

fishing, registration of foreign vessels 15.9.3

floodgates argument
economic loss, 12.1.44, 13.3.2, 13.3.12
revival of argument, 13.5.10
secondary economic loss, 13.7.9
unfounded, 13.3.19

flooding, 5.1.1, 20.1.1–8
caused by building of dams, 20.1.8, 20.1.4
design of golf club, 20.10.1–6
foreseeability, 20.1.3
water pipes, 5.3.1–8, 5.5.1–6

foreseeability, 8.3.9–11
economic loss, 13.2.3
flooding of neighbours' property, 20.1.3
inevitable accidents, 5.10.5, 6.5.4, 22.7.1–4
nature of accidents, 8.5.1–6
safe place of work, 19.3.3–4
second accident, 10.7.2
standard of care, 8.6.2, 9.1.8
thin skull rule, 11.3.1–10
third party damages, 12.1.8
vandalism, 12.1.43, 12.1.44

forgery, 2.1.12

fraud, passing-off 7.1.13

French law
concept of fault, 12.1.44
quasi-delict, 5.9.5

funeral expenses, 1.3.15, 1.4.8

general practitioners, vicarious liability of health boards, 14.1.8, 14.1.27-29

goodwill, meaning, 7.1.5

health and safety at work *see* **manual handling operations; safe means of access; safe place of work; safe plant and equipment; safe system of work**

Heineccius, Johan, 5.9.6

heritable property
dangers, 17.4.2–3
defects, 17.4.2
duties of property, 5.5.2, 5.5.4, 12.1.1–44
flooding of neighbours' property, 20.1.1–8
liability *ex domino soli*, 5.5.4, 12.2.5
nuisance on neighbouring land, 5.1.1–10, 5.2.4, 5.3.1–8, 5.4.2
use *in aemulationem vicini*, 5.11.1–3

hire, title to sue manufacturers of equipment, 13.9.1–10

hire-purchase
recovery of goods, 6.2.2
spuilzie, 6.1.4
title to goods, 6.3.1–13
title to sue for damages to moveables, 13.10.2
hotels, Hotel Proprietors Act 1956, 6.7.1–8
hypothecs, title to sue for damages to moveables, 13.9.9, 13.10.2
industrial diseases
deaths, 1.3.7
legal aid, 1.11.8
industrial disputes, 3.3.1, 3.3.6
conspiracy, 7.11.2
intimidation, 7.11.1–2
inevitable accidents, 5.10.5, 6.5.4
heart attacks, 22.7.1–4
inference
damage to neigbouring property, 5.5.2
injuries resulting from breaches of statutory duty, 24.5.1–8
negligence, 5.10.1
open doors of train carriages, 24.3.1–7
primary facts, 10.6.3
innkeepers
duty of care, 6.5.2
Hotel Proprietors Act 1956, 6.7.1–8
innuendoes, 21.1.1–5, 21.3.1–4, 21.13.6
insurance
asbestos-related diseases, 1.2.1
domicile of insurers, 23.2.1
road traffic accidents, 20.6.11, 22.4.2
intelligence services, duty of confidentiality, 4.3.1–9
interdicts, passing off, 7.2.3, 7.3.1–7
interest
damages, 1.4.32–33
rates on asbestos-related claims, 1.3.26
intimidation, 7.11.1–2, 7.12.1
intrusions, 2.1.12, 5.2.3
jurisdiction
special jurisdiction 23.2.1–17
supply of defective goods 2.10.1–4
jury trials, 9.4.2, 19.1.2
Justinian's Institutes 5.9.2
land *see* **heritable property**
latent defects, 17.4.4, 20.10.1–6
law reform
asbestosis, 1.1.1–3
defenders' tactics in personal injury cases, 1.3.1
non-patrominial loss, 1.4.37–42
personal injuries, 1.3.24–72
spuilzie, 6.1.5–7
Lawburrows, recent use, 2.6.3
legal aid, industrial diseases, 1.11.8
legal personality, unborn children, 22.9.4

legislation
wrongful legislation under EU law, 15.9.1–38
wrongful subordinate legislation, 15.9.37
Lex Aquilia, 2.7.3, 2.7.5, 6.8.2
liability *see* **strict liability**
liens, title to sue for damages to moveables, 13.9.5, 13.9.9, 13.10.2
limitation of actions
court discretion, 20.12.8
defences, 20.12.1–15
diseases, 20.13.2
starting date, 20.12.6
local authorities
breach of statutory duties, 5.1.1, 5.1.11, 17.4.2
burst water pipes, 5.3.1–8
loss of services, 1.3.15, 1.4.8
loss of society, 1.3.16, 1.4.9
babies' death resulting from anti-natal injuries, 22.9.1
case law, 1.4.20–27
continuation in law, 1.4.48
increase of awards, 1.4.48–50
insufficiency of awards, 1.4.39, 1.4.30
level of awards, 1.4.14, 1.4.18
nature and purpose of awards, 1.4.18–19
past and future suffering, 1.4.38
quantum of damages, 1.3.20, 1.3.37, 1.3.34
loss of support, 1.3.15, 1.4.8
lucrum cessans, 2.1.5
malice, conspiracy, 7.5.16, 7.5.18
malitiis non est indulgendum, 5.11.4
mandates, vicarious liability, 22.4.2
manual handling operations, 15.5.1–10, 15.7.1–6
duty to provide training, 15.5.9
risk of injury, 15.7.3
marriage
inducement to breach of promise, 7.7.1–5, 7.9.5
law reform, 7.8.2
medical negligence, 9.3.1–4, 14.1.1–32
causation, 10.1.1–8, 10.6.4
criteria for deviation from normal practice, 9.3.4
England and Wales, 9.3.2
mesothelioma, 1.1.1
delaying tactics by defenders, 1.3.21–23
diagnosis, 1.1.3
failure to diagnose, 1.11.10
level of awards, 1.4.16
victims, 1.5.4, 1.6.1–3
molestation, 2.1.12

motorcars
  reputation of dealers, 21.13.1–13
  restrictive covenants, 7.9.1–7
moveable property *see also* **defective goods; product liability**
  hire purchase, 6.3.1–13
  spuilzie, 6.1.1–7
  wrongful interference, 6.1.1–4
mutual gables, 5.11.1–6
national interest
  disclosures by members of intelligence services, 4.3.4–8
  obligations of confidentiality, 4.21
nautae, caupones, stabularii, 2.1.10, 6.5.2
necessary services, 1.3.11
negligence *see also* **professional negligence**
  animals, 18.1.6
  basis of Scottish actions for reparation, 3.1.4
  Bell's Principles, 2.5.3
  breach of statutory duties, 15.1.1–10
  burst water pipes, 5.3.1–8
  consumer law, 8.1.1–24
  hire purchase, 6.3.1–13
  inference, 5.5.1–6, 5.10.1
  nuisance, 5.1.5–10, 5.2.2
  onus of proof, 5.3.4, 5.4.2
  ownership of land, 5.3.1–8
  recognised principles, 13.3.6
  snails in ginger beer bottles, 8.1.1–24
negotiorum gesto, 12.2.5
neighbours
  aemulatio vicini, 5.11.1–4
  identification, 8.1.5, 13.7.6
  nuisance, 5.1.1–10, 5.2.4, 5.3.1–8, 5.4.2
nervous shock
  guidelines, 8.4.3–4
  primary and secondary victims, 8.4.5
  road traffic accidents, 8.3.1–13
no-fault compensation, 1.11.11
non-patrimonial loss
  definition, 1.4.19
  law reform, 1.4.37–42, 1.4.48–51
  no executry transmission, 1.4.10
  statutory damages, 1.3.35–40
novus actus interveniens, 10.7.2, 12.1.30
nuisance
  common law, 5.1.1, 5.1.3, 5.1.8
  land, 5.3.1–8, 5.4.2, 5.5.1–6
  neighbouring land, 5.1.1–10, 5.2.4, 5.3.1–8, 5.4.2
  sports, 5.4.5
  strict liability, 5.1.5–10, 5.2.2, 5.2.5
occupiers' liability
  1960 Act, 16.1.1-3
  application to roads and streets, 16.2.4

burden of proof, 16.2.2
damage to neighbouring land, 5.1.2–10, 5.4.2
danger notices, 16.4.2
duty of care to neighbours against third party damage, 12.1.40, 12.2.5
England and Wales, 16.2.3
fencing of railway lines, 16.5.1–8
liability to trespassers, 16.3.2, 17.4.3
meaning of occupier, 16.2.1
railway transformers, 16.3.1–4
standard of care, 16.3.2
whether absolute liability, 5.7.1–6
onus of proof see **burden of proof**
optional procedure, reparation actions, 1.3.25
passing-off
  burden of proof, 7.1.3–4
  fraudulent intent, 7.1.13
  get-up of goods, 7.1.5–11
  interdicts, 7.2.3, 7.3.1–7
  meaning, 7.1.1–2
  requirements of actions, 7.3.7
  Scotch Whisky Association, 7.2.2
patrimonial loss, 1.3.11
  after death, 1.4.8
  executry transmission, 1.3.17, 1.4.10
personal injuries
  defenders' tactics, 1.3.1
  duplication of damages, 1.4.43–45
  heads of damages, 1.3.11–12
  law reform, 1.3.24–72
  quantification of damages after death, 1.4.56–57
  Scottish Law Commission report, 1.4.1–72
  statistics, 1.3.4–5
  survey of legal practice, 1.3.2–3
  unborn children, 22.9.1–7
pleadings, lack of specification, 5.3.4–8
pneumoconiosis, causation, 10.3.1–5
police
  forceful removal of detainees' clothing, 3.3.13
  powers of arrest, 2.11.2, 3.3.4, 3.3.6–8
  powers of detention, 2.11.2, 3.3.1–14
post traumatic stress disorder, 8.4.7
Praetor's Edict, 2.1.10, 6.5.1–7
prescription, defences 20.10.1–6
primary economic loss
  building defects, 13.3.1–30
  faulty house valuation, 13.1.1–12
  Junior Books controversy, 13.5.1–12
  Junior Books revival in Scottish courts, 13.6.1
  meaning, 13.2.2

occupiers' claims on subcontractors, 13.3.1–30
privacy
actio injuriarum or convicium, 21.14.3
debate, 21.14.5
differences between Scots and English law, 21.14.3
influence of European Convention on Human Rights, 21.14.4
private international law
1995 Act, 23.5.1
choice of law, 23.4.1
jurisdiction, 2.10.1–4
special jurisdiction, 23.2.1–17
privilege
reports of court proceedings, 21.14.7
statutory privilege under 1996 Defamation Act, 21.14.7
privity of contract, 13.5.6
rigidity, 13.5.9
Scots law, 13.5.12
probability, meaning, 12.1.26
product liability, 8.1.1–24
1987 Consumer Protection Act, 17.1.1–9
defences, 17.3.1, 17.3.5, 17.4.5
design defects, 17.3.5
development risks, 17.3.1, 17.4.5
meaning of damage, 17.3.1
meaning of defect, 17.3.1
meaning of product, 17.1.2, 17.3.3
problems of the 1987 Act, 17.3.1–6
strict liability, 17.3.6
surviving role of common law, 17.2.2
United States, 17.4.2
professional negligence *see also* **medical negligence**, 9.3.1–4
accountants, 13.2.3, 13.2.6
standards, 9.4.3
surveyors, 13.1.1–12
proof *see* **burden of proof; corroboration; inference;** *res ipsa loquitur*
property *see* **heritable property; moveable property**
provisional damages, asbestosis, 1.4.16, 1.10.3
provocation, assault, 3.1.1–5
proximity, 12.1.44
building society surveyors to house purchasers, 13.1.6
checklist to found duty of care, 13.3.20, 13.5.6
economic loss, 13.2.3, 13.3.3–4
foundation of duty of care, 13.3.13, 13.3.17, 13.6.2–3
house builders, 13.2.6, 13.3.3–4
manufacturers to consumers, 8.1.6

public bodies
duty of care to public, 14.2.2–3
liability of health officials, 14.1.1–32
liability to public in exercise of discretionary powers, 14.1.19–21, 14.2.3
public interest
disclosures by members of intelligence services, 4.3.4–8
obligations of confidentiality, 4.21
public policy, 14.2.3, 20.6.2
common criminal enterprise, 20.6.3, 20.6.7, 20.6.12, 20.8.1–8
quae quasi ex delicto nascuntur, 5.9.2
quantum of damages
house valuation, 13.2.4
loss of society, 1.3.20, 1.3.37, 1.3.34
quasi-delicts, 2.5.3, 2.8.3, 2.9.3, 2.10.4, 5.2.3, 13.3.1
Bell's Principles, 5.9.5
French law, 5.9.5
meaning in Scots law, 5.9.1–4
Roman quasi delicts and land use, 5.7.1–3
qui facit per alium facit per se, 19.1.4, 19.1.5
racial discrimination, 7.6.3
railways
fencing of lines, 16.5.1–8
protection of transformers, 16.3.1–4
reasonable care, meaning, 12.1.26
reasonable practicability, burden of proof, 15.7.4
recompense, 6.1.7
registered designs, 7.1.3
remoteness of damages, 5.2.6, 8.3.1–13, 8.6.2
loss of employees' services, 11.1.1–6
practical expediency, 13.7.8
thin skull rule, 11.3.1–10
reparation
meaning, 2.11.2
Stair's Institutions, 2.1.9, 2.1.1–3
res ipsa loquitur, 5.1.2, 5.3.5–6, 5.8.2, 8.1.19, 17.2.2
explosions, 24.1.1–4
limitation of principle, 24.3.7
meaning, 24.1.2
open doors of train carriages, 24.3.6
restitution, or spuilzie, 6.1.5, 6.1.7
restraint, Stair's Institutions, 2.1.6
restraint of trade 7.9.3–4, 7.10.4
restrictive covenants, inducement to breach, 7.9.1–7
retrospective legislation, Damages Bill, 1.5.2, 1.9.16–17, 1.9.7–8, 1.10.15, 1.11.13–17

risks
acceptance, 16.5.8, 18.3.3, 20.6.1
assessment, 15.7.5
development risks, 17.3.1, 17.3.5,
17.4.5
manual handling operations, 15.7.3
road traffic accidents
contributory negligence, 20.4.1–4,
20.5.2
drivers without licences, 2.8.1–8
ex turpi causa non obitur actio, 20.8.1–8
heart attacks, 22.7.1–4
insurance, 20.6.11, 22.4.2, 22.8.2
nervous shock, 8.3.1–13
volenti non fit injuria, 20.6.1–12, 22.4.3
roads, application of occupiers' liability,
16.2.4
safe means of access
standard of care, 15.3.1–10
statutory duties, 19.5.1
safe place of work, statutory duties,
19.3.1–4
safe plant and equipment, 2.8.1, 19.1.9
safe system of work *see also* **manual**
handling operations, 19.1.1–9
working with animals, 18.1.2, 18.1.8
Scotch Whisky Association, passing-off,
7.2.2
Scottish Law Commission
failure to consult claimants, 1.11.10
memorandum on spuilzie, 6.1.1–7
recommendations on effect of death
on damages, 1.4.46–72, 1.7.2
report on effect of death on damages,
1.4.1–72, 1.11.10
report on the obligation of confidence,
4.1.1–3
secondary economic loss, 6.2.1
damaged electricity supply cable,
13.7.1–7
meaning, 13.2.2
title to sue for damages to moveables,
13.9.1–10
Secretary of State
duty of public information, 14.1.16
liability for actions of public bodies,
14.1.10–25
sewerage
maintenance, 5.1.10–11
statutory duty of local authorities, 5.1.1
sic utere tuo ut alienum non laedas, 5.5.6
snails, in ginger beer bottles, 8.1.1–24
solatium, 1.3.12
elements, 1.4.58–61
extinguishment of claim after death,
1.3.18, 1.4.11
level of awards, 1.4.15

loss of life expectancy, 1.4.62–66, 1.9.5,
1.9.11–12
meaning, 1.4.5, 1.4.24–25
personal nature of claim, 1.4.53, 1.4.68
transmissibility after death, 1.3.27–30,
1.4.35–36, 1.4.52–55, 1.4.67–72,
1.9.2
whether patrimonial asset, 1.4.34
specificatio, doctrine, 6.3.13
speculative actions, 1.11.5–6
spoliatus ante omni est restituendus, 6.1.1
sports, nuisance 5.4.5
spuilzie, 2.1.12, 2.6.3
Erskine's Institutes, 6.1.2
hire purchase goods, 6.1.4
law reform, 6.1.5–7
remedies, 6.1.1–4
title to sue, 6.2.2
whether fallen into disuse, 6.1.1, 6.1.3
wrongful interference in interests in
moveable property, 6.2.1
stable keepers, Praetor's Edict, 2.1.10,
6.5.2–6
Stair's Institutions, 2.1.1–12, 5.9.6, 18.1.6
separation of concepts of delict and
punishment, 2.5.4
standard of care, 9.1.1–11
building, 13.3.5
foreseeability of accidents, 8.6.2, 9.1.8
medical care, 9.3.1–4
occupiers' liability, 16.3.2
professional negligence, 9.4.7
safe means of access, 15.3.1–10
subjective test, 9.1.5
statistical evidence, causation, 10.6.4
statutory duties *see also* **employers'**
liability; occupiers' liability;
product liability
breaches, 10.3.4, 22.4.3
breaches by local authorities, 5.1.1,
5.1.11, 14.2.2
coal mining, 15.1.1–10
difference with common law duty of
care, 15.4.2
standard of care, 15.3.1–10, 15.5.1–10,
15.7.1–6
windows, 15.2.2
strict liability
animals, 5.2.3, 5.10.3, 18.5.4
consumer law, 5.10.3
defence of *damnum fatale,* 20.2.4
dog bites, 18.4.2, 18.5.3
England and Wales, 18.1.4
failure to implement directives,
15.9.11, 15.9.25, 15.9.29, 15.9.33
householders, 5.7.1–6
nuisance, 5.1.5–10, 5.2.2, 5.2.5

product liability, 17.3.6
statutory duty of local authorities, 5.1.2
surveyors
drop in house prices, 13.2.4
negligence, 13.1.1–12
thin skull rule, 11.3.1–10
third party damages, 12.1.1–44
title to sue
damages to moveables, 13.9.1–10
manufacturers by consumers, 8.1.16
spuilzie actions, 6.2.2
torts 1.4.47
conversion, 6.1.7
distinction with law of contract, 13.5.9
meaning, 2.8.4
trade
economic embargoes, 7.5.1–23
restraint of trade, 7.9.3–4, 7.10.4
trade marks, 7.1.3, 7.1.5
trade unions
conspiracy, 7.5.1–23
role in occupational disease claims, 1.11.2, 1.11.8, 1.11.12
training, manual handling operations, 15.5.9, 24.7.1
trespass, 3.3.1–4, 5.2.3, 8.5.5
interference with dangerous things on trespassed land, 12.1.33
occupiers' liability, 16.3.2, 17.4.3
ultra vires, subordinate legislation, 15.9.37
unfair contract terms, 13.2.5
United States
economic loss, 17.4.1
law of privacy, 21.14.4
manufacturers' negligence, 8.1.10
product liability, 17.4.2
vaccination, risks, 14.1.1–32
valuation, surveyors, 13.1.1–12, 13.2.4

vandalism, duty to prevent, 12.1.1–44
verbal injuries *see also convicium*; **defamation**
motor dealer, 21.13.1–13
or *convicium*, 21.13.2
or defamation, 21.13.4, 21.13.13
vicarious liability, 5.7.3
Bell's Principles, 2.5.4
company directors, 22.3.1–4
defective premises, 19.1.4
defective systems of work, 19.1.1–9
delegation of duty of care, 19.1.3
employees' heart attacks, 22.7.1–4
for employers' independent contractors, 26.6.4
health boards for actions of general practitioners, 14.1.8, 14.1.27–29
Home Office for Borstal officers, 14.1.18
lorry driver on unauthorised route, 22.1.1–5
mandates, 22.4.2
meaning of 'scope of employment', 22.1.2, 22.5.11–19
multiple employers, 22.5.1–19
plant and equipment, 19.1.4
Stair's Institutions, 2.1.10
violent profits, 6.1.1
remedies, 6.1.7
restatement of principle, 6.1.7
volenti non fit injuria, 16.3.4, 16.5.8, 20.7.2
common law and statutory duty, 20.6.3
road traffic accidents, 20.6.1–12, 22.4.3
water pipes
common property, 5.13.1–3
flooding, 5.3.1–8, 5.5.1–6